PENGUIN BOOKS

THE DELUGE

'This book is the best example of the "grand strategy" genre since
The Rise and Fall of the Great Powers . . . a bold reconceptualization
of the making and breaking of the liberal international order'
John Bew, *New Statesman*

'A remarkable new synthesis which draws on [Tooze's] two particular
areas of expertise, Eurasia and especially Germany, and the global
financial system revolving around London . . . the great strength of
his book is that he invites us to look at familiar events in unfamiliar
ways . . . Tooze's account brims with contemporary resonances . . . the
general public and policymakers alike will – must! – turn to Adam
Tooze for instruction' Brendan Simms, *Tablet*

'It is particularly refreshing to read Adam Tooze's book . . .
it confirms his stature as an analyst of hugely complex political
and economic issues . . . Tooze's book covers a huge geographical
sweep . . . he shows himself a formidably impressive chronicler
of a critical period of modern history, unafraid of bold judgements'
Max Hastings, *Sunday Times*

'Interesting, engaging and very readable . . . he has also delivered, for
the first time, a clear and compelling rationale as to why it is actually
worth going back and looking at the era of the First World War at this
particular moment in time . . . *The Deluge* reminds us why we write
history and why we should read it' Neil Gregor, *Literary Review*

'Frequently compelling . . . *The Deluge* contains some surprising
revelations and is bound to be of interest to specialists and
non-specialists alike' Robert Gellately, *Times Higher Education*

'What Adam Tooze has done – a huge, formidable achievement – is to
reconstruct a vast global web, and to show how the slightest vibrations
on its threads had consequences everywhere, almost regardless of
individual fears and hates or venomous ideologies. The breadth of
his scholarship also frighteningly illuminates the fragility of peace'
Sinclair McKay, *Daily Telegraph*

'A bold and persuasive reinterpretation of how the US rose
to global pre-eminence and along the way it recasts the story
of how the world staggered from one conflagration to the next . . .
The Deluge offers us a genuinely global revision of the conventional
view of the 1920s, one which shows how weak the enemies of the
new pax Americana really were . . . Tooze's brilliant account also
offers much food for thought for any observer of the current
international scene' Mark Mazower, *Guardian*

ABOUT THE AUTHOR

Adam Tooze is Barton M. Biggs Professor of History and Director of
International Security Studies at Yale University. He taught for many
years at the University of Cambridge. His last book, *The Wages of
Destruction*, was universally acclaimed as one of the most important
books written on the Third Reich. It was shortlisted for the Duff Cooper
Prize and won both the Longman-History Today Book of the Year Prize
and the Wolfson Prize for History.

ADAM TOOZE

The Deluge

*The Great War and the Remaking of
Global Order, 1916–1931*

PENGUIN BOOKS

PENGUIN BOOKS

UK | USA | Canada | Ireland | Australia
India | New Zealand | South Africa

Penguin Books is part of the Penguin Random House group of companies
whose addresses can be found at global.penguinrandomhouse.com.

First published by Allen Lane 2014
Published in Penguin Books 2015
008

Typeset by Jouve (UK), Milton Keynes
Printed in Great Britain by Clays Ltd, St Ives plc

A CIP catalogue record for this book is available from the British Library

ISBN: 978-0-141-03218-4

www.greenpenguin.co.uk

MIX
Paper from
responsible sources
FSC® C018179

Penguin Random House is committed to a
sustainable future for our business, our readers
and our planet. This book is made from Forest
Stewardship Council® certified paper.

For Edie

Most troublesome questions are thus handed over, sooner or later, to the historian. It is his vexation that they do not cease to be troublesome because they have been finished with by statesmen, and laid aside as practically settled ... It is a wonder that historians who take their business seriously can sleep at night'.

Woodrow Wilson[1]

The chronicle is finished. With what feelings does one lay down Mr. Churchill's two-thousandth page? Gratitude ... Admiration ... A little envy, perhaps, for his undoubting conviction that frontiers, races, patriotisms, even wars if need be, are ultimate verities for mankind, which lends for him a kind of dignity and even nobility to events, which for others are only a nightmare interlude, something to be permanently avoided.

J. M. Keynes reviewing Winston Churchill's book
The Aftermath[2]

Contents

Introduction

ONE
The Eurasian Crisis

TWO
Winning a Democratic Victory

THREE
The Unfinished Peace

FOUR
The Search for a New Order

Conclusion

List of Illustrations

List of Maps

The dismemberment of China, c. 1911

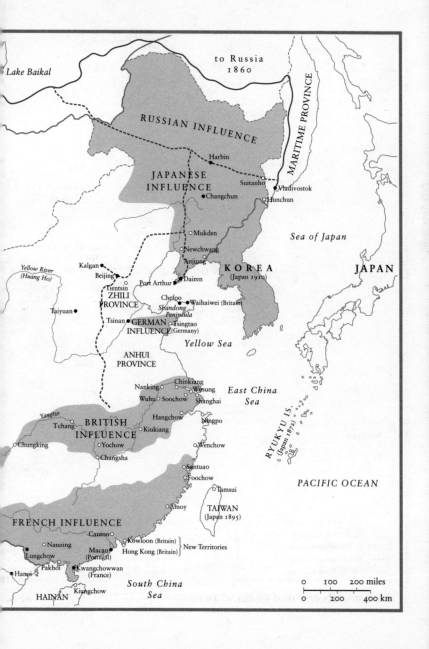

Lake Baikal

to Russia
1860

RUSSIAN INFLUENCE

MARITIME PROVINCE

Harbin

JAPANESE
INFLUENCE

Suitanho
Vladivostok

Changchun
Hunchun

Mukden

Sea of Japan

Newchwang

Anjiung

KOREA
(Japan 1910)

JAPAN

Yellow River
(Huang Ho)

Kalgan
Beijing

Tientsin
ZHILI
PROVINCE

Port Arthur
Dairen

Chefoo
Waihaiwei (Britain)

Taiyuan

Shandong
Peninsula

Tsinan
Tsingtao
(Germany)

GERMAN
INFLUENCE

Yellow Sea

ANHUI
PROVINCE

Nanking
Chinkiang

Wusung

Wuhu
Soochow

Shanghai

East China
Sea

Hangchow
Ningpo

Yangtze

Tchang
BRITISH
INFLUENCE

Kiukiang

Chungking
Yochow

Changsha

Wenchow

RYUKYU IS.
(Japan 1872)

Santuao

Foochow

PACIFIC OCEAN

Tamsui

Amoy

TAIWAN
(Japan 1895)

FRENCH INFLUENCE

Canton

Nanning
Kowloon (Britain)

Lungchow
Macao
(Portugal)
Hong Kong (Britain)
New Territories

Pakhoi
Kwangchowwan
(France)

Hanoi
Kiungchow

South China
Sea

HAINAN

0   100   200 miles

0   200   400 km

European territorial changes resulting from the First World War

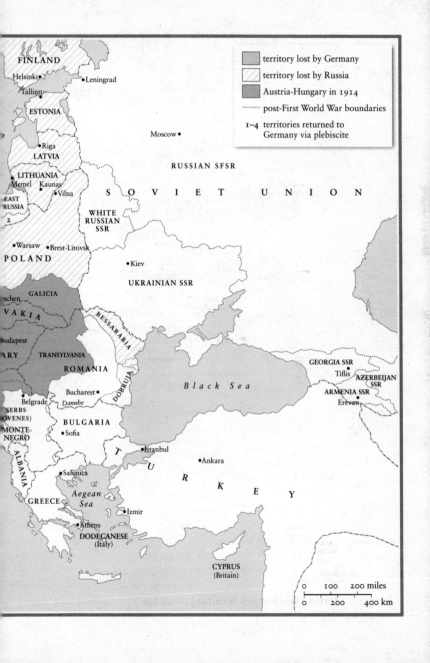

FINLAND
Helsinki•
•Leningrad
Tallinn•
ESTONIA

•Riga
LATVIA
•LITHUANIA
Memel •Kaunas•
EAST •Vilna
RUSSIA
2
•Warsaw •Brest-Litovsk
POLAND

Moscow •

RUSSIAN SFSR

S O V I E T   U N I O N

WHITE
RUSSIAN
SSR

•Kiev
UKRAINIAN SSR

GALICIA
...schen
VAKIA
BESSARABIA
...udapest
TRANSYLVANIA
ARY
ROMANIA
DOBRUJA
•Belgrade
Bucharest •
Danube
SERBS
(OVENES)
BULGARIA
MONTE-
NEGRO •Sofia
ALBANIA
•Salonica
GREECE
Aegean
Sea
•Istanbul
•Athens
DODECANESE
(Italy)

Black Sea

GEORGIA SSR
Tiflis•
AZERBEIJAN
SSR
ARMENIA SSR
Erevan•

T
U
R
•Ankara
K
E
Y
•Izmir

CYPRUS
(Britain)

territory lost by Germany
territory lost by Russia
Austria-Hungary in 1914
post-First World War boundaries
1–4 territories returned to
    Germany via plebiscite

0   100   200 miles
0   200   400 km

List of Figures and Tables

Acknowledgements

This book was born in the wake of my last project with Simon Winder and Clare Alexander. I am grateful to them both as well as to Wendy Wolf for setting me on my way. My new agents in the US, Andrew Wylie and Sarah Chalfant, saw the project to its conclusion. Knowing that 2014 was bound to be a crowded anniversary year, *The Deluge* was shepherded to prompt publication thanks to the combined efforts of Simon, Marina Kemp, my copy-editor Richard Mason, the indexer Dave Cradduck and the production team at Penguin headed by Richard Duguid. I am deeply grateful for their friendly professionalism and commitment to the project.

Writing books is not easy, but some books are harder to write than others. This was not an easy book. Those who have friends and colleagues to help them must count themselves lucky, and I am truly so. In England I was fortunate to have Bernhard Fulda, Melissa Lane, Chris Clark, David Reynolds, Matt Inniss and David Edgerton as conversational companions and readers of the manuscript. After moving to Yale in 2009, I discovered a good fortune that was even greater. Beyond strong individual friendships I found intellectual community.

Community is woven of many threads. Above all I have been sustained by a brilliant group of graduate students and soon-to-be colleagues who have inspired and energized me in ways I have never before experienced. Grey Anderson, Aner Barzilay, Kate Brackney, Carmen Dege, Stefan Eich, Ted Fertik and Jeremy Kessler have constituted a shifting and constantly renewing conversation extended over the years since 2009. The momentum and sleepless energy that we have generated in this group has been extraordinary. It has been a true joy and privilege to share this experience. Long may it continue.

Yale is a varied intellectual ecotope and my second circle is made up of friends and colleagues in international history and at International Security Studies, the outfit that I inherited in 2013 from the great Paul Kennedy. Directors need associate directors. Amanda Behm's exemplary work as my Associate Director at ISS was crucial to allowing me to finish this book in 2013. Not that ISS is a two-person show. Among the wider cast of characters tied to international history at Yale, my colleague Patrick Cohrs and Amanda's predecessor as Associate Director, Ryan Irwin, stand out as particularly important in influencing this book.

Finally, I want to thank my colleagues in History, in Political Science, German Studies and the Law School who have taken time to discuss or comment on chapters, or who have shared moments of inspiration, illumination or encouragement. Laura Engelstein made me feel at home at Yale and reassured me about my grasp of Russian history. Tim Snyder, Paul Kennedy and Jay Winter contributed to a memorable debate about an early position paper. Julia Adams hosted a fascinating conversation at the Transitions seminar. Karuna Mantena provided a sounding board for the issues of India and liberalism. Scott Shapiro and Oona Hathaway's enthusiasm for international law and the peaceful order of Kellogg-Briand is infectious. John Witt provided a model of scholarly companionship over many early mornings at Blue State Café. Conversations with Bruce Ackerman helped me to solidify my reading of the Wilsonian moment. Paul North pushed me to justify a reformist position in modern politics. Seyla Benhabib articulated a defence of such a position more brilliant than I could possibly offer. Ian Shapiro's delightful enthusiasm for my last book encouraged me enormously.

On top of all this, successive cohorts of undergraduate students at Yale to whom I taught aspects of interwar international history have offered valuable suggestions and input. I think in particular of Ben Alter, Connor Crawford, Benjamin Daus-Haberle, Eddie Fishman and Teo Soares. They all left their mark on this text, in some cases literally. Ben and Teo both provided valuable editorial assistance, as did Ned Downie, Isabel Marin and Igor Biyurkov, my trusty assistant at ISS.

Away from home base in Cambridge and Yale, the first paper I gave on this project was to Hans-Ulrich Wehler's legendary seminar at Bielefeld University. It was a privilege to appear in that forum. Early on, I received extremely useful comments from the American History seminar in Cambridge. The last paper I gave in Britain was at James Thompson's invitation to the History seminar at Bristol University. Peter Hayes and Deborah Cohen offered me a podium at Northwestern University, Geoff Eley at a fascism workshop at Notre Dame. Charlie Bright and Michael Geyer shared in the excitement of a workshop at

Yale. Dominique Reill and Hermann Beck fuelled a fascinating discussion at the University of Miami. At the Great Depression Conference at Princeton in early 2013, Barry Eichengreen reacted with exemplary grace to my critique of *Golden Fetters*. Nothing could have been more encouraging. At the University of Pennsylvania, Jonathan Steinberg, Dan Raff and Michael Bordo all helped me to firm up my take on American hegemony in the interwar period. Jonathan's enthusiastic commentary on my work has accompanied me throughout my career for almost 20 years. His friendship and that of Marion Kant has been a great gift. Harold James and other contributors to a National Intelligence Council Analytic Exchange in Washington DC in January 2013 offered an entrée to a new world of American policy debate. At a workshop on Techno-Politics in the Age of the Great War 1900–30, hosted by the IFK centre for advanced studies in Vienna, I was particularly fortunate to get feedback from Hew Strachan, Jay Winter and once more from Michael Geyer. Special thanks to Jari Eloranta for last-minute assistance with data.

Twenty-two years ago in the PhD programme at the LSE I met Francesca Carnevali. In all the years that followed we read each other's work. We were the most intimate of friends. Francesca was, of course, among the first to read drafts of this book. She and Paolo Di Matino, her incomparable husband, whom I am honoured to count as a friend and colleague, shared with me their extraordinary energy, hospitality and love whenever I could visit Birmingham. The fact that Francesca is gone leaves a gaping hole in our world.

Francesca looked forward. The future and the new were her greatest sources of solace. Since 2009 in New Haven, Annie Wareck and Iain York have for me given a new meaning to the idea of friendship. They and their wonderful sons, Zev, Malachai and Levi, have brightened and warmed our time beyond measure.

Becky Conekin supported me in finishing this book, as I was proud to support her in finishing her own brilliant work on Lee Miller. This reciprocity sustained us in almost twenty years of being together. I hope that one day she can feel as proud as I do of what we accomplished.

This book is dedicated to our darling daughter Edie, who was and is the light of my life.

New Haven, November 2013

Introduction

The Deluge: The Remaking of World Order

On Christmas Morning 1915, David Lloyd George, the erstwhile radical liberal, now Minister of Munitions, rose to face a restless crowd of Glaswegian trade unionists. He had come to demand a further round of recruits for the war effort and his message was suitably apocalyptic. The war, he warned them, was remaking the world. 'It is the deluge, it is a convulsion of Nature . . . bringing unheard-of changes in the social and industrial fabric. It is a cyclone which is tearing up by the roots the ornamental plants of modern society . . . It is an earthquake which is upheaving the very rocks of European life. It is one of those seismic disturbances in which nations leap forward or fall backward generations in a single bound.'[1] Within four months his words were echoed from the other side of the battle-lines by the German Chancellor Theodore von Bethmann Hollweg. On 5 April 1916, six weeks into the terrible battle of Verdun, he confronted the Reichstag with the stark truth. There was no way back. 'After such dramatic events history knows no status quo.'[2] The violence of the Great War had become transformative. By 1918, World War I had shattered the old empires of Eurasia – Tsarist, Habsburg and Ottoman. China was convulsed by civil war. By the early 1920s the maps of eastern Europe and the Middle East had been redrawn. But dramatic and contentious as they were, these visible changes acquired their full significance from the fact that they were coupled to another deeper, but less conspicuous shift. A new order emerged from the Great War that promised, above the bickering and nationalist grandstanding of the new states, fundamentally to restructure relations between the great powers – Britain, France, Italy, Japan, Germany, Russia and the United States. It took geostrategic and historical imagination to comprehend the scale and significance of this power transition. The new order that was in the making was defined in large part by the absent presence of its most defining element – the new power of the United States. But on those endowed with such vision, the prospect of this tectonic shift exerted an almost obsessive fascination.

Over the winter of 1928–9, ten years after the Great War had ended, three such contemporaries – Winston Churchill, Adolf Hitler and Leon Trotsky – all had occasion to look back on what had happened. On New Year's Day 1929 Churchill, then serving as Chancellor of the Exchequer in the Conservative government of Stanley Baldwin, found time to finish *The Aftermath*, the concluding volume of his epic history of World War I, *The World Crisis*. For those familiar with Churchill's later histories of World War II, this last volume comes as a surprise. Whereas after 1945 Churchill would coin the phrase 'a second Thirty Years War' to describe the long-running battle with Germany as a single historical unit, in 1929 he struck a very different note.[3] Churchill looked forward to the future, not in a spirit of grim resignation, but with considerable optimism. Out of the violence of the Great War it seemed that a new international order had emerged. A global peace had been built on two great regional treaties: the European Peace Pact initialed at Locarno in October 1925 (signed in London in December) and the Pacific Treaties signed at the Washington Naval Conference over the winter of 1921–2. These were, Churchill, wrote, 'twin pyramids of peace rising solid and unshakable . . . commanding the allegiance of the leading nations of the world and of all their fleets and armies'. These agreements gave substance to the peace that had been left unfinished at Versailles in 1919. They filled out the blank check that was the League of Nations. 'The histories may be searched,' Churchill remarked, 'for a parallel for such an undertaking.' 'Hope,' he wrote, 'now rested on a surer foundation . . . The period of repulsion from the horrors of war will be long-lasting; and in this blessed interval the great nations may take their forward steps to world organization with the conviction that the difficulties they have yet to master will not be greater than those they have already overcome.'[4]

These, unsurprisingly, were not the terms in which either Hitler or Trotsky would capture their vision of history ten years after the war. In 1928 the war veteran and failed-putschist-turned-politician, Adolf Hitler, as well as contesting and losing a general election, was negotiating with his publishers over a follow-up to his first book, *Mein Kampf*. The second was intended to collect his speeches and writings since

1924. But since his book sales in 1928 were as disappointing as his electoral performance, Hitler's manuscript never went to press. It has come down to us as his 'Second Book' ('Zweites Buch').[5] Leon Trotsky for his part had time to write and reflect, because after losing his struggle with Stalin, he had been deported first to Kazakhstan and then in February 1929 to Turkey, from where he continued his running commentary on the revolution that had taken such a disastrous turn since the death of Lenin in 1924.[6] Churchill, Trotsky and Hitler make for an incongruous, not to say antipathetic, grouping. To some it will seem provocative even to place them in the same conversation. Certainly they were not each other's equal as writers, politicians, intellectuals or moral personalities. All the more striking is the way in which at the end of the 1920s their interpretations of world politics complemented each other.

Hitler and Trotsky recognized the same reality that Churchill did. They too believed that World War I had opened a new phase of 'world organization'. But whereas Churchill took this new reality as cause for celebration, for a communist revolutionary like Trotsky or a national socialist such as Hitler it threatened nothing less than historical oblivion. Superficially, the peace settlements of 1919 might seem to advance the logic of sovereign self-determination that originated in European history in the late Middle Ages. In the nineteenth century this had inspired the formation of new nation states in the Balkans and the unification of Italy and Germany. It had now climaxed in the break-up of the Ottoman, Russian and Habsburg empires. But although sovereignty was multiplied, its content was hollowed out.[7] The Great War weakened all the European combatants irreversibly, even the strongest amongst them and even the victors. In 1919 the French Republic may have celebrated its triumph over Germany at Versailles, in the palace of the Sun King, but this could not disguise the fact that World War I confirmed the end of France's claim to be a power of global rank. For the smaller nation states created over the previous century, the experience of the war was even more traumatic. Between 1914 and 1919, Belgium, Bulgaria, Romania, Hungary and Serbia had all faced national extinction as the fortunes of war swung back and forth. In 1900 the Kaiser had brashly claimed a place on the world stage. Twenty years later Germany was reduced to squabbling with Poland over the boundaries of Silesia, a dispute overseen by a Japanese viscount. Rather than the subject, Germany had become the object of *Weltpolitik*. Italy had joined the war on the winning side, but despite solemn promises by its allies, the peace reinforced its sense of second-class status. If there was a European victor it was Britain, hence Churchill's rather sunny assessment. However, Britain had prevailed not as a European power but as the head of a global empire. To contemporaries the sense that the British Empire had done relatively less badly out of the war only confirmed the conclusion that the age of European power had come to an end. In an age of world power, Europe's position in political, military and economic terms was irreversibly provincialized.[8]

The one nation that emerged apparently unscathed and vastly more powerful from the war was the United States. Indeed, so overwhelming was its pre-eminence that it seemed to raise once more the question that had been expelled from the history of Europe in the seventeenth century. Was the United States the universal, world-encompassing empire similar to that which the Catholic Habsburgs had once threatened to establish? The question would haunt the century that followed.[9] By the mid-1920s it seemed to Trotsky that 'Balkanized Europe' found 'herself in the same position with respect to the US' that the countries of south-eastern Europe had once occupied in relation to Paris and London in the pre-war period.[10] They had the trappings of sovereignty but not its substance. Unless the political leaders of Europe could shake their populations out of their usual 'political thoughtlessness', Hitler warned in 1928, the 'threatened global hegemony of the North American continent' would reduce them all to the status of Switzerland or Holland.[11] From the vantage point of Whitehall, Churchill had felt the force of this point not as a speculative historical vision, but as a practical reality of power. As we shall see, Britain's governments in the 1920s again and again found themselves confronting the painful fact that the United States was a power unlike any other. It had emerged, quite suddenly, as a novel kind of 'super-state', exercising a veto over the financial and security concerns of the other major states of the world.

Mapping the emergence of this new order of power is the central aim of this book. It requires a particular effort because of the peculiar way in which America's power manifested itself. In the early twentieth century, America's leaders were not committed to asserting themselves as a military power, beyond the ocean highways. Their sway was often exercised

indirectly and in the form of a latent, potential force rather than an immediate, evident presence. But it was nonetheless real. Tracing the ways in
which the world came to terms with America's new centrality, through
the struggle to shape a new order, will be the central preoccupation of this
book. It was a struggle that was always multidimensional – economic,
military and political. It was one that began during the war itself and
stretched beyond it into the 1920s. Getting this history right matters
because we need to understand the origins of the Pax Americana that
still defines our world today. It is crucial too, however, to understanding
the huge second spasm of the 'second Thirty Years War' that Churchill
would look back upon from 1945.[12] The spectacular escalation of violence unleashed in the 1930s and the 1940s was a testament to the kind
of force that the insurgents believed themselves to be up against. It was
precisely the looming potential, the future dominance of American
capitalist democracy, that was the common factor impelling Hitler,
Stalin, the Italian Fascists and their Japanese counterparts to such radical action. Their enemies were often invisible and intangible. They
ascribed to them conspiratorial intentions that enveloped the world in
a malign web of influence. Much of this was manifestly unhinged. But
if we are to understand the way in which the ultra-violent politics of
the interwar period was incubated in World War I and its aftermath,
we need to take this dialectic of order and insurgency seriously. We
grasp movements like fascism or Soviet communism only very partially
if we normalize them as familiar expressions of the racist, imperialist
mainstream of modern European history, or if we tell their story backwards from the dizzying moment in 1940–42, when they rampaged
victoriously through Europe and Asia and the future seemed to belong
to them. Whatever comforting, domesticated fantasies their followers
may have projected onto them, the leaders of Fascist Italy, National
Socialist Germany, Imperial Japan and the Soviet Union all saw themselves as radical insurgents against an oppressive and powerful world
order. For all the braggadocio of the 1930s their basic view of the Western Powers was not that they were weak, but that they were lazy and
hypocritical. Behind a veneer of morality and panglossian optimism
the Western Powers disguised the massive force that had crushed Imperial Germany and that threatened to enshrine a permanent status quo.
To forestall that oppressive vision of an end of history would require

an unprecedented effort. It would be accompanied by terrible risks.[13] This was the terrifying lesson that the insurgents derived from the story of world politics between 1916 and 1931, the story recounted in this book.

I

What were the essential elements underpinning this new order that seemed so oppressive to its potential enemies? By common agreement the new order had three major facets – moral authority backed by military power and economic supremacy.

The Great War may have begun in the eyes of many participants as a clash of empires, a classic great power war, but it ended as something far more morally and politically charged – a crusading victory for a coalition that proclaimed itself the champion of a new world order.[14] With an American president in the lead, the 'war to end all wars' was fought and won to uphold the rule of international law and to put down autocracy and militarism. As one Japanese observer remarked: 'Germany's surrender has challenged militarism and bureaucratism from the roots. As a natural consequence, politics based on the people, reflecting the will of the people, namely democracy (*minponshugi*), has, like a race to heaven, conquered the thought of the entire world.'[15] The image that Churchill chose to describe the new order was telling – 'twin pyramids of peace rising solid and unshakable'. Pyramids are nothing if not massive monuments to the fusion of spiritual and material power. For Churchill, they provided a striking analogue to the grandiose ways in which contemporaries conceived of their project of civilizing international power. Trotsky characteristically cast the scene in rather less exalted terms. If it was true that domestic politics and international relations would no longer be separate, as far as he was concerned, both could be reduced to a single logic. The 'entire political life', even of states like France, Italy and Germany, down to 'the shifts of parties and governments will be determined in the last analysis by the will of American capitalism ...'[16] With his usual sardonic humour, Trotsky evoked, not the awesome solemnity of the pyramids, but the incongruous spectacle of Chicago meat-packers, provincial senators and manufacturers of condensed milk lecturing a Prime Minister of France, a British Foreign

Secretary or an Italian dictator about the virtues of disarmament and world peace. These were the uncouth heralds of America's drive toward 'world hegemony' with its internationalist ethos of peace, progress and profit.[17]

But however incongruous may have been its form, this moralization and politicization of international affairs was a high-stakes wager. Since the wars of religion in the seventeenth century, conventional understanding of international politics and international law had erected a firewall between foreign policy and domestic politics. Conventional morality and domestic notions of law had no place in the world of great power diplomacy and war. By breaching this wall, the architects of the new 'world organization' were quite consciously playing the game of revolutionaries. Indeed, by 1917 the revolutionary purpose was being made more and more explicit. Regime change had become a precondition for armistice negotiations. Versailles assigned war guilt and criminalized the Kaiser. Woodrow Wilson and the Entente had pronounced a death sentence on the Ottoman and Habsburg empires. By the end of the 1920s, as we shall see, 'aggressive' war had been outlawed. But, appealing as these liberal precepts might have been, they begged fundamental questions. What gave the victorious powers the right to lay down the law in this way? Did might make right? What wager were they placing on history to bear them out? Could such claims form a durable foundation of an international order? The prospect of war might be terrible to contemplate, but did declaring a perpetual peace imply a profoundly conservative commitment to upholding the status quo, whatever its legitimacy? Churchill could afford to talk in sanguine terms. His nation had long been one of the most successful entrepreneurs of international morality and law. But what if, as a German historian put it in the 1920s, one were to find oneself amongst the disenfranchised, amongst the lower breeds in the new order, as 'fellaheen' amidst the pyramids of peace?[18]

For true conservatives the only satisfactory answer was to turn back the clock. They demanded that the liberal train of moralistic international organization should be reversed and international affairs returned to an idealized vision of a *Jus Publicum Europaeum* in which the family of European sovereigns lived side by side in a non-judgemental, non-hierarchical anarchy.[19] But not only was this a mythic history, with little bearing on the reality of international politics in the eighteenth and nineteenth centuries. It ignored the force of Bethmann Hollweg's message to the Reichstag in the spring of 1916. After this war, there was no way back.[20] The true alternatives were starker. One was a new kind of conformity. The other was insurgency, epitomized in the immediate aftermath of the war by Benito Mussolini. In Milan in March 1919 he launched his Fascist Party by denouncing the emerging new order as 'a solemn "swindle" of the rich', by which he meant Britain, France and America, 'against the proletarian nations', by which he meant Italy, 'to fix forever the actual conditions of world equilibrium . . .'[21] Instead of a reversion to an imaginary *ancien régime*, he held out the promise of further escalation. What reared its ugly head with this politicization of international affairs was the kind of irreconcilable conflict of values that had made the religious wars of the seventeenth century or the revolutionary struggles at the end of the eighteenth century so lethally violent. Given the horrors of World War I there must either be perpetual peace, or a war even more radical than the last.

Though the danger of such confrontation was clearly real, the severity of this risk depended not only on the resentments that were stirred up and the ideologies that were pitted against each other. In the end, the risks involved in seeking to create and uphold a new international order depended on the plausibility of the moral order to be imposed, its chance of gaining general acceptance on its own merits, and the force mustered to support it. After 1945 in the global Cold War clash between the United States and the Soviet Union, the world would witness the logic of confrontation taken to its extreme. Two global coalitions, self-confidently proclaiming antagonistic ideologies, each armed with massive arsenals of nuclear weapons, threatened humanity with Mutually Assured Destruction. And there are many historians who want to see in 1918–19 a precursor to the Cold War, with Wilson squaring off against Lenin. But though this analogy may be tempting, it is misleading in that in 1919 there was nothing like the symmetry that prevailed in 1945.[22] By November 1918 not only was Germany on its knees, but Russia too. The balance of world politics in 1919 resembled the unipolar moment of 1989 far more than the divided world of 1945. If the idea of reordering the world around a single power bloc and a common set of liberal, 'Western' values seemed like a radical historical departure, this is precisely what made the outcome of World War I so dramatic.

Defeat in 1918 was all the more bitter for the Central Powers, because in the course of World War I, as we shall see, the military initiative had seemed to shift repeatedly back and forth. Through remarkable staff work, the Kaiser's generals were repeatedly able to establish local superiority and to threaten breakthroughs: in 1915 in Poland, at Verdun in 1916, on the Italian front in the autumn of 1917, on the Western Front as late as the spring of 1918. But these battlefield dramas should not divert us from the underlying logic of the war. Only against Russia did the Central Powers actually prevail. On the Western Front, from 1914 down to the summer of 1918, the record was one of frustration. And one central factor helps to explain this, the balance of military materiel. From the summer of 1916 onwards when the British Army brought an enormous transatlantic supply line to bear on the European battlefield, it was only ever a matter of time before any local superiority established by the Central Powers was turned into its opposite. They were worn down in an attritional struggle. Though a thin crust of resistance held even in the final days of November 1918, the collapse thereafter was near total. When the great powers gathered at Versailles in an unprecedented global assembly, Germany and its allies were prostrate. In the months that followed, their once proud armies were disbanded. France and its allies in central and eastern Europe were masters of the European scene. But this, as the French were acutely aware, was no more than a start. On the third anniversary of the Armistice, in November 1921, an exclusive club of leaders gathered for the first time in Washington DC to accept a global order defined by America in unprecedentedly stark terms. At the Washington Naval Conference, power was measured in the currency of battleships, doled out, as Trotsky mockingly put it, in 'rations'.[23] There would be none of the ambiguity of Versailles, nor the obfuscations of the League of Nations Covenant. The rations of geostrategic power were fixed in the ratio of 10:10:6:3:3. At the head stood Britain and the United States, who were accorded equal status as the only truly global powers with a naval presence throughout the high seas. Japan was granted third spot as a one-ocean power confined to the Pacific. France and Italy were relegated to the Atlantic littoral and the Mediterranean. Beyond these five, no other state reckoned in the balance. Germany and Russia were not even considered as conference participants. This it seemed was the outcome of World War I: an all-encompassing global order, in which strategic power was more tightly held than nuclear weapons are today. It was a turn in international affairs, Trotsky remarked, analogous to Copernicus's rewriting of the cosmology of the Middle Ages.[24]

The Washington Naval Conference was a powerful expression of the force that would underwrite the new international order, but in 1921 there were already some who wondered whether the great 'castles of steel' of the battleship era were truly the weapons of the future. Such arguments, however, were beside the point. Whatever their military utility, battleships were the most expensive and technologically sophisticated instruments of global power. Only the richest countries could afford to own and operate battle-fleets. America did not even build its full quota of ships. It was enough that everyone knew that it could. Economics was the pre-eminent medium of American power, military force was a by-product. Trotsky not only recognized this, but was eager to quantify it. In an era of intense international competition, the dark art of comparative economic measurement was a characteristic preoccupation. In 1872, Trotsky believed there had been rough parity between the national wealth of the United States, Britain, Germany and France, each possessing between 30 and 40 billion dollars. Fifty years later the disparity was clearly enormous. Post-war Germany was impoverished, poorer, Trotsky thought, than it had been in 1872. By contrast, 'France is approximately twice as rich (68 billions); likewise England (89 billions); but the wealth of the US is estimated at 320 billion dollars.'[25] These figures were speculative. But what no one disputed was that at the time of the Washington Naval Conference in November 1921, the British government owed the American taxpayer $4.5 billion, whilst France owed America $3.5 billion and Italy owed $1.8 billion. Japan's balance of payments was seriously deteriorating and it was anxiously looking for support from J. P. Morgan. At the same time, 10 million citizens of the Soviet Union were being kept alive by American famine relief. No other power had ever wielded such global economic dominance.

If we turn to modern-day statistics to plot the development of the world economy since the nineteenth century, the two-part storyline is clear enough (Fig. 1).[26] Since the beginning of the nineteenth century the British Empire had been the largest economic unit in the world. Sometime in 1916, the year of Verdun and the Somme, the combined output

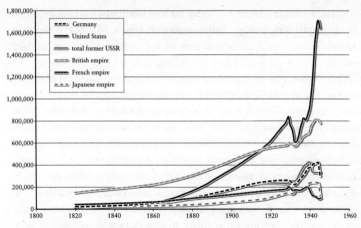

Figure 1. The GDP of Empires (PPP-adjusted 1990 dollars)

of the British Empire was overtaken by that of the United States of America. Henceforth, down to the beginning of the twenty-first century, American economic might would be the decisive factor in the shaping of the world order.

There has always been a temptation, particularly on the part of British authors, to narrate nineteenth- and twentieth-century history as a story of succession, in which the United States inherited the mantle of British hegemony.[27] This is flattering to Britain, but it is misleading in suggesting a continuity in the problems of global order and the means for addressing them. The problems of world order posed by World War I were unlike any previously encountered – by the British, the Americans or anyone else. But, on the other side of the balance sheet, American economic power was of a different quantity and quality from that which Britain had ever deployed.

British economic preponderance had unfolded within the 'world system' created by its empire, stretching from the Caribbean to the Pacific, expanding through free trade, migration and capital export across a vast 'informal' span.[28] The British Empire formed the matrix for the development of all the other economies that made up the advancing frontier of globalization in the late nineteenth century. Faced with the rise of major national competitors, some imperial pundits, advocates of a 'greater Britain', began to lobby for this heterogeneous conglomerate to be forged into a single, self-enclosed economic bloc.[29] But thanks to Britain's entrenched culture of free trade, a preferential imperial tariff would only be adopted amid the disaster of the Great Depression. The United States was everything that the champions of imperial preference longed for, but the British Empire was not. The United States began as a heterogeneous collection of colonial settlements that in the early nine-teenth century had developed into an expansive and highly integrative empire. Unlike the British Empire, the American Republic sought to incorporate its new territories in the West and the South fully into its federal constitution. Given the cleavage in the original founding of the eighteenth-century constitution, between the free-labour North and the slave-labour South, this integrative project was fraught with risks. In 1861, within a century of its birth, America's rapidly expanding polity shattered into a terrible civil war. Four years later the Union had been preserved but at a price no less terrible in proportional terms than that paid by the major combatants in World War I. In 1914, just over fifty years on, the American political class consisted of men whose child-hoods were deeply scarred by that bloodshed. What was at stake in the peace policy of Woodrow Wilson's White House can only be under-stood if we recognize that the twenty-eighth President of the United States headed the first cabinet of Southern Democrats to govern the country since the Secession. They saw their own ascent as vindication of the reconciliation of White America and the refounding of the American nation state.[30] At a terrible cost America had forged itself into some-thing unprecedented. This was no longer the voraciously expansive empire of the westward movement. But nor was it Thomas Jefferson's neo-classical ideal of a 'city on a hill'. It was something judged impos-sible by classical political theory. It was a consolidated federal republic of continental scale, a super-sized nation state. Between 1865 and 1914, profiting from the markets, transport and communications networks of Britain's world system, the US national economy grew faster than any economy had ever grown before. Occupying a commanding position on the coastline of the two largest oceans, it had a unique claim and capacity to exert global influence. To describe the United States as the inheritor of Britain's hegemonic mantle is to adopt the vantage point of those who in 1908 insisted on referring to Henry Ford's Model T as a 'horseless carriage'. The label was not so much wrong, as vainly anachronistic. This was not a succession. This was a paradigm shift, which coincided with the espousal by the United States of a distinctive vision of world order.

This book will have much to say about Woodrow Wilson and his successors. But the most elementary point is easily stated. Having formed itself as a nation state of global reach through a process of expansion that was aggressive and continental in scope but had avoided conflict with other major powers, America's strategic outlook was different from either that of the old power states like Britain and France or their newly arrived competitors – Germany, Japan and Italy. As it emerged onto the world stage at the end of the nineteenth century, America quickly realized its interest in ending the intense international rivalry which since the 1870s had defined a new age of global imperialism. True, in 1898 the American political class thrilled to its own foray into overseas expansion in the Spanish-American War. But, confronted with the reality of imperial rule in the Philippines, the enthusiasm soon waned and a more fundamental strategic logic asserted itself. America could not remain detached from the twentieth-century world. The push for a big navy would be the principal axis of American military strategy until the advent of strategic air power. America would see to it that its neighbours in the Caribbean and Central America were 'orderly' and that the Monroe Doctrine, the bar against external intervention in the western hemisphere, was upheld. Access must be denied to other powers. America would accumulate bases and staging posts for the projection of its power. But one thing that the US could well do without was a ragbag of ill-assorted, troublesome colonial possessions. On this simple but essential point there was a fundamental difference between the Continental United States and the so-called 'liberal imperialism' of Great Britain.[31]

The true logic of American power was articulated between 1899 and 1902 in the three 'Notes' in which Secretary of State John Hay first outlined the so-called 'Open Door' policy. As the basis for a new international order these 'Notes' proposed one deceptively simple but far-reaching principle: equality of access for goods and capital.[32] It is important to be clear what this was not. The Open Door was not an appeal for free trade. Amongst the large economies, the United States was the most protectionist. Nor did the US welcome competition for its own sake. Once the door was opened, it confidently expected American exporters and bankers to sweep all their rivals aside. In the long run the Open Door would thus undermine the Europeans' exclusive imperial domains. But the US had no interest in unsettling the imperial racial hierarchy or the global colour-line. Commerce and investment demanded order not revolution. What American strategy *was* emphatically directed towards suppressing was imperialism, understood not as productive colonial expansion nor the racial rule of white over coloured people, but as the 'selfish' and violent rivalry of France, Britain, Germany, Italy, Russia and Japan that threatened to divide one world into segmented spheres of interest.

The war would make a global celebrity out of President Woodrow Wilson, who was hailed as a great path-breaking prophet of liberal internationalism. But the basic elements of his programme were predictable extensions of the Open Door logic of American power. Wilson wanted international arbitration, freedom of the seas and non-discrimination in trade policy. He wanted the League of Nations to put an end to inter-imperialist rivalry. It was an anti-militarist, post-imperialist agenda for a country convinced of the global influence that it would exercise at arm's length through the means of soft power – economics and ideology.[33] What is not sufficiently appreciated, however, is how far Wilson was willing to push this agenda of American hegemony against all shades of European and Japanese imperialism. As this book will show in its opening chapters, as Wilson drove America to the forefront of world politics in 1916, his mission was to ensure not that the 'right' side won in World War I, but that no side did. He refused any overt association with the Entente and did all he could to suppress the escalation of the war that London and Paris were pursuing and which they hoped would draw America onto their side. Only a peace without victory, the goal that he announced in an unprecedented speech to the Senate in January 1917, could ensure that the United States emerged as the truly undisputed arbiter of world affairs. This book will argue that despite the fiasco of that policy already in the spring of 1917, despite America's reluctant engagement in World War I, this would remain the basic objective of Wilson and his successors right down to the 1930s. And it is this which holds the key to answering the question that follows. If the United States was bent on instituting an Open Door world and had formidable resources at its disposal to achieve that goal, why did things go so badly awry?

II

This question of the derailment of liberalism is the classic question of interwar historiography.[34] The wager of this book is that the question takes on a new aspect precisely if we start from an appreciation of quite how dominant the victors of World War I led by Britain and the United States actually were. Given the events of the 1930s this is all too easy to forget. And the immediate answer given by propagandists of Wilsonianism did suggest the opposite.[35] Even before it occurred, they were anticipating the failure of the Versailles peace conference. They depicted Wilson, their hero, in tragic terms, vainly trying to extricate himself from the machinations of the 'old world'. The distinction between the American prophet of a liberal future and the corrupt old world to which he brought his message was fundamental to this storyline.[36] In the end Wilson succumbed to the forces of that old world, with British and French imperialists in the lead. The result was a 'bad' peace that was in turn repudiated by the American Senate and much of the public, not only in America but throughout the English-speaking world.[37] Even worse was to follow. The rearguard action put up by the old order not only blocked the route to reform. In so doing it opened the door to even more violent political demons.[38] With Europe torn between revolution and violent counter-revolution, Wilson found himself facing Lenin in a foreshadowing of the Cold War. The spectre of Communism in turn animated the extreme right. First in Italy and then across the continent, most lethally in Germany, fascism came to the fore. The violence and increasingly racialized and anti-Semitic discourse of the crisis period 1917–21 hauntingly foreshadowed the even greater horrors of the 1940s. For this disaster the old world had no one to blame but itself. Europe, with Japan figuring as its apt pupil, truly was the 'Dark Continent'.[39]

This storyline has dramatic force and has spawned a remarkably rich historical literature. But beyond its usefulness for historical writing, it matters because it actually informed transatlantic arguments about policy-making from the turn of the century onwards. As we shall see, the attitudes of the Wilson administration and his Republican successors down to Herbert Hoover were powerfully shaped by this perception of European and Japanese history.[40] And this critical narrative was attractive not only to Americans but to many Europeans as well. For radical liberals, socialists and social democrats in Britain, France, Italy and Japan, Wilson provided arguments to use against their domestic political opponents. It was really during World War I and its aftermath, in the mirror of American power and propaganda, that Europe discovered a new sense of its own 'backwardness', a point driven home with even greater force after 1945.[41] But the fact that this historical vision of a Dark Continent violently resisting the forces of historical progress had actual historical influence, also harbours risks for historians. The heartbreaking fiasco of Wilsonianism has cast a long shadow. The Wilsonian construction of interwar history saturates the sources to such an extent that it requires a conscious and sustained effort to hold it at bay. This is what gives such a powerful corrective value to the testimony of the incongruous trio with whom we began – Churchill, Hitler and Trotsky. Their vision of the aftermath of the war was quite different. They were convinced that a fundamental change *had* come over world affairs. They were also agreed that the terms of this transition were being dictated by the United States, with Britain as its willing accessory. If there was a dialectic of radicalization operating behind the scenes that would throw open the door of history to extremist insurgency, as of 1929 it was obscure to both Trotsky and Hitler. It took a second dramatic crisis, the Great Depression, to unleash the avalanche of insurgency. Once the extremists were given their chance, it was precisely the sense that they faced mighty opponents that animated the violence and lethal energy of their assault on the post-war order.

This brings us to the second major strand of interpretation of the interwar disaster, which we will call the crisis of hegemony school.[42] This line of interpretation starts exactly where we do here, with the crushing victory of the Entente and the United States in World War I, and asks not why the main thrust of American power was resisted, but why the victors, those who held such a preponderance of power in the wake of the Great War, did not prevail. After all, their superiority was not imaginary. Their victory in 1918 was no accident. In 1945 a similar coalition of forces would impose an even more comprehensive defeat on Italy, Germany and Japan. Furthermore, after 1945 the United States in its sphere went on to organize a highly successful political and economic order.[43] What had gone wrong after 1918? Why had American policy miscarried at Versailles? Why had the world economy imploded in 1929? Given the starting point of this book, these are questions that we cannot escape and they too resonate down to the present day. Why does 'the West' not play its winning hands better? Where is the capacity for management and leadership?[44] Given the rise of China, these questions have an obvious force. The problem is to find the right standard by which to judge this failure and to provide some compelling explanation for the lack of will and judgement that are the serious shortcomings of rich, powerful democracies.

Faced with these two basic explanatory options – the 'Dark Continent' versus the 'failure of liberal hegemony' schools – the ambition of this book is to seek a synthesis. But to achieve that is not a matter of mixing and matching elements from both sides. Instead, this book seeks to open the two main schools of historical argument to a third question, one that reveals their common blind spot. What the historical schemas offered by both the 'Dark Continent' and the 'hegemonic failure' models of history tend to obscure is the radical novelty of the situation confronting world leaders in the early twentieth century.[45] This blind spot is inherent in the crude 'new world, old world' schema of the Dark Continent interpretation. This ascribes novelty, openness and progress to 'outside forces', be they the United States or the revolutionary Soviet Union. Meanwhile, the destructive force of imperialism is vaguely identified with an 'old world' or an 'ancien régime', an epoch that in some cases is seen stretching back to the age of absolutism, or even further into the depths of blood-soaked European and East Asian history. The disasters of the twentieth century are thus ascribed to the dead weight of the past. The hegemonic crisis model may interpret the interwar crisis differently. But it is even more dramatic in its historical sweep and even less interested in acknowledging that the early twentieth century may actually have been an era of true novelty. The strongest versions of the argument insist that the capitalist world economy has since its inception in the 1500s depended on a central stabilizing power – be it the Italian city states, or the Habsburg monarchy, or the Dutch Republic, or the Victorian Royal Navy. The intervals of succession between these hegemons were typically periods of crisis. The interwar crisis was merely the latest such hiatus, in the interval between British and American hegemony.

What neither of these visions can encompass is the unprecedented pace, scope and violence of change actually experienced in world affairs from the late nineteenth century onwards. As contemporaries quickly realized, the intense 'world political' competition into which the great powers entered in the late nineteenth century was not a stable system with an ancient lineage.[46] It was legitimated neither by dynastic tradition nor by its inherent 'natural' stability. It was explosive, dangerous, all-consuming, attritional, and in 1914 no more than a few decades old.[47] Far from belonging in the lexicon of a venerable but corrupt 'ancien régime', the term 'imperialism' was a neologism that entered widespread use only around 1900. It encapsulated a novel perspective on a novel phenomenon – the remaking of the political structure of the entire globe under conditions of uninhibited military, economic, political and cultural competition. Both the Dark Continent and the hegemonic failure models are therefore based on a faulty premise. Modern global imperialism was a radical and novel force, not an old-world hangover. By the same token the problem of establishing a hegemonic world order 'after imperialism' was unprecedented. The scale of the problem of world order in its modern form had first crowded in on Britain in the last decades of the nineteenth century, as its far-flung imperial system faced challenges from the heartland of Europe, the Mediterranean, the Near East, the Indian subcontinent, the huge land mass of Russia, and Central Asia and East Asia. It was Britain's world system that had knit these arenas together, and brought their crises into global synchrony. Far from presiding triumphantly over this panorama, the scale of this challenge had forced Britain into a series of strategic improvisations. Threatened by the emergent powers of Germany and Japan, Britain had abandoned its offshore position and opted instead to commit itself to understandings in Europe and Asia, with France, Russia and Japan. Ultimately, in World War I the British-led Entente would prevail, but only by further intensifying its strategic entanglements and extending them around the world through the global reach of the British and French empires and across the Atlantic to the United States. The war thus bequeathed an unprecedented problem of global economic and political order, but no historical model of world hegemony with which to address it. From 1916 the British themselves would attempt feats of intervention, coordination and stabilization to which they had never aspired in the empire's Victorian heyday. Never was British imperial history more closely entwined with world history and vice versa, an entanglement that continued perforce into the post-war period. As we shall see, despite the limited resources at its disposal, Lloyd George's government in the post-war years played a quite unprecedented role as the pivot of European finance and diplomacy. It was also his downfall. The train of crises that reached their nadir in 1923 ended Lloyd George's tenure as Prime Minister and exposed for all to see the limits of Britain's hegemonic capacity. There was only one power, if any, that could fill this role – a new role, one that no nation had ever seriously attempted before – the United States.

When President Wilson travelled to Europe in December 1918 he took with him a team of geographers, historians, political scientists and economists to make sense of the new world map.[48] The spatial sweep of the disorder confronting the major powers in the wake of the war was vast. Throughout the length and breadth of Eurasia the war had created an unprecedented vacuum. Of the ancient empires, only China and Russia were to survive. The Soviet state was the first to recover. But the temptation to interpret the 'stand off' between Wilson and Lenin in 1918 as an anticipation of the Cold War is a further instance of the refusal to recognize the exceptional situation created by the war. The threat of Bolshevik revolution was certainly present in the minds of conservatives all over the world after 1918. But this was a fear of civil war and anarchic disorder and it was in large part a phantom menace. It was in no way comparable to the awesome military presence of Stalin's Red Army in 1945, or even the strategic heft of Tsarist Russia before 1914. Lenin's regime survived the revolution, defeat at the hands of Germany and civil war, but only by the skin of its teeth. Communism was throughout the 1920s fighting from the defensive. It is questionable whether the United States and the Soviet Union were on the same footing even in 1945. A generation earlier, to treat Wilson and Lenin as equivalent is to fail to acknowledge one of the truly defining features of the situation – the dramatic implosion of Russian power. In 1920 Russia appeared so weak that the Polish Republic, itself less than two years old, decided that this was the time to invade. The Red Army was strong enough to ward off that threat. But when the Soviets marched westwards they suffered a crushing defeat outside Warsaw. The contrast to the era of the Hitler–Stalin Pact and the Cold War could hardly be more stark.

Given the astonishing vacuum of power in Eurasia from Beijing to the Baltic, it is hardly surprising that the most aggressive exponents of imperialism in Japan, Germany, Britain and Italy sensed a heaven-sent opportunity for aggrandizement. The uninhibited ambitions of the arch-imperialists in Lloyd George's cabinet, or General Ludendorff in Germany, or Goto Shinpei in Japan, provide ample material for the Dark Continent narrative. But violent as their visions clearly were, we must be attentive to the nuance of their war-talk. A figure such as Ludendorff was under no illusion that his grand visions of the total redesign of Eurasia were expressions of traditional statecraft.[49] He justified the scale of his ambition precisely on the basis that the world was entering a new and radical phase, the ultimate or the penultimate phase in a final global struggle for power. Men like these were no exponents of any kind of 'ancien régime'. They were often highly critical of traditionalists who in the name of balance and legitimacy shrank from seizing the historic opportunity. Far from being exponents of the old world the most violent antagonists of the new liberal world order were themselves futuristic innovators. They were not, however, realists. The commonplace distinction between idealists and realists concedes too much to Wilson's opponents. Though Wilson may have been humiliated, the imperialists also found themselves on the back foot. Already during the war the problems inherent in any truly grandiose programme of expansion had become amply apparent. As we shall see, within weeks of its ratification in March 1918 the Treaty of Brest-Litovsk, the ultimate imperialist peace, was repudiated by its own creators who found themselves struggling to escape the contradictions of their own policy. Japanese imperialists raged impotently against the refusal of their government to take decisive steps to subordinate all of China. The most successful imperialists were the British, their main zone of expansion in the Middle East. But this was truly the exception that proves the rule. Amidst the rivalry of British and French imperial demands, the entire region was reduced to chaos and disorder. It was World War I and its aftermath that made of the Middle East the strategic albatross it has remained to this day.[50] On the better-established axes of British imperial power, towards the White Dominions, Ireland and India, the main line of policy was one of retreat, autonomy and Home Rule. It was a line pursued inconsistently and with considerable reluctance, but nevertheless it was unmistakable in its direction.

Whereas the familiar narrative of Wilsonian failure pictures the American President as caught up in the irrepressible aggression of old-war imperialism, the actual situation was that the former imperialists were of their own accord arriving at the conclusion that they must search for new strategies appropriate to a new era, after the age of imperialism.[51] A number of key figures came to embody this new *raison d'état*. Gustav Stresemann brought Germany into a cooperative relation with both the Entente powers and the United States. The British Foreign Secretary Austen Chamberlain, the eldest son of the Edwardian imperialist firebrand Joseph Chamberlain, shared a Nobel Peace Prize with Foreign Minister Stresemann for their tireless efforts toward a European settlement. The third to receive a Nobel Prize, for the Locarno Treaty, was Aristide Briand, the French Foreign Minister and ex-socialist for whom the 1928 Pact to Outlaw Aggressive War was named. Kijuro Shidehara, Japan's Foreign Minister, embodied the new approach to East Asian security. All of them orientated themselves towards the United States as the key to establishing a new order. But to identify this shift too closely with individual figures, however significant, is to miss the point. These individuals were often ambiguous exponents of transformation, torn between their personal attachment to older modes of policy-making and what they perceived to be the imperatives of a new age. What made the likes of Churchill confident that the new order was robust and what made Hitler and Trotsky so despondent was precisely that it seemed to be founded on foundations more solid than the force of individual personality.

It is tempting to identify this new atmosphere of the 1920s with 'civil society' and the plethora of internationalist and pacific NGOs that sprang up in the wake of World War I.[52] However, the tendency to identify innovative moral entrepreneurship with international peace societies, cosmopolitan congresses of experts, the passionate solidarity of the international women's movement, or the far-flung activities of anti-colonial activists, backhandedly reinstates the well-worn stereotypes about the recalcitrant persistence of imperialist impulses at the heart of power. Conversely, the powerlessness of the peace movement licenses the cynical realists in their hard-bitten insistence that, in the final analysis, it is only power that counts. The wager of this book is different. It seeks to locate a dramatic shift in the calculus of power, not external to, but within the government machinery itself, in the interaction between military force, economics and diplomacy. As we shall see, this was most obviously the case in France, the most maligned of the 'old world powers'. After 1916, rather than remaining mired in ancient grudges, we will see that Paris's overriding aim was to forge a novel, Western-orientated Atlantic alliance with Britain and the United States. It would thus free itself from the odious association with Tsarist autocracy on which it had relied since the 1890s for a dubious promise of security. It would bring France's foreign policy into line with its Republican constitution. This search for an Atlantic alliance was the novel preoccupation of French policy that after 1917 unified individuals as far apart as Georges Clemenceau and Raymond Poincaré.

In Germany the scene is dominated by the figure of Gustav Stresemann, the great statesman of the Weimar Republic's stabilization period. And from the climactic Ruhr crisis of 1923 onwards, Stresemann was no doubt crucial to anchoring Germany's Western orientation.[53] But, as a nationalist of a Bismarckian stripe, he was a late and hard-won convert to the new international politics. The political force that sustained every single one of his famous initiatives was a broad-based parliamentary coalition with which Stresemann in its inception had been bitterly at odds. The three members of this coalition, the Social Democrats, Christian Democrats and progressive Liberals, were the leading democratic forces of the pre-war Reichstag. All three shared the distinction of having been, at one time, bitter foes of Bismarck. What brought them together in June 1917 under the leadership of Matthias Erzberger, the populist Christian Democrat, were the disastrous consequences of the U-boat campaign against the United States. As we shall see, the first test of their new policy came as early as the winter of 1917–18. When Lenin sued for peace, the Reichstag coalition sought as best they could to deflect the heedless expansionism of Ludendorff and to shape what they hoped would be a legitimate and therefore sustainable hegemony in the East. The notorious Treaty of Brest-Litovsk will emerge from this book as comparable to Versailles, not in its vindictiveness, but in the sense that it too was a 'good peace gone bad'. What marked the argument within Germany over the victorious peace of Brest-Litovsk as a significant overture to the new era of international politics, is the fact that it was always as much about the domestic order of Germany as about foreign affairs. It was the refusal of the Kaiser's regime either to make good on promises of domestic reform or to craft a viable new diplomacy that prepared the ground for the revolutionary changes of the autumn of 1918. When Germany faced defeat in the West, it was, as we shall see, the Reichstag majority that dared, not once, but three times between November 1918 and September 1923 to wager the future of their country on subordination to the Western Powers. From 1949 down to the present the Reichstag majority's lineal descendants, the CDU, SPD and FDP, remain the mainstays both of democracy in the Federal Republic and of their country's commitment to the European project.

In this nexus between domestic and foreign policy, and in the choice between radical insurgency and compliance, there are remarkable parallels in the early twentieth century between Germany's situation and that of Japan. Threatened in the 1850s by outright subordination to foreign power, facing Russia, Britain, China and the United States as potential antagonists, one Japanese response was to seize the initiative and to embark on a programme of domestic reform and external aggression. It was this course, pursued with great effectiveness and daring, that earned for Japan the sobriquet of the 'Prussia of the East'. But what is too easily forgotten is that this was always counterbalanced by another tendency: the pursuit of security through imitation, alliance and cooperation, Japan's tradition of new, Kasumigaseki diplomacy.[54] This was achieved first through the partnership with Britain in 1902 and then through a strategic modus vivendi with the United States. Simultaneously, however, Japan was undergoing domestic political change. The alignment between democratization and a peaceful foreign policy was no more simple in Japan than it was anywhere else. But during and after World War I, Japan's emerging system of multi-party parliamentary politics acted as a substantial check on the military leadership. It was the importance of this linkage that in turn raised the stakes. By the late 1920s, those calling for a foreign policy of confrontation were also demanding a domestic revolution. It was in the 1920s in Taisho-era Japan that the bipolar quality of interwar politics was most manifest. So long as the Western Powers could hold the ring in the world economy and secure peace in East Asia, it was the Japanese liberals who held the upper hand. If that military, economic and political framework was to come apart, it would be the advocates of imperialist aggression who would seize their opportunity.

The upshot of this reinterpretation is that contrary to the Dark Continent narrative, the violence of the Great War was resolved in the first instance not into the Cold War dualism of rival American and Soviet projects, nor into the no less anachronistic vision of a three-way contest between American democracy, fascism and Communism. What the war gave rise to was a multisided, polycentric search for strategies of pacification and appeasement. And in that quest the calculations of all the great powers pivoted on one key factor, the United States. It was this conformism that filled Hitler and Trotsky with such gloom. Both of them hoped that the British Empire might emerge as a challenger to the United States. Trotsky foresaw a new inter-imperialist war.[55] Hitler already in *Mein Kampf* had made clear his desire for an Anglo-German alliance against America and the dark forces of the world Jewish conspiracy.[56] But despite much bluster from the Tory governments of the 1920s, there was little prospect of an Anglo-American confrontation. In a strategic concession of extraordinary significance, Britain peacefully ceded primacy to the United States. The opening of British democracy to government by the Labour Party only reinforced this impulse. Both the Labour cabinets over which Ramsay MacDonald presided, in 1924 and 1929–31, were resolutely Atlanticist in orientation.

And yet despite this general conformity, the insurgents were to get their chance, which brings us back to the essential question posed by the hegemonic crisis historians. Why did the Western Powers lose their grip in such spectacular fashion? When all is said and done, the answer must be sought in the failure of the United States to cooperate with the efforts of the French, British, Germans and the Japanese to stabilize a viable world economy and to establish new institutions of collective security. A joint solution to these twin problems of economics and security was clearly necessary to escape the impasse of the age of imperialist rivalry. Given the violence they had already experienced and the risk of even greater future devastation, France, Germany, Japan and Britain could all see this. But what was no less obvious was that only the US could anchor such a new order. Stressing American responsibility in this way does not mean a return to a simplistic story of American isolationism, but it does mean that the finger of enquiry must be pointed insistently back at the United States.[57] How is America's reluctance to face the challenges posed by the aftermath of World War I to be explained? This is the point at which the synthesis of the 'Dark Continent' and hegemonic failure interpretations must be completed. The path to a true synthesis lies not only in recognizing that the problems of global leadership faced by the United States after World War I were radically new and that the other powers too were motivated to search for a new order beyond imperialism. The third key point to establish is that America's own entry into modernity, presumed in such a simple way by most accounts of twentieth-century international politics, was every bit as violent, unsettling and ambiguous as that of any of the other states in the world system. Indeed, given the underlying fissures within a formerly colonial society, originating in the triangular Atlantic slave trade, expanded by means of the violent appropriation of the West, peopled by a mass migration from Europe, often under traumatic circumstances, and then kept in perpetual motion by the surging force of capitalist development, America's problems with modernity were profound.

Out of the effort to come to terms with this wrenching nineteenth-century experience emerged an ideology that was common to both sides of the American party divide, namely exceptionalism.[58] In an age of unabashed nationalism, it was not Americans' belief in the exceptional destiny of their nation that was the issue. No self-respecting nineteenth-century nation was without its sense of providential mission. But what was remarkable in the wake of World War I was the degree to which American exceptionalism emerged strengthened and more vocal than ever, precisely at the moment when all the other major states of the world were coming to acknowledge their condition as one of interdependence and relativity. What we see, if we look closely at the rhetoric of Wilson and other American statesmen of the period, is that the 'primary source of Progressive internationalism . . . was nationalism itself'.[59] It was their sense of America's God-given, exemplary role that they sought to impose on the world. When an American sense of providential purpose was married to massive power, as it was to be after 1945, it became a truly transformative force. In 1918 the basic elements of that power were already there, but they were not articulated by the Wilson administration or its successors. The question thus returns in a new form. Why was the exceptionalist ideology of the early twentieth century not backed up by an effective grand strategy?

What we are pushed towards is a conclusion that is hauntingly reminiscent of a question that still faces us today. It is commonplace, particularly in European histories, to narrate the early twentieth century as an eruption of American modernity onto a world stage.[60] But novelty and dynamism existed side by side, this book will insist, with a deep and abiding conservatism.[61] In the face of truly radical change,

Americans clung to a constitution that by the late nineteenth century was already the oldest Republican edifice in operation. This, as its many domestic critics pointed out, was in many ways ill-adjusted to the demands of the modern world. For all the national consolidation since the Civil War, for all the country's economic potential, in the early twentieth century the federal government of the United States was a vestigial thing, certainly by comparison to the 'big government' that would act so effectively as the anchor of global hegemony after 1945.[62] Building a more effective state machinery for America was a task that progressives of all political stripes had set for themselves in the wake of the Civil War. Their urgency was only reinforced by the disturbing populist upsurge that followed the economic crisis of the 1890s.[63] Something had to be done to insulate Washington from the alarming rise in militancy that threatened not only the domestic order but America's international standing. This was one of the principal missions both of Wilson's administration and its Republican predecessors early in the twentieth century.[64] But whereas Teddy Roosevelt and his ilk saw military power and war as powerful vectors of progressive state construction, Wilson resisted this well-trodden, 'old world' path. The peace policy that he pursued up to the spring of 1917 was a desperate effort to insulate his domestic reform programme from the violent political passions and the wrenching social and economic dislocation of the war. It was in vain. The calamitous conclusion to Wilson's second term in 1919–21 saw the coming apart of this first great twentieth-century effort to remake American federal government. The result was not only to unhinge the Versailles peace treaty but to precipitate a truly spectacular economic shock – the worldwide depression of 1920, perhaps the most underrated event in the history of the twentieth century.

If we bear these structural features of America's constitution and political economy in mind, then the ideology of exceptionalism can be seen in a more charitable light. For all its celebration of the exceptional virtue and providential importance of American history, it carried with it a Burkean wisdom, a well-founded understanding on the part of the American political class of the fundamental mismatch between the unprecedented international challenges of the early twentieth century and the peculiarly constrained capacities of the state over which they presided. Exceptionalist ideology carried with it a memory of how recently the country had been torn apart by civil war, how heterogeneous was its ethnic and cultural make-up, and how easily the inherent weaknesses of a republican constitution might degenerate into stalemate or full-blown crisis. Behind the desire to keep a distance from the violent forces unleashed in Europe and Asia, there lay a recognition of the limits of what the American polity, despite its fabulous wealth, was actually capable of.[65] For all their forward-looking vision, progressives both of Wilson's and Hoover's generation were fundamentally committed not to a radical overcoming of these limitations, but to preserving the continuity of American history and reconciling it with the new national order that had begun to emerge in the wake of the Civil War. This then is the central irony of the early twentieth century. At the hub of the rapidly evolving, American-centred world system there was a polity wedded to a conservative vision of its own future. Not for nothing did Wilson describe his goal in defensive terms, as one of making the world safe for democracy. Not for nothing was 'normalcy' the defining slogan of the 1920s. The pressure this exerted on all those who sought to contribute to the project of 'world organization' will be the red thread that runs through this book. It connects the moment in January 1917 when Wilson sought to end the most calamitous war ever fought with a peace without victory, to the depths of the Great Depression fourteen years later, when the all-consuming crisis of the early twentieth century claimed its last victim – the United States.

The tumultuous, blood-soaked events recorded in these pages turned the proud national histories of the nineteenth century on their head. Death and destruction broke the heart of every optimistic Victorian philosophy of history – liberal, conservative, nationalist, and Marxist as well. But what was one to make of this catastrophe? For some it betokened the end of all meaning in history, the collapse of any idea of progress. This could be taken fatalistically, or as a licence for spontaneous action of the wildest kind. Others drew more sober conclusions. There was development – perhaps even progress, for all its ambiguity – but it was more complex, more violent than anyone had expected. Instead of the neat stage theories projected by nineteenth-century theorists, history took the form of what Trotsky would call 'uneven and combined development', a loosely articulated web of events, actors and processes developing at different speeds, whose individual courses were interconnected in labyrinthine ways.[66] 'Uneven and combined development' is not an elegant phrase. But it well encapsulates the history we tell here, both of international relations and of interconnected national political development, stretching around the northern hemisphere from the United States to China by way of Eurasia. For Trotsky, it defined a method both of historical analysis and of political action. It expressed his dogged belief that whilst history offered no guarantees, it was not without logic. Success depended on sharpening one's historical intelligence so as to recognize and seize unique moments of opportunity. For Lenin, similarly, a key task of the revolutionary theorist was to identify and attack the weakest links in the 'chain' of imperialist powers.[67]

Taking the side, not of the revolutionaries, but of the governments, the political scientist Stanley Hoffmann, writing in the 1960s, offered a rather more graphic image of 'uneven and combined development'. He described the powers, great and small, as members of a 'chain gang', a lurching, shackled-together collective.[68] The prisoners were differently proportioned. Some were more violent than others. Some were single-minded. Others exhibited multiple personalities. They struggled with themselves and with each other. They could seek to dominate the entire chain, or to cooperate. As far as the chain would give, they could enjoy some degree of autonomy, but in the end they were locked together. Whichever of these images we adopt, they have the same implication. Such an interconnected, dynamic system can be understood only by studying the entire system and by retracing its movements over time. To understand its development, we must narrate it. That is the task of this book.

ONE

The Eurasian Crisis

I

War in the Balance

Viewed from the trench lines of the Western Front, the Great War could appear static – a struggle waged over a handful of miles at the cost of hundreds of thousands of lives. But this perspective is deceiving.[1] On the Eastern Front and in the war against the Ottoman Empire the battle-lines were fluid. In the West, though the front line barely moved, this stasis was the result of massive forces locked in a precarious balance. From one month to the next the initiative shifted from one side to other. As 1916 began, the Entente were planning to crush the Central Powers between a concentric series of assaults delivered in sequence by the French, British, Italian and Russian armies. It was in anticipation of this onslaught that the Germans on 21 February seized the initiative in launching its assault on Verdun. By attacking a key point in the French fortress chain they would bleed the Entente to death. The result was a life-and-death struggle which by the early summer had sucked in more than 70 per cent of the French Army and threatened to turn the Entente's concentric strategy into little more than a series of ad hoc relief operations. It was to seize back the initiative that at the end of May 1916 the British agreed to bring forward their first major land offensive of the war, on the Somme.

As the combatants strained to the limit, their diplomats worked urgently to drag more countries into the maelstrom. In 1914 Austria and Germany had lured Bulgaria and the Ottoman Empire onto their side. In 1915 Italy came in on the side of the Entente. Japan had joined the cause in 1914, snapping up Germany's Chinese concessions in Shandong. By the end of 1916 Britain and France were luring the Japanese navy out of the Pacific to do escort duty against Austrian and German submarines in the eastern Mediterranean. Vast amounts of cash and every conceivable means of diplomatic pressure were brought to bear on the last remaining central European neutral, Romania. If it could be flipped into the Entente camp it would pose a mortal threat to the soft underbelly of the Austro-Hungarian monarchy. But there was only one power in 1916 that could truly transform the balance of the war, the United States. Whether in economic, military or political terms, its stance was decisive. It was only in 1893 that Britain had seen fit to upgrade its legation in the American capital to the status of a full embassy. Now, less than a generation later, European history seemed to hang on the posture that Washington would adopt towards the war.

I

The success of the Entente's strategy depended on combining a devastating series of concentric military offensives with the slow economic strangulation of the Central Powers. Before the war the British Admiralty had prepared plans not only for a naval blockade but also for an annihilating financial boycott of all central European trade. But, in August 1914, in the face of fierce protests from America, they shrank from the rigorous enforcement of these plans.[2] The result was an uneasy standoff. Britain and France compromised the effectiveness of their ultimate maritime weapon. But the blockade even in its partial form was hugely unpopular in the United States. The American navy regarded the British blockade as 'untenable under any law or custom of maritime war hitherto known ...'[3] But even more politically charged was the German response. In an effort to turn the tables on the Entente, in February 1915 the Kriegsmarine deployed its U-boats in the first all-out assault on transatlantic shipping. They managed to sink almost two ships per day and an average of 100,000 tons per month. But the shipping resources of Britain were deep and if continued for any period of time this assault seemed bound to force America into the war. The *Lusitania* in May and the *Arabic* in August 1915 were only the best-known casualties. Anxious to avoid further escalation, at the end of August the Kaiser's civilian government retreated. With the backing of the Catholic Centre Party, the progressive Liberals and the Social Democrats, Chancellor Bethmann Hollweg issued orders to restrict the U-boat campaign. Just as the Entente could not properly enforce its blockade for fear of antagonizing America, Germany's counterstroke miscarried for the same reason. Instead, in the spring of 1916, the German navy tried to break the maritime deadlock by luring the British Grand Fleet into a North Sea trap. On 31 May 1916 in the battle of Jutland, 33 British and 27 German capital ships clashed in the largest naval confrontation of the war. The result was inconclusive. The fleets slunk back to base, henceforth to exert their influence from offstage as massive, silent reserves of naval power.

In the summer of 1916, as the Entente struggled to regain the initiative on the Western Front, the politics of the Atlantic blockade remained unresolved. When the French and British sought to tighten their grip by blacklisting American firms charged with 'trading with the enemy', President Wilson could barely contain his anger.[4] It was 'the last straw', Wilson confessed to his closest advisor, the urbane Texan Colonel House, 'I am, I must admit, about at the end of my patience with Great Britain and the allies.'[5] Nor did Wilson content himself with expostulation. The American Army might be small, but even in 1914 the American fleet was a force to be reckoned with. It was the fourth largest in the world and unlike the Japanese or the German navies it actually had a proud memory of having clashed with the Royal Navy in 1812. To the followers of Admiral Mahan, America's great theorist of naval power from the gilded age, the war presented a priceless opportunity to outbuild the Europeans and to establish undisputed control over the oceanic waterways. In February 1916 President Wilson fell in with their demands, launching a campaign to gain congressional approval for the construction of what he boasted would be 'incomparably the greatest navy in the world'.[6] Six months later, on 29 August 1916, Wilson signed into law the most dramatic naval expansion plan in American history, appropriating almost $500 million over three years to build 157 new vessels, including 16 capital ships. Less dramatic, but no less consequential in the long run, was the establishment in June 1916 of the Emergency Fleet Corporation to oversee the construction of a merchant shipping fleet to rival that of Britain.[7]

When in September 1916 Colonel House and Wilson discussed the likely impact of America's naval expansion on Anglo-American relations, Wilson's view was blunt: 'let us build a navy bigger than hers and do what we please'.[8] The reason that threat was so ominous for Britain was that, once roused, the United States, unlike Imperial Germany or

Japan, clearly had the means to make good on it. Within five years America would be acknowledged as Britain's naval equal. From the British point of view, in 1916 the war thus took on a fundamentally new aspect. As the twentieth century began, containing Japan, Russia and Germany had been the chief priorities of imperial strategy. Since August 1914 all that counted was the defeat of Imperial Germany and its allies. In 1916, Wilson's evident desire to build an American naval force equal to that of Britain raised an alarming new prospect. Even at the best of times a challenge by the United States would have been intimidating. Given the demands of the Great War it was a nightmarish prospect. Nor were America's naval ambitions the only fundamental challenge facing the Europeans in 1916.[9] The rising economic power of America had been evident from the 1890s, but it was the Entente's battle with the Central Powers that abruptly shifted the centre of global financial leadership across the Atlantic.[10] In so doing, it redefined not only the locus of financial leadership, but what that leadership actually meant.

All the main European combatants began the war with what were by modern standards remarkably strong financial balance sheets, solid public finances and large portfolios of foreign investments. In 1914 fully a third of British wealth was held in private overseas investment. As the war began, the mobilization of these domestic and imperial resources was compounded by an immense transatlantic financing operation. This involved all the governments of Europe, but above all the British in a new form of international action. Before 1914, in the era of Edwardian high finance, London's leading role was generally acknowledged. But international finance was a private affair. The conductor of the gold standard orchestra, the Bank of England, was not an official agency but a private corporation. If the British state was present in international finance, its influence was subtle and indirect. The UK Treasury remained in the background. Under the extraordinary pressures of the war, these invisible and informal networks of money and influence were quite abruptly solidified into a claim to hegemony of a far more concrete and overtly political kind. From October 1914 the British and French governments put the weight of hundreds of millions of pounds of government loans behind the 'Russian steam roller' that was to crush the Central Powers from the east.[11] Following the Boulogne agreement of August 1915, the gold reserves of all three major Entente Powers were pooled and used to underwrite the value of sterling and the franc in New York.[12] Britain and France in turn assumed responsibility for negotiating loans on behalf of the entire Entente. By August 1916, in the wake of the terrible cost of the Verdun battle, France's credit had sunk to such a low ebb that it fell to London to underwrite the entire New York operation.[13] A new network of political credit had been created in Europe with London at its centre. But this was only one leg of the operation.

In accounting terms the financing of the Entente's war effort involved an enormous reshuffling of national assets and liabilities.[14] To provide collateral, the UK Treasury organized a forced purchase scheme for private holdings of first-class North American and Latin American securities, which were exchanged for domestic UK government bonds. The foreign assets, once in the hands of the UK Treasury, were used to provide security for billions of dollars' worth of Entente borrowing from Wall Street. The liabilities that the UK Treasury incurred in America were counterbalanced in Britain's national balance sheet by vast new claims on the governments of Russia and France. But to imagine this gigantic mobilization as the effortless redirection of an existing network underplays the historic significance of the shift and the extreme precariousness of the financial architecture that emerged. After 1915, the Entente's war borrowing upended the political geometry of Edwardian finance.

Before the war billions had been lent by private lenders in London and Paris, the rich core of Imperial Europe, to private and public borrowers in peripheral nations.[15] As of 1915, not only had the source of lending shifted to Wall Street, it was no longer railways in Russia or diamond prospectors in South Africa queuing up for credit. The most powerful states of Europe were now borrowing from private citizens in the United States and anyone else who would provide credit. Lending of this kind, by private investors in one rich country to the governments of other rich developed countries, in a currency not controlled by the government borrower, was unlike anything seen in the heyday of late Victorian globalization. As the hyperinflations after World War I were to demonstrate, a government that had borrowed in its own currency could simply print its way out of debt. A flood of new banknotes would wipe out the real value of the war debt. The same was not true if Britain or France borrowed in dollars from Wall Street. The most powerful states in Europe became dependent on foreign creditors. Those creditors in turn extended their confidence to the Entente. By the end of 1916, American investors had wagered two billion dollars on an Entente victory. The vehicle for this transatlantic operation, once London took charge in 1915, was a single private bank, the dominant Wall Street house of J. P. Morgan, which had deep historic ties to the City of London.[16] This was a business operation for sure. But it was coupled on the part of Morgan with an unabashedly anti-German, pro-Entente stance and a backing within the United States for President Wilson's loudest critics, the interventionist forces within the Republican Party. The result was a quite unprecedented international combination of public and private power. In the course of the gigantic Somme offensive over the summer of 1916, J. P. Morgan spent more than a billion dollars in America on behalf of the British government, no less than 45 per cent of British war spending in those crucial months.[17] In 1916 the bank's purchasing office was responsible for Entente procurement contracts valued in excess of the entire export trade of the United States in the years before the war. Through the private business contacts of J. P. Morgan, supported by the business and political elite of the American Northeast, the Entente was carrying out a mobilization of a large part of the US economy, entirely without the say-so of the Wilson administration. Potentially, the Entente's dependence on loans from America gave the American President huge leverage over their war effort. But would Wilson actually be able to exercise that power? Was Wall Street too independent? Did the Federal government have the means to control the activities of J. P. Morgan?

In 1916 the question of war finance and America's relations with the Entente became embroiled in the debate that had been raging for more than a generation over the governance of American capitalism. In 1912, forty years after it had recommitted itself to the gold standard in the aftermath of the Civil War, the United States had still lacked a counterpart to the Bank of England, the Bank of France or the Reichsbank.[18] Wall Street had long lobbied for the establishment of a central bank to act as a lender of last resort. But banking interests were far from happy when in 1913 Wilson signed into existence the Federal Reserve Board. For the tastes of the Wall Street interests, notably J. P. Morgan, Wilson's Fed was far too politicized.[19] It was not a truly 'independent' institution on the model of the privately owned Bank of England. In 1914, as war broke out in Europe, the new system had survived its first test. The Fed and the Treasury intervened to prevent the closure of the European financial markets from causing a collapse on Wall Street.[20] Between 1915 and 1916 the American economy was driven upwards on a vast export-led industrial boom. To meet the needs of the European war, the factory towns of the Northeast and the Great Lakes were sucking in labour and capital pell-mell from all across the United States. But that only increased the pressure on Wilson. If the boom was allowed to proceed unchecked, America's investment in the Entente war effort would soon become too big to be allowed to fail. The American government would in fact lose the freedom of manoeuvre that promised to give it such power in 1916.

Might the Entente for its part have done better to rely rather less on the resources of the United States? Germany after all fought the war without the benefit of such largesse.[21] But that comparison demonstrates precisely what the importance of American imports actually was (Table 1). After the draining battles at Verdun and on the Somme in the summer of 1916, Germany remained on the defensive on the Western Front for almost two years. The Central Powers limited themselves to less expensive operations on the Eastern and Italian fronts. Meanwhile, the blockade took a heavy toll on their civilian populations. From the winter of 1916–17 the city dwellers of Germany and Austria were slowly starving. Ensuring the supply of food and coal to the home front was not an incidental consideration in World War I, it was an essential factor in deciding the eventual outcome.[22] Economic pressure took time to force the issue, but in the end its influence was decisive. When the Germans launched their last great offensive in the spring of 1918, a large

Table 1. What the Dollars Bought: The Share of Vital War
Materials Purchased by the UK Abroad, 1914–18 (%)

	shell cases	aeroengines	grain	oil
1914	0	28	65	91
1915	49	42	67	92
1916	55	26	67	94
1917	33	29	62	95
1918	22	30	45	97

part of the Kaiser's army was too hungry to sustain the offensive for long. By contrast, the relentless offensive energy of the Entente in 1917 – the French offensive in Champagne in April, the Kerensky offensive in the East in July, the British assault in Flanders in July – and the final drive in the summer and autumn of 1918, would have been impossible both in military and political terms without North American backing. In London, at least until the end of 1916, there were voices calling for Britain to escape dependence on American loans. But they were by the same token calling for a negotiated peace. They were overridden by the advent of the Lloyd George coalition government in December 1916 committed to delivering a 'knock-out blow'. What no one seriously contemplated was continuing the war at full force without relying on supplies and credit from the United States. From 1916, once the Allies had taken up their first billion dollars in credit in their first major effort to break the Central Powers through concentric assaults, the momentum was cumulative. The assumption behind all subsequent offensive planning was that it would be sustained by substantial transatlantic supplies. And this then reinforced the dependence. As the billions piled up, maintaining payments on the outstanding debts, avoiding the humiliation of a default, became overriding preoccupations both during the war itself and even more in its aftermath.

II

In any case, the transatlantic struggle over the future course of the war was never merely economic or military. It was always eminently political. It was on politics that the willingness to continue the war depended and this too was a transatlantic question. But here the contours of the argument were far less clear-cut than they were with regard to economic and naval power. The image that we have of the relationship between American and European politics in the early twentieth century is profoundly shaped by the later experience of World War II. In 1945 well-fed, self-confident GIs appeared in Europe amidst the ruins of war and dictatorship as heralds both of prosperity and democracy. But we should be careful in projecting this identification of America with an alluring synthesis of capitalist prosperity and democracy too far back into the early twentieth century. The speed with which the United States claimed pre-eminent political leadership was as sudden as the emergence of its naval and financial power. It was a product of the Great War itself.

Not surprisingly, against the backdrop of its terrible civil war, America's democratic experiment had attracted mixed reviews in the half century that separated 1865 from the outbreak of 1914.[23] The newly unified Italy and Germany did not look to America for constitutional inspiration. Both had their own home-grown tradition of constitutionalism. Italy's liberals modelled themselves on Britain. In the 1880s the new Japanese constitution was modelled on a blend of European influences.[24] During the heyday of Gladstone and Disraeli, even in the United States the first generation of political scientists, the young Woodrow Wilson amongst them, looked across the Atlantic to the Westminster model.[25] Of course, the Union side had its own heroic narrative with Abraham Lincoln as its great tribune. But it was only after the shock of the Civil War had dissipated that a fresh generation of American intellectuals could affirm a new, reconciled national narrative. As the western frontier closed, the continent was unified. The Spanish-American War of 1898 and America's conquest of the Philippines in 1902 added swagger. The industrial dynamism of the United States was unprecedented. Its agricultural exports brought abundance to the world. But, among the progressive reformers of the gilded age, America's self-image was ambiguous. America was a byword for urban graft, mismanagement and greed-fuelled politics, as much as for growth, production and profit. In search of models of modern government, it was to the cities of Imperial Germany that American experts made pilgrimage, not the other way around.[26] Looking back from 1901, Woodrow Wilson himself remarked that though 'the nineteenth century' had been 'above all others a century of democracy ... the world' was 'no more convinced of the benefits of democracy as a form of government at its end than it was at its beginning ...' The stability of democratic republics was still in question. Though the commonwealths 'sprung from England' had the best track record, Wilson himself admitted that the 'the history of the United States ... has not been accepted as establishing their tendency to make government just and liberal and pure'.[27] Americans themselves had reason to trust in their own system, but as far as the wider world was concerned, they still had much to prove.

Nor should we assume that with the outbreak of war the tables were immediately turned. Until the death toll became unbearable, the European combatants saw the great mobilization of August 1914 as a miraculous vindication of their nation-building efforts.[28] None of the combatants were full-blown democracies in a late twentieth-century sense, but nor were they ancien régime monarchies or totalitarian dictatorships. The war was sustained if not by patriotic ecstasy then at least by a remarkably extended consensus. Britain, France, Italy, Japan, Germany and Bulgaria all fought the war with their parliaments in session. The Austrian parliament reopened in Vienna in 1917. Even in Russia the early patriotic enthusiasm of 1914 brought a revival of the Duma. On both sides of the front line, soldiers were above all motivated to defend the systems of rights, property and national identity in which they felt themselves to have a profound stake. The French fought to defend the Republic against a hereditary foe. The British volunteered to do their bit to defend international civilization and put down the German menace. The Germans and Austrians fought to defend themselves against French resentment, Italian treachery, the overbearing demands of British imperialism and the worst menace of all, Tsarist Russia. Though open calls for mutiny were suppressed and though strikers could find themselves incarcerated or drafted to dangerous sectors of the front, open talk of negotiated peace was commonplace in a way that would have been unthinkable on either side in the latter stages of World War II.

When the British government was reconstructed in December 1916 under Prime Minister Lloyd George, it was precisely so as to reassert the ultimate goal of delivering a 'knock-out blow' to Germany, against increasingly vocal calls for a compromise peace. Most of the important cabinet seats were claimed by the Tories, but the Prime Minister himself was a liberal radical with a sure instinct for the popular mood. Already in May 1915 his predecessor Asquith had introduced trade unionists into the British cabinet. Early twentieth-century European politics was more inclusive than it is often given credit for. In France, the socialists were an essential part of the Union Sacrée, the cross-party alliance that saw the Republic through the first two years of the war. Even in Germany, though the government remained in the hands of the Kaiser's appointees, the Social Democrats were the largest party in the Reichstag. Chancellor Bethmann Hollweg consulted with them routinely after August 1914. When in the autumn of 1916 generals Hindenburg and Ludendorff put the war economy into top gear, they relied on the co-opted support of the trade unions.

The reaction of Americans of Teddy Roosevelt's stripe to this spectacle of European mobilization was not one of superiority, but of awed admiration.[29] As Roosevelt put it in January 1915, the war might be 'terrible and evil, but it is also grand and noble'. Americans should 'assume' no 'attitude of superior virtue'. Nor should they expect Europeans to 'regard' them as 'having set a spiritual example ... by sitting idle, uttering cheap platitudes, and picking up their trade, whilst they had poured out their blood like water in support of ideals in which, with all their hearts and souls, they believe'.[30] For Roosevelt, if America was to vindicate its emergence as a legitimate great power, it must prove itself in the same struggle, by throwing its weight behind the Entente. But to Roosevelt's immense frustration, the pro-war forces were a minority in America even after the sinking of the *Lusitania* in May 1915. Millions of German-Americans preferred neutrality, as did many Irish Americans. Jewish Americans were hard pressed not to celebrate the advances of the Imperial German Army into Russian Poland in 1915, where they brought welcome relief from Tsarist anti-Semitism. Neither the American labour movement nor the remnants of the agrarian populist movement, which had assembled around Wilson's bid for the presidency in 1912, were pro-war. Wilson's first Secretary of State was none other than William Jennings Bryan, the evangelical fundamentalist, pacifist and anti-gold standard radical of the 1890s. He was profoundly suspicious of Wall Street and its connections to European imperialism. As the clock ticked towards the July crisis of 1914, Bryan toured Europe signing a series of mediation treaties that would avoid the possibility of American involvement in a war. When war broke out he advocated a truly comprehensive boycott of private lending to either side. Wilson overrode this proposal and in June 1915, following the sinking of the *Lusitania*, Bryan resigned in protest when Wilson threatened Germany with hostilities if it did not cease U-boat attacks. But Wilson himself was anything but a pro-interventionist.

Before he was hailed as a world-famous liberal internationalist, Woodrow Wilson rose to prominence as one of the great bards of American national history.[31] As a professor at Princeton University and the author of best-selling popular histories, he had helped to craft for a nation still reeling from the Civil War a reconciled vision of its violent past. One of Wilson's earliest memories of childhood in Virginia was of hearing the news of Lincoln's election and the rumours of a coming civil war. Growing up in Augusta, Georgia, in the 1860s – what he would describe to Lloyd George at Versailles as a 'conquered and devastated country' – he experienced from the side of the vanquished the bitter consequences of a just war, fought to its ultimate conclusion.[32] It left him deeply suspicious of any crusading rhetoric. Nor was it just the Civil War that scarred Wilson. The peace that followed was, if anything, even more traumatic. Throughout his life he would denounce the Reconstruction era that followed, the effort by the North to impose a new order on the South that enfranchised the freed black population.[33] In Wilson's view it had taken America more than a generation to recover. Only in the 1890s had something like reconciliation been achieved.

For Wilson as for Roosevelt the war was a test of America's new self-confidence and strength. But whereas Roosevelt wanted to prove the manhood of the US, for Wilson the war raging in Europe challenged his nation's moral equilibrium and self-restraint. By America's refusal to become embroiled in the war, its democracy would confirm the nation's new maturity and immunity to the inflammatory wartime rhetoric that had done such harm fifty years earlier. But this insistence on self-restraint should not be misunderstood for modesty. Whereas interventionists of Roosevelt's ilk aspired merely to equality – to have America counted as a fully fledged great power – Wilson's goal was absolute pre-eminence. Nor was this a vision that scorned 'hard power'. Wilson had thrilled in 1898 to the excitement of the Spanish-American War. His naval expansion programme and his assertion of America's grip on the Caribbean approaches was more aggressive than that of any predecessor. In order to secure the Panama canal, Wilson in 1915 and 1916 did not hesitate to order the occupation of the Dominican Republic and Haiti, and intervention in Mexico.[34] But thanks to its God-given natural endowments, America had no need of extensive territorial conquests. Its economic needs had been formulated at the turn of the century by the 'Open Door' policy. The US had no need of territorial domination, but its goods and capital must be free to move around the world and across the boundaries of any empire. Meanwhile, from behind an impenetrable naval shield it would project an irresistible beam of moral and political influence.

For Wilson the war was a sign of 'God's providence' that had brought the United States 'an opportunity such as has seldom been vouchsafed any nation, the opportunity to counsel and obtain peace in the world . . .' – on its own terms. A peace accord on American terms would permanently establish the 'greatness' of the United States as 'the true champions of peace and of concord'.[35] Twice, in 1915 and 1916, Colonel House was despatched to tour the capitals of Europe to offer mediation, but neither side was interested. On 27 May 1916, only weeks before the British began their Wall Street-financed offensive on the Somme, Wilson spelled out his vision of a new order in a speech to a gathering of the League to Enforce Peace, at the New Willard Hotel in Washington.[36] Agreeing with the Republican internationalists who hosted the event, Wilson pronounced himself willing to see the United States join any 'feasible association of nations' that would underwrite a future peace. As twin foundations of that new order, he called for freedom of the seas and limitations of armaments. But what differentiated Wilson from most of his Republican rivals was that he coupled this vision of America's role in a new world order with an explicit refusal to take sides in the current war. To do so would be to forfeit America's claim to absolute pre-eminence. With the war's 'causes and its objects', Wilson announced, America was not concerned.[37] In public he was content to remark simply that the war's origins were 'deeper' and more 'obscure'.[38] In private conversation with his ambassador in Britain, Walter Hines Page, Wilson was blunter. The Kaiser's U-boats were an outrage. But British 'navalism' was no lesser evil and posed a far greater strategic challenge for the United States. The atrocious war was, Wilson believed, not a liberal crusade against German aggression, but a 'quarrel to settle economic rivalries between Germany and England'. According to Page's diary, in August 1916 Wilson 'spoke of England's having the earth and of Germany wanting it'.[39]

Even if 1916 had not been an election year and even if Morgan had not been one of the most prominent backers of the Republican Party, the enmeshing of a large part of the American economy on the side of the Entente at the behest of pro-British bankers would have posed a dramatic challenge to Wilson's administration. As the electoral campaign entered its final stages, the tensions produced within the United States by the war boom came to a dangerous head. Since August 1914 the huge credit-fuelled boost in exports had driven up the cost of living. The much-vaunted purchasing power of American wages was melting away.[40] It was the American worker who was paying for business war-profiteering. Over the summer Wilson approved moves by the populist wing in Congress to impose a tax on exports to Europe. In the last days of August 1916, in response to the threat of a general strike on the railway network, he intervened on the side of the unions, forcing Congress to concede the eight-hour day.[41] In response, American big business rallied as never before around the Republican presidential campaign. The Democrats, for their part, pilloried the Republican Charles Hughes as the 'war candidate' in the service of Wall Street profiteers. After this poisonous campaign that produced the biggest electoral turnout in American political history, the manner of Wilson's victory did little to calm the savagely partisan mood. Though Wilson won a solid popular majority, in the Electoral College he prevailed only thanks to California by a margin of just 3,755 votes. Wilson thus became the first Democrat to be re-elected as President for a second term since Andrew Jackson in the 1830s. As far as the Entente and their backers in America were concerned, it was a sobering outcome. A large part of the American public had declared its desire to stay outside the conflict.

III

Given Wilson's re-election, to count on American acquiescence in the growing economic demands of the Entente war effort was clearly risky. But the conflict had a dynamic of its own. With the German onslaught on Verdun reaching its horrific climax, the Entente decision to bring forward the first major British offensive on the Somme was taken on 24 May 1916, three days before Wilson first announced his vision of a new world order at the New Willard Hotel.[42] Though the British offensive failed to achieve a breakthrough, it threw the Germans onto the defensive. Meanwhile, on the Eastern Front the Entente's grand strategy came close to decisive success. There, the might of the Imperial Russian Army, backed by the financial and industrial capacity of the Entente, could be brought to bear against the tottering Habsburg Empire. On 5 June 1916 the energetic cavalry commander General Brusilov hurled the cream of the Russian Army against the Austro-Hungarian lines in Galicia. In a remarkable few days of fighting, the Russians laid waste to

Habsburg military power. But for an urgent injection of German troops and military leadership, the southern half of the Eastern Front would have collapsed. The shock to the Central Powers was so dramatic that it threatened to unleash a chain reaction.

On 27 August Romania finally abandoned its neutrality and declared war on the side of the Entente. Instead of the wagons of Romanian oil and grain, on which the Central Powers had come heavily to depend, a fresh enemy army of 800,000 drove westwards into Transylvania. Improbable though it may seem, in August 1916 it was not President Wilson but Prime Minister Bratianu in Bucharest who appeared to hold the fate of the world in his hands. As Field Marshal Hindenburg commented in retrospect: 'Truly, never before was a state as small as Rumania, handed a role of such world historic significance at such an opportune moment. Never before have potent great powers like Germany and Austria been exposed in such a way to a state which had perhaps only one twentieth of their population.'[43] At the Kaiser's HQ the news of Romania's entry into the war 'fell like a bomb. William II completely lost his head, pronounced the war finally lost and believed we must now ask for peace.'[44] The Habsburg ambassador in Bucharest, Count Ottokar Czernin, predicted 'with mathematical certainty the complete defeat of the Central Powers and their allies if the war were continued any longer'.[45]

In the event, Romania defied the odds in its favour. A German-led counter-attack turned defeat into victory. By December 1916, with German and Bulgarian forces converging on Bucharest, the Romanian government and what was left of its army found themselves as refugees in Russian Moldavia. But it is this dramatic train of events that forms the essential backdrop to the confrontation between the Entente, Germany and Woodrow Wilson over the winter of 1916–17. Berlin's path towards escalation was marked out at the end of August 1916 when the Kaiser replaced Erich von Falkenhayn, the discredited mastermind of Verdun, with Field Marshal Hindenburg and his chief of staff, Erich Ludendorff, as the Third Supreme Army Command (3. OHL). Having over the previous two years been confined exclusively to the war against Russia, for Ludendorff and Hindenburg a close inspection of the Western Front came as a severe shock. The German effort at Verdun had been huge. But the extraordinary intensity of the British Somme offensive set a new benchmark. In response, Hindenburg and Ludendorff's first move was to hunker down into a defensive posture. If they were to have any hope of matching the Entente's globalized war effort, Germany would need a new mobilization of its own. Dubbed the 'Hindenburg programme', it was designed to double ammunition output within the year. Its targets were met, though at a huge cost to the home front. In the meantime, it was this same defensive rationale that led the 3. OHL to back the navy in calling for the U-boats to be unleashed. If Germany was to survive, the transatlantic supply lines had to be severed. Hindenburg and Ludendorff would not launch an attack immediately. They would give Bethmann Hollweg a chance at peace mediation. The German socialists needed to be reassured that they were supporting a purely defensive war.[46] The risks of escalating the U-boat war were obvious. Americans would be antagonized. But to continue to hold back was simply to play into British hands. In economic terms, North America was fully committed to the Entente in any case.

Not surprisingly the Entente, who faced the daunting task of raising a further billion dollars' worth of loans in the United States in the near future, were rather less sanguine about the inevitability of American support. Nevertheless for Britain and France, even more than for the Germans, a negotiated peace was unattractive. After two years of war, Germany's armies occupied Poland, Belgium, much of northern France and now Romania. Serbia had been erased from the map. In London in the autumn of 1916 it was the argument over strategic priorities in the third year of the war that brought down the Asquith government.[47] Ironically, those who were most open to Wilson's idea of a negotiated peace were those who were most suspicious of the long-term rise of American power. This was particularly true of old-school liberals, such as the British Chancellor Reginald McKenna. As he warned the cabinet, if they continued on their current course 'I venture to say with certainty that by next June [1917] or earlier the President of the American Republic will be in a position, if he so wishes, to dictate his own terms to us.'[48] McKenna's desire to avoid falling further into dependence on America was the obverse of Wilson's distaste for European politics. As seen from both sides, the best way to minimize future entanglement was to halt the war as soon as possible. But by December 1916, McKenna and Asquith were out of office. In came Lloyd George at the head of a coalition dedicated to defeating Germany decisively. Ironically, though the posture of the coalition was fundamentally out of kilter with Wilson's desire to end the war, it was the most Atlanticist in its basic commitments.[49] As Lloyd George informed Robert Lansing, Wilson's Secretary of State, he looked forward most enthusiastically to a permanent international order founded on the 'active sympathy of the two great English-speaking nations'.[50] As he put it to Colonel House earlier in 1916, 'if the United States would stand by Great Britain the entire world could not shake the combined mastery we would hold over the seas'.[51] Furthermore, the 'economic force of the United States' was 'so great that no nation at war could withstand its power . . .'[52] But, as Lloyd George had been arguing already since the summer of 1916, American loans established not simply Britain's subordination to Wall Street, but a condition of mutual dependence. The more that Britain borrowed in America and the more it purchased, the harder it would be for Wilson to detach his country from the fate of the Entente.[53]

2

Peace without Victory

As 1916 drew to a close, both blocs of European combatants were preparing to take huge risks on the assumption that the financial entanglement between America and the Entente would sooner or later force Washington to align itself on the side of the Entente. Nor was this a secret of state. The assumption was widely shared. In his exile in Zurich the Russian radical, Vladimir Ilyich Lenin, was in June 1916 putting the final touches to what was to be one of his most famous pamphlets, 'Imperialism, the Highest Stage of Capitalism'.[1] This cast commonplace assumptions about the necessity of American involvement into an iron-clad theoretical dogma. According to Lenin, states in the age of imperialism were drawn into the fight as tools of national business interests. On this logic it was apparent that Washington must sooner or later declare war on Germany. What none of these speculations could account for, however, was the remarkable course of events between November 1916 and the spring of 1917. The American President, re-elected with a mandate to keep America out of the war, tried to do something far more ambitious. He attempted not just to preserve neutrality but to end the war on terms that would place Washington in a position of pre-eminent global leadership. Lenin may have declared imperialism to be the highest stage of capitalism, but Wilson had other ideas.[2] So, it turned out, did the combatants. If a return to the pre-war world of imperialism was impossible, revolution was not the only alternative.

I

Throughout October 1916 the banking house J. P. Morgan was in urgent discussions with the British and the French over the future of Allied finance. For their next season of campaigning, the Entente proposed to raise at least 1.5 billion dollars. Realizing the enormity of these sums, J. P. Morgan sought reassurance both from the Federal Reserve Board and from Wilson himself. None was forthcoming.[3] As Election Day on 7 November approached, Wilson began drafting a public statement to be delivered by the governor of the Federal Reserve Board warning the American public against committing any more of their savings to Entente loans.[4] On 27 November 1916, four days before J. P. Morgan planned to launch the Anglo-French bond issue, the Federal Reserve Board issued instructions to all member banks. In the interest of the stability of the American financial system, the Fed announced that it no longer considered it desirable for American investors to increase their holdings of British and French securities. As Wall Street plunged and sterling was offloaded by speculators, J. P. Morgan and the UK Treasury were forced into emergency purchasing of sterling to prop up the British currency.[5] At the same time the British government was forced to suspend support of French purchasing.[6] The Entente's entire financing effort was in jeopardy. In Russia in the autumn of 1916 there was mounting resentment at the demand by Britain and France that it should ship its gold reserves to London to secure Allied borrowing. Without American assistance it was not just the patience of the financial markets but the Entente itself that would be put at risk.[7] As the year ended, the war committee of the British cabinet concluded grimly that the only possible interpretation was that Wilson meant to force their hand and put an end to the war in a matter of weeks. And this ominous interpretation was reinforced when London received confirmation from its ambassador in Washington that it was indeed the President himself who had insisted on the strong wording of the Fed's note.

Given the huge demands made by the Entente on Wall Street in 1916, it is clear that opinion was already shifting against further massive loans to London and Paris ahead of the Fed's announcement.[8] But what the cabinet could not ignore was the open hostility of the American President. And Wilson was determined to raise the stakes. On 12 December the German Chancellor, Bethmann Hollweg, without stating Germany's own aims, issued a pre-emptive demand for peace negotiations. Undaunted, on 18 December Wilson followed this with a 'Peace Note', calling on both sides to state what war aims could justify the continuation of the terrible slaughter. It was an open bid to delegitimize the war, all the more alarming for its coincidence with the initiative from Berlin. On Wall Street the reaction was immediate. Armaments shares plunged and the German ambassador, Johann Heinrich von Bernstorff, and Wilson's son-in-law, Treasury Secretary William Gibbs McAdoo, found themselves accused of making millions by betting against Ententeconnected armaments stocks.[9] In London and Paris the impact was more serious. King George V is said to have wept.[10] The mood in the British cabinet was furious. The London *Times* called for restraint but could not hide its dismay at Wilson's refusal to distinguish between the two sides.[11] It was the worst blow that France had received in 29 months of war, roared the patriotic press from Paris.[12] German troops were deep in Entente territory in both East and West. They had to be driven out, before talks could be contemplated. Nor, since the sudden swing in the fortunes of the war in the late summer of 1916, did this seem impossible. Austria was clearly close to the brink.[13] When the Entente met for their war conference in Petrograd at the end of January 1917, the talk was of a new sequence of concentric offensives.

Wilson's intervention was deeply embarrassing, but to the Entente's relief the Central Powers took the initiative in rejecting the President's offer of mediation. This freed the Entente to issue their own, carefully worded statement of war aims on 10 January. These demanded the evacuation of Belgium and Serbia, and the return of Alsace Lorraine, but more ambitiously they insisted on self-determination for the oppressed peoples of both the Ottoman and Habsburg empires.[14] It was a manifesto for continued war, not immediate negotiation, and it thus raised the inescapable question: how were these campaigns to be paid for? To cover purchases in the US running at $75 million per week, in January 1917 Britain could muster no more than $215 million in assets in New York. Beyond that, it would be forced to draw down on the Bank of England's last remaining gold reserves, which would cover no more than six weeks of procurement.[15] In January, London had no option but to ask J. P. Morgan to start preparing to relaunch the bond issue that had been aborted in November. Once more, however, they had reckoned without the President.

At 1 p.m. on 22 January 1917 Woodrow Wilson strode towards the rostrum of the US Senate.[16] It was a dramatic occasion. News of the President's intention to speak was only leaked to the senators over lunch. It was the first time that a President had directly addressed that august body since George Washington's day. Nor was it an occasion only on the American political stage. It was clear that Wilson would have to speak about the war and in so doing he would not merely be delivering a commentary. Commonly, Wilson's emergence as a leader of global stature is dated a year later to January 1918 and his enunciation of the so-called '14 Points'. But it was in fact in January 1917 that the American President first staked an explicit claim to world leadership. The text of his speech was distributed to the major capitals of Europe at the same time that it was delivered in the Senate. As in the 14 Points speech, on 22 January Wilson would call for a new international order based on a League of Nations, disarmament and the freedom of the seas. But whereas the 14 Points were a wartime manifesto that fit snugly into a mid-century narrative of American global leadership, the speech that Wilson delivered on 22 January is a great deal harder to assimilate.

As the door to the American century swung wide in January 1917, Wilson stood poised in the frame. He came not to take sides but to make peace. The first dramatic assertion of American leadership in the twentieth century was not directed towards ensuring that the 'right' side won, but that no side did.[17] The only kind of peace with any prospect of securing the cooperation of all the major world powers was one that was accepted by all sides. All parties to the Great War must acknowledge the conflict's deep futility. That meant that the war could have only one outcome: 'peace without victory'. It was this phrase that encapsulated the standpoint of moral equivalence with which Wilson had consistently staked his distance from the Europeans since the outbreak of the war. It was a stance that he knew would stick in the gullet of many in his audience in January 1917.[18] 'It is not pleasant to say this . . . I am seeking only to face realities and to face them without soft concealments.' In the current slaughter the US must take no side. For America to ride to the assistance of Britain, France and the Entente would certainly ensure their victory. But in so doing America would be perpetuating the old world's horrible cycle of violence. It would, Wilson insisted in private conversation, be nothing less than a 'crime against civilization'.[19]

Wilson was later to be accused of the idealistic belief that the League of Nations could by itself ensure peace, of shrinking moralistically from the question of power. The failure to face up to the question of international enforcement was denounced as the birth-fault of internationalist 'idealism'. But in that sense Wilson was never an idealist. What he called for in January 1917 was a 'peace made secure by the organized major force of mankind'. If the war ended in a world divided between victors and vanquished, the force necessary to sustain it would be immense. But what Wilson aspired to was disarmament. At all costs he wanted to avoid the 'Prussianization' of America itself. This was why a peace without victory was so essential. 'Victory would mean peace forced upon the loser . . . It would be accepted in humiliation, under duress, at an intolerable sacrifice, and would leave a sting, a resentment, a bitter memory upon which terms of peace would rest, not permanently, but only as upon quicksand . . .' 'The right state of mind, the right feeling between nations, is as necessary for a lasting peace as is the just settlement of vexed questions of territory or of racial and national allegiance . . . Any peace which does not recognize and accept this principle will inevitably be upset. It will not rest upon the affections or the convictions of mankind.'[20] It was precisely to create the necessary conditions for a peace that could be upheld without a costly international security system that Wilson in January 1917 was calling for an end to the war. The exhaustion of the warlike spirits of all the powers, the demonstration by example that war had lost its utility, would make the League self-supporting.

But if this was what Wilson meant by a peace of equals, it had a further implication. Wilson is famous as the great internationalist amongst American presidents. However, the world he wanted to create was one in which the exceptional position of America at the head of world civilization would be inscribed on the gravestone of European power. The peace of equals that Wilson had in mind would be a peace of collective European exhaustion. The brave new world would begin with the collective humbling of all the European powers at the feet of the United States, raised triumphant as the neutral arbiter and the source of a new form of international order.[21] Wilson's vision was neither one of gutless idealism nor a plan to subordinate US sovereignty to international authority. He was in fact making an exorbitant claim to American moral supremacy, rooted in a distinctive vision of America's historic destiny.

II

Unlike the response to the 14 Points in 1918, the reaction to Wilson's call for a 'peace without victory' in January 1917 was distinctly mixed.[22] In the US the President was cheered by his progressive and left-wing supporters. By contrast much of the Republican Party reacted with fury to what they understood as an unprecedented partisan intervention by the executive branch. Following the bitterly contested election of 1916, the President's address was, one Republican fumed, a 'stump speech delivered from the throne', an unprecedented abuse of the Senate as a platform for a partisan executive branch.[23] Another member of the audience was left with the impression that Wilson 'thinks he is the President of the world'. Charles Austin Beard, the noted progressive historian, commented to *The New York Times* that the only conceivable reason Wilson would have taken such an initiative was that, as in 1905 when President Roosevelt mediated the Russo-Japanese War, one of the sides in the conflict was on the point of bankruptcy and needed urgently to end the struggle.[24] That Wilson meant to bankrupt them was precisely what the Entente feared. For Paris and London the questions raised by Wilson's speech went beyond constitutional niceties. His vision threatened to drive a wedge into the solidarity of the Allied home front that had so far enabled the war to be continued in large part on a volunteer basis without draconian domestic repression. What was even more alarming was that Wilson was entirely aware of what he was doing. 'Perhaps I am the only person in high authority amongst all the peoples of the world,' the President proclaimed before the Senate, 'who is at liberty to speak and hold nothing back.' 'May I not add,' he went on, 'that I hope and believe that I am in effect speaking for liberals and friends of humanity in every nation and of every program of liberty?' Indeed, Wilson went further: 'I would fain believe that I am speaking for the silent mass of mankind everywhere who have as yet had no place or opportunity to speak their real hearts out concerning the death and ruin they see to have come already upon the persons and the homes they hold most dear.'

It was here that the true import of Wilson's address became clear. The American President was calling into question the representative legitimacy of all of the combatant governments. And on the Entente side, the far from silent organizations that claimed to represent that 'mass of mankind' responded to Wilson's cue. As Wilson spoke on 22 January the British Labour movement was meeting in Manchester – 700 delegates, including a minister in Lloyd George's new government, representing two and a quarter million members, more than four times the number at their first meeting in 1901.[25] The general tone of the discussion was patriotic. But at the mention of Wilson's name the anti-war faction organized in the Independent Labour Party burst into a well-orchestrated ovation.[26] Though this earned them a reprimand from *The Times*, the *Manchester Guardian* applauded.[27] In the French chamber on 26 January, 80 Socialist deputies called on the government to express its agreement with Wilson's 'elevated and reasonable' sentiments.[28]

All of this ought to have presented a truly historic opportunity for Germany. The American President had weighed the war in the balance and had refused to take the Entente's side. When the blockade revealed what Britain's command of the seaways meant for global trade, Wilson had responded with an unprecedented naval programme of his own. He seemed bent on blocking any further mobilization of the American economy. He had called for peace talks whilst Germany still had the upper hand. He was not deterred by the fact that Bethmann Hollweg had gone first. Now he was speaking quite openly to the population of Britain, France and Italy, over the heads of their governments, demanding an end to the war. The German Embassy in Washington fully understood the significance of the President's words and desperately urged Berlin to respond positively. Already in September 1916, after extended conversations with Colonel House, Ambassador Bernstorff had cabled Berlin that the American President would seek to mediate as soon as the election was over and that 'Wilson regards it as in the interest of America that neither of the combatants should gain a decisive victory'.[29] In December the ambassador sought to bring home to Berlin the importance of Wilson's intervention in the financial markets, which would be a far less dangerous way of throttling the Entente than an all-out U-boat campaign. Above all, Bernstorff understood Wilson's ambition. If he could bring the war to an end he would claim for the American presidency the 'glory of being the premier political personage on the world's stage'.[30] If the Germans were to thwart him, they should beware his wrath. But such appeals were not enough to halt the logic of escalation that had been set in motion by the Entente's near breakthrough in the late summer of 1916.

Hindenburg and Ludendorff were the generals who had saved Germany from Russia in 1914 and conquered Poland in 1915. But they owed their rise to the Supreme Command to the crisis of the Central Powers in August 1916. This experience of near disaster defined the politics of the war in Germany from this moment onwards. In 1916, Germany had sought to bleed France dry at Verdun, but out of concerns about America it had withheld the U-boats. The Entente had survived. Over the summer of 1916 the blows dealt to Austria had been near fatal. Given the force mobilized by the Entente in the meantime, any further restraint would be disastrous. The leading figures in Berlin never took seriously the idea that Wilson might actually manage to stop the war. Whatever the nuances of American politics, they insisted its economy was ever more committed on the Entente side. The effect was self-fulfilling. By acting on their deterministic beliefs about American politics, the Kaiser's strategists tore the ground from beneath Wilson's feet. On 9 January 1917, overriding the hesitant objections of their Chancellor, Hindenburg and Ludendorff rammed through the decision to resume unrestricted U-boat warfare.[31] Within less than two weeks the depths of their miscalculation were to become obvious. Even as Wilson strode to the Senate rostrum on 22 January 1917 to call for the war to be brought to an end, Germany's U-boats were battering their way through winter seas to assume battle stations in a wide arc surrounding the British and French Atlantic coastline. As Ambassador Bernstorff informed the State Department in anguished terms, it was too late for them to be recalled. At 5 p.m. on 31 January he handed Secretary of State Lansing the official declaration of unrestricted submarine warfare against the supply lines of the Entente in the Atlantic and the eastern Mediterranean. On 3 February, Congress approved the breaking of diplomatic relations with Germany.

The German decision cast 'peace without victory' into historical oblivion. It drove America into a war that Wilson detested. It robbed him of the role to which he truly aspired, the arbiter of a global peace. The resumption of unrestricted submarine warfare on 9 January 1917 marked a turning point in world history. It forged another link in the chain of aggression stretching back to August 1914 and forward to Hitler's relentless onslaught between 1938 and 1942, which held fast the image of Germany as an irrepressible force of violence. Already at the time unrestricted U-boat warfare was the subject of anguished self-examination. As Bethmann Hollweg's diplomatic advisor, Kurt Riezler, noted in his diary, 'the fate that hangs over everything suggests the thought that Wilson may in fact have intended to pressure the others and had the means to do so and that that would have been 100 times better than the U Boat war'.[32] For nationalist liberals such as the great sociologist Max Weber, one of the most penetrating political commentators of the day, Bethmann Hollweg's willingness to allow the military's technical arguments to override his own better judgement was damning evidence of the lasting damage done to Germany's political culture by Bismarck.[33]

But if we allow the peculiar pathology of German political history alone to explain the derailment of 'peace without victory', we understate the significance of the rift between Washington and the Entente over the winter of 1916–17. Wilson's challenge was not to Germany in particular, but to European power as a whole. Indeed his challenge was principally directed at the Entente. From the Somme offensive of July 1916 onwards, it was the Entente that took the initiative in replying to Wilson's obvious desire for a negotiated peace, by widening and intensifying the conflict. The fact that this caused Germany to tip America into the Entente's camp should not obscure the fact that the Entente too was running huge risks. To compound the irony, the Entente ran them on assumptions that were complementary to those on which Germany committed itself to its disastrous course of aggression. If London and Paris entwined America ever more into their war effort, Wilson's hand would be forced. But it was, in fact, only Germany's anticipation of that logic that made it real. This would be obscured by hindsight, but it was not forgotten by contemporaries. It would return to haunt them in the politics of the armistice in October 1918. But even after the opening of the U-boat campaign it was not clear that all was decided.

III

Following the severing of diplomatic relations with Germany, there were many in Wilson's administration, perhaps most notably Secretary of State Lansing, who now wanted to commit completely to the Entente. America, he demanded, should align itself with its 'natural' allies in the cause of 'human liberty and the suppression of Absolutism'.[34] The pro-Entente voices in the Republican Party led by Teddy Roosevelt were in full cry. The British government was only too keen to seize this opportunity of a transatlantic political alliance. Having belatedly come to the realization that, as their ambassador to Washington put it, 'Morgans cannot be regarded as a substitute for the proper diplomatic authorities in conducting negotiations likely to affect our relations with the United States', London hurriedly dispatched a Treasury team to Washington in the hope of initiating government-to-government contact.[35]

Atlanticism came easily to the Entente by 1917.[36] Since before the war, starting with the Second Moroccan Crisis at Agadir in 1911, it had become increasingly commonplace to stress the political solidarity of Britain and France against the bullying imperialism of Germany. Deeply disappointed by the failure of his hopes for an Anglo-German rapprochement, Lloyd George came to see France as 'Britain's ideological counterpart in Europe'. Upholding their alliance against the 'throned Philistines of Europe' was essential.[37] In his wartime speeches Lloyd George did not hesitate to associate British democracy with the European revolutionary tradition. The knock-out blow to Imperial Germany, he promised, would deliver 'liberté, egalité, fraternité' for all.[38] To assert a common Atlantic heritage in the struggle for liberty and freedom was simply the next step in this chain of historical and ideological associations.

Such thinking came even more easily to French Republicans. Already before the war, many in the Third Republic had looked upon the Entente with Britain as a 'liberal alliance' that would help France offset its regrettable dependence on an alliance with the autocracy of Tsarist Russia.[39] When André Tardieu, one of Prime Minister Georges Clemenceau's closest collaborators, was dispatched to Washington in May 1917, his mission was to deliver an appeal for the 'two democracies, France and America' to stand together in proving the point that 'republics are in no way inferior to monarchies when they are attacked and have to defend themselves'.[40] And there were, of course, plenty of voices in the United States willing to chime in. In the spring of 1917, French delegations to Washington and New York were feted as the heirs of Lafayette who had helped to win freedom for the colonists in 1776. But what both the Entente strategists and the Germans had not reckoned with was the White House and the substantial body of American opinion that President Wilson represented. Despite German aggression, America was not yet at war, and the President and his circle continued to cold-shoulder the Entente.[41]

Wilson's reluctance to become involved in the European conflict derived in part from his belief that wider issues were at stake. As we shall see in chapter 5, in the spring of 1917 the President was deeply preoccupied with events in China. Japan's role as an ally of the Entente disturbed him greatly. Over the winter of 1916–17 the strategy of American leadership that lay behind his call for a peace without victory was explicitly spelled out in racial terms. Given China's vulnerability and the dynamic expansion of Japanese power, what was at stake for Wilson in suppressing the self-destructive violence of European imperialism were not just the petty quarrels of the old world, but nothing less than the future of 'white supremacy on this planet'.[42] As the US cabinet met to debate the news from Europe in late January 1917, one witness recorded Wilson's thought as follows: The President was 'more and more impressed with the idea that "white civilization" and its domination in the world rested largely on our ability to keep this country intact, as we would have to build up the nations ravaged by the war. He said that as this idea had grown upon him he had come to the feeling that he was willing to go to any lengths rather than to have the nation actually involved in the conflict.'[43] When Wilson said it would be a 'crime against civilization' for America to allow itself to become sucked into the war, it was 'white civilization' that he had in mind. In Britain there were plenty who shared Wilson's racial vision of world history. But it was precisely so that Britain could concentrate its main force in Asia, they believed, that Germany must be tamed. The war in Europe was not a distraction from the worldwide struggle, it was an essential part of it. Why then was the President so reluctant to see America's essential interests engaged? Despite the efforts by the Entente to align their cause with the values of America, Wilson remained deeply sceptical. And if we trace the development of Wilson's political personality back to its origins in the nineteenth century, it becomes clear why.

As a conservative Southern liberal, Wilson's view of history was shaped by two great events: the disaster of the Civil War, and the drama of the eighteenth-century revolutions as interpreted by the writings of the Anglo-Irish conservative, Edmund Burke.[44] In 1896 Wilson contributed a glowing preface to one of Burke's most famous speeches on 'Conciliation with the Colonies'. Originally delivered in 1775, Burke's oration became for Wilson a statement of a fundamental distinction. Whereas Burke showered praise on the freedom-loving American colonist, he 'hated the French revolutionary philosophy and deemed it unfit for free men'. Wilson heartily agreed. Looking back over a century of revolution, he denounced the legacy of that philosophy as 'radically evil and corrupting. No state can ever be conducted on its principles. For it holds that government is a matter of contract and deliberate arrangement, whereas in fact it is an institute of habit, bound together by innumerable threads of association, scarcely one of which has been deliberately placed ...' Contrary to the delusional idea that self-determination could be realized in a single revolutionary spasm, Wilson insisted that 'governments have never been successfully and permanently changed, except by slow modification operating from generation to generation'.[45] With the French experiences of 1789, 1830, 1848 and 1870 in mind, Wilson in an earlier essay had opined that: 'democracy in Europe has acted always in rebellion, as a destructive force ... It has built such temporary governments as it has had opportunity to erect ... out of the discredited materials of centralized rule, elevating the people's representatives for a season ... but securing almost as little as ever of that everyday local self-government which lies so near to the heart of liberty'.[46] Even in 1900 he saw in the French Third Republic a dangerously unsteady descendant of absolute monarchy, the 'eccentric influence' of which had brought the entire project of democracy in the modern world into disrepute.[47]

True freedom was for Wilson indelibly rooted in the deep-seated qualities of a particular national and racial way of life. Failure to recognize this was the source of a profound confusion about American identity itself. Americans of the gilded age, Wilson remarked, were apt to think of themselves as having lost the revolutionary ardour which they imagined to have propelled the founding fathers. They thought of themselves as inoculated by 'experience ... against the infections of hopeful revolution'. But this sense was based on an 'old self-deception'. 'If we are suffering disappointment, it is the disappointment of an awakening'. Those who romanticized America's eighteenth-century revolution 'were dreaming'. In truth, 'The government which we founded one hundred years ago was no type of an experiment in advanced democracy ...' Americans 'never had any business harkening to Rousseau or consorting with Europe in revolutionary sentiment'. The strength of democratic self-determination, American-style, was precisely that it was not revolutionary. It had inherited all its strengths from its forebears. 'It had not to overthrow other polities; it had only to organize itself. It had not to create, but only to expand self-government... It needed nothing but to methodize its way of living.'[48] In words that were to echo through his views about World War I, Wilson insisted: 'there is almost nothing in common between popular outbreaks such as took place in France at her great Revolution and the establishment of a government like our own ... We manifested one hundred years ago what Europe lost ... self-command, self-possession.'[49] He thus gave his peculiar personal inflection to the general sense of alienation with which many Americans regarded the 'old world'. What Wilson was determined to demonstrate amidst the crisis of the world war was that America had not lost the 'self-possession' he prized above all else.

Wilson was no doubt more comfortable with the British than the French and wrote eloquently about the merits of the British constitution. But precisely because Britain was the nation from which America's own political culture had historically derived, it was essential for Wilson that Britain itself must remain fixed in the past. The thought that it might be advancing along the path of democratic progress, alongside rather than behind America, was deeply unsettling. The fact that the Prime Minister who took office weeks after Wilson's re-election, Lloyd George, was perhaps the greatest pioneer of democracy in early twentieth-century Europe, was lost on the White House. Wilson was only too happy to fall in with radical critics who denounced the Prime Minister as a reactionary warmonger.[50] Colonel House, when he visited London, much preferred dealing with Tory patricians, such as Lord Balfour and old-school Liberal Grandees like Sir Edward Grey, who fitted Wilson's aspic image of British politics far better than the populist Lloyd George.

IV

Faced with this wall of stereotypes, it was tempting for the Europeans to respond with their own version of the stylized transatlantic difference. At Versailles, Georges Clemenceau was to remark that he found Wilson's sanctimoniousness easier to stomach when he reminded himself that the American had never 'lived in a world where it was good form to shoot a Democrat'.[51] But Clemenceau, perhaps out of politeness, perhaps from sheer forgetfulness of his long career, failed to note that he and Wilson did in fact share a common point of reference in a truly violent period of political struggle not in Europe, but in America itself. Though half a century in the past, the Civil War spoke directly to the deepest source of Wilson's discomfort with the rhetoric of just war so eagerly taken up in the spring of 1917 by both the Entente and their cheerleaders in America.

If Wilson's Southern childhood was marked by the Civil War, Clemenceau was defined by his inheritance of the French revolutionary tradition.[52] His father had been arrested for resisting the Bonapartist usurpation of the 1848 revolution and narrowly escaped deportation to Algeria. In 1862 Clemenceau himself served time in the infamous Mazas jail for seditious activity. In 1865, broken hearted and with nothing to hope for in Napoleon III's France, Clemenceau shipped out to that great battleground of nineteenth-century democratic politics, Civil War America. With his recently minted medical degree he meant to volunteer as a medic in the service of Lincoln's Union Army, or to make a life for himself as a frontiersman in the American West. Instead, he settled in Connecticut and New York and over the following years produced for the liberal newspaper *Le Temps* a remarkable series of reports on the bitter struggle over the effort to complete the defeat of the South by means of comprehensive reconstruction. True to his convictions, Clemenceau saw Reconstruction as a heroic effort to complete a victorious just war with a 'second revolution'. It was a battle that concluded, to Clemenceau's delight, with the passage of the Fifteenth Amendment in February 1869, promising voting rights for African Americans. For Clemenceau, the radical Republican abolitionists were the 'noblest and finest men of the nation', inspired by 'all the wrath of a Robespierre'.[53] Coming from Clemenceau, this was the highest compliment. The partisans of Reconstruction were fighting to save the United States from 'moral ruin' and 'misfortune' in the face of abusive, self-interested heckling from Southern Democrats.

Amongst that crowd was to be found Woodrow Wilson, who as a young man impressed all his acquaintances with his dogged adherence to the Southern cause. As the author of best-selling popular histories in the 1880s and 1890s, Professor Wilson concluded his triumphant narrative of the American nation state with a celebration of the reconciliation between North and South, which had condemned Reconstruction and consigned the black population to a disenfranchised underclass. For Wilson, the heroes of Clemenceau's reports were the architects of a 'perfect work of fear, demoralization, disgust and social revolution'. In their determination to 'put the white South under the heel of the black South', the advocates of Reconstruction had inflicted on the Southern states a policy 'of rule or ruin'.[54] One cannot help wondering what the future American President might have thought if during his adolescence as a young Southerner he had happened to stumble across the following lines dispatched to Paris in January 1867 by the future leader of wartime France: 'If the Northern majority weakens and the nation's representatives let themselves be persuaded in the interests of conciliation or of States' Rights to let the Southerners reenter Congress easily, there will be no more internal peace for a quarter of a century. The slavery party of the South combined with the Democrats of the North will be strong enough to defeat all the efforts of the abolitionists, and the final and complete emancipation of the coloured people will be deferred indefinitely.'[55] As the first Southerner to be elected President since the Civil War, Wilson owed his career to that postponement of justice.

If Clemenceau was too distracted in 1917 to spend much time dredging up memories half a century old, for Wilson's American opponents the historic resonances of 'peace without victory' were too strong to resist. The German declaration of U-boat warfare on 30 January 1917 overshadowed not just Wilson's Senate speech but also one of the most savage attacks upon it by Teddy Roosevelt.[56] He was quick to identify the conservative historical lineage of Wilson's stance on the war. In the colonial era, it had been the 'Tories of 1776', Roosevelt reminded his listeners, who had wanted compromise with Britain, who had 'demanded peace without victory'. In the agonizing final stages of America's own civil war, in 1864 it had been the so-called 'Copperheads' who 'demanded peace without victory . . .'[57] Now 'Mr Wilson' was asking 'the world to accept a Copperhead peace of dishonor; a peace without victory for the right; a peace designed to let wrong triumph; a peace championed in neutral countries by the apostles of timidity and greed.'[58] The Copperheads were the faction of the pro-slavery Democratic Party that clung to political survival in the North during the Civil War, notably in Lincoln's home state of Illinois. At the climax of the struggle in 1864 they had advocated a compromise peace with the rebellious slaveocracy of the South. The partisans of a total Northern victory had named them after a venomous snake.

V

As March began in 1917, America was not yet at war. To the frustration of much of his entourage, the President still insisted that it would be a 'crime' for America to allow itself to be sucked into the conflict, since it would 'make it impossible to save Europe afterwards'.[59] In front of the entire cabinet he rejected Secretary of State Lansing's contention that 'an essential of permanent peace was that all nations should be politically liberalized'.[60] Wilson wanted the world pacified, for sure. A peace without victory would see to that, but a country's political complexion was a different matter. It was an expression of its inner life. To think that a country could be 'liberalized' at a stroke from without was to fall into the fallacy of French revolutionary thought. A nation must be given time and the protection of a new international order to develop of its own accord. Under the ideological cloak of a liberal crusade Wilson feared that the old-world vice of militarism would find fertile new soil in America. 'Junkerthum . . . would creep in under cover of . . . patriotic feeling'.[61] He continued to insist that 'probably greater justice would be done if the conflict ended in a draw'.[62] It was only as the full extent of Germany's disastrously ill-timed lurch into aggression became clear that Wilson was finally forced to abandon his position of moral equivalence. The U-boats were not the last word.

In late February 1917 British intelligence plucked a top-secret telegram from the transatlantic wires. In it the German Foreign Office authorized its embassy in Mexico City to propose an anti-American

alliance to the Mexican government of General Carranza in conjunc-
tion with Japan. In exchange for military assistance from Germany,
Mexico would launch an immediate attack on Texas, New Mexico and
Arizona.[63] By 26 February, Washington was informed. The news became
public a day later. Amongst pro-German circles in the US, the initial
response was one of disbelief. As the American-German activist George
Sylvester Viereck protested to the newspaper proprietor William Ran-
dolph Hearst at the end of February 1917, 'the alleged letter ... is
obviously a fake; it is impossible to believe that the German Foreign
Secretary would place his name under such a preposterous document ...
the Realpolitiker of the Wilhelmstrasse would never offer an alliance
based on such ludicrous propositions as the conquest by Mexico of
American territory ...'[64] In Germany too there was astonishment. For
the Reich to be offering Texas and Arizona to Mexican 'brigands' whilst
simultaneously angling for an alliance with Japan, the leading German
industrialist Walther Rathenau wrote to General Hans von Seeckt, was
'too sad even to laugh about'.[65] But however hallucinogenic these associations may have appeared, the bizarre German scheme to seize the
military initiative in the western hemisphere was the logical extension
of Berlin's *idée fixe* that America was already committed to the Entente
and that a declaration of war was under any circumstances inevitable.
Despite Wilson's obvious unwillingness to go to war, on Saturday
3 March 1917 the German Secretary of State, Arthur Zimmermann,
publicly acknowledged the authenticity of the reports.

Added to the now-routine sinking of American ships by German
U-boats, the refusal of Berlin even to deny this unprovoked aggression
left Wilson with no option. On 2 April 1917 he went before the Senate
to demand a declaration of war. For men like Roosevelt and Lansing
the declaration of war was simply a relief. Germany had demonstrated
once and for all its true, aggressive character. For Wilson, by contrast, to
be forced to abandon his vision of 'peace without victory' and to throw
his country's weight onto the side of the Entente was a stomach-churning
reversal. As one of his most insightful biographers puts it, in characteristically exalted terms, Wilson's declaration of war was his 'Gethsemane'.[66]
Certainly, there were tones of Lutheran heroics in the final lines of his
address to the Congress: 'America is privileged to spend her blood and
her might for the principles that gave her birth and happiness and the
peace which she has treasured. God helping her, she can do no other.'

But what was Wilson committing himself to? Even as he entered the war, he held back.

America was joining the war to 'vindicate the principles of peace and justice in the life of the world as against selfish and autocratic power and to set up amongst the really free and self-governed peoples of the world such a concert of purpose and of action as will henceforth insure the observance of those principles . . .' 'A steadfast concert for peace can never be maintained except by a partnership of democratic nations,' Wilson continued. 'No autocratic government could be trusted to keep faith within it or observe its covenants.' In such a struggle, it was 'no longer feasible or desirable' for America to remain neutral. This appeared to concede the argument to Lansing and Roosevelt, who had always insisted that it was impossible for America to uphold a position of equivalence between the two sides. But examined closely, there was a remarkable selectivity in Wilson's declaration. He did not include Germany's main allies, the Ottomans or Habsburgs, in his declaration of war or his denunciation of autocracy. Nor did he squarely endorse the Entente powers as representatives of democracy or examples of self-government. His objectives were stated in abstract and prospective terms. Having failed in his effort to force an end to the war from without, Wilson was determined to shape the order of a new world from within. But to do so he had to preserve his distance. Rather than formally allying America with the Entente, Wilson insisted on his detached status as an 'associate'.[67] At the crucial moment, this would give him the freedom he needed to throw his weight onto the scales, not behind London and Paris, but so as to restore America's role as the arbiter of global power.

3

The War Grave of Russian
Democracy

On 6 April 1917 America entered the war, swinging the balance of force decisively in favour of the Entente. It retrospect it would come to seem a foreordained turn in world history. But at that very moment, it became obvious what extraordinary risks the Entente had been running in escalating the war in the face of American opposition. It became clear how finely balanced the war had been and how much traction Woodrow Wilson's January appeal for a 'peace without victory' might have acquired, if only he had been able to keep America out of the war a few months longer. On 20 March 1917, the same day that Wilson reluctantly agreed with his cabinet to ask Congress for a declaration of war, Washington instructed its embassy in Petrograd to recognize the new Provisional Government of Russia.[1]

After a week of strikes and demonstrations and the refusal of the Petrograd garrison to follow orders, on 15 March the Tsar had abdicated. With the authority of the Romanov dynasty in tatters, the Tsar's brothers refused to take the throne.[2] As America moved toward war, Russia was not yet officially a Republic, but the Provisional Government that had constituted itself from progressive elements of the Duma, the Tsar's rump of a parliament, announced that a Constituent Assembly, elected on a 'universal basis', would meet within the year. Following the example of its illustrious American and French precursors, this revolutionary Convention would decide the most fundamental and contentious questions bequeathed by the old regime – the political constitution of the country, the land question, and future relations between Russia and the tens of millions of non-Russians gathered under the oppressive rule of the Tsars. In the meantime the chief new sources of revolutionary legitimacy were the assemblies known as Soviets, which constituted themselves on the initiative of radical soldiers, workers and peasants in every city, town and village. By the early summer these Soviets would hold their own national congress and enter into a coalition with the Provisional Government.

Though permanent constitutional change awaited the Constituent Assembly, there was an overwhelming and immediate consensus about certain features of the new order. Freedom was the watchword of the revolution. The death penalty was abolished. All restrictions on assembly and free speech were lifted. The civil equality of Jews and other ethnic and religious minorities was proclaimed. Feminist demonstrators loudly and successfully demanded that women, as well as men, must elect the Constituent Assembly. Order number one of the Petrograd Soviet granted to the rank and file of the Russian Army the same catalogue of rights now enjoyed by other citizens. Brutal corporal punishment was outlawed. Even desertion was no longer punishable by death. Soldiers were granted the full freedom of political discussion and organization. In a breath-taking reversal, Russia, formerly the autocratic bugbear of Europe, was remaking itself as the freest, most democratic country on earth.[3] The question was: What implications did this great victory for democracy have for the war?

I

To men like Robert Lansing, Wilson's Secretary of State, this was the moment of truth.[4] Since 1916 he had been the most influential advocate within the administration of the cause of the Entente. Britain and France's reliance on the armies of the Tsarist autocracy had been the biggest obstacle to his championing of the cause of the 'democratic Entente'. Now, as Lansing put it to his cabinet colleagues, 'the revolution in Russia . . . had removed the one objection to affirming that the European war was a war between democracy and absolutism'.[5] And in his declaration of war, Wilson himself welcomed the 'wonderful and heartening things that have been happening within the last few weeks in Russia'. The foreign autocracy that had ruled Russia had been 'shaken off and the great, generous Russian people have been added in all their naive majesty and might to the forces that are fighting for freedom in the world . . .'[6] London and Paris were swept with enthusiasm for a democratic Russia. Georges Clemenceau shared Lansing's excitement about the prospects for a transatlantic democratic coalition. In the spring of 1917 he welcomed the coincidence of America's declaration of war and the overthrow of the Tsar in terms that were nothing short of ecstatic: 'the supreme interest of the general ideas with which President Wilson sought to justify his actions', in declaring war, 'is that the Russian Revolution and the American Revolution complement each other in a miraculous way, in defining once and for all the moral stakes in the conflict. All the great peoples of democracy ... have taken that place in the battle that was destined for them. They work for the triumph not of one alone, but of all.'[7] Russia's democratic revolution would re-energize the war effort, not end it.

And these hopes were not entirely misplaced. In the spring of 1917 the Russian revolution was first and foremost a patriotic event. Of all the scurrilous rumours spread about the Tsar and Tsarina, by far the most damaging were those alleging treacherous contacts with their cousins in Germany. How else was one to explain the Tsar's obstinate refusal to embrace the uplifting spirit of reform and mobilization that had swept Russian liberals and even many Russian socialists to his side in August 1914? On the Northern Front Russia's armies had suffered heavy defeats at the hands of the Germans. But not everything had gone wrong in Russia's war. In 1915 its armies had thrashed the Turks. In the summer of 1916 General Brusilov's devastating offensive had crippled the Austrians and tipped Romania onto the side of the Entente. It was the failure to make good those victories that turned draft riots, agrarian protest and strikes into a political revolution. With the Tsar out of the way, there could be no talk of surrender. Anyone who insulted the revolutionary patriotism of the great, grey-coated mass of peasant soldiers, who dominated every assembly in Petrograd, ran the risk of lynching.[8] Revolutionary honour and the sacrifice of millions of dead were at stake. Furthermore the strategists in the Provisional Government and the Petrograd Soviet had to consider the wider consequences. If Russia entered into separate negotiations with Imperial Germany, the Allies would surely retaliate by cutting off the flow of credit from London, Paris and New York. A peace in the East would allow the Germans to concentrate all their forces on winning a crushing victory in the West. Then they would turn back against Russia.

But if capitulation was not an option, nor could the revolution continue the Tsar's war. The men who dominated the early phase of the revolution – figures such as Alexander Kerensky, the Labourite social democrat shuttling between the Provisional Government and the Soviet, or Irakli Tsereteli, the charismatic Georgian Menshevik internationalist who led foreign policy discussion in the Petrograd Soviet – had no desire to continue the war for the conquest of imperialist objectives such as the Dardanelles. What the revolution needed was a peace with honour, a peace without defeat. Furthermore, if this was not to be a separate peace Kerensky and Tsereteli needed to bring the rest of the Entente along. Russia's democratic revolutionaries thus faced precisely the dilemma that Wilson had been struggling with only a few weeks earlier – how to end the war in a way that would offer no encouragement to triumphalism but inflict no stinging defeat on either side. Furthermore, Russia's revolutionaries were aware of this parallel. Though it had been directed primarily to London and Paris, the significance of Wilson's challenge to the Entente over the winter of 1916–17 had not been lost on the Russians. As stated by Nikolai Sukhanov, one of Tsereteli's Menshevik colleagues in the Soviet, the first demand of the Soviet in 1917 should be to revoke the belligerent answer that the Entente had given to Wilson's Peace Note of December 1916.[9] On 4 April, the day the US Senate voted for war with Germany, the executive committee of the Petrograd Soviet laid down a peace formula with three key demands: self-determination, no annexations and no indemnities. The Russian Army would remain in the field until assured of a peace on those terms, a peace without selfish victory, but a peace that would bring honour to the revolution precisely by denouncing the Tsar and by placing Russia at the forefront of world 'democracy'.

Within days the 'Petrograd formula' had been adopted by the Provisional Government. In May its pro-Entente Foreign Minister, the liberal Pavel Miliukov, was removed at the behest of the Soviet, for his adherence to traditional, 'annexationist' war aims.[10] The Soviet's policy of 'revolutionary defensism' was one not of dogmatic socialist dictatorship but of compromise. Defence of the revolution was a posture around which Kerensky and Tsereteli hoped to rally all the 'live forces' in Russian politics: Marxists, agrarian Social Revolutionaries and liberals. The Bolsheviks barely figured in the discussion. Lenin was waiting in exile for his transport to be organized by the Kaiser's secret service. The Bolsheviks on the spot were an undistinguished group who were tempted to fall in with the Soviet majority. Lenin did not return to Petrograd until the night of 16 April, when in his famous 'April theses' he immediately announced his hostility to any agreement between the revolutionary Soviet and the inherited authority of the Provisional Government.[11] Any compromise was a betrayal of the revolution.

Over the coming year Lenin was to do his violent best to ensure that Tsereteli and Kerensky were swept into the dustbin of history. But their position should be taken seriously. Revolutionary defensism was a patriotic strategy. Democratic Russia would not surrender to Imperial Germany. But Lenin's opprobrium notwithstanding, it was revolutionary too. To advocate peace in the spring of 1917 was not to advocate the pre-war status quo, but to call for the political transformation of Europe. It was the Petrograd Soviet that loudly proclaimed what had been left tacit in Wilson's Senate address. Given the sacrifices already made by all sides by 1917, a 'peace without victory' could only be contemplated by a government willing to break with the past. It implied the utter futility of the most costly war in history. It required governments willing to dissociate themselves, like Wilson, from the question of war guilt and to criticize imperialism on all sides. Only such a government could accept a peace without victory as something other than a humiliation. It was precisely for that reason that the political class of Britain and France had so doggedly resisted Wilson's call. They could not accept his moral equivocation. They understood that they had no place in his vision of the political future. Ill-timed German aggression had tipped Wilson onto their side. But if the Russian revolution had started a few months earlier, if Germany had postponed its decision to resume unrestricted U-boat warfare until the spring, or if Wilson had been able to stay out of the war until May, what might have been the result? Could the war have continued? Might democracy in Russia have been saved? As the departing German ambassador to Washington Count Bernstorff noted in agonized retrospect: If Germany over the winter of 1916–17 had 'accepted Wilson's mediation, the whole of American influence in Russia would have been exercised in favour of peace, and not, as events ultimately proved, against' Germany. 'Out of Wilson's and Kerensky's Peace programme', Germany could surely have rescued a peace offering all that 'we regarded as necessary'.[12] It is these unfathomable counterfactuals that give such vast significance to the near coincidence between the Russian revolution and the American entry into the war. But even with

Wilson on the side of the Entente, the Russian revolution sent shock-waves through both sides. It came close over the summer of 1917 to bringing the war to an end with something like a 'peace without victory'.[13] It was a bitter irony that it was America's entry into the war that did more than anything else to put paid to that possibility. The consequences for Europe and for Russia in particular would be momentous.

II

After the terrible third winter of the war, the energy that had carried the combatants through 1916 was ebbing away. On the Eastern Front there had been no serious fighting since the overthrow of the Tsar. Whilst they waited to see whether a separate peace could be arranged with the revolutionary government, the Germans held off from any offensive. Within Germany, the Russian revolution had shaken popular resolve to continue the struggle. Defending Germany against the aggression of autocratic Tsarism had been the main motive for the Social Democratic Party to support the war. With the Russian revolutionaries renouncing any annexationist intentions, that was now thrown into doubt. On 8 April 1917 at the insistence of Chancellor Bethmann Hollweg, who was desperate to hold the SPD behind his government, the Kaiser issued his Easter proclamation, promising immediate constitutional reform in Prussia at the end of the war. One-man-one-vote would replace the three-tier-class voting system that had hitherto excluded the left from the Prussian state parliament that controlled two-thirds of Germany. But it was too little too late. In mid-April 1917 the SPD, the great mother-ship of European socialism, split.[14] The more radical left wing gathered within the Independent Social Democratic Party (USPD), demanding an immediate peace on the terms now being offered by the revolutionary Soviet in Petrograd, a resolution enthusiastically endorsed by 300,000 striking workers in the great industrial centres of Berlin and Leipzig. The Majority SPD (MSPD) continued to give their support to the national war effort, but they insisted more urgently than ever that it must remain a defensive struggle. Through neutrals and with the indulgence of the Reich government they took the lead in opening negotiations with their socialist comrades in Russia.

These tremors within the political fabric of the Central Powers were all the more significant because they coincided with the spectacular failure of the Entente's latest bid for military victory. On 18 April 1917, after softening up operations by the British, the French Army once more crashed into the German line. But despite the optimism radiated by their youthful new commander General Nivelle, the attack failed. The German lines held and French morale drained away. On 4 May the first units in the French Army refused orders. Within days, mutiny had spread to dozens of divisions. Whilst the ruthless General Pétain struggled to restore order, the French Army was paralysed. Paris did its best to cover up the crisis and there was no corresponding reaction in the British trenches. But by May 1917 a wave of discontent had engulfed the British Isles. In the House of Commons 32 Liberal and Labour MPs voted demonstratively in favour of a motion calling for peace on the basis of the Petrograd formula.[15] Meanwhile, industrial districts of Britain were wracked by what was by far the most serious bout of industrial unrest seen since the start of the war.[16] Hundreds of thousands of skilled engineering workers ignored the instructions of the official trade unions and laid down their tools. In early June, Lloyd George, rather than celebrating the prospect of a great democratic crusade, was scaring the cabinet with talk of a British Soviet. Fearful of a popular backlash, the House of Windsor let it be known that the homeless Romanovs were not welcome at Buckingham Palace. As George V confided to a confidant, there was too much 'democracy in the air'.[17]

The mounting sense of paralysis gripping the Entente was heightened by the impact of the U-boat blockade. Between February and June 1917 the Germans sank over 2.9 million tons of shipping. To maintain its own imports, Britain cut back the allocation of tonnage to Italy and France. Struggling to contain the collapse in morale, Paris was forced to prioritize food imports over the needs of armaments production.[18] In Italy, which was even more dependent on foreign supplies, the situation was truly critical. By the early summer of 1917 Italian coal deliveries were running at half the required level.[19] On 22 August 1917 food stocks had reached such a low ebb in Turin, the heart of Italy's war economy, that shops were closed for all but a few hours per day. Whilst strikers closed the railway network, crowds led by anarcho-syndicalist agitators looted, attacked police stations, and torched two churches. The army cordoned off the city. Eight hundred rioters were arrested and an uneasy calm was restored, but not before 50 workers and 3 soldiers had been killed.

However, despite the impact they were having on the Entente, as far as Berlin was concerned, the U-boats were a deep disappointment. In January 1917 the navy had promised that Britain would be starving before the year was out. By the summer it was clear that despite the losses they were inflicting, Germany simply did not have enough submarines to overcome the merchant fleet that the Entente was able to mobilize from every corner of the earth. The dawning realization of this defeat completed the profound political reorientation in Germany. With both wings of the SPD now more vociferous than ever in their calls for peace, in early July 1917 they were joined by spokesmen both for the populist wing of the Catholic Centre Party and the progressive Liberals. The outlines of this coalition had been visible since the 1912 Reichstag election, when the three parties that had once been the antagonists of Bismarck gained almost two-thirds of the popular vote. The Social Democrats, Christian Democrats and progressive Liberals now formed a standing committee to press their demands for democratization at home and a negotiated, non-annexationist peace.[20] On 6 July the Reichstag majority found its voice when Matthias Erzberger, the leading spokesman of the left wing of the Centre Party, who in 1914 had been amongst the most boisterous advocates of expansive war aims, made a dramatic call for Germany to face the consequences of the failure of the U-boat campaign. Germany must seek a negotiated peace.[21] Bethmann Hollweg scrambled to contain the crisis by extracting from the Kaiser another promise of democratization in Prussia after the war. But it was not enough. The Chancellor had failed to resist the disastrous escalation of the U-boat war and must now pay the political price. He was dismissed and on 19 July the Reichstag voted by a large majority to approve a peace note. This called for a 'peace of understanding' and the 'permanent reconciliation of peoples', which could not be based on 'forced territorial acquisition' or 'political, economic or financial oppression'. They called for a new and equitable international order based on the liberal principles of free trade, the freedom of the seas, and the establishment of an 'international judicial organization'. Though the Reichstag majority avoided any direct echo of either Petrograd's or Wilson's language, there was no mistaking their general concordance. The Russians, Erzberger hoped, would be won over 'in a matter of weeks'.[22]

Peace without victory was no longer merely a slogan or wishful thinking. Given the exhaustion of all the European combatants, by the summer of 1917 it seemed increasingly a fact. And in early May the Russian revolutionaries looked poised to take advantage. The Provisional Government had been recognized by the United States and the Entente. Given the huge sacrifices it had made, Russia as a loyal member of the alliance was within its rights to ask for the question of war aims to be reopened. Meanwhile, the Petrograd Soviet, as an unofficial body, was free to pursue a parallel campaign of international solidarity and peace propaganda. Pressure from within the Entente itself, both from above and below, would achieve what Wilson could not. It would force London and Paris to negotiate, allowing Russia to escape the choice between an odious separate peace and fighting the war to an imperialist finish. In April 1917 British and French delegations, headed by leading figures in their respective Labour and Socialist parties, travelled to Petrograd charged by their governments with the mission of convincing the Russians to stay in the war. They found the revolutionary defensists set firmly against a separate peace with Germany, but insistent that the Entente must reconsider its war aims. Both Arthur Henderson and Albert Thomas, leading pro-war socialists in Britain and France respectively, were deeply concerned about the possible derailment of the democratic revolution in Russia. In the hope of warding off the Bolsheviks, they agreed to persuade their comrades at home to attend the international socialist conference that Petrograd had called to meet in Stockholm on 1 July.[23] The French Socialists duly withdrew their ministers from the French cabinet. But, after General Pétain had restored order to the Western Front by court-martialling several thousand French mutineers, Paris was not about to risk further pacifist contamination. The passports of the French Socialists were summarily cancelled and Lloyd George's government promptly followed suit. The effect was to split the British labour movement, between the pro-war majority and a vocal oppositional minority that now stretched beyond the ranks of the Independent Labour Party.

To the Russian Socialists, the obduracy of London and Paris came as little surprise. What was more disappointing was the attitude of Washington.[24] Even following America's entry into the war, the revolutionary defensists still counted on Wilson for support. And Wilson fully appreciated their dilemma. He regarded the secret Entente agreements of 1915 and 1916 in which Imperial Russia was entangled as odious. He knew, as he put it to a British confidant, that the Russians 'in setting up their new government and working out domestic reforms' might arrive at the point at which they found 'the war an intolerable evil and would desire to get to an end of it on any reasonable terms'. When the Petrograd Soviet issued its formula for peace that so obviously echoed Wilson's own 'peace without victory' appeal, it caused real embarrassment in Washington.[25] If Wilson had been able to throw the weight of the United States behind Petrograd's call for peace, the effect might have been dramatic. But the headlong aggression of Germany in the spring of 1917 appears to have convinced Wilson that so long as Imperial Germany remained a threat, there was no prospect of calming the militarist impulse in Britain and France.[26] Germany and thus the old world as a whole could be tamed only through force. To ensure that this pacification did not become another imperialist war of conquest, America must have leadership of the war effort. It was one thing for the President of the United States to arbitrate a world settlement, it was quite another to allow the Russian revolutionaries to dictate the pace of peace politics. Nothing good could come of an undisciplined socialist peace conference in Stockholm in which America had no substantial voice. Having been forced to opt for war, Wilson was not about to lose control of the politics of peace. When the Russian government made its official appeal for the Entente to revise their war aims, London and Paris were only too happy to let Wilson be the first to reply. On 22 May the American President issued a response to the Russian people in which he began by reaffirming the deadly menace posed by Imperial Germany. The apparent willingness of the Kaiser's government to accept reform was designed 'only to preserve the power they have set up in Germany . . . and their private projects of power all the way from Berlin to Baghdad and beyond'. Berlin remained at the centre of 'a net of intrigue directed against nothing less than the peace and liberty of the world. The meshes of that intrigue must be broken, but cannot unless wrongs already done are undone. . .'[27] A lasting peace could not simply reinstate the status quo ante 'out of which this iniquitous war issued . . . that status must be altered in such a fashion as to prevent any such hideous thing from ever happening again'. The vital precondition was that Germany must be defeated first. And there must be no hesitation '. . . we may never be able to unite or show conquering force again in the great cause of human liberty. The day has come to conquer or submit . . . If we stand together, victory is certain and the liberty which victory will secure. We can afford then to be generous, but we cannot afford then or now to be weak . . .'

This resonant language of Republican militancy, so at odds with Wilson's stance of only a few months earlier, pleased London and Paris enormously. The Foreign Secretary, Arthur Balfour, remarked gleefully that Wilson's volte-face had been necessary to 'counteract [the] effect which some of his earlier [pacifist] pronouncements have apparently had in Russia'.[28]

With France and Russia on the point of exhaustion, it was Britain that led the effort to re-energize the war and for this, American assistance was indispensable. In the summer of 1917 the greatest threat to the British war effort were not the U-boats, nor the threat of a Soviet in Leeds, but the very real possibility of default on the loans contracted in Wall Street since 1915. In this regard the American declaration of war provided immediate relief. Already by the end of April, Washington had provided Britain with an unprecedented official advance of $250 million, pending congressional approval of as much as $3 billion in loans. As it turned out, Congress took longer than expected, which only served to highlight the state of complete dependence into which the Entente had slipped. In the last days of June, Britain came within hours of insolvency.[29] But with the US as a co-belligerent, there was no longer any real risk of disaster. The Entente had moved from its precarious reliance on the vagaries of the private capital market, to the new ground of openly political government-to-government lending. It was this backing that allowed Britain's Field Marshal Haig to begin preparing a huge new offensive drive. The preparatory barrage for what was to become infamous as the Passchendaele offensive began on 17 July. Over a two-week period over 3,000 British guns delivered 4.238 million rounds onto the German trenches. At an estimated cost of $100 million this storm of steel was a further demonstration of the potency of the transatlantic war effort.[30] In military terms the assault aimed to sweep the Germans from their toehold on the Flanders coastline. But the offensive's rationale was eminently political. Passchendaele was an expression of the British government's grim determination to silence once and for all the talk of peace without victory.[31]

For Russia's democratic revolutionaries this show of belligerence was a disaster. If neither London nor Washington would countenance this talk of peace, this left Petrograd with two options. The Petrograd Soviet might have embraced the risky course of entering into separate peace talks with Germany. In July, if it had not already been otherwise committed, it could have seized on the Reichstag peace resolution, and challenged the rest of the Entente to respond. Despite his distaste both for the Germans and the Russian socialists, could Wilson really have refused such an appeal? What would have been the impact in Britain and France? In the House of Commons, the Independent Labour Party was demanding a positive response to the Reichstag note. The discontent of the workforce was undeniable.[32] But in Russia neither the Provisional Government nor the majority in the Soviets could bring themselves to take a first step toward Germany. To usher in the new revolutionary era by suing for a separate peace would be a fundamental betrayal. Russian democracy could have no future in isolation.

Was there a more radical alternative? On the left wing of the revolution the Bolsheviks were a growing force. Lenin was making waves with his violent hostility to any compromise between the forces of the revolution and the hangovers from Tsarist-era liberalism and parliamentary conservatism that still clung to ministerial positions in the Provisional Government. His slogan was 'all power to the soviets'. Only with power securely in the hands of the revolution would it be possible to formulate a clear choice between a truly democratic peace and a revolutionary continuation of the war. For Lenin, the Petrograd Soviet's peace formula was not enough. Self-determination and no annexations might sound like progressive principles, but why should a revolutionary accept the endorsement of the pre-war status quo implied by 'no annexations'?[33] The only truly revolutionary formula was unqualified support for 'self-determination'. Whereas liberals and reformist progressives shrank from such a formula because of the violence and inter-ethnic conflict it could easily stir up, Lenin espoused the slogan precisely because he expected it to unleash a whirlwind. The harbinger of the future, as far as Lenin was concerned, was the uprising that had taken place a year earlier in Dublin. On Easter Monday 1916, 1,200 Sinn Fein volunteers had taken on the British Army in a sacrificial act, which as we shall see was to turn Irish politics on its head and set the stage for the open struggle for independence. Whereas more orthodox Marxists dismissed Sinn Fein as suicidal putschists who lacked substantial working-class backing, for Lenin they were a vital pointer to the revolutionary future: 'To imagine that social revolution is *conceivable* without revolts by small nations in the colonies and in Europe, without revolutionary outbursts by a section of the petty bourgeoisie *with all its prejudices* . . . to imagine all this is to *repudiate social revolution* . . .' Anyone, who expected a '"pure" social revolution', made only by the working class, would '*never* live to see it . . . We would be very poor revolutionaries if, in the proletariat's great war of Liberation for socialism, we did not know how to utilise *every* popular movement . . .'[34] Lenin demanded an immediate revolutionary peace. But, as anyone familiar with his writings would soon realize, this slogan was easily misunderstood. Lenin wanted urgently to halt the all-consuming, imperialist World War that was threatening to extinguish any hope of historical progress. But he wanted this peace only because he hoped that it would unleash an even more encompassing international class war – the 'proletariat's great war of Liberation'. A revolutionary peace concluded by an all-Soviet Russian regime would cause an uprising of the German proletariat. That liberals and Mensheviks shrank from such a course, fearing that it would unleash civil war in Russia, was precisely what marked it for Lenin as the correct revolutionary line. He was no pacifist. His aim was to turn meaningless imperialist slaughter into historically progressive class war. But what even Lenin did not dare to advocate in the summer of 1917 was a separate peace, a peace at any price with the Kaiser's regime.[35]

Barring that, what was the alternative? Petrograd might simply have adopted a defensive posture. The Germans certainly showed little sign of wishing to take military advantage of Russia's disorder. In the hope that the Russians would come round to a separate peace Ludendorff refrained from any offensive operations in the East. When the first high-level American mission headed by Elihu Root visited Petrograd in June 1917, it too recommended inaction. So long as Russia remained loyal to the Entente, America was willing to provide aid. On 16 May the US Treasury agreed to provide the Provisional Government with an immediate loan of $100 million. Supplies were piled high at Vladivostok, if only they could be moved along Russia's disintegrating railway system. To address this bottleneck Wilson authorized the immediate despatch of a technical railway mission to restore the capacity of the Trans-Siberian railway. In July the railway commission authorized the procurement in the US of 2,500 locomotives and 40,000 wagons.[36] Perhaps it was not yet too late to stabilize Russian democracy as part of a joint war effort against Germany.

But the prospect of hunkering down in the ragged trench lines to hold out for another season of indecisive campaigning went fundamentally against the spirit of revolutionary Petrograd. There was a serious risk that if the army was left inactive throughout the summer, the Provisional Government would lose whatever capacity it still had to counteract Bolshevik subversion. The signs that the British were already discounting Russia as a military force were deeply ominous. Whatever Petrograd did, they had to bring the Entente along with them, but what leverage could they exercise if they were no longer an active participant in the war? Like Wilson, Russia's democratic revolutionaries were forced to gamble that they could alter the course of the war from within. To force the rest of the Entente to take seriously Russian democracy's appeals for a negotiated peace, in May 1917 Kerensky, Tsereteli and their colleagues set themselves frantically to rebuilding the army as a fighting force. They were not unrealistic enough to imagine that they might defeat Germany. But if Russia could deliver the kind of blow against Austria that Brusilov had pulled off in 1916, the Entente would surely have to listen. It was an extraordinary wager that reveals, not the timidity, but the desperate ambition of the February revolution.[37]

III

Certainly Russia was not suffering from any shortage of materiel. Thanks to its own mobilization efforts and the now abundant Allied supply line, the Russian Army of the early summer of 1917 was better equipped than at any previous point in the war. The question was whether its soldiers would fight. In May and June, Kerensky, Brusilov and a hand-picked group of political commissars waged a desperate struggle to rouse the Russian Army from its apathy and to counteract the increasingly pervasive influence of Bolshevik agitators preaching Lenin's heretic gospel. It was the revolutionary democrats of February 1917, not Lenin and Trotsky, who first introduced political commissars to the Russian Army, to deliver the slogans of the revolutionary war effort. In his memoirs Kerensky describes the breathless moment on 1 July 1917 as the barrage lifted ahead of the fateful assault: 'Suddenly there was a deathly hush: it was zero hour. For a second we were gripped by a terrible fear that the soldiers might refuse to fight. Then we saw the first lines of infantry, with their rifles at the ready, charging toward the frontlines of German trenches.'[38] The army advanced. In the south, under the dynamic command of the young war hero, Lavr Kornilov, they made inroads against the shaky Habsburg forces. But where Bolshevik subversion was most serious, in front of the Germans in the north, the majority of the troops refused orders and remained in their trenches. On 18 July, with the Russians off balance, Germany counter-attacked.

The result was to pivot not just Russian but German history as well. At the very moment, on 19 July 1917, that Erzberger introduced the peace resolution in the Reichstag, the premise on which he made his challenge to the Kaiser's regime was overturned. The U-boats might have failed, but in the East, the German Army was poised to win the war. Within hours of the German assault, the Russian defences collapsed and a rout ensued. Whilst the British got bogged down in the terrible slaughter of Flanders, on 3 September 1917 the Kaiser's army marched triumphantly into Riga, once the capital of the Teutonic knights. In a mirror image of events in the autumn of 1916, when the Entente had seemed close to victory, this time it was the prospect of German triumph that obliterated the possibility of a negotiated peace. Within days of their entry into Latvia, Hindenburg and Ludendorff began shuffling seven of their crack Baltic divisions thousands of kilometres to the south, to positions on a tightly concentrated sector surrounding the Italian town of Caporetto.[39] On 24 October, German shock troops crashed through the Italian lines. Swinging south towards Venice, they unhinged an entire segment of the front line.[40] Within a matter of days the Italian Army suffered 340,000 casualties, of whom 300,000 were taken prisoner. A further 350,000 soldiers retreated in disarray. With the Germans and Austrians advancing on Venice, 400,000 civilians fled in terror. Italy survived the crisis. A government of national unity took office in Rome. French and British reinforcements poured in. The Austro-German advance was halted on the Piave river line. But in Germany militarism had gained a new lease on life. The summertime parliamentary onrush of Erzberger, the SPD and the Reichstag majority was halted. Hundreds of thousands of enraged nationalists flocked into the newly formed German Homeland Party (Deutsche Vaterlandspartei), determined to prevent the traitorous democrats from sabotaging the final push for victory.[41]

In Russia, the impact of the failure of Kerensky's democratic war effort was even more dramatic. The advocates of revolutionary defensism were humiliated. The peasant soldiers, many of whom had reluctantly steeled themselves for one last offensive, now abandoned the cause en masse. On 17 July, as the tide on the battlefield was about to turn, radicalized military units in the garrisons around Petrograd marched on the centre of the city to put an immediate end to the war. They acted seemingly without orders from Bolshevik headquarters, but as the demonstrations escalated, Lenin and the party leadership threw themselves behind the rebellion. The uprising was not put down until the following day. The revolution was now openly and violently divided against itself. Despite their profound commitment to democratic freedoms, the Petrograd Soviet had no option but to order the mass arrest of the Bolshevik leadership. It was the first time that any such measures had been used since the overthrow of the Tsar. Fatally, however, the Provisional Government did not disarm the rebellious garrison units that formed the real base of Bolshevik strength, nor were they willing to decapitate the Bolshevik organization. The death penalty remained taboo.

Having survived an attack from the left wing, the main danger to Russian democracy was now from the right. With Brusilov's reputation in tatters, the obvious Bonapartist pretender was General Kornilov, who Kerensky had approved as commander-in-chief.[42] After weeks of open conspiracy, on 8 September 1917 Kornilov mounted his coup, only to find himself foiled by precisely the same force that had doomed the summer offensive. The mass of the army was no longer willing to take orders for decisive action. Kornilov was arrested. But who was to govern? Kerensky, who had launched the disastrous offensive and appeared to have colluded with Kornilov, was utterly discredited. Tsereteli and the Mensheviks on the Executive Committee of the Petrograd Soviet were struggling for legitimacy. They could not resist calls for the release from prison of notorious Bolshevik agitators, such as Trotsky and Alexandra Kollontai. The last resort was the Constituent Assembly. Due to tactical manoeuvrings and the formidable difficulties of staging a general election in a country the size of Russia at a time of war and civil disorder, the date for the Constituent Assembly elections had been repeatedly put back. In August it was irrevocably fixed for 25 November. It is commonly said that it was a dangerous power vacuum that opened the door to Lenin in the autumn of 1917. But what really defined the situation and compelled Lenin and Trotsky to act was the prospect that the Constituent Assembly would soon fill that vacuum with a potent source of democratic authority. On 23 October, during a conspiratorial meeting in Petrograd, Lenin blurted out: 'Now was the moment for seizing power, or never ... it is senseless to wait for the Constituent Assembly that will obviously not be on our side ...'[43]

As far as the Bolsheviks were concerned, the Constituent Assembly elected on the basis of universal suffrage, including the bourgeoisie as well as workers and peasants, could never be anything more than a cloak for bourgeois power. 'All power to the Soviet' had been Lenin's slogan from the start. After the embarrassment of the Kornilov putsch, the all-important Petrograd Soviet was firmly under the sway of the Bolsheviks. With Trotsky in command, Petrograd voted to call a full session of the All-Russian Congress of Soviets to meet on 7 November. This national congress would provide a plausible substitute for the Constituent Assembly. But by the same token, the Bolsheviks were less certain of their grip on the All-Russian Congress than they were of their hold over the Petrograd Soviet. Lenin had not forgotten the scorn heaped on his 'peace' policy by the majority of Mensheviks and Social Revolutionaries at the summer session of the All-Russian Congress. To ensure that there was no repeat, Trotsky planned to launch a pre-emptive coup, overthrowing the remnants of the Provisional Government and installing an all-socialist government in Petrograd, thus facing Lenin's critics with a fait accompli. On the evening of 6 November, one day before the All-Russian Congress of Soviets was due to meet, Red Guards occupied every key point in the city. After a largely unopposed seizure of power, at 10.40 p.m. on the evening of 7 November (25 October old style) Lenin felt confident enough to allow the All-Russian Congress to convene. It promptly overturned the prevailing majority of Mensheviks and Social Revolutionaries and voted in a new Central Executive Committee dominated by Lenin and his comrades. On the day after the coup, Lenin proposed that the Constituent Assembly elections be cancelled altogether. There was no need for such an exercise in 'bourgeois democracy'. But he was overruled by the Bolshevik Executive Committee, which decided that to flout the democratic hopes of the February revolution so openly would do more harm than good.[44]

The elections duly went ahead in the last week of November (Table 2). Too frequently overlooked, they deserve to stand, not only as a monument to the political capacities of the Russian people, but as a milestone in the history of twentieth-century democracy. At least 44 million Russians cast a vote. To date it was the largest expression of popular will in

Table 2. The Biggest Event in Democratic History: The Outcome of
the Russian Constituent Assembly Election, November 1917

	millions	% tabulated votes
Socialist Revolutionaries (agrarian)	15.9	38
SD Bolshevik	9.8	24
SD Menshevik	1.4	3
minor socialist	0.5	1
Constitutional Democrats, Kadets (liberal)	2.0	5
other non-socialist parties	1.3	3
Ukrainian (mainly SR)	4.9	12
Islamic parties	0.9	2
other nationalities	1.7	4
unclassified	3.4	8
	41.8	100

history. Almost three times as many Russians voted in November
1917 as Americans had done in the 1916 presidential election. Not until
the 1940s was any Western election to outdo this spectacular event.
Turnout ran at just short of 60 per cent. Participation was somewhat
higher in the 'backward' countryside than in the cities. There was little
or no evidence of fraud. The Russian electorate cast their ballots in a
manner that clearly reflected both the basic structure of Russian society
and the course of national political events since February 1917. As the
foremost historian of this long-forgotten episode comments: 'We may
conclude . . . that there was nothing fundamentally wrong with the election . . . When burghers vote for property rights, soldiers and their wives
for peace and demobilization, and peasants for land, what is there about
the spectacle that is abnormal or unreal?' They may have had little
experience of democracy, but 'in an elemental way, the electorate' of
revolutionary Russia 'knew what it was doing'.[45]

Taken together, the parties of the revolution – the agrarian Socialist
Revolutionaries and their Ukrainian sister party, the Mensheviks and
the Bolsheviks – commanded almost 80 per cent of the vote. The parties
of revolutionary defensism – the Socialist Revolutionaries (SRs) and
Mensheviks – were still the most popular, even after the Bolshevik coup.

But by the autumn of 1917 their positions were painfully incoherent. By contrast, a large and energetic minority clustered around the urban areas and above all around Petrograd, giving their backing to the Bolsheviks. Since the spring of 1917, the SRs and Mensheviks had been imploring the Bolsheviks to form a broad-based revolutionary coalition. But this was of no interest to Lenin and Trotsky. Instead, they allied themselves opportunistically with the extreme left wing of the agrarians, the Left SRs, whose advocacy of class war was even more militant than their own. The first meeting of the Constituent Assembly was postponed until January 1918 and in the meantime the Bolsheviks set about consolidating a Soviet regime and making good on Lenin's most popular slogan: 'Land, Bread and Peace'.

IV

In the aftermath of the coup, in a last desperate bid to save Russia's democratic revolution, Viktor Chernov, the veteran leader of the agrarian Social Revolutionaries, appealed to London, Paris and Washington to provide him with a sensational foreign policy breakthrough, with which to answer Lenin's seductive promise of an immediate peace. But he hoped in vain. There was no reaction. After the revolutionary contagion had threatened to spread westwards in the summer, the Allies had decided to quarantine the Russian menace. In Washington, at least, there was some sense of the scale of the impending disaster. Following the collapse of the Kerensky offensive in early August 1917, Colonel House had written to Wilson that he felt an urgent move towards an immediate peace was vital: 'It is more important . . . that Russia should weld herself into a virile Republic than it is that Germany should be beaten to her knees. If internal disorder reaches a point in Russia where Germany can intervene, it is conceivable that in the future she may be able to dominate Russia both politically and economically. Then the clock of progress would indeed be set back.' If, on the other hand, democracy were to be 'firmly established' in Russia, House urged, 'German autocracy would be compelled to yield to a representative government within a very few years.'[46] For the sake of progress, America must use its leverage to impose an immediate peace on the basis of the status quo ante, together with some face-saving 'adjustment' over Alsace Lorraine.

Paris might object, but House thought it likely that France would in any case 'succumb' that winter. Wilson faced 'one of the great crisis [sic] that the world has known'.[47] House prayed that Wilson would 'not lose this great opportunity'.[48] Before rivers of American blood were spilled, before Washington's engagement became irrevocable, he should renew the project of peace without victory.

If House had come to his appreciation of the strategic importance of a democratic Russia in May, rather than in mid-August 1917, if Wilson had been willing to respond constructively to the peace feelers of the revolutionary defensists, or to signal his acceptance of a separate peace, perhaps democracy in Russia might have been saved. But neither response was ever forthcoming. America's entry into the war shut the door on the peace and Wilson refused to reopen it. Colonel House's insights into the geopolitics of progress were out of season. At the end of August, Wilson contemptuously swatted aside a peace initiative from the Vatican, insisting, to the indignation of his former supporters, that no peace could be negotiated with the Kaiser's regime.[49] The last desperate appeals from Russia received no reply. As the leading historian of the doomed agrarian party has commented, we will never know whether the determination of the Allies to continue the war 'killed outright'[50] the possibility of a democratic alternative to the Bolsheviks, or 'merely created an atmosphere in which that idea could not live. But that it was one or the other, there can be no reasonable doubt.'[51] As the Bolshevik Red Guards occupied the Winter palace, Kerensky made his escape in a convoy under the protection of the American embassy flag.

4

China Joins a World at War

On 21 July 1917 in the immediate aftermath of the collapse of Kerensky's offensive in Russia, the liberal American journalist and China-hand Thomas Franklin Fairfax Millard, whose weekly *Review of the Far East* was published in Shanghai, laid down a remarkable challenge to Washington:

> Yes, it is very inconvenient for democracy, at the time when the issue of a world-war is narrowing down to a test of the fate of democracy, to have two great nations like Russia and China trying republicanism for the first time, and under precarious conditions ... but just because the local and general conditions are rather unfavourable, and further because of the linking of these experiments with the cause of democracy throughout the world by reason of the war, it becomes virtually impossible for the US to remain a mere spectator of the course of events in Russia and China. Action to hearten, encourage, and support Russia already has been taken by the US government. Action to hearten, encourage, and support China in her effort to maintain a Republic ought to be devised and undertaken without delay.[1]

By the 1940s we are used to seeing Chinese and Soviet Russian history as conjoined under the sign of Communism. But in 1917 for a fleeting moment, a different kind of connection seemed possible. China and Russia would join the United States in a democratic coalition. What seemed to beckon, if only the will could be found to grasp the opportunity, was the intoxicating prospect of a liberal future for Eurasia. Nor, as we shall see, was this merely the imagining of a lone American journalist. In China just as in Russia, what was at stake in 1917 was the future of a republican revolution. As in Russia this domestic struggle became intertwined with the global war. And just as in Russia, a year that began with a surge of patriotic republican enthusiasm ended in a disastrous descent towards civil war. As a result, by the end of 1917, though the Western Front remained deadlocked, the political order in the vast expanse of Eurasia was shaking from end to end.

I

The crisis in Beijing that prompted Millard to his startling call for action was precipitated in February 1917 by Woodrow Wilson's decision to break off diplomatic relations with Germany and his invitation to the other neutral powers to join him in doing so. Wilson took his stand in the name of 'just and reasonable understandings of international law and the obvious dictates of humanity', and bluntly stated that he took it 'for granted' that all other neutrals would 'take the same course'.[2] For the Chinese political class this was a direct challenge. Even less than the United States had China been able to insulate itself from the conflict. In September 1914 Japan had abruptly occupied the German concession in the city of Qingdao on the Shandong Peninsula. As of 1916 Chinese volunteers were doing labour service for the Entente. While Germany intensified its U-boat campaign in the first days of March 1917, 500 Chinese labourers drowned when the French troopship *Atlas* was torpedoed. Was Beijing not under the same obligation as Washington to protect its citizens against German aggression? Not to have joined Washington in taking a stand would have amounted to a humiliating admission of incapacity. Furthermore, it would have been to miss out on a heaven-sent opportunity to align the fledgling Chinese Republic with the United States and thus to complete the political transformation that began with the Chinese revolution in the winter of 1911–12.[3]

The fact that the centuries-old Ch'ing dynasty finally collapsed in February 1912 to be replaced by a republic marks one of the true turning points in modern history. Republicanism had arrived in Asia. It caused consternation amongst conservatives in China. But it also came as a nasty shock to the Japanese, who after the Meiji Restoration had as recently as 1889 settled on a monarchical constitution modelled on that of Imperial Germany. After thousands of years of dynastic rule China might not seem to be propitious soil for a republic. It was easy then, as now, for Chinese strongmen to find Western academics happy to confirm that Asian values 'required' authoritarian leadership.[4] But throughout decades of turmoil China's transition from monarchy to republic was to prove remarkably durable.[5] The first Chinese general election of 1913 was held under a franchise restricted to men over the age of 21 with elementary education. But by the standards of the day that was hardly ungenerous. Even allowing for the failure of the majority of the Chinese electorate to turn out, the 20 million votes cast made this one of the largest democratic events on record.[6] Furthermore, despite rampant corruption, the leading party of the revolution, the Guomindang, achieved a clear majority for its republican and parliamentary programme.

Before they could exploit their victory, however, the Guomindang's parliamentary leader was gunned down by an assassin linked to President General Yuan Shi-kai. After a short-lived rebellion, concentrated mainly in the southern provinces, Sun Yat-sen and the rest of the Guomindang leadership fled into exile. Yuan prorogued the parliament and suspended the provisional constitution drafted by the revolutionaries. Backed by a foreign loan brokered by London and Japan, but boycotted by Wilson's administration in Washington, Yuan attempted to initiate a fresh authoritarian turn. Yuan, who had come to national prominence in the last years of the empire as the commander of the New Model Army in North-Central China, was a military modernizer who had no faith in new-fangled constitutions.[7] But what he did not reckon with was the opposition of the majority of the Chinese political class. When over the winter of 1915–16 Yuan made a bid to install himself as monarch, the result was nationwide revolt.[8] By the spring of 1916 the southern provinces, the traditional counter-weight to Beijing, abetted by Japanese agents provocateurs, were in open opposition, demanding a federalist constitution.[9] More threateningly, the younger leaders of Yuan's own militarist grouping, General Duan Qirui of Anhui province and General Feng of Zhili, declared against their former patron. China's energetic new press mounted a furious nationalist clamour against Yuan's bid for absolute power.[10] Realizing that he was risking national disintegration and thereby opening the door to Japanese and Russian intervention, Yuan humiliatingly renounced any monarchical ambition and appointed General Duan as his Prime Minister. Duan was certainly no liberal. He had received his military training in Germany and was loyal to Yuan's vision of authoritarian consolidation. But he was what the Germans would later dub a *Vernunftrepublikaner*, a republican out of realism.[11]

When the discredited Yuan died suddenly in June 1916, he was succeeded as President by Li Yuanhong, one of the figureheads of the original uprising of 1911 and the Guomindang's preferred candidate for president back in 1913. Li's first move was to restore the constitution of 1912 and to recall the parliament that Yuan had disbanded with its substantial majority of Guomindang MPs. Under the leadership of the Vice Chairman of the Senate, the Yale-educated C. T. Wang, the parliament set to work drafting a new constitution. In February 1917 the parliament voted to disestablish Confucianism as an official religion. A new generation of Western-influenced intellectuals took charge of Beijing University, including the first generation of Chinese Marxists. Briefly, it seemed as though Chinese politics might be entering a period of constructive reform. A foreign policy that aligned the Chinese Republic with President Wilson seemed the ideal complement to this policy of republican consolidation.

Against Japan and the European imperialists, America had emerged as the great hope of many Chinese. As the youthful nationalist student Mao Zedong wrote to a friend in early 1917: 'Japan is our country's strong enemy.' Within 'twenty years', Mao was convinced, 'China would have to fight Japan, or go under'. Sino-American friendship, by contrast, was fundamental to the nation's future. 'The two Republics East and West will draw close in friendship and cheerfully act as reciprocal economic and trade partners.' This alliance was 'the great endeavour of a thousand years'.[12] America's ambassador in Beijing, the progressive political scientist Paul Reinsch, was only too happy to encourage such talk. Though he was temporarily without telegraph connection to Washington, in early February 1917 Reinsch on his own initiative offered China a loan of $10 million to enable it to make war preparations and follow America in breaking off relations with Germany.[13] But as both Reinsch and the British Embassy reported, there was deep anxiety in Beijing. To remain inactive might be humiliating. To join in an association with America was certainly tempting. But because the United States had set itself so publicly apart from the Entente, how would France, Britain and above all Japan interpret a Chinese alignment with it? As Reinsch reported to Secretary of State Lansing, President Li and

Prime Minister Duan were hesitating because they feared that if China was to become a combatant and if this were to require a 'more adequate military organization', this would enable the Japanese to demand a 'mandate' from the Allies 'to supervise such organization'.[14] If Beijing refused, could China count on America's support? Much now depended on President Wilson.

By contrast with the enthusiasm of the American Embassy in Beijing, the mood in Washington was cautious. On 10 February 1917, having read the cables from Reinsch, Wilson commented to Lansing: 'these and earlier telegrams about the possible action of China make my conscience uneasy. We may be leading China to risk her doom.' '... (I)f we suffer China to follow us in what we are now doing,' the President went on, 'we ought to be ready to assist and stand by her in every possible way ... can we count on the Senate and on our bankers to fulfil any expectations we may arouse in China?'[15] Secretary of State Lansing concurred.[16] Any move to strengthen China's own military capacity was bound to be considered a 'menace that would justify Japan in demanding control'. If Washington were to encourage an independent Chinese effort, Lansing cautioned, they would have to be 'prepared to meet Japanese opposition'.[17]

II

For liberal China Hands such as Ambassador Reinsch or Millard, a confrontation with Japan was not unwelcome. But as we have seen, Wilson harboured deep fears about the global racial balance. In his vain struggle to preserve American neutrality, he felt himself to be the guardian of 'white civilization'. With Europe divided this was not the moment for confrontation in the East. Racial fantasies aside, Japan was certainly a force to be reckoned with. Since the Meiji Restoration it had racked up a formidable track record of aggression.[18] In 1895 Japan had humiliated China, extracted formidable reparations, and prised Korea away. In 1905, now as an ally of Britain, it had inflicted a humiliating defeat on Russia. In August 1914 a request from British Foreign Secretary Grey orchestrated by Japan's Foreign Minister Kato had licensed Tokyo's hasty declaration of war on Germany and its incursion into Shandong. On the lower reaches of the Yellow River within striking distance of Beijing, it was revered as a holy site of all three of China's major religious traditions – Confucianism, Taoism and Buddhism: its occupation was a new and devastating blow to Chinese prestige.

Worse was to follow. To gain the protection of the other members of the Entente, Yuan Shi-kai asked to be invited to declare war on Germany too. But Japan vetoed any show of Chinese independence. Instead, in January 1915, Tokyo handed Beijing a list of 21 demands that were soon to acquire global notoriety as one of the most flagrant expressions of imperialism produced by the war. The first four sections of the 21 Points were familiar expressions of sphere-of-influence diplomacy – a forceful restatement of familiar Japanese objectives in securing their interests in Northern China and Manchuria, contiguous with their colony of Korea. The notorious Section V demands, by contrast, were a claim to hegemony over the central administration in Beijing, its army and financial administration, that would have given Japan rights superior to all other powers throughout China.[19] Because they challenged all the interested powers, the Section V demands were bound to be controversial in the West. But what no one in Japan, nor even amongst President Yuan's inner circle in Beijing, had reckoned with was the patriotic indignation of the Chinese public.[20] As news of the Japanese claims leaked out, 40,000 demonstrators marched in protest in Beijing. The nation was swept by a boycott campaign against Japanese goods. Fashionable Chinese women dropped the Tokyo hairstyles that had come into vogue after Japan's triumph over Russia. Beijing University students resolved to recite the 21 Points every day to remind themselves of the stain on their national honour. At a stroke, what the Japanese had intended as a regional *coup de main* had turned into an international scandal. Whilst British diplomats struggled to prevent China and Japan coming to blows, the *Washington Post* broadcast the full details of the 21 Points to its indignant readership. There were speeches of protest in Congress denouncing Japan as the 'Prussia of the East'.

There certainly were political forces in Japan willing to live up to this billing. The circle around *genro* Yamagata, the most influential survivor of the founding Meji generation, speculated more or less openly about the mistake that Japan had made in joining the side of the Entente. Convinced that Japan would in the long run face a confrontation with the United States, they favoured a conservative alliance with autocratic Tsarist Russia, a relationship that was consolidated by a secret treaty over the summer of 1916. But though scepticism about Japanese intentions toward China was certainly warranted, anti-Japanese outrage easily blinded Western observers to the ambiguity of imperialist politics in Japan. Facing a collapsing regime in China and competing with an aggressively expansionist autocracy in Russia, imperialism often went hand in hand in Japan with reform-minded liberalism. This was all the more the case once Japanese expansion was underwritten by the Anglo-Japanese alliance. Up until 1914, Japan's economic development and public finances depended to an extraordinary extent on the City of London. Nor was Japan in its domestic politics the authoritarian power-house of liberal, anti-imperialist cliché. Following the death of the last Meiji Emperor in July 1912, four cabinets succeeded each other in short succession, buffeted by elite infighting and popular protest. Prime Minister Okuma, who took office in April 1914, was steeped in the prejudices of his era and his class, but he had also been exposed to Western political thought and, in the early years of the Meiji, had been counted as a champion of a British-style constitutional monarchy. Coming out of retirement in 1914 to stabilize the crisis of the new Taisho era, Okuma formed a cabinet that featured a number of eye-catching members, including true heroes of Japanese liberalism such as Ozaki Yukio, the 'god of Japanese constitutionalism', who served as his Minister of Justice. His main backing in the Diet came from the party known as the Doshikai. Among the disparate factionalism of Japanese party politics, the Doshikai stood out for their consistent adherence to an economic policy of liberal orthodoxy, the pillars of which were the gold standard and Japan's intimate relationship with London. This connection was personified by Foreign Minister Kato, who had served as Japan's ambassador to Britain. After the war, the Doshikai were to morph into the main liberalizing force in Japanese parliamentary politics. In 1925 they were to carry through the introduction of full manhood suffrage.

The fact that these changes occurred without violent overthrow should not lead us to underestimate their significance. When compared to the Chinese Republic's rough-hewn exercise in democracy, Japan's elections up to 1919 were staid affairs involving an electorate of no more than 1 million out of a population of 60 million. But from the turn of the century popular interest in politics dramatically revived. Newspaper circulation grew exponentially from 1.63 million copies per day in 1905 to 6.25 million in 1924.[21] From the outbreak of war with Russia in 1905, Japan was repeatedly convulsed by waves of popular agitation. For Japanese intellectuals, deeply influenced by European historical thinking, it was evident that Japan as much as China was caught up in a tidal wave of historical change. The question was what implications it should have for foreign policy.

When Okuma and Kato launched Japan into the war they, like the advocates of war in China, did so with a sense of historic purpose that went beyond mere imperial aggrandizement. Invoking Sir Edward Grey and the Anglo-Japanese Treaty to justify the declaration of war allowed Kato to sideline the more conservative figures in the Japanese establishment around *genro* Yamagata. Looked on in this light, the 21 Points were a further effort by Kato to maintain the respectability of Japanese foreign policy in Western eyes by containing the even more radical, racialized visions of confrontation that were circulating within the imperial military establishment. The gamble backfired horribly. Though Beijing was forced into humiliating concessions, Tokyo could not uphold the hugely controversial Section V demands in the face of international protest. Britain negotiated a compromise between Tokyo and Beijing. Foreign Minister Kato, one of the great hopes of Japanese liberalism, resigned, and from the summer of 1915 until Yuan's death a year later, Japanese policy towards China lurched towards a new and dangerous adventurism. Rather than pursuing the vain search for international respectability, the rump of the Okuma cabinet allowed itself to be persuaded by Vice Chief of Staff Tanaka Giichi to commit itself to a radical attack on the central authority of Beijing. Japan would eliminate China from the menacing strategic configuration in the Pacific by a ruthless policy of divide and rule, squeezing Yuan to make humiliating concessions, whilst sponsoring nationalists such as Sun Yat-sen to rebel against him. But although by the spring of 1916 Tanaka had managed to push China to the brink of civil war, this did little in a positive sense to secure Japan's long-term strategic position.

In the summer of 1916 the fiasco of the liberal version of Japanese imperialism opened the door to a new government headed by General Terauchi, a bull-necked militarist and ruthless former governor of Korea. Unlike Okuma, Terauchi was openly hostile to any move toward the liberalization of the Japanese constitution. He took office declaring that his government would 'transcend' parliamentary control and no area of policy was more sensitive than foreign policy. Facing what it believed to be a threat on an oceanic scale from the United States, the Terauchi government was insistent that Japan must go beyond a regional policy of spheres of interest. It was not enough for Japan to carve out its place in Manchuria, alongside British emplacements in Central China and France in the South, let alone to engage in the kind of destructive divide and rule tactics pursued by Tanaka.[22] Instead, to confront the threat from across the Pacific, Tokyo must intensify its effort to place all of China under Japanese influence, thereby excluding the Western Powers altogether from the region. But the scandal of the notorious Section V of the 21 Points had taught a lesson. In pursuing this enormously ambitious agenda, Japan must use new tools. The new programme was not without a military dimension. Japan would seek long-term intergovernmental military agreements. But henceforth Japanese policy in China would be directed through the national government in Beijing and the lead would be taken by bankers, principally the shadowy associate of Interior Minister Goto Shinpei, Nishihara Kamezo.[23]

The enormous centrifugal forces that upended the structures of pre-war finance in the Atlantic were also at work in the Pacific. By 1916, Japan's balance of payments was so strong and the Entente's financial position so desperate that Tokyo was in the truly unprecedented position of lending money to the Entente (Table 3). The first loan was for 100 million yen to pay for Russian purchases of Japanese-made rifles on British account. Japan would exert leverage over Beijing by becoming its chief source of foreign finance. And this shift to a strategy of long-term financial hegemony was further reinforced by Japan's internal politics. Despite their pretensions to 'transcendence', Prime Minister Terauchi and his authoritarian friends needed support in parliament.[24] To counterbalance the criticism of ousted Foreign Minister Kato and the biting attacks of radical liberals such as Ozaki Yukio, Terauchi's purportedly independent conservative government was in fact dependent on the gentry party of provincial Japan, the Seiyukai. Their redoubtable leader, Hara Takashi, was no progressive. He resisted the rising tide of democracy in Japan and was only too happy to profit from a rigged election in 1917 to establish a huge majority in the Diet. He scoffed at the aspirations of Chinese nationalism. But of one central feature of the new world Hara was unshakably convinced – the dominant power of the future was the United States. America's indignant reaction to the 21 Points had made clear that Japan must consider its China policy carefully.

Table 3. From Deficit to Surplus to Deficit: Japan's Fragile Balance of Payments, 1913–29 (in millions of yen)

| | current account | | | capital balance sheet | | | | | |
	balance	trade balance	shipping income	net debt/ asset position	Japanese foreign debts	Japan loans to Chinese government	government loans to France, Russia, Britain	other private foreign investments	specie-holding abroad
1899–1913	-951	-1409	270	-1223	2069	60		540	246
1914	9.56	-5	39						212
1915	265	176	50						379
1916	575	371	158				263		487
1917	784	568	274				443		643
1918	868	294	455				575		1135
1919	107	-74	368	1399	1822	236	575	1085	1343
1920	-393	-388	268						1062
1921	-307	-361	140						855
1922	-98	-268	111						615
1923–1929	-1022	-2259	906	-738	2549	94		1717	0

Japan must be aware of its limits. China's sheer bulk counselled caution. As Foreign Minster Motono Ichiro put it in December 1916: 'There are those who say that we should make China a protectorate or partition it, and there are those who advocate the extreme position that we should use the European war to make China completely our territory . . . but even if we were able to do that temporarily, the (Japanese) Empire lacks real power to hold on to it very long'.[25] A Chinese warlord put the same point rather more crudely. For all their aggression, the Japanese were 'not sure' that they could 'swallow' China. 'We are weak, we are stupid, we are divided, but we are innumerable, and in the end, if they persist, China will burst the Japanese stomach.'[26]

III

Such was the delicately poised situation into which Wilson's appeal to the neutral powers exploded in early February 1917. How would Japan and China react? The American Embassy at least had no doubts about its mission. To consolidate the Chinese Republic and ward off Japan's influence, Beijing must join Washington in an immediate break with Germany. For five days straight in early February, Ambassador Reinsch and his team belaboured Prime Minister Duan and President Li. As one of his staff put it, Reinsch was at the head of a 'flying wedge of muscular and determined American citizens who drove China relentlessly over the line of self-sufficiency and into world affairs'.[27] It was this aspiration to membership in the international community that resonated through the announcement duly issued by Beijing on 7 February. Faced with Germany's violation of international law, 'China for the sake of its status in the world should not remain silent. China will take this opportunity to enter a new era of diplomacy, become an equal member of the international community, and through a firm policy, win favorable treatment from the Allies.' The British Embassy informed London that the majority of the cabinet and 80 per cent of China's newspaper-reading public were in favour. From the nationalist South, the Republican newspaper *Chung-Yuan Pao* declaimed: 'This is the time for action. We must range ourselves on the side of justice, humanity and of international law . . .'[28] But within days of the Chinese break with Germany, these hopes were to suffer a shattering disappointment. Far from embracing the Chinese

Republic in its desire to enter the war, President Wilson and Secretary of State Lansing drafted a polite, but discouraging response: 'The American government highly appreciates disposition of China but does not wish to lead it into danger. It regrets practical inability to give any present assurances . . . The Chinese government, therefore would do well to consult its representatives in the Allied countries. Ignorance of Japan's attitude also suggests caution.' To offset the dispiriting impact of this message, Wilson asked Reinsch to express verbally his sincere support for Chinese independence.[29] But despite Reinsch's over-eager promises, and despite the fact that as of April 1917 $3 billion were in the pipeline for the Entente, not even $10 million were approved for China.[30]

A very different message emerged from Japan. Since 1914 Tokyo had adopted a negative attitude toward China's participation in the war against Germany. Now, Terauchi's cabinet was eager to put its new strategy of comprehensive hegemony to the test. On 13 February Nishihara arrived in Beijing with the mission to bring China into the war on Japanese terms. Not to be outdone by Reinsch, the Japanese played on China's demand for international respect. Nishihara encouraged China to make substantial demands of the Europeans, including a ten-year suspension of the indemnity imposed after the suppression of the Boxer rebellion, permission to establish a viable tax base for the Chinese national government by raising customs tariffs, as well as the right to station units of the Chinese Army in the territory of the foreign Legation for the duration of war. Furthermore, unlike his American rivals, Nishihara had the means to deliver on his promises. Within days of his arrival in China he was in negotiations over large loans. On 28 February 1917 Nishihara received Tokyo's approval for an initial tranche of 20 million yen ($10 million), to be disbursed immediately on declaration of war against Germany.

As far as Tokyo was concerned, its new strategy in China seemed to be paying handsome dividends. The Americans appeared surprisingly easy to intimidate. Given the perilous state of the war in Europe, the British and French were willing to concede virtually anything Japan demanded.[31] In January 1917, in exchange for the despatch of a Japanese flotilla to the eastern Mediterranean to help combat the Austro-German U-boat menace, they secretly approved Japan's retention of Germany's rights in Shandong after the end of the war. The real problem for Japan in its search for a policy beyond the imperialism of spheres of interest was, as it turned out, the Chinese. In Tokyo it might seem that the choice was between a policy of divide and rule and one of sponsoring the consolidation of a cooperative Chinese national government. But the awakening of Chinese nationalism confronted Tokyo with a fundamental dilemma. In 1915 Japan's 21 Points had united China against Japan. The unintended effect of Tokyo's new policy of working concertedly with the Beijing government was to discredit their Chinese collaborators and to unleash precisely the kind of disintegration that General Tanaka's secret agents had worked so hard to manufacture through subversive means in 1916. As news leaked out that Prime Minister Duan had accepted Japan's generous offer of loans, a wave of nationalist opposition began to build. From his rebel base in Southern China, Sun Yat-sen let it be known that he opposed entering the war. Echoing the fears that Prime Minister Duan himself had expressed to the Americans, Sun insisted, that 'Whether a country can promote her status' by means of war, depended 'on the strength she has gained. For China, to join the allies will result in domestic disorder rather than improvements.'[32]

The battle for the future of the Chinese Republic began in April 1917, with America's declaration of war on Germany. Prime Minister Duan responded by convoking a conference of military governors in Beijing, who agreed that China must follow suit. But he was now anxious about the reaction of parliament, which though it had voted to break off relations might not support a declaration of war by a government beholden to Japan. With characteristic tact, his warlord friends decided to surround the parliament with an armed mob of their retainers. Outraged by this blatant act of intimidation, the Guomindang majority agreed that a declaration of war was essential on patriotic grounds, yet declared that China could go to war to defend its honour, only once Duan and his pro-Japanese clique had resigned. When Duan refused, President Li dismissed him. Duan's military cronies left Beijing announcing that they would raise a rebellion. But Li was in no mood to compromise. The warlords' challenge to the parliament was illegitimate and would either lead to 'a partition of the country' or risked reducing China to a 'protectorate [of Japan] like Korea'.[33] In fact, sticking as best it could to the principles of its new policy, Tokyo exercised considerable restraint, turning down several requests from Duan for aid. Japan wanted to deal with an authoritative government. It was

President Li who precipitated the final collapse by summoning to Beijing one of the most reactionary of the warlords, Zhang Xun, who he apparently believed could serve as a counterweight to the two major militarist groupings that had emerged from Yuan Shi-kai's power bloc: Prime Minister Duan's Anhui clique and General Feng's Zhili power base. Zhang, however, had his own ideas. He occupied the imperial palace and proclaimed the restoration of the Ch'ing dynasty. President Li was placed under house arrest from which he had to be rescued by Japan's embassy guards.

With Li having invited the chaos, the door was open for Tokyo to intervene directly in Beijing in the name of the integrity of the Chinese Republic. Nishihara released a generous dole of funds to the Zhili wing of the Northern militarist group whose troops promptly reoccupied the capital, routing General Zhang's forces. The Anhui and the Zhili cliques divided power between them. Duan was restored as Prime Minister. Feng, the leading commander of the Zhili faction, replaced Li as President. However, refusing to accept the return of the twice-discredited militarists to Beijing, in the summer of 1917 the Guomindang members of the parliament decamped to the South where they constituted a rebel nationalist government headed by their long-time leader Sun Yat-sen. Meanwhile in Beijing on 14 August, the anniversary of the Boxer uprising, Duan rammed a declaration of war through what was left of the Beijing parliament. He had made his country a party to the war, thereby securing the place at the peace conference that many in China's political class saw as a priceless entry ticket to the international arena. He had also put paid, once and for all, to monarchical restorationism in China. But, with two separate governments in the North and South, China's thirty-year era of disintegration and civil war had begun.

In this conflict, all the sides looked to outside help. With Britain and France tied down in Europe, Russia consumed by revolutionary turmoil and Japan firmly committed to the Northern militarists, the Southern nationalist government turned to the United States. Serving as the Foreign Minister of the Southern government was Wu Tingfang, a distinguished servant of the Ch'ing dynasty and former ambassador to the United States, the first Chinese to be called to the Bar in London's Lincoln's Inn. In July 1917, Wu, who the American press sometimes referred to as the Benjamin Franklin of China, appealed directly to Washington.[34] 'In view of the present dangerous situation and the attitude of the rebellious tuchuns (military governors), I earnestly request that President Wilson, as the defender of the cause of democracy and constitutionalism all the world over, be moved to make a public statement on the subject of the American attitude toward China and earnestly support President Li Yuan-Hung.'[35]

But, despite the strong liberal credentials of men like Wu, the White House refused to take sides.[36] In the summer of 1917, as the Chinese parliament stood face to face with the warlords over the question of the declaration of war, Secretary of State Lansing let it be known that 'The entry of China into war with Germany – or the continuance of the status quo – are matters of secondary consideration.' 'The principle necessity for China is to resume and continue her political entity, to proceed along the road of national development on which she has made such marked progress. With the form of government in China, or the personnel which administers that government, the US has an interest only in so far as its friendship impels it to be of service to China. But in the maintenance by China of one central united and alone responsible government, the United States is deeply interested . . .'[37] This was profoundly humiliating. At the beginning of the year, the Chinese political class had thrilled to the idea that by joining the coalition against Germany they might gain recognition in the advance guard of the family of nations. Now, Lansing was openly asserting China's unreadiness for any such alliance and refusing to take sides in China's internal struggles. By contrast, Imperial Japan had picked a side and was shepherding China into the war under an authoritarian regime. If Duan and the militarists were given their authoritarian head, government in China would certainly be 'central, united and alone responsible', but was this the kind of regime that would really be in the interest of the United States? Furthermore, whatever its superficial solidity, could such a government really produce a lasting settlement of China's political future?

Amidst the chaos of Beijing's factional politics, what Washington refused to acknowledge was that serious issues of principle were at stake. In an open letter published from Shanghai en route to joining Sun Yat-sen's breakaway Southern government, Wu Tingfang addressed himself once more to America: 'The war in Europe is being fought . . . to put an end to Prussian militarism,' he insisted. 'And I want the Americans here to understand that China's present troubles are due to exactly the same causes.' Drawing on his Gladstonian background, the new language of liberal internationalism came fluently to Wu: 'We are engaged in a struggle between democracy and militarism ... I ask Americans to be patient and give China a chance. Democracy will triumph ... I hope to see the day when the stars and stripes and fire-coloured flag of China will be intertwined in an everlasting friendship.'[38] The point was made even more forcefully by C. T. Wang, former vice president of the Senate and one of the authors of the 1917 constitution. Wang pilloried the stark difference in America's attitude towards European and Asian affairs: 'It is becoming rather ridiculous, at a time when America is engaged in a world-war ... with the avowed principal object of saving democratic principle of government from being smothered by autocratic militarism, that the power and influence of the US should be applied in one place abroad, and should not be applied in another place abroad.' 'A primary requisite is that, as between reversion to an archaic monarchy, or the retention of a military oligarchy, or a graduated advance toward genuine republicanism, the influence of the United States ought to be thrown definitely to bring about the latter alternative. If this leads to quasi-interference in Chinese politics, then that responsibility must be faced.'[39]

In the wake of the summer crisis in Beijing, Washington did show some signs of formulating a more concerted policy towards China and Japan. But as far as the Chinese nationalists were concerned, the upshot of those deliberations was hardly reassuring. Rather than engaging China, Lansing chose to deal with Japan. In November 1917, without consulting Beijing, Lansing and the Japanese ambassador Viscount Ishii issued a public statement that affirmed the Open Door policy in China – the principle of equal access for all foreign trade and investment – but also recognized Japan's 'special interest' in Northern China on account of its geographic proximity.[40] China's ambassador in Washington, Wellington Koo, a graduate of Columbia Law School, promptly protested that it was unacceptable for Japan and America to be conferring over the future of China without Chinese involvement. Had he been party to private conversations within the Wilson administration, Koo would have been even more indignant. In September, Colonel House had proposed to Wilson that the vast population of China be placed under the administration of an international mandate, made up of three trustees nominated, with 'Chinese consent', by the USA, Japan and the 'other powers'. China, he felt, was 'in a deplorable condition. The prevalence of disease, the lack of sanitation, a new system of slavery, infanticide, and other brutal and degenerate practices make the nation as a whole a menace to civilization. There is no administration of justice worthy of the name, and the intercommunication is wholly inadequate . . .' The international 'trusteeship' would 'last for an agreed upon number of years, but long enough to put China in order, develop a civilization and purchasing power, and take her out of the backward nations and make her a blessing rather than a menace to the world'.[41]

Compared to this kind of fantasy, Japan's strategy was at least based on the elementary recognition that the Beijing government must be dealt with directly as a partner in power. But, by the same token, Japan now faced the consequences that America wished to avoid. Japan had taken sides in a civil war and its involvement was escalating the conflict. Japan's Chinese allies were engaged in a high-stakes wager. They were gambling that the resources Japan would place at their disposal would be sufficient to overcome the opposition that that support aroused. As Duan told Nishihara in one of their early interviews in February 1917, his intention was to use Japanese aid to push through 'administrative reforms', which meant, Nishihara informed Tokyo, that Duan intended to crush his political enemies and to bring all of China under his sway. Shortly after the declaration of war on Germany in August 1917, Duan explained to ambassador Reinsch that his first aim was to 'make the military organization in China national and unified, so that the peace of the country shall not at all times be upset by local military commanders'.[42] As one of the leading experts on warlordism has remarked, one of the great ironies of the period is that disorder in China was driven not by overt particularism, but by the excessive ambition to national unification.[43] Flush with Japanese funds, in October 1917 Duan launched the first of the North-South campaigns for military unification that were to convulse the country for the next ten years. But in pursuing this military strategy Duan failed to secure the backing of the rival Zhili military faction, headed by President Feng. After the Zhili had sabotaged his campaign to reconquer Hunan province, the fulcrum of central China, Duan was forced to resign. Nor were the Japanese entirely unhappy to see him go. The unification of China under a military strongman was an ambiguous prospect to say the least, and Hara feared that it might finally push the Americans into action. Instead, Tokyo set itself in 1918 to brokering a reconciliation between North and South that would quieten liberal calls for intervention and perhaps do something to restore Japan's battered international image.[44]

Given the delicately balanced political situation within Japan itself, a determined move by the United States at this moment might well have produced an accommodating reaction. Despite the dark ruminations on the part of some Japanese imperialists, there was no majority in Tokyo for a confrontation with Washington. The election of 1917 had given Hara and his Seiyukai the majority they needed to hold the radical anti-Westerners in line. If America had been able to deliver funds in China on the scale that Nishihara had mobilized, it might well have tilted the balance quite decisively. As Jeremiah Jenks, the globe-trotting financial economist, put it, in an urgent letter to Wilson: 'One percent' of the $3 billion earmarked for the Entente 'would put China into position to straighten out her own internal affairs . . .' 'Five per cent' would have emancipated China from Japan altogether, enabling China to establish itself as a 'very important factor in actually fighting the war . . .'[45] At the end of 1917, six years after the overthrow of the Ch'ing dynasty, there were signs that Washington was finally about to put some financial muscle behind its strategy in Asia. Lansing proposed that $50 million would be provided for military reconstruction and the development of the Southern railway network. A further $100 million would help to stabilize the Chinese currency. The funds were be raised by an international bankers' consortium with Wall Street taking the lead.[46] Wilson approved the scheme and the War Department was keen on the idea of moving an army of 100,000 Chinese soldiers to France. But no money ever flowed.

When Lansing and Wilson had first discussed the Chinese dilemma in February 1917 they had mentioned Congress and Wall Street as potential obstacles. When Lansing floated his loan plan in December 1917 it was immediately sunk by Secretary of the Treasury Macadoo. He did not want to ask Congress for authorization for a major government loan to China and he didn't want a Chinese funding drive to compete with Liberty Bonds. When Macadoo finally did agree to a loan it was to be on an entirely private basis to the sum of only $55 million. But with no coherent American strategy in sight, J. P. Morgan promptly announced that it had no interest in China loans except in cooperation with Japan.[47] Japan could deliver influence and even a modicum of security in its sphere of interest, likewise the British in central China and the French in the South. America's resources were potentially far greater, but Washington's refusal to commit to any coherent vision of Chinese political development stopped the flow of funds.

IV

In the spring of 1917 America's entry into the war had seemed to many to herald a transnational crusade for liberal republicanism. But by the end of 1917 the hope that Washington had either the capacity or the will to orchestrate such a sweeping campaign had already been shaken. The failure to produce a constructive policy of engagement in China was no doubt in part explicable in terms of racial and cultural prejudice. It would not be until the end of the 1920s that the United States took Chinese nationalism seriously. But this refusal was not confined to China. As the experience of Russia suggests, there was a more general failure on the part of Washington over the summer of 1917 to take up the challenge of managing the kind of global democratic campaign that Wilson had seemed to promise. In China and Russia, where revolutionary republican projects were immediately at stake, there was a bewildering mismatch between political rhetoric and the effective deployment of resources. The statement issued by Lansing on the need to prioritize the coherence of the Chinese state over participation in the war might well have been extremely welcome if it had been directed to Petrograd in July 1917. But it was only far later in the summer that Colonel House among others realized the enormous strategic importance of protecting the democratic experiment in Petrograd. Conversely, if the kind of financial and logistical support poured into Russia through Vladivostok had been directed to China, it could not but have had a dramatic impact on the force-field of Sino-Japanese relations. As we shall see, the pattern would repeat itself in Europe. In 1918 Wilson would raise great hopes by promising democratic Germany a liberal peace, only for those expectations to be dashed.

There is a pattern here. In truth, despite the appearance Wilson created of speaking to them directly, China, Russia and Germany were objects of his strategy. They were not his real interlocutors. Transformation in such alien places was no doubt welcome, but it was at best a long-term process and one from which America should keep its distance. Wilson's public rhetoric, his diplomacy and strategy were not directed to them, but to containing the dangerous association he had been forced to enter into with the British Empire, the rampaging Japanese, and the vindictive and unpredictable French, an association all the more dangerous because the Machiavellian imperialists of the old world had so many powerful and self-interested friends in America itself, in Congress and on Wall Street. It was Wilson's determination to preserve the upper hand over this network of forces closer to home, not the uncertain prospects for progress in faraway places in Asia or Europe, that dominated every other consideration.

5

Brest-Litovsk

On 2 December 1917 in a gloomy barracks complex in western Russia, representatives of the Bolshevik regime and the Central Powers – the Germans, Austrians, Turks and Bulgarians – sat down to negotiate a peace. Four months later they concluded the notorious Brest-Litovsk Treaty that stripped Russia of territories inhabited by 55 million people, a third of the empire's pre-war population, a third of its agricultural land, more than half its industrial undertakings and mines that had produced almost 90 per cent of its coal. Brest-Litovsk has gone down in history as a stark symbol both of the excesses of German imperialism and Lenin's stop-at-nothing determination to deliver peace.[1] But it was a twisted road on which the Bolsheviks and the Central Powers travelled to the final brutal peace on 3 March 1918.[2] Surprisingly, for a treaty that is generally remembered as an act of imperial rapacity of Hitlerite proportions, the negotiations were prolonged and substantive, and the language they were couched in was the language of self-determination.[3] From the Bolsheviks this was to be expected. Lenin and Trotsky, the commissar for foreign affairs, were after all famous exponents of the new principles of international relations. But in fact at Brest it was the Germans as much as the Soviets who sought to craft a modern peace in the East, based on the new standards of legitimacy, or at least it was the German Foreign Secretary Richard von Kühlmann and his backers in the Reichstag majority who did. Quite deliberately they sought to seize the initiative by establishing a liberal order in the East to replace the autocratic empire of the Tsar.

That such a peace would mean a large loss of territory for Russia was hardly surprising. As Lenin himself had forcefully argued, if the principle of self-determination was taken seriously it trumped any claim to preserve the territorial status quo.[4] By what right could the Bolsheviks, who were violently consolidating their coup in Petrograd, claim the territories conquered by the Tsar? By Lenin's own estimates more than half the populations of eastern Europe were oppressed nationalities.[5] As draconian as the final treaty was from a Russian point of view, only a very small portion of the territory removed from Russia was directly annexed by Germany. Instead, Brest gave birth to the precursors to the Baltic states in their modern form, an independent Ukraine and a Transcaucasian Republic.[6] Of course, in 1918 all of these polities fell willy-nilly under the 'protection' of Imperial Germany. Consequently it has been commonplace to dismiss them as mere 'puppets' of German imperialism. But in doing so, we fall in with the invective of the Bolsheviks. Since 1991, all of these creations of the 'Brest-Litovsk moment', and more, have come to be regarded as legitimate members of the family of nations. Now as then Poland and the Baltic states look to protectors in the West. Today they are keen members of an American-dominated NATO and the European Union, in which Germany is the dominant force. If they are not more anxious about their security, it has much to do with the early twenty-first-century map of Eurasia, on which Russian power is even more drastically circumscribed than it was at Brest. Compared to either the Tsarist past or the post-Soviet future, the vision of a Brest-style peace in the East was not inherently illegitimate. What discredited it was the failure of Berlin to sustain a consistently liberal policy. The suspicion of bad faith hanging over Berlin had the effect both of making the Bolsheviks appear as victims and of handing the initiative back to the Western Powers.

In January 1918, in response to the German-Bolshevik talks at Brest, both Lloyd George and Woodrow Wilson felt obliged to make powerful statements of the liberal world order they envisioned for the post-war period. Of the two statements it was Woodrow Wilson's 14 Points manifesto that would echo around the world. But far from challenging Lenin and Trotsky, as Cold War legend would have it, Wilson chose to conciliate them. In the process, by portraying Lenin and Trotsky as potential partners in a democratic peace and a unitary 'Russian people' as the victim of German aggression, Wilson helped to consolidate the black legend of Brest. Meanwhile, as democrats in Berlin and Vienna looked on in horror, Bolshevik revolutionary tactics combined with the most aggressive impulses of German militarism to eviscerate any attempt to create a legitimate order in the East.

I

True to their promise of delivering an immediate end to the fighting, it was the Bolsheviks who, at the close of November 1917, asked the Germans to enter into negotiations. But on what terms could peace be made? In the spring of 1917 Lenin had been the sternest critic of the revolutionary defensists and their 'Petrograd formula' for a democratic peace, savaging the soft-minded compromises between the conservative doctrine of 'no annexations' and the revolutionary slogan of 'self-determination'. But now that the Provisional Government had been overthrown, what was the alternative? The answer was no more clear in November 1917 than it had been six months earlier. Certainly, Lenin in the first weeks of his new regime did not dare to say out loud that his policy might amount to accepting a separate peace on any terms the Germans would offer. Nor did the Central Powers demand this sacrifice. In acquiescing to an armistice, Germany agreed to negotiate on whatever version of the Petrograd peace formula the Bolsheviks could square with their conscience. Furthermore, Germany did not demand that Russia formally break ranks with the Entente. Instead, Russia and Germany issued a joint declaration, inviting all the other combatants to join the talks. In accordance with the requirements of the 'new diplomacy', the negotiations at Brest were to be carried out with an unusual degree of publicity.[7] To spread their message, the Bolsheviks were even permitted regular fraternization sessions with German troops. At Brest the atmosphere was a strange mixture of old-school aristocratic chivalry and revolutionary innovation. The talks were the first great-power conference in the modern era in which a woman, Anastasia Bizenko, an ex-Social Revolutionary terrorist turned Bolshevik, served as a plenipotentiary for the Soviet side.

It is tempting to dismiss this surprising beginning as a propaganda charade. But that is seriously to underestimate the forces that were in play. The Bolshevik grip on power in November 1917 was truly precarious. Lenin and Trotsky's partners in power, the Left Social Revolutionaries, were no friends of the Entente, but like all the other parties of the February revolution they rejected any idea of a separate peace with the Kaiser. Like the majority of the Bolshevik Party's own activists, they clung to the idea that if acceptable terms could not be agreed, they would proclaim a 'revolutionary war', summoning the insurgent energies of both the Russian and German people for united resistance against imperialism. In December 1917 the divisions within the German home front were more and more evident. Since the first major wave of strikes in April 1917, industrial unrest had boiled throughout the summer. The Reichstag majority that had passed the peace resolution remained in being.[8] In November the parliamentarians asserted themselves by turfing out Georg Michaelis, the puppet Chancellor whom Hindenburg and Ludendorff had installed to replace Bethmann Hollweg. This time the parliamentarians insisted on a substantial figure, Georg Hertling, former Prime Minister of Bavaria and the first of a long line of Christian Democrats to govern twentieth-century Germany. For his deputy, the Reichstag majority chose one of their own, the progressive liberal Reichstag deputy Friedrich von Payer.

Germany had set out on a road to 'parliamentarization'. But would these first steps be enough to quiet popular unrest? And, if they did satisfy the left, might that provoke a backlash from the right? Since August 1917 the ultra-nationalist Homeland Party (Vaterlandspartei) had been mobilizing the right wing of German politics to fight the war to a victorious finish; if this required an open military dictatorship, so much the better.[9] The Vaterlandspartei, though it exhibited populist fascistoid traits, never in fact managed to break out of the pre-war nationalist milieu. But what now concerned the leaders of the Reichstag majority was the prospect that a dogged rearguard action by the German right wing would stall any further reform and provoke a radicalization on their exposed left flank. In the autumn of 1917 support for the breakaway anti-war Independent Social Democratic Party (USPD) was clearly surging. There could no longer be any doubt that the most vocal section of the German working class, perhaps a majority, were demanding a negotiated peace, an end to martial law, democratization in Prussia and an immediate improvement in food rations. Germany's food situation in the coming winter was truly alarming. As Friedrich Ebert, one of the most energetic leaders of the majority Social Democrats, spelled out to his colleagues in the Reichstag on 20 December 1917, 'in April and May we will be faced with a void. So nothing but shortened bread rations to 110 grams per day. That is impossible.'[10] With Russia suing for an armistice, the fabled granary of the Ukraine beckoned in the East. But to gain access to those desperately needed supplies, short of wholesale occupation, Germany and Austria needed a trade deal. Whereas the Bolsheviks could be satisfied with an armistice, it was the Central Powers who needed a substantive peace settlement as quickly as possible.

Before the war, Germany's Foreign Secretary Kühlmann had made a name for himself as a 'liberal imperialist' and he understood that he had to take these domestic pressures seriously. What the German home front needed was a prompt and profitable peace that was in tune with the Reichstag's peace declaration of July 1917. The German right wing, however, were incensed even by the armistice terms. With the German Army victorious, how could Kühlmann agree to bind Germany to a peace formula proposed by Russian revolutionaries? Why did decisive military victory not give Germany a completely free hand? To the Vaterlandspartei the answer was obvious. As the arch-conservative baron Kuno von Westarp put it in a Reichstag committee, what was at work, both at home and abroad, was the corrosive influence of 'democracy'.[11] On 6 December the Prussian conservatives made their stand. Defying public appeals for a bold gesture of enlightened reform by the Kaiser himself, the Prussian House of Lords voted down the proposal for manhood suffrage.[12] As one of Ludendorff's closest collaborators, Colonel Max Bauer, commented approvingly, why should Germany lay down the lives of its best sons 'only to drown under Jews and Proles'?[13]

For the German right, the line was clear. Democratization was a prelude to capitulation. More sophisticated exponents of German strategy could see other possibilities. For men such as Matthias Erzberger, or Bethmann Hollweg's close collaborator Kurt Riezler, democratization at home was the only possible basis on which Germany could pursue a great-power policy capable of matching that of Britain and the United States.[14] The stalwart commitment of the vast majority of the Social Democratic Party had demonstrated the powerful force of German working-class patriotism. But if democracy would give the projection of German power a new energy and legitimacy, it would also impose its own self-limiting logic, restraining the tendency toward heedless territorial acquisition. Adding territory through annexation might satisfy a crude military conception of security. But even with the limited powers conceded to the Reichstag by the Bismarckian constitution, accommodating the Polish minority had presented worrying problems. If one contemplated Germany's future as a democratized *Volksstaat*, or people's state, how were large territories to be incorporated whose populations were linguistically, culturally and religiously alien? Germany did not want to find itself in the situation of the Westminster Parliament, with a resentful Irish minority holding the balance of power. As far as Chancellor Hertling was concerned, the conclusion was obvious. 'We want to remain a nation state don't we, and do not want to integrate such alien population splinters.'[15]

On the extreme right, pan-German ideologues might imagine a future in which Germans lorded it over a million-strong helot class. The radical leader of the pan-Germans, Heinrich Class, was even willing to contemplate mass clearances of native populations to create land in the East 'free of people'. Such fantasies were encouraged in 1917 by the flight of a large part of the pre-war population.[16] In Courland, one of the prime targets of German annexiationists, more than half of the pre-war Latvian population of 600,000 souls had fled by 1918.[17] The methods that Turkey had used to dispose of its Armenian population were no secret to the German political class. But most viewed the Turkish example with revulsion. Even diehard conservatives dismissed pan-German talk of enslaving the Belgian population and clearing the East as dangerous and impractical.[18] During the debate over the peace resolution in July 1917 Erzberger announced to a cheering Reichstag that it would be far cheaper to provide insane-asylum beds for the pan-Germans than it would be to indulge their imperialist delusions. As a spokesman for the Social Democratic Party declared, the times were long gone when 'peoples can be distributed, divided and shoved together like a herd of sheep'.[19]

Since the publication of Friedrich Naumann's much misunderstood book on the vision of a unified *Mitteleuropa* in October 1915, there had been a lively discussion of a zone of German hegemony in central Europe, based on some kind of federative imperialism.[20] Gustav Stresemann, the nationalist liberal, called for Germany to consolidate a bloc of 150 million consumers, on the basis of which it might hope to face the power of American industry.[21] At that point Russia had still been in the fight. Once Tsarist power collapsed in 1917 and America entered the war, it was obvious to the more intelligent strategic thinkers in Germany that there was no better means with which to dynamite the Tsarist Empire than for Berlin to espouse the demand for self-determination.[22] Ironically, the Bolsheviks agreed. Within ten days of seizing power on 15 November (2 November old style), Lenin and his trusted lieutenant

Joseph Stalin had issued their Declaration of the Rights of the People of Russia, which appeared to grant the right to self-determination up to and including secession.[23] To Foreign Secretary Kühlmann the Brest-Litovsk negotiations thus seemed to offer an opportunity to found a new order in the East not merely on Germany's undoubted military dominance, but on the emphatic embrace of a new principle of legitimacy. Germany would secure power on a continental scale not through annexation, but through the formation of an economic and military bloc of smaller eastern European states under German protection. The autonomous Polish entity carved by Germany and Austria out of Russian territory in the autumn of 1916 was a start. While in economic and military terms the new Poland would be bound tightly and irrevocably to Germany, in the social and cultural sphere it would be given the freedom 'to express itself nationally'.[24] As Chancellor Bethmann Hollweg had put it in 1916, 'the times are no longer for annexation, but rather for the cuddling up [sic] of smaller state-entities to the great powers, to mutual benefit'.[25] If only Germany were willing to embrace self-determination and domestic reform, Eduard David, a leading Social Democrat, explained to General Max Hoffmann at his headquarters in Brest, it could exceed even the wildest ambitions of Wilhelmine *Weltpolitik*. In cooperation with Russia and a cluster of new Eastern states, Germany would escape the narrowness of mere *Mitteleuropa*, extending its influence over all of Eurasia, from the Persian Gulf to the Indian Ocean and the Pacific.[26]

Such a vision was self-serving of course. But the advocates of this alternative version of German hegemony should not be dismissed either as dupes or as forerunners of Nazi empire.[27] Their opponents on the German right regarded them as a real threat. The bitterness of the nationalist vitriol poured on Philipp Scheidemann, the leader of the SPD, for his advocacy of a German version of a democratic peace was shocking even to hardened veterans of the Bismarckian era. During the battles over the Brest-Litovsk Treaty, Erzberger twice risked prosecution in the military courts for his defence of Lithuanian and Ukrainian independence.[28] Even men like Chancellor Bethmann Hollweg and staffers such as Kurt Riezler were not merely cynical. They believed that history refuted the choice, supposed by simplistic advocates of nationalism, between slavery and full, unfettered sovereignty. For most, full sovereignty was always a chimera. Even neutrality was an option only under exceptional circumstances. As Woodrow Wilson had discovered, even the greatest power could uphold it only through isolation. For most the real choice was one between hegemons. The Baltic states, if broken away from Russia, would inevitably fall into the orbit of another great power, if not Germany or Russia, then Britain. What the more far-sighted strategists in Imperial Germany were advancing was a vision of negotiated sovereignty in which economic and military independence was pooled by smaller states with larger states.[29]

The fact that the proposal was coming from Imperial Germany should not lead us to dismiss it out of hand. In light of twentieth-century experience the legitimacy of such a vision can hardly be denied in principle. Since 1945 it has formed an essential building block of the relative peace and prosperity established in Europe and East Asia.[30] Furthermore, this vision of a new order in eastern Europe was tied to a programme of domestic reform that would not have left Imperial Germany unchanged. At Brest the Germans were arguing not only over a new order in eastern Europe. They were engaged in a struggle over Germany's own political future.[31] But if we grant that the terms of the armistice on 2 December 1917 were not empty, if the espousal of the Petrograd formula by the German side was not mere verbiage, then this makes it all the more important to explain how relations between Germany and the Bolsheviks degenerated into a brutal power struggle – and how by the summer of 1918 the Kaiser's armies found themselves in occupation of a zone of Russian territory almost as extensive as that conquered by Hitler's Wehrmacht on its march to Stalingrad in 1942.

II

Beginning on 22 December 1917 the first round of formal peace talks at Brest went eerily well.[32] The agreement on the armistice principles of 'self-determination, no annexations and no indemnities' held. On Christmas Day the Central Powers and the Bolshevik negotiators issued a communiqué announcing their agreement on the basic principles of a peace of no annexations and a withdrawal of occupying forces, a formula to which they still hoped the Entente might adhere. Anticipating the imminent announcement of a long-awaited peace, large crowds gathered in Vienna. As was the intention of both sides, the success of the talks wrong-footed the Entente. If a peace could be made in the East on liberal terms, why was the Western Front still consuming thousands of men by the day? Trotsky added to the Entente's embarrassment by publishing the full text of the secret London Treaty of 1915, which revealed the imperialist carve-up with which London and Paris had purchased Italy's entry into the war. Already in November, London and Washington had agreed on the need to make a new statement of war aims. But it soon became clear that neither the French nor the Italians would tolerate any such flexibility.[33] The Italians were reeling from Caporetto. In Paris, Georges Clemenceau had come into office determined to prosecute the war to the end, not to open a divisive debate about the peace. When London hosted the first Inter-Allied Conference attended by the United States at the end of November 1917, the risk of a humiliating dispute over war aims was thought so severe that the plenary sessions were restricted by Clemenceau's forceful chairmanship to no more than eight minutes.[34] Both Wilson and Lloyd George concluded that they would have to take the initiative independently.

But if the situation in Washington and London was tense, anyone close to the Brest negotiations could sense that there too a storm was waiting to break. As was always clear to the more sophisticated operators on the German side, the much-hailed Christmas Day declaration was not a selfless German gift to the Bolsheviks, but an explosive charge placed beneath the Russian Empire. As a basic preliminary both sides had agreed to withdraw their combat forces from the contested areas of Russia. The Bolsheviks convinced themselves that by this agreement the Germans had miraculously conceded the status quo of 1914, prior to holding plebiscites in the contested regions. It was this same misinterpretation that fuelled the vicious attacks on Kühlmann from the German right. In fact, the German negotiators never had any intention of leaving it up to Lenin and Stalin to extend their idea of self-determination throughout the pre-war territory of the Russian Empire. As far as Kühlmann was concerned, following their liberation from the oppressive rule of the Tsar, the populations of Poland, Lithuania and Courland had made a de facto declaration of independence. They no longer belonged to Russia and did not fall under the terms of the Christmas Day agreement regarding troop withdrawal. Under German protection these nationalities had exercised their right to opt out of the civil war that Lenin was openly advocating.[35]

Kühlmann had entangled his opposite numbers in a web. But it was woven as much of Bolshevik self-deception as of German deceit. In taking the first dangerous steps towards a separate peace, it suited Lenin and Trotsky only too well to present the negotiations as an unexpected triumph. But the jubilation on the Soviet side following the apparently generous Christmas Day agreement was such that the leadership of the German delegation began to worry that, once the Bolsheviks were forced to confront the true nature of the agreement, the shock would derail the entire peace process. General Hoffmann, the highest-ranking German officer at the talks, who liked to think of himself as an honest exponent of Realpolitik, opposed both to the excesses of the pan-German annexationists and the sweet-talking obfuscation of German liberals, was ill at ease with Kühlmann's manipulative approach. It was with some relish that he took on the task of bringing home to the Soviets over luncheon on 27 December what was in fact in store for them. The territories to which the Christmas Day agreement applied, the territories from which the German Army would progressively withdraw and to which the principle of self-determination would then be applied, were not the border regions occupied by Germany since 1915, but those further to the north and east, including Estonia and segments of Belorussia and Ukraine that had been occupied only in the final phase of the German advance. The result was a public relations disaster that permanently discredited the Brest-Litovsk peace. The 'deceit' of German imperialism was revealed. Whilst Lloyd George and Wilson put the finishing touches to their liberal war manifestos, allied propagandists had open season. General Hoffmann became internationally notorious as an extreme exponent of militarism. Whatever the rights or wrongs of the Polish, Ukrainian, Lithuanian or Latvian causes, however dubious the counter-claims of the Bolshevik regime, the espousal of self-determination by Imperial Germany now appeared as nothing more than a manipulative ruse. Events in Berlin and Vienna over the following weeks should have been enough to demonstrate that far more was at stake.

With Vienna entering its third year of slow starvation, the optimistic Christmas Day announcement from Brest had raised great hopes. When, over the following days, it emerged that thanks to the clumsy rapacity of the 'Prussian militarists', the Austrian population might starve for months to come, the reaction was immediate. On 14 January, Vienna was swept by enormous mass strikes.[36] Ottokar, Count Czernin, the Austrian representative at Brest, was forced to threaten Kühlmann that soon it would be Vienna not the Bolsheviks who were looking for a separate peace. But Kühlmann was boxed in. Hindenburg and Ludendorff were oblivious to the disastrous political consequences of their aggression. When the Kaiser agreed with the Brest negotiating team to redraw Germany's eastern boundary in such a way as to minimize the number of undesirable new Polish inhabitants in the Reich, Ludendorff and Hindenburg threatened to resign. On 8 January 1918, when the majority parties met to discuss the possibility of a new Reichstag resolution to reaffirm Germany's commitment to the principles of a liberal peace, Erzberger commented that they now had a double threat to deal with. Germany's workers were threatening to strike, but if the Kaiser's generals were not granted a military dictatorship, they too seemed ready to rebel.[37]

And yet, the tensions in Berlin were as nothing compared to the situation in Petrograd. In January 1918, as the illusion of a cheap peace evaporated, the Bolsheviks were finally forced to face the seriousness of their situation. In 1917 the much maligned revolutionary defensists had refused to contemplate separate peace talks with Germany, precisely because they had foreseen the dilemma that Lenin and Trotsky now found themselves in. To refuse to come to terms with Germany risked a disastrous invasion. But if they accepted a humiliating peace they would have to brace themselves for civil war. The Bolsheviks, as always, comforted themselves with the thought that Germany would soon erupt in revolution. Trotsky responded by raising the stakes and issuing a radical peace appeal to the world, challenging the Entente to apply self-determination to Ireland and Egypt.[38] The news from Vienna was certainly encouraging. But Lenin had come to a sober conclusion.[39] Knowing the condition of the Russian units stationed in front of Petrograd, he rejected the idea of a revolutionary war of resistance as a pipe dream. The Soviet regime would have to make a separate peace, however ruinous the terms. This would be disowned by the Left SRs. It would be rejected by leading Bolsheviks such as Nikolai Bukharin and Trotsky as well. Whatever the attitude of the rank-and-file soldiery, amongst the revolutionary leadership peace at any price was never a popular slogan.

Anxious to exploit the dilemma now facing the Bolsheviks, American and Entente representatives in Petrograd began to wonder whether Germany's aggression might not offer a chance to reconstruct a 'democratic war' alliance. Trotsky certainly seemed amenable. In the last days of 1917, Edgar Sisson, Wilson's personal emissary in Russia, cabled Washington that: 'Obvious, of course, to you that disclosure German trickery against Russia in peace negotiations promises to immensely open up our opportunities for publicity and helpfulness . . . If the President will restate anti-imperialist war aims and democratic peace requirements of America, I can get it fed into Germany in great quantities . . . and can utilize Russian version potently in army and everywhere.'[40] As if in answer, on 8 January Wilson issued what was soon to become his most famous wartime declaration – the 14 Points. They were to echo down the twentieth century as a manifesto of international liberalism, supposedly heralding American backing for self-determination, democracy and a League of Nations. They are often described as America's opening salvo in the great ideological contest of the century. But this interpretation has more to do with the stark polarities of the later Cold War than the realities of 1918. What Wilson was trying to do in January 1918 was to untangle a confusion that since 1917 had become nearly complete.[41] In the course of the last year he himself had been forced to abandon his own 'peace without victory' formula, thereby forcing Russia's democrats to fight a war they could only lose. Lenin and Trotsky, the chief beneficiaries of that disaster, were negotiating on the basis of the peace formula proposed by their despised democratic opponents. Meanwhile, the Reichstag majority and its vision of a peace based on self-determination had been made to seem like a mere smokescreen for the true intentions of German militarism. The initiative was thus handed back to the Entente and to Wilson. The 14 Points with which the President responded to this contorted situation were no radical manifesto. Neither of the two key terms usually ascribed to Wilsonian internationalism – democracy and self-determination – appear anywhere in the text.[42] What Wilson was attempting to do was respond to the disastrous situation created over the last 12 months by the derailment of his policy first for peace and then for war. He did so in terms that reflected not his radicalism, but his conservative evolutionary liberalism.

Five of the 14 Points restated the liberal vision of a new system of international politics to which Wilson had been committed since May 1916. There must be an end to secret diplomacy. Instead, there must be 'open covenants of peace openly arrived at' (Point 1), freedom of the seas (Point 2), the removal of barriers to the free and equal movement of trade (Point 3), disarmament (Point 4). The fourteenth point called for what would soon be known as the League of Nations, 'a general association of nations ... under specific covenants for the purpose of affording mutual guarantees of political independence and territorial integrity to great and small states alike' (Point 14). But this international framework did not promise or require from its members any particular type of domestic constitution. Nowhere in the 14 Points does Wilson mention democracy as a norm. Rather he stressed the freedom of nations to choose their own form of government. This, however, was not stated in terms of an emphatic act of self-determination. The phrase 'self-determination' appears nowhere either in the 14 Points or in the speech with which Wilson delivered them to Congress on 8 January 1918. In January of that year it was the Bolsheviks and Lloyd George who tossed this explosive concept into the international arena. Wilson would not adopt it until later in the spring.[43]

With regard to the colonial question, what concerned Wilson were not the rights of the oppressed people so much as the violence of inter-imperialist competition. Point 5 called for the claims of the rival powers to be settled not by war, but by 'a free, open-minded, and absolutely impartial adjustment'.[44] As far as the subordinate populations themselves were concerned, Wilson called simply for the 'observance of the principle that in determining all questions of sovereignty ... the interests of the populations concerned must have equal weight with the equitable claims of the government whose title is to be determined'. Quite apart from the fact that the claims of the colonial powers were thereby given no less weight than those of the subordinate populations, it was significant that Wilson spoke here of the interests, not the voice, of those populations. This was entirely compatible with a deeply paternalistic view of colonial government.

The significance of this choice of words becomes clear when it is contrasted with what Wilson had to say about the territorial question at issue in the European war. Here too he invoked not an absolute right to self-determination but the gradated view of the capacity for self-government that was typical of conservative nineteenth-century liberalism. At one end of the scale he called for Belgium to be evacuated and restored (Point 7), 'without any attempt to limit the sovereignty which she enjoys in common with all other free nations'. Alsace-Lorraine was to be returned and any occupied French territory was to be 'freed' from German domination (Point 8). Italy's boundaries were to be adjusted 'along clearly recognizable lines of nationality' (Point 9). But with regard to the peoples of the Habsburg and Ottoman empires (Point 12), the Balkans (Point 11) and Poland (Point 13), the tone was more paternalistic. They would need 'friendly counsel' and 'international guarantees'. What this foreign oversight would guarantee was not 'self-determination' but 'security of life and an absolutely unmolested opportunity of autonomous development'. This is the muted socio-biological vocabulary typical of Wilson's world view. There was no 'French' radicalism in the 14 Points.

It was near the halfway stage of his manifesto (Point 6) that Wilson addressed the situation in Russia. Given the events since November 1917, one might have expected him to be at pains to draw a sharp distinction between the Russian people and the Bolshevik regime that had violently usurped the right to represent them. Secretary of State Lansing in private memoranda to Wilson was demanding that America should denounce Lenin's regime 'as a despotic oligarchy as menacing to liberty as any absolute monarchy on earth'.[45] But no such distinction was made in the 14 Points. On the contrary, Wilson extended to the Bolsheviks praise of a kind he had never offered to the Provisional Government. Whereas in May 1917 Wilson had lined up with the Entente in lecturing Alexander Kerensky and Irakli Tsereteli on the need to continue the war, he now characterized the Bolshevik delegation, who were about to agree a separate peace, as 'sincere and in earnest'. The spokesmen of the Russian people, the Bolsheviks, were speaking, Wilson opined, in the 'true spirit of modern democracy', stating Russia's 'conception of what is right, of what is humane and honorable for them to accept . . . with frankness, a largeness of view, a generosity of spirit, and a universal human sympathy, which must challenge the admiration of every friend of mankind . . . whether their present leaders believe it or not, it is our heartfelt desire and hope that some way may be opened whereby we may be privileged to assist the people of Russia to attain their utmost hope of liberty and ordered peace.' Echoing the Bolshevik negotiating position at Brest, Wilson called for the peace to begin with the withdrawal of all foreign forces, so as to allow Russia the 'unhampered and unembarrassed opportunity for the independent determination of her own political development and national policy'. What is striking about this formulation was precisely Wilson's unproblematic use of the term 'Russia' and 'national policy' with regard to an empire that was in the process of violent decomposition.[46] At the moment when the 14 Points began to circulate around the world, nationalist movements in Ukraine, the Baltic and Finland were dissociating themselves from the Soviet regime to which Wilson was giving such fulsome praise.[47] And yet so overwhelmingly favourable were his comments directed towards Petrograd that one New York columnist leapt to the conclusion that Washington was about to extend official recognition to Lenin's government. This was premature. But it was certainly a more plausible reading of the 14 Points than the later interpretation, which saw Wilson's statement as the opening salvo in the first phase of the Cold War.

As for Germany, throughout the tumultuous summer of 1917 Wilson had stuck to the position to which he had swung around in April. The Reichstag majority were not to be trusted. Their reformist professions and their peace resolutions were a cover for German imperialism. This was the same basis on which Wilson had rejected the advances of the revolutionary defensists from Petrograd and had boycotted the Stockholm process. Now, belatedly, in January 1918, in presenting his 14 Points to Congress, the President did acknowledge that there was a struggle going on within German politics between 'the more liberal statesmen of Germany and Austria' and the 'military leaders who have no thought but to keep what they have got'. On the outcome of that struggle, he declared, 'the peace of the world' would depend.[48] Wilson seems to have hoped that his 14 Points once adopted by the Austrian and German opposition might have opened the door to general peace talks. But he was too late. If he had been willing to contemplate general negotiations in the summer of 1917, it might have radically altered the complexion of politics in both Russia and Germany. We can only imagine how Russia's struggling Provisional Government might have acted if they had dreamt in June or July that a bid for an immediate peace would receive the kind of praise that Wilson was now showering on Trotsky. With America only just having entered the war and the democratic enthusiasm in Russia at full spate, the political pressure such a peace move would have exerted on London and Paris would have been immense. But by early 1918 the balance of power in Germany had shifted against the Reichstag majority and the Entente were more adamant than ever. Whatever the propaganda success of the 14 Points, they could not be used to negotiate with Germany in the shadow of Brest-Litovsk.[49] As a result, in January 1918 it was the Bolsheviks to whom Wilson brought relief. Their propagandists saw to it that the Russian text of Wilson's declaration was plastered all over Petrograd. Lenin had it telegraphed to Trotsky as a token of his triumphant success in pitting the imperialists against each other.[50]

6

Making a Brutal Peace

Two days after President Wilson had issued his bland proclamation of support for the 'Russian' people, on 10 January 1918 the representatives of independent Ukraine arrived at Brest-Litovsk to make their own peace claim. This changed the political complexion of the talks. In the first weeks of negotiations there had been general agreement on the Petrograd formula. Self-determination was the order of the day. The indignation unleashed by the revelation of what Foreign Secretary Kühlmann intended this to mean cast Germany in a bad light. But the territories at issue in the first round of talks were the Baltic states. Though they were the prized demands of German annexationists, they were, in the final analysis, small fry and in any case already under the uncontested control of the Kaiser's armies. From a safe distance, the Soviets could denounce the hypocrisy of German imperialism. They were not forced to show their own hand. The Wilsonian rendition of the Bolsheviks as sincere and earnest advocates of a democratic peace victimized by German imperialism remained credible. Ukraine was a problem on a different scale. It was a strategic asset of the first rank, the disposition of which would decide the future of Russian power and shape of the new order in the East. As 1918 began, Ukraine was controlled neither by the Germans nor by the Bolsheviks. Here, their rival visions of a new order would clash directly and the full complexity of the moral and political balance would become apparent.

I

It is tempting to say that in Ukraine during the winter of 1917–18 there was a power vacuum, except that to speak in such terms is to prejudge

the issue. After the overthrow of the Tsar, in Kiev, as in the rest of Russia, a revolutionary authority had established itself. Unlike in Petrograd
the revolutionaries in Ukraine had immediately set up a rudimentary
parliamentary forum, the Rada. In this assembly the parties inclined to
nationalism, led by the local brand of agrarian Social Revolutionaries,
had a clear majority. But no significant voices made a claim to independence. The Ukrainian revolutionaries were anxious to play their
part in the 'triumph of justice . . .' in Russia. After all, where else 'in the
world was there such a broad, democratic, all-embracing order? Where
was there such unlimited freedom of speech, of assembly, or organization as in the new, great revolutionary state.'[1] Over the summer of
1917 the liberals in the Provisional Government had stalled Kiev's
demands for real autonomy.[2] But the politicians of Ukraine awaited the
Constituent Assembly, which would surely decide in favour of a federal
constitution. It was the breakdown of legitimate authority in Petrograd
that forced Kiev into a declaration first of national autonomy and then
in December 1917 of outright independence. Whatever its differences
might have been with the Provisional Government, the Rada could not
accept the Bolsheviks' claim to speak on its behalf. The Central Powers
were only too happy to agree. They promptly extended an invitation to
Kiev to join the talks at Brest.

For the Bolsheviks this raised a terrifying prospect. In the pre-war
years, Ukraine had accounted for one-fifth of total world exports of
grain, a share twice that of the United States. Petrograd and Moscow
needed that grain as much as did Vienna and Berlin. Ukraine was no less
vital to Russia's future as an industrial power. The region produced all
of Russia's coking coal, 73 per cent of its iron and 60 per cent of its
steel. Ukraine's manganese was exported to all the blast furnaces of Europe.[3] If an independent government established itself in Kiev this would
be a huge blow to the Soviet regime. Furthermore, unlike the baronial
assemblies that were providing the Germans with a fig leaf of legitimacy
in the Baltic and Poland, the Rada could not be dismissed as a creature
of foreign power. At Brest, the Bolsheviks had so far managed to present
themselves as the champions of national liberation against German
aggression. But already in December as the first exchanges between the
Soviet authorities and Kiev deteriorated into hostility, the all-important
qualification to Lenin and Stalin's endorsement of self-determination
became apparent. The Bolsheviks approved self-determination, but only

insofar as it was the 'revolutionary masses' who were in control. In the eyes of the Bolsheviks, the Ukrainian Rada was nothing more than an assembly of property owners serviced by their Menshevik and Social Revolutionary lackeys. By early 1918 the Bolshevik agitator Karl Radek was inciting the Petrograd population, 'if you want food . . . cry "death to the Rada!"'. By 'its Judas-like treachery' in accepting the invitation of the Central Powers, the Ukrainian parliament had 'dug its grave'.[4] As the Ukrainian delegation arrived in Brest, a hand-picked anti-Rada Bolshevik government was directing a ragtag army of mercenaries against Kiev. After the shadow-boxing over the Baltic, the real stakes in the Eastern peace were about to become clear.

On 12 January, after sitting through an infuriating lecture from the Soviets on the 'legitimate' procedures for self-determination, General Max Hoffmann, who since the Christmas crisis had been pilloried in the international press as the archetypal German militarist, lost his temper. Why, he demanded to know, should the representatives of Imperial Germany take lessons in legitimacy from the Bolsheviks, whose own regime was 'based purely on violence, ruthlessly suppressing all who think differently'.[5] The Bolsheviks were already attacking the national Constituent Assembly of Ukraine. If the Germans were to evacuate the Baltic, the same would happen there. But Trotsky was unabashed. His retort was a classic dose of Marxist state theory: '. . . the General is completely right when he says that our government is founded on power. All history has known only such governments. So long as society consists of warring classes the power of the government will rest on strength and will assert its domination through force.' What the Germans were objecting to in Bolshevism was 'the fact that we do not lock up the strikers, but the capitalists who lock out the workers, the fact that we do not shoot the peasants who raise their claim to the land, but that we arrest the large landowners and officers who want to shoot the peasants . . .' And, Trotsky went on, the 'violence' that Bolshevism applied, 'the violence that is supported by millions of workers and peasants and that is directed against a minority which seeks to keep the people in servitude; this violence is a holy and historically progressive force.' Reading the transcript from Brest, the Kaiser added in the margin: 'For us the opposite!'[6]

Trotsky's statement was of such stark clarity that it echoed down the century. If he was right and if government was always ultimately founded on violence, how could political action ever be squared with a moral standpoint? If taken at face value, the implications of this irreconcilability between the pragmatic demands of power and the imperatives of morality were either tragic or revolutionary.[7] On either view, short of a world-changing revolution, no compromise, no civilizing of the violent foundations of power could be taken seriously. For the Brest talks, this remarkably frank exchange spelled a disastrous degeneration. How could a peace negotiated between actors with such diametrically opposed views, who could agree only on the historical efficacy of force, ever be anything more than an armed truce? As the German and Ukrainian advocates of a constructive peace looked on, the revolutionary cynicism of Trotsky and the Realpolitik of General Hoffmann combined to empty the principle of self-determination of any substantial meaning. Together they ended the negotiations as a search for agreement and reduced them instead to a naked trial of strength.

Within days of Trotsky's revealing retort, the Bolsheviks provided a vivid demonstration of their uncompromising commitment to violence as a means of making history. On the morning of 18 January, the negotiations were halted to allow Trotsky to return to Petrograd with a map showing the full extent of Germany's demands. But the first item on the Bolsheviks' agenda that day was not the peace, but the final liquidation of the democratic revolution in Russia. The date of 18 January 1918 had been set for the first meeting of the Constituent Assembly. As Trotsky was haggling with the Germans in Brest, heavily armed Red Guards were sweeping anti-Bolshevik protestors from the streets of the Russian capital, killing several dozen.[8] The Assembly opened at 4 p.m. and promptly elected Victor Chernov, leader of the Social Revolutionaries, the winners of the election, as its president. Outside, Red Guard cannons were trained on the Assembly building. Inside, the majority faced the continuous, raucous barracking of the Bolshevik faction, with Lenin and the rest glaring down from the balcony. Despite the attempt at intimidation, the Assembly persisted in hearing speeches by the leaders of the February revolution, including the Georgian Menshevik Irakli Tsereteli, who since being declared an outlaw had been living in hiding. He warned that if the Constituent Assembly were 'destroyed . . . then . . . civil war shall come to suck the life blood of democracy'. The Bolsheviks 'would . . . open the door to counterrevolution'.[9] In the early hours of the morning of 19 January, as the Bolshevik delegation contemptuously withdrew, leaving the closing of the chamber to the janitorial staff and Red Guards, the Russian Constituent Assembly voted into effect the egalitarian land law that had been the prized ambition of generations of Russian radicals. As the lights went out, Chernov could be heard solemnly proclaiming the birth of the 'Russian Democratic Federated Republic'.[10]

The Assembly was never to reopen. Its violent suppression was a shattering blow to the democratic hopes once placed in the revolution. As Maxim Gorky wrote, 'For almost a hundred years the finest Russians have lived by the idea of a Constituent Assembly ... in the struggle for this idea, thousands of the intelligentsia and tens of thousands of workers and peasants have perished ...'. Now, Lenin and his regime of People's Commissars had 'given orders to shoot the democracy that demonstrated in honor of this idea'.[11] But the Bolsheviks were unabashed. *Pravda*'s headlines denounced Chernov and Tsereteli as 'The hirelings of bankers, capitalists, and landlords ... slaves of the American dollar.'[12] Lenin offered a chilling obituary for parliamentary politics. Under the title 'People from Another World', he described the anguish he felt at having to attend even one meeting of the Constituent Assembly.[13] It was for him the experience of a nightmare. 'It is as though history had accidentally ... turned its clock back, and January 1918 became May or June 1917!' To be plunged from the 'real', 'lively' activity of the Soviet of workers and soldiers into the world of the Constituent Assembly, was to be plunged into a 'world of saccharine phrases, of slick, empty declamations, of promises and more promises based ... on conciliation with the capitalists'. 'It was terrible! To be transported from the world of living people into the company of corpses, to breathe the odour of the dead, to hear those mummies with their empty "social" ... phrases, to hear Chernov and Tsereteli, was simply intolerable.' The elected delegates of the Social Revolutionaries, who had braved Bolshevik intimidation to applaud the appeal to unite against the threat of civil war, Lenin mocked as the un-dead, who after sleeping in their coffins for the last six months, had arisen to mechanically applaud the counter-revolution. The Bolsheviks and the men of the February revolution were now on different sides of the barricades. Against those who called for peace, Lenin hailed 'the class struggle that has become civil war, not by chance ... but inevitably ...' Lenin, of course, was making his own inevitabilities. Nothing was more likely to provoke a civil war than the attempt to found a one-party dictatorship on a humiliating, separate peace with Germany.

Furthermore, nothing was more likely to isolate that dictatorship from Russia's allies in the Entente than the decision, anticipated in London and Paris since December 1917, and finalized by the Presidium of the Central Executive Committee on 3 February 1918, to repudiate Russia's massive foreign debts: $4.92 billion piled up in the pre-war era, $3.9 billion since the start of the war, the latter sum formally guaranteed by the British and French governments. The Soviet government's refusal to accept responsibility for the liabilities of its predecessor was, as London protested, a challenge to the 'very foundations of international law'. The Bolsheviks responded that the loans to the Tsar's government were part of an imperialist web designed to make Russia the servant of Western capitalism. The Russian people had 'long since redeemed' anything they owed, with 'a sea of blood and mountains of corpses'. Henceforth the issue of debt repudiation would pose a fundamental obstacle to any rapprochement between the Soviet regime and the Western Powers. Lenin and Trotsky had burned their boats.[14]

II

Meanwhile at Brest, faced with the full demands of the Central Powers, the Bolshevik strategy was one of delay and it fell to Trotsky to manage the strategic retreat. If the outcome of the negotiations depended ultimately on brute force, then clearly the Central Powers had the upper hand, but not entirely so. In the East the Germans might have military predominance, but in the wider war time was not on their side. To capitalize on their victory over Russia, Ludendorff and Hindenburg were now planning a massive effort in the West. Given the timetable for what must surely be Germany's final offensive, the High Command urgently needed to settle the situation in Russia. Furthermore, though Trotsky and the left of the Bolshevik Party exaggerated the prospect of a revolutionary overthrow, the solidity of the home front in both Germany and Austria was now seriously in question. The massive strikes that swept Austria in January 1918 culminated in a mutiny of the Austrian fleet in the Adriatic.[15] In Germany too, tensions were rising to an unbearable pitch. On 28 January, a week after the protests in Vienna had ebbed away, the factory cities of Germany were swept by an unprecedented wave of industrial action. The strikers' demands were openly political – a reasonable peace with Russia and domestic political reform, an end to martial law and the abolition of Prussia's three-tiered electoral system. For the first time the Majority SPD leadership felt compelled to throw its full weight behind the strike movement.[16] Not that there was any suggestion that the strikes were pro-Bolshevik. The violence in Russia led both the MSPD and the USPD to distance themselves from Lenin. Democracy, not a dictatorship of the proletariat, was their goal. But despite the moderation of these demands, the strike split the SPD from its bourgeois friends in the Reichstag majority. With the Vaterlandspartei baying from the right, the Catholic Centre Party and the Liberals could ill afford to associate too closely with the 'disloyal' Socialists. Just as the negotiations at Brest reached their most critical point, just as President Wilson was demanding to know who spoke for Germany, the progressive Reichstag coalition was in disarray.[17]

In the first days of February, in the hope of rescuing something from the wreckage of their vision of a legitimate order in the East, Kühlmann and Count Czernin, Austria's chief negotiator, made one last effort to force Trotsky to take seriously the question of self-determination. First they staged a confrontation between the main Soviet delegation and the delegation of the Rada. Predictably, the Bolsheviks launched into vituperative denunciation. But with the Germans holding the ring, the Ukrainian delegates were not cowed. 'The government of the Bolsheviks, which has broken up the Constituent Assembly and which rests on the bayonets of hired red guards, will never elect to apply in Russia the very just principle of self-determination, because they know only too well that not only the republic of the Ukraine, but also the Don, the Caucasus, Siberia, and other regions do not regard them as their government, and that even the Russian people themselves will ultimately deny their right.'[18] Trotsky was visibly embarrassed by this retort. But his answer to the Rada was the same as the answer he had given to Hoffmann. Troops loyal to the Soviet had just captured Kiev. With the Rada government in flight, the territory actually represented by their articulate young representatives at Brest was little larger than the conference room in which they were currently sitting. This was true enough. But, as should have been obvious, if it came down to a simple trial of strength, it was General Hoffmann, not Trotsky, who held by far the strongest cards. Confident of their ability to create a fait accompli, the Central Powers ignored Trotsky's threats and ended the session by formally recognizing the Rada delegation.

The Austrians, however, needed more than this. Given their utterly depleted state, they required not only a formal treaty with a vestigial Ukrainian government, but a workable grain-delivery contract. With Bolshevik forces occupying much of northern Ukraine, Count Czernin could not abandon his efforts to reach an agreement with Trotsky. This meant that they had to return to the question of the Baltic states and establish ground rules for what was actually meant by self-determination. On 6 February in a personal meeting with Trotsky, Czernin elaborated the basis for a compromise over the assemblies that would bring self-determination to the Baltic. Why should they not include elements approved by both the Central Powers and the Soviets? Trotsky refused to be entrapped in such constructive talk. Whatever concessions the desperate Austrians were offering, in the hands of his imperialist antagonists, Trotsky insisted, the principle of self-determination could never be anything more than an ideological snare. As to the peace, he was no fool. Trotsky understood that the Germans could take what they wanted. Given this reality, what concerned him was not what the Germans took, but how they took it. 'Russia could bow to force, but not to sophistry. He would never . . . admit German possession of the occupied territories under the cloak of self-determination, but let the Germans come out brazenly with their demands . . . and he would yield, appealing to world opinion against an act of brutal brigandage'. As the German radical Karl Liebknecht wrote from prison, from the point of view of the revolution the result of the Brest-Litovsk Treaty was 'not nil, even if it' resulted in a 'peace of forced capitulation'. Thanks to Trotsky 'Brest-Litovsk has become a revolutionary tribunal whose decrees are heard far and wide . . . it has exposed German avidity, its cunning lies and hypocrisy'. But it had exposed not only General Hoffmann and Ludendorff. Even more important for Trotsky, as for Liebknecht, was 'the annihilating verdict' that the peace would pass on the reformist illusions of Germany's democratic majority.[19] As in Russia, there must be no compromise, no hypocrisy, no possibility of a democratic peace short of total revolution.

The room for agreement in any meaningful sense of the word had now been exhausted. On 10 February the Central Powers announced to the Russian delegation that they had signed a separate peace with Ukraine, which the Soviet delegation must recognize. The treaty with Ukraine provided Berlin and Vienna with the right to purchase the entire grain surplus. But the Ukraine was neither to be starved nor robbed. Nor would the Central Powers be permitted to buy grain on credit. It was to be paid for by deliveries of industrial goods.[20] And the Ukrainian negotiating team, representing a government that was in flight on a train provided to them by the Germans, were able to extract remarkable concessions. Vienna was so desperate for a peace that Count Czernin agreed to upgrade the Ukrainian minority within the Austro-Hungarian Monarchy by creating a new province of Ruthenia with full cultural rights.[21] Even more remarkably, Czernin agreed to the secession to Ukraine of the city of Cholm, which had previously been promised to the Polish state whose right to self-determination the Austrians and Germans had notionally acknowledged in November 1916. By the first weeks of 1918, Germany and Austria needed the Ukrainians more than they needed the Poles.

Having invited a trial of strength, the Bolsheviks now faced a critical decision. To the conventionally minded there were only two choices. Overwhelmingly the most popular option in Petrograd and Moscow, if not on the front line amongst the troops themselves, was to refuse the German terms and to relaunch the war. No Russian government had ever surrendered. The revolution should not be the first. A majority on the party's Central Committee supported Trotsky's idea of rebuilding Russia's links to the Entente.[22] Nikolai Bukharin and other purists on the Bolshevik left counted on the revolutionary energy of the Russian peasants and workers. From Lenin such talk attracted nothing but sardonic scorn. The hopes of a revolutionary war were 'capable of giving satisfaction to those who crave the romantic and the beautiful', but failed completely 'to take into consideration the objective correlation of class forces . . .'.[23] Lenin now openly demanded a peace at any price. Trotsky had seen too much of Russia's dilapidated Northern Front not to appreciate the force of Lenin's point. But unlike Lenin, Trotsky thought that there might be a third position between Bukharin's revolutionary war and Lenin's ruinous peace. Counting not on revolution in Germany, but on the ability of the Reichstag majority to prevent a resumption of fighting, Trotsky proposed simply to end the talks by announcing that Russia was unilaterally abandoning the war. On 22 January, after Lenin's appeal for an immediate settlement was rejected by the Executive Committee of the party, Trotsky narrowly won its backing for his daring new strategy. Rather than recognizing the treaty with Ukraine, on 10 February Trotsky broke off the negotiations declaring: 'No peace. No war.' In Petrograd, there was an euphoric reaction. If Trotsky had not delivered 'peace without victory' – the great hope of 1917 – he had, at least, secured an end to the fighting without the explicit acknowledgement of defeat.[24]

III

Everything now depended on the response of the Germans. Following Trotsky's startling declaration, the Bolshevik delegation was delighted to see their relentless tormentor General Hoffmann reduced to spluttering expostulation. The idea of unilaterally and one-sidedly suspending a war was simply 'unheard of ... unheard of'.[25] As Kühlmann's legal experts confirmed, in three thousand years of international law there had been only one single precedent of a Greek city state during the classical period refusing both to continue fighting and to make peace.[26] Trotsky had gambled that the moderate forces in Germany would be strong enough to hold back the militarists. And if something like Trotsky's strategy had been attempted in the summer of 1917, when the momentum had been on the side of the Reichstag majority, perhaps a stand-pat strategy of 'No peace. No war' could have been made to stick. But in February 1918 Trotsky overestimated the strength of the progressive coalition in Germany, which his own negotiating tactics had done so much to undermine.

The climactic confrontation came on 13 February at a conference at the Kaiser's residence in Bad Homburg. As Trotsky had hoped, Chancellor Hertling and Foreign Secretary Kühlmann argued strongly against any resumption of hostilities.[27] The home front would be profoundly disillusioned by any fresh bloodletting in the East. Surely every available man was needed in the West. But Ludendorff, seconded by General Hoffmann, was adamant. If Trotsky would not talk, the German military would create facts. There was no need for long-winded discussions let alone any further consultation with the German parliament. As far as the Kaiser was concerned, the mere mention of the Reichstag was enough to trigger an outburst that was profoundly symptomatic of the crisis-ridden atmosphere pervading Germany. There could be no question of the elected politicians interfering in questions of peace and war, the Kaiser ranted. What was at stake was a struggle of the widest dimensions and Germany must proceed with utter ruthlessness. A few days earlier Bolshevik radio stations had begun broadcasting an appeal for the revolutionary overthrow of the Hohenzollern dynasty. The Kaiser responded in kind, '(W)e must . . . strike the Bolsheviki dead as soon as possible . . .'[28] Recalling happier days of big-game hunting, he remarked: 'Bolsheviki are Tigers, encircle them, shoot them down.'[29] What haunted the Emperor was the prospect of Britain and America taking advantage of the power vacuum in the East. 'Russia organized in Anglo-Saxon hands is great danger . . . Bolsheviki must be disposed of. On this the following suggestion . . . we should give aid to Estonia. The Baltic must appeal for help against robbers. We will then provide assistance (analogue to Turkey in Armenia). Form a Baltic gendarmerie that will restore order . . . policing action, but not war.'[30] The atrocities perpetrated by the 'special police' units of the Young Turks were well known in Germany. So the import of these remarks is chilling.

To cap it all, the Kaiser abruptly revealed further insights into the dark forces that he suspected were at work. The 'Russian people', he opined, had been 'delivered to the vengeance of the Jews, they [Bolsheviki] are in touch with all the Jews of the world. Freemasonry too . . .'.[31] A second record of the same meeting added a wider dimension of conspiracy. 'Wilson,' the Kaiser declaimed, 'has proclaimed the removal of the Hohenzollern as a war aim and is now supporting the Bolsheviki, along with the entire international Jewry – Grand Orient Lodge.'[32] In the Kaiser's mind, it seems that Wilson's conciliatory remarks toward the Bolsheviks in his 14 Points address had conjured up the fantasy of a world Jewish conspiracy with its tentacles in both Washington and Petrograd. After this outburst, the discussion was adjourned to allow the Kaiser to take a restorative stroll.

Over the brunch buffet, Vice-Chancellor Friedrich von Payer, the progressive liberal who acted as the representative of the Reichstag majority in the Reich government, sought solace from Foreign Secretary Kühlmann. According to Kühlmann's memoirs, von Payer was quite beside himself. 'He [Payer] said to me that he had thought, through his many years of parliamentary experience, to have some insight into the decisive matters of state. But today's meeting had opened his eyes for much of which he previously had no idea.' The 'great contradictions and profound abysses within the life of the German state' revealed by the Kaiser's outburst had left him 'deeply shaken'. Kühlmann replied that he 'had been a long time acquainted with these abysses. But it was impossible for a statesman entrusted with matters of life and death, even in utter frankness to give the leading parliamentarians a clear view and to present to them the difficulties with which they had to struggle step by step.'[33]

In truth, the Kaiser's anti-Semitic flare-up on 13 February was no one-off. Over the winter of 1917–18 he had come increasingly under the influence of extremist nationalist propaganda and his daily notes to his subordinates were now commonly laced with diatribes against 'Jewish subversives'. Even more seriously, in the weeks before the Bad Homburg conference Ludendorff had finally confronted the question of what to do with the large Polish and Jewish populations in the Polish territory he was determined to annex. His solution was taken from the pages of pan-German fantasy. As many as 2 million people would be uprooted from their homes, with particular care being taken to ensure that the large and politically dangerous Jewish population was neutralized. Ludendorff hoped that they might be 'caused to emigrate' to the United States.[34] Overarching the increasing radicalism of Ludendorff's vision was not just the assumption of hostility toward the Jews and the need to erase the revolutionary threat posed by Bolshevism, but the assumption that the present war would not be the last. His increasingly excessive demands were driven by the vision that the current war was a preliminary to an even larger all-out confrontation with the Western Powers that would occupy generations to come. In the short term the Bad Homburg conference gave the German militarists the licence they needed. On 18 February the German advance resumed.

IV

'The whole of Russia,' General Hoffmann mused in his diary, 'is no more than a vast heap of maggots – a squalid, swarming mess.'[35] His army moved south and eastwards down intact railway lines virtually unopposed. By early March, Kiev was in German hands. Trotsky's gamble had spectacularly backfired. Bourgeois circles in Petrograd were eagerly anticipating the arrival of the Kaiser's troops, whilst the Social Revolutionaries with their dangerous proclivity for assassination railed at Lenin's betrayal of the revolution. The leadership of the Bolshevik Party was deeply split. The only common denominator was the ever more draconian demand for revolutionary discipline and mobilization. On 14 February the Red Army was called into being and Trotsky put himself at the head of the mobilization.[36] On 21 February all of Russia was placed under the terrible dictate of a new revolutionary decree, which threatened all saboteurs and collaborators with summary execution. All able-bodied members of the bourgeoisie were declared liable for conscription into forced labour battalions.[37] Faced with the unstoppable German advance, after two days of debate Lenin persuaded the Bolshevik Central Committee to accept the peace terms that had been on offer at Brest at the beginning of February.[38] But this was no longer enough. The Germans now demanded a completely free hand in determining the mode of self-determination in those territories under their control and an immediate peace between the Soviet regime and Ukraine.

On 23 February the Bolshevik Committee met once again, but even Lenin's threat of resignation was not enough to carry a majority. His motion to accept the increased German demands was passed only after Trotsky, who was serving as chair, abstained. In the Petrograd Soviet, the inner bastion of the revolution, Lenin faced embittered opposition both from the Social Revolutionaries and the left wing of his own party. But Lenin was relentless. Like the soldiers of World War I, who had had to set aside their heroic visions of war, he insisted that revolutionaries must come to terms with a new, disenchanted vision of historical progress: 'The revolution is not a pleasure trip! The path of revolution leads over thorns and briars. Wade up to the knees in filth, if need be, crawling on our bellies through dirt and dung to communism, then in this fight we will win. . .'[39] By the end of the night Lenin's motion was carried by the narrow margin of 116 to 85, with 26 abstentions.

On 26 February, having received news of the Bolshevik surrender, the Germans halted within a few days' march of the Soviet capital. Four days later, running a gauntlet of hostility from the local Russian population, the grizzled old Bolshevik Grigori Sokolnikov returned to Brest-Litovsk ready to accept whatever terms were offered. Embarrassed by how far things had degenerated since their first relatively cordial meetings, the German and Austrian diplomats had hoped to soften the brutality of the proceedings by setting up a series of subcommittees, in which they would spin out technical discussions of the peace terms. But to their consternation, the Bolshevik delegation refused to go through the motions of giving serious consideration to the treaty text. Any further talk would merely have legitimized a settlement, which, as both sides frankly acknowledged, rested on nothing but force. They signed the document as it was placed in front of them and departed.

Lenin's decision to buy time by means of the Brest-Litovsk Treaty was certainly the severest test to which the internal party discipline of the Bolsheviks was ever subjected. Though the imminent threat of German invasion had secured the majority that Lenin needed, a furious debate now raged over ratification. Bukharin, Karl Radek and Alexander Kollontai had formed a breakaway faction known as the Left Communists, dedicated to resisting Lenin's 'obscene' peace. The Seventh National Congress of the Bolshevik Party, held in Petrograd on 7 March whilst German aircraft flew overhead, was a dismal and bitter affair.[40] Only 47 voting delegates attended, representing no more than 170,000 party members out of a notional total of 300,000. Once more Lenin assailed the Left Communists for their irrational, romantic vision of history. Their posture was that of the 'aristocrat who, dying in a beautiful pose, sword in hand, said: "Peace is disgraceful, war is honourable."' By contrast, Lenin cast himself as the voice of the people, arguing from the 'point of view of . . . every sober-minded peasant and worker' who knew that such a peace was merely a moment for 'gathering forces'.[41] Lenin carried the party majority, but the Left Communists were unreconciled and Trotsky continued to abstain. To console themselves for accepting Lenin's odious peace, the delegates rallied around a resolution promising the 'most energetic, mercilessly decisive and draconian measures to raise the self-discipline and discipline of the workers and peasants of Russia', to prepare them for the 'liberationist, patriotic socialist war' that would drive out the German oppressors.[42]

In this historic epoch of violence and confusion, Lenin insisted, when the temptation to revolutionary self-immolation was ever present, clearheadedness and rigorous analysis were at a premium. It was to impose that leadership that Lenin demanded a series of important changes to clarify the party's position and to set it determinedly on its revolutionary path.

The traditional title of Social Democracy, still proudly born by Karl Marx and Friedrich Engels, was clearly no longer appropriate. Having dissolved the Constituent Assembly, the Soviet regime must break openly with the 'standards of "general" (i.e. bourgeois) democracy'. Lenin acknowledged only one relevant precursor, the Paris Commune of 1871. The party's title would henceforth reflect that proud heritage. Whereas liberals hypocritically talked of universal human rights, a properly Communist regime must make clear that 'liberties and democracy' were '*not* for all, but *for* the working and exploited masses, to emancipate them from exploitation . . . The exploiters should expect only "ruthless suppression".'

The climax of Lenin's campaign came at the All Russian Congress of Soviets. Having abandoned Petrograd, the Congress met in Moscow – the 1,232 delegates, 795 Bolsheviks, 283 Left Socialist Revolutionaries, 25 Socialist Revolutionaries of the Centre and no more than 32 Mensheviks.[43] On 14 March, Lenin delivered an impassioned oration in which he called upon Russia to 'size up in full, to the very bottom, the abyss of defeat, partition, enslavement, and humiliation into which we have been thrown', all the better to steel the will for 'liberation'. He promised that if they could only gain time for reconstruction the Soviet regime would 'arise anew from enslavement to independence . . .'. The motion for ratification was carried by the huge Bolshevik majority. But the Left Socialist Revolutionaries voted solidly against it and then resigned from the Council of People's Commissars in which they had shared power since the November revolution. Of the Left Communists, 115 abstained and refused any further participation in internal party business. The Brest-Litovsk Treaty, the negotiations for which had begun under the sign of the Petrograd Soviet's democratic peace formula, had become the driving force behind Lenin's one-party dictatorship.

The mirror image of that brutal process unfolded simultaneously in Germany. On 17 March 1918, Berlin played host to a ghostly ceremony in which a delegation of German gentry from Courland, Latvia, formally petitioned the Kaiser to assume the mantle of Archduke.[44] The Baltic was to become a playground of neo-feudalism. The following day, more than three and a half months after negotiations had begun at Brest-Litovsk and in a very different political climate, the Reichstag met to debate the ratification of the treaty. Matthias Erzberger tried to rally his partners in the Reichstag majority with an emergency resolution demanding respect for the right of self-determination for Poles,

Lithuanians and Latvians. He even attempted to make further approval of war credits conditional on the government's agreement.[45] But there was no denying the triumph of the right. Gustav Stresemann, who since 1916 had been amongst the foremost advocates of unrestricted U-boat warfare, now declared that in the East the German Army had demonstrated that 'the right of self-determination does not apply! I do not believe in Wilson's universal League of Nations; I believe that after the conclusion of peace it will burst like a soap-bubble.'[46]

But despite this triumphalism, by the spring of 1918 not even a victorious peace of stupendous dimensions could restore the national unity that had launched the German war effort in August 1914. The USPD denounced Brest as a Peace of Violation (*Vergewaltigungsfrieden*). For the SPD, the once loyal Eduard David spoke fiercely against the short-sightedness of the Kaiser's government. Germany had gambled away a unique opportunity to found a lasting new order in eastern Europe. 'The grand perspective of arriving at a friendly neighbourly relationship with all of eastern Europe encompassing both politics and economics has been buried.'[47] Though Erzberger has frequently been taken to task for voting in favour of the Brest treaty, his support was strictly conditional. As he stated in preliminary discussions in Reichstag committee: 'The Eastern peace will not be worth the paper on which it is written, if the right to self-determination of the Poles, Lithuanians and Courlanders is not implemented quickly, loyally and honestly.'[48] When it came to the vote on 22 March, the SPD abstained and the USPD voted against the motion. There was nothing like the popular excitement that had accompanied the first news of the Christmas agreement at Brest a few months earlier. Though the reduction of Russian power was a huge gain for Germany, the peace in the East had not brought an end to the war. Instead, victory in the East had become the platform for a last bid for victory in the West.

V

Since the previous autumn Hindenburg and Ludendorff had been gathering their forces for an offensive. Over the winter, the German armies on the Western Front were increased from 147 to 191 divisions whilst those on the Eastern Front were stripped from 85 to 47. For the first time since 1914 the Germans in the West would not be outnumbered. Through skilful diversionary tactics and by concentrating almost half the German Army on the British sector, on 21 March 1918 Ludendorff managed to raise the odds in his favour at the point of attack to 2.6:1. Beginning at 4.40 a.m., 11,000 guns and mortars delivered a devastating five-hour barrage against the British front line around St Quentin, followed by a concentrated thrust by 76 divisions across a 50-kilometre front.[49] Winston Churchill, who witnessed the attack, described it as 'the greatest onslaught in the history of the world'.[50] Never had so much manpower or firepower been concentrated on a single battlefield. By nightfall the leading German assault teams had penetrated to a depth of 10 kilometres. At Amiens it seemed that the Kaiser's army might split the Western Front in two.

On 23 March the Emperor declared a day of national celebration and marked the occasion by unleashing the first barrage from the gargantuan Big Bertha guns against Paris. His Imperial Majesty was in a buoyant mood, announcing to his entourage that 'when an English parliamentarian comes pleading for peace, he will first have to bow down before the Imperial standard, because what was at stake was a victory of monarchy over democracy'.[51] And though he did not say so, the Kaiser clearly meant to exact the same tribute from Germany's parliamentarians as well. The impetus of the progressive Reichstag majority had been halted. But by the same token, it was now clear that the imperial government was waging war against the will of a large part, perhaps a majority, of the German people. The cost was appalling. On the first day of what was to prove the Kaiser's last battle, Germany suffered 40,000 killed and wounded, its heaviest casualties of the entire war. Amongst the dead on the second day was Ludendorff's own stepson.[52] When the liberal Prince Max von Baden asked the general to explain the outlook if Germany were not to achieve decisive success, Ludendorff replied simply 'well then, Germany will perish'.[53] Kaiser Wilhelm had failed to make a legitimate peace in the East and had failed to carry through a constructive reform of the Bismarckian constitution. The fate of the Emperor and his regime was now hanging on the verdict of the battle.

7

The World Come Apart

On the evening of 14 May 1918, Lenin addressed the Central Executive Committee of the All Russian Congress of Soviets. The terms that he chose to describe the international situation were both drastic and uncharacteristically surreal. Socialism in Russia, he declaimed, inhabited an 'oasis amidst a raging sea of imperial robbery'.[1] The imperialists themselves had lost control of the war. The survival of the Soviet regime itself was the best evidence for this. To Lenin it was obvious that the capitalist powers must have an overriding common interest in the destruction of his regime. What prevented them from cooperating to snuff out the Russian revolution was the force-field of imperial rivalries. In the East, Japan was held in check by the United States. In the West, the life-and-death struggle between Britain and Germany prevented either from moving against Petrograd. At any moment, all the forces of imperialism might coalesce and turn against the Soviet regime. But just as suddenly, imperialist rivalry in some far-flung part of the world might trigger a new feud amongst them. True revolutionaries must face the possibility that if the imperialist war continued unchecked, it might lead to the total annihilation of civilization and an end to the possibility of any kind of progress.[2]

This scenario of capitalism in its final stage consuming itself in an orgy of imperialist destruction is one of the hallmarks of Lenin's political thinking. As Lenin insisted with characteristic clarity, if this struggle was as unpredictable as he claimed, it unhinged any linear notion of historical development, which normally served Marxist revolutionaries as their warrant. The course of history that Marxist theory had 'naturally' imagined 'as straight, and which we must imagine as straight in order to see the beginning, the continuation and the end', was 'in real life ... never ... straight'. It was 'incredibly involved'. Huge 'zig zags' and 'gigantic', complex 'turns' were unleashed as millions of people began the agonizing process of making their own history under conditions far from their own choosing.[3] Not economics but violence was the defining feature of this epoch. In Russia, a civil war had already begun that was 'interwoven with a whole series of wars'. The Soviet regime must brace itself for 'a whole era of ... imperialist wars, civil wars inside countries, the intermingling of the two, national wars liberating the nationalities oppressed by the imperialists and by various combinations of imperialist powers ... This epoch, an epoch of gigantic cataclysms, of mass decisions forcibly imposed by war, of crises, has begun ... and it is only the beginning.'[4] In such apocalyptic circumstances, the ordinary political logic of Marxism was inverted. As Lenin put it in a truly astonishing statement to the party at the end of April 1918: 'If we as a single troop of the world proletariat, as the first troop ... have moved into the lead, it is not because this troop is better organized ... it has moved to the first place, because history is not developing rationally.'[5] Bolshevism's victory was an expression of history's lack of logic, an island-oasis, a surreal slip of Minerva's tongue.

Lenin's vision of imperialist war as inferno has echoed down from World War I to the present day, in broad-brush critiques of modern civilization that continue to command an influential audience. But he himself was far too politically minded to tarry very long with such dark vistas. His interpretation of world affairs was at the service of a political strategy. In 1918 his vision of the Soviet regime as an island-oasis amidst a raging storm of imperial competition was the basis for his claim to dictatorship. It took a unique type of historical insight and political resilience to withstand the stresses of this moment. To survive, the Soviet Union must accept a peace at any price with whomever held power in Germany. This was a painful compromise, as Lenin himself freely admitted. But all the greater was the credit claimed for Lenin when his tactics paid off, the Soviet Union survived, and Germany went down to defeat.[6] What this triumphalist narrative ignores is how fundamentally Lenin misread the political logic of the war and how close that misreading brought his regime to extinction.

I

Lenin's separate peace at Brest-Litovsk was bound to antagonize Russia's former allies in the Entente. Back in December 1917, Britain and France had already begun discussing intervention to restore an Eastern Front against Germany. But they could ill afford to move significant forces from the West, and as the German offensive began in the spring their situation became truly desperate. Instead they urged Japan to take the initiative. And there were certainly expansionists in Japan who hoped that the Terauchi government would strike.[7] In March 1918 as Germany imposed its will at Brest, the fiercely aggressive Interior Minister Goto Shinpei demanded that Japan should seize the opportunity to force its way into Siberia with an army of 1 million men, enough to deter any future attempt by the West to compete with Japan in East Asia. Goto was deeply unsettled not so much by the Soviet regime as by the enthusiastic global response to Wilson's 14 Points. 'If we probe the real intentions of the USA further,' Goto insisted, 'it embraces what I call moralistic aggression. It is, in other words, none other than a great hypocritical monster clothed in justice and humanity.' To counter this expansive ideological attack, nothing less than total mobilization and the suppression of all liberal dissent within Japan was necessary to prepare the nation for leadership in the inevitable 'world war' between Asia and the West.[8] But the majority of the cabinet did not share Goto's aggressive vision. Japan would not be strengthened by becoming embroiled at the behest of the British and French in the wastelands of Siberia. Furthermore, any large-scale operation in Russia's Pacific provinces would have to be squared with the Terauchi government's strategy of cultivating good relations with Beijing.

Within days of the Bolshevik seizure of power, the Japanese ambassador to China proposed a far-reaching military agreement. Japan would provide a backbone of military expertise and equipment for the Chinese Army. Together, Japan and China would take control of the orphaned Russian railway network in the Far East.[9] In December 1917 Nishihara Kamezo, Japan's financial representative in China, called for a 'fundamental union' of Japan and China to ensure 'eastern self-sufficiency' and to 'prevent for all time, the intrusion of European power in the Japan sea'. The elder statesman Yamagata Aritomo called for an alliance so close that Japan and China could act 'as if one country with different bodies but of the same mind'.[10]

Ominous as such talk of a pan-Asian, anti-Western bloc sounded, Goto and his ilk did not have a free hand. As progressives such as Yoshino Sakuzo noted, there was a striking lack of popular support in Japan for military action.[11] In the Diet, the advocates of aggression faced opposition from the likes of the radical liberal Ozaki Yukio, who seized on Wilson's 14 Points to highlight the fact that whereas 'the western allies are trying to destroy militarism, the Terauchi cabinet is trying, at home and abroad, to strengthen and protect it'.[12] Following the rigged election of 1917, the liberal opposition were in no position to dictate terms. But Hara Takashi's huge conservative Seiyukai majority exercised its own form of restraint. Hara was unshakeable in his conviction that 'the future of Japan depends on the close relationship with the US'.[13] And his position was all the stronger for the fact that it was shared by the liberal elder statesman Prince Saionji and Baron Makino.[14] They did not rule out the pursuit of Japanese interests in Asia. But they demanded tact. Whereas Goto and Ozaki both conflated the strategic and domestic conflicts between Japan and America, one for conservative the other for liberal ends, Hara worked on the assumption that if Japan were willing to act cooperatively, America was most unlikely to challenge Japan's domestic order and might well turn a blind eye to its sponsorship of authoritarian militarism in China. Hara did not oppose Japanese military intervention in Siberia. But if the militarists acted without the green light from Washington, he would abandon Terauchi to the mercies of the radicalized opposition.

How would America decide? As the struggle over the Brest-Litovsk Treaty swung one way and then the other, there was a powerful faction in Washington led by Secretary of State Lansing who saw Bolshevism in precisely the terms that Lenin imagined – as a natural ideological enemy of the US that must be stamped out. What was coming 'to the surface' in Russia, Lansing presciently observed, was 'in many ways more to be dreaded than autocracy'.[15] Whereas Tsarism had been 'the despotism of ignorance', Lenin's was an 'intelligent despotism'. Wilson himself was more worried about the Japanese. Panicked by exaggerated French reports that the Japanese were about to act, Wilson on 1 March 1918 signalled his willingness to approve a joint Entente action. But only a day later he reversed this decision under the influence of an urgent memo from William Bullitt, one of his most radical advisors. For Bullitt, what was at stake was the rationale for America's entry into the war. Wilson had joined the war in the hope of turning the Entente in a more progressive direction. He could not, therefore, hand off moral responsibility for an intervention in Russia.

'In Russia today,' Bullitt insisted 'there are the rudiments of a government of the people, by the people, and for the people.' The real threat to democracy lay not in Lenin's *Sovnarkom* (Council of People's Commissars), but in the forces of reactionary imperialism that were alive within the Entente as much as in the Central Powers. 'Are we going to make the world safe for this Russian democracy,' Bullitt demanded, 'by allowing the allies to place Terauchi in Irkutsk, while Ludendorff establishes himself in Petrograd?'[16] On 4 March 1918, Bullitt's arguments prevailed. The President swung back firmly against any Allied intervention.[17] Not only did Wilson retract his support for intervention, on the advice of Bullitt and Colonel House he renewed the attempt to enlist the Russian revolution in a democratic alliance against reactionary Germany. Wilson appealed directly to the Congress of Soviets, which was meeting on 12 March to hear Lenin's arguments for ratification of the Brest-Litovsk Treaty. Under even more incongruous circumstances than in January, Wilson restated the message of the 14 Points. Ignoring the fact that the Congress of Soviets was standing in for the repressed Constituent Assembly, Wilson expressed 'every sympathy' for Russia's effort to 'weld herself into a democracy'. He demanded that she be left free of 'any sinister or selfish influence, which might interfere with such development'. But as House spelled out, what Wilson was actually thinking of went beyond Germany and Brest. 'My thought is . . . to seize this opportunity to clear up the far eastern situation but without mentioning Japan in any way. What you would say about Russia and against Germany could be made to apply to Japan or any other power seeking to do what we know Germany is attempting.'[18]

Behind the scenes in March 1918 Trotsky was in virtually daily conversation with Bruce Lockhart and Raymond Robins, the enthusiastic representatives of Britain and the United States, about a rapprochement between the Soviet regime and the Western Powers. In the north at Murmansk in the second week of March a small detachment of British troops was landed to protect Allied stores against seizure by the advancing German Army.[19] But at the Congress of Soviets Leninist rigour prevailed. There could be no compromise with a liberal hypocrite like Wilson. The Congress issued a truculent revolutionary riposte that was intended, in the words of Lenin's devoted follower Alexander Zinoviev, 'as a slap in the face of the American President'. Whilst Wilson's message thus fell on deaf ears amongst the Soviets, the hint was not lost on the more perceptive members of the Japanese cabinet. On 19 March, at the insistence of Hara, the interventionists in Tokyo were once more overruled. Nothing would be done without America's explicit approval.[20] When an over-eager Japanese naval unit made an impromptu landing in Vladivostok, it was immediately countermanded by Tokyo. On 23 April, humiliated by his inability to force through a policy of aggressive intervention in Siberia, Foreign Minister Ichiro Motono, the senior hawk in Terauchi's cabinet, resigned. He was replaced by Goto Shinpei who was, if anything, even more aggressive. But he had no greater room for manoeuvre than his predecessor. As President Wilson put it to the British representative Sir William Wiseman, the 'US government held the key to the situation . . .', 'the Japanese government would not intervene' without Washington's 'sanction'.[21] What Wilson did not acknowledge, any more than Lenin, were the forces that gave him that influence – the solid parliamentary majority in Japan who were determined to steer their country away from violent fantasies of oceanic struggles with the West, toward an accommodation with America.[22]

II

Lenin feared the Japanese but he could do little about them. The Bolshevik grip on eastern Russia was too tenuous to allow a coherent policy to be developed in that region. By the same token, the mounting tide of anti-Bolshevik activity in the Far East did not immediately challenge the Communists' grip on the core of Russian territory. The cornerstone of Lenin's survival strategy was the Brest-Litovsk Treaty with Germany. But this involved a contradiction. In the process of negotiating the treaty the Bolsheviks had done everything they could to empty it of legitimacy. But how could a treaty that the weaker party so flagrantly disowned have any binding force on the stronger party? The obvious cynicism of the Bolsheviks only encouraged similar attitudes on the German side. Why should Germany not act as the ruthless imperialist that it was being typecast as? And if not Germany, why not its allies?

In the spring of 1917 the German High Command had halted their Turkish allies on the South-Eastern Front. In this period of respite a fledgling Transcaucasian Republic had constituted a makeshift parliament, the Siem, in Tiflis to represent the formerly Russian provinces of Georgia, Armenia and Azerbaijan. Under the same terms as the Ukrainians they had been invited in December 1917 to join the conference table at Brest. But unlike Ukraine, the revolutionaries of the Caucasus refused the invitation. They would not even sit at the same table as the traitorous Bolsheviks. When the deliberations at Brest broke down, this made them fair game. Mindful of the horrors perpetrated against the Armenians since 1915, the German Foreign Office quickly reiterated to Constantinople that what was needed was a military offensive, not a resumption of the massacre.[23] But Berlin's pleas were in vain.[24] When the Soviets scuttled back to the negotiating table at Brest in the first week of March, Turkey demanded not only the border of 1913 but all of the territory taken by the Tsars since the 1870s. With hundreds of thousands of terror-stricken Armenians fleeing before General Enver Pasha's army, even this was no longer enough. Since the resumption of hostilities, Turkish blood had been spilled. There had been massacres of Muslim villagers too. If the Transcaucasian Republic wanted peace, it would have to purchase it at the price of Armenian territory. On 28 April, with the Germans looking on, the Turks calmly informed the Armenian members of the Transcaucasian delegation that unless their demands were met the genocidal Ittihadist commandos would complete the total annihilation of their people.[25]

To assert at least some control over their rampaging allies, the Germans despatched General Hans von Seeckt, the future leader of the Weimar Republic's Reichswehr, as an observer on the Caucasus front line. But Seeckt soon became intoxicated by the vistas opened up by the Russian collapse. 'As I stood on the rails that lead via Tiflis to Baku,' Seeckt wrote home, 'my thoughts wanted to go further, beyond the Caspian, through the cotton fields of Turkestan to the Olympian mountains. And if, as I hope, the war will continue for some time, we may yet beat on the doors of India.'[26] At the German Foreign Office an excitable official noted that if Germany was able to gain a foothold in the region, 'even the idea of a land route to China ... would move from the realm of adventurous fantasy into that of real calculation'.[27] But as General Enver Pasha reached out for Azerbaijan and the oil fields of Baku, what concerned Berlin more than China was the risk that pan-Turkic aggression might invite British intervention from Persia. Whilst Armenia was sacrificed to the Turks, Germany would build a base in the region by offering Georgia, with its advantageous coastline on the Black Sea and rich deposits of metal ores, a protectorate. With the Turkish Army advancing north, this was more than the Georgians could refuse. On 26 May they broke ranks, abandoned the Transcaucasian Siem and declared full independence. To the Armenians, the Georgian delegation expressed their regret at the horrible fate that awaited them. But 'we cannot drown with you,' the Georgians informed them. 'Our people want to save what they can. You too, are obligated to seek an avenue for agreement with the Turks. There is no other way.'[28]

Into a few hundred square miles of barren and mountainous land granted to the Armenian reservation, 600,000 people crowded. Half of them were penniless refugees who had been on the move since 1915. Turkish artillery was within easy range of the makeshift capital of Erevan. With no access to the sea and no railway system, the Turks closed the territory throughout the summer months to ensure that none of the abandoned fields just beyond the reservation's borders could be harvested.[29] As one German military representative on the spot reported to Berlin, the Turks were clearly intending to 'starve the entire Armenian nation'.[30] Meanwhile, in the relative safety of Tiflis, the German flag was raised alongside that of Georgia. General Otto von Lossow, the Kaiser's representative, signed a provisional agreement providing Germany with rights to Georgian manganese ore and access to the port of Poti. With German troops having occupied the Crimea and seized much of the Russian Black Sea Fleet, German engineering teams in the Caucasus began inspecting the railway system to establish the viability of Ludendorff's latest fantasy, which was to freight a light flotilla of the German navy including a dismantled U-boat cross-country to the port of Baku, where they would establish German naval supremacy over the landlocked Caspian Sea.[31] From his Caucasus bridgehead Ludendorff mused about launching attacks on Britain's position in the Persian Gulf.

This, however, was music of the far-distant future. The immediate prize of the Brest-Litovsk Treaty was supposed to have been the establishment of Ukraine as a substantial client state and economic partner of the Central Powers.[32] Having occupied the agrarian heartland in the spring advance, the Germans by early May 1918 had added the Donets industrial region to their zone of occupation. Already in December 1917 a businessmen's committee had been formed in Berlin to evaluate the possibilities of German investment in the East. But that was a long-term proposition. The most pressing priority was grain. In 1918 Austria and Germany confidently expected at least 1 million tons from their new ally. But by the end of April it had become clear that 'exploiting' the bread basket of the Ukraine would present more problems than these fantasies allowed. If they were to avoid the enormous costs of a full-scale occupation, Austria and Germany needed a cooperative local authority to collaborate with them. Having been driven out of Kiev, only to be restored courtesy of the German Army, the Rada needed a breathing space to re-establish itself. But the scale and urgency of Germany and Austria's economic demands made this impossible.[33]

In Ukraine, as in the rest of revolutionary Russia, the only way to secure popular legitimacy was to cede possession of the land to the peasants.[34] Over the summer of 1917 a nationwide land grab had redistributed the gentry's estates. In the Constituent Assembly election, the peasants had voted in their millions for the party that promised a village-based agrarian future, the Social Revolutionaries. The SRs were reliable allies against the Bolsheviks, but their land policy ran directly counter to the interests of the Central Powers. To maximize the surplus available for export, they needed cultivation to be concentrated in large, market-orientated farms. For the Rada to have presided over the restoration of the great estates for the sake of its German protectors would have discredited it completely. For the Germans themselves to reverse the agrarian revolution by force would have required hundreds of thousands of troops from the Western Front that Ludendorff could ill afford. If the Germans had been able to barter desirable manufactured goods in exchange for grain deliveries, this conflict might have been alleviated. Under the Brest-Litovsk Treaty, Germany had committed itself to trading grain for industrial goods. But under the strain of the war effort, goods for export were in desperately short supply.[35] To purchase the grain they needed, the Central Powers resorted to the short-term expedient of simply ordering the Ukrainian National Bank to print whatever currency they required. This gave them purchasing power and avoided requisitioning, but within a matter of months it rendered the currency worthless. As General Hoffmann noted from Kiev: 'Everyone is rolling in money. Roubles are printed and almost given away ... the peasants have enough stocks of corn to live on for two or three years, but they will not sell it.'[36] Having reached this point, there was no alternative but to resort to coercion.

In early April, Field Marshal Hermann von Eichhorn, the German occupation commander, issued a decree requiring compulsory cultivation of all land. However, the Field Marshal acted without the approval of the Rada and the deputies refused to ratify the decree. Within days, the German military decided against diplomacy. In a *coup d'état* they ousted the Ukrainian National Assembly and installed a so-called Hetmanate under the Tsarist cavalry officer Pyotr Skoropadskyi.[37] Only six weeks after the ratification of the Brest-Litovsk Treaty, under the pressure of economic necessity, the German military had unilaterally abandoned any residual claim to be acting as the protector of the legitimate cause of self-determination. Skoropadskyi spoke virtually no Ukrainian and filled his cabinet with conservative Russian nationalists. The real power-holders in Germany seemed to have lost interest in the project of creating a viable Ukrainian nation state. Instead, they appeared to be readying Kiev as the launching pad for a conservative reconquest of all of Russia.

If these threats from the south were not menacing enough, by May Lenin's regime faced an even more direct attack from the north. Along with the other Baltic states, Finland had declared independence from Russia in December 1917. In line with Lenin's nationalities policy, Petrograd had given its blessing. But at the same time it directed local Bolsheviks with strong trade union support to seize control of Helsinki. By the last week of January, Finland was plunged into civil war. In early March 1918 as German troops marched into Ukraine, the Kaiser and Ludendorff settled on a plan for a joint German-Finnish force that would first wipe out the Finnish Bolsheviks before continuing the march south towards Petrograd. Icy weather delayed the arrival of General von der Goltz's German expeditionary force until early April. But when they joined up with the Finnish White Guards of General Mannerheim they made up for lost time.[38] By 14 April, after heavy fighting, they had cleared Helsinki of Red Guards. As a token of German appreciation, von der Goltz disbursed food aid to the cheering burghers of the city.[39] The civil war ended on 15 May, but the killing did not. Following a reprisal shooting of White prisoners of war by Red Guards, the Finnish-German combat group unleashed a 'White terror' that by early May had claimed the lives of more than 8,000 leftists. At least 11,000 more would die of famine and disease in prison camps.[40] In the spring of 1918, Finland became the stage for the first of a series of savage counter-revolutionary campaigns that were to open a new chapter in twentieth-century political violence.

In the first week of May 1918, with the terror in full swing, Mannerheim and his German auxiliaries pushed menacingly towards the Russian fortress of Ino guarding the northern gateway to Petrograd. To the Soviets it seemed as though the Kaiser and his entourage had thought better of the compromise they had settled for at Brest. Why after all should Germany allow itself to be constrained by a mere treaty, one furthermore that the Soviets themselves had dismissed as nothing more than a scrap of paper? If Lenin's strategy of balancing between the imperialist powers was to work, he would have to go beyond merely ratifying Brest. After signing the treaty he had tacked away from the Germans, encouraging Trotsky to cultivate close contacts with the emissaries of the Entente and the United States in Petrograd and Moscow.[41] Now in early May he embarked on a second desperate gamble. If the Brest-Litovsk Treaty was no longer enough to satisfy German imperialism, Lenin would put more flesh on the bare bones of the peace.

On 6 May he called a night meeting of the party's Central Committee and demanded that his Comrades, who had agreed to the Brest treaty with such reluctance, must now swallow further concessions.[42] Anticipating opposition from the left wing of his party, Lenin returned to the attack, pouring acid contempt on the 'childishness' of the Left Communists. As Lenin insisted with characteristic impatience, 'nobody, except Menshevik blockheads of the first order', had 'ever expected' the course of historical development by itself 'to bring about "complete" socialism smoothly, gently, easily and simply'.[43] But even by his standards the new turn in policy was dizzying. On 14 May Lenin proposed that the German imperialists should be offered a comprehensive plan of economic cooperation.[44] By way of justification he offered what was surely the weirdest of his many modifications of orthodox Marxism. The need for a close alliance between the Russian revolution and Imperial Germany, he argued, arose out of the twisted logic of history itself. History had by 1918 'taken such a *peculiar course* that it has given birth ... to two unconnected halves of socialism existing side by side, like two future chickens in the single shell of international imperialism'. Brought together by the Brest-Litovsk Treaty, Soviet Russia and Imperial Germany were those twin chickens. To overcome the split between the political conditions for socialism, realized in Russia, and the economic conditions, realized in Germany, the shell of the treaty must be filled with a substantial economic alliance. Lenin promised his colleagues that Germany's legendary wartime economic organization, established by the electrical engineering magnate Walther Rathenau, was 'the most striking embodiment of the material realisation of the economic, the productive and the socio-economic conditions for socialism'. Through an economic and political alliance this organizational and technical potential would be harnessed to the political radicalism of the Bolsheviks.[45]

Nor was Lenin wrong to count on the cupidity of the Germans. The Berlin Foreign Ministry, with its distinctly economistic vision of German policy, seized eagerly on his proposal, calling together a standing committee of industrialists, bankers and politicians to consider the possibility of taking financial and technical control of Russia. As Lenin had hoped, Krupp and Deutsche Bank were licking their lips. But on sober inspection the dish was less appetizing than promised. Though Russia presented spectacular long-term opportunities, to take advantage of them would require huge investments that could be financed only with difficulty in wartime. Nor could the millions of tons of steel required for reconstruction come from Germany. Reconstruction would have to begin by restarting Russia's own blast furnaces, which by the summer of 1918 had been largely blown out.[46]

Lenin was not so naive as to underestimate these difficulties. Nor was it consistent with his strategy of 'balancing' to make such an offer only to the Germans. Russia's debts to Britain and France were already too large to make them promising targets for Lenin's manipulative tactics. But America's representatives in Moscow, above all the ubiquitous Colonel Robins, were fascinated by the prospects. On 20 April 1918 Robins cabled the American ambassador, urging that a decision be made. Unless Washington planned to offer Lenin 'organized opposition', he insisted that there must be 'organized cooperation'. As Robins telegraphed to America's reluctant ambassador, the stakes could not be higher. Russia's reconstruction was the 'largest economic and cultural enterprise remaining in the world'.[47] The question was whether this would take place 'under either German or American supervision and support'.

On 14 May, the same day that he put forward his dramatic plan for an embrace of German imperialism, Lenin provided the departing Colonel Robins with a prospectus for future economic cooperation with the United States. As Lenin acknowledged, for many years to come Germany would be too preoccupied with its own post-war recovery to be able to return to its pre-war role as Russia's main industrial supplier. 'Only America,' Lenin insisted, 'can become that country.'[48] Russia urgently needed railway equipment, farm machinery, electrical generators and mining equipment. There were huge construction projects across Russia. In exchange Russia would be able to offer annual exports of at least 3 billion gold roubles of oil, manganese and platinum as well as animal hides and furs. But on his return to Washington, Robins found no audience. President Wilson dismissed his emissary as someone 'in whom I have no confidence whatever'.[49] Lenin's effort at balancing had broken down. His dramatic lurch towards the Germans had tilted the balance on the Allied side decisively in favour of Robins's first option: organized opposition.

In truth, Lenin's efforts at balancing after May 1918 were misguided in a more fundamental sense. The idea that he could buy off German aggression through economic concessions was a figment of his ideological imagination. What limited Ludendorff's aggression was not Soviet diplomacy but the demands on German military resources made by the Western Front and the reassertion within Germany of a precarious political equilibrium. Since 1917, the Reichstag majority had been arguing for a durable and profitable peace in the East. In February 1918, following Trotsky's bizarre abandonment of the negotiations, they had lost the battle to prevent the resumption of hostilities. But, once the Reichstag had solemnly ratified the Brest-Litovsk Treaty in March, for the Kaiser and the military leadership to have simply ignored it and to have overturned the Soviet regime would have been an affront of historic proportions to the German parliament. Furthermore, what would have been the strategic rationale for such aggression? As Foreign Secretary Kühlmann pointed out, however odious the Bolsheviks might be, 'armed intervention against the revolution does not, as such, belong to the tasks of German policy'.[50] Speaking to the Reichstag Foreign Affairs Committee on 22 May, Kühlmann made clear that he had serious doubts about using the Skoropadskyi regime in Ukraine to launch an authoritarian restoration in Russia. Germany's strategic aim must be to keep Ukraine independent and the Tsarist Empire divided, even if this meant tolerating the Bolsheviks in Petrograd. 'It may seem strange for conservative and militarist Germany to support a socialist government in another country. But our interests dictate that we should do everything to prevent an imminent restoration of Russian unity. A unified Russia was bound to be pro-Entente.'[51] Nor did Kühlmann endorse Ludendorff's thrust into the Caucasus. He described the Caspian naval adventure simply as 'flaming madness'.[52]

The fact that Kühlmann was willing to speak in such frank terms to a committee of the Reichstag was indicative of the divisions within Germany opened up by the bruising peace-making process at Brest. In February 1918 the Foreign Secretary had privately shared his dismay with Vice-Chancellor Payer. By May the authoritarian behaviour of the German military in the East was so overt as to demand a public response. On 8 May Matthias Erzberger launched another of his sensational attacks on the Wilhelmine establishment, denouncing the high-handed behaviour of the German Army in the Ukraine. Fed by Erzberger's contacts in Kiev, the liberal *Vossische Zeitung* published eyewitness reports of the scandalous events surrounding Skoropadskyi's coup. German soldiers had stormed the Rada, a sovereign national parliament with which only a few weeks earlier the Reichstag had ratified a solemn treaty. A revolver had been pointed at the head of the Ukrainian president, the venerable historian Mykhailo Hrushevsky. Members of the Rada had been subjected to humiliating body searches. Cabinet ministers were arrested by German troopers. The newly minted Hetman was a reactionary Cossack. With such high-handed brutality Germany had forfeited any chance of establishing a legitimate and productive hegemony in the East. 'A German soldier can no longer show himself unarmed in Kiev. . . .', Erzberger lamented, '. . . the railway men and workmen are planning a general strike . . . the peasants would not deliver any grain, and bloodshed must be reckoned with in the event of requisitioning'.[53] Instead of the 1 million tons promised under the peace treaty, the Ukraine delivered no more than 173,000 tons to the Central Powers in 1918.[54] But it was not bread alone that was at stake. The question that concerned Erzberger and his colleagues in the Reichstag majority was who controlled the Reich.[55] In future Erzberger demanded all measures in the East should be subject to the approval of Germany's civilian government. There must be a complete ban on military interference in the internal affairs of Ukraine and the Baltic states, to which Germany had extended formal recognition.[56]

Predictably, nationalist members of the Reichstag greeted Erzberger's intervention with outrage. Gustav Stresemann, the leading voice amongst the nationalist liberals, insisted that Erzberger's proposed civilian control must be rejected since it would undermine the German government and would serve as 'confirmation of (President) Wilson's point that Germany was a military autocracy, with which the Entente powers were unable to negotiate'.[57] Those speaking for the motion could only agree, but drew the opposite conclusion. The authoritarian threat was real and it had to be stopped. Despite encouraging news from the Western Front, Ludendorff and Hindenburg knew that they could not act in complete disregard of the civilian authorities in the Reich. On 18 May after an urgent intercession by Chancellor Hertling, Ludendorff agreed to halt the Finno-German march on Petrograd.[58] As in Japan, civilian political control asserted itself as a basic safety catch against the more radical fantasies of the German imperialists. Despite its odious reputation and fragile legitimacy, the Brest-Litovsk Treaty served as the main line of defence against a further radicalization of the war. Ironically, the chief beneficiaries of this precarious equilibrium were the Bolsheviks. Whether it could hold would depend on the escalation unleashed by the aggression of both sides.

8

Intervention

On 16 May 1918, in a brief lull between the German attacks in the West, a British general staff memorandum envisioned a truly apocalyptic scenario. Assuming that Hindenburg and Ludendorff, courtesy of Lenin, were able to press-gang 2 million men from the Russian provinces, the Central Powers would be able to continue the war at least until the end of 1919. Germany, the British staffers speculated, would come to resemble 'the conditions of the ancient Roman empire, with legionnaires fighting on her frontiers and slaves working at home, both recruited from subject races'. Unlike the Western Powers, the 'hunnish' Germans were 'not hampered ... by any standards of Christianity ... the Germans are frankly pagan and opportunist, and will not hesitate to employ any such methods that may be necessary for their purpose. Starvation and flogging, backed by machine-guns, soon produce the required effect in a community of illiterates with centuries of serfdom behind them.'[1] Six weeks later, at the height of the final German offensive in the West, the British government informed America that 'unless Allied intervention is undertaken in Siberia forthwith', Germany would impose its hegemony over all of Russia. In that case, even with a full-scale commitment by America, the Entente would 'have no chance of being ultimately victorious' and would run a 'serious risk of defeat in the meantime'.[2]

It was not, as Lenin imagined, the revolutionary threat posed by Communism that brought down upon his regime the intervention by the Entente, Japan and the United States. The scenario that haunted the Allies and impelled them to action *was* a ghostly premonition of the future. But what was on their mind was not the spectre of revolution or an anticipation of the Cold War, but a foretaste of the summer of 1941 when the military triumphs of the Wehrmacht threatened to extend Hitler's slave empire throughout Eurasia. The prospect that terrified the British and the French in 1918 was not the spectre of Communism as such, but the threat that under Lenin, Russia would become an auxiliary of German imperialism. It was Lenin's lopsided policy of balancing culminating in his lurch towards Germany in May 1918 that made the push for intervention irresistible.

I

Lenin's desperate determination to solidify the Brest-Litovsk Treaty came as a shock to those representatives of the Entente still in Russia, who since the winter had been working frantically to maintain relations between the two sides. Reversing his previous advocacy of cooperation with the Bolsheviks, Bruce Lockhart, Britain's chief representative, now advised London that with Lenin in command, Russia would never escape the German grip. The Entente must launch a massive military intervention, if necessary even without the cooperation of Russian anti-Bolsheviks. But there was no difficulty on that score. On 26 May the Socialist Revolutionaries, the party with the strongest claim to a popular majority in both Russia and Ukraine, declared their support for armed foreign intervention. The Left Socialist Revolutionaries would not consort with the Entente, but were in open opposition. During the Tsarist period they had been pioneers in the bloody art of political terrorism. On 30 May, claiming to have evidence that hit squads were active in the capital, Lenin declared martial law. After a wave of arrests, all representatives of the Mensheviks and Socialist Revolutionaries were expelled from the Central Executive Committee of the All-Russian Congress of Soviets.[3]

In Petrograd and Moscow the Bolsheviks were able to retain control. But across the far-flung territory of Russia the Soviet regime was openly challenged. By the spring of 1918 the global linkage of politics and strategy from the Baltic to the Pacific had become almost commonplace. Even so, it must have come as a surprise to find the fate of Siberia hanging on the decision of a Czech professor, who from exile in Washington found himself in command of armies operating on battlefronts stretching from Flanders to Vladivostok. The professor in question was the sociologist and philosopher Tomas Garrigue Masaryk. The forces at his command were several divisions of patriotic Czech prisoners of war who had been mobilized in 1917 by Alexander Kerensky to bolster the fragile Russian front line against their hated national enemy, the Austrians. Following the Brest peace talks, the Czechs had reaffirmed their loyalty to the cause of the Entente and whilst still deep inside Russia had placed themselves under the command of Marshal Foch in France. This disciplined and highly motivated force, 50,000 strong, determined to continue the fight against the Central Powers even a thousand miles from their homes, now menaced both the Bolsheviks and the German forces stretched thinly across southern Russia. When Trotsky issued the order for the Czechs to be disarmed, it was assumed, not surprisingly, that he was acting on German instructions. Armed clashes between the Czechs and Red Guards broke out at railway junctions across Siberia. By the end of May virtually the entire transcontinental artery was in the hands of Masaryk's legion.

To advocates of intervention in Britain and France, the Czechs seemed like an army parachuted from heaven. However, with an eye to the post-war peace, Masaryk would not act without approval from President Wilson, whose position on the question of Czech independence was notoriously ambiguous.[4] In the 14 Points, in the hope of keeping open the door to a separate peace with Vienna, Wilson had abstained from any mention of the Czech cause. It was not until the ratification of the Brest-Litovsk Treaty, and the even more draconian peace imposed on Romania in May 1918, that Wilson was willing openly to endorse national autonomy for the Czechs and their South Slav brethren. Even then, this did not translate into any eagerness to see the Czechs in Siberia used against the Bolsheviks. Wilson was seconded in this reluctance by Masaryk, who continued to profess his sympathy for the 'revolutionary democracy' in Russia. It was not until early June, with the drastic British strategic appreciations in hand, that Secretary of State Lansing managed to persuade Masaryk that the Czech Army, rather than withdrawing towards Vladivostok, could do a vital service to the Allies by establishing a blocking position along the Trans-Siberian railway.[5] Coached by Lansing, Masaryk demanded as his quid pro quo a Wilsonian death sentence on the Habsburg Empire.

The stakes of the intervention in Siberia were growing ever higher. Just as Lansing and Masaryk were bartering the end of the Habsburg dynasty against Czech assistance in Siberia, William Bullitt, Wilson's radical advisor, was making one last effort to stop the intervention. 'We are about to make one of the most tragic blunders in the history of mankind,' Bullitt wrote to Colonel House. The advocates of intervention were typical exponents of imperialism. Following a violent counter-revolutionary intervention, 'how many years and how many American lives' would it 'take to re-establish democracy in Russia?'[6] There was no question that Bullitt was closer to Wilson in spirit than was Lansing. But whereas less than six weeks earlier, with regard to Japanese intervention, Wilson had boasted of his grip over the Japanese, Lenin's abrupt embrace of Germany had robbed him of his grip. He could not hold back the momentum for intervention if its principal rationale was anti-German rather than anti-Soviet.

On 30 June 1918 Britain and France publicly proclaimed their support for Czech national aspirations, citing as their justification the 'sentiments and high ideals expressed by President Wilson'. Once more, Wilson was entangled in the logic of his own ideological programme and the experience drove him to the point of distraction. Speaking to his cabinet in June 1918 he remarked that the Allied war advocacy of intervention in Russia left him lost for words. 'They propose such impractical things to be done immediately that he often wondered whether he was crazy or whether they were.'[7] When a US Treasury official reported after a visit to Europe that the British Prime Minister, Lloyd George, was openly mocking the idea of a peace based on the League of Nations, the President replied: 'Yes I know that Europe is still governed by the same reactionary forces which controlled this country until a few years ago. But I am satisfied that if necessary I can reach the peoples of Europe over the heads of their rulers.'[8] Once more, Wilson's reluctance to intervene was bringing to the fore the politics of 'peace without victory'. But with Germany apparently about to establish control over all of western Russia, Wilson could not uphold the position of moral equivalence that this stance implied. On 6 July he took the initiative. Without prior consultation with either Japan or Britain, Wilson announced that the Allied intervention would be directed through Siberia and would take the form of two contingents of 7,000 men, supplied by the US and Japan. Their mission was neither to take the offensive against Germany nor to overthrow the Bolsheviks, but simply to screen a Czech withdrawal to Vladivistok.

In London, Lloyd George was incensed. After months of dangerous vacillation, Wilson had taken it upon himself unilaterally to fix the terms of the intervention and to do so in a manner which, though bound to provoke the Bolsheviks, was quite insufficient to overthrow them. The inadequate intervention amounted, as Bruce Lockhart would later comment, to a 'paralytic half-measure, which in the circumstances amounted to a crime'.[9] Certainly, Lloyd George was in no mood to take lessons from Wilson on democracy. In a furious telegram to the British Embassy in Washington the British Prime Minister rejected the supposition that Britain's intentions were reactionary. Lenin's recent move toward the Germans had shifted the terms of the debate entirely. Whereas it might once have been possible to oppose intervention on the grounds that it gave encouragement to reactionary forces, now Lloyd George insisted 'I am interventionist just as much because I am a democrat as because I want to win the war.' The 'last thing' Lloyd George 'would stand for, would be the encouragement of any kind of repressive regime' in Russia 'under whatever guise'.[10] Only a democratic Russia would provide a real buffer against the German threat. As Britain's Chief of the Imperial General Staff had put it, 'unless by the end of the war democratic Russia can be reconstituted as an independent military power, it is only a question of time before most of Asia becomes a German colony, and nothing can impede the enemy's progress towards India, in defence of which the British empire will have to fight at every disadvantage'. As Lloyd George insisted, Russia's political complexion would define the post-war order. 'Unless by the end of the war Russia is settled on liberal, progressive and democratic lines', neither the 'peace of the world' nor more specifically 'the peace and security of the Indian frontier' could be assured.[11] But, as he admitted regretfully, 'we can do nothing without the US'.[12] In light of that inconvenient truth, the British war cabinet agreed to swallow its objections and give its support to Wilson's half-hearted Siberian mission, hoping that force of circumstance would lead, in due course, to a more adequate scale of operation.

II

If the British had been able to see inside Ludendorff's staff offices in the summer of 1918, they would have found ample fuel to feed their fears. Up to the end of June, Chancellor Hertling was able to hold the line established in mid-May, blocking military advances in the East. This position was communicated to the Bolsheviks, enabling them to concentrate their trusty Latvian regiments, fighting as they believed for their independence, against the Czechs, who were fighting for theirs.[13] But the equilibrium in Germany was precarious. In late June a memo prepared by Ludendorff's staff, on 'The Aims of German Policy' (*Ziele der deutschen Politik*), made clear the extent to which German military policy had radicalized since Brest. Ludendorff's aim was no longer merely to exercise hegemony over the periphery of the former Tsarist Empire, leaving the Bolsheviks in the rump of Russia to their own ruinous devices. In a mirror image of Lloyd George's vision of a democratic bastion in Russia, Ludendorff aimed to reconstruct an integral Russian state that thanks to its conservative political make-up could be counted on as a 'reliable friend and ally ... that not only poses no danger for Germany's political future, but which, as far as possible, is politically, militarily and economically dependent on Germany, and provides Germany with a source of economic strength'.[14] The peripheral states of Finland, the Baltic, Poland and Georgia would remain under German protection. The return of Ukraine to Moscow would be bartered against German economic control over Russia as a whole. Harnessed to the Reich, Russia would provide the means for Germany to exert its domination throughout Eurasia. It would provide the hinterland for an economically self-sufficient, politically authoritarian 'world state structure' (*Weltstaatengebilde*), capable of competing head on with the 'pan-American bloc' (*panamerikanischen Block*) and the British Empire.[15]

This new strategic vision was formally adopted during the last great strategic discussion at the Kaiser's headquarters at Spa in early July 1918.[16] But as Kühlmann had pointed out to the Reichstag, the idea of reconstructing a conservative Russian nation state under German auspices was fraught with contradictions.[17] Early contacts with suitable figures amongst the anti-Bolshevik Russians, most notably the Kadet Pavel Miliukov, ousted as Russian Foreign Minister by the Petrograd Soviet in May 1917, led to the conclusion that no self-respecting Russian patriot would ever accept the terms of the Brest-Litovsk Treaty, let alone Ludendorff's even more expansive vision.[18] Furthermore, as Kühlmann and the Reichstag anxiously pointed out, the German military were alarmingly unclear about how their expansive visions of hegemony in the East were to be reconciled with the demands of the war in the West. Though wave upon wave of attacks had stretched the Allied lines in France near to breaking point, it was obvious that Germany was nearing the end of its strength. Ominously, the Kaiser had greeted the thirtieth year of his rule on 15 June with an apocalyptic speech. In the war everything was at stake. There was no room for compromise in the West any more than there was in the East. 'Either the Prusso-German Germanic Weltanschauung – justice, freedom, honour, and morals – be respected, or the Anglo-Saxon Weltanschauung will triumph and that means sinking into the worship of mammon. In this struggle one Weltanschauung will be destroyed.'[19]

Such language is of course irresistibly reminiscent of Hitler's infamous 'Table Talk' tirades of the 1940s. But tempting as such comparisons are, they obscure the radical difference in political circumstance between 1918 and 1941. Even at the height of World War I, the safeguards of nineteenth-century constitutionalism continued to function. Less than ten days after the Kaiser had made his apocalyptic address, he was directly contradicted in front of the Reichstag by his Foreign Secretary.[20] Germany must realize, Kühlmann insisted, that in light of the 'incredible magnitude' to which the war had expanded, it was unrealistic to expect that the country could impose in the West the kind of one-sided peace (*Diktatfrieden*) that had been possible at Brest. Final and ultimate military victory, as Ludendorff seemed to envision it, was out of the question. How could Germany ever hope to achieve a complete defeat of the United States or the British Empire? The Reich would have to negotiate. Indeed, as the battle in the West turned against Germany, a negotiated peace was the very best that Germany could hope for. Speaking for the SPD, Eduard David, once amongst the most prominent advocates of a liberal peace in the East, drove the point home. The forces demanding a further escalation of the war were 'the remnants of the feudal order' in Europe, of which 'the strongest and most influential remnant' was no longer in Russia, but in 'East Elbia'.[21] The following day, compounding the mounting sense of confusion, Hindenburg and Ludendorff held a press conference at which Germany's military leadership publicly disowned the position of the Reich's Foreign Secretary. The war, the military leadership insisted, could still be won by a crushing victory in the West. The issue of the SPD's daily newspaper, *Vorwärts*, which had dared to publish Kühlmann's words, was impounded.

Kühlmann's political career was over. On 9 July 1918, despite having the backing of the Reichstag majority, he was replaced by Paul von Hintze, an unswerving follower of the Kaiser.[22] But the domestic opposition to Ludendorff's imperial fantasies in the East remained solid. Chancellor Hertling promised the Reichstag that whatever the new Foreign Secretary's personal proclivities, his government would not turn Belgium into an insuperable obstacle to peace. Germany required only that it should be properly neutralized. Furthermore, he remained committed to the Brest-Litovsk Treaty. Both Hertling and Vice-Chancellor Payer would resign if any steps were taken beyond the treaty. But this was no longer enough for the SPD, which despite voting for another round of war credits withdrew its support from the Hertling government. The Social Democrats had entered into a coalition with the Centre Party and Liberals in the summer of 1917 on the basis of a common peace platform. But not only had the Hertling government taken the collapse of the strike wave in January 1918 as the signal for a punitive programme of wage and ration cuts, it had also completely failed to deliver a foreign policy in conformity with the demands of that platform. When, a year earlier, the SPD had thrown its weight behind the Reichstag's peace resolution, American troops had only been trickling into France. Now hundreds of thousands were pouring in every month.[23] At a moment of such national emergency, how could the SPD be expected to tolerate the scandalous situation in which Germany had no coherent foreign policy and warmongers were permitted to dictate the nation's course according to their irresponsible whims?

III

Though neither Ludendorff nor Lenin attributed any inherent significance to the Brest-Litovsk Treaty, its formal legality provided Germany's politicians with the crucial check they needed to restrain the escalating radicalization of the Kaiser's regime.[24] As Foreign Secretary Hintze put it to an eager group of nationalist deputies, 'The Brest peace is ... not to be budged.'[25] But in insisting on adherence to the legal frame of the treaty, it was the civilians in Germany who were begging the question.

How long could advocates of legality uphold a treaty with a regime like that of Lenin? The Bolsheviks themselves had not hidden their contempt for the treaty. When Lenin attempted to fill the agreement with more meaning he did so by adding economic inducements for German business. But to what lengths would he have to go to sustain his embrace of German imperialism against the violent domestic opposition it aroused in Russia?

On 4 July 1918 the body that was still recognized as the supreme authority in revolutionary Russia, the Fourth All-Russian Congress of Soviets, met in Moscow for the first time since the inauguration of Lenin's new foreign policy. An unprecedentedly overt campaign of intimidation and election rigging had ensured a solid Bolshevik majority. But it had not silenced the opposition. Over-confident in his command, Lenin entrusted the task of presenting the new phase of rapprochement with Germany to the urbane Georgy Chicherin, a direct descendant of one of the Tsar's ambassadors at the Congress of Vienna. With Count Mirbach the German ambassador seated in the royal box as a guest of honour of Sovnarkom (the Council of People's Commissars), Chicherin began a bland overview of the new pro-German, Leninist orthodoxy. But as the audience reacted to his speech, the Congress threatened to descend into chaos. A representative of the Ukrainian peasant resistance sprang onto the stage to make an impassioned oration against the violence of the German occupation. Hurling threatening gestures in the direction of the German guests, the Left Socialist Revolutionaries broke into an anti-Leninist chorus of 'Down with Brest! Down with Mirbach! Down with the lackeys of Germany!'[26] Trotsky from the chair did his best to calm the embarrassing scene. But, in the end, he was forced to resort to naked threats. Delegates who engaged in acts of provocation, he warned, would be subject to immediate arrest. The following day Lenin appeared before the Congress to defend his policy in person. But the rebellious Left Socialist Revolutionaries were not cowed. Rather than promoting Soviet power, Lenin's policy of ever closer accommodation with Berlin was leading to a 'dictatorship of German imperialism'. Count Mirbach's presence at the Congress of Soviets, the hallowed assembly of the Russian revolution, was a flagrant admission of this subservience. Undaunted by the howling Leninist majority, the Left Socialist Revolutionaries demanded the renunciation of the Brest-Litovsk Treaty.

The next day they made good on their threats. Assassins posing as Cheka agents entered the German Embassy and shot dead Count Mirbach. The intention was clearly to drive a wedge between Russia and Germany. After some hesitation the Latvian Red Guards put down the feeble attempt at an uprising by the Left Socialist Revolutionaries. The Germans reacted as the Russian opposition had hoped. They demanded further humiliating concessions, including the deployment to Petrograd of a full battalion of 650 German infantry as embassy guards. This threw even Lenin into a rare bout of depression. To agree to such demands would confirm the accusations that the Bolsheviks were reducing Russia to the status of a 'little oriental state', where Western embassies could demand the protection of their own legation guards.[27] As a concession, the Germans agreed to send the troops to Moscow unarmed and in plain clothes. Meanwhile the Bolsheviks responded with brutal repression. Though the Cheka never arrested the individuals responsible for the killing, it was in the summer of 1918, as the struggle over Lenin's policy toward Germany reached its height, that the terror apparatus of the Soviet state began to take institutional shape. In early July, as White forces drove westwards from their bases in Siberia flanked by the Czechs, the Cheka carried out its first mass executions.[28] On the night of 16–17 July all members of the Romanov imperial family were murdered: Tsar Nicholas II, his wife Alexandra, their four daughters and son. By early August, Lenin was calling for 'merciless mass terror against kulaks, priests and White guards' and the establishment of a more permanent apparatus of 'concentration camps' to deal with 'unreliable elements'. In the 'life and death struggle' for the survival of the revolution, *Izvestia* declaimed, there were 'no courts of law' to appeal to, merely the injunction to kill or be killed.[29] With British forces in the north and Japanese and American forces in the Pacific readying themselves to attack, the civil war that the Bolsheviks had deliberately provoked was threatening to merge with the wider global struggle.

On 29 July 1918 Lenin gave the party's Central Committee a truly drastic appraisal of the situation. Encircled by a 'forged chain' of Anglo-French imperialism, Russia had been 'sucked back into the war'. The fate of the revolution now depended 'entirely upon who will carry off the victory ... the entire question of the continued existence of the USSR ... has been reduced to this military question'.[30] When pressed by the British representative Bruce Lockhart as to whether this amounted to a declaration of war against the Entente, Lenin was evasive. But behind the scenes the Bolsheviks had made their choice. Following through the logic of the policy adopted since May, Lenin was clasping the Germans ever closer. On 1 August with Lenin's personal approval Chicherin approached Mirbach's successor as ambassador, the prominent nationalist politician Karl Helfferich, to ask Germany to intervene with military force to stabilize the Murmansk front, where the British were establishing an anti-Soviet base.[31] A day later, having confirmed that this extraordinary request did indeed come from the Kremlin, Helfferich forwarded the message to Berlin. First Lenin had moved to tighten relations with Germany. That had made it impossible for Woodrow Wilson to continue to resist the call for intervention. Now, the intervention that Wilson had been forced to approve triggered Lenin into inviting Germany to transform the uncomfortable modus vivendi of Brest into active military cooperation. As Rosa Luxemburg, the great tribune of the German radical left and long-time critic of Lenin, was to put it, in one of her most devastatingly perceptive attacks, this was 'the final stage' of the 'path of thorns' that the Russian revolution had been forced to travel towards 'an alliance between the Bolsheviks and Germany'.[32]

Ludendorff, not surprisingly, leapt at the chance of directing German and Finnish forces against the British in northern Russia. To scare the Reichstag into line, General Hoffmann was peddling dark visions of an encircling Entente position that would run from Murmansk by way of the Volga to Baku and Baghdad.[33] But Ludendorff had his limits. 'A military alliance and a fighting shoulder to shoulder with the Bolsheviks, I consider out of the question for our Army.'[34] German intervention must go hand in hand with a political reorganization of Russia. This would start with the German occupation of Petrograd and Kronstadt. Given the prevailing anarchy in Russia, Ludendorff thought that six divisions would be enough to give military backing to a new, popular Russian regime. By mid-August the Germans were in top-secret staff talks with the Finns and Russian experts about what was now dubbed Operation Capstone (Schlussstein). Some 50,000 troops were moving to advanced positions ready for an assault that was to sweep by way of Petrograd towards the British positions at Murmansk.[35]

Lenin's regime was teetering on the edge of a complete capitulation to Germany. And this impression was only reinforced when on 27 August

1918 the two sides finalized the Supplementary Treaty to Brest-Litovsk. In exchange for German protection, the Soviet regime offered indemnities not included in the original Brest Treaty to the sum of 6 billion marks ($1.46 billion). The Governorates of Livonia and Estonia were formally removed from Russian territory, consolidating German hegemony in the Baltic. The Communists also agreed to recognize the independence of Georgia, Germany's protectorate in the Caucasus, and to supply at least 25 per cent of the oil from Baku to the Central Powers once Azerbaijan was back in Soviet hands.[36] Under the terms of the treaty, Germany and Finland agreed to abstain from any assault on Petrograd in exchange for a guarantee that the Bolsheviks would see to it that all the Entente forces were driven out of Soviet territory. In the event that the Soviet regime was unable to make good on this obligation, secret clauses provided for German and Finnish intervention.

The trigger for Operation Capstone was built into the treaty. Crucially, however, the German Foreign Office made sure that any Finnish-German deployment must be at the explicit invitation of the Soviet side. It was up to the Communists to surrender Petrograd to Ludendorff. Of course, Lenin was in no position to enforce any such conditions. The Red Guards could have offered no more than token resistance to a concerted German-Finnish attack. It was the civilian authorities in Berlin who served as the real check. Already in early August the Foreign Office extracted from Ludendorff a promise that he would act only within the terms of the Supplementary Treaty.[37] It was this restraint that saved Lenin's regime from a military entanglement with Imperial Germany, which, as Rosa Luxemburg put it, would have meant the 'moral bankruptcy', if not the outright destruction, of the revolution. The formal authorization for the occupation of Petrograd never came. Instead the German Foreign Office, over protests from Ludendorff, agreed to supply 200,000 rifles, 500 million rounds of ammunition and 70,000 tons of coal so the Soviets might defend themselves.[38]

But the willingness of the German civilian authorities to hold the line on the fragile legal ground of Brest had not yet faced its sternest test. Sensing the growing vulnerability of the Bolshevik regime, the terrorist teams of the Left Socialist Revolutionaries raised the stakes. Three days after the Supplementary Treaty to Brest was initialled, on 30 August, Lenin was in an industrial suburb of Moscow delivering the new and drastic slogan that had replaced his promises of peace – 'Victory or death!' As he left the Mekhelnson armaments works, he was hit in the neck and shoulder by an assassin's bullets. In a simultaneous attack the Petrograd Cheka chief Moisei Uritsky was killed. The policy of repression that had been gathering force since July was now transformed into the open proclamation of the 'Red Terror'. In Petrograd alone 500 political prisoners were shot on the spot. Thousands more were to follow. Hostages were taken across the country. Anyone suspected of counter-revolutionary activity was liable to arrest and detention in one of the growing network of prison camps. At the end of July, Lenin had refused British representative Lockhart a formal declaration of war. Now on 1 September 1918 the British Embassy was stormed and hostages were taken. A military attaché was killed. Henceforth Soviet Russia was to be governed as a 'military camp'. A revolutionary military council headed by Trotsky took over much of the business of the party's Central Committee.[39]

The ruthless bloodshed of the Red Terror added dramatic impetus to those in Germany calling for a decisive anti-Bolshevik intervention. The Reichstag majority opposed ratifying the Supplementary Treaty that was bound to unite Russia in patriotic opposition to Germany and the Bolsheviks.[40] Sensing that he might yet get his chance, Ludendorff put the troops preparing for Operation Capstone on maximum readiness. Additional air units were moved from the West. On 8 September 1918 a team of German and Finnish military engineers began exploring the transport routes around Petrograd in the direction of Murmansk. How long the Foreign Office could have upheld its opposition to Ludendorff's aggression is far from certain. Coming hard on the heels of the supplementary agreement to Brest, the Red Terror placed the German Foreign Service in a truly invidious position. The embassy, which had moved from Moscow back to Petrograd, found itself at the centre of what one of the horrified diplomats described as a 'St Bartholomew's Day Massacre'. The desperate Russian bourgeoisie, many of whom looked to the Germans for protection, discovered that they had been 'sold to the devil' for the paltry sum of 6 billion marks.[41]

When Erzberger criticized the Supplementary Treaty to Brest in conversation with liberal Vice-Chancellor Payer, Payer admitted that the Reich's government was so uncertain of its position that it no longer

1. Too proud to fight: Colonel House and Woodrow Wilson, 1915

Irish Rebellion, May, 1916.
Sackville Street in ruins.

2. The aftermath of the Easter Rising, Dublin, 1916

3. German troops marching into Bucharest, December 1916

4. Would-be Emperor: Yuan Shi-Kai, 1916

5. Men and women queuing to vote for the Russian Constituent Assembly, November 1917

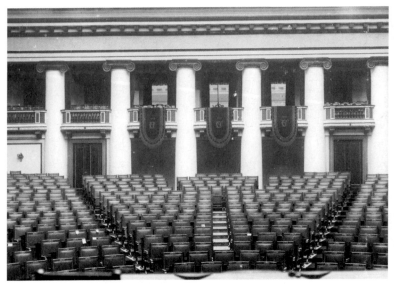

6. Waiting for Russian democracy: the Tauride Palace, meeting place of the Constituent Assembly, January 1918

7. American and French troops with Renault FT light tanks, 1918

8. A blindfolded Russian negotiator with Habsburg troops en route to Brest-Litovsk

9. Prince Leopold of Bavaria signing the Brest-Litovsk Treaty, March 1918

10. German troops in Kiev, August 1918

11. Poster for the eighth German war loan, March 1918

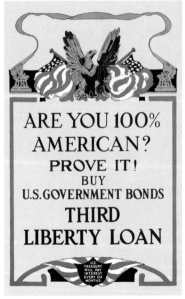

12. Poster for the Third US Liberty Loan, April 1918

13. The revolution comes to Berlin: Kiel marines on the Friedrichstrasse, 7 November 1918

14. The SMS *Hindenburg* sailing into Scapa Flow to surrender, 21 November 1918

15. Woodrow Wilson welcomed on arrival at Dover, 26 December 1918

16. Clemenceau, Wilson and Lloyd George at Versailles

planned to submit the text of the treaty to the Reichstag for ratification. Foreign Secretary Hintze would sign it and apply retrospectively for an indemnity for this breach of the constitution.[42] Mirbach's outspoken replacement, the nationalist Karl Helfferich, was not satisfied with such makeshifts. On 30 August he resigned in protest, denouncing the apologetic stance of the German government. The defenders of the Brest Treaty in Berlin were perpetrating a 'systematic misrepresentation' of a regime that 'in its excesses was barely exceeded by the Jacobins'. Helfferich would not stand for the 'ostensible treatment' of Lenin's regime as a government on the same footing as that of Germany. He could not be party to the effort to 'solidarize, or at least to give the appearance of solidarizing with the regime . . .'. For the Reich's government to condone Bolshevik violence was disastrous not only for Russia. It would undermine morale on the German home front.[43] But despite Helfferich's protest, the Foreign Office clung to the Brest Treaty as a 'kind of protection', as one Reichstag deputy put it, 'against the German military'.[44] The alternative of allowing Ludendorff a free hand in the East, to wage the kind of counter-revolutionary campaign recently witnessed in Finland, was simply too awful to contemplate. Germany's demoralized diplomats were instructed to avoid any public statements against the Bolsheviks and to intercede against acts of terror only when German citizens were at risk.

On 24 September 1918, in the sorry culmination of Germany's bankrupt policy, Foreign Secretary Hintze deliberately misled the Reichstag with regard to events in Russia. Responding to questions about the terror being perpetrated by a government with which Germany was now in what amounted to an alliance, Hintze replied 'in Greater Russia the cauldron of revolution continues to boil . . . certainly acts of terror are committed; but that they are going on on the scale reported in the press is most unlikely . . .'. The Foreign Office had made 'specific enquiries and have been officially informed, that the reported figures (of executions) are on the whole greatly exaggerated'.[45] Confronted with daily evidence of violence, the German consul in Petrograd could only bite his tongue. As Hintze himself later admitted, his deliberate obfuscation of the true character of the Bolshevik regime could be justified only by reference to 'higher political concerns'.

IV

The politics of intervention in the summer of 1918 are indicative of quite how seriously the liberal cause had derailed since the moment in July 1917 when the Petrograd Soviet's democratic peace offensive came so agonizingly close to coinciding with the Reichstag's peace resolution. By May 1918 progressives in Germany and the United States found themselves clinging to a bad peace with an increasingly odious Soviet regime as the only way to prevent a further escalation of violence. Lenin for his part, whilst insisting that he was playing one imperialist power off against the others, in fact slid ever further across the line that separated a regrettable separate peace from a truly discreditable alliance with German imperialism. As for Ludendorff, he wanted nothing more than to crush the Soviet regime to death. But he was prevented from acting by the German government and the Reichstag majority, which had no love for either the Bolsheviks or the arbitrary rule of the German military in the East, yet saw Brest as the best way to contain a further escalation.

Given this confused situation, it is hardly surprising that it was the advocates of intervention in London, Paris and Washington who had the better of the argument. Lenin's ever more transparent alignment with Germany allowed them to establish a clear political and strategic position. The Bolshevik regime, odious in its own right, was allied with German militarism and autocracy. Interventions by Japanese, American, British and French forces, combined with local Russian support, would strike against both enemies. It was an intervention, as Lloyd George and Lansing insisted, in which strategic imperatives and the pursuit of democracy were inseparable. The war fused the two together, and if the war in the West had continued much longer it is hard to see how the Bolshevik regime could have survived. There was plenty of Japanese manpower available for deployment and the Japanese military knew how to seize their moment. Overriding the hesitancy of the parliamentary politicians, by November they had poured 72,000 troops into Siberia.[46] What halted that escalation, what saved the Bolsheviks from an open capitulation to Ludendorff that would have robbed them of any historic legitimacy, was the suddenness of Germany's defeat in the West.[47] This not only prevented the realization of Operation Capstone, but it also took the wind out of the sails of Allied intervention almost as soon as it began.

TWO

Winning a Democratic Victory

9

Energizing the Entente

Between 21 March and 15 July 1918 five waves of German attacks hurled themselves against the Allied lines in northern France. By early June the Germans seemed once more to have Paris within their reach. Frantic preparations were made to evacuate the government to Bordeaux. But on 18 July the French counter-attacked and in a matter of days the momentum shifted decisively. The Kaiser's exhausted and hungry army reeled back towards the borders of the Reich. By September, Canadian, British, South African and Australian forces had driven decisively through the Hindenburg line. It was a spectacular military victory and it was won by the Entente.[1] The key defensive battles of the spring and early summer were fought by the British and French virtually unaided. America's military effort during the Allied counter-offensive was more significant, but General John Pershing's army required many more months of combat experience to mature into a war-winning force. America made its truly decisive contribution in the sphere of economic mobilization. But as the war in the East demonstrated, neither the military nor the economic effort would have mattered if the Entente Powers had not maintained their political coherence. Russia was disintegrating into civil war. The Habsburg and Ottoman empires were tottering. By the summer of 1918, the future of the imperial regime in Germany was more and more openly questioned. When Germans came to analyse and explain their own defeat, it was above all around this political factor that their thoughts circled. It was the flip-side of the notorious 'stab in the back' legend. They attributed an enormous influence to Allied propaganda and to the demagogic genius of Lloyd George and Clemenceau. What Germany had lacked was a populist, democratic

'Führer'.[2] But potent as the charisma of Lloyd George and Clemenceau no doubt was, to focus on their personalities would be to understate the forces in play.

The crises that shook both the French and Italian war efforts in 1917 were profound. The French mutiny and the Italian collapse at Caporetto were on a par with anything suffered by Tsarist Russia prior to the revolution. Both France and Italy responded with repression in the first instance. Thousands of French mutineers were court-martialled, an exemplary few were executed. In Italy the reprisals following the disaster at Caporetto were wholesale. It is possible in both cases, indeed it has become commonplace in recent historical writing, to trace forward from these moments of crisis to the escalation of political violence, war and further trauma that befell both countries over the coming decade.[3] It was the extraordinary effort required to carry the war through 1917 and to its conclusion that led to the radical polarizations, extreme rhetoric, and the personal animosities and passions that motivated both the first onrush of extremism in the immediate aftermath of the war and its second coming in the 1930s.[4] In Italy the lingering fury at the humiliating collapse in November 1917 echoed through the machismo of Mussolini's Fascist movement.[5] But by itself this does not explain Mussolini's ascent to power, let alone the overthrow of the French Third Republic. To draw a straight line from the crisis of 1917 to the fascism and collaboration in the Europe of 1940 does no justice to the success achieved by the Entente war effort. In the Entente's survival and eventual victory in November 1918 coercion and censorship certainly played a role. The Entente Powers were also richer, and better located strategically. But their political survival was also owed to the fact that they had deep reserves of popular support to draw on and that their political class managed to respond to the crisis of the war in a way that the Central Powers did not, by promising a further widening of democracy at home and greater enfranchisement in the colonial sphere.

I

Between March and November 1917 the French war effort staggered through a profound crisis. Following Woodrow Wilson's appeal for a peace without victory and the Petrograd peace initiative, the Socialist

Party abandoned the government and the cross-party Union Sacrée collapsed. Three cabinets fell in short succession. By the autumn it seemed that France might be drifting toward a peace on whatever terms could be obtained from Germany. With democracy in Russia fighting for its life, there were voices in London and Washington that favoured sacrificing France's obstinate demand for the return of Alsace-Lorraine to achieve a quick settlement. But a majority of the French public were still determined to continue the war. On 16 November 1917 the period of uncertainty was brought to an abrupt end when Clemenceau took office as Prime Minister and announced his new priorities: 'total war [*guerre integrale*] . . . war, nothing but war'.[6]

After his return from America in 1870, Clemenceau had made his mark in 1871 as one of the radical deputies who refused to ratify the peace with Bismarck and voted instead for a fight to the finish. But as a militant patriot he had no desire to narrow the political base of the Republic. The Socialists demonized his role in breaking the first major wave of syndicalist strikes in 1906, which he considered a menace to the Republic. But Clemenceau himself was never anything other than a man of the left. In 1917 he courted Socialists as cabinet members.[7] But the party held him at arm's length. Albert Thomas, the reformist labour leader, recently returned from Petrograd, harboured his own prime ministerial ambitions. In the end, despite continued harassment in the Chamber of Deputies, Clemenceau took two Socialists into his government not as cabinet members but as commissioners. Meanwhile, the trade union leadership, with whom Clemenceau entertained workman-like relations, were given the clear signal that rather than making appeals for peace, they should vent the frustration of their members in demands for wage increases. For Clemenceau inflation was a small price to pay for a united national war effort. To silence talk of peace yet further, Clemenceau hurled accusations of defeatism and worse at a wide range of potential challengers from the left.

There was personal animosity at stake in Clemenceau's prosecution of figures such as Joseph Caillaux and former Interior Minister Louis Malvy. But above all Clemenceau, modelling himself on his Athenian hero Demosthenes, was driven to demonstrate that France's will to resist would not be broken, that as a republic it could seize the historic opportunity to stand beside Britain and the United States in a transatlantic, democratic coalition against the Central Powers.[8] For the French

Republic to waver at such a moment would be a betrayal of its historic mission. Clemenceau's insistence on 'war, nothing but war' was intended to silence not only the pacifists. He was no more patient toward contentious discussions of over-ambitious war aims. Between 1915 and the spring of 1917 the diplomats of Tsarist Russia had repeatedly urged the French to enter with them into agreements for the division not only of the Ottoman Empire, but of Germany as well.[9] In 1916, facing the full force of the Verdun assault, the cabinet of Aristide Briand had cheered itself by weighing up a partition of Germany between a French-sponsored Rhineland and a Russian land-grab in the East. But for the collapse of Tsarism in March 1917, this objective might well have become established as official policy. As Clemenceau well understood, in the new age of international politics such ideas would have hung like an albatross around the neck of French diplomacy.

To see what damage such vaulting ambition might have done both to French internal politics and its relations with its allies, one need only turn to Italy. Whereas Clemenceau successfully silenced discussion of the post-war order, Italian politics between 1915 and 1919 was torn apart by a clash between different visions of its place in the future international system.[10] Under the terms of its pre-war alliances Italy in 1914 ought to have entered on the side of the Central Powers. Instead, in the London Treaty of 1915 it obtained generous promises of imperial gains from the Entente. By 1917, with both Wilson and the Russian revolutionaries calling for a liberal peace, these were to become notorious. After the disaster at Caporetto they seemed not only ludicrously out of kilter with Italy's military means, but positively hurtful to the national war effort. In November 1917 Vittorio Orlando, the new liberal Prime Minister, called on Italians to emulate the Roman Republic's recovery from its shattering defeat at Cannae (216 BC). He formed a broad-based cabinet and despite the anti-war stance of the Italian Socialist Party, refused to carry out a wholesale crackdown. This enabled him to cultivate close relations with the pro-war Socialists, headed by the pro-Wilsonian Filippo Turati. Leonida Bissolati, an agrarian radical, former editor of *Avanti* and decorated war veteran, was charged with implementing an eye-catching package of welfare benefits. His efforts were flanked by the highly energetic Finance Minister Francesco Nitti, frequently referred to as 'l'Americano', who set aside hundreds of millions of lire for the support of ex-servicemen.[11] Meanwhile Italy's savers rallied to the cause, subscribing an unprecedented 6 billion lire to the war loan issued in January 1918. But Italy did not survive by its own means alone. In the desperate weeks in October and November, troops and equipment from France, Britain and the United States had poured into Italy. In thousands of villages and towns Italian-American friendship was celebrated in improvised processions not infrequently featuring the Virgin Mary with the Stars and Stripes in her hand.[12] In the Italian Army itself, Wilsonian propagandists collaborated eagerly with the newly created Servizio P, which for the first time attempted to bridge the huge social and cultural gulf between the Italian officer class and the rank and file.

Orlando thus restored a measure of social peace. But the Italian war effort remained under a cloud of political uncertainty due to the manner in which the country had entered the conflict.[13] Parliament had not been appraised of the details of the London Treaty, but rumours were enough to suggest that Italy's political leaders, above all Foreign Minister Sidney Sonnino, had made their country complicit in an odious example of old world imperialism. On 13 February 1918 these fears were fully confirmed when the full text was read out in the Italian Chamber of Deputies. The effect was explosive. There was outrage even on the government benches, as ministers learned for the first time of the discreditable, annexationist demands for which Italy had been fighting. Giovanni Giolitti, the pre-war leader of Italian liberalism, who had opposed the alliance with the Entente in 1915, demanded that the war be brought to an end immediately. But this was not the only option. If only it abandoned its old-fashioned and unrealistic imperialist ambitions, pro-Entente socialists and liberals saw no reason why Italy's strategic interests could not be made compatible with the new era of self-determination.[14] As we have seen, by the spring of 1918 the Entente and the United States were coming around to the view that the Habsburg Empire must be dismantled.[15] Just as German progressives had hoped to fashion a liberal hegemony in the East, Italian progressives foresaw a future in which Italy would play the role of promoter and protector of self-determination throughout south-eastern Europe, a vision that harked back to the legendary nineteenth-century Italian patriot and pan-European, Giuseppe Mazzini.

In April 1918, with London's active encouragement, the pro-war anti-annexationist wing of Italian politics played host in Rome to a

Congress of the Oppressed Nationalities from across the Habsburg Empire. Prime Minister Orlando was clearly attracted by this vision, but in his effort to hold together a broad-based coalition he did not dare to drop Sonnino, the father of the London Treaty.[16] In the pre-war period Sonnino had been among the most prominent advocates of reform in Italian politics. The furore over the London Treaty drove him into the arms of the right. In a mirror image of the extremist Patriotic Party in Germany, 158 deputies, a third of the chamber, banded together in support of Sonnino in the so-called Fascio for National Defence, determined to prevent any backsliding. For internationally minded progressives, Sonnino's dogged adherence to the odious London Treaty risked reducing Italy to 'an anachronism'.[17] Sonnino, one pro-Entente socialist fumed, 'does not see that in this way he discredits his own politics ... putting Italy in the dock again under the accusation of Machiavellianism'. Sonnino was blind to 'major world currents, outside of which there are no grand politics'.[18]

If the contradictions between democracy and empire were becoming a source of political tension by 1917–18, one might have expected Britain to be their most notable victim. And both at home and in the empire, London certainly did face enormous challenges. But in the face of these, it was Britain that drove the Allied war effort into the ghastly fourth year of the war.[19] It was Britain that emerged from the conflict with its political system most intact and with the majority of its strategic objectives met. Between 1916 and 1922 Britain was to occupy perhaps the most prominent position of leadership in both world and European affairs in its history. This outcome was due in large part to its favourable initial conditions. Britain was beyond the immediate reach of the Central Powers and had the resources of its empire to fall back on. But this triumph was also a testament to the adaptive capacities of the British political class. Lloyd George, like Clemenceau, was the advocate of a full-throated war effort. The harassment of those suspected of non-conformity or resistance on the home front was relentless. On the Western Front, discipline in the British ranks was notoriously harsh. But this coercion was combined with the hallmarks of Lloyd George's pre-war political persona. Between 1906 and 1911 in the Liberal government of Prime Minister Asquith, it had been Lloyd George who had carried the radical flag, taking the fight to the House of Lords and breaking their veto over the budget, pushing through redistributive taxation, introducing a social insurance system and guaranteeing the right of trade unions to free collective bargaining.

Before he became the scourge of conservatism at home, Lloyd George had made his name as a radical anti-imperialist. In 1901, in the midst of the Boer War, speaking to a raucous crowd in Birmingham, the heartland of jingoist nationalism, he had demanded that the empire must free itself of 'racial arrogance'. It must reshape itself as a realm of 'fearless justice' held together by a common commitment to national freedom. 'We ought,' Lloyd George insisted, 'to give freedom everywhere – freedom in Canada, freedom in the antipodes, in Africa, in Ireland, in Wales and in India. We will never govern India as it ought to be governed until we have given it freedom.'[20] Despite the repeated cycles of promise and disappointment that littered its history, the seemingly contradictory idea of a 'liberal empire' was not empty nor, at the beginning of the twentieth century, was it historically moribund. The fact that Lloyd George could initiate dramatic change, in wartime, at the head of a coalition in which most of the key positions were occupied by Tories, is testament to imperial liberalism's renewed relevance in an age of dramatic global transition.

II

That there was no time to lose was made horribly evident by the escalation of tension in Ireland.[21] When they were swept into office in 1906, the Liberals had been committed to making good on Gladstone's long-deferred promise of Home Rule – autonomy for Ireland within the United Kingdom. This gained them the support of the parliamentary party of moderate Irish nationalism, who after Asquith's electoral setbacks in 1910 actually held the balance of power in the House of Commons. Though undeniably a territory of colonial settlement, indeed the origin of British colonialism, Ireland, unlike the rest of the empire, had an integral place in the constitution of the United Kingdom. At Westminster, it was spectacularly over-represented. Of the 670 MPs returned in the last pre-war election, 103 were elected by Irish constituencies, of whom 84 were members of the moderate nationalist Irish Parliamentary Party led by John Redmond.[22] But any move to Home Rule would provoke violent resistance from the Protestant community that held a solid majority in Ulster, Ireland's Northern province, and who were fiercely committed to remaining under the direct rule of London.

By the spring of 1914, the Irish crisis was tearing the British state apart. With the encouragement of the Tory Party and the covert endorsement of the British monarch, the army in Ireland gave notice that regardless of the will of Parliament, they would not impose Home Rule on Ulster. So serious were the rumours of civil war that in July 1914 the British Foreign Office thought it best to warn Berlin that they should not count on Ireland to distract Britain from coming to the aid of France. Despite the open threat of mutiny in August 1914, the Asquith government pushed Home Rule through Parliament, but immediately suspended implementation. The postponement was a sop to the Unionists at the expense of Irish nationalism, but believing that the war was the first test of responsible Home Rule, Redmond threw his party behind the war effort. It was this policy of compromise and delay that opened the door to the radical nationalist minority who had gathered before the war in the Sinn Fein movement. On Monday 24 April 1916, Dublin was laid waste by rifle and artillery fire as extreme Irish nationalists launched a suicidal assault on British power.[23] It took a week of bitter fighting to quell the rebellion. London's embarrassment was compounded by the brutal repression meted out by army commanders on the spot. Though the uprising was crushed, the result, as the insurgents had hoped, was a strategic disaster for British rule. At a stroke they had restored Britain's fading image as the brutal oppressor and destroyed the credibility of Redmond and the moderates.

If Home Rule was unmanageable, by 1916 London was haunted by the thought that the empire might soon face 'another Ireland', in India. As in Ireland, the search for a liberal answer to the question of imperial overlordship in India had been given new energy by the accession of a Liberal government in 1906. In 1909 a system of legislative councils had been introduced to incorporate a larger part of the Indian elite into running the Raj. But by 1916 it was clear that this formula was losing its grip. In May 1916 the Anglo-Irish agitator and disciple of theosophy Annie Besant began to spread her influence from Madras across India, regaling crowds of tens of thousands in Bombay with rousing tales of the Dublin uprising.[24] The radical Hindu leader Bal Gangadhar Tilak revived his fundamentalist wing of Indian nationalism and joined in the clamour for Home Rule. At Allahabad in the spring of 1916, leaders of the Hindu-dominated Indian National Congress and the Muslim League issued an unprecedented joint declaration calling for far-reaching constitutional change. This cooperation was consolidated in December at Lucknow when an agreement was reached under which the rights of the Muslim minority would be protected by means of separate electoral colleges.[25] These inter-communal agreements were profoundly unsettling to the British. Protecting the 80 million Muslims of the subcontinent was one of the fundamental justifications for British rule. If, unlike in Ireland, the majority and minority could make common cause against London, then the end of the Raj might be approaching far faster than anyone had imagined.

It was against the backdrop of this double crisis in India and Ireland that Lloyd George took office in December 1916 determined to widen the political base of the imperial war effort. The centrepiece of this strategy was the creation of a unified Imperial War Cabinet, in which imperial statesmen such as Jan Smuts of South Africa were given a very prominent role. But Lloyd George also insisted that Satyendra Prassano Sinha, the chair of the 1915 meeting of the Indian National Congress, should attend the Imperial Cabinet as a full member, in his capacity as 'representative of the Indian people'.[26] As Secretary of State for India, the liberal conservative Austen Chamberlain remarked to Viceroy Chelmsford that Sinha was 'the nearest approximation which India can produce under present circumstances to a prime minister . . . the status of India in the Empire is thus fully recognized and an advance has been made such as Indians indeed hoped for, but scarcely expected, a few months ago'.[27] As a further concession, in early March 1917 the government of India announced to general applause that it had secured the right to impose a protective tariff on the import of British manufactures of cotton goods, one of the most eagerly anticipated benefits of self-rule. For British liberals this undermined the entire logic of empire. What purpose was there in clinging to far-flung territories, if they were allowed to retreat into economic self-sufficiency? But Lloyd George was relentless. Parliament must give India what it wanted.[28]

But economic and political concessions were no longer enough. By the spring of 1917, it had become clear that London would have to do something unprecedented. It would have to define in solemn and public terms the ultimate goal of its rule in India. Austen Chamberlain explained to his cabinet colleagues on 22 May 1917: 'The constant harping on the theme that we are fighting for liberty and justice and the rights of people to direct their own destinies, the revolution in Russia [the February revolution] and the way in which it has been received in this country and elsewhere, the reception of the Indian delegates here, and the position given to India in the councils of the empire – has strengthened the demand for reform and has created a ferment of ideas . . .' If Britain failed to come forward with sufficiently bold proposals, it risked throwing the 'moderate element – such as it is – into the hands of the extremists'.[29] Then Britain would be forced to respond with violence. Its moderate collaborators would be discredited and India would fall into the hands of their home-grown version of Sinn Fein.

By the summer of 1917 the first steps in this disastrous delegitimizing cycle were already being acted out by the overstretched governors of Indian provinces, who ruled territories the size of European countries. Unaware of the dramatic concessions being contemplated in London, on 24 May 1917 Governor Pentland of Madras, the home base of Annie Besant's protest movement, issued an abrupt statement denying any possibility of Home Rule. The result was a storm of protest. From Bengal, Governor Ronaldshay, who faced the most serious threat of terrorist violence, suggested that to quell dissent an extension of wartime security powers might be required, triggering the establishment of a committee of inquiry on repressive powers chaired by Justice Rowlatt. On 16 June Pentland placed Besant under house arrest.[30] This played directly into the hands of the radicals. Home Rule agitation spread across the Indian political class. Mohandas Gandhi, recently arrived from South Africa, threw himself into the struggle, calling for a petition with a million peasant signatures.[31] In an audience with Viceroy Chelmsford, Gandhi warned that Home Rule, which only months earlier had appeared an outlandishly radical demand, was 'in a fair way towards commanding India's identity . . .'[32]

III

With Ireland in open rebellion and the political temperature rising in India, in the spring and summer of 1917 the British government faced a mounting crisis at home as well. The strikes of early May, involving hundreds of thousands of workers in defiance of the official trade union leadership, were unprecedented. The government's response was to arrest the leading shop stewards under pre-emptive Defence of the Realm powers.[33] In January the Independent Labour Party had cheered Wilson's 'peace without victory' speech, and in the summer their conference in Leeds passed resolutions supporting a negotiated peace on the basis of the Petrograd formula, by a majority of two to one. There was no real threat of revolutionary overthrow, however it was clear that it was not just the legitimacy of the empire which needed to be addressed, but that of the Westminster political system as a whole. There had not been an election in Britain since 1910. A poll would be postponed until the end of the war, but before then the parties would have to decide on which electorate their mandate would be based.

Edwardian Britain, in the pre-war years, had witnessed spectacular struggles over votes for women and some murmurings about a further extension of the working-class franchise. In 1910 not quite two-thirds of the male population was entitled to vote, with disenfranchisement in poor urban districts rising to over 60 per cent.[34] After a war that had taken the lives of hundreds of thousands of men from those same districts, this was no longer a sustainable position. According to conventional expectations any substantial widening of the electorate would tilt the political balance decisively toward the Liberals and the emerging Labour Party. But unlike in Imperial Germany, the democratization of Britain was not allowed to become a matter for ruinous confrontation between democratic and anti-democratic forces. In February 1918, with barely a ripple of public argument, Britain passed the largest franchise reform in its history.

Many observers at the time and since have attributed the smooth passage of this dramatic reform to intelligent procedural solutions.[35] A cross-party parliamentary conference had begun discussing the issue in the autumn of 1916. Headed by the Speaker of the House of Commons, the patrician Tory moderate James Lowther, it conducted itself as the very model of sophisticated compromise. By early 1917 the cross-party conference had already agreed on manhood suffrage. Within a matter of months it agreed a compromise formula on female suffrage that would enfranchise millions of women, but maintain an overall male majority in the electorate. The only issue that was hotly debated in Parliament was the proposal to introduce an element of Proportional Representation. Designed to give a voice to minorities, it was Lloyd George who got this conservative provision dropped. The avoidance of conflict was striking. But it invites a question: What allowed a fundamental process of constitutional change to appear as little more than a procedural adjustment, 'pre-chewed political baby food', as one conservative fundamentalist commented?[36] Beneath this idealized image of discursive agreement lay something more fundamental: a clear commitment by the leadership of both established parties to secure the legitimacy of the political process by ensuring that the reforms appeared neither as a bribe nor as a concession extracted by coercive threats. Across the political divides, there was an interest in maintaining Britain's self-image as a peaceable kingdom, stabilized by successive waves of top-down reform.[37] Behind this well-cultivated facade, however, it is clear that tables were thumped and points of principle clashed. The threat of open public protest was essential to maintaining the momentum of reform. Crucially, a solid coalition between democratic feminists, the Labour Party and the trade union movement made clear that any measure to enfranchise soldiers and male war workers that did not include votes for women would be unacceptable. Conversely, feminist activists were sufficiently committed to their alliance with Labour that at the crucial moment in early 1917 they chose to support manhood suffrage, even though they gained only a restricted female franchise.

The sense that they faced an unstoppable inevitability led the Tories to take the initiative themselves. In August 1916 it was the patrician Lord Salisbury who introduced the emotively entitled Trench Voting Bill. To avoid panicking the party's suburban base, Tory Central Office kept to themselves alarming calculations about the likely increase in young working-class voters and enfranchised trade unionists. Meanwhile, the Tory leadership worked hard to silence embarrassing outbursts of openly anti-democratic sentiment from within their own ranks.[38] The press, with Lord Northcliffe leading the way, rallied to the democratic consensus. By 1917, in the pages of *The Times*, opposition to the franchise was painted as divisive and ipso facto unpatriotic.

The result was a process of historic change that appeared to move of its own accord. As Lord Bryce, the eminent constitutionalist, commented to his colleague A. V. Dicey in September 1917, the contrast with the struggles over the great Reform Act of 1866 was stark. Then, both sides of the argument had assumed 'that fitness' for the franchise 'had to be proved', Now, 'when one talks to the young sentimental woman suffragist he [sic] sees no relevance in the enquiry whether the great mass of women know or care anything about politics. It is quite enough for him that they are human beings. As such they have a right to vote.'[39] Meanwhile on the left, militant advocates of suffrage were left to wonder at a mysterious transformation for which a decade of activism and protest had doubtless prepared the way, but that now seemed to be moving of its own accord. As the militant suffragist Millicent Fawcett put it to a triumphant suffragist and Labour rally in the spring of 1917: 'The result of the Speaker's Conference was an illustration of the deathless energy and vitality of the suffrage movement. The Conference had been initiated by an anti-suffragist, presided over by an anti-suffragist and consisted at first of fifty percent anti-suffragists; though the brew seemed distinctly anti-suffrage, when the tap was turned – suffrage came out.'[40]

Throughout the British franchise reform debate overt references to the wider world were scarce. As the 'mother of parliaments' Westminster took no lessons from foreigners. That 'foreign' influences were abroad in British politics at all was indicative of the seriousness of the crisis. But despite this strategic parochialism, by 1917 international concerns were more or less openly entering into the discussion of the British constitution. In his retrospective account of the Speaker's Conference, Lowther himself made a revealing admission. He 'felt very strongly' that to 'renew' the 'party and domestic polemics' over the franchise that had wracked the pre-war era, 'would bring discredit upon Great Britain in the face of her Dominions and colonies, at the very moment when the nation should be occupied in the consideration of large and novel problems . . . As time went on I became more and more impressed with the soundness of this view, and frequently pressed it upon my colleagues when there seemed to be any danger of a breakdown.'[41] To Lowther, as to other British conservatives, resistance to democracy had become an anachronism.

IV

Whilst the Lloyd George government steered through the domestic crises of the summer of 1917, in India matters were coming rapidly to a head. In July, Chamberlain resigned as Secretary of State for India. He thereby accepted responsibility for the disastrous Mesopotamian campaign of 1915 that had been the independent responsibility of the government of India and the Indian Army. As his replacement Lloyd George chose not a conservative, but a Cambridge-educated liberal, Edwin Montagu, the assimilated scion of a prominent Jewish banking family. To Montagu the situation was clear. Britain must reclaim 'the courage and sureness of touch which rendered us famous as Empire builders'. Otherwise, it would 'make a series of Irelands' across the world.[42] The administration of the Raj had become too rigid and bureaucratic. It could not merely rely on its reputation for efficiency. In the words of the foremost historian of British imperial strategy, it had 'to become political, to argue its case, to win over opinion'.[43] For this, a statement of purpose was essential and it seemed to Montagu that by 1917 the only acceptable slogan was 'self-government'.[44] Montagu did not imagine Home Rule for 240 million Indians as a single nation state. 'As a goal,' he proclaimed, '. . . not one great Home Rule country, but a series of self-governing provinces and principalities, federated by one central government'. Nor was he in a hurry. Montagu still believed that self-government was a project that would be realized over 'many years . . . many generations'.[45] Such qualifications were the staple of nineteenth-century justifications of empire. But as Montagu took office the credibility of this gradualist approach to reform was fraying. As he wrote to Chamberlain in the summer of 1917, they must promise 'self-government' now. To do anything less would only arouse bitter disappointment. Better to make no announcement. But, in that case, they must steel themselves for 'grim repression on a growing scale and the alienation of many, if not all, the moderates'.

By August the decision could no longer be put off. Without British concessions to show for their pains, the moderates would be completely routed at the upcoming annual meeting of the Indian National Congress. With no more time to lose, it was former Viceroy and arch-conservative Lord Curzon who proposed a compromise. India should be promised neither self-government nor self-determination, but 'the fuller realisation of responsible government'. What Curzon wished to imply by stressing responsibility remains mysterious. Perhaps he meant to warn against 'irresponsible' Indian opposition.[46] He may have wished to restate the familiar British self-justification of protecting India from an upper-caste Hindu tyranny. Whatever Curzon's intention, the formula allowed Montagu to present the House of Commons on 20 August 1917 with a historic statement. The ultimate objective of the Raj was the 'increasing association of Indians in every branch of the administration, and the gradual development of self-governing institutions, with a view to the progressive realisation of responsible government in India under the aegis of the British crown'. In India the moment at which such a tepid pronouncement might have roused real enthusiasm had passed. Nevertheless, the implications were momentous. As Montagu admitted to Chamberlain, if they had simply promised 'self-government', that might have been construed to mean that India could be placed under a 'Hindu dictator'. 'Responsible government' clearly meant that any such ruler would have to be 'responsible to some form of parliamentary institution'.[47]

In India itself, Viceroy Chelmsford knew that he needed to deliver a more concrete gesture. Overruling opposition from the provincial governors, he ordered Annie Besant's release from house arrest. In the autumn of 1917 it was not London but the cause of Home Rule that claimed a great victory. December 1917 saw the incongruous spectacle of Besant, an elderly Anglo-Irish woman presiding triumphantly over the most agitated mass meeting the patrician Indian National Congress had ever witnessed. Indian nationalism was becoming a mass movement.

After the Versailles Treaty it was to become a commonplace that simple liberal nostrums such as 'self-determination' were ill-adjusted to complex historical realities. But whatever the complications of Silesia or the Sudetenland, they paled by comparison with the problem facing Secretary of State Montagu in his attempt to devise a system of 'responsible' self-government for India. The task involved devising a constitution for an entire subcontinent, an extraordinarily diverse slice of humanity, divided along lines of religion, ethnicity, caste and class. Not only that, but it involved facing the contradiction between the constitution of the Raj, which the British were not afraid to call 'autocratic', and the demands of representative government. Within weeks of making his historic announcement Montagu was writing in a state of some gloom to the Viceroy, 'the more I think of the subject, the more I realize the extraordinary difficulties of the position . . . Is there any country in the world that has attempted a half-way house in this, or a quarter-way house? An autocratic and independent executive is common. Self-governing institutions are now (I don't ever quite know why), accepted as the only proper form of government. How can you unite the two? Can you have a form of government administered by an alien agency partly responsible to the people of that country itself?'[48]

The ground plan of this 'quarter-way house' was worked out between Montagu, Chelmsford, the leadership of the Congress and the Muslim League over the winter of 1917–18. The particulars, especially regarding electoral provisions, were further elaborated in Westminster committee and shepherded through Parliament by Sinha, who became the first Indian to be raised to the peerage, in 1919. Governmental authority in India was divided between a central executive, provincial governments and local authorities. Central and provincial governments were to be answerable to legislative councils constituted in part through nomination and in part through electorates of varying size. Significantly, by 1922, the British relinquished all official control over local government in India and the urban franchise was rapidly expanded.[49] At the provincial level, the equivalent of medium-sized European states, the make-up of the electorate varied, with special representation being granted to landowners and urban business interests. To prevent upper-caste domination, separate electoral colleges were provided for non-Brahmins. Throughout, the electorate was to be split between Hindu and Muslim on the formula agreed by the Congress and the Muslim League at Lucknow in 1916. As Montagu and Chelmsford acknowledged, these compromises were far from any liberal ideal. But they were not merely reactionary either, as is evidenced by the solution adopted for the female franchise. This was to be determined at a provincial level, with the result that in the elections to the Madras state legislature more women were entitled to vote than in all but a handful of the most liberal European nations.

The Montagu-Chelmsford reforms were soon to be swamped by the massive popular mobilization of 1919. But in the spring of 1918 the report jointly written by Montagu and Chelmsford could still claim to be a powerful restatement of the basic agenda of liberal empire. Responsible government must be the goal of British rule in India, the report insisted, because it was the 'best form of government' that the British themselves 'knew'.[50] Upholding a racial double standard in India was not tenable in the long run. Despite the differences that segmented Indian society, its unity was growing. Illiterate peasants were maturing into responsible citizens. Britain must gamble that the best way to hasten the growth of the capacity for self-government was to transfer responsibility to the Indians themselves, the exercise of which would 'call forth the capacity for it'. Meanwhile, the troublesome nationalists should not be repressed, but acknowledged as Britain's own 'children'. Their desire for 'self-determination' was the 'inevitable result of education in the history and thought of Europe'. In the long run British rule could only be legitimate if it satisfied the 'desires which it creates'. Nor should London expect gratitude and react resentfully when it was not shown. Things were past the point at which Britain could expect plaudits from its grateful imperial subjects. But it should not be deterred by protest or discontent. As one official was later to put it, 'the gradual change from Autocratic to responsible Government cannot be effected without taking risk'.[51] Britain should persist with its liberal programme sustained by the 'faith that is in us'.

Despite profound reservations, the Indian political class, once more, fell in with this appeal.[52] Down to the end of the war Gandhi could be found travelling across India, recruiting volunteers for the war effort of the liberal empire. Home Rule, he insisted, meant not independence, but that Indians 'should become ... partners in the Empire', like Canada and Australia.[53] The radical Hindu nationalist Tilak called on his fellow Indians to view British war bonds as the 'title deeds of Home Rule'.[54] When the great popular uprising against British rule began in 1919, it was not triggered by discontent at the inadequacy of the Montagu-Chelmsford proposals. It was sparked by outrage at the fact that the trust which the Indians had once more placed in that settlement had been violated by precisely the kind of draconian measures that liberals such as Montagu were desperate to avoid.

V

Long-simmering nationalist resentments, long-standing liberal promises, and the pressure of the war were the main drivers of the crises facing the Lloyd George government in 1917. Russia's democratic revolution of the spring of 1917 – not the Bolshevik coup – added further pressure. But how did America figure in this constellation? During her period of house arrest in the summer of 1917, Annie Besant imagined herself at the centre of a worldwide network. She appealed to Australia to reject London's call for conscription. Besant had copies of the journal she kept during her internment sent to sympathizers in Japan and the US, so that 'England's allies might put pressure upon her not to trample in India on the principles for which they were all fighting in Europe. If the American press take up the matter as we hope it may, the Indian government will not be able to cover up its deeds ... The British democracy will hear via the United States of the war upon liberty declared by the Indian government, and the president of the (United) States may interfere on behalf of India ...'[55] But appealing as it may be to construct a 'Wilsonian moment' in India, it existed, if it existed at all, in the minds of no more than a handful of nationalists.[56] What would link Indian politics to the world was the internal politics of the empire – London, Ireland and imperial policy in the Middle East. The same could not be said for Ireland. It looked less to the rest of the empire than across the Atlantic. As a result, the Irish question, with all its ramifications for British politics, became entangled to a quite extraordinary degree in London's relations with Washington.

In 1916 there was no public more susceptible to the appeal of Sinn Fein than the Irish community of the United States.[57] And if there was any population in the United States to which Wilson's 'peace without victory' stance made immediate and intuitive sense it was Irish Americans. Facing bitter competition from Sinn Fein it was John Dillon, the deputy leader of the hitherto moderate Nationalist Party, who demanded to know from London: 'How can you face Europe? How can you face America tomorrow, and pose as the champions of oppressed nationalities? What answer will you have when you are told, as you will be told at the peace conference, "go home and put your own house in order".'[58] America's entry into the war relieved but did not lift this pressure. In his speech to Congress on 2 April 1917 Wilson placed the United States on the side of democracy against untrustworthy autocracies. But he left open where the Entente were to be situated. In correspondence with London, it was the Irish impasse that he highlighted as the only obstacle to 'an absolutely cordial cooperation' between the US and Britain. Following the overthrow of Tsarism, all that was needed to demonstrate that 'the real programme of government by the consent of the governed had been adopted everywhere in the anti-Prussian world' was Home Rule.[59]

Something had to be done. But what? If the British Liberals had seen a way to deliver Home Rule without unleashing a civil war in Ireland, they would have seized on it long since. Speaking in the House of Commons in March 1917, Lloyd George reiterated that as far as London was concerned the question had already been decided by Parliament in August 1914. It was now up to the Irish themselves to agree on how to implement Home Rule. In the spring of 1917 one option considered in London was to bring Australian and Canadian pressure to bear as advertisements for the benefits of autonomous self-government within the empire. But the Ulster Protestant influence was too strong in Canada and the Irish Catholic element too powerful in Australia. The Irish question was internal not just to British politics but to the politics of the entire empire.[60] Was the United States the decisive external force with which one might break the deadlock? In light of America's importance to the imperial war effort, the leaders of the Conservative Party had been forced already in 1916 to accept that there could be no more talk of a Protestant mutiny in Ulster. It was left to die-hard Unionists like Lord Selborne to rail against the 'idea that we are to change our constitution because of the force of American public opinion'.[61]

To work out an all-Irish compromise, Lloyd George convened a Constitutional Convention meeting in Dublin. But this was no longer enough to satisfy the more radical wing of Irish nationalism. Sinn Fein and its allies boycotted the Convention, demanding that the Irish question be put to the post-war peace conference, 'an unpacked jury of the nations of the world' that 'England could not coerce or cajole'.[62] Even the moderate Nationalists, who did agree to attend the Convention, were now making demands that amounted to the kind of Dominion status enjoyed by Canada or Australia. Meanwhile the Unionists agreed to concede Home Rule to the South but only in exchange for a permanent exemption for Ulster. This would satisfy the Protestant majority but would trap hundreds of thousands of Catholics as a disadvantaged and resentful minority in Northern Ireland. If London were to impose a compromise solution, if necessary with force, how would Washington react? If Washington demanded Home Rule, perhaps Lloyd George might enlist Wilson in sharing responsibility for the disagreeable choices that lay ahead. Throughout the bitterly contested deliberations of the Constitutional Convention, the British supplied the White House with the same confidential reports that were received by George V in Buckingham Palace.[63] The message was clear. The hopes of American intervention were fuelling intransigence on the Nationalist side. Unless the full force of both London and Washington was put behind a compromise, Ireland faced permanent partition between a 'majority and a minority each relying upon the doctrine of self-determination . . .'[64]

It was the war that forced the issue. As Germany's spring offensive crashed into the Allied lines in March 1918, manpower was the imperative of the moment. Sinn Fein refused any war service on behalf of the British state. But the British Labour movement made clear that it would not accept a last levy of men from London and Manchester, if Dublin and Cork remained exempt. The only way to give even a shred of legitimacy to conscription in Ireland was to move immediately to Home Rule. This, however, would require the South to accept the exemption of Ulster and Ulster to accept that this exemption could only be temporary. Fearing the worst, prior to the final decision, Foreign Secretary Arthur Balfour took the remarkable step of first contacting the White House to elicit the President's opinion. Aware that this constituted an unprecedented opening of the internal affairs of the United Kingdom to the views of the American government, Balfour thought it necessary to explain that Irish conscription was only 'apparently' a 'purely domestic' matter. If a decision on this question were to upset the balance of opinion in the US, it might have important ramifications for the Alliance.[65] In the event, the White House resisted the British invitation to share responsibility for an Irish settlement. Colonel House merely made a perfunctory reply reiterating the need for Home Rule. But hardliners in Whitehall viewed these proceedings with less equanimity. One noted imperialist fumed that Balfour's enquiry was 'a document' the likes of which he 'never thought to see an English statesman put his name to'. By washing their dirty linen in front of the Americans, the British cabinet had stooped to asking Wilson and House 'to make up their minds for them'. But injurious though it may have been to national pride, neutralizing the possibility of a disavowal from the White House was essential. When Lloyd George announced Irish conscription to the House of Commons on 16 April 1918, he was able to present it not only as the quid pro quo for Home Rule. He was also able to reassure Parliament that this resolution was fully consistent with 'that principle of self-determination for which we are ostentatiously fighting', and that London could expect a 'full measure of American assistance'.[66]

When Curzon had addressed the House of Lords in May 1917, he had held out the prospect that the harmonious resolution of the Irish question would 'pave the way for that world cooperation of the three greatest liberty-loving nations on earth – namely, France, the United States of America, and ourselves . . .'. 'The settlement of the Irish question' would thus emerge 'as a great world factor of capital importance . . .'.[67] Washington's grudging response to the Home Rule compromise of April 1918 fell far short of that grandiose vision, and with good reason. Ireland's political future was in no way resolved. Sinn Fein was preparing to resist conscription with force. The path to partition and a bloody civil war was clearly marked. But London's painstaking elaboration of the Home Rule formula had done enough to prevent any serious breach with Washington. Wilson denied Sinn Fein its demand that Ireland should be debated at the Versailles peace conference. It remained a matter internal to the British Empire.[68] At least in this minimal sense America was cooperative. How far America would underwrite Britain's wider effort to reconstruct its empire remained a question still to be resolved.

VI

The most consequential effort to explore how far America might go was made in the Middle East, the main zone of imperial expansion during the war.[69] From the mid-nineteenth century British policy in the region had been torn between the desire to protect the Suez canal, by shielding the ailing Ottoman Empire against Tsarist expansion, and liberal indignation over 'Turkish atrocities' in the Balkans. Turkey's decision to join the Central Powers in October 1914 turned London's policy in a decidedly turkophobic direction. In December, London declared a protectorate over Egypt, triggering the Russians into expansive claims on Ottoman territory, which Britain and France sought to contain in the spring of 1916 with the so-called Sykes-Picot agreement.[70] This allocated a slice of northern Mesopotamia, Syria and Lebanon to France. Palestine proper was to be internationalized as a buffer zone. Britain would secure the extended eastern flank of Egypt with naval bases in Gaza and Haifa. In 1917 Russia's collapse, France's enfeeblement and the recovery of Britain's military position in Mesopotamia came together with the new imperial focus of Lloyd George's cabinet, to produce a far more aggressive strategy. In the eyes of Curzon and Viscount Alfred Milner the outcome of the war should be the total suppression of imperialist competition by the assertion of British control over the eastern Mediterranean and East Africa, establishing a British Monroe Doctrine in the Indian Ocean and its approaches. It was to be an all-empire project. The Indian Army played a decisive role in all the campaigns against the Turks.[71] In 1917 London weighed up the possibility of giving Germany's East African colonies to India as its own mandate.[72] The Admiralty was abuzz with schemes to base squadrons of an imperial navy in the Indian Ocean and the Pacific.

Conceived at first at a moment of triumph, at the height of the crisis that followed the Brest-Litovsk Treaty and Ludendorff's Western offensive in the spring of 1918, this encompassing vision of empire became instead the vision of a defensive redoubt to which Britain would retreat if France collapsed and control of the continent fell to a rampant Germany.[73] This made it all the more pressing to decide how such expansionism might be squared with the dominant power of the future, the United States. As Milner put it, 'the remaining free peoples of the world, America, this country and the Dominions' must be 'knit together in the closest conceivable alliance'.[74] How could this ambition conform with Wilson's opposition to any imperial expansion in the Middle East? Washington had refused even to declare war on Turkey.

Meanwhile the overthrow of the Tsar had transformed Russia's politics. In May 1917 the distinguished patriotic liberal, Pavel Miliukov, was forced by the Petrograd Soviet to resign as Foreign Minister, for upholding the Russian demands on the Ottoman Empire. If a democratic Russia was now calling only for international supervision of the Black Sea Straits, how could Britain justify its claims? If, as one Middle East hand put it in the summer of 1918, 'open annexation is no longer practical and out of kilter with declaration of allies', Britain must make itself into the vanguard of self-determination.[75] In 1915 London had officially espoused the cause of the Armenian minority. In the summer of 1916 Britain sponsored a rebellion in Arabia. In 1917 it was to address the specific challenges posed by the Russian revolution and the rise of American power that British imperial strategists took up the cause of Zionism.[76]

Since 1914 a handful of Zionist activists in Britain and America had been urging London to assume the mantle of their protector. This was flattering to men such as Balfour and Lloyd George, steeped as they were in Old Testament religion. But it was a far from obvious association. Britain's own Jewish population was small and highly assimilated. In 1914 the central office of the international Zionist organization was headquartered in Germany and had declared itself ostentatiously neutral. In 1915 Zionists both in Europe and America had been unable to hide their enthusiasm when the Kaiser's armies drove the Tsar's army out of western Poland. Though it is hard to credit in retrospect, the promise of a new regime of toleration in the East was one of the aspirations associated by German-speaking Jews with the Brest-Litovsk moment. When Lloyd George took office in December 1916 it was precisely to redress this imbalance, to win 'world Jewry' back for the cause of the Entente, that British Zionists began pursuing a new alliance with the British Empire. By the spring of 1917 influential voices in London were calling for the Zionist cause to be added to the Armenians and Arabs as British clients. Finally, in August, as General Allenby's troops readied themselves for a drive to Jerusalem, the small coterie of Zionists in Britain led by Chaim Weizmann were asked by the Foreign Office to draft a declaration in favour of a Jewish home in Palestine.

The proposal was vigorously debated in cabinet, with heated opposition coming from Curzon, who regarded Russia, not the Turks, as the main threat, and from Edwin Montagu, Secretary of State for India. Preoccupied as he was with his momentous declaration on Indian policy, Montagu could not but regard with horror the casual manner in which Britain, the ruler in India of the largest Muslim population on earth, was proposing to affront the Ottoman Empire. This was bound to consolidate the ominous alliance between the Muslim League and the Hindu Home Rulers. But Montagu spoke not only in his capacity as Secretary of State. He was also a prominent member of assimilated Anglo-Jewry. As such, Montagu deeply resented the Zionist claim to represent the entire 'Jewish people' and he was acutely sensitive to the anti-Semitic reflexes amongst his Gentile colleagues that Weizmann was turning so eagerly to his advantage.[77]

First and foremost, the British cabinet was considering patronage of the Zionist cause because they credited 'world Jewry' with power to influence affairs both in the United States and in revolutionary Russia. In 1917 the openly anti-Semitic Petrograd correspondent of *The Times* stoked widespread speculation about the role of the Jews in the overthrow of the Tsar. The assumed influence of the New York Jewish lobby, echoing similar anxieties about the power of the Irish-American machine, reflected a by no means flattering conception of the working of American democracy. The Zionist activists themselves did nothing to discourage these crude ideas. Spokesmen for 'world Jewry' was precisely what they aspired to be. Opponents of Zionism within the American Jewish community found themselves portrayed as a reactionary moneyed elite fighting the democratic aspirations of the 'Jewish masses'. The news that the huge Zionist organizations in revolutionary Russia had, in fact, voted overwhelmingly to disown any aggressive demands on the Ottoman Empire was suppressed.

Once again, the United States was the crucial factor. Would Wilson take up the role assigned to him? When in August 1917 the President proved unenthusiastic about a Palestine declaration, the British cabinet pulled back. It was not until October that Wilson's equivocation was overcome by persistent lobbying from within his inner circle.[78] In light of these overriding 'political considerations' Curzon withdrew his objections. Montagu was outvoted and the cabinet approved Balfour's short declaration announcing Britain's sponsorship of Jewish aspirations to a National Home in Palestine. It was despatched to Lord Rothschild as the presumptive leader of Anglo-Jewry, on 2 November 1917.

VII

On 20 November 1917, with the French and Italian governments reeling and his own leadership in question, Lloyd George personally welcomed the first American government delegation to visit wartime Britain at a joint conference with the British War Cabinet. The meeting was staged not in the usual Cabinet Room in Number 10 Downing Street, but in the Treasury Board Room next door, from where, Lloyd George informed his guests, Lord North had in the 1770s 'decided and directed' the ill-fated policy that drove the American colonists to rebellion. That had been, Lloyd George admitted, 'a cardinal error'.[79] Britain had learned its lesson. Whilst the war in Europe might be in disarray, Britain was rebuilding its empire in the image of a liberal future. The programme of change in India and the new policy in the Middle East were tokens of Lloyd George's determination to remake the empire as a 'great commonwealth of nations'. Nine days later the British and American parties joined sixteen other delegations at the Inter-Allied Conference in Paris. Despite the challenge laid down by the Bolsheviks and Germans at Brest-Litovsk, the French and Italians in their weakened state refused to allow any discussion of broader war aims. Lloyd George's response to this impasse was telling.

His first reaction was to despatch the charismatic South African General Jan Smuts to Switzerland for secret discussions with the Austrians, who were clearly desperate and might perhaps be lured out of their dependence on Germany. The message that Smuts conveyed to the Austrians was indicative of the British self-conception at the time. If Austria would abandon Germany, Smuts assured the Austrian envoy, London would 'assist Austria' in giving 'the greatest freedom and autonomy to her subject nationalities ...'. 'If Austria could become a really liberal empire ... she would become for central Europe very much what the British Empire had become for the rest of the world ...', a benevolent liberal guardian.[80] It was a fantasy no doubt, but one that had taken on real force.

But in response to the publicity fanfare from Brest-Litovsk, secret diplomacy was not enough. On 5 January 1918, Lloyd George used the occasion of a national meeting of Labour organizers at Methodist Central Hall in London, the same venue that would host the first meeting of the UN General Assembly in 1946, to make a major statement on the war aims of the British Empire. The speech was drafted in close consultation with the pro-war wing of the Labour Party and representatives of the empire. The Entente, Lloyd George proclaimed, was an alliance of democracies fighting for a democratic peace. 'The days of the Treaty of Vienna,' the Prime Minister announced, are 'long past'.[81] It would be a peace, he openly declared, of self-determination, ensuring that governments ruled by the consent of the governed. It would restore the sanctity of treaties and would be underwritten by an international organization to see to it that peace was preserved and the burden of armaments was lifted. Whilst Wilson was still labouring over his 14 Points address, it seemed that Lloyd George had beaten him to it. Would it be Lloyd George, the champion of 'British democracy', who claimed for himself the ideological leadership of the war against Germany? The question was not fanciful. As Colonel House later admitted, 'when the Lloyd George speech came out ...', the mood in the White House was 'depressed'.

Wilson was scheduled to address Congress a few days later, but following Lloyd George, what did he have to add? House was undaunted: 'I insisted that the situation had been changed for the better rather than for the worse.' Lloyd George had merely cleared the air of any potential quarrel between the US and London. It was all the more 'necessary for the President to act ... after the President had made his address, it would so smother the Lloyd George speech that it would be forgotten and that he, the President, would once more become the spokesman for the Entente, and indeed ... for the liberals of the world'.[82] House was proved right. And the willingness of world opinion not only to give far greater attention to Wilson's 14 Points, but to read into his text phrases that Lloyd George rather than Wilson had actually uttered, was a harbinger of things to come. But it should not be allowed to obscure the point that if the leaders of the British Empire emerged in a confident mood in November 1918, it was because they felt they had secured the foundations of the empire as a key pillar of the emerging, liberal world order.

10

The Arsenals of Democracy

France, Britain and Italy contained the crisis of political legitimacy that felled Russia and would soon tear the Central Powers apart. But what kept the populations of the Entente off the streets and drove their armies across the line was a remarkable economic effort. Even the richest combatants in World War I were not affluent by modern standards. Pre-war France and Germany had per capita incomes roughly comparable to those of Egypt or Algeria today, but had access to far less sophisticated technologies of transport, communications and public health. And yet despite such limitations, the major combatants were by 1918 committing 40 per cent or more of total output to the destructive purposes of the war. It was a defining moment in reshaping the modern understanding of economic potential. Back in 1914 conventional liberal wisdom had insisted that the globalization of the world economy would make prolonged war impossible. The collapse of trade and finance would bring the fighting to a halt within months. That crisis had indeed arrived in the autumn of 1914, when financial markets seized up and the stocks of ammunition ran low. Both were overcome through decisive state intervention. Central banks took charge in the money markets of New York, London, Paris and Berlin.[1] Imports and exports were tightly regulated. Scarce raw materials and food were rationed. Far from limiting the combat, industrial mobilization and technological innovation acted as a flywheel on the war.[2] This enormous effort spawned three new visions of modern economic power, two of which have remained as part of the commonplace iconography of the war; the third, significantly, was largely erased from memory.

The first economic model spawned by the war was that of the self-sufficient, state-planned national economy. In May 1918 Lenin justified his turn toward Germany by citing that country as the non plus ultra of economic and industrial modernity.[3] It was in Germany, he insisted, that a form of state capitalism had been born which would provide the stepping stone to the socialist future. Walther Rathenau, the CEO of the international electrical engineering group AEG, became renowned as the exponent of a new mode of organized capitalism, in which corporate organization would be merged seamlessly with the power of the state.[4] This identification of Germany as the epitome of an organized planned economy was ironic, since by 1916 the organizational and productive inferiority of the German war effort was already starkly apparent. In the autumn of 1916 the Hindenburg armaments programme was conceived as a vain effort to outdo Lloyd George's triumphs as Munitions Minister in Britain.[5] By 1918 the productive capacities of the Entente and the Americans, the cooperation they managed to sustain and their willingness to take considerable risks, all combined to give the Allies a crushing superiority.[6] In every dimension it was the Allied armies that pushed the battlefield into a new technological era. When the climactic assault on the Hindenburg line began on 8 August 1918, 2,000 Allied aircraft provided smothering air superiority. The German squadrons, led amongst others by the youthful Hermann Goering, were outnumbered five to one. On the ground the imbalance was even more severe. By 1917 every major attack by French or British infantry could count on the support of hundreds of tanks. The Germans never fielded more than a handful. But the truly decisive difference was in firepower. Artillery war reached its apotheosis in 1918. On 28 September 1918, in preparation for the final push through the German defensive line, British artillery unleashed 1 million shells in a single, continuous day-long barrage – 11 shells per second for 24 hours.[7]

In November 1918 Germany's planned economy surrendered in the face of a second even more powerful economic vision – a triumphant model of 'democratic capitalism'. At the heart of the democratic war effort stood the much-heralded economic potential of the United States. World War I marked the point at which America's wealth stamped itself dramatically on European history. The globetrotting engineer and philanthropist Herbert Hoover was the first great ambassador of American abundance. His food-relief organization operated first in occupied Belgium and then across all of war-torn Europe. Meanwhile, Henry Ford's rise to global prominence as the prophet of a new era of mass-produced prosperity coincided almost exactly with the war. Ford introduced his legendary $5 per-day wage on his Model T production lines in January 1914.[8] Following Wilson's declaration of war, Ford outdid himself in his extraordinary promises: 1,000 two-man tanks per day, 1,000 midget submarines, 3,000 aero engines per day, 150,000 complete aircraft. None of these ever materialized. Europeans, notably the British, the Germans, the French and the Italians, were the great mass-producers of aircraft in the early twentieth century. But Ford's legend was as robust as his car. By the winter of 1917 it was not incongruous for Britain's General Allenby to credit his celebrated march on Jerusalem to 'Egyptian labour, camels and the Model T'.[9]

American 'productivism' soon established itself as one of the guiding ideologies of the early twentieth century. Greater productivity per hour promised an escape from hard political choices, opening the door to a new era of domestic and international harmony. It was a vision that suited socialists as well as liberals and found recruits even amongst the new breed of 'reactionary modernists'.[10] But as a self-declared ideology we should treat 'productivism' and the associated fable of American abundance with the caution it deserves. The celebration of American productive power was exaggerated. It tempts historians to project the dominant position that American mass-manufacturing had established by the 1940s anachronistically into an earlier era. As an ideology it obscures the interests that it served and, with its emphasis on tangible, material goods it deflects attention from the true locus of American power, which in 1918 was founded above all on money not on things. In the economic sphere even more distinctly than in politics we see the sudden overshadowing of European history by the prospective dominance of the United States. If we look more closely at the way in which America's resources were actually funnelled into Europe, what we see is both the purposefulness with which that shadow was cast and the as yet fragile facade from which it was projected.

I

From the summer of 1917 Entente military planning was based on the assumption that 1 million American soldiers would arrive in Europe by the end of 1918.[11] But at the beginning of the year only 175,000 had crossed the Atlantic, out of which General Pershing had managed to form only two oversized infantry divisions. In the United States droves of would-be Doughboys had signed up. But they were training with wooden rifles and obsolete machine guns. They had none of the heavy weaponry that ruled the European battlefield. Nor, in early 1918, was America in any position to supply its new army with advanced armaments from its own factories. Though the US had made huge deliveries of war supplies, the Entente's orders had been concentrated on raw materials, semi-finished products, explosives, gunpowder and ammunition.[12] The actual weapons of war continued to be designed and finished by the Europeans. Once American armaments production did begin to be ramped up, it was based on European types. Ford's main contribution, rather than the thousands of tanks he promised, was to devise a low-cost process for mass-producing the cylinders required by the Liberty aero-engine that American engineers had scrambled together from French, British, Italian and German designs. Despite the already legendary prowess of Detroit, there was too little time for America's distinctive new system of mass-manufacturing to have a truly decisive impact.[13] The year 1918 should not be confused with 1944. In 1918 it was the American Army that fought with French weapons, not the other way around. Three-quarters of the aircraft flown by the US Air Service were of French origin.[14]

The fact that the Americans would begin their apprenticeship on the Western Front as pupils of the British and French was no surprise and this transatlantic division of labour was efficient. But there was one rate-limiting factor that constrained any American contribution – shipping. When the commitment of 1 million American soldiers was made, it was understood that they would be shipped to Europe predominantly in American vessels. But due to infighting in Washington, little was done in 1917 to actually build cargo ships. By the end of the year the American general staff disposed of only 338,000 tons of shipping. To tip the manpower balance decisively by the summer they would need to concentrate at least ten times that figure.[15] The ensuing struggle casts a stark light on relations between the Wilson administration and its European associates during the final crisis of the war.

The effective monopoly over the world's shipping fleet established by Britain and its allies after 1914 was a direct challenge to Wilson's vision of an American-led world order. The Shipping Act passed in September

1916 was intended to sponsor the construction of an American merchant navy to rival that of Britain.[16] These, however, were peacetime measures and the rival American interests were slow to agree on the details. Once the U-boat war forced America's hand in April 1917, it was the Federal government that took emergency powers to build and operate a publicly owned merchant fleet. But by then the British had pre-emptively cornered every free slipway and dry dock in the United States. In response, Wilson placed a moratorium on any further foreign orders. Outstanding British and French orders were bought out by the US government. Finally, in October 1917 all steel-hulled cargo ships in the United States were placed under Federal control. On this basis, the Emergency Fleet Corporation launched an epic ship-construction programme. With their familiar combination of showmanship, entrepreneurial energy and technical vision, America's industrial barons competed in meeting ever more excessive targets. Some $2.6 billion later, the results were impressive. In the last six months of 1918 American shipyards delivered as much as the entire world had launched in 1913 – 100 ships on 4 July 1918 alone (Independence Day).[17] But by the third quarter of 1918 the military crisis had already passed.

During the truly critical period, between March and July 1918, when the American Army was desperately needed in France, American shipyards produced virtually no additional cargo capacity. Not only that, even at the height of the crisis, the Wilson administration did not give clear priority to the needs of the European war. Of the ships requisitioned by the Federal government, only a fraction were actually allocated to troop transport. As the Germans advanced to within artillery range of Paris in April 1918, Wilson was still insisting that America must maintain its growing presence on the profitable Brazil and Japan trading routes. The burden was placed instead on the British and French fleets. Already in January the British had imposed a stomach-churning shift in priorities. To free enough capacity to transport 150,000 American soldiers per month, food imports were slashed.[18] When the German offensive tore into the Allied lines on 21 March, even more drastic measures were required. Turning the tables on Wilson, it was now Lloyd George who, over the head of the laggardly President, appealed directly to the American public. Wilson was so incensed that he even considered having the British ambassador recalled. 'I fear,' he expostulated on one occasion, 'I will come out of the war hating [the] English.'[19] But the

American military authorities responded. In the month of May, 250,000 men were moved, 1.788 million men in all between February and November 1918, at least half of them on British ships.

The bottleneck of shipping reduced the transatlantic war economy to the most primitive economic trade-off: men against things. To maximize capacity American soldiers were shipped virtually without equipment. Britain and France supplied the fresh American divisions with all their rifles, machine guns, artillery, aircraft and tanks. Indeed, they had to feed them from their own depleted stocks. This human cargo was America's major contribution to the military victory – a fresh crop of healthy, well-fed young men of prime fighting age, the likes of which had become depressingly rare in Europe.[20] Due to their lack of combat experience, most of America's army could not be thrown directly into the front line. But they were a promise of ultimate victory and a strategic cushion against the possibility of a German breakthrough. On the Italian front a single American regiment was deployed, in a purely propagandistic role. Its three battalions of 1,000 strapping young men from Ohio were moved rapidly from town to town, parading in changing uniforms so as to create the impression of tens of thousands of reinforcements.[21]

What actually enabled the huge transatlantic movement was the remarkable system of inter-Allied economic cooperation that the Entente had devised since 1915. Originally confined to the financing and purchasing of wheat, then the distribution of coal, inter-Allied cooperation extended in the autumn of 1917 to the common regulation of all-important shipping capacity.[22] The Allied Maritime Transport Council, based in London, was made up of representatives of all the combatant governments, headed by Britain and France. Though each delegate owed primary loyalty to his national government, they collectively constituted an inter-governmental authority capable of making decisions affecting the lives of literally every inhabitant of Europe, whether civilian or soldier. Given the extremity of their situation, by early 1918 it was the Entente Powers, not Wilson, who were exploring radical new forms of cooperation and coordination. In halting Germany's final onslaught, the Entente created precedents for inter-governmental cooperation that went beyond anything ever realized in the League of Nations. From 1916, France, Russia and Italy all borrowed on British credit. In 1916 an economic conference had met in Paris to sketch a bold vision for long-term Allied economic cooperation against common enemies. In November 1917, following the Caporetto disaster, the Supreme War Council was established. By April 1918 British and French soldiers were fighting under one supreme command. In May, Marshal Foch's coordinating powers were extended across the entire length of the Western Front from the North Sea to the eastern Mediterranean. Meanwhile, British and French rations were weighed against each other in common purchasing and shipping plans. Through the involvement of a generation of businessmen, engineers and technocrats, such as the Briton Arthur Salter and his close colleague and friend, the Frenchman Jean Monnet, this cooperation was to provide the inspiration for the project of the European Union led by the functional integration of the European Coal and Steel Community (ECSC) after World War II.[23]

This third economic model spawned by the war, the model of inter-Allied cooperation, was eclipsed in historical memory by its two chief competitors – Germany's planned economy and America's capitalist abundance.[24] Nor was this any coincidence. The victor states were liberal political economies that chafed at state regulation.[25] And this opposition from within France, Italy and Britain found an eager echo in Washington.[26] The Wilson administration regarded the inter-Allied institutions with profound suspicion. Before the war, breaking open the cartel arrangements and protective trade regimes of Europe's empires had been the chief purpose of the Open Door policy. Alarmed by the bold demands of the Paris conference of 1916, which Washington viewed as a project of global cartelization and the absolute negation of the Open Door, American resistance amounted to something akin to open hostility.[27] Americans who spent too long working within the inter-Allied organizations were held at arm's length for fear that they had become 'out of touch with the American situation . . . and become European in their views'. Wilson believed that it took only six months for Americans working in London to become 'Anglicized'.[28] In practice, however, every American intervention in Europe – Hoover's relief programme for Belgium no less than Pershing's independent American Army – was dependent on the cooperative logistical apparatus established by the Entente. In 1918, if Belgium continued to be fed, it was not only on account of Hoover's organizational genius, or America's largesse, but because the inter-Allied shipping agency placed the priority of American relief shipments even above the needs of the home fronts of France, Britain and Italy.[29]

II

Given the profoundly uncooperative behaviour both of General Pershing and the Wilson administration, it became commonplace in Britain to discuss the strategic balance on the Western Front as a zero sum game. If the war were won in 1918, it would be a triumph for the British Empire. If the war dragged on into 1919, Britain, like France, would find itself utterly depleted. Even if huge new levies of manpower could be raised in India or Africa, victory would be claimed by the Americans. Some even began to wonder whether Britain and France might not be better off without the American military contribution. Winston Churchill reacted with a characteristic appeal to Atlantic unity. 'Quite apart from the imperious military need, the intermingling of British and American units on the field of battle and their endurance of losses and suffering together may exert an immeasurable effect upon the future destiny of the English-speaking people,' he opined. It would 'afford us perhaps the only guarantee of safety if Germany emerges stronger from the War than she entered it'.[30]

Other, cooler heads pointed out that fantasies of independence were vain in any case. Whether victory was won in 1918 or 1919, whether or not a large American army was involved, the Entente were dependent on the United States. Behind Detroit's aero-engines and Pittsburgh's steel was something less tangible but ultimately decisive, dollar credits. Since 1915 Wall Street had bankrolled the Entente. Even without the abrupt intervention of the Federal Reserve Board in November 1916 and despite the sympathetic cooperation of J. P. Morgan, the limit of the Entente's credit would undoubtedly have been reached in the course of 1917. But instead, overriding the limit of the private capital market and replacing it with a radically new geometry of financial and economic power, one rich democracy, the United States, channelled huge public loans to London, Paris and Rome. It was this direct financing out of US public credit that helped to give the Entente its crucial margin of advantage over Germany. On 24 April 1917 Congress laid the foundation for long-term funding in the form of the Liberty Loan authorization. The initial authorization of funds for the American war effort was for $5 billion, of which as much as $3 billion were allocated for loans to the Entente. Unlike American troops, American money flowed quickly. By

July 1917 Treasury Secretary William McAdoo had already advanced $685 million to Britain.[31] At the time of the armistice in 1918 just over $7 billion had been taken up. By the spring of 1919 the maximum limit of $10 billion had been reached.

Money defined all the other problems. Prior to April 1917, to economize on dollar spending, a large part of British shipping had been tied up on the very long haul to Australia. After April 1917, with an abundant supply of dollars, purchasing and shipping could be concentrated on the far more efficient transatlantic route. The link between public credit and export promotion was a further defining feature of the new relationship with America. Up to April 1917 the Entente had borrowed in the United States to fund purchases from the US and overseas. A condition attached to all US congressional appropriations was that the dollars lent must be spent exclusively in America. After April 1917 the US Federal government was operating a gigantic, publicly funded export scheme. The American fiscal apparatus and the productive capacity of American business were harnessed together as never before. No previous 'financial hegemony' exercised by Spain, Holland or Britain between the seventeenth and nineteenth centuries had ever exercised anything approximating this scale or degree of coordination. The Inter-Allied Supply Council, formed unlike the other inter-Allied agencies at the behest of Washington, worked under the close supervision of an assistant secretary to the US Treasury and funnelled orders directly to the US War Industries Board.[32]

As critics like John Maynard Keynes, the brilliant young economist advising the UK Treasury, had predicted, delivering the knock-out blow to Germany put Britain at the mercy of the United States. Lloyd George had willingly courted this risk, expecting America to understand its own interests in an Atlantic alliance. But as Keynes was to experience first hand in Washington in the summer of 1917, the reality of transatlantic partnership was less reassuring than the rhetoric of a democratic alliance might suggest. To Keynes it seemed that the Wilson administration positively relished the opportunity to reduce Britain to a state of 'complete financial helplessness and dependence'.[33] That dependence expressed itself at its most basic level in the monetary system. Before the war, the international gold standard had been anchored to the gold parity of the pound sterling. After 1914, though it could no longer be freely converted at home, sterling remained nominally attached to gold and in

New York the exchanges continued to function. For the Entente Powers it was vital to maintain the value of their currencies against the dollar. They couldn't credibly promise to repay their dollar debts if the lira, the rouble, the franc or sterling were depreciating violently. The dollar costs of debt service would become exorbitant. In January 1917, in a confidential memo for the Treasury, Keynes advised strongly against leaving the gold standard: 'we have made a fetish of the gold standard. We have taken immense pride in it ... To point out the depreciation of the German exchanges and the stability of our own has been our favourite form of propaganda.'[34]

Keynes, characteristically, hit upon the central point. The dependence of the Entente on the United States was not necessary. Like Germany, the Entente could have tried to fight the war without American resources. But this would have been a very different kind of war than that for which London, Paris and Petrograd had planned in early 1917. London's decision to lead the Entente toward Wall Street was taken as part of the deliberate high-risk strategy, as part of an all-out effort to deliver the 'knock-out' blow. And it did serve to give the Entente an impressive material preponderance both on the battlefield and in terms of the material conditions of the home front. But once the decision to engage the US was adopted, once it was made into both a cornerstone of military strategy and of Entente propaganda, it created an immense dependence, and the Wilson administration both before and after American entry into the war was conscious of this. In the spring of 1917 Wilson's Treasury Secretary (and son-in-law) William McAdoo made quite clear that he aimed to replace sterling with the dollar as the key reserve currency.[35] As a first move, McAdoo proposed that no funds from congressionally approved Liberty Loans should be used to support either sterling or the franc. Nor should London be permitted to use such funds to repay overdrafts that it had contracted with J. P. Morgan during Wilson's credit freeze over the winter of 1916–17. This put London under terrible pressure. First at the end of June, and then again at the end of July 1917, Britain came within hours of default.[36] The near panic this caused in London and on Wall Street was enough to convince the Wilson administration that even if the dollar was to replace sterling in the long run, in the short term defending sterling was the cheapest way to prop up the Entente war effort. But this guarantee was limited to the duration of the war. When hostilities ended, the Entente would be left to its fate. The US dollar would emerge as the only global currency still securely based on gold.

The fact that American support was limited to the bilateral dollar-sterling rate was significant in light of monetary relations within the British Empire. The empire had two lopsided monetary pillars, the first being sterling based on gold supplied in large part from South Africa. The second was the Indian rupee based on an uneasy silver-currency standard. The war put this structure under extreme pressure. Britain's imports from the Dominions and India surged, whilst its exports to the empire were throttled to a bare minimum. The empire accumulated large surplus claims on Britain, but given its desperate need for dollars and gold, London could not permit the empire to indulge in an import boom from third markets, such as the US. Within days of the outbreak of war, London declared a monopoly on the output of South Africa's gold mines, setting an artificially low official price and raking in exorbitant fees for shipping and insurance. South African banks attempting to sell gold directly to the US at higher market prices were subject to sanctions and a vicious propaganda campaign denouncing them for collaboration with the enemy.[37] Despite protests from the mining corporations who were in effect being forced to provide a subsidy to the British war effort, the price was held until the end of the war. The result was to concentrate one of the world's main supplies of gold in London, but also to provoke bitter nationalist protests. In the Transvaal mining region vociferous Boer activists demanded that South Africa must take full control of its own gold, establishing refineries and its own mint.

Whereas in South Africa attention focused on a single key commodity produced by gigantic, British-owned mining corporations, employing a minority workforce of white miners, in India, wartime financial relations were potentially even more explosive, involving as they did the relations between the British and a population of 240 million people largely dependent on agriculture for their subsistence. The 'economic drain' on India had long been a staple of nationalist argument.[38] Whatever the merits of the case prior to 1914, once the war began, 'the drain' took on a manifest reality. From the autumn of 1915 the balance of trade shifted decisively in India's favour. Under normal circumstances this would have triggered either expanded Indian imports or an inflow of precious metals. But instead, to prevent India's purchasing power from spilling over into a huge surge in 'unnecessary' imports, wartime controls were extended to the subcontinent.[39] Held in bank accounts in London, India's export earnings were invested in British war bonds. In effect, India was enrolled in an involuntary war-saving programme, a commitment made all the more painful because the government of India was simultaneously slashing spending on long-promised investments such as primary education to make room for war costs.[40]

In early 1916 the Indian currency was officially uncoupled from silver. Henceforth, the backing for the rupee would be the British government bonds held in London in India's name. On the assumption that sterling retained its pre-war value, these bonds would be redeemable after the war for bullion or goods. But, in the likely event of a post-war devaluation, India would suffer a commensurate loss. In the meantime, India was awash with currency no longer backed by any metallic equivalent. Even at the best of times, Indian peasants were extremely reluctant to hold paper currency. With the risk of inflation becoming more and more obvious, the remaining silver stocks disappeared from the market. This in turn made it harder to sustain the fiction that the flood of paper rupees would eventually be redeemable in specie. As a countermeasure, in April 1916 the government of India began feeding silver purchased in the United States into circulation.[41] But, given its desperate shortage of dollars, this could never satisfy demand. Nor did America's entry into the war bring any immediate relief. Instead, in September 1917, Washington insisted that if India was providing Britain with deliveries on credit, then the same privilege must be extended to the US as well. The United States extracted a rupee credit equivalent to $10.5 million from India.

By early 1918 the Indian currency system was close to collapse. In Bombay political discussion of the Montagu-Chelmsford reforms was overshadowed by tumultuous scenes on the exchanges as merchants scrambled to cash their rupee notes for the dwindling stock of silver. Given London's precarious position, only the United States had the resources to underwrite the monetary system of the Raj. On 21 March Washington announced that it would throw open for sale the enormous silver reserves of the US. Under the Pittman Act the sale of 350 million ounces of silver was approved, at the fixed price of one dollar per ounce. The government of India was authorized to use its funds in London to replenish its silver stocks from the American official reserves.[42] In effect India was uncoupled from sterling and moved to a silver-dollar basis, with the rupee valued at approximately a third of an ounce of silver, or 35.5 cents. Against sterling the rupee promptly appreciated from 16 pence per rupee to 18 pence. This devaluation of sterling raised the cost of imports to Britain. But the political relief was huge. As the Indian currency controller warned, a failure by London to meet the demand for silver would have been a greater blow to the Raj than a military defeat, or even a 'German landing in Norfolk'.[43]

II

World War I ratified the emergence of the US as the dominant force in the world economy. The rivalrous talk in London and Washington could give the impression that the issue at stake was the question of how America would succeed to Britain's position of pre-eminence. But that seriously understated the novelty of the situation created by the war. In its pomp Victorian Britain had never commanded the kind of leverage over Prussia, or Napoleon III's France, or Alexander III's Russia, that Washington was accumulating. In their struggle to defeat Germany, the Entente entered into an unprecedented period of dependence on the United States. This new asymmetrical financial geometry signalled the end to the great-power competition that had defined the age of imperialism. It did so in a double sense. On the one hand, the Entente's transatlantic war effort defeated Germany. But at the same time it raised the US to a position of unprecedented dominance, not over its Caribbean satrapies or the Philippines, but over Britain, France and Italy, the great powers of Europe. In its basic outline this was exactly the kind of unilateral power to which Woodrow Wilson had aspired with his strategy of 'peace without victory'. Whether it would actually give Washington the leverage that he hoped for would depend on three questions: Would the democracies of Europe cooperate in their submission to the financial demands of their new creditor? Would Washington be able to block the efforts of the European Powers to enrol the United States in their own, more multilateral vision of a new international economic order? And would America's own institutions prove adequate to the challenge of an entirely new kind of financial leadership?

That there would be need for such leadership was by 1918 painfully evident. Despite American support, the underlying weakness of the

British, French and Italian currencies was unmistakable. And their anxious gyrations were superimposed on a more basic global trend: inflation. The post-war hyperinflation that wracked the Weimar Republic in 1923 is the stuff of legend. But it was not a unique experience. In the aftermath of the war, Poland, Austria and Russia all suffered devastating hyperinflations. And it was not until 1920 that the trajectory of these countries diverged fundamentally from that of the other combatants. Between 1914 and 1920, inflation swept the world. In Sierra Leone the price of a cup of rice rose fivefold.[44] In Harare the real wages of African workers halved.[45] In Egypt, as in India, the metallic basis of the currency was replaced by the dubious backing of British government debt. The money supply promptly doubled, leading to a disastrous surge in the urban cost of living (Table 4).[46]

Price changes on this scale triggered bitter social conflicts over shares of purchasing power and wealth. Producers of goods that were in high demand and those who could set their own price generally did well out of the war. On the other hand purchasers with sufficient clout, such as the British Empire, could fix the market to their advantage. Britain not only set the price for South African gold. It also rigged the price of Egyptian cotton.[47] In all of the combatant economies, indispensable war workers were able to extract premium wages. But this, in turn, increased the incentive for employers and the war-planning authorities to dilute the male workforce with underpaid female labour. As inflation accelerated, battles over income shares expanded into a generalized war of all against all. Most dangerously, peasant farmers became increasingly unwilling to exchange their crops for devalued currency. Only the promise of industrial goods would coax them out of a retreat into self-sufficiency. In 1917 it was riots on the bread lines that toppled the Tsarist monarchy. By 1918 much of central Europe was starving and the entire economy of the Indian Ocean and Pacific was facing a dramatic rice crisis.[48] In Japan, just as it launched its controversial intervention in Siberia in August 1918, the government of Prime Minister Terauchi Masatake was toppled by an extraordinary wave of rice riots that swept from fishing villages to the industrial towns of the coast and from there to Tokyo itself.[49]

The ultimate driver of this inflationary wave was monetary expansion originating at the heart of the global monetary system in Europe and the US. As war expenditure surged, in none of the combatant countries did taxes keep up. The state skimmed off purchasing power by

Table 4. The Wartime Dislocation of the Global Price System: Wholesale Prices (1913 = 100)

	1913	1914	1915	1916	1917	1918	1919	1920	1921
European combatants									
France	100	102	140	189	262	340	357	510	346
Netherlands	100	105	145	222	286	392	297	281	181
Italy	100	95	133	201	299	409	364	624	578
Germany	100	106	142	153	179	217	415	1486	1911
European neutrals									
Spain	100	101	119	139	160	204	195	222	190
Denmark	100	112	143	189	250	304	326	390	
Norway	100	115	159	223	341	345	322	377	269
Sweden	100	116	145	185	244	339	330	347	211
British Empire									
UK	100	99	123	161	204	225	235	283	181
Australia	100	106	147	138	153	178	189	228	176
Canada	100	100	109	134	175	205	216	250	182
New Zealand	100	104	123	134	151	175	178	212	205
India	100	100	112	125	142	178	200	209	183
South Africa	100	97	107	123	141	153	165	223	160
Egypt	100	98	103	128	176	211	231	312	173

(continued)

Table 4. The Wartime Dislocation of the Global Price System: Wholesale Prices (1913 = 100)

	1913	1914	1915	1916	1917	1918	1919	1920	1921
Western hemisphere									
USA	100	97	107	128	170	203	203	197	123
Peru	100	105	125	160	195	217	227	238	
Asia									
Japan	100	96	97	117	149	196	240	258	201
China	100	91	97	117	133	148	155	147	134

issuing government bonds repayable long after the end of the war. But much surplus purchasing power remained in circulation. Furthermore, a large part of the bonds were purchased not by savers but by banks. Rather than immobilizing household funds, the bonds provided the banks with a safe investment that could be resold for cash to the central bank – the Bank of England, Bank of France or Reichsbank. Like a cash deposit, the bonds therefore served as the basis for a pyramid of credit-creation. The central banks were transformed into inflationary pumps. The entire sterling zone of the British Empire was swept up in the inflation issuing from London, the Treasury and the Bank of England. Through these same mechanisms, rapid inflation came even to the heart of the new structure of financial power, the United States.

The story of American war finance was told by boosters of Wilsonianism as the story of the Liberty Bond.[50] Before the war no more than 500,000 wealthy Americans had invested regularly in government debt. By the end of the war Treasury Secretary Russell Leffingwell claimed that 20 million American citizens had signed for Liberty Bonds and perhaps as many as 2 million Americans had joined the volunteer sales force that reached virtually every community in the country. Over $30 billion were raised. This huge popular mobilization was presented by the Wilson administration as a fundamental advance in democracy and a break with the bad old days of Wall Street domination. In fact, it was in many cases a coercive mobilization with huge pressure being exerted, particularly on recent immigrants, to prove themselves 100 per cent American. Stiff prison sentences were handed out for anyone daring even to question the official Liberty Bond propaganda. If it had been matched by an equivalent amount of private saving, the Liberty Bonds would have served as a solid, non-inflationary foundation for the entire Allied war effort. This was certainly the rhetoric that would surround the loans in later years. Millions of ordinary Americans had sunk their hard-earned savings into the Allied war effort and must therefore be repaid. But though the Liberty Bonds certainly bulked large in the popular imagination and were undeniably vital to the collective war effort, their relationship to real saving was far from straightforward. Saving by American households and businesses actually slumped in 1918. In large part, therefore, the flow of funds to the Federal government was provided by an increase in bank credit. Desperate as they were to prevent any dislocation in America's fragile banking system, the Treasury and the Fed underwrote this monetary expansion. Reserve requirements were loosened. In advance of the issue of each tranche of Liberty Bonds the Treasury anticipated the proceeds by releasing huge volumes of short-term Treasury certificates directly to the banks. These were supposed to be redeemed out of the dollars raised from the sale of the Liberty Bonds. But in practice vast portfolios of certificates remained with the banks, putting the Treasury under constant pressure to refinance (Table 5).[51]

With government expenditure surging, and private demand not substantially contained, compensation might have come, as it was to do in World War II, through an increase in actual economic activity. The expanded flow of purchasing power might then have been matched by additional goods and services. In the first years of the war the procurement orders of the Entente had had this effect on the American economy, driving up employment and output.[52] But in 1916 productive expansion reached its limit. Measured in prices of 1914, American GDP rose fractionally over the following two years from $41.3 billion in 1916 to only $42.9 billion in 1918, before relapsing to $41 billion in 1919.[53] Despite the propagandistic bluster, there was no substantial increase in either output or productivity. With an expanding flow of demand competing for a static volume of output, the result was inevitable. The war was paid for through an inflation tax. Whereas real output barely increased, between 1916 and 1920 nominal national income surged from $43.6 billion to $82.8 billion. Prices doubled. In 1914 Ford had caused a worldwide sensation with his $5 per-day wage. By the late summer of 1917 that was no more than a bare minimum. As the cost of living surged, real wages lagged behind.[54] Between 1914 and 1916 the profits earned by American export industry were nothing short of phenomenal.[55] As labour unions struggled to maintain their members' real earnings, they unleashed an unprecedented wave of labour disputes that shook America between 1917 and 1919.

Far from serving as the stable anchor of a new international economic order, the effect of the wartime mobilization on the US economy was profoundly destabilizing. Both the American public and key decision-makers in the Wilson administration came to experience their country no longer as standing detached and pre-eminent above the global crisis, but as dangerously enmeshed within it. The stage was set for the post-war backlash.

Table 5. A Low-Growth War Economy: The United States, 1916–20

	$ billion, current prices				$ billion, 1914 prices				% share of GNP		
	GNP	federal spending	War dept. and Navy	savings	GNP	federal spending	War dept. and Navy	savings	federal spending	War dept. and Navy	savings
1916	43.6	0.7	0.3	7.0	41.3	0.7	0.3	6.6	2	1	16
1917	49.9	2.1	0.7	7.0	42.1	1.8	0.6	5.9	4	1	14
1918	61.6	13.8	7.0	4.4	42.9	9.6	4.9	3.1	22	11	7
1919	65.7	19.0	11.3	7.6	41.0	11.8	7.0	4.7	29	17	12
1920	82.8	6.1	1.7	5.6	41.0	3.0	0.8	2.8	7	2	7

11

Armistice: Setting the Wilsonian Script

The battle on the Western Front turned decisively against Germany in the first weeks of July 1918. On 22 July Ludendorff ordered a general retreat from the Marne salient. Since the beginning of the year the German Army had lost 900,000 men. Fresh American troops were arriving at a rate of 250,000 per month. Twenty-five powerful divisions had already formed in France. Fifty-five more were building on the other side of the Atlantic.[1] From week to week the balance would tilt more and more severely against Germany. This did not, however, imply an immediate end to the war. It was not until October that the German Army began to disintegrate. Faced with far more overwhelming odds, Hitler's regime would use every means of coercion and propaganda to rally the Reich for an apocalyptic last stand. There were those in Germany in 1918 who wished to do the same. If they had gained the upper hand, 1919 might have witnessed the kind of inferno that laid waste to much of Germany and central Europe in 1944–5. Instead, thanks to decisions taken by the remnants of the Kaiser's regime, the majority parties in the Reichstag and hundreds of thousands of ordinary Germans, the war was brought to an end on the morning of 11 November 1918.

To this day, the decision for peace in November 1918 is not given its due as a remarkable victory for democratic politics. This was hardest for Germany. But the armistice was controversial also in London, Paris and Washington. Their leaders too had to choose peace. Were they right to settle for an armistice rather than fighting on to an outright German surrender? By October Germany's defences were collapsing. If the war had been continued even for a few weeks, the Entente might have ended the year by imposing an unconditional surrender. Instead Germany managed not only to rescue itself from the jaws of absolute defeat but, to a surprising degree, to define the politics of the peace. For sure, Germany was no longer in a position to claim the 'peace of equality' promised by Wilson in January 1917. Nevertheless, in the course of negotiating the armistice, Berlin quite deliberately wrote Wilson and his promise of a peace without defeat back into the heart of the script.

I

After the failure of the last German offensive in July and the immediate French counter-attack, it was the British push towards Amiens that knocked Germany onto the ropes. After 8 August, 'the black day of the German Army', Ludendorff and Hindenburg never regained their balance.[2] But thanks to wishful thinking and the tangled lines of communication between Berlin and the Kaiser's headquarters at Spa, it wasn't until the second week of September that the true severity of the military situation began to dawn on Germany's politicians. In November 1917 the Reichstag majority had installed the Christian Democrat Georg von Hertling as Chancellor. He was expected to protect civil rights on the home front, to democratize Prussia, and to craft a sustainable and legitimate peace in the East. He had failed to deliver on every front. The result of the fiasco of Brest-Litovsk was to rob Germany of any credibility as an international actor. As Friedrich Ebert of the Socialist Party charged in Reichstag committee: 'We are pursuing a policy that is internally dishonest. One takes what one can get! And speaks of reconciliation and negotiations . . . at the political level we face nothing but a field of rubble!'[3] In mid-September 1918 Austria appealed openly for peace and yet Hertling's government refused to react. With its allies collapsing, it was clear that Germany needed to negotiate, but it would need a new government to do so. Of course, both the British and Americans had stated that they expected regime change in Germany. Even the conservatives around the Kaiser were now growing used to the idea that they might have to concede a democratic facade. But power was slipping from their grasp. To the Reichstag majority parties, currying favour with the West was not the point. They demanded power because the existing regime was politically bankrupt. Only the Liberals, Centre Party and SPD appeared to be capable of formulating a coherent foreign policy and backing it with the necessary popular support. Like Russia's revolutionaries of February 1917, their aim was not to surrender. On the contrary, by putting the home front on a democratic basis they hoped to negotiate from a position of relative strength.[4] When Matthias Erzberger on 12 September 1918 first summoned the SPD to join the Centre Party in a new Reich government, the leading Liberal spokesman Friedrich Naumann chose a telling historical analogy. He hoped that the entry of the socialists into government would bring to the Reich the same rush of patriotic excitement with which the French radical Léon Gambetta had re-energized resistance to Bismarck's invading armies in the autumn of 1870.[5]

In the first days of October the liberal Prince Max von Baden took office as Chancellor on a governmental platform agreed between the SPD, Liberals and Centre Party. Internally his government promised the democratization of Prussia, an end to martial law, and a fully parliamentary constitution in the Reich. A peace on the basis of a League of Nations was a logical complement to this domestic reformism. Berlin offered the full restoration of Belgium and complete autonomy for all the territories liberated from the Tsar. But if peace was refused, the new government of Germany would launch a democratic levée en masse and steel itself to fight to the finish.[6] That such a government would appeal to President Wilson for mediation was not surprising. But it was not an automatic choice. The new Chancellor distrusted the American President. Von Baden was particularly opposed to any unilateral approach to Washington. London and Paris could not help but regard any such move as an attempt to gain bargaining advantage by setting the Entente and America against each other. It would be interpreted as further evidence of Berlin's bad faith. It was not the way for a government to start whose watchword was credibility and coherence. If Germany was serious about making peace, it must seek it directly with the powers whose armies were about to win a crushing victory in the field, Britain and France, not attempt to gain leverage by parlaying with their American associate.[7]

This hostility to Wilson was shared by prominent voices in the SPD. From the right of the party, Albert Suedekum drafted a memo arguing that the real enemy both of Germany and of Europe as a whole was American capitalism. Wilson 'was openly aspiring to the role as arbiter of the world'.[8] His aim was to humble all of Europe, reducing the continent to a collection of national republics all of which were economically dependent on America. The only way for Europe to escape this collective 'violation' was for the SPD to seek to settle the terms of a European democratic peace with the Socialists in France and the British Labour Party.

But this was not the majority view amongst the spokesmen of the Reichstag majority. In August 1918 Matthias Erzberger finished his book *Der Völkerbund: Der Weg zum Weltfrieden (The League of Nations: The Path to World Peace)*.[9] Erzberger's aim was to persuade the German public that contrary to the prevailing view Wilson was not merely a hypocrite, but in fact the representative of a tradition of liberalism deeply rooted in American democratic and anti-militarist politics. Furthermore, despite the bellicose rhetoric of the British and French governments, the League of Nations idea had genuine friends there as well. Imperial Germany had put itself in the wrong already before 1914 by flouting the Hague conference on international arbitration. Germany must not surrender the new politics of peace to its enemies. It must claim the idea of a league of peace as part of its own national history, in such forerunners as the medieval Hanseatic League and in philosopher Immanuel Kant's speculations on an order of perpetual peace. Furthermore, after the experience of this war who could doubt that Germany had a vested interest in peace? If the war ended with a League, Erzberger insisted, Germany would have won far more than it would be losing.[10] As far as Philipp Scheidemann and the SPD were concerned, the war had demonstrated beyond doubt that as far as Germany was concerned, war had lost its utility as a means of politics. Whatever the triumphs of its soldiers, Germany could not prevail against a global coalition.[11] Instead, Germany should commit itself to compulsory international arbitration overseen by a League with a strong executive. Erzberger foresaw a League reinforced by the weight of world public opinion and sustained by a common underpinning of Christian and democratic values. Public opinion was a nebulous thing no doubt. But it was a force that Germany's militarists had for too long ignored. In October all 50,000 copies of Erzberger's first edition were sold within a matter of weeks.[12]

Above all, however, Germany's internationalism was Atlanticist. On 12 September 1918, two weeks before the final crisis broke on the Western Front and Max von Baden took office, Erzberger insisted to his colleagues in the Reichstag that they must espouse the League as the first step toward a 'great gesture across the ocean, to Wilson'.[13] And despite the Chancellor's anti-Americanism this was the strategy that prevailed.[14] On 6 October von Baden asked Wilson to negotiate a peace on the basis of the principles laid out in the 14 Points: self-determination, no annexations, no indemnities. The dramatic implications of this move were not lost on Berlin. Germany was humbling itself. In a desperate effort to secure its survival, Germany was exploiting Wilson's evident desire to establish America as the arbiter of world affairs. The possibility that Berlin might actually take up Wilson's offer of 'peace without victory' had been the nightmare of Entente strategy ever since the Peace Notes of December 1916. Until the autumn of 1918, political divisions within Germany had made it impossible for Berlin to avail itself of this option. The Reichstag's peace appeal of July 1917 had been overshadowed by Germany's military triumph over Russia. The effort to make a progressive peace at Brest-Litovsk had been derailed by the disastrous interaction between the German militarists and the Bolsheviks. In the autumn of 1918 the German bid for a liberal peace would once again come close to fiasco. In November the politics of the armistice negotiations would unleash first a mutiny and then a revolution, but not before Berlin had given Wilson the chance to force the hand of London and Paris. In defeat, Germany conferred on Wilson the position that the Entente had worked so hard to deny him. It was the armistice that once more transformed the President from a combatant into the arbiter of European affairs. On the brink of collapse Germany allowed Wilson to fashion the script that has defined the story of the peace ever since.

II

On 27 September 1918, sensing that the end was nigh, Wilson used the occasion of the Fourth Liberty Bond drive in New York to set out once more in a speech the basic outlines of a 'liberal' peace. A 'secure and lasting peace' could be obtained only by sacrificing 'interests' to 'impartial justice'. The one 'indispensable instrumentality' of this peace would be a League of Nations. In his new effort to formulate the basis for a peace, known as the 'five particulars', Wilson documented once more the reluctance with which he had entered into the coalition against

Germany. The League could not be formed during the war since that would make it into an instrument of the victors. The new order must offer impartial justice for both victors and vanquished. No special interests ought to prevail over the common interests of all. There could be no special understandings within the league. There could be no self-interested economic combinations, nor any continuation of warlike boycotts or blockades. All international agreements must be entirely public. Once more Wilson claimed to be giving voice to the 'unclouded' thoughts 'of the mass of men', and he challenged the leaders of Europe, if they dared, to voice their dissent from his principles. Unsurprisingly, whereas London and Paris were silent, Max von Baden's government eagerly signalled its complete agreement. In the first armistice note addressed to Wilson on 7 October, Berlin offered negotiations on the basis of his speech of 27 September, plus the 14 Points.

It becomes far easier to understand the course of events after October 1918 if we acknowledge at the outset that Wilson was always highly sceptical about the democratization process in Germany. The American President was the very opposite of the universalist for which he is too often mistaken. For Wilson, genuine political development was a gradual process deeply determined by profound ethno-cultural and 'racial' influences. Regarding Germany he held simplistic views. Ever since the summer of 1917 he had been convinced that the 'military masters' of Germany were pursuing a two-pronged strategy: '. . . stand pat if they win, yield a parliamentary government if they lose'.[15] For this reason the fate of the Reichstag majority and the Weimar Republic were incidental to Wilson's calculations. At the Paris Peace Conference he made every effort to avoid meeting the German delegation. 'He would not have minded,' Wilson remarked, 'meeting the old blood and iron people of the old regime, but he hates the thought of seeing these nondescript creatures of the new . . .'.[16] 'Nondescripts' like Ebert and Erzberger might take a few steps in the right direction, but it would take years if not decades for true self-government to take root in Germany. For Wilson, the negotiations with Germany were above all a lever through which to gain purchase on the victors. Now that Germany was on the brink of defeat, it was French and British imperialism that Wilson believed posed the main threat to his vision of a new world order. It was for this reason that, though American troops in their hundreds of thousands were fighting side by side with the Entente, he chose to respond to

Berlin unilaterally without consulting either London or Paris. Wilson asked the Germans to give more details of their position, to which the Max von Baden government responded delightedly that it wholeheartedly accepted every one of the 14 Points and was willing to withdraw German troops from all occupied territories under the supervision of a 'mixed commission'.

In October 1918 Britain and France were faced with an extraordinary situation. At the moment of military triumph it seemed that Wilson was abruptly veering back toward the vision of US pre-eminence as an arbiter in world affairs that had first confronted them in January 1917. Tensions between Washington and the European capitals had risen seriously since the spring of 1918. The Entente had been furious over Wilson's laggardly reaction to Ludendorff's final assault. Over the summer, relations had worsened over the question of intervention in Russia. Similarly, though London was rather more firmly committed to the League of Nations than Washington turned out to be, Wilson and Lloyd George were already arguing over its design. Within Wilson's inner circle, the talk about the Europeans was relentlessly hostile. On the European side, even the official minutes record the indignation of the British cabinet at Wilson's effrontery in opening unilateral peace talks with Berlin. Less discreet records of Lloyd George's meetings in early October report furious outbursts. Wilson was acting alone. He was letting Germany off the hook and he was doing it all in the name of progress and justice. When even *The Times* hailed Wilson's peace notes as a great liberal gesture, Lloyd George could barely contain himself.[17] Nor was it only in Europe that memories of 'peace without victory' were reawakened. In the US as well, the Republicans were demanding not an armistice but an unconditional surrender.

Anxious about the anger stirred by his unilateral diplomacy, but determined to seize the opportunity that Germany was offering him, Wilson raised the stakes. On 14 October in his response to Max von Baden's second armistice notice, the President demanded proof that Germany was really on the road to democracy. The implication was clear: the Kaiser must go. Once again Wilson's concern was as much for public opinion at home as for any real change in Germany. He needed to appear both forceful and liberal at the same time. But as far as London and Paris were concerned, this too was a serious misstep: In Germany, making democratization a condition of peace was bound to have a counter-productive effect; the advocates of reform would look like puppets of the enemy. The European Allies were right.

In Berlin, the impact of Wilson's second note was dismaying. The Max von Baden government remained committed to negotiations with Washington. By late October the military situation was so dire that the Reichstag majority had abandoned any idea of a popular campaign of resistance to an Allied invasion. But on the German far right, Wilson's demand for the Kaiser's abdication was incendiary. Defying the will of the civilian government, Ludendorff travelled to Berlin to make a protest and to rally the forces of the right for a final battle in defence of the Kaiser's imperial standard. On 26 October Max von Baden dismissed him. The navy was not so easily tamed. Under the cover of preparing for a relief operation along the Flanders coastline, the German Admiralty gave orders for a last, massed sortie into the North Sea in search of an apocalyptic confrontation with the British navy. It was this suicidal mutiny by the officer class that brought on the final collapse. In the first days of November 1918 the crews of the fleet at Kiel refused to follow their mutinous officers' orders. As the news spread by telephone and telegraph, their courageous example inspired a wave of revolution across Germany.

Over the winter of 1917–18 at Brest-Litovsk the aggression of German militarists had sabotaged the Reichstag's effort to broker a legitimate peace in the East and sparked strikes in Berlin and Vienna that splintered the democratic opposition. Now the attempt by the right wing to sabotage a peace in the West resulted in the full-scale breakdown of the Kaiser's regime. Thanks to the insubordination and irrationality of the German ultra-nationalists, the attempt by German parliamentarians to manage an orderly democratic exit from the war came close to disaster. As reports of mutiny and rebellion poured in from across Germany in the first days of November, the von Baden government, with its authority crumbling around it, waited with bated breath for news from the West. Would Wilson be able to strong-arm the Entente into accepting the armistice terms to which Germany had so eagerly agreed? Would the Allies come to the table before the German state was torn apart by the clash between the revolution from the left and the right-wing fronde? By 4 November, as it appeared that London and Paris were holding out and Germany's military defences were disintegrating before their eyes, Berlin was in a state of repressed panic.

III

From a German point of view it would later seem that the combination of Wilsonian liberal moralism, designed to trick Germany into an armistice, followed by the dagger thrust of Franco-British aggression delivered at Versailles, was a dastardly tactical combination arranged by the Machiavellian genius of Anglo-American imperialism. That is not how it seemed from the vantage point of either London or Paris. In October 1918, Wilson opened negotiations with Berlin entirely without coordination with the Entente. To gain some grip on the situation, London and Paris demanded that Wilson dispatch to Europe a senior representative capable of formulating the final armistice terms in cooperation with them. On 27 October in Paris they duly confronted Colonel House.[18] The British, French and Italians at first threatened to take a hard line, refusing to associate themselves with any peace that incorporated the 14 Points since those too had been a unilateral presidential announcement. The French and Italians did not object to the idea of a League of Nations, but did not want it written into the peace. The British objected to a general commitment to uphold the freedom of the seas. Rather than accept such a disabling limitation, they would prefer to fight the war to a finish on their own. The German peace notes had reopened fundamental differences between Wilson and the Entente. In the autumn and winter of 1918, as victory was imposed, Wilson on several occasions chose to remind those around him of his basic position. His aversion to European power politics did not discriminate between land and sea. '[A]t one time if it had not been for his realization that Germany was the scourge of the world, he would have been ready to have it out with England.'[19] With Germany defeated, that moment had perhaps arrived. In the American cabinet in late October, when one of his colleagues warned him against forcing the Entente to accept a peace they did not want, Wilson had shot back 'they needed to be coerced'. Coerced they undoubtedly were.[20]

The exchange of notes with Germany had raised intense public excitement. The casualties during the final battles of 1918 were as terrible as any in the entire war. Not only did this add to war weariness, it made the question of manpower all the more pressing. In the first days of November 1918, Georges Clemenceau was forced to conclude a deal with the Senegalese leader Blaise Diagne which promised political rights for native Senegalese in exchange for a levy that would give France the shock troops it needed to claim part of the victory in 1919.[21] In Ireland things had gone beyond the point of compromise. If the war continued into the winter, London faced the prospect of having to press-gang hundreds of thousands of rebellious Fenians. Despite their bellicose rhetoric, neither Clemenceau nor Lloyd George wanted war for its own sake. Even though they were unaware of Germany's near complete collapse, it was clear that they had gained a historic victory. If they fought on into 1919 they might hope to impose an unconditional surrender on Germany, but it would be American forces that would claim a far greater share of the credit. If France and Britain made peace now, they could look forward to being hailed as heroes. The only thing that could possibly jeopardize their triumph would be a botched attempt to sabotage an armistice, from which they would emerge looking like reactionary opponents of Wilson's vision of peace and democracy.[22]

Furthermore, though Colonel House had instructions to 'coerce' the Europeans, he was, in fact, far more willing to make concessions than Wilson. In exchange for an acceptance of the 14 Points as the basis for the peace, House agreed that it should be up to the Commander-in-Chief of the Allied armies, General Foch, to lay down the military terms of the armistice. To France's satisfaction, Foch insisted on the complete disarmament of the German military and the withdrawal of the German Army east of the Rhine. Allied forces would take up positions in the Rhineland and occupy bridgeheads on the eastern side of the river. These were provisional demands, not a final peace, but Foch was surprised when they were accepted. He had thought them so radical that Berlin was bound to decline, thus giving him the chance to push the war to a truly conclusive victory.

As far as Britain was concerned, House went even further. He agreed to allow the British Empire to formulate its objections as an explicit set of reservations to the final note sent to the Germans. This was galling but it at least gave the British a more solid legal position. Britain could accept a peace that required no punitive indemnities. But in a war that had spread ruination across much of the world it was not equitable to restrict compensation to just those territories that the German Army had physically devastated. The armistice note therefore specified that Germany would be held to account for all the costs inflicted by its aggression, a far more all-encompassing rubric. The second reservation concerned freedom of the seas. Britain did not dispute the legitimate maritime interests of its partners. Since 1917 it had been urging the Wilson administration to consider a naval partnership.[23] Failing a bilateral Treaty, London had proposed a four-way agreement including Japan and France. But to neutralize the oceans would give unrestricted licence to aggressors. The defeat of Germany had pivoted on control of the Atlantic. If the League of Nations was to have a powerful mechanism of economic sanctions, it would depend on an effective naval blockade. The only secure foundation for a liberal world order was to eliminate the threat posed by aggressive powers and to place the main global traffic arteries in the hands of states that could be trusted. Colonel House did not concede the principle but allowed the British to write their reservations into the terms of the armistice. Once the British and Americans agreed, Clemenceau had no option but to fall into line.

On 5 November the German government was informed of the armistice terms. In Berlin the relief was profound. At that very moment the Bismarckian state was being swept away by the revolution. On 9 November the German Republic was declared not once but twice, first by the more radical then by the more moderate wing of German social democracy. By 10 November the German Army was in such disarray that the armistice delegation at Compiègne could no longer communicate safely with its own headquarters at Spa. It was not until 2 a.m. on 11 November that the delegation led by Erzberger received confirmation from Berlin that the new revolutionary government upheld their authority to sign the ceasefire. Under such circumstances, for the Entente to have accepted the 14 Points as the basis of the future peace was an astonishing triumph for the diplomacy initiated by the Reichstag majority in early October. If the French and British had realized how close to the precipice of disintegration Germany stood, they could easily have derailed Wilson's coup. Within days the revolutionary avalanche would have left Germany completely unable to resist a further military advance. Instead, the German government had allowed Wilson to define the politics of peace.

IV

Those who sympathized with Wilson's vision have ever since construed the Armistice as a founding document of the new era, a promise to the world and to Germany of a 'liberal peace'. Critics of the eventual Versailles peace spoke of covenants, contracts and constitutions.[24] Indeed, Wilson invoked nothing less than divine inspiration. But, in truth, this construction was a rearguard action, a rhetorical effort to bolster the extremely precarious political foundations of the peace.[25] The manner in which Wilson had conducted his unilateral negotiations with Berlin in October 1918, the ways in which Britain and France had been coerced into accepting the Wilsonian terms, left the Armistice that followed on a weak footing. This was well understood by those in Berlin, including von Baden himself, who doubted the wisdom of a one-sided approach to Wilson. It was shouted furiously behind closed doors in London and Paris. Within the White House, Wilson had overridden critics in his own cabinet. The hair-raising coincidence of Germany's military and political collapse with the armistice talks only added to the force of the point. The accusation later made by the likes of John Maynard Keynes, that Germany had been tricked, that the Entente had obtained an armistice on false pretences from a valiant and still combative foe, inverts reality. Up to the end the Entente continued to treat the German state as a sovereign counterpart, whilst the Reich was, in fact, collapsing into chaos. Between 9 and 11 November 1918, it was the Germans who negotiated at Compiègne as though they represented a government and an army capable of continuing the struggle, when in fact both were in a state of dissolution. The Germans would protest their betrayal, but in light of what happened across Germany in the first two weeks of November, as far as the British and French were concerned, this was merely further evidence of their bad faith.[26]

Wilson was engaged in a high-stakes wager. He was choosing to forego imposing a peace of his design by force of American arms. He was gambling that an armistice made on the basis of his 14 Points would hold the Entente in check. For this to succeed, Wilson needed to rally public opinion and he needed above all to control Washington, the new hub of global power. But it was precisely there, in the week prior to the Armistice, that Wilson lost his grip. In America, despite the impending military victory, the mood was intensely contentious. Whereas Clemenceau and Lloyd George could not afford to challenge Wilson openly, the same was not true of the President's domestic political opponents. Wilson's willingness to enter into a unilateral exchange of telegrams with Berlin, precisely at the moment when tens of thousands of American soldiers were laying down their lives in north-eastern France in the forest of Argonne, caused outrage. On 7 October, Republicans in the Senate initiated a debate demanding complete victory. Henry F. Ashurst of Arizona called for the Allies to drive 'a wide pathway of fire and blood from the Rhine to Berlin'. Not surprisingly, such references to General Sherman's march on Atlanta disturbed Wilson. He invited Ashurst to a personal conference at which he revealed his true strategic purpose. Whereas an unconditional German surrender would unleash British and French power, Wilson insisted that he was 'thinking now only of putting the United States into a position of strength and justice. I am now playing for 100 years hence.'[27] Wilson's opponents were not swayed. On 21 October, Senator Miles Poindexter introduced a motion calling for Wilson to be impeached if he continued to negotiate with the Germans.[28] Days later both ex-presidents Taft and Roosevelt did what no European dared to do – they publicly disowned the 14 Points. As Theodore Roosevelt put it with characteristic style, 'let us dictate peace by the hammering of our guns ... and not chat about peace to the accompaniment of the ticking of typewriters'.[29]

This was not idle posturing. Washington was in the midst of mid-term election fever. As in the presidential election of 1916, the partisanship was intense. On 21 October the *Rocky Mountain News* gave voice to a new narrative of rabid, anti-Wilsonian politics, denouncing 'Bolsheviks in the democratic party'.[30] In a three-hour address to a New York audience Roosevelt suggested that Wilson's willingness to deal with a German government stacked with Social Democrats and allied with Lenin revealed his true sympathy for 'Germanized socialists and the bolshevists of every grade'.[31] In reply, on 26 October, Wilson was tempted into a disastrous gamble. Forced to play an unusually pronounced role in a mid-term race, the President announced to the electorate that 'your vote this year will be viewed by the nations of Europe from one standpoint only. They will draw no fine distinctions. A refusal to sustain' the Democrat majority would be 'read as a refusal to sustain the war and to sustain the efforts of our peace commission to secure the fruits of war'.[32] It was an appeal fully in line with Wilson's vision of presidential leadership. But it was a shockingly presumptuous break with precedent and it was widely seen as having tipped the electoral balance against him. On 5 November 1918 the Republicans won majorities in both houses of Congress. Wilson's bitter opponent Henry Cabot Lodge emerged as Senate majority leader and chair of the Foreign Relations Committee.

There is no question that much of the invective hurled at Wilson and the Democrats in 1918 was irresponsible. It spread like a virus through the American political system, helping to prepare the ground for the delirious Red Scare in 1919. The accusation that Democrats sympathized with socialism and were ipso facto unpatriotic has echoed through demagogic right-wing discourse in America down to the present day. But this should not obscure the substance of the disagreement. Wilson's unilateral diplomacy was an extraordinary power play. It was motivated not by his concern for German democracy but by a desire to subordinate Britain and France to his particular vision of American power. Wilson's Republican critics envisioned a very different peace. As Roosevelt confirmed to British Foreign Secretary Lord Balfour, America should stand 'for the unconditional surrender of Germany and for absolute loyalty to France and England in the peace negotiations . . . America should act, not as an umpire between our allies and our enemies, but as one of the allies bound to come to an agreement with them.' 'While we gladly welcome any feasible scheme for a League of Nations, we prefer that it should begin with our present allies, and be accepted only as an addition to and in no sense a substitute for the preparedness of our own strength and for our own defenses.'[33] To a journalist friend Roosevelt spoke of a working agreement between the British Empire and the United States that he was now content to call 'an alliance'.[34] Wilson's main Republican opponents were no more isolationists than Clemenceau and Lloyd George were reactionaries. What they had in common was their rejection of Wilson's peculiar vision of American global leadership. Their concept of a post-war order would be based on a privileged strategic alliance between the United States and the other states they recognized as partners in an exclusive democratic club, above all Britain and France. This was a vision that was both menacing to Germany and profoundly distasteful to Wilson. In this respect his alignment with Berlin was no mere figment of the partisan imagination.

12
Democracy Under Pressure

Between October and December 1918 the old world of Europe collapsed. Revolution swept away not only the Habsburgs and the Hohenzollern, but along with them the royal houses of Bavaria, Saxony and Württemberg, eleven Duchies and Grand Duchies, and seven smaller German principalities. They were not much lamented. Germany, Austria and Hungary all declared themselves republics, as did Poland and Czechoslovakia, Finland, Latvia, Lithuania and Estonia. One of the remarkable things about interwar Europe, whatever its other political challenges, was the impotence of restorationist monarchism. The only exception to republican rule was the new South Slav state of Yugoslavia, built around the Serbian royal house that was relegitimized as the anchor of national identity in the course of the war. But the fall of dynasties was, as the Russian revolution had demonstrated, only the first phase. What would come next? As in Russia in 1917, in central Europe during the autumn of 1918 it was social democrats and liberals who dominated the scene. True communists were a tiny minority everywhere. Nevertheless, it was easy to imagine the Soviet regime lurking expectantly to the East. A day after the republic was declared in Berlin, the chief Soviet newspaper, *Pravda*, called for 10 November 1918 to be celebrated as a national holiday to mark the uprising of the German working class. Was this the signal for world revolution?

Certainly, as Woodrow Wilson embarked for Europe on the first ever such tour by an American President, he imagined himself as the centre of a global storm. 'The conservatives do not realize what forces are loose in the world at the present time,' Wilson lectured his staff in December 1918 onboard the SS *George Washington*. 'Liberalism is the only thing that can save civilization from chaos – from a flood of ultra-radicalism that will swamp the world . . . Liberalism must be more liberal than ever before, it must even be radical, if civilization is to escape the typhoon.'[1] If Russia offered one vision of global revolution, to many Wilson seemed to offer another. Having been written into the Armistice, the 14 Points now acquired an extraordinary global currency. In Korea, China and Japan demonstrators carried Wilson's slogan on their banners. In the mountains of Kurdistan, the Turkish nationalist leader Kemal Ataturk found himself confronted with the worldly younger sons of tribal chieftains insisting that Turkish-Kurdish relations be settled on the basis of the 14 Points.[2] In the deserts of Libya the local Berber resistance, negotiating in the name of the newly founded Tripolitanian Republic, lectured their Italian foes that 'the age of imperialism had waned and that what had been possible in the nineteenth century was no longer possible in the second decade of the twentieth century'. They made peace on strictly Wilsonian terms and celebrated the occasion with a cavalcade of motor vehicles featuring effigies of the League of Nations.[3]

The widening of political horizons heralded by such incidents was dramatic. It speaks to our global age in much the same way that the image of a stand-off between Lenin and Wilson spoke to historians writing in the era of the Cold War.[4] But the worldwide revolution of 1919 is an event that did not happen, either in its Wilsonian or Leninist varieties. In Europe, revolution spread neither as far nor as wide as it had done three generations earlier in 1848.[5] The defeat of radical socialism in 1919 was even more decisive than the setback suffered by Europe's Liberals in 1848. Wilson's 'revolution' ended in a notorious fiasco. Lenin and Wilson died within weeks of each other in early 1924 as deeply disappointed men. True believing Wilsonians and fellow travellers of Leninism have ever since derived dramatic conclusions from this failure. The aborted or failed revolution of 1918–19, it is said, shaped the rest of the twentieth century. It was the conservatism, the rancorous nationalism, the inveterate imperialism of the 'old world' that frustrated both Lenin and Wilson and made impossible any true break with the past.[6] Instead, the violence of the Great War was stitched together with the even greater violence that was to come.

But the narrative of failure, whether Marxist-Leninist or Wilsonian, should not blind us to the forces that did work their way through the crisis. If there was no revolution, there was no comprehensive counter-revolution either. Though they did not conform to either the Leninist or the Wilsonian script, very powerful forces of change had been unleashed by the war. If the outcome was more conservative than the adherents of Wilson and Lenin hoped for, what must be acknowledged is the ambiguous influence these self-proclaimed champions of progress had in helping to bring about that disappointing result.

I

In November 1918, as he recovered from the near-fatal wound inflicted by his enraged assassin, Lenin, far from thinking himself on the revolutionary offensive, was in a state of deep anxiety. Though he was delighted to see the spread of the revolution from its Russian beginnings to a world movement, it was for him a moment of unprecedented danger. Since seizing power Lenin had imagined himself balancing Imperial Germany against the overwhelming power of the Entente. Now the German counterweight was gone. As Lenin commented, 'when Germany is being torn apart by the revolutionary movement at home, the British and French imperialists consider themselves masters of the world'.[7] The intervention in Russia that had begun in July 1918 would surely intensify. As to the German revolution itself, Lenin was just as cautious as he had been about the February revolution in Russia. The patriotic German Socialists who had taken power in November were no better than the 'liberal imperialists' of the Entente. The precipitate withdrawal of German troops from Ukraine allowed Bolshevik forces to seize control of Kiev. Trotsky was rapidly mobilizing hundreds of thousands of men in the newly formed Red Army. But the challenge faced by Lenin and Trotsky was enormous. With or without the Treaty of Brest-Litovsk, great swaths of what had once been the Tsarist Empire had declared independence. Japanese, American, British and French troops held bridgeheads stretching from the far north to the Crimea and Siberia. Substantial counter-revolutionary armies were gathering on every side – General Yevgeny Miller's forces in the north behind a British screen at Archangel; Nikolai Yudenich's army in the Baltic, collaborating with the Finns, the Germans and Estonians; Anton Denikin's Volunteer Army in the south with Cossack and Anglo-French support; Alexander Kolchak's army in the east, which took over the positions held by the Czech Legion in Siberia.[8] Far from looming over western Europe, there had not been a time in two centuries when Russian power seemed so reduced and hemmed in.

There were voices amongst the Entente who, as Lenin imagined, wanted to destroy the Soviet regime completely. For Winston Churchill, soon to take over as Secretary of State for War, the Bolshevik menace had to be eradicated. As he telegraphed in January 1919, 'What sort of Peace shd [sic] we have, if all of Europe and Asia from Warsaw to Vladivostok were under the sway of Lenin?'[9] On 29 December 1918 France had announced a comprehensive blockade designed to weaken the Soviet regime fatally. But if the politics of revolutionary internationalism were hemmed in, so too were the politics of counter-revolution.[10] The intervention in July had been triggered not, as Lenin imagined, by hostility toward the Bolsheviks, but by his apparent determination to throw his regime into the hands of Imperial Germany. Rather than uniting capitalist imperialism against the Communist regime, it was Germany's surrender that saved the Soviet government. The Armistice not only spared Lenin the odium of an ever closer alliance with Ludendorff. It also took the impetus out of the intervention almost before it began. Furthermore, with the Germans on the retreat, it was now the White, anti-Bolshevik forces, not the Bolsheviks, who appeared to patriotic Russians as the lackeys of foreign power.

When the governments of the major powers convened at the Quai d'Orsay in Paris on 16 January 1919 to discuss the Russian situation, Lloyd George made clear his position.[11] He did not doubt that the Bolsheviks were at least as 'dangerous to civilization' as the militarists of Germany. A case could be made for their outright destruction. But given the growing strength of the Red Army, that was no longer a minor undertaking. It would require an invasion by at least 400,000 men. Amidst the universal desire for demobilization, no one in the room was willing to commit the necessary resources. To end the war with Germany only to begin an all-out assault on Russia would stir up outrage in the West. As Lloyd George commented to the British war cabinet: 'Our citizen army will go anywhere for Liberty, but they could not be convinced', whatever the Prime Minister himself believed, 'that the suppression of Bolshevism was a war for liberty.'[12] The 10,000 sailors of the French navy sent to the Crimea had already mutinied.[13] The Entente could continue the policy of blockade. But, Lloyd George went on, there were 150 million civilians in Russia. The policy of blockade was not a 'health cordon, it was a death cordon'. And it would not be the Bolsheviks who died, but those Russians whom the Entente wanted to help. That left only one alternative: to negotiate. But with whom and under what circumstances?

Lloyd George favoured summoning all the warring Russian parties to Paris 'to appear before' America and the great powers of the Entente 'somewhat in the way that the Roman Empire summoned chiefs of outlying tributary states ...'. But the staunchly anti-Bolshevik French would hear nothing of it. They would 'make no contract with crime'.[14] Nor would they abandon their anti-Bolshevik allies in Russia. France had more to lose in Russia than any other power. Eventually, agreement was reached on the proposal to invite all the Russian parties to a conference quarantined on the Princes' Islands in the Sea of Marmara. Georges Clemenceau agreed only to avoid a break with Britain and America.

On the Soviet side the idea of negotiating with Wilson and the Entente reopened the wounds of Brest-Litovsk. Trotsky opposed any talks. The Red Army fought on, regardless of the calls for a ceasefire. But Lenin signalled that he was willing to talk. The collapse of the planned conference was therefore blamed on the Whites who, with the encouragement from hardliners in London and Paris, refused the invitation to parlay. This reopened the door to the interventionists. Between 14 and 17 February 1919, with Lloyd George absent from Paris, Churchill attempted to gain American backing for a military solution. But both Wilson and Lloyd George refused. Instead, Wilson dispatched one of his most radical advisors, William Bullitt, to Russia. He held intensive conversations with Georgy Chicherin and Lenin, but by the time Bullitt returned to the West in late March, the conference was too preoccupied with the German peace to want to address the hugely controversial issue of Russia. Meanwhile, Lloyd George retreated into arguing that if Russians were as profoundly anti-Bolshevik as was often claimed, they ought to put paid to Lenin themselves. Woodrow Wilson too preferred to let the Russians fight it out. By May the worst fear of revolutionary contagion had passed.

The pressure either to come to terms with or to eliminate the Soviet threat altogether would have been more serious if there had been a real risk of a new Russo-German alliance. But over the winter of 1918–19,

Lenin was far more interested in conciliating the Entente than he was in cultivating relations with Germany's new republic, and the feeling was amply reciprocated. The war had spoken its verdict. Whatever the far-flung fantasies of revolutionaries and counter-revolutionaries, the centre of power lay in the West, not the East.[15] Neither of the two wings of German socialism, the SPD and the USPD, was friendly to the dictatorship in Russia. Lenin's regime and the chaos unfolding in Russia were distasteful reminders of the miscarriage of German policy in the East. It was no surprise that Germany's new republic moved rapidly to close the Soviet embassy in Berlin and to wave aside the offer of Russian grain deliveries. Nor was it a coincidence that the two most direct political challenges to the Soviet regime both came from within the left in Germany. On the far left Rosa Luxemburg called for an uprising of the German working class that would unleash a genuine Marxist revolution, putting Lenin's top-down dictatorship in the shade.[16] From the centre ground Karl Kautsky, long the pope of the SPD's orthodox Marxism, denounced the Soviet Terror and called for socialists to acknowledge their stake in the institutions of parliamentary democracy.[17]

Establishing Germany's own democracy was the first order of the day.[18] The SPD and their friends in the Reichstag majority wanted to push as soon as possible toward elections to a Constituent Assembly, the date being set for the third week of January 1919. But for the USPD and the small minority even further to the left, this threatened the entire revolution. As Rosa Luxemburg put it, 'To resort to the National Assembly today is consciously or unconsciously to turn the revolution back to the historical stage of bourgeois revolutions' – it was to hand the revolution back to its enemies.[19] Holding Germany's elections in January would freeze the new status quo. If Germany was to have a true revolutionary moment, it must not re-enact the French revolution of 1789, but move forward immediately to a Soviet system, the promise of the future. To Luxemburg's horror, when Germany's Congress of Soviets met in Berlin in December 1918 the vast majority of the delegates voted for democratization. They wanted socialization of heavy industry and thoroughgoing reform of the army. But above all they wanted the Constituent Assembly. With this endorsement the SPD pressed ahead to hold elections in the third week of January. And to make doubly sure, they consolidated their position with two 'understandings'. One was between trade unions and employers, to preserve the functioning of Germany's economy.[20] The other was between the provisional government and the remnants of the army command. On a charitable reading, what united these understandings was the determination to ensure that there would be no descent into 'Bolshevik conditions' in Germany, no chaos or civil war.[21] What the SPD feared was a second instalment of the disorder that had swept through Germany in the week before 9 November 1918.

This fear was, as it turned out, not entirely misplaced. But it was precisely the clumsy efforts by the government to assert control that brought on the chaos. When revolutionary soldiers' units in Berlin refused to vacate the centre of the city and demanded their pay, the result, over the Christmas and New Year holiday, was serious street fighting in the German capital. Meanwhile, with Rosa Luxemburg and Karl Liebknecht in the lead, the Spartakist faction coalesced on 1 January 1919 with other ultra-left groups to form the German Communist Party (KPD). It would take the lead where both the MSPD and the USPD were failing. When the dismissal of the mutinous left-leaning police president of Berlin triggered huge street demonstrations on 5 January, this tiny group decided, against the vote of Luxemburg, that the time had come for action. Small and weakly armed squads of Communists and sympathizers from the USPD set up barricades and occupied the offices of the SPD's newspapers, an open act of defiance in the centre of the capital. How would the provisional government respond? When Gustav Noske, the Peoples' Commissioner for Military Affairs, demanded that the uprising be put down, Friedrich Ebert as head of the SPD retorted that he should 'do it himself!' To which Noske, according to his own memoirs, responded: 'So be it! Someone has got to be the bloodhound!'[22] After mediation failed, on the morning of Saturday 11 January, regular army troops under Noske's command blasted their way through the barricades to the Reich Chancellery. There Ebert made an appearance, thanking the troops for their part in enabling the National Assembly to go ahead despite the resistance of an irresponsible minority, who had courted civil war. Fifty-three leading members of the revolutionary committee were taken prisoner, put on trial, and eventually acquitted in the summer of 1919. Karl Liebknecht and Rosa Luxemburg, the most hated figures on the far left, were not so fortunate. They were seized on 15 January, bludgeoned, and shot to death. It was this murder, not the violence of the uprising, in which perhaps as many as 200 people died, that tarnished the image of

Noske's politics of order. This was not republican discipline. It was counter-revolutionary barbarity licensed by the SPD. The news of the murders sent a wave of horror through the ranks of the party. There were calls for the government to resign. But Noske's response was hard-boiled: 'War is War.'[23]

The violent clashes were a disaster for the German far left. But they were not a prelude to a military dictatorship. A week after the suppression of the Spartakist uprising on 19 January 1919, 30 million men and women, over 83 per cent of Germany's adult population, cast their votes for the Constituent Assembly. It was by far the most impressive democratic display anywhere in the Western world in the aftermath of World War I. Three million more Germans voted than in the US presidential election of 1920, though Germany's population was 61 million versus the 107 million of the United States. The SPD topped the poll with 38 per cent of the vote. For a society as internally divided as Germany this was remarkable. It was more than any party had ever won in German history. It was more than Hitler was to garner at the peak of his electoral popularity in 1932. No party would exceed this share of the vote until the triumphs of Konrad Adenauer at the height of the post-war economic miracle in the 1950s. But it was far short of a majority and the SPD's putative partners in a government of socialist unity, the far left USPD, added only 7.6 per cent. By this point, thanks to the violence in Berlin, a coalition between the SPD and the USPD was out of the question in any case. They had taken up opposite sides in an unequal civil war.

Although the vote of January 1919 was a vote against a socialist republic, it was not a vote for reaction. In setting its face against the socialist adventurism of the far left, the SPD affirmed its commitment to the strategy it had pursued since the summer of 1917. Together with the Catholic Centre Party and Progressive Liberals, the SPD would form a democratic majority so substantial that it could marginalize both the extreme left and the extreme right. In the last pre-war election, in 1912, the three parties of the Reichstag majority – the SPD, Centre Party and Progressive Liberals – had won two-thirds of the vote. On 19 January 1919 together they commanded a massive 76 per cent of the vote. The German electorate had delivered a resounding majority not for socialist revolution but for democratization and the diplomacy that had achieved such a remarkably favourable armistice. The right wing, including the Bismarckian National Liberals of Gustav Stresemann's ilk, was reduced to less than 15 per cent of the vote. Spurred on by this dramatic result, the majority parties set about drafting a capacious republican constitution that would incorporate both liberal freedoms and the basic demands of social democracy. With the ranks solidified they braced themselves to face the peace.

II

Back in 1871, after crushing the Paris Commune a republic had imposed itself with force against the demand for socialist revolution. In 1919 the same violent verdict was delivered in Germany. What implications did this have for European socialism and its role in post-war reconstruction? Two weeks after the German elections, on 3 February, both the SPD and the USPD dispatched delegates to the first post-war conference of the Second Socialist International, in Berne.[24] As the successor to the pre-war International, it was attended by 26 national parties. It was the first time since 1914 that German and Austrian delegates confronted their former comrades from the French Socialist Party and the British Labour movement. Through a display of refound unity, the organizers hoped to rally support for a politics of democratic transformation that refused the violence of the Bolsheviks. They also hoped to add their weight to President Wilson's efforts to craft a 'democratic peace'. As he embarked on several weeks of tours through the capitals of the Entente in December 1918, Wilson had made clear that he welcomed the support of the European left. On his arrival in France it was the Socialist Party that took the lead in welcoming the President. When on 27 December he was hosted at Buckingham Palace he appeared in pointedly plain attire and struck a resolutely Cromwellian pose. His message was blunt: 'You must not speak of us who come over here as cousins, still less as brothers; we are neither. Neither must you think of us as Anglo-Saxons, for that term can no longer be rightly applied to the people of the US. Nor must too much importance in this connection be attached to the fact that English is our common language ... no, there are only two things which can establish and maintain closer relations between your country and mine: they are community of ideals and of interests.'[25] Wilson made no secret of the fact that, as far as he was concerned, the community of values was embodied far more in the opposition Labour Party than Lloyd George's coalition.

It was no coincidence therefore that the British Labour movement was amongst the leading forces behind the Wilsonian agenda of the Berne conference.[26] But the conference itself, far from mobilizing an imposing wave of opinion, was a shambles. What became painfully apparent were the multiple fault lines running through European socialism, which threatened to reduce it either to civil war, as in Germany, or to a state of near paralysis. The Italian Socialists were the only party to have come through the war united around a radical agenda. But that meant they refused to attend the Berne conference. They would have no truck with an assembly of 'national chauvinists', most of whom had betrayed the cause of internationalism by supporting their national war efforts. Instead, the Italian Socialists became one of the first western European parties to take up Lenin's invitation to join the new Third International, the Communist International or Comintern, which held its first sparsely attended meeting in Moscow on 19 March 1919. The French Socialist Party also managed to preserve its organizational unity, but, as its performance at the Berne conference was to reveal, only at the expense of complete ideological and practical incoherence.

At the opening session, the right wing of the French socialist delegation, the so-called 'patriotic' socialists, who had served in French governments until the crisis of 1917, monopolized the meeting by demanding to recap the fateful events in July 1914. Where had their German comrades been when it counted? Given the rancour left by the war, this was predictable. But it was fundamentally at odds with the Wilsonian internationalism officially professed by the organizers with their rhetoric of a 'peace of equals', or the stance of Ramsay MacDonald of the British Independent Labour Party, who blamed the Franco-Russian alliance as much as the Germans for the outbreak of war. The two days of bludgeoning debate between the right wing of the French socialists and the majority SPD came close to derailing the entire conference. The SPD were happy to condemn the folly of the Kaiser, but only as one imperialist among others. What did the German socialists have to apologize for? Should they have surrendered in August 1914 to Franco-Russian imperialism, or to the threat of starvation by the British? They came to Berne as a party that had overthrown the Kaiser and made a revolution. Why should they humble themselves before

French comrades who had done nothing to break with their own country's imperialist past? If the French wanted to settle the Alsace-Lorraine question on democratic grounds, let there be a plebiscite. But the patriotic wing of the French socialist delegation would not hear of it. As Wilson himself had acknowledged, Alsace-Lorraine was not a question of self-determination, but simply of restorative justice.[27]

By comparison with the recalcitrant patriotism of the right wing of both the French and German socialist parties, Kurt Eisner, the spokesman of the German left-wing USPD, cut a brilliant figure. The acting Prime Minister of Bavaria, alone amongst all the delegations, was willing to condemn not only imperialism in general, but to admit his nation's principal culpability.[28] It was this willingness to break the patriotic ranks that in 1919 would transform the USPD into the acceptable face of German democracy, as far as the Allies were concerned.[29] But by the same token it made Eisner and his comrades disastrously unpopular with the German electorate. In early 1919, faced with the guns of the Freikorps paramilitaries, the USPD shifted further to the left, adopting the Bolshevik slogan of all power to the Soviets and flirting with affiliation to Lenin's Comintern. The party paid the price, and not only in votes. On 21 February, 11 days after the end of the Berne conference, having accepted the verdict of his party's crushing defeat in the National Assembly election, Eisner was on his way through the streets of Munich to submit his resignation as Prime Minister when he was gunned down by a right-wing assassin.

The subject of violence was on the agenda at Berne. But what preoccupied the majority of the conference was not the, as yet, sporadic attacks from the right. What concerned them was the systematic class terror openly advocated by Lenin and Trotsky. The organizers wanted to follow Kautsky, who attended the conference as a delegate for the USPD, in distancing European socialism from this violent dogma. The social democratic Second International would soon dispatch a delegation to give encouragement to the embattled republic of Georgia, where social democracy was struggling to establish itself against the looming threat of the Red Army. But at Berne, there was no unity on the question of Bolshevism. After the right wing of the French Socialist Party had monopolized the first two days with their anti-German campaign, it was now the turn of the French left wing to unite with the radical fringe of the Austrian Socialist Party to block any common resolution on the question of dictatorship in Russia.

The one motion at Berne that did not provoke protests from one or other wing of the French Socialists was the vote of approval for Wilson's promise of a progressive peace and the League of Nations. There were, of course, good reasons for reformist Social Democrats to take this stand. A strong League of Nations would provide the international mediation that had been so tragically lacking in July 1914. A coordinated international approach to labour legislation would remove cut-throat foreign competition as the most telling argument against national welfare measures. It made sense for a gathering of labour movements to demand that the League of Nations be based on properly democratic principles. But the spokesmen of the radical left could easily have found reason, as the Leninist Comintern was soon to do, to dismiss any such talk as 'bourgeois internationalism'. In Berne, the left wing stayed their hand. Whatever their other differences, if there was one thing German and French socialists of every stripe could agree on, it was their delight in the shadow that Wilson was casting over the 'imperialists', Clemenceau and Lloyd George.[30]

No doubt negative stereotyping can serve a useful purpose in fostering political cohesion, and Wilsonian internationalism might have helped to weld together the disunited European labour movement as a democratic force. But though it did salve the wounds, socialist Wilsonianism was too weak a force to restore the unity sundered by the war and the Bolshevik seizure of power. With Lenin consolidating his grip in Russia, the idea that a unified left, stretching from Rosa Luxemburg to Gustav Noske, could gain a democratic majority anywhere in central or western Europe, was a mirage. In many places, a democratic programme of national reform did command a majority. However, it was one built not on a unified socialist bloc, but, as Germany demonstrated, on a decision by the right wing of social democracy to drop the far left and to opt for a coalition with Christian Democrats and Liberals.[31] This was a painful choice. As the German example demonstrated, it could have lethal repercussions for the far left, all the more so if they gave repression a chance by espousing the rhetoric and the practice of Leninist civil war. Wilsonianism did not make it any easier. By casting suspicion on the likes of Erzberger, Clemenceau and Lloyd George, Wilsonian rhetoric helped to discredit precisely the figures on whom the prospects for a broad-based progressive coalition, in fact, depended. By offering moderate social democrats the false hope of a radical internationalism that was not Bolshevism, Wilsonianism made broad-based progressive coalitions less, not more, thinkable. Nowhere were the ironic consequences more evident than in Britain, the least Bolshevik and most Wilsonian of Europe's labour movements.

III

In Britain a more or less explicit alliance between the mainstream Liberal Party and organized Labour had been a mainstay of radical reform since the 1870s. In 1914 the vast majority of the Labour movement had rallied to the war. Since December 1916, Lloyd George had made sure always to include a trade union representative in the inner circle of his war cabinet. But the peace debate unleashed by Wilson in 1917 put this incorporation under real pressure. Since 1914 Ramsay MacDonald had led a small minority in opposition to the war, entertaining close relations with the Union of Democratic Control, the British grouping of radical liberals that served as a sounding board for Woodrow Wilson. In 1917 this anti-war bloc gathered far greater weight when the formerly pro-war Labourite Arthur Henderson abandoned the Lloyd George government over its refusal to allow him to attend the Stockholm peace conference. Lloyd George's January 1918 declaration of war aims was an effort to hold the Labour Party behind the war, but with Henderson in the lead the labour movement was now preparing to compete not as a Liberal auxiliary, but as an alternative government.[32] With the franchise having been vastly expanded, there seemed no reason why Labour should not claim a majority of the electorate that was now overwhelmingly working class.

In due course, these predictions were to be confirmed. The fact that between 1923 and 1945 Britain was to elect a Labour government three times on a platform committed to a British form of socialism, ought to be counted amongst the more remarkable peaceful transitions of modern political history. But it was only in 1945 that Labour on its own was in a position to win an outright majority. Both in 1923 and 1929 the Labour governments depended on Liberal support. In 1918 the party's overconfidence was to exact a high price. When Lloyd George decided to call a quick post-war election and offered Labour candidates safe seats on his coalition ticket, the party leadership refused. Counting on their new national organization, contesting almost half the seats, Labour expected to make dramatic gains and wanted to draw a clean line between itself and the government it now denounced as warmongering.[33] Instead, on 14 December, the government scored a crushing electoral victory. Lloyd George and his Tory coalition partners virtually eliminated the rump of the Liberal Party led by former Prime Minister Herbert Asquith. Of 300 Labour candidates only 57 entered the House of Commons.

Ironically, rather than being celebrated as a triumph of democratic reform, the first election under Britain's new comprehensive franchise became notorious as a triumph of jingoist nationalism. Under the shadow cast by Wilson, the 'khaki election' was greeted by a barrage of criticism not from the right, but from the left. Faced with the 'degradation of this Parliament' Ramsay MacDonald, who had lost his seat, despaired altogether of human nature.[34] Lloyd George and his Tory partners had, it seemed, found a way to turn democracy into a vehicle for reaction. Lloyd George, the staunch opponent of the Boer War, stood accused of pandering to the basest instincts of nationalism. The sense of having been cheated was only amplified by the arbitrariness of Westminster's first-past-the-post constituency system. Although Asquithians, Liberals and Labour gained more than one-third of the electorate, they won only one-eighth of the seats.[35] But though this rankled, the vagaries of the Westminster system were predictable and they did not make the system inherently conservative. In 1906 it had given the Lib-Lab coalition a landslide. During the reform debates of 1917, it was the Conservatives who had pushed for proportional representation, wanting to protect themselves against what they took to be the inevitable working-class majority under a universal franchise. But though the electorate did indeed expand by two-thirds in 1918 as compared with 1910, what the government had not reckoned with was the suicidal incompetence of their opponents. In 1918 the Labour Party made no arrangement with the Asquithian Liberals, thus splitting the opposition vote, with predictable results.

The Coalition, however, was under no illusion about the actual popular mood. Jingoistic demonstrations and newspaper headlines aside, they knew that there was no tidal wave of nationalist enthusiasm behind the government. Despite Lloyd George's encouragement of the 'trench vote', the vast majority of the soldiers were too exhausted and apathetic to turn out. The Conservatives gained their huge share of the House of Commons seats from only 32.5 per cent of the electorate, a lower share than in any British election in the twentieth century other than the historic defeats of 1945 and 1997. Of course, this was in part an effect of their coalition agreement with Lloyd George. But the Tory leadership were convinced that Lloyd George was essential as a shield against the rise of Labour.[36] And the modest electoral share was to prove a persistent feature of Tory electoral fortunes in the 1920s, a decade in which they broke the 40 per cent threshold only once. Despite the superficial dominance of the Coalition in Parliament, it was clear that the ground was shifting. In the election in Britain on 14 December 1918, the trade unions were strong enough to pay for half of Labour's candidates.[37] And this was backed outside Parliament by a truly unprecedented wave of labour mobilization.

The upsurge in working-class militancy between 1910 and 1920 was a phenomenon that swept the entire world.[38] Rather than seeing it as a mere epiphenomenon of the socialist revolution that did not happen, it deserves to be seen as a transformative event in its own right. In the United States, in the last 18 months of Wilson's presidency, it was to unleash a veritable right-wing panic. In France, the delegates to the Versailles peace conference witnessed street battles on May Day 1919. By the summer of 1919 Rome appeared on the point of losing control of much of urban Italy. The surge of militancy in Britain may not have been so radical in its rhetoric, but it was nevertheless formidable. Whilst the British Empire was still battering at the Hindenburg line, the Lloyd George government faced a police strike and a serious railway stoppage.[39] So worrying was the situation that the government authorized local police forces to call on military assistance (Table 6).[40]

With the war at an end, repression gave way to a major dose of conciliation. On 13 November 1918 Lloyd George signalled generosity by promising to maintain the real purchasing of wages at their armistice level. But wage increases were no longer the only trade union demand. Across Europe, America and even in the ranks of the nascent Asian labour movement, the eight-hour day was as much a symbol of the new order as the League of Nations. In December, facing the threat of a

Table 6. War, Inflation and Labour Militancy, 1914–21:
The Number of Strikes

	1914	1915	1916	1917	1918	1919	1920	1921
Denmark	44	43	66	215	253	472	243	110
France	672	98	314	696	499	2026	1832	475
Germany	1233	141	240	562	532	3719	3807	4455
Italy	905	608	577	470	313	1871	2070	1134
Netherlands	271	269	377	344	325	649	481	299
Russia	3534	928	1288	707				
Spain	212	169	237	306	463	895	1060	373
Sweden	115	80	227	475	708	440	486	347
UK	972	672	532	730	1165	1352	1607	763
USA	1204	1593	3789	4450	3353	3630	3411	2835

general railway strike, Lloyd George forced his Conservative cabinet colleagues to agree to the introduction of the eight-hour day at full pay. Clemenceau followed suit in the spring of 1919, as did the Weimar Republic. The third major trade union demand was for the state to assume control of key industries. In Britain the key battleground's were the coalmines, which were overwhelmingly most important source of fossil fuel not only for the UK, but for much of the rest of Europe. The so-called 'Triple Alliance', a coalition of railway workers, dockers and miners, had the capacity to paralyse not just Britain but the entire inter-Allied supply network.

Unlike the political leadership of the Labour Party, however, the trade unions displayed a clear sense of the realities of power. They knew their own strength, but they also appreciated that an all-out strike would leave the government with no option but to resort to force. As Ernest Bevin, the leader of the powerful Transport Workers' Union, put it, if the 'Triple Alliance' were to activate their threat, 'I think it must be civil war, for I cannot see how it is possible, once all the TU are brought in, for the government to avoid fighting for the supremacy and power, and I do not believe that our people, if they knew what it meant, would be prepared to plunge into it.'[41] Given the failure of the Labour Party in the elections, Lloyd George would have Parliament behind him. Both sides had too great a stake in Britain's self-image as a 'peaceable kingdom' to risk such a clash. Instead, both the unions and the Lloyd George coalition preferred to haggle.

On 24 February 1919, to placate the Triple Alliance, Lloyd George persuaded the Miners' Federation of Great Britain to agree to a Royal Commission on nationalization. In November 1918 the Prime Minister had signed up his reluctant Tory partners to a platform boldly entitled a 'Democratic Programme of Reconstruction'. With remarkable frankness the Conservative Party leader Andrew Bonar Law spelled out to the patrician Lord Balfour the logic of this arrangement. It might be tempting for the Tories to break with their erstwhile nemesis, Lloyd George. But if they did so they risked facing a 'combined Liberal and Labour party . . .'. Even if the Conservatives were able to muster a majority on their own, the resulting polarization would be highly dangerous. 'The only chance . . . of a rational solution' to the vast array of reconstruction problems was that they should be addressed by a government that was drawn not from one 'section' of British society but from elements of all the main camps. Then there would 'at least be a chance that the reforms, which undoubtedly will be necessary, should be made in a way which was as little revolutionary as possible'.[42] At crucial moments Lloyd George reminded his cabinet colleagues of this basic political insight. After what they had spent on securing victory in the war, it was nonsense to squabble over hundreds of millions needed to secure domestic peace. If the war had lasted another year, would they not have somehow or another raised another £2 billion? Compared to that, '£71 million was cheap insurance against Bolshevism'.[43]

Of course, wartime spending habits could not be continued indefinitely. On 30 April 1919, Chancellor Austen Chamberlain presented Parliament with a budget that cut public spending in half.[44] But whereas military spending was slashed, one-fifth of the budget was set aside to subsidize bread prices and railway fares and to pay for war pensions and other costs of demobilization. Never before had welfare spending been given such clear priority over imperial defence.

Before the war Lloyd George had proved himself as one of the great architects of modern democracy, in his struggle with the House of Lords over the creation of a modern progressive tax system. His challenge back then had been to find a democratic basis on which to pay both for increased welfare spending and the naval arms race with the Kaiser's Germany. In 1919, having contributed to the defeat of Germany, his government faced a fiscal crisis of unimagined proportions. In 1914 British public debt had stood at only £694.8 million. Five years later the figure had mounted to a dizzying £6.142 billion, of which £1 billion was owed to America, and not in sterling but in dollars (Table 7).[45] Already in 1919 debt service amounted to 25 per cent of the budget and would in the foreseeable future rise to something closer to 40 per cent. These burdens were heavy, but Britain was rich. The load both of domestic and foreign debt on France and Italy was proportionally even heavier. According to contemporary estimates public debt contracted during the war came to 60 per cent of pre-war national wealth in Italy as opposed to 50 per cent in Britain and only 13 per cent in the US.[46]

On 11 December 1918, in an impromptu speech in Bristol, Lloyd George had made his most inflamatory statement of the 'khaki' election campaign. When it came to reparations, he announced to a cheering crowd, the Germans should not expect to get off easily – 'we shall search their pockets'.[47] With this resort to populism, Lloyd George's critics alleged, the Prime Minister opened the door to disaster at the Versailles peace conference. But to see his speech as mere demagoguery ignores

Table 7. The New Hierarchy of Financial Power: An American Assessment of Budget Positions Ahead of Versailles, December 1918 (billion $)

	Germany	GB	France	Italy	USA
total national wealth of all kinds (pre-war)	75.0	75.0	60.0	20.0	250.0
annual national income pre-war	10.0	11.0	7.0	3.0	40.0
government debt before war	1.2	3.5	6.6	2.9	1.0
government debt at the end of the war	40.0	40.0	28.0	12.0	23.0
interest charges on post-war debt (no sinking fund)	2.0	2.0	1.4	0.6	1.0
current income from taxation	1.9	4.0	1.5	0.9	4.0
pre-war savings	2.5	2.5	0.9	0.4	5.0
pre-war trade balance	−0.4	−0.7	−0.3	−0.2	0.7
pre-war spending on army	0.3	0.1	0.2	0.1	0.1
pre-war spending on navy	0.1	0.2	0.1	0.1	0.2

the reality of the financial crisis and the unprecedented severity of social conflict. Despite the talk of a Wilsonian peace without indemnities on the Labour left, reparations were not a simple left-right issue. If repayment of the war debts was not to stymie any effort to create a fairer society by means of public education, social insurance and public housing – the agenda shared by new liberals and reformist socialists across Europe – some additional source of funding had to be found. As John Maynard Keynes, later one of the arch-critics of reparations, admitted in the spring of 1919, the 'intense popular feeling . . . on the question of indemnities . . .' was not based on 'any reasonable calculation of what Germany can, in fact, pay'. It was based on a very 'well-founded appreciation of the intolerable situation' that would arise for the European victors if Germany did not carry a substantial fraction of the burden.[48] When Lloyd George, the father of Britain's system of social insurance, spoke of searching the Germans' pockets for reparations, what he was promising anxious middle-class taxpayers was that these immense new burdens would not be borne by them alone.

Of course, to Lloyd George's critics this was precisely the demagoguery: to link widows' pensions with German reparations. A liberal peace was perfectly compatible with domestic reform so long as governments had the courage to impose heavy taxation on their own wealthy elites.[49] A capital levy, a tax on wealth as opposed to income, was much discussed in Britain in 1919, as it was in France and Germany. It was given serious attention by some of the most influential economists of the day, including in His Majesty's Treasury, the bastion of economic orthodoxy.[50] As their pre-war track records demonstrated, neither Clemenceau nor Lloyd George was averse to soaking the rich. But to carry such a radical measure would have required precisely the kind of broad-based radical coalition between Liberals and Labour that neither the French Socialists nor the British Labour Party would contemplate. It was the failure of the left to offer a viable alternative majority that foreclosed more radical financial options.

In any case, the fact that a capital levy was not widely adopted did not mean that Europe's elite escaped unscathed. Everywhere tax rates were pushed to unprecedented levels. Despite the failure of ambitions to outright revolution, whether through inflation or taxation, one of the consequences of World War I was to initiate an unprecedented levelling of wealth across Europe. This was not a shift limited to one country.

None of the major European combatants would ever be the same again. More than that, it was an interlinked process. Through reparations and the vast international debts accumulated during the war, the governments and societies of Europe were interlocked as never before. On 27 May 1919, France's unfortunate Finance Minister Louis-Lucien Klotz found himself calling upon the Chamber of Deputies to approve painful tax increases, so as to demonstrate to 'our allies that France still knows how to make the sacrifices the situation demands, and thus deserves ... the maintenance of the agreements in the military, economic, and financial sphere, which have produced the victory of right over might'.[51]

Taxation was no longer a strictly national matter. To impose heavy reparations on Germany was one way out of that dilemma. But it was not the only way. The war had been won by the US and the Entente through cooperation. For the economies most severely wounded by the war, the great hope was that this mutual assistance might be extended into peacetime. In 1918 Britain and France had both proposed plans for a post-war economic organization to secure them during the period of reconstruction.[52] These plans extended unprecedented commitments to their national populations. As the French socialist Léon Blum noted, for the first time in history promises had been made by the war-fighting states to compensate their citizens for the damage done.[53] This had international as well as domestic implications. It was in this spirit that the French Minister of Commerce, the solidarist and social reformer Etienne Clémentel, wrote to Clemenceau in December 1918, expressing his confidence that 'our new ally the United States will certainly come around to this way of thinking and will agree that the complete reconstruction of the North of France and Belgium is in essence everyone's business, the primordial task of the economic league of free peoples'.[54] It was at Versailles that this wager would be put to the test.

THREE

The Unfinished Peace

13

A Patchwork World Order

On 18 January 1919 the long-awaited peace conference convened in the Hall of Mirrors in Louis XIV's palace at Versailles outside Paris. It was fifty years to the day that the first emperor of the new Germany had been proclaimed on the same spot. With revolution seething across central Europe, with an army of 12 million American and Entente soldiers waiting on the defeated enemy's borders for their demobilization, it might have seemed obvious to start with a general discussion of a European peace. But three weeks earlier, on the British leg of his grand tour, President Wilson had already made clear his refusal to fall in with this sense of priority. America, he had told his English audience, was 'not now interested in European politics' or 'merely in the peace of Europe'. America was interested in 'the peace of the world'.[1] As if to put the old world in its place, the first decision of the Supreme Council on 25 January was not to begin the conference with Europe, but to appoint a Commission consisting of representatives of the five great powers – the US, Great Britain, France, Italy and Japan – together with delegations from China, Brazil, Serbia, Portugal and Belgium – to draft the Covenant of a League of Nations. The full Commission convened for its first meeting on Monday 3 February in Colonel House's suite, Room 351 of the Hotel Crillon overlooking the Place de la Concorde. Ever since the end of the seventeenth century there had been talk of a League of peace. Now the first draft of the League of Nations was put together in a matter of a fortnight, in a dozen sessions, held in the evenings, lasting a total of perhaps 30 hours. On 14 February an exhausted Woodrow Wilson delivered the first draft of the Covenant to a crowded Plenary meeting of the peace conference at the Quai d'Orsay.

After several months of revisions it would form the first part of the Treaty of Versailles.

As one of his biographers remarked, 'February 14 1919, would seem to be the climactic day towards which Wilson's life had supremely moved'.[2] Wilson deliberately placed himself at the centre of the drama, chairing all but one of the Commission meetings. It was his triumph. It would also be his defeat. The President's hopes for a new world, so the Wilsonian propagandists told the story, were wrecked by the avarice of Europe and Japan.[3] It was they who mangled the President's vision until it became easy prey for his enemies at home. But the story of the League as Woodrow Wilson's crusade against the vices of old world imperialism was self-defeating. It refused to acknowledge the fact that in early 1919 Britain, France and Japan were all looking to the peace conference to answer the question of how a new world order would be shaped. They had interests to defend and ambitions to pursue, but they had been severely shaken by the war and the upheavals at both ends of Eurasia. The fact that the imperialist practices of the pre-war period could not continue was obvious. The age of imperialist *Weltpolitik* had proved ruinously dangerous. Nor despite the loose talk of 'old world' or 'traditional' imperialism was head-on rivalry between the major powers in every arena of the world an ingrained habit. It dated to the 1880s. What Britain, France and Japan aspired to construct, no less than the American delegation, was a new order of security. The drafting of the League Covenant was for them the moment at which Wilson would answer the fundamental question of the post-war world: what could they expect from the United States? The answer they received was incoherent. For its most perceptive critics the fundamental defining feature of the League was not its internationalism, nor the logic of imperial power that it cloaked, but its failure to respond to the challenges of the twentieth century by explicitly laying out a new model of territorial or political organization.[4] Wilson himself insisted that the League Covenant must not be confining, it must 'not be a straitjacket'. It was a 'vehicle of power, but a vehicle of power which may be varied at the discretion of those who exercise it and in accordance with the changing circumstances of the time'.[5] The question that haunted the rest of the world was who would have the power to exercise that discretion, to wield that power.

I

As far as Wilson and his entourage were concerned, an important battle-line with the Europeans was drawn already at the end of 1918. In early December as the USS *George Washington* carried the President across the Atlantic to Europe, the attitude in Wilson's circle toward the old continent hardened. Wilson fumed at British resistance to 'freedom of the seas', he inveighed against the plot by France, Great Britain and Italy to 'get everything out of Germany' that they could. Wilson was 'absolutely opposed'. As he put it to journalists in his entourage: 'A statement that I once made that this should be a "peace without victory" holds more strongly today than ever.'[6] How would the 'old world' reply?

On 29 December, Prime Minister Clemenceau rose to address the Chamber of Deputies. For months he had been plied with questions. Was the government committed to the 14 Points? Did it support the League of Nations? Unlike Wilson and Lloyd George, Clemenceau had preserved a profound silence over war aims. Now, finally, he rounded on his hecklers.[7] He paid his respects to the hopes inspired by the League, but he declared that the fundamentals of security remained the same. France must look to its military strength, its borders and its allies. At a stroke, the French Premier appeared to have defined the coming argument. For Joseph Tumulty, Wilson's chief of staff, Clemenceau's speech vindicated the President's controversial decision to attend the Paris conference in person. The stage was set for the 'final issue between balance of power and league of nations'.[8] But to accept the Wilsonian reading of Clemenceau is to miss the point. Clemenceau was no conventional advocate of old school Realpolitik. The transatlantic security system he had in mind was neither old-fashioned nor reactionary. In fact it was unprecedented.[9] Since the spring of 1917 he had been hailing the unique historic opportunity to align the three great democratic powers and thus to make a peace that would see 'justice fortified'.[10] Clemenceau was sceptical about talk of disarmament and arbitration as panaceas. But what really worried him about the League was that it would allow Britain and the United States the freedom to retreat into self-satisfied isolation, leaving France alone. To guard against either prospect, the most internationally minded French republicans, men like Léon Bourgeois, the French negotiator on the League of Nation's commission, argued that the League must become a multilateral democratic alliance with powerful collective security provisions. Insofar as there was a truly strong internationalist vision on offer in the League of Nations Commission in early February 1919, it was put forward, not by Wilson, but by the representatives of the French Republic.[11]

For Britain no less than for France the strategic relationship with the United States was crucial. As Lloyd George put it, the 'reality' of the League as an organization of global peace must be grounded in the 'cooperation between Great Britain and the USA'.[12] By comparison with the French, the British preferred a minimal organizational architecture for the League precisely because they wanted to use it as a flexible vehicle for their alliance with Washington. But, as was true for the French, what the British were proposing was radically new. Not since Spain and Portugal had divided up the New World in 1494 with the Treaty of Tordesillas had there been a strategic vision of comparable scope. As far as both French and German observers were concerned, the prospect of such an Anglo-American condominium was regarded as ushering in the end of Europe as an independent locus of global political power.[13]

What of the fourth great power? In the course of the Congressional 'Treaty Fight' in 1919, denunciations of Japan's imperialism would do lasting damage to the reputation of the Versailles Treaty. Japan's track record was notorious. The eagerness with which the Japanese Army rushed 75,000 men into Siberia in the autumn of 1918, ten times the number reluctantly agreed by Wilson in the summer, was just the latest demonstration of its aggression. But the irony was that precisely at this moment the trend of Japanese politics was running strongly in the opposite direction. In September 1918, following the nationwide rice riots, Terauchi Masatake's Conservative cabinet had collapsed. As leader of the largest parliamentary party, Hara Takashi was appointed Prime Minister, the first commoner to hold that position in Japan's modern political history.[14] Hara was no progressive. But the cornerstone of his conservative strategy was the search for an accommodation with the United States. Hara found important allies in the liberal barons Saionji Kinmochi and Makino Nobuaki, who headed the delegation to Paris. In France in the 1870s Saionji had become acquainted with Clemenceau in radical liberal circles. The venerable baron was selected to head the delegation on account of his popularity with the Japanese public.[15] But Makino too was a convert to the new rules. 'The respect for peace and rejection of high handedness are trends of the world today,' Makino insisted. Given that 'Americanism' was now 'being propounded across the earth', Japan could not continue its policy of militarist aggression toward China.

Nor was this merely a matter of elite strategy. Public opinion carried an increasingly heavy weight, a factor that was easily underestimated by Western observers. A powerful democratic agitation was sweeping across Japan, which by 1925 would force the introduction of male suffrage. The Japanese professoriate, students in their tens of thousands, and the readership of Japan's burgeoning broadsheet press were politicized as never before. For Japan's most influential liberal thinker, Yoshino Sakuzo, it was clear that the victory of November 1918 had delivered the Hegelian verdict of history. The war had brought the triumph of liberalism, progressivism and democracy over authoritarianism, conservatism and militarism. Once a prominent liberal imperialist, Yoshino now embraced the principle of 'no annexations' and the League of Nations as representing 'the prevailing world trend for greater international justice by consolidating democracy internally and establishing equality externally'.[16] But Japan's era of popular political mobilization was not confined to the left. Popular nationalism too experienced a dramatic revival. They too demanded to know: would the peace offer their country a legitimate and equal place in the new world order?

II

By the time they arrived in Paris in January 1919, the American delegation understood the practical necessity of collaborating with the British Empire. Even before the meetings of the Commission began, American and British negotiators had agreed the disposal of the German and Ottoman empires by means of the mandate system and had prepared a draft Covenant for the League. As Wilson put it, 'it would be good politics to play the British game "more or less" in formulating the League Covenant in order that England might feel her views were chiefly to be embodied in the final draft'.[17] The basic constitution was clear. There would be a League Council and a General Assembly. Sovereignty and territorial integrity would be protected. There would be collective enforcement action. It was over the all-important details of the Covenant that opinions differed. The British position as articulated by Robert Cecil was clear. To be functional, the Council must be small. The great powers must at all times maintain the majority of votes. No great power should find itself unwillingly 'dragged' into a major international confrontation on account of the petty resentments of a smaller League member. There must be no repetition of Sarajevo. The Council's decision must therefore be taken unanimously, which again put a premium on having a compact decision-making body.

True to this conception, the first joint Anglo-American draft restricted membership in the League's inner council to the five great powers.[18]. Other League members were to be summoned as and when the great powers needed their advice. Not surprisingly, this offended the 'lesser nations'. By the second meeting of the Commission, as the minutes coyly record, the discussion had become 'very animated'.[19] To force their point the delegates of the smaller states, over the objection of both the Americans and the British, insisted that the drafting Commission be expanded to include four additional members – Greece, Poland, Romania and Czechoslovakia. Though to the British it seemed 'most unreal' to insist on the absolute equality of states and though the practical advantages of an intimate council of the great powers were obvious, Cecil was a true-believing internationalist and the overriding purpose of the League was to act as a 'voice of the world', affirming the 'equality of the powers'.[20] Wilson, as chair of the Commission, was non-committal. He did not openly distance himself from the British. He insisted that there were compelling reasons for the great powers to have special representation. After all, the burden of enforcing any League decisions would fall disproportionately on them. Furthermore, if the question of interest was what should decide representation, then the great powers, by virtue of their worldwide activities, were 'always interested'. By contrast, after the creation of the League the smaller states had even less reason for independent diplomacy than before, since they could live contentedly in the knowledge that their fundamental interests were protected by the international community.[21] But, as everyone was well aware, Wilson's own first draft of the Covenant had provided for the smaller powers to have a significant voice in the Council, and as chair-man he happily opened the floor to critical contributions from Serbia, Belgium and China.[22]

Faced with this wall of opposition, Cecil accepted that the draft would have to be redone, but this begged the question of how the dis-tribution of seats within the Council was to be characterized. A number of delegates were uncomfortable with the distinction between great and small powers, let alone Wilson's even more invidious tripartite distinc-tion between 'great', 'middling' and 'minor' powers. Furthermore, the Belgian delegation pointed out that any such system of classes suggested the possibility that 'other powers might take shape and be properly described as great powers ...'. Provision would have to be made to promote rising powers to permanent Council membership and to counterbalance their addition by adding smaller members. In reply, Cecil asked whether the Belgians were thinking of Germany as a poten-tial future member of the Council. This provoked general consternation and prompted Ferdinand Larnaude, the second French delegate, to ram home what was really at stake for France. Given Cecil's train of thought, Larnaude 'thought that the use of the general terms "great" and "small" power was inadvisable'. The League was 'the outcome of this war'. Of course, the Big Five were not the only ones to have made a contribution. 'But the matter is not one to be discussed in the abstract or on the basis of sentiment; but a thing of cold fact; and the fact is that the war was won by Great Britain, France, Japan, Italy and the United States. It is essential that the League be formed around these effective powers ...'[23] 'During the course of the war,' continued the second French delegate, Bourgeois, 'the five nations had made a league of nations after a sort; they have fought, actuated by a single idea. Now it is important that it be made known to the world that they are creating this League under the influence of a single idea.'[24]

Finally on 13 February 1919, at the ninth meeting of the Commis-sion, the ratio was fixed in line with Wilson's original conception at five to four in favour of the great powers.[25] In a general sense this tilted the compromise toward the idea of the League not as a vehicle for great-power governance but as the representative assembly of the 'family of nations', the venue, as Paul Hymans the Belgian delegate put it, to affirm 'the dignity of nations'.[26] The Covenant also now avoided any categorical distinction between great and small powers. The Big Five were simply listed by name as permanent members. The rest of the Council was to be chosen from amongst 'the other member states'. In the draft agreed in February no justification was offered for the status of the Big Five, neither their size nor their role in the war being mentioned. No distinction was drawn between great and small powers, or allies, auxiliaries and vanquished. The Covenant avoided any reference to the actual hierarchy of global power. By the same token, no criteria were specified that would allow an argument for change to be made in terms of the wording of the Covenant itself.

The same clash of visions recurred on every issue of the Covenant. Who, for instance, should be eligible for membership in the League? In Wilson's own first drafts of the Covenant, he had included 'popular self-government' as a criterion to be met by applicant members, which would have made the League an association of democracies. But this clause was cut out by the legal experts. In the third meeting of the Commission on 5 February, Wilson sought to remedy this by requiring that 'only self-governing states' could in future become members of the League. In reply Bourgeois made a characteristically forceful intervention. Self-government by itself was not adequate. 'Whether the form of government is republican or monarchical,' he went on, 'makes no difference. The question ought to be, is this government responsible to the people?'[27] What was truly at stake for the French was the political 'character' of the League and its members. To impose the stiffest possible test they demanded that any vote for admission should be unanimous. Speaking for Britain, Cecil's approach was characteristically flexible. Self-government, he opined, was a 'word' that was 'hard to define, and it is hard to judge a country by this standard'. Crucially, Britain very much wanted to have India included, and though it was making progress towards self-government, the Commission was not willing to grant that India already qualified. This embarrassment was resolved by making India an original signatory of the Covenant to which the qualifications required of new applicants did not apply. After Jan Smuts came up with that procedural fix, Cecil was happy to agree to any formula approved by Wilson. If Germany was the main anxiety, the British felt it was best to avoid general formulae at all. On paper, after all, it could not be denied that the Reichstag had been a 'democratic institution'.

Furthermore, 'in a few years' time the Reichstag could have converted Germany into a constitutional government, in the true sense of the word'. To impose stiff entrance criteria for the former enemy powers, Cecil suggested that the article be amended to permit the League to 'impose on any States seeking admission such conditions as it may think fit'. This would allow the League to 'say to some State, you are too military; to another you are too despotic etc'.[28]

Disconcertingly, though it was he who was moving the amendment, Wilson refused to clarify his own terms. As he willingly admitted, he had 'spent twenty years' of his 'life lecturing on self-governing states and trying all the time to define one', but he despaired of ever being able to provide a watertight definition. In the end it came down to a kind of practical wisdom. He could, Wilson insisted, 'recognize' such a constitution 'where I see it'. One should not be misled by the Reichstag or the formidable apparatus of German electoral politics. Regardless 'of how it appeared on paper, no one would have looked at the German government before the war, and said that the nation was self-governing'.[29] When the French proposed taking up Cecil's idea of tailoring the requirements to specific applicants, Wilson responded with an even more disconcerting admission. It would be unwise, he interjected, to insist too firmly on very exclusive membership criteria, because that might involve setting up 'standards that we have not always lived up to ourselves'. 'Even all the states now here associated were not regarded by all other states as having good characters.'[30] This only served to heighten French alarm. For a republican of Clemenceau's stripe, it was perverse to turn the impossibility of achieving international consensus into a reason for retreating into minimalist relativism. Precisely because the world was likely to be riven with conflict, democrats must distinguish their friends from their enemies and learn to stand together. This was why the League should be equipped with clear membership criteria and effective enforcement mechanisms. But the British and Americans resisted any move in the French direction. In the end the Commission settled for a compromise that satisfied no one. Any talk of democracy or constitutionalism or responsible government was abandoned in favour of an amendment that simply required candidates for admission to be 'fully self-governing'. This clearly ruled out colonies but left open the question of members' internal constitutions.[31]

III

In the discussion of the League's enforcement mechanisms, the difference in underlying visions became even more pointed. The French insisted that if it was to offer a truly effective security guarantee, the League must dispose of an international army. It must have a permanent general staff and a tough regime of supervised disarmament. If implemented, this would have made Marshal Foch's supreme command over Allied forces, instituted at the final moment of crisis in the spring of 1918 and still operative in the spring of 1919, into the model for a permanent military apparatus. But this was unacceptable to both the British and Americans. When the French had the temerity to press the issue, the British revealed the power balance that was to define the scope for compromise over the League. On the morning of 11 February, Robert Cecil rounded on Léon Bourgeois, 'speaking very frankly but in private', he reminded him that 'Americans had nothing to gain from the League', that the 'offer that was made by America for support was practically a present to France, and that to a certain but to a lesser extent this was the position of Great Britain' as well. 'If the League of Nations was not successful,' Cecil warned, Britain would withdraw from the negotiations and make an offer of a separate 'alliance between Great Britain and the United States'. With the darkest fear of French policy laid bare on the table, 'the meeting adjourned for lunch'.[32] Now that the British were acting as the enforcers, Wilson could adopt a more conciliatory tone. He gladly conceded to the French that the recent war had 'made apparent the absolute necessity of the unity of command ... but the unity of command only became possible because of the immediate and imminent danger which threatened civilization. To propose to realise unity of command in time of peace, would be to put forward a proposal that no nation would accept ...'[33] 'We must make a distinction between what is possible and what is not.'[34]

Behind the scenes the familiar role assignment at Versailles was reversed. It was Wilson's realism that turned the French from radical internationalists into defenders of the status quo. If their futuristic internationalist vision was rejected, then France's minimum negotiating goal was to soften the disarmament provisions of the League Covenant so that they did not operate in such a lopsided fashion as to jeopardize

French security. When the British and Americans called for an end to conscription, France replied that conscription was a 'fundamental issue of democracy', a 'corollary of universal suffrage'.[35] The result was a lowest common denominator compromise that suited the British and Americans far better than their allies. Under Article 8, the target level for disarmament was to be adjusted with 'special regard to the geographical situation' of each state. The 'fair and reasonable' level of forces that would be allowed to each member was to be determined by the Council according to an unspecified procedure. There was to be a 'full and frank interchange of information' about armaments between states, but no inspection or 'control'. Instead of a standing army, the League would be equipped with a 'permanent Commission' to advise on disarmament and 'military and naval questions'.

The security regime provided by the Covenant centred on Article 10, which required the High Contracting Parties to 'respect and preserve as against external aggression the territorial integrity and existing political independence of all states'. But contrary to the claims later made by Wilson's Republican opponents, the Covenant provided no automatic enforcement mechanism. It was up to the discretion of the Council to 'advise upon the means by which this obligation shall be fulfilled'. The true substance of the Covenant lay in the procedural mechanism it specified for delaying and mediating conflict. No party was to go to war before submitting the case to arbitration (Article 12). A ruling was to be delivered within six months. The warring parties were to respect a further three months' waiting period before engaging in conflict. If a ruling was reached the terms were to be published, providing the basis for an emerging body of international law (Article 15). Only a unanimous report by the members of the Council other than the parties to the conflict would have binding force. No member of the League was permitted to declare war on a party to a conflict that was complying with a unanimous Council recommendation. A failure to comply with this arbitration procedure would be considered an act of aggression against all other members of the League and would license sanctions under Article 16. These included a complete and immediate economic blockade and the interdiction of all communications between citizens of the Covenant-breaking state and the rest of the world. The Executive Council was placed under a duty to consider joint military and naval action, but it was not required to take action. In the event that the

Council was not unanimous, it was required merely to publish the opinions of both the majority and the minority. The attempt by the Belgians to give binding force to a mere majority vote of the Council was warded off by the British with Wilson's backing. A no-vote in the Council could not be overridden. No great power could be forced to take action by the League.

To minimize their commitments yet further and to avoid becoming sucked into the defence of an indefensible status quo, the British had insisted that the League should have the right to adjust boundaries where appropriate. But this risked turning the League Council into the court of appeal for every revisionist and irredentist cause in the world. So, instead, under Article 24 it was the Body of the Delegates that was given the responsibility 'from time to time' to 'advise the reconsideration by States members of the League, of treaties which have become inapplicable, and of international conditions of which the continuance may endanger the peace of the world'. But no procedure was specified by which such advice should be formulated, nor did the Covenant spell out the consequences of such a finding. Under Article 25, signatories were required to void any treaties incompatible with the League Covenant, but, again, no procedure was specified by which a conflict between new and old commitments might be resolved.

From the point of view of those who had hoped to create a robust international security regime, this was deeply disappointing. But as far as Wilson was concerned, the mistrust and insecurity that animated these discussions was the wrong place to start. 'It must not be supposed,' Wilson insisted, 'that any of the members of the League will remain isolated if it is attacked ... We are ready to fly to the assistance of those who are attacked, but we cannot offer more than the condition of the world enables us to give ... When danger comes, we too will come, and we will help you, but you must trust us. We must all depend on our mutual good faith.'[36] Bourgeois and Larnaude were too polite to point out that less than four years earlier President Wilson had declared himself 'too proud' to fight, or that, even at the moment of greatest danger in the spring of 1918, America's soldiers had hardly 'flown' to the defence of France. Instead, the French asked for some token of the 'mutual good faith' to which Wilson so eloquently appealed to be written into the Covenant. Should it not include some explicit statement of solidarity, acknowledging the blood spilled in common in the war? But on this the French were repeatedly thwarted by the British and Americans. They insisted that the League should not be 'burdened' with the rancour of the war. But if wartime solidarity was not to be invoked, what was the common bond to which Wilson was appealing?

As a substitute, Bourgeois suggested that the League of Nations should invoke the legacy of the pre-war Hague Peace Arbitration Treaties. That experience had taught bitter lessons. The advocates of internationalism had to stand together, because their project was not, as Wilson fondly imagined, supported by an irresistible groundswell of public opinion. The advocates of The Hague Treaties, Bourgeois reminded the Commission, had had 'jokes and raillery' heaped on them by 'opponents of Right', self-proclaimed 'realists' and narrow-minded exponents of national egotism. They had faced a barrage of criticism from those who had 'tried to cast discredit on the first great enterprise for the organization of right in the world'. And Bourgeois finished with a heartfelt appeal: 'I foresee, I announce and I want it to be written in the minutes that, against the work we are now undertaking, the same criticisms and the same raillery will be made, and that they will even try to say that this work is useless and ineffective.' Such denunciations were not inconsequential. The mocking criticism directed against The Hague Treaties had helped to erode the support of those 'who ought to have been the staunchest upholders'. Given this fragility, as Larnaude insisted, 'Not to mention The Hague Conference is not only ingratitude, but it is something more, it may be a disregard of the interest we have, not to deviate from the conventions which have truly played a part in this war.'[37] But the British were not moved. Standing in for Wilson as chairman, Cecil dismissed the whole issue as merely a 'question of form'. Colonel House also objected, but on different grounds. Since the US Congress had ratified The Hague Convention only with reservations, even to mention The Hague in the League Covenant was a 'question of form' that might raise 'vast and very difficult' problems.

IV

Clemenceau was no simple-minded realist when it came to international affairs. On the contrary, in early April 1919 he would make an impassioned appeal for the Versailles Treaty to set a dramatic precedent by bringing the Kaiser to trial as an international criminal.[38] But the frustration that Larnaude and Bourgeois experienced in the Commission confirmed Clemenceau in his suspicion that the League was a lost cause as far as France was concerned. Making the best of a bad situation, Clemenceau joined the British and Americans in distancing himself from Bourgeois' impractical demands, all the better, he hoped, to consolidate the trilateral transatlantic pact with Britain and America that was his true goal.[39] Provided that a democratic alliance was in place, France could live with an empty League. The real risk from the point of view of Paris was that the League might have become an exclusive Anglo-American duopoly. Both at the time and since, critics would argue that the League served as a convenient vehicle for the upholding of an Anglo-American imperium.[40] But what substance was there to these claims? Certainly the British hoped to turn the League into the forum for a transatlantic condominium and this vision was attractive to at least some Republican senators.[41] But the attitude of the Wilson administration was not encouraging. And they were least encouraging where it mattered most – regarding money and ships.

There was some talk over the winter of 1918–19 from the Entente side of making the League into the vehicle for an international financial settlement. But as we shall see, those plans were rapidly quashed. Wilson's stance on naval affairs was, if anything, even more worrying. In advance of his visit to London in December, he gave a carefully scripted interview to The Times in which he spoke of the need for 'the most generous understanding between the two great English-speaking Democracies'.[42] But what did this mean for the future organization of naval power? In his independent armistice exchanges with the Germans in October 1918, Wilson had reiterated the call for the freedom of the seas that was anathema to the British. To further increase the pressure, in late October he asked Congress to appropriate funds for a second three-year naval spending programme. And in unguarded moments on the passage to Europe in early December he made clear what this meant. If Britain would not come to terms, America would 'build the biggest Navy in the world, matching theirs and exceeding it ... and if they would not limit it, there would come another and more terrible and bloody war and England would be wiped off the face of the map'.[43] When Wilson arrived in Europe there seemed little prospect of Britain gaining either of its main objectives: a cordial power-sharing agreement with the United States, or recognition by the US of the exceptional naval needs of a worldwide empire. Caught between these conflicting impulses, by the end of March 1919 relations between the naval officers of the two sides had degenerated to such an extent that the admirals threatened war and had to be restrained from assaulting each other.[44]

In this tense situation, the League of Nations discussion did bring relief on at least one crucial point. As Wilson himself was forced to admit, it was contradictory both to insist on the creation of a League of Nations with the power to impose an international blockade and to declare the freedom of the seas an absolute principle. The Royal Navy would clearly play a crucial role in imposing the sanctions required by the League. The 'joke', Wilson admitted, was 'on him'. Talk of the freedom of the seas was quietly shelved. But would the British and American navies be able to cooperate? Was Wilson determined to push ahead to build the largest navy in the world? If the US acted unilaterally and aggressively, could Britain afford not to respond? It would make a mockery of the League of Nations if it began not with disarmament but with the greatest arms race the world had ever seen. But as the Versailles peace talks began, America's wartime shipbuilding programme was belatedly hitting its stride.[45] Any suggestion of the need to limit naval construction was apt to be interpreted as a symptom of European presumption. The result was a truly ironic inversion.

Since 1916 Wilson had argued that America needed to threaten to build a huge navy to force the British to accept the terms of the new order. As the peace conference entered its fortnight of deepest crisis, in late March 1919 Lloyd George turned the tables on him. Wilson had returned from Washington in an embarrassing situation. His conversations with congressional leaders had made clear that the Covenant would not pass without an explicit inclusion of the Monroe Doctrine. Britain had no objection, for it had been one of the original instigators of the doctrine. And the Royal Navy had been its de facto upholder throughout the nineteenth century. But America's claim to naval dominance was profoundly disturbing, and not just to Britain. In the first week of April as the conference reached deadlock, Lloyd George made clear that there would be no British signature on an amended Covenant including the Monroe Doctrine unless Wilson agreed to refrain from an all-out naval arms race.[46] Cecil was horrified at what he deemed Lloyd George's cynicism. But his indignation did little to dent Downing

Street's logic: 'The first condition of success for the League of Nations is ... a firm understanding between the British Empire and the United States of America and France and Italy that there will be no competitive building up of fleets or armies between them. Unless this is arrived at before the Covenant is signed, the League of Nations will be a sham and a mockery.'[47] Rather than Wilson using American naval armaments to force Britain to fall into line with his vision of a new international order, it was Britain that held Wilson's Covenant hostage to curb American naval armaments. Lloyd George agreed to approve an amended Covenant on 10 April only after Wilson conceded that America would reconsider the 1918 naval programme and would engage in regular talks on armaments plans.[48] Thus the blank canvas of the League was filled, if not with an Anglo-American alliance, then at least with a commitment to avoid confrontation.

14

'The Truth About the Treaty'

For France the peace talks had started badly. In the League of Nations Commission the British and Americans collaborated to block the French vision of the League. The Covenant that was to form the global framework for the post-war order contained few if any of the provisions that would be necessary to secure peace in Europe. In the struggle over the Armistice in the autumn of 1918, the British had had enough leverage to ensure that their single most important objective was met: the German Fleet was interned in Scapa Flow. By comparison, France was forced to look for its security to the draconian armistice conditions, which had to be renewed month by month. The story of Versailles was in large part defined by France's efforts to have its interests recognized. The result by June 1919 was a treaty that in the words of Jacques Bainville, France's most influential right-wing historian and publicist of the interwar period, was 'too kind for all that it was cruel'.[1] How had this come about? The answer first to hand was to think in terms of an unhealthy compromise between two sides. The French were responsible for the draconian measures, whereas Britain and America preened themselves as the advocates of a more liberal peace. 'Too cruel' was the judgement above all of British liberals like John Maynard Keynes. Bainville, like many of his compatriots, thought the peace 'too kind'.[2]

Not surprisingly, this simple assignment of roles has provoked rebuttal. Were the French really vindictive, the British and the Americans really liberal in their approach to Germany? Beyond this question of role assignments, are there perhaps deeper reasons for the fraught quality of Versailles? Perhaps the kindness and cruelty of Versailles are symptomatic of the unsteady emotional economy of moralistic liberalism.[3]

The fury of a just war generated punitive impulses that over time were always likely to become distasteful, setting up a no less unstable backlash, this time in the spirit of appeasement.[4] After all, a just peace could mean both hanging the Kaiser and restraining the unreasonable Poles. But in seeking to explain Versailles's Janus face, Bainville looked beyond the emotional cycle of crime and punishment to a deeper historical and structural feature of the peace. Whether it was cruel or kind, what struck Bainville most about the Versailles settlement was that it extended the principle of national sovereignty across all of Europe, including to Germany. Despite the disaster unleashed by Bismarck's creation of 1871, an integral and sovereign German nation state was taken for granted as a basic element in the new order. For Bainville this assumption was the hallmark of sentimental nineteenth-century liberalism.[5] The bizarre mixture of cruelty and kindness that characterized the peace was the direct result of Clemenceau's effort to reconcile the security needs of France with his romantic attachment to the principle of nationality. Whatever we may think of Bainville's politics, the force of his point can hardly be denied. Across the sweep of modern history since the emergence of the modern nation state system in Europe in the seventeenth century, the assumption of German national sovereignty marks the treaty of 1919 as unique. Most, if not all, of the problems peculiar to the Versailles Treaty system arose from it.

I

Given the French insistence on demilitarizing the Rhineland, occupying strategic bridgeheads, subjecting Germany to international inspection and stripping it of its border territories, it may seem perverse to insist that German sovereignty was a defining feature of the Versailles peace. When it suited his negotiating tactics, Clemenceau was happy to unleash the exponents of an even more radical solution. But as Bainville with his acute sense of French political history well understood, for a man of Clemenceau's disposition, German nationality could not really be denied. Self-determination as a universal aspiration was not an idea imported to an uncomprehending Europe by an American President. Since the first French Republic had embarked on the revolutionary wars of the 1790s, the question of how to accommodate French security with the rights of other people to self-determination had been an abiding preoccupation. Furthermore, as radical republicans like Clemenceau regretfully acknowledged, France's long history of aggression had played a disastrous role in inciting the furies of German nationalism. Above the mirrors at Versailles the friezes celebrated Louis XIV's rampages across the Rhine. The first French revolutionaries had thought of themselves as breaking with the legacy of Bourbon power. They announced themselves as liberators of an enslaved Europe. But the just war of the revolution soon gave way to Napoleonic imperialism. The tragic torsion imparted to European history by the degeneration of the French revolution was fundamental to Clemenceau's distinctively republican view of history.[6] The Congress of Vienna of 1815 had imposed peace on Europe, but it had denied the national aspirations of Germany. The disastrous denouement came in the 1860s when the vainglorious ambition of Bonaparte's nephew opened the door to Bismarck. If the France of Napoleon III had no friends in 1870, it was for good reason. Clemenceau did not bemoan the defeat of a regime that had imprisoned both him and his father. The disaster was that Germany's wounded pride was now slaked by Prussia's aggression. Clemenceau had many brutal and prejudiced things to say about Germans. But he did not deny that the Huns of 1914 were in no small part the product of France's own twisted history.

It was not, of course, the singular responsibility of the French to have denied German national aspirations. The fragmenting of German sovereignty was a defining feature of every general settlement of European affairs both before and after 1919. The Treaty of Westphalia in 1648, which ended the Thirty Years War, acknowledged the sovereignty of the emerging nation states of Europe, led by France, but relegated the German lands to the Holy Roman Empire, divided along lines of religion into hundreds of principalities, dukedoms and free cities. Though the map was tidied up in the wake of the Napoleonic occupation of Germany, the same basic pattern held in 1815. Invidious comparisons have often been drawn between the shabby treatment of the demoralized German delegates in Paris in 1919 and the hospitable welcome that had once been extended to Talleyrand, the representative of the defeated France at the Congress of Vienna. But this is utterly beside the point. Talleyrand represented the restored, legitimist Bourbon dynasty. In 1815 even the quietest pretension to German unity had been silenced by the secret police forces of Austria, Prussia and Russia. As recently as 1866, during the crisis that would lead to the Austro-Prussian War, the French statesman Adolphe Thiers could declare that the 'greatest principle of European politics' was that Germany must consist of independent states, bound together by no more than a federation.[7] It was against this backdrop that Clemenceau made what at first may seem an incongruous claim: '... the Treaty of Versailles can make this boast ... that it did conceive, and even in part bring about, certain relations founded on equity between nations that had been ground against one another by successive outbreaks of historical violence'.[8] A consolidated German nation state would stand after Versailles at the heart of Europe. Furthermore, as one could hardly fail to notice even from the most casual inspection of the post-war map, due to the simultaneous collapse of the three eastern empires, Germany not only survived the war. In defeat in 1918 it bulked far larger than it had done in victory in 1871.

Could the existence of a German nation state have been reversed? In 1918 there was excited talk amongst journalists, senior military figures and even in the Quai d'Orsay of a 'new Westphalia'. Perhaps France could regain the dominant position it had enjoyed under Louis XIV. Perhaps German nationalism could be curbed or turned against itself. After all, the unification of Germany was a work of violence. In 1849 Prussian troops had crushed a patriotic liberal revolution in southern Germany. In the summer of 1866, in what is commonly but misleadingly referred to as the Austro-Prussian War, Prussia had faced not Austria alone, but a coalition consisting of Saxony, Bavaria, Baden, Württemberg, Hesse, Hanover and Nassau. Over 100,000 Germans had been killed or wounded in what amounted to a North-South civil war. Why should a state, united so recently and with such violence, not be disassembled? But attractive as such visions may have been for anyone thinking from a narrowly French perspective, they ignored the consolidation of German national sentiment since 1871. As Clemenceau recognized, German patriotism was not a figment of the romantic liberal imagination. It was a fact, dramatically reaffirmed by the war. More fundamentally, fantasies of a re-division of Germany begged the question of force. Even if France acting alone might sponsor the separation of the Rhineland, how could it hope to sustain such a partition? The treaties of Westphalia and Vienna were Europe-wide agreements upheld by collective guarantees. It was not impossible to imagine such a solution in the twentieth century. A division of Germany was precisely what was imposed after 1945. But the conditions that made the partition of Germany after World War II into a stable feature of the European order for almost two generations illuminate the full extent of the dilemma facing France in 1919.

The reconstruction of West Germany after World War II has gone down in history as a warrant for the possibility of successful 'regime change'. It also frequently serves as a foil against which to contrast the 'failure' of 1919. But one should not underestimate the massive commitment of money and political capital involved in the reconstruction after World War II, resources that all the victorious powers found far harder to mobilize after World War I. Nor should one prettify the coercive international framework within which such reconstruction was accomplished. The peace settlement after 1945 was far more drastic in its implications for German sovereignty than anything contemplated in 1919. It was World War II that made true many of the horrors envisioned by enraged nationalists after World War I. The country was occupied with massive force. Its territory was torn apart. Eleven million Germans were ethnically cleansed from the contested borderlands in the East. The casualties still defy precise enumeration. But resentful nationalists claim as many as 1 million German civilian victims of this exodus. Hundreds of thousands of women were raped. Reparations and occupation costs were extracted from every part of Germany. War criminals were hunted down. Several thousand were executed, tens of thousands imprisoned and permanently debarred from public life. In both the Eastern and Western zones the entire political, legal, social and cultural system was subject to intrusive and widely resented re-engineering. It was a reconstruction whose success and legitimacy was eventually acknowledged only in the Federal Republic, never in East Germany. Even in West Germany it took the effort of several generations of engaged citizens who doggedly and often with considerable bravery insisted on the need to break with their country's past. The Communist dictatorship in the East had to rely on one of the most intensive police states in history. The entire story was given a happy ending only in 1989 with the collapse of Soviet power and reunification. But even in 1990, the 'Two Plus Four' negotiations that ratified reunification demonstrated not so much the restoration of complete German sovereignty as the multiple conditions to which it continues to be subject through NATO and the European Union.

The unprecedented commitment of the Western Powers was one crucial precondition in enabling this remarkable trajectory. But a no less indispensable element in the equation was the massive coercive force of the Red Army. After 1945 it was the very real threat of a Soviet takeover that drove West Germany willy-nilly into the arms of the West and kept it there. And this too marks 1919 as a singular moment in European history. Since the eighteenth century, Russia had overshadowed German history.[9] Germany's military defeat of Russia in 1917 removed this basic parameter of European power politics. For France as for Germany this had dramatic implications. In the 1890s it was the common fear of the unified Reich that had brought Tsarist autocracy and republican France together in an incongruous alliance. For French strategists of Clemenceau's ilk this was always profoundly uncongenial. The coincidence of the Russian revolution with America's entry into the war in 1917 made both impossible and unnecessary any resumption of a Franco-Russian alliance against Germany. Instead, the French Republic would place its security on a far more congenial basis by means of a political and strategic alliance with the United States and Britain. This transatlantic democratic alliance would be strong enough both to accommodate and to control a unified Germany. To the East, Germany would be safely separated from Russia by Allied sponsorship of the substantial new states of Poland and Czechoslovakia. The fundamental question was whether France could extend into the peace its epoch-making wartime cooperation with Britain and America.

By the autumn of 1918 both London and Washington had agreed to the French claim that Alsace-Lorraine should be restored without a plebiscite. In January 1919 when addressing the French Senate, President Wilson appeared to go further. France, he declaimed, stood 'at the frontier of freedom'. It would 'never again' have to face a 'lonely peril' or have to ask 'the question who would come to her assistance'. France should know that 'the same thing will happen always that happened this time, there shall never be any doubt or waiting or surmise, but that whenever France or any other free people is threatened the whole world will be ready to vindicate its liberty'.[10] Setting aside the memories of 'too proud to fight' and 'peace without victory', if the notion of a 'frontier of freedom' was more than an empty phrase it had radical implications. It implied a specific, absolute, territorial demarcation between different spheres of political value – on the one side freedom, on the other side its enemies. It was the kind of language that President Truman would adopt in 1947 to justify containment, the Marshall Plan and NATO. But Wilson, to the profound regret of the French, showed no recognition of the import of his words. In the League of Nations Commission he reverted only a few weeks later to a language of moral equivalence. Over the League Covenant the French chose to retreat. When it came to Germany, they could not.

II

The first French goal was to disarm Germany. On this, the Americans abstained and the disagreements with the British were technical. They were settled in February 1919 by agreeing both to ban conscription and to limit the German Army to a force of 100,000 lightly armed volunteers. The next French goal was to ensure that what remained of the German Army was pushed well back from its frontier. To the north of Alsace, they wanted to transfer the coal-mining region of the Saar to French control. Its pits would provide France with the coal of which it had been robbed when the retreating German Army flooded the pits of France's northern industrial region. As the Rhine flowed further north towards Holland, the German Rhineland extended west of the river. Generalissimo Foch and the baying pack of nationalist opinion demanded that it should be separated from Germany to form a separate republic which could either be grouped together with Belgium and Luxemburg or neutralized. During the war Clemenceau had silenced all such talk, but on 25 February 1919 he permitted his closest advisor, André Tardieu, to ventilate the radical case in front of the conference. But Clemenceau chose his moment carefully. He avoided a direct confrontation with Wilson, who was absent from Paris selling the League to Congress. On Wilson's return on 14 March the stage was set for the climactic crisis of the peace conference. Wilson was horrified by the scale of the French demands. But Clemenceau was adamant. Fearing that the conference would collapse in an embarrassing debacle, Lloyd George suggested a dramatic solution. He proposed to Wilson that the British Empire and the United States should offer France a trilateral security guarantee. Though this was a dramatic departure for both countries and though such a separate military alliance was in contradiction with several of Wilson's well-known pronouncements on the League, the President was persuaded that he must consent or see the conference and with it the League Covenant fail.[11]

The significance of this offer was not lost on Clemenceau. By contrast with the territorial fixation of France's soldiers, he placed a pre-eminent value on the political alliance between the three Western democracies.[12] He understood that such a gesture by Britain and the United States was without precedent. He recognized that in any future war against Germany it gave France the best hope of eventual victory that it could possibly hope for. But after a few days of deliberation Clemenceau returned to the meeting of the Big Three to restate his demands. The Rhineland would remain as part of Germany. But it must be demilitarized and subject to joint occupation by the Allies. Allied forces must hold bridgeheads on the east bank of the Rhine, from which the German Army would be required to retreat at least 50 miles. Whether or not the Saar was separated from Germany, its coal must be reserved for France. The reaction from the British and the Americans was indignation. Lloyd George and his advisors withdrew to a mansion in Fontainebleau to draft a major restatement of the 'liberal' aims of the peace, distancing themselves from France and crafting the script for a generation of appeasement.[13] On 7 April Wilson threatened to abandon Paris altogether.[14] Ever since, Clemenceau's failure to respond more cooperatively to the offer of a security pact has served critics of the peace as the best illustration of his bad faith. But this once more fails to take seriously what the French were saying.

The fundamental French objective was to protect their country not just against the general menace of German power, or even against the prospect of defeat, but against the threat of invasion and occupation.[15] Of course the French would never forget their experiences in 1870 and 1914. But here too they were making a more general point of considerable novelty. Before the war, the conventions of international law had been developing in such a way as to insulate civilian life as far as possible from war fighting. It was this development that allowed liberal theorists such as the oft-derided Norman Angell to argue that, provided the conventions of international law were respected, from the point of view of the civilian population it ought to make little difference which civilized government they lived and worked under.[16] But it was precisely those laws of war that the Kaiser's armies had systematically violated in their occupation of Belgium and northern France. Allied propaganda was prone to exaggeration, but the Germans did not even attempt to deny that they had executed several thousand Belgian and northern French civilians, whom they chose to regard as illegal combatants.[17] Nor did they deny that during their retreat to the Hindenburg line they had laid waste to a large part of northern France. Captured German documents from 1917 and 1918 convinced the French that this had been done not only for tactical advantage but to cripple their economy permanently.[18]

The loss to France was spectacular. In an area of devastation that amounted to only 4 per cent of the country, the Germans managed to do damage totalling between 2 and 3 billion dollars.[19] To the profound frustration of the French and Belgians, when he arrived in Europe Wilson refused to tour the devastated areas, apparently because he feared that it would upset his emotional equilibrium.[20] The French could not afford the luxury of such detachment. For them, Germany's turn against the developing norms of international civility was a clear warning. This made clear that it was no longer enough for the French government to guard against defeat. It had an imperative obligation to protect its citizens against another German occupation. This was a novel territorial problem that required a territorial solution. It must be at the aggressor's expense.

On 8 April, after days of fraught bargaining, the Big Three avoided an open breakdown.[21] The Saar was placed under a complex League of Nations administration with the right to opt either for return to Germany or accession to France in a plebiscite to be held in 1934. For the duration, the output of the coal mines would go to France. The Rhineland was to be fully demilitarized and subject to Allied occupation for 15 years. A phased withdrawal would be conditional on the German fulfilment of their other obligations under the Versailles Treaty and on Britain and the United States making good on their security guarantee. As Clemenceau was later to insist, he had won all that France could hope for.[22] He had his hand on the German collar. He had the backing of Britain and America. Should they withdraw, it would be a disaster for France. But at least Paris would have the right under the terms of the treaty to entrench its position in the occupied areas. What Clemenceau hoped was that he had secured these guarantees whilst cementing rather than weakening the wartime alliance. The cooperation with Britain and America enjoined by the treaty was almost as important to him as its anti-German elements. British and American contingents would stand guard over Germany alongside the French Army. Overseeing German disarmament would be a shared responsibility. 'Responsibility' for Clemenceau was the key word. He did not believe in the binding force of treaties unless woven together with 'drive . . . beliefs, thoughts', and the 'will' to bring 'interests traditionally opposed and sometimes even contradictory' into a common purpose. This is what the Allies had achieved since 1917. If this wartime partnership could be turned into an 'indestructible alliance in the peace', France would be as secure as it could possibly be.[23] What Clemenceau characteristically did not allow for was the damage done by his own pugnacious stand. He had antago-nized both Britain and the United States, and whilst his cabinet gave their approval to the treaty on 4 May, he had not reconciled a large and vocal element of French opinion to what they still regarded as a naive, liberal peace.[24]

III

These tensions were compounded by the effort to construct a security system in the East. To guard against the strategic disaster of a Russo-German rapprochement, France needed to construct a solid cor-don of East European nation states. But no 'cruelty' of the peace rankled the Germans more deeply than the border settlement in the East, and anglophone observers all too easily sympathized. As one American mili-tary observer remarked in April 1919: 'In Central Europe the French uniform is everywhere . . . the imperialistic idea has seized upon the French mind like a kind of madness and the obvious effort is to create a chain of States, highly militarized, organized as far as possible under French guidance . . .'[25] Poland, Romania and Czechoslovakia appeared as France's guard dogs. But to be discussing the issue in these terms was to hand the Germans a propaganda victory from the start. As Wilson himself retorted to critics of the territorial settlement, Versailles was 'a severe treaty in the duties and penalties it imposes upon Germany, but . . . it is much more than a treaty of peace with Germany. It liberates great peoples who have never before been able to find the way to liberty.'[26] Clemenceau struck the same attitude. The theme of the peace was national liberation. The peacemakers were thinking 'less around the old than around the new'.[27] In central Europe that was inevitably at the expense of the incumbent powers.

In the Czech case, to view the question as a German question at all was to start by granting the pan-German case. When it was incorporated into the Habsburg Monarchy in 1526, the kingdom of Bohemia had included a large swath of German-speaking people in its western region, later to become notorious as the Sudetenland. This territory was economically important and now constituted a natural defensive barrier for any Czech state. Its prosperous population had by 1913 grown to 3 million and had remained ethnically and linguistically German. But never in its history had any of this land belonged to any of the states that were forged into the German Reich in 1871. On the grounds of self-determination the American delegation were sceptical about handing the territory to Czechoslovakia. To arrogate it to Austria would create a bizarre geographic configuration. But to attach it to Germany would be to hand the defeated Reich a major territorial gain at the expense of the Entente's Czech allies. This was out of the question as far as Clemenceau and Lloyd George were concerned.[28] If Germany and Czechoslovakia later chose to exchange territories on terms agreeable to Prague, that would be up to them and the League – it was not a matter for the peacemakers. In truth, it took an Austrian pan-German of Hitler's ilk to make the Sudetenland into a grievance. The Weimar Republic did not press the case very hard.

The truly explosive question was the Polish-German boundary and the most painful question of all concerned Silesia.[29] It too had once belonged to the Bohemian Crown and thus to the Habsburgs, only for it to be seized in 1742 by Frederick the Great in the most notorious of all his opportunistic campaigns. By that point, Lower Silesia had already been thoroughly 'Germanized'. But in Upper Silesia there was a large Polish population. To further complicate matters the region was the hub of the industrial revolution in eastern Europe. The economic map had been transformed by German capital and technology combined with the entrepreneurial energy of its aristocratic magnates. Seven German feudal dynasties owned one-quarter of Silesia and most of its immense reserves of metal ores and coal. If a newly created Polish state was to have any real economic independence, it must have these industrial resources. For the same reason Poland needed access to the sea, which required carving a corridor through ethnic German territory to the Baltic shoreline at Danzig.

The positions were predictable. The Poles, backed by the French, wanted the most generous settlement possible including the transfer of the city of Danzig and all of Upper Silesia to Poland.[30] The British and Americans resisted, arguing that this would do too much violence to the principle of self-determination. The arguments began in February 1919 and continued until days before the signing of the Versailles Treaty in June. Danzig, the port city that commanded the mouth of the Polish corridor to the Baltic, was removed from German sovereignty. But on the insistence of Lloyd George and Wilson, it was not allocated to Poland. Instead it was placed under League of Nations administration as a 'Free City'. The corridor was tailored to Poland's disadvantage to keep the size of the German ethnic minority to a minimum. On the insistence of Lloyd George, the question of deciding the final boundary in Upper Silesia was postponed at the last minute, to be settled by a plebiscite.[31] Contrary to the unfounded assertions of later critics, notably John Maynard Keynes, the peacemakers did not irresponsibly ignore the disruption to an integrated industrial system caused by drawing national boundaries. The treaty of separation between Germany and Poland was one of the most comprehensive and technical settlements in the annals of diplomacy.[32] Never before in Europe's long history of territorial rearrangement had such careful consideration been given to squaring both general principles of justice and the imperatives of power with complex territorial realities. Never before had the interests of different national and ethnic groups, both political and economic, been so carefully weighed in the balance. Through painstaking committee work, the peacemakers sought to align national borders so that railways were allocated as conveniently as possible to national territories.[33] Elaborate provisions were put in place to ensure that Poland could not starve Germany of coal. The minutiae of central European history were made the concern of the entire international community. The final League report on the Silesian question was drafted by delegates from Belgium, Brazil, China and Spain. A Japanese viscount acted as rapporteur. Set against the long and bitter history of territories such as Silesia, it is hard to avoid the conclusion that Versailles lived up to its claim to have married diplomacy with expert decision-making in a new and enlightened fashion.

Once more, the contrast with the period after 1945 is sobering. Between 1918 and 1926 roughly half the German population of what was now Polish territory chose to emigrate.[34] After the Potsdam Conference of 1945 the proceedings were far more brutal. Within three years the entire German population of much of eastern Europe had been violently expelled at the point of a gun. In Silesia that amounted to 3 million people. Almost 100,000 people were confirmed dead, with another 630,000 recorded as missing, or 'fate unknown'.[35] The same treatment was meted out to the inhabitants of the Sudetenland.

But such horrors lay in the future. In 1919 German outrage was inconsolable. The Weimar Republic was never reconciled to the new boundaries with Poland. But the resentment of the defeated Germans is by itself no proof of injustice. If the Poles and the Czechs were to have effective self-determination, what was the alternative? As Lord Balfour put it, the extinction of Poland had been 'the great crime' of *ancien régime* power politics.[36] When he heard the Germans complaining of the abuse of their rights in the East, Clemenceau recalled the Polish exiles he had known and the stories they told of Prussian schoolmasters beating Polish children for reciting the Lord's Prayer in their Slav tongue.[37] There was a clear and justified sense that Versailles was not merely creating a strategic *cordon sanitaire* in the East, but righting historic wrongs. When the Germans claimed that the Entente was bent on the destruction of their nation, Balfour rejected the accusation. What the Entente was challenging was the 'rather artificial creation of the modern Prussia, which includes many Slav elements which never belonged to Germany until about 140 years ago, and ought, really, not to belong to Germany at this moment'.[38] It was regrettable, but 'inevitable', Wilson acknowledged, that as tens of millions of Poles, Czechs and Slovaks asserted independence, those Germans who chose to remain in areas of historic colonization would find themselves in the unenviable position of being ruled by Slavs.[39] Precisely how many Germans suffered that dreadful fate and how that number compared to the Poles remaining under German sovereignty remains a matter of arcane dispute. Certainly the figure of 4.5 million 'Germans' lost in the East should be treated with suspicion.[40]

Furthermore, as the different reactions to the problem of German ethnic minorities in Czechoslovakia and Poland suggest, much depended on which Slavs were involved. The Czech national cause was the best represented of the post-war claimants. President Tomas Masaryk was married to an American Unitarian feminist. He had spent much of the war in the US and was one of the most fluent exponents anywhere of the new language of international liberalism. Together with Foreign Minister Edvard Benes he did his best to contain the aggressive asser-tion of territorial claims against Hungary and Poland that accompanied independence for the Czech nation. As a result Czechoslovakia earned a reputation as the model citizen of the post-war era.[41] It helped that the largest political force amongst the Sudeten Germans were the left-wing Social Democrats who were skilfully and decisively integrated into the new multi-ethnic polity.[42] Independent Czechoslovakia had a formid-able economic base and Prague's management of the post-war financial issues contrasted pleasingly with the chaos amongst its neighbours. As citizens of the Czechoslovak Republic, the Sudeten Germans could count themselves fortunate to have escaped the starvation, violence and economic disorder suffered by their ethnic compatriots in Austria and Germany.

The same could not be said of Poland. The challenges facing that new state were monumental. The Polish Republic had to be assembled out of the territories of three defunct empires – German, Austrian and Rus-sian – with radically different political traditions and wildly mixed populations. By 1919 the Polish lands were poor, overpopulated and ravaged by years of fighting. A supreme effort of determined and wise political leadership would have been required to construct a successful nation state on such foundations. The preconditions were not promis-ing. The Polish political parties were legendary for their infighting. A deep fissure ran between the ethnic nationalism of the National Democrats predominant in Russian Poland, whose chauvinism and anti-Semitism were notorious, and the more progressive nationalism of Austrian and German Poland, whose leading figurehead was the renegade socialist Jozef Pilsudski.[43] Their bitter disagreements spilled over into an adven-turist foreign policy that led Poland to wage no fewer than six wars between 1918 and 1920, including attacks on the Baltic states, the Ukraine and a near-fatal assault on the Soviet Union.[44] At the same time, to integrate the new nation, Poland launched a dramatic programme of welfare spending without the financial means to support it. The result was ruinous inflation.[45]

There were good reasons, therefore, for Germans to regret their incorporation into the Polish Republic. But fundamentally the German hostility toward any solution to their border disputes with Poland was rooted in something other than mere rational calculation. It expressed a deep strain of ethnic prejudice and racial animosity. The mere thought of being ruled by Poles was enough to send a shiver through the soul of any authentic German nationalist. The year 1919 saw not just a rearrangement of boundaries in Europe. It was truly a post-colonial moment. Established hierarchies of politics, culture and ethnicity were overturned. This sense of revolutionary change in turn helps to explain the attitude of suspicion and fear shared by those who had to decide the Polish question at Paris.[46]

On 25 March 1919, at the height of the crisis between the Big Three, Poland was a key issue in the Fontainebleau meeting from which Lloyd George hoped to relaunch the British claim to moral leadership. Interpreted in terms of the emotional cycle of liberalism, the Fontainebleau memorandum was the moment at which guilt gained the upper hand. For the sake of peace, Germany must be given a more generous settlement. The greatest danger, Lloyd George announced, was to create in the East a new Alsace-Lorraine. 'I cannot conceive of any greater cause of future war,' he was happy to state, 'than that the German people, who have certainly proved themselves one of the most vigorous and powerful races in the world, should be surrounded by a number of small states, many of them consisting of people who have never previously set up a stable government for themselves, but each of them containing large masses of Germans clamouring for reunion with their native land. The proposal of the Polish Commission that we should place 2,100,000 Germans under the control of a people which is of a different religion and which has never proved its capacity for stable self-government throughout its history must, in my judgement, lead sooner or later to a new war . . .'[47] In more unbuttoned moments Lloyd George referred to the Poles as 'hopeless'. Lord Cecil regarded them as 'orientalised Irish'. Jan Smuts resorted to his South African idiom. As far as he was concerned the Poles were simply 'kaffir'.[48]

It was to calm anxieties about east European self-determination that

Smuts originally proposed the patronizing foreign oversight of the mandate system. This proved unacceptable to everyone in the region. But
international supervision nevertheless formed an essential element of
the 1919 treaty in central Europe.[49] In Danzig as well as in Fiume on the
Adriatic the irreconcilable conflict of national claims was resolved
through internationalization. In the summer of 1919, Poland was forced
to agree to a minority protection regime that became a model for the
rest of eastern Europe in the 1920s. At the League of Nations a standing
committee system was set up to ensure that the new minorities were
given the chance to appeal against persecution, a system of which the
Germans were to make aggressive and highly effective use. The provisions for the plebiscite that would decide the fate of Silesia in March
1921 were extraordinarily elaborate. Some 15,000 Allied troops over-
saw the territory and hundreds of international officials were deployed.[50]
Virtually the entire population voted and when the Poles resorted to an
uprising, Allied forces restored order and removed the Polish rebels
from the large swath of German territory. Once more it was the League
of Nations that was handed the unenviable task of making the final partition. Inevitably, it fell far short of satisfying Germany. But it was
certainly no capitulation to Poland.

IV

The indignant response of the Germans to the peace was not surprising.
Defeat was a disaster. The consequences were shocking. The 'Wilsonian'
armistice won in the nick of time in November 1918 had misled the
German public into imagining that they would be treated as equal partners in shaping the peace. To discover that the armistice negotiations
were part of a larger power play between Washington and the Entente,
and that a 'peace of equals' meant that henceforth German interests
would be treated on an equal footing with those of Poland, was nightmarish. But painful as it was, German discomfort was only the most
radical manifestation of the traumatic adjustment that all the European
powers were undergoing in the wake of the war. Clemenceau might
insist that Versailles conceded to Germany its dream of the nineteenth
century, its claim to a nation state. But in light of the consequences of

the war, this assertion begged so many questions that it was hard not to suspect him of bad faith.

The war had been precipitated by an age of imperialist rivalry, which by the 1890s had left behind the idea that mere national sovereignty was enough. What counted was the global stage. With the era of global competition having being declared over, Germany stood alone, shorn of its overseas territories and its navy. A republican of Clemenceau's ilk would, of course, reply that a large landlocked European nation could well do without an ill-assorted collection of African and Pacific possessions.[51] But he did not think of France's own future in such provincial terms. For France, beyond imperialism there was a brighter future. Paris had made serious and far-reaching proposals for a strong League of Nations. Those had been foiled. But at least France was acknowledged as a permanent Council member by right. If Paris had its way, Germany might never be admitted to the League. And what would admission to the League mean, if it was merely a vehicle for Anglo-American hegemony?[52] To be just another member of a general assembly of nations was not what Weltpolitik had promised at the turn of the century. Precisely so as to insure against that fate, Clemenceau looked beyond the League to a trilateral transatlantic alliance with Britain and the United States.

But that only raised further questions for Germany. Faced with such an overwhelmingly powerful and futuristic coalition in the West, what did Germany's bare European sovereignty amount to? In response, it was tempting for Germany to look to the East. But there, too, it was to be hemmed in. Under the oversight of Asians and Latin Americans, German and Polish votes were cast into the same ballot box. The cruelty and kindness of the Versailles Treaty were felt so acutely because in them were intertwined historically anachronistic visions of international order. In a global age the naked sovereignty acknowledged for Germany had come to seem like a badge of second-tier status. The more imaginative critics of the peace saw Germany as the victimized test subject for new forms of hollowed-out, depoliticized sovereignty.[53] What Germans' resentment made it hard for them to acknowledge was that this painful adjustment was in varying degrees the prospect facing all the European states.

15

Reparations

In the first days of April 1919, as the peace conference entered its critical stage, the question of reparations became ever more central to the architecture of the peace. The payments mattered not only in financial terms. They provided a running test of German compliance with the Versailles Treaty. The notorious war-guilt clause, Article 231, actually stated not Germany's guilt, but its 'responsibility' for the damage suffered by the Allies due to 'the war imposed upon them by the aggression' of the Central Powers. France for its part counted on the joint responsibility of the Allies for enforcing payment. The eventual withdrawal of the occupying forces in the Rhineland and the return of the Saar were both conditional on Germany meeting its reparations obligations. France and the Allies would leave German soil 15 years after it began making regular payments. If Germany did not pay, France would not leave, so at least Clemenceau reassured the French Chamber of Deputies. Under the terms of the Armistice, the parties of the Reichstag majority never disputed Germany's obligation to make good the damage done by the Kaiser's armies. Nor did they dispute that the sums would run to tens of billions of pre-war, full-value Goldmarks. But despite this basic agreement, there was a yawning gap between what the French and the British, even at their most moderate, felt entitled to demand and the sum that Germany, even in its moments of greatest cooperativeness, was willing to offer.

Furthermore, from the German point of view there was a quality to the reparations demands – the remorseless, inescapable weight of debt – that made them in some ways even more odious than the territorial provisions of the treaty. Unlike the loss of territory, which directly affected only the border regions, reparations touched every man, woman and child in Germany. They burdened the entire nation literally every day. Their weight would not be lifted for generations to come. Nationalist propagandists spoke of reparations as bondage and slavery.[1] The nightmare of Senegalese troops in the Rhineland occupation force raping German women had its more rarefied counterpart in political commentary, which saw Germany reduced by reparations to a semi-colonial status. The imposition of these foreign debts seemed to threaten Germany with relegation to the netherworld of third-class states – the Ottoman Empire, Persia, Egypt and China – which in the age of imperialism had retained the vestiges of sovereignty, but were in practice subordinate to foreign oversight and financial control.[2]

Nor were these fears without their echo on the French side. There were those who did fantasize about turning the Saar into a coal colony. In incautious moments there was talk in Paris of 'ottomanizing' the Reich.[3] These echoes of the age of imperialism are crucial to understanding why Germany reacted with such outrage to the financial claims against it. But like their obverse, namely Clemenceau's insistence that German sovereignty was respected by the peace, they imposed on the situation after World War I a vision that was out of date. It wasn't simply the inherent implausibility of viewing Germany as a French imperial possession, a story that had been played to its violent conclusion already in the Napoleonic era. The truly misleading aspect was to view Germany's situation under the Versailles Treaty in isolation from the global force-field in which all the European combatants now found themselves. Ironically, since it was the Entente that had constructed the new geometry of international finance, France's future position of subordination was already more definitely marked out by the spring of 1919 than was that of Germany.[4]

I

For the Entente there was nothing that was clearer in the wake of the war than that its economic and financial position had changed forever. For the French the shock was no doubt severest of all.[5] Before the war Paris had been second only to London as a source of international credit. Now France was a needy borrower. One prong of the French response was to rebalance the European economy at the expense of Germany. French heavy industry would be strengthened above all by deliveries of German coal and the ore from Alsace-Lorraine.[6] But this effort at European industrial rebalancing was combined with a wider vision that foresaw the extension of inter-Allied and transatlantic cooperation beyond the end of the war. In strategic terms this was in line with Clemenceau's insistence on the absolute priority of the three-way transatlantic democratic alliance. But whereas Clemenceau's mind roamed over centuries of European history and his rhetoric was that of nineteenth-century radicalism, the vision pushed by his Commerce Minister Étienne Clémentel was of a modernist, technocratic character.[7] Following the resolutions of the London economic conference of 1916, Clémentel envisioned a global collaboration between France, Britain and the US to secure joint control over key raw materials.[8] As he put it at the London conference, Clémentel hoped that the war would usher in nothing less than 'the beginning of a new economic era, one which permits the application of new methods, founded on control, on collaboration, on everything that can introduce some order into the process of production ... a new order of things, which will mark one of the great turning points in the economic history of the world'.[9]

Whereas the French vision of a military alliance of the Western democracies pointed forward to NATO, Clémentel's vision anticipated European integration.[10] Amongst his collaborators was the young businessman Jean Monnet, who spent the war based in London, helping to perfect the inter-Allied system of shipping control. After 1919 Monnet was to join his wartime colleague Arthur Salter for a stint at the economic commission of the League of Nations. Following a spell of entrepreneurial activity in China, Monnet joined de Gaulle in London in 1940, where he worked once again on questions of inter-Allied economic cooperation, emerging in 1945 as the godfather of French industrial modernization. In 1950 Monnet was to become renowned as the architect of the European Coal and Steel Community.[11] Fifty years later in his *Memoirs*, Monnet looked back with regret on what he saw as the missed opportunity of 1919. At this moment Europe might have taken a bold step toward industrial cooperation. 'It was to take many years and much suffering before Europeans began to realize that they must choose either unity or decline.'[12]

But it was the American position at least as much as the European that was to change between 1919 and 1945. Both future President Harry S. Truman and his fabled Secretary of State, George Marshall, saw combat in France in 1918. Returning to Europe in 1945, they hustled Paris into leading the rest of the continent toward cooperation and integration. Jean Monnet was amongst their most active collaborators. Back in 1919 the Wilson administration took a very different line. Washington set itself firmly against Clémentel and his integrationist schemes. Already on 21 November 1918, Treasury Secretary William McAdoo cabled the American representatives in London calling for them to cut back the functions of the inter-Allied bodies to a minimum, 'thus concentrating all important negotiations and decisions in Washington'.[13] Herbert Hoover, who had responsibility for food supplies, promised that the United States would 'not agree to any programme that even looks like inter-Allied control of our economic resources after peace'.[14] The proposal for a permanent joint wheat-purchasing scheme filled him 'with complete horror'. As far as the Wilson administration was concerned, the inter-Allied structures promoted by the French were really 'arrangements, which the English' would 'set up in London for provisioning the world with our foodstuffs and on our credit'.[15] The only guarantee that 'justice' would be done 'all around', Hoover insisted, was for America to act alone.

The sooner wartime regulations were stripped away, the sooner the unfettered movement of capital and goods would resume. Prosperity and peace would return and American pre-eminence would assert itself in its God-given medium. Markets and business would replace politics and military power.[16] But the consequences of this push to depoliticize the world economy were perverse. Far from taking politics out of economic life, the result was to drive Europe ever more deeply into the greatest financial and political entanglement of all – reparations. On 5 February 1919 Clémentel confronted the Economic Drafting Committee of the Council of Ten with the clear choice. France was willing to approve a moderate peace. But this depended on instituting 'by means of measures based on common agreement, an economic organization designed to assure the world a secure recovery . . .'. If not, the 'guarantee' of 'security' would have to be provided by a 'peace of reprisals and punishments'.[17]

11

Superficially the question was simple: how much reparation would the Allies demand? No answer was given at Versailles because the Big Three could not agree on a figure that seemed both realistic and politically acceptable. In this argument the chief roadblock to agreement were not the French, but the British. The basis for a Franco-American agreement was visible from the start. The restitution of the damage done by the Kaiser's army had been explicitly vouchsafed in the armistice terms. This was not even seriously disputed by the Germans. The bill for French reconstruction was agreed amongst the Allies at approximately 64 billion Goldmarks ($15 billion). Allowing for uncontentious claims by other parties, France announced it would settle for an overall total for all countries as low as 91 billion Goldmarks – providing it was allocated the lion's share. Paris was also happy to approve a far larger figure, provided that France's priority was acknowledged by an allotment of at least 55 per cent. In January 1919 French and American experts converged on a figure of 120 billion Goldmarks ($28.6 billion), within striking distance of the final figure of 132 billion Goldmarks that was eventually to be settled upon in London in May 1921.

Given the fact that its main claim was undisputed, the French priority was to obtain payment as quickly as possible. The reconstruction of northern France could not wait. Millions of people needed to be rehoused, villages rebuilt, farmyards restocked and industry set back on its feet. In the first instance, this would have to be financed either out of the savings of the French people or by loans from London or New York. By 1922, the French government had already advanced the equivalent of $4.5 billion for pensions and reconstruction in the devastated regions on a reparations account filled in the main through domestic loans. The crucial question was how soon Germany would assume the burden of financing.[18]

The British situation was entirely different. Britain had not suffered significant damage to its territory. But London had incurred huge losses to its shipping, it had run down its capital stock and borrowed on a gigantic scale to fund the entire Entente. For Britain the essential point was distributional. It needed to ensure that the wealth which had made London the hub of the Entente war effort did not leave it carrying a disproportionate burden for decades to come. The risk was that the spectacular damage to France and Belgium would be made good whilst the less visible attrition Britain had suffered would go unacknowledged. Furthermore, Britain needed to ensure that Germany did not emerge from the war as an even more formidable competitor than it already had been before. At its simplest, in the spring of 1919 the objective of the Lloyd George government was to impose a final total that was impressive and to ensure that Britain was allocated at least one-quarter of whatever Germany actually paid. If this proved unattainable then London would block any specific agreement, postponing a final settlement until the dust of the post-war crisis had settled. The initial demand formulated in December 1918 by the most hawkish experts that Lloyd George could muster was for a crushing total of 220 billion Reichsmarks.[19] At more than five times the best-known estimate of German pre-war national income, this figure was so exaggerated that it came to haunt Lloyd George as a symbol of his bad faith. It clearly took him by surprise as well. To maintain the balance of the European economy, Britain needed Germany hobbled but not crushed. The figure agreed in Paris between the French and Americans of only 120 billion Reichsmarks would have imposed a debt burden on Germany that was more sustainable, but by the same token it implied a British share that was dangerously lean. If the final figure was going to be a disappointment, Lloyd George preferred to postpone the bad news.

When the French would not agree to reduce their percentage share, Lloyd George shifted the argument to an in-depth discussion of the specific types of damage. This was the point at which the British introduced the battering ram of pensions. As the father of National Insurance in Britain, the subject was dear to Lloyd George's heart. But for the American legal team, the British insistence on the inclusion of pensions came to stand as a symbol of the betrayal of the armistice commitments. Berlin had agreed to pay for reconstruction and for damage caused by the aggression of the Kaiser. To include the costs arising from Allied welfare payments was going too far. On 1 April 1919 President Wilson himself was called upon to adjudicate. The ensuing debate is often taken to be a typical instance of Wilson's capitulation to European guile. After sitting through hours of argument, the President, according to the notes taken by Thomas W. Lamont, a partner in J. P. Morgan, gave voice to his frustrations: 'Logic! Logic! . . . I don't give a damn for logic. I am going to include pensions!' Was this the moment at which the President abandoned Germany to the rancour of Britain and France? Lamont was clearly anxious that his notes might be taken this way. So he included the explanation that the President's expostulation was not an 'off-hand utterance'. Wilson was not expressing a 'contempt for logic, but simply an impatience with technicality; a determination to brush aside verbiage and get at the root of things.' And there was 'not one of us in the room whose heart did not beat with a like feeling ...'.[20] The question at hand could not be settled 'in accordance with strict legal principles ...'. Wilson had no patience for the doctrine of original intent. 'He was ... continuously finding new meanings and the necessity of broad application of principles previously enunciated even though imperfectly, and that he felt that justice would be done by compelling the enemy to make good ...'[21] Regardless of the wording of the Armistice, why should war widows not be compensated? On 1 April Wilson gave his personal approval to the British push to expand the class of possible claims.

But this ad hoc approach had consequences. If all pension claims were admitted, the result was to inflate the sum to an impossible figure. This risked provoking the Germans into an outright rejection. So, instead, final agreement was postponed. To offset the immediate costs of reconstruction, Germany would deliver a substantial sum in 1919 and 1920 – in the order of $5 billion – for the immediate use of the Allies, much of it in kind.[22] These deliveries would be overseen by a Reparations Commission that by 1 May 1921 would also have the task of fixing the final total. The schedule of repayment would stretch to at least 1951. Should the annuities prove excessive, the Germans would have a right to appeal. In the meantime Germany would issue IOUs to the value of 20 billion Goldmarks to cover its obligations up to 1921 and a further 40 billion Goldmarks to cover the sums due by the 1930s ($4.8 billion and $9.6 billion respectively). A further tranche of 40 billion Goldmarks would be called upon if German economic conditions improved sufficiently.[23] Ideally, the French hoped to be able to sell these claims to investors in exchange for the dollars it urgently needed. But to ensure that it could control any such attempt to market the reparations bonds, America insisted that it must have a seat on the Reparations Commission and that a unanimous decision should be required in advance of any such sale.

III

This was obviously a makeshift arrangement. But it was a compromise agreed by all sides. Woodrow Wilson himself helped to broker the deal. All the major Entente powers signed. But what had they agreed?[24] Insofar as the financial settlement at Versailles had any substance beyond the immediate payments imposed on Germany, it consisted in an agreement between the United States, France and Britain to go on negotiating. Writing in December 1921, John Maynard Keynes, the British economist, former Treasury advisor and vocal critic of the Versailles Treaty, acknowledged the political logic behind this compromise. The reparations settlement was not wise, nor in every respect practical. In some respects it was clearly dangerous, but, with more than two years distance from the events, Keynes was able to admit that 'public passions and public ignorance play a part in the world of which he who aspires to lead a democracy must take account; . . . the Peace of Versailles was the best momentary settlement which the demands of the mob and the characters of the chief actors conjoined to permit'. If a truly safe and workable treaty could not be made in 1919, it was up to the skill and courage of the world's political leaders to construct one over the years to come.[25] Two years earlier, having resigned his position at the Treasury in a state of utter despair, Keynes had been in a far less patient mood. No single individual did more to undermine the political legitimacy of the Versailles peace than Keynes with his devastating book *The Economic Consequences of the Peace*, published in December 1919.

Generations of economists have picked apart the flaws in Keynes's argument.[26] But his critique stands both as a reflection of and as a major contributor to the mood of disillusionment that followed Versailles. Combining the authority of an economic expert, the colour of an insider and magnificent rhetorical force, Keynes's book sold in the hundreds of thousands. It was quoted verbatim in the Republican assault on Wilson's treaty in the US Senate. Both Lenin and Trotsky recommended Keynes as essential reading to the Comintern.[27] He was welcomed with open arms in Germany and helped to poison yet further the atmosphere between London and Paris. Superficially, of course, Keynes stood on Germany's side. But it was far from obvious, even from a German standpoint, whether he did not do more harm than good. His influence encouraged those in Germany who insisted that any payment was impossible, when a good faith effort to honour the treaty, even if it had fallen short, might well have steered the Weimar Republic away from the ruinous crisis of 1923.[28] Of course, the point is not that Keynes was personally responsible for the ensuing disaster. The point is that rather than reading Keynes as a guide to the reparations problem, we should see *The Economic Consequences of the Peace* as symptomatic of the crisis that is the central preoccupation of this book.

Keynes was perhaps the most outspoken member of that liberal faction within the British political class for whom the war was an agonizing symptom of a deeper malaise.[29] Even whilst serving at the very heart of the British war effort, on secondment from King's College, Cambridge, to the UK Treasury, Keynes was struggling with profound personal doubt. In 1916 he sought exemption from military service not on the grounds of his war work, but as a conscientious objector. As a civil servant he was barred from publishing under his own name, but under a pseudonym in April 1916 he contributed a strongly argued article in support of the pro-peace stand of the Independent Labour Party, spelling out an argument that in some respects anticipated Wilson's call for 'peace without victory'. But Keynes was not so much a Wilsonian as the mirror image of a Wilsonian. He opposed Lloyd George and those dedicated to delivering the knock-out blow precisely because they were leading Britain headlong into ever greater dependence on America. Whereas Wilson sought to insulate America from the aggressive impulses of the 'old world', Europe, for Keynes, stood for a fragile blend of capitalism with true personal and cultural freedom.[30] He saw none of this in America, even in its progressive version. What Wilson and Keynes had in common was a desire to preserve distance. The reality that faced them in 1919, however, was entanglement. If we compare the narrative of the peace provided by *The Economic Consequences* with what Keynes himself contributed as an expert to the peace conference, we get some sense of the contortions that were necessary to maintain at least the hope of disentanglement.

Keynes's best-seller was a book about Europe written from the vantage point of Britain, which, as Keynes insisted, stood 'outside' the continental crisis.[31] Keynes's message was addressed to the British government, appealing for it to take leadership. But what is striking is the way in which he edged around the question of America's part in the disaster. In chapter 3 Keynes delivered his devastating sketch of the Big Three as a bestiary of democratic vice. Wilson appears as the priggish Presbyterian preacher, Lloyd George as the quicksilver opportunist, but Clemenceau is the true villain of the piece – a wizened Frenchman who had imbibed the politics of Bismarck. This picture, however, is preserved in its simplicity only by excluding any treatment of the details of reparations from the stylized group portrait. It is only in the following chapters that Keynes addresses the treaty terms and reparations. Here his argument is subtly but significantly different. The main emphasis is on the point-by-point critique of every excessive demand made on Germany. But this is framed by a question. Could things have turned out differently?

Keynes argued that the only way that the crisis might have been defused was for Britain and America to have arrived at a general economic settlement in a preliminary discussion. Once again, his stress is on the British. But here, at least, Keynes goes beyond the personal critique of Wilson. The problem was that the American delegation had arrived at Paris without a properly worked-out economic plan.[32] What such a joint Anglo-American proposal might have involved does not emerge until the very end of Keynes's ferocious polemic. The first remedy he proposed was a reduction of the demands on Germany. But this, Keynes acknowledged, could only be justified in connection with a far wider financial rearrangement. Again he placed the onus on Britain to lead the way in abandoning all financial claims on Germany. But this, in turn, would have to be followed by a general cancellation of all inter-Allied debts and a new $1 billion loan, which would enable reparations to be paid and world trade to be restarted. As harsh as was his criticism of French demands, Keynes acknowledged at the end of his book that to consider a reparations reduction in isolation without allowing for a reduction of inter-Allied debts would be profoundly unjust.[33]

But in *The Economic Consequences of the Peace* Keynes never connected his outline of an alternative financial architecture with his furious personal polemic against the folly of Clemenceau and Lloyd George, or his historical account of how reparations came to be imposed. He presented his alternative plan as though it were an entirely novel idea, a great opportunity that had been missed at Versailles. His hundreds of thousands of readers across the world were left unaware of the fact that projects for a general reordering of the international economy, indeed Keynes's very own proposals, had been considered at Versailles and rejected, not by Paris but by Washington. By the time of publication, in the hope of achieving a constructive revision of the peace, Keynes no doubt wished to avoid recriminations with the Americans. Furthermore, he shared Wilson's deep distrust of the French. But the result was grossly to misrepresent the politics of the peace-making process.

As Keynes acknowledged, what gave London its scope for strategic action was that it could afford to separate the question of what to demand from Germany from the question of settling its debts with the United States. The rest of the Entente did not have this luxury. Early in 1919 the Italians, who in relation to their modest national income were carrying the most unbearable level of foreign debt, suggested that as a prelude to the peace Washington might consider a general reapportionment of the costs of the war.[34] The logic was simple. If the United States, by far the richest and least indebted of any of the combatants, were to grant substantial, well-publicized concessions to its European allies, they could afford both financially and politically to moderate their claims on Germany. Clemenceau's government promptly associated itself with this call. America's reaction was no less swift. On 8 March 1919, Treasury Under-Secretary Carter Glass cabled Paris that any such proposal would be treated as a veiled threat of default. Under such circumstances Washington could not be expected to consider any new credits. Washington insisted that Clemenceau should make a public commitment to refrain from any further demands for debt relief.[35] When, in April 1919, faced with the impasse in the Versailles negotiations, the French resumed their calls for concessions, they were reminded that Clemenceau's promise had been read into the congressional record. Paris was instructed in humiliating terms to put its financial household in order.[36]

To the British, these clashes between America and France were far from unwelcome. As Lloyd George wrote to London, the Americans were forming the view that 'the French have been extraordinarily greedy ... and ... in proportion to their increasing suspicion of the French is their trust of the British'.[37] Yet the British could not fault the logic of the French and Italian proposals. It was Keynes's task at the Treasury to prepare the British response, which was presented to the Americans at the end of March. As Keynes acknowledged, a complete cancellation of inter-Allied claims would impose a loss of £1.668 billion on the US. But Britain as a large net creditor to the Entente would also bear a substantial loss, running to £651 million. The chief beneficiaries would be Italy, which would be relieved of £700 million in debt, and France, which would be granted £510 million in debt relief. Among the great powers there was absolutely no precedent for such enormous transfers of monies, but in light of the relative strength of the Allied economies and the damage they had suffered in the war, this did not seem unreasonable. All the arguments that Keynes would later deploy with such dramatic effect against reparations were first put to use in March 1919 in an effort to persuade Washington of the disastrous consequences of upholding the entangling network of inter-Allied war debts. Keynes was quite frank about the desperate situation in which France found itself. If Britain and America were to insist on full repayment, 'victorious France must pay her friends and allies more than four times the indemnity which in the defeat of 1870 she paid Germany. The hand of Bismarck was light compared with that of an ally or of an associate.'[38] How were the populations of Europe to be brought to accept an infuriatingly inadequate reparations settlement, if not by means of generous concessions from those who could afford to make them?

What Keynes did not tell the readers of *The Economic Consequences of the Peace* was that the proposals he presented at the end of the book, like those of the French and the Italians, were immediately vetoed by Washington. The Americans wanted no linkage. To maximize its influence the Wilson administration wanted to deal with each Allied debtor bilaterally and to move as quickly as possible toward the restoration of free international trade and private finance. It was precisely to rebut this American vision of a rapid return to the Edwardian free-market status quo that Keynes wrote the first draft of the elegant historical narrative that would later frame his best-selling book. The American vision of a quick restoration of liberal capitalist finance was, Keynes insisted, based on a weak grasp of history. It was undeniable that before the war large-scale private lending had animated the financial markets of the world. London had been the hub of that system, Wall Street a client. But as Keynes pointed out, this system was no more than fifty years old and it was 'fragile'. It had 'only survived because its burden on the paying countries has not so far been oppressive' and because its material benefits were obvious. Loans were tied to 'real assets' such as railways, and as debts between private borrowers and lenders they were 'bound up with the property system more generally'. Crucially, international loans had been seen as promises of progress. Prompt debt service ensured the prospect of larger loans on more generous terms in future. Those who after World War I were calling for a rapid return to private finance were arguing 'by analogy ... that a comparable system between governments' could be made a 'permanent order of society', this despite the fact that the war had left obligations that were 'far vaster' and of 'definitely oppressive scale'. These debts corresponded in daily life to 'no real assets' and were unrelated in any direct way to the system of private property. To attempt an immediate return to laissez-faire liberalism was both unrealistic and dangerous. Given the massive labour unrest convulsing the industrial regions of Britain, France, Germany and Italy, policy-makers should not forget that, even 'capitalism at home, which engages many local sympathies, which plays a real part in the daily process of production, and upon the security of which the present organization of society largely depends, is not very safe'.[39]

Despite the force of these arguments and despite the unsatisfactory direction that the reparations negotiations were taking, the Americans would not hear of any dramatic debt-reduction plan. It was in response to their stonewalling that Keynes developed his second major proposal for international reconstruction – an international loan consortium. In *The Economic Consequences of the Peace* he touted the idea of an international loan of $1 billion, about £200 million.[40] Six months earlier at Versailles he had been more ambitious. To get the cycle of repayment going, Keynes proposed that Germany should be enabled to issue almost six times as much, £1.2 billion in foreign bonds.[41] Out of the proceeds, Germany would settle the most pressing demands of its wartime trading partners, allowing it to uphold its creditworthiness. Some £724 million would be used to settle its immediate reparations obligations. The rest of the Allies would provide Germany with £200 million in working capital with which to pay for the import of food and raw materials it urgently needed. To make the bonds attractive they would offer 4 per cent interest tax free. The international bonds would have absolute priority over all claims on the German government and they would be recognized as first-class collateral by all central banks. In the first instance the £1.2 billion in bond issue would be backed by the guarantee of the defeated powers collectively. But behind this guarantee would stand a consortium of the wartime Allies. The members of this consortium in turn would be answerable to the League of Nations. Unlike Clémentel, Keynes's aim was not to create an elaborate long-term structure of government control to replace free trade or private lending. But he was scathing about those who believed that 'with the early removal of obstacles in the form of the blockade and similar measures to free international intercourse, private enterprise may be safely entrusted with the task of finding the solution'. The problem of restoring Europe was simply 'too great for private enterprise, and every delay puts this solution further out of court'. The governments of Europe and America must act to restore basic lines of credit so that private initiative might then take over, otherwise those countries most in need of credit would be caught in a vicious circle of economic crisis, political uncertainty and diminished creditworthiness.[42] If the liberal economy was to be saved, if unpolitical international markets were to be restored, the precondition was a political masterstroke.

The American financial experts closest to the European situation fully understood this logic (Table 8). On 29 March 1919 Lamont of J. P. Morgan drafted a strongly worded letter to Treasury Secretary Russell C. Leffingwell. 'America holds the key,' he began. 'In the hands of the Secretary of the Treasury today, I believe is the power to conclude a real and lasting peace; if he fails to exercise that power, no one can foresee the consequences – consequences with almost as terrible results for America as for the rest of the world.' The letter was never sent.[43] But on 1 May 1919 Lamont did join forces with the economics expert Norman Davis to cable Washington, calling on the Treasury to do anything that it could 'prudently and safely' do.[44] But by contrast with the sympathetic voices of the bankers, a very different tone prevailed amongst those closest to the Wilson administration. Already on 11 April 1919 Hoover counselled Wilson that a sound post-war order could not be built on the wartime alliance between the United States, Britain and France. If America did not distance itself, the result would be an endless series of demands. If, on the other hand, Washington were to use its muscle to force Britain and France to moderate their reparations demands, then that would make the US appear as the friend of Germany. The only option was to withdraw altogether from entanglement. If the Allies were left with sole responsibility for their actions, they would refrain from making the unreasonable demands that they might make under US

Table 8. The Heavy Hand of the 'Associate': Allied Indebtedness to the United States (million $)

	pre-Armistice loans	post-Armistice loans	sale of war supplies and relief loans	net principal owed in February 1922	net interest accrued by February 1922	total net debt to US, February 1922
Great Britain	3,696	581		4,166	261	4,427
France	1,970	1,027	407	3,358	197	3,555
Italy	1,031	617		1,648	145	1,793
Belgium	172	177	30	378	29	407
Russia	188	5	5	193	25	218
Yugoslavia	11	16	25	51	5	56
Romania		25	13	36	4	40
Greece		15	15	15	1	16
total Allies	7,068	2,458	480	9,845	667	10,512

protection. Dissociating America from its former allies was crucial if the League of Nations was not to become 'a few neutrals gyrating around' an 'armed alliance'. That was bound to drive the 'central Empires' and Russia 'into an independent league'. Hoover then went on to spell out more clearly than Wilson ever did the underlying political logic of their shared vision of offshore American power. The 'necessary European revolution' was, in Hoover's view, not 'yet over'. America should admit to itself that it did not 'have the stomach to police it'. It should guard against becoming associated with a 'storm of repression of revolution'. The fact that it was Britain, France and Italy who were asking for concessions, not Germany, Austria or Hungary, appeared not to matter to Hoover. Even with its former allies America should not accept 'terms of coordination ... that would make our independence of action wholly impossible'. The United States was 'the one great moral reserve in the world' and it must preserve that moral capital intact. If the Europeans were not willing to accept the 14 Points in their entirety, America should 'retire from Europe lock, stock and barrel' and concentrate its 'economic and moral strength' on the rest of the world.[45] This was not isolationism. It was Wilsonian purism, a rejection of an entanglement with Europe in the interest of American world leadership.

The official American response to the Keynes plan was less insulting than their reaction to the French. But the rejection was no less decisive.[46] The Treasury denounced the plan as yet another European effort to turn America into the chief reparations claimant and as a threat to America's own creditworthiness.[47] Keynes's scheme would leave the world awash with dubious debt, accelerate inflation, and perpetuate the role of the state in the world economy, which was the root of so much discord.[48] The irresistible congressional pressure for tax cuts ruled out any write-down of US war loans to Europe.[49] Washington was not blind to the fact that to demand immediate repayment of the inter-Allied debts would cause a dramatic crisis. In September 1919 the Wilson administration announced a two-year moratorium on the payment of interest on inter-Allied debts.[50] But Washington made clear that this was a unilateral concession, not to be regarded as part of any grand bargain. Both principal and interest would eventually be paid in full. The Treasury reiterated its warning against any attempt by debtors to form a common front. It would negotiate with each European power separately. There would be no linkage between war debts and reparations.

Meanwhile France was running desperately short of dollars. In the autumn several large municipal loans came dangerously close to default in New York.[51] The US Treasury gave its grudging assent to a new French approach to Wall Street, but emphasized that American investors would expect at least 6 per cent in interest and would expect to be repaid in dollars, not devalued francs. In fact, the Treasury was far too optimistic. From Wall Street, Paris learned that given the unresolved overhang of $3 billion in inter-Allied loans, it would have difficulty negotiating even short-term credits. The governors of the Federal Reserve thought that the French would be lucky to attract lenders even at the punishing interest rate of 12 per cent. Given the whip hand exercised by the US Treasury, a peace whose terms were defined by the private capital markets was coming to look from a European point of view ominously like a 'peace without victory'.

16

Compliance in Europe

Reflecting on his first failure to overturn the post-war order, in his prison cell in Landsberg in early 1924, Adolf Hitler described in *Mein Kampf* how he awoke in November 1918, half blinded in a military hospital, to discover that the Armistice had been declared and that Germany was dissolving in revolution. He resolved to become a politician so as to fight the new world that had come so suddenly into existence.[1] Benito Mussolini was already a politician before the war. But the war transformed him too, as it transformed Hitler. Though Mussolini was to succeed where Hitler failed in taking advantage of the post-war crisis, in their methods and their basic historical vision they were in profound agreement. Modern Italy and modern Germany had been made barely three generations earlier, during the convulsive mid-nineteenth-century disintegration of Europe's post-Napoleonic order. What was to unite Hitler and Mussolini was their common reaction to the world crisis unleashed by World War I. The reality of world power as represented by the Big Three at Versailles was what they had to contend with. As Lloyd George commented to one of Wilson's inner circle in May 1919, 'as long as America, England and France stand together, we can keep the world from going to pieces'.[2]

The question that haunted both Hitler and Mussolini was what history held in store for Germany and Italy if Lloyd George was right. Neither Mussolini nor Hitler began their post-war careers by scorning the Western democracies, as the braggadocio of the 1930s might suggest. In the aftermath of World War I they regarded the Western Powers with a mixture of awe, fear, envy and resentment. In the spring of 1919 Mussolini spoke of Italy as a 'proletarian nation'.[3] The economic and military might of the Big Three was obvious. But democratic politics was not moribund in 1919 either. There had never been anything like Woodrow Wilson's global celebrity. Yet it was not Wilson who Mussolini and Hitler regarded as the model of a truly popular modern politician, but Lloyd George.[4] For both Mussolini and Hitler, it was Britain's war leader who had fashioned a demotic, popular ideology that energized an entire empire. It was to the Western Powers, the all-mighty defenders of the new order, that the future belonged, unless the insurgents could rally against their oppressive power.

In the fateful weeks between March and June 1919, Mussolini and Hitler were still faces in a crowd, Mussolini's somewhat more prominent. But in both Italy and Germany the nationalist groundswell was broad-based. Millions clamoured that their nations must not accept the place allotted to them in the new order being devised at Paris. They must attempt to assert their autonomy before it was too late. Nevertheless when the time came on 28 June 1919, the representatives of both Italy and Germany signed the Versailles Treaty. In the arguments between Britain and France and the United States we see what gave the peace its amorphous shape. In the struggles in Germany and Italy over acceptance we see the forces that held the peace in place.

I

After warding off the last Austrian offensive on the Piave river line in the summer of 1918, the Italian armies had bided their time before launching a crushing offensive on 24 October, the anniversary of Caporetto. In a matter of days the Austro-Hungarian Army collapsed and the Habsburg Empire disintegrated. Over the winter of 1918–19 the problem facing the Italian political class was what to make of this hard-won victory. In the first half of 1918 it had still seemed as though Prime Minister Orlando might move decisively to the center-left, making Italy the sponsor of self-determination throughout the Adriatic. But by December Sidney Sonnino was still in place as Foreign Minister and the broad-based coalition that Orlando had assembled in the wake of the Caporetto disaster was disintegrating. Both Bissolatti, the leading pro-war socialist, and Orlando's pro-American Finance Minister, Francesco Nitti, resigned. The supporters of the annexationist London Treaty were in full cry. But the far left was rallying as well. The space for compromise was rapidly shrinking. President Wilson attracted large crowds when he visited Italy in January 1919. But when, shortly after Wilson's departure, Bissolati attempted to present his vision at a League of Nations at rally in Milan, he was howled down by a mob with Mussolini to the fore.[5]

In 1918 the London Treaty had remained a domestic political issue. In 1919 it became an international *cause célèbre*, a test of the significance of the new international politics. Wilson was not unaccommodating to Italy. He enjoyed the company of Orlando. Sonnino had an upright reputation as an honest dealer. To the dismay of his purist supporters, Wilson was willing to offer Italy an extremely generous settlement at the expense of defeated Austria, giving Rome full command of the Brenner Pass along with its German-speaking population.[6] But the London Treaty was odious. Under its terms, for the sake of Italy's aggrandizement alone 1.3 million Slavs, 230,000 Austrians and tens of thousands of Greeks and Turks would have been transferred to Italian sovereignty. But Sonnino was unmovable. Virtually alone amongst the conference participants he refused even to pay lip-service to the new norms.[7] Though it might now be denounced by President Wilson, the London Treaty had been a solemn undertaking between Italy, Britain and France. Was a treaty to be dismissed as a mere scrap of paper, for which Italy had laid down the lives of more than half a million of its young men? For what had the Entente fought the war, if not for the sanctity of treaties? What terrified London and Paris was that if Rome had stuck to this line, they would have been faced with a stark choice between one regime of international legitimacy and another – the sanctity of treaties on the one hand and the emerging norms of a new liberal order on the other. The prospect of a head-on clash between the Europeans and Wilson left the conference in a state of deep agitation. For Lloyd George it would have been nothing less than a 'catastrophe if the European powers and the United States' had been divided by this legacy of the past.[8]

It was precisely because they realized the conflict facing them that both Britain and France had so actively supported the democratic interventionist wing of the Italian wartime coalition. If Rome would relinquish the territories promised in 1915, they offered instead to support Italian claims to influence in the Adriatic on the grounds of self-determination – by way of the Italian enclaves dotted along the eastern Adriatic coastline since the Middle Ages. Ironically, it was as part of this alternative, liberal programme of war aims that the democratic interventionists first raised the claim to the Italianate port city of Fiume, which under the Treaty of London had been assigned to Croatia. This exclusion had long rankled with Italian nationalists and over the winter of 1918–19 the demand for Fiume was taken up by Orlando. Though this helped to pacify the nationalist mob, in Paris the result was damaging incoherence. In an outrageously assertive memorandum presented to the Versailles conference on 7 February 1919, Rome claimed both its rights under the Treaty of London and Fiume, on grounds of ethnic self-determination.[9]

Fiume may have been an Italian town, but its hinterland was clearly Slav. Furthermore, it was the only major port city of the new Yugoslav state. President Wilson was willing to impose a severe peace on what was left of Austria. But the interests of Yugoslavia, an Entente ally, had to be defended. Wilson's experts were adamant that to make any concession to Italy would be to succumb to the worst habits of the 'old order'.[10] Britain was desperate not to clash with Wilson and was sponsoring the new Yugoslavia. Orlando's demand for both the honouring of the London Treaty and Fiume gave Arthur Balfour, the Foreign Secretary, the chance he needed. It was not London but Rome that was overturning the spirit and the letter of the 1915 agreement. In light of the Italian demand for Fiume, Britain no longer felt bound by the embarrassing terms of the London Treaty.[11] The French were more vulnerable to Italian pressure than the British. But to exploit that weakness Rome would have needed to act fast. Once the Big Three had reached agreement on Germany in early April, Clemenceau set his face against Italy. On 20 April as Orlando realized his predicament, there were embarrassing scenes as the Italian Prime Minister was reduced to tears.[12] On 23 April at Wilson's insistence, France and Britain jointly declared that Fiume would remain as part of Yugoslavia.

This was followed by a further unprecedented step. Over the head of the official delegation of a friendly government President Wilson issued a manifesto to the Italian people. America was 'Italy's friend', the American President declared. The two countries were 'linked in blood as well as in affection'. But America had been privileged 'by the generous commission of her associates ... to initiate the peace ...' and 'to initiate it upon terms she had herself formulated'. The United States was now under a 'compulsion' to 'square every decision she takes a part in with those principles'. Wilson chose not to mention the fact that in October 1918 Italy had protested the armistice negotiations and argued against the inclusion of the 14 Points. Now he asked Italians to accept that America was bound. 'She can do nothing else. She trusts Italy, and in her trust believes that Italy will ask nothing of her that cannot be made unmistakably consistent with those sacred obligations.'[13]

This direct appeal to the Italian population was the most dramatic expression of Wilson's distance from Europe's political institutions. If the British were regarded as imperialist recidivists and the French as 'selfish', the Wilsonian attitude toward the Italian political class was little short of contemptuous. In the wake of the military disaster at Caporetto in October 1917, US propaganda had been welcomed into Italy by the Orlando administration both as a sign of the new government's liberalism and as a substantial contribution to morale.[14] By August 1918 American speakers in southern Italy claimed to have encountered audiences that 'worshipped' the name of Wilson and had memorized entire passages from his speeches. To Charles Merriman, the chief of US propaganda, it seemed that Wilson should simply bypass the 'unpopular stench' that was 'called government' in Italy. If he put himself forward to the Italian population as their true leader, Wilson 'could so easily capture the whole situation for himself and do it in a perfectly legitimate and natural way'. All he had to do was to 'come down and play moral politics to the crowded and expectant galleries'.[15] The Wilsonians had hoped to put this to the test during the President's tour of Italy in January 1919, but Orlando denied Wilson the chance to address the adoring crowds in Rome. Now Wilson was making up for lost time. For his press secretary Ray Stannard Baker, Wilson's challenge to Rome marked the 'greatest moment of the Conference', bringing 'to the surface' the 'two forces which have so long been struggling in secret'.[16] Nor was Wilson content to rely on public diplomacy. On 23 April, whilst he approved an urgent $100 million credit for France, he ordered the suspension of any further financial assistance for Italy.[17] When Stannard Baker warned Orlando's aides that America would soon be ending support for the lira, the President applauded.[18]

The point was not lost on Orlando. Wilson, he spluttered, had 'addressed himself directly to the people of Italy along the lines which he had used to eliminate the Hohenzollerns as the ruling class of Germany'.[19] As was clear to all present at the conference, the American

President had challenged the Italian Prime Minister's right to speak for his people.[20] On the evening of 24 April, Orlando and Sonnino quit Paris to hold counsel with the cabinet and the Italian parliament.[21] In truth, both men were increasingly isolated not only in Paris, but within the Italian political class. Sonnino was no longer radical enough for the far right. Orlando had ruined his credentials with the left. But dissatisfaction with the government was emphatically not the same as being willing to accept an American President dictating terms to Italy. Even pro-war, pro-American voices such as Bissolati or the socialist Salvemini were indignant. They had not imagined that a 'peace of equals' would imply that Italy would be placed on the same footing as the rough and ready nation state of Yugoslavia. As Salvemini saw it, Wilson was venting on Italy his frustration at the shipwreck of his larger vision at the hands of Britain and France. Why did Wilson not have the courage to explain to the American people that if they demanded recognition of the Monroe Doctrine, other nations were entitled to the consideration of their regional interests too?[22] Wilson was 'remaking his virginity' at Italy's expense.[23]

With tempers running high, the Chamber of Deputies gave Orlando a resounding vote of confidence. In Rome there were outrages against the American flag. The embassy, Red Cross and YMCA buildings had to be placed under armed protection.[24] But this did not resolve the impasse in Paris. Orlando waited to be invited back to the conference. But no call ever came. Italy was important, but in truth it was not indispensable to the new order. The League of Nations Covenant was slightly amended to allow Italy to join at a later stage. The Big Three presented Germany with the peace treaty on 7 May and Orlando and Sonnino were left to slink back to Versailles without fanfare. They returned because not to do so would have turned Italy's victory into a dangerous isolation on the international stage. At the very least the country was in desperate need of coal deliveries from Britain and financial relief from America.[25] In 1913 Italy's coal imports had run at a rate of 900,000 tons per month. In the last two years of the war they had been throttled to barely 500,000 tons.[26] Its grain imports were similarly starved. Italy desperately needed the cooperation of its wartime allies. But as several further humiliating rounds of argument were to reveal, the Italians would be granted neither the full extent of the London Treaty nor the national totem of Fiume.

Orlando and Sonnino's position was untenable, and on 19 June they both resigned. They were replaced by a cabinet headed by 'L'Americano', Francesco Nitti, who promptly signed the Versailles Treaty with Germany. Striking a refreshing tone of reasonableness, the new Prime Minister pointed out that the treaty provision barring any move to unify Germany and Austria would mean that whatever the terms of the settlement with Yugoslavia, Italy's borders would be the most secure in Europe. But Nitti was boxed in by his predecessor's pandering to the nationalists. He could not simply abandon the claim to Fiume. Instead, his government proposed the neutralization of the city and its hinterland under the League of Nations. On 12 September 1919 this provoked the ultra-nationalist poet-demagogue Gabriele d'Annunzio into launching an occupation of Fiume at the head of a force of several thousand volunteers. The army was too unreliable for Nitti to order d'Annunzio expelled. So instead he called a general election in the hope that a truly representative national parliament would give him the support necessary to carry through the overdue reorientation of Italian foreign policy.

The election result on 16 November 1919 vindicated Nitti's government in at least one sense. The right-wing cheerleaders of the Fiume coup were crushed. Of the 168 members of the Fascio of national defence that had rallied around Sonnino in the final year of the war, only 15 were returned. Mussolini's first attempt to launch Fascism as a parliamentary party ended in humiliation. In Turin his movement won only 4,796 votes to the 170,315 cast for the Socialists and 74,000 for the Catholic Popolari. Mussolini himself was briefly arrested.[27] But Nitti's Liberals themselves suffered shattering losses. From controlling 75 per cent of the seats in parliament their share fell to just over 40 per cent. Like most forward-thinking Italians, Nitti hoped that he might be able to govern in cooperation with the moderate wing of the Socialist Party. And it was the left that triumphed in the polls, winning over 30 per cent of the seats. But at its party conference in Bologna in October 1919 the Italian Socialist Party (PSI), fatefully, had voted three to one in favour of joining Lenin's radical Comintern.[28] Fired by their surging electoral success and a huge wave of strikes and land seizures, the most intransigent wing of the PSI expected an imminent revolution. That in turn opened the door to Mussolini's second coming, no longer as a journalist or parliamentary politician, but as the leader of a new breed of right-wing enforcers, dedicated to destroying the Italian social-ist movement physically. Unfortunately for Nitti, the reformist socialists who might have helped to avoid this escalation did not break away from their radical comrades until 1922. Instead, Nitti remained in office only thanks to the toleration of the new Popular Catholic Party, which had secured a solid 20 per cent of the vote at its first attempt. Faced with strikes and land seizures, Nitti clung to the guiding idea of both his business and political career. If European liberalism was facing a pro-found crisis, it must look to support from the New World. The political and economic crises afflicting Italy could only be resolved with the help of the United States. Throughout the war Nitti had worked to secure finance and supplies from the US. Now he hoped that by riding out the storm of Fiume and forcing his countrymen to accept the 'mutilated vic-tory', Italy would gain acceptance as a favoured partner in a new world order, the centre of which would be on Wall Street.

II

In May 1919 the Versailles peace process entered its final, critical phase. On the morning of 8 May, as the German cabinet met to consider the terms of the peace that been presented to them overnight, President Friedrich Ebert called on his colleagues to curb 'the passion' that 'trem-bled through' all those present. They must calmly consider the document in front of them.[29] Otto Landsberg, the Social Democratic Minister of Justice who was responsible for preserving public order, called for a state of siege. By dampening the popular reaction this would maximize the government's freedom of manoeuvre and limit the political damage if it was forced to accept the humiliating terms. Both Philipp Scheide-mann for the Social Democratic Party and Matthias Erzberger for the Centre Party understood the need not to provoke the Entente. But both were furious at the terms offered to them. Furthermore, they feared that unless they took a strong stance against the treaty the position of their friends in the Progressive Liberal Party would become untenable as their bourgeois support moved to the right. Germany's first democratic government therefore opted to place itself at the head of a wave of orchestrated patriotic indignation.[30] The risk that the extreme right would take control of the theatre of outrage was obvious. But after the election of January the governing coalition of SPD, Centre Party and Left Liberal Party had reason to believe that they had support from every segment of German society. To create a suitably sombre mood, an immediate ban was declared on inappropriate theatrical performances and popular entertainments.[31]

On the afternoon of 12 May, Scheidemann, the veteran leader of the majority Social Democrats and first Chancellor of the German Republic, who as an itinerant teenage printer 'on the tramp' had once been reduced to begging a meal from Count Bismarck's soup kitchen, solemnly declared to the National Assembly that the Versailles Treaty was 'unacceptable [*unanehmbar*]'.[32] The hand that signed it would wither. Across Germany public opinion rallied in well-choreographed mass protests. The trade union leadership proclaimed the treaty a death sentence. Earlier in the year the USPD had made some headway in broaching the question of German war guilt. A confidential commission of inquiry had been set up to investigate the events of the July crisis of 1914. It had already produced damning evidence of German complicity in Austria's provocative ultimatum to Serbia.[33] But now any thought of publishing the incriminating findings was silenced.[34] The trade union leader Carl Legien declared that the Versailles peace terms dispelled any doubt about the true nature of the war. Whatever the guilt of the Kaiser and his entourage in starting the war, the people of Germany must now unite against the rapacious imperialism of the Entente. As Foreign Secretary Graf Brockdorff put it, the Republic should work to bring together 'workers, bourgeois and civil servants' in united opposition to the peace.[35]

Amidst the patriotic uproar, on 29 May the German government submitted a skilfully worded counter-proposal that sought to minimize territorial losses by making concessions on disarmament and reparations.[36] No party of the first Weimar coalition had any principled objection to disarmament. On Erzberger's urging, they embraced the abolition of conscription and agreed to reduce the army to 100,000 professional soldiers within three years.[37] In return they asked that Germany should be given a security guarantee by the League of Nations, which should take up the cause of disarmament across the board. The cabinet also agreed to make a substantial initial offer of reparations.[38] With the French and British unable to reach agreement on a final total, Germany offered 100 billion Goldmarks ($24 billion), starting with an initial tranche of 20 billion Goldmarks.[39] On closer inspection the offer was far less generous than it at first seemed. Whilst the French faced enormous up-front costs for reconstruction, the Germans were offering annual payments of only 1 billion Goldmarks. During the long wait for repayment, the principal was to carry no interest. Berlin also claimed credit for large quantities of requisitioned goods. More constructively, they asked for foreign credits to enable the cycle of trade and repayment to begin. Financing the reparations, the Germans hoped, would become a mechanism for their reintegration into the global economy.[40] At least as far as posterity was concerned, this counter-offer was a triumph. In his *Economic Consequences of the Peace* John Maynard Keynes made the German offer into his benchmark of reasonableness.[41] In early June 1919 Berlin came close to repeating the feat of October 1918 by splitting the coalition arrayed against them. This time it was not Wilson but Lloyd George who made a disruptive last-minute appeal for more generous terms. Recognizing that Poland was by far the most sensitive issue, London insisted that the division of Silesia must be settled by plebiscite. But this was as much as either Wilson or Clemenceau was willing to concede. On 16 June the Germans were handed back the treaty and told that they must give their assent within a week or face invasion. Though the Allies had demobilized the bulk of their armies, in June 1919 they still had the equivalent of 44 combat-ready divisions, more than enough to overwhelm any possible resistance.[42] The German situation was truly desperate. But even at this moment of crisis the Reich retained its sovereignty. The peculiar agony of Versailles was that it forced the vanquished to will their own defeat as a conscious choice.

Amongst the officer class and Junker barons of Prussia, the peace terms triggered the threat of open rebellion.[43] The territory to be handed to the Poles was Prussian heartland.[44] Why should Prussia accept a ruinous and humiliating peace in the East, where they had won a triumphant victory? There was talk of the legendary Graf David von York, who at Tauroggen in December 1812 had defied his King and had thrown the weight of patriotic Prussia behind Russia in its fight against Napoleon.[45] The state government of Prussia half-heartedly warned against acts of desperation. But it made clear that if the Reich failed to defend the 'vital interests [*Lebensinteressen*]' of the state of Prussia, then the 'healthy elements' would have no choice but to break away. A newly founded Eastern State (*Oststaat*) would create the launching pad for a future 'resurrection of the German Empire'.[46]

The position of the Foreign Office and the majority of the Weimar coalition was reflected in the memorandum drafted by the German peace delegation on 17 June.[47] They too advised rejection. The peace was insupportable because its terms were deliberately calculated to violate German self-respect. It was impractical. It was at odds with the terms of the Armistice. It was in bad faith because it asked Germany to admit against the truth its sole responsibility for the war and to recognize as a just peace what was in fact an act of violence. Honesty, the delegation insisted, was the only lasting foundation for a peace. It was not consistent with this basic axiom to sign a treaty that Germany was convinced it could not fulfil. By refusing to engage in direct face-to-face negotiations, the Allies had betrayed their own lack of conviction in the justice of their cause. For the Liberal Democrats, Hugo Preuss, the architect of the Weimar constitution, declared that accepting the treaty would be akin to committing suicide for fear of death. Prime Minister Scheidemann announced that if the Allies wanted to impose the treaty, they should come to Berlin themselves to do their own dirty work. So long as it remained true to itself, Scheidemann insisted, 'even a Germany that has been torn apart will find itself back together'.[48] This was a repeated refrain in 1919. If Germany agreed to be its own executioner, it would rob itself of any hope of regeneration. For the sake of the future, it must uphold its honour and accept the consequences, however disastrous. Unlike the Oststaat fantasists, the cabinet never contemplated armed resistance. But surprisingly serious consideration was given to Scheidemann's vision of simply abandoning German sovereignty to the Allies. Germany would surrender itself whilst declaring its faith that 'the progressive, peaceful development of the world will soon bring us a non-partisan court of justice, in front of which we will ask for our rights'.[49]

It took the level-headed courage of Matthias Erzberger to point out the dangers involved in a flirtation with Trotsky's tactic of 'No Peace. No War.' The French and British would never be foolish enough to fall in with Scheidemann's fantasy. They would not relieve the Germans of the burden of governing themselves in the face of defeat. They would not occupy the whole of Germany. They would simply lop off those assets that were profitable, reducing the rump to a state of impoverished chaos. The League of Nations was an attractive court of appeal. But this neutral arbiter would only be called into existence through Germany's ratification of the treaty. If German liberals still hoped for a 'progressive, peaceful development' of world politics, they would have to make a painful down-payment, by choosing the path of cooperation rather than confrontation.[50] However unjust and dishonest the terms, the Versailles Treaty did at least offer the chance of preserving the German nation state intact. As Erzberger sensed in his democratic bones, what the vast majority of the population yearned for was not national heroics but peace. This was dramatically confirmed at an emergency meeting of the prime ministers of the 17 member states of the Reich, at which Bavaria, Württemburg, Baden and Hesse spoke strongly in favour of acceptance.[51] It might be painful for Prussia to cede territory to Poland, but if the Reich did not comply with the peace it would be the west and south that would face a French invasion. In this regard, as Brockdorff commented with ill-concealed scorn, Erzberger's demagoguery knew no bounds. He had 'let it be discretely known,' Brockdorff sneered, 'that he did not want to dilate on the rape of German women by Senegalese and negro troops, but that the invasion would inevitably lead to the collapse and disintegration of the Reich'.[52]

This was distasteful, no doubt. But Erzberger and the other advocates of acceptance, notably Eduard David, his long-time associate on the right wing of the SPD, were dogged in their commitment to securing the future of the Reich. If Berlin failed to respond to the German population's desire for peace, there would be disaster. In October 1918 the Reichstag majority had taken responsibility for opening armistice negotiations and despite the mutinous heroics of the navy and the socialist revolution, they had at least avoided an unconditional surrender or wholescale occupation. If the Reichstag majority did not steel itself for a further act of courage, Germany was once again threatened with disaster. A government led by the USPD, the one party that had forsworn any loyalty to the continuity of the German state, would sign a humiliating peace on terms congenial to either the Entente or Moscow. The result would be an all-out civil war. Germany would follow Russia toward disintegration and anarchy. Insofar as there was a specific scenario fuelling the violence against the left in post-war Germany, it was not the fear of the overthrow of capitalism so much as this nightmare of a rerun of Trotsky's disastrous gamble in western Europe. If maintaining the integrity of the Reich was the uppermost goal, then the only option was to take the step that Tsereteli and Kerensky had not dared to take in the summer of 1917. Germany must fashion a broad-based national government to accept a humbling peace.[53] The question was how to find the necessary majority for acceptance.[54]

Throughout early June, General Wilhelm Groener and Defence Minister Gustav Noske struggled day by day to stem the mounting tide of military rebellion.[55] Their efforts allowed the civilian politicians to have the last word. When President Ebert put the question to Prime Minister Scheidemann's cabinet on 18 June, the result was a split. Erzberger and the two other Centre Party members voted to approve the treaty. But the Social Democrats were divided, with Prime Minister Scheidemann voting against, along with Foreign Minister Brockdorff and three other Liberal Democrats. The meeting ended inconclusively at 3 a.m.[56] A few hours later a majority of the SPD parliamentary party voted to accept the treaty with conditions. But since there was no prospect of the Allies accepting any conditions, the only effect of the vote was to render the position of Prime Minister Scheidemann untenable. He had pledged to reject the treaty and was forced to resign. With four days to go to the Allied deadline, Germany had no government. In the National Assembly the parties continued vainly to discuss conditions.[57]

The naval officer corps, whose recklessness had precipitated the final collapse in November 1918, gave a more emphatic response. On the morning of 21 June 1919, with the Kaiser's Ensign flying, Rear Admiral Ludwig von Reuter replied to the peacemakers at Versailles by ordering the scuttle of the German High Seas fleet interned in the British naval base of Scapa Flow. Though British marines struggled to prevent this violation of the Armistice, killing nine German seamen in the process, the Germans managed to sink the vast bulk of the Kaiser's navy – 15 battleships, 5 cruisers and 32 destroyers – the largest loss of ships on any single day in the annals of naval history. Back in Germany, Field Marshal Hindenburg insisted that his soldiers' honour dictated a similar course. Though they would be overwhelmed in the West, the German Army should retreat to a defensive bastion in the East and resume the struggle. President Ebert, in choosing Scheidemann's replacement, kept his options open by nominating a solid trade union patriot, Gustav Bauer, who had previously spoken strongly against the treaty.

It was not until 12 noon on 23 June, the final day of grace, that President Ebert finally accepted that the oppositional forces had no majority. Both the SPD and the Centre Party, the parties on which the Republic depended, were profoundly split. The minimal national solidarity necessary to enable democratic politics to function hung by the most tenuous of threads. As Ebert, Bauer and the government ministers condemned by default to take responsibility for the treaty left the final all-party conference, the rejectionist leader of the Liberal Democrats recorded that he was suddenly seized by 'a sense of responsibility'.[58] In an important concession, which was henceforth to define those who accepted the basic parameters of democratic politics in the Weimar Republic, the Democrats and at least some of the Nationalists gave an assurance to their colleagues that despite their differences, they would respect the patriotic motives of those who took responsibility for signing the peace. It was a fragile commitment soon renounced by an irresponsible nationalist backlash, but on 23 June 1919 the mere promise was enough. At 3.15 p.m. with only hours remaining, the National Assembly delivered the crucial vote. No names were recorded. Nor was the Assembly asked directly to approve the Versailles Treaty. A 'large majority of the Assembly' was declared to have confirmed the cabinet's view that it had authority to sign. Ninety minutes later the Allies were formally notified.

Whilst Paris celebrated, Berlin faced the disillusioned reality of defeat.[59] Warnings from General Groener and Defence Minister Noske were enough to abort an attempted coup by Prussian guards units at the end of July.[60] But amongst the advocates of an Oststaat, the kernel of a putschist movement had formed. In the autumn of 1919 the nationalists built momentum by launching vituperative public attacks against the SPD and Erzberger, which by the following spring would drive Erzberger out of politics amidst corruption allegations. The stab-in-the-back legend began to develop real momentum. The critical moment was reached in March 1920 when, under the disarmament clauses of the treaty, it came time to disband the paramilitary Freikorps units.[61] On 13 March, Wolfgang Kapp, one of the original organizers of the *Vaterlandspartei* that had spearheaded the rally against peace in 1917, and General Walther von Lüttwitz, the orchestrator of the Freikorps, led their men in a march on Berlin. They demanded a non-party ministry dominated by soldiers and an end to compliance with the treaty. They also wanted immediate national elections, which they believed would sweep away the left-wing National Assembly that had been an aberration of the immediate post-war moment. As it turned out, the electoral calculation of the putschists was not entirely awry. But their practical preparations were woeful. Kapp had few influential friends in Berlin. Furthermore, the putschists had fundamentally misjudged the balance of real force that underpinned the Weimar Republic. During the revolutionary upheaval of November 1918 the trade unions had played a deliberately low-key role, preferring to dampen down shop-floor radicalism. But faced with a direct attack on the Republic, their response was decisive. A nationwide general strike paralysed the country. By 17 March the putsch was over.

For a few days the labour movement celebrated the triumph of workers' power. All the governing parties of the Republic, including the Liberal Democrats, were required to sign up to a manifesto reaffirming the call for state ownership of key industries.[62] Gustav Noske and other SPD leaders contaminated by collaboration with the Freikorps were forced out. There was excited talk of a new government of socialist unity. But even if they had been able to collaborate, the USPD and the SPD fell well short of a majority in the National Assembly. And, as quickly as it had arisen, the fantasy of left unity was dispelled when in the Ruhr, the heartland of German heavy industry, the anti-Kapp general strike transformed into a rolling socialist uprising. By 22 March communist militants had formed into Red Guard detachments and seized control of the industrial cities of Essen and Duisburg. A desperate effort was made at mediation, but with 50,000 of its own men under arms, the radical left now wanted a trial of strength.[63] Amidst bitter fighting and gruesome reprisals, tens of thousands of pro-government troops, spearheaded once more by the Freikorps, retook the Ruhr. The government side suffered at least 500 dead. Over 1,000 insurgents were killed, the majority of whom were executed after capture.

The Kapp putsch and the subsequent Ruhr uprising revealed how close Germany had come to civil war. It also confirmed Erzberger's nightmare of foreign intervention. The Ruhr was part of the demilitarized western territory of Germany. In reaction to the entry of German army units, the French seized control of the city of Frankfurt. But astonishingly, despite this escalating violence, the well-habituated machinery of German democratic politics continued to function. Elections were the one wish granted to the putschists. Two months after the fighting ended in the Ruhr, on 6 June 1920 almost 28.5 million men and women voted for the first Reichstag of the Weimar Republic. The 80 per cent turnout delivered a body blow to the founding parties of the Republic. From a commanding share of 75 per cent the 'Reichstag majority' coalition of SPD, Centre Party and Democratic Liberals slumped to less than 45 per cent. Punishing the SPD for its complicity with the counter-revolution, the voters of the left made the USPD into the second largest party in the Reichstag. Meanwhile, the intransigent nationalists of the German National People's Party (DNVP) surged to 15 per cent, as well as the conservative right had done in any German election since the days of Bismarck. A huge fund of democratic political capital had been wasted in 1919–20, but the result did not overturn the founding compromises of the Republic. A vote for the USPD was as likely to be a vote for a more radical democratic Republic as it was for a dictatorship of the proletariat. The Leninist Communist Party scored a derisory 2 per cent.

The big winners of the election were the nationalist liberals of the DVP. Their leading spokesman was Gustav Stresemann, who had made himself infamous during the war as one of the most uproarious exponents of Wilhelmine imperialism. Following the revolution Stresemann had suffered a nervous collapse and in March 1920 he came perilously close to complicity with the Kapp putsch.[64] But with the passing of that crisis he gained a new sense of purpose. What 1919–20 taught was that the advocates of acceptance of the Versailles Treaty had been correct. For the foreseeable future the fate of Germany hung on the fate of the Republic and its ability to come to terms with the former enemies in the West. Like Erzberger, Stresemann understood that the decisive power was above all the United States. But whereas Erzberger had gambled on the fickle politics of Wilsonian liberalism, Stresemann would place his bet, like Francesco Nitti in Rome, on what he believed to be a more durable force, the strategic interest of American business in the future of the European economy.[65]

17

Compliance in Asia

At the signing ceremony on 28 June 1919 the Chinese were the only delegation to stay away. Since the first week of May the Versailles conference had reduced the largest country in the world to uproar. The transfer by the conference of Germany's Shandong concession to Japan was to go down in the epic of modern Chinese nationalism as a founding moment. China became at once the victim of both Japanese aggression and Western hypocrisy.[1] But this morality tale of Chinese martyrdom and Japanese aggression was always incomplete. The high stakes involved for both sides had been made evident by the crisis precipitated by China's entry into the war in 1917 and the fraught politics of the Siberian intervention. The attempt to make peace in 1919 forced basic questions about Asia's future back onto the global agenda.

I

In tune with the 'spirit of the times', Japan's new post-war government had dispatched a pro-Western, liberally inclined delegation to the peace conference.[2] The year 1918 ended with Prime Minister Hara Takashi drawing down one-third of the Japanese contingent in Siberia. Meanwhile, though Hara brought the activist China-hand Tanaka Giichi into his cabinet as Defence Minister, the policy of cooperation with Beijing remained firmly in place. General Duan, Japan's pawn in 1917, was gone. Instead, Tokyo had encouraged peace talks in Shanghai between North and South, enabling China to send a unified delegation to Versailles. But what road would a unified Chinese state take?

The government in Beijing after the fall of Duan showed little sign of rebelling against Japanese tutelage. From the South, Sun Yat-sen looked for recognition wherever he could get it. In January 1919 he sought to interest the leaders of global capitalism in a remarkable plan for comprehensive economic development.[3] But he could not even get an acknowledgement from the White House. America's ambassador in Beijing, Paul S. Reinsch, continued his anti-Japanese agitation. However, his own visions for China's development, like those circulating in Washington, were deeply patronizing, involving large-scale international supervision. In early 1919 Japan agreed to join the international loan consortium, seeming to suggest an end to its high- pressure financial diplomacy of the war years. Its sole reservation was that its prime Manchurian railway assets should be exempted from consortium oversight.

The British, given their enormous stake in China, viewed the prospect of a clash between Japan and America with considerable anxiety. London was reluctant to abandon its Japanese ally and uncertain of America's true intentions. It was left to Britain's ambassador in Beijing, Sir John Jordan, to advocate a new policy in Asia based on building a fresh relationship with China. He hoped to neutralize and internationalize all foreign concessions in China, abolishing spheres of interest, thus rendering 'such terms as open door and China's integrity realities and not the meaningless expressions they too often are at present'. 'Without sacrifices on the part of the powers who acquired or inherited leased territories of 1898, no solution of the China problem seems possible,' Jordan insisted. It was up to the United States and Britain to lead the world toward a system that would 'guarantee economic freedom and military security . . .'[4] Whilst London and Washington weighed up their options, Jordan feared that the initiative might pass to the Japanese.

In January 1919 the Counselor to the State Department, Frank Polk, put a dark construction on Japan's new support for Chinese unity in a report to Secretary of State Robert Lansing.[5] At Versailles he warned they might join together to mount an all-out attack on Western privileges in Asia. With Japanese backing, Beijing would demand a wholesale treaty revision. Such claims were fully consistent with the new language of a liberal international order, but they were demands that 'the white powers could not meet' without forfeiting their grip on East Asia.[6]

Given this uncertainty, the Americans were only too happy to turn the Paris negotiations into a stage for a confrontation between Japan and China. On 27 January, at President Wilson's insistence, the Chinese delegation was in attendance when Japan bluntly presented its demands for Germany's treaty rights in Shandong. The Americans then coached the most articulate element in the Chinese delegation, headed by the American-trained Wellington Koo, representing the Northern government in Beijing, to formulate a set-piece of liberal outrage directed against Tokyo. Koo rejected Japanese claims to German privileges as unwarranted intrusion on the rights of a nation of 400 million people. Putting on display his American legal training, Koo invoked the principle of *rebus sic stantibus*, insisting that a treaty could be overturned if the conditions under which it were signed were overturned. The Western delegations were impressed by his fluency and within days, as the news of the hearings in Paris spread eastwards, the Beijing government received messages of support from across China.[7] The original intention of the Chinese political class in joining the war had been to secure a seat at the table. Now, with American approval, it appeared that China would score a great diplomatic triumph over Japan.

But what Koo failed to acknowledge was that Japan was not demanding the German rights by force majeure. In compliance with its new policy of cultivating good relations with Beijing, in September 1918 the Terauchi government had gained the signature of Chinese Prime Minister Duan to an understanding that conferred on Japan the right to maintain a garrison in Shandong in exchange for a further tranche of Nishihara's financial largesse and a promise that Japan would back China's campaign to revise the entire structure of unequal treaties.[8] Meanwhile, Britain and France had conceded Tokyo's claim already in January 1917 in exchange for Japanese naval assistance in the Mediterranean. The revelation of these commitments by Beijing, Paris and London brought the first debate on the Shandong question to an embarrassing standstill.

For the representatives of Tokyo the first days at the Versailles peace conference had come as a painful shock. The Japanese had acknowledged Wilson's 14 Points, but they had not anticipated that the entire conference would be framed in liberal terms. They had certainly not expected to be made to plead their case in front of the Chinese. What were the West's intentions? Were they seriously interested in a more equitable international order, or were they, as the Japanese right wing suspected, intending 'to freeze the status quo and hold in check the development of second-rate and lower-ranked nations'?[9] It was this uncertainty that gave crucial salience to the Japanese demand for race equality to be written into the League Covenant. As the Western strategists suspected, this had pan-Asian appeal and would allow Japan to offset its image as an imperialist aggressor. But above all this was a question of domestic politics.[10] In the wake of the rice riots of 1918 the complexion of Japanese politics had irrevocably changed. The masses were agitated. After touring Europe and the United States in 1919, the leading parliamentary liberal Ozaki Yukio returned to Japan convinced that only universal suffrage could channel the forces of change in a constructive direction.[11] But it was not only the left that drove Japan's new era of popular political mobilization.[12] Popular nationalism too experienced a dramatic revival. The significance of the demand for racial non-discrimination for the Hara government in the spring of 1919 was precisely that it was the only issue on which the militants of both left and right could agree. How would the West respond?

Already on 9 February the American legal expert David H. Miller recorded a frank exchange between Colonel House and Lord Balfour on the question of the upcoming Japanese motion. To pre-empt the Japanese, House sought to persuade Balfour to accept an amendment to the Covenant's preamble that would include a quotation taken from the Declaration of Independence to the effect that all men were created equal. 'Colonel H's view was that such a preamble, however little it squared with American practice, would appeal to American sentiment, and would make the rest of the formula more acceptable to American public opinion.'[13] Balfour's response was striking. The claim that all men were created equal, Balfour objected, 'was an eighteenth-century proposition which he did not believe was true'. The Darwinian revolution of the nineteenth century had taught other lessons. It might be asserted that 'in a certain sense . . . all men of a particular nation were created equal'. But to assert that 'a man in Central Africa was created equal to a European' was, to Balfour, patent nonsense. To this remarkable broadside, House offered no immediate rebuttal. He was not about to disagree about Central Africa. But he pointed out that 'he did not see how the policy toward the Japanese could be continued'. It could not be denied that they were a growing nation who had industriously exploited their own territory and needed room to expand. They were refused outlets in 'any white country', in Siberia and in Africa. Where were they to turn? 'They had to go somewhere.' Balfour did not question this fundamental premise of the age. Dynamic populations needed space into which to expand. Indeed, as a staunch advocate of the Anglo-Japanese alliance, Balfour 'had a great deal of sympathy' for the Japanese predicament. But with Central Africa on his mind, he could not admit the general principle of equality. Other ways must be found of satisfying Japan's legitimate interests. In any case, Balfour was clearly interpreting the proposal far more expansively than the Japanese ever intended it. The idea that Japan might be speaking on behalf of Africans would no doubt have caused indignation in Tokyo. What was at stake were European-Asian relations and specifically the right of Asians to join Europeans in the settlement of the remaining open territories of the world.[14]

Blocked at the first attempt, the Japanese delegation could not settle for a simple rejection. At the end of March they presented a new, watered-down version of their proposal, eliminating any reference to race and demanding only non-discrimination on a national basis. But they now found themselves caught in the labyrinthine internal politics of the British Empire. It was the authority of the British delegates – Robert Cecil and Lord Balfour – that had blocked the first Japanese amendment. But, when pressed, the British insisted that it was not they but the Australians who were the real obstacle. This further raised the pressure on the Japanese delegation. How were they to explain to the Japanese public that a principle of such obvious importance had failed as a result of the objections of a country as insignificant as Australia? But London stood by the White Dominions and on this occasion Wilson was only too happy to back Australia up. In light of attitudes in California on the Asian issue it was hugely convenient to let the British Empire provide the first line of resistance.[15] There was no prospect whatsoever of Congress approving a Covenant that limited America's right to restrict immigration.

The affair reached its discreditable climax on 11 April at the final meeting of the League of Nations Commission. The Japanese had now retreated to demanding nothing more than an amendment to the preamble, calling for the 'just treatment of all nationals'. On this basis they could count on a clear majority in the Commission. As the French put it, they had no wish to cause embarrassment to London, but 'it was impossible to vote for the rejection of an amendment, which embodied an indisputable principle of justice'. When the Japanese put the question, their opponents were so shamefaced that they asked that their No votes not be officially recorded. As Cecil's notes reveal, only the notoriously anti-Semitic Polish delegate Roman Dmowski voted with the British, forcing Wilson to use his power as chairman to block the amendment by ruling that it required unanimity.[16] Despite the clear majority in favour, the Japanese proposal was dropped.[17] Whereas House was pleased to celebrate a demonstration of 'Anglo-Saxon tenacity, with Britain and American alone against the majority', the affair clearly left a nasty taste in Cecil's mouth.[18]

II

The peace-making process in Asia never recovered from the humiliation dealt to Japan over the League of Nations Covenant.[19] On 21 April, ten days after the racial equality proposal was vetoed by the Americans and the British, the diplomatic advisory council met in Tokyo to chart their strategy for the final round of negotiations. In light of the humiliation over the Covenant, the council concluded that Japan must threaten to abandon the conference if it was not granted Germany's Chinese concession on the Shandong Peninsula. Early on in the negotiations in Paris, Japan had secured its fair share of Germany's Pacific Island colonies. It had joined Britain and France as a mandatory power. But China was a matter of even greater import. As Foreign Minister, Viscount Uchida cabled the delegation 'to maintain our government's dignity there shall be no room for conciliatory adjustment'.[20]

Predictably enough, when they returned to the matter in late April, the Western Powers proposed that Shandong should be 'internationalized'.[21] Some mandate-like structure should be devised. The mandate model had been proposed by Jan Smuts to deal with central Europe, but had been rejected there. In January it had been used to distribute the fragments of the German and Ottoman empires between the British Empire, the French and the Japanese. But Shandong was a different matter altogether. Japan angrily rejected any such idea.[22] Mandates were for 'colonies ... where the native peoples still lacked modern civilization ... in cases like China, a country with a developed culture', quite different principles applied.[23] More constructively, the Japanese delegation were at pains to explain to Wilson that they represented a government that belonged to the 'moderate' wing of Japanese politics. They were willing to consider a fundamental revision of the international order in East Asia, but this made it particularly regrettable that they were being made the scapegoat of Chinese nationalism. The Western Powers could not defend Beijing's rights in the name of the equality of states and at the same time allow the Chinese delegation to disregard, on grounds of incompetence, treaties signed by their own government only months earlier. As one of Japan's delegates put it to Robert Lansing, was it not 'ridiculous for a nation of 400 millions to go around complaining that they had signed a treaty under duress'.[24] Japan was asking no more than that China honour its contractual commitments. If Japan was not accorded its rights, its representatives would depart from the peace conference. Unlike the Italians they did not muddy their case with additional claims. And they could count on sympathy both from the British and the French. Saionji appealed particularly to his old friend Georges Clemenceau to appreciate the pressure that he was under on the home front.[25]

Wilson was desperate not to lose both the Japanese and the Italians from the conference in a single week.[26] He did not pay the Japanese population the double-edged compliment he paid the Italians by appealing to them over the heads of their own government. On 22 April the argument shifted decisively in Japan's favour. The Chinese delegation were told that though they had the sympathy of the Western Powers, they must consider themselves bound by their prior treaty with Japan.[27] To moderate the blow, on a suggestion from Britain, a compromise was reached under which Japan publicly stated its desire to inherit only the economic privileges granted to Germany in Shandong and renounced any intention of assuming permanent administrative control of the territory.[28] But given the charged emotions on both sides, this was far from enough. Even an apologetic delegation from Wilson could not dissuade the Chinese from issuing a formal protest to the Council of Four, invoking the 14 Points.[29]

Given the vested interest of the Chinese elite in international recognition at almost any price, the matter might well have rested there, had it not been for the reaction in China itself. Since Japan's humiliating 21 Points ultimatum in 1915, the cities of China had witnessed wave upon wave of nationalist protest. When the news of Japan's success over Shandong reached China on 4 May 1919, the anger it unleashed expressed the entire frustration experienced since the revolution.[30]

Given what had been revealed in Paris about Beijing's arrangements with Japan, it is no surprise that this was directed inwards as well as outwards. The key slogan of the protests faced both ways: 'externally, let us struggle for sovereignty; internally throw out the traitors'.[31] In the capital the residence of Cao Rulin, China's Finance Chancellor and the chief conduit for the Nishihara loans from Japan, was burned to the ground. Of the total student population of Beijing at the time, half are believed to have participated in the uprising, including many from the Women's Teachers' College.[32] Nor was it only young radicals who took up the cause. The warlords and politicians who had been meeting sporadically in the North-South peace conference brokered by Japan immediately called a special session from which they instructed the Paris peace delegation that 'if the peace conference should ... refuse to uphold China's position, we 400 million Chinese people ... will never recognize it'.[33]

These unprecedented protests placed the diplomats in Paris in an impossible position. Koo was desperate to secure for China a position as a founding member of the new order. But he could not sign the Versailles Treaty without reservations on Shandong. Wilson and Lloyd George ruled this out. Making an exception for the Chinese risked derailing the entire conference. The Beijing Foreign Ministry was forced to inform the indignant provinces that the balance of interests suggested that China should sign the treaty anyway. Once League of Nations membership was secured, the Chinese assumed that the other nations would vote them into the League's Council, from where they might seek redress. But the reaction to this proposal was a further round of student demonstrations and strikes. With Beijing under martial law, over one thousand patriotic protestors were detained. By early June, the conservative Chinese President Xu Shichang was scandalized to see a noisy crowd of young women outside his residence demanding the release of their incarcerated male classmates. In solidarity, the merchant community formed a nationwide business association and announced a boycott of Japanese goods.[34] In Shanghai protests in foreign-owned textiles plants brought out perhaps as many as 70,000 workers in what was the first overtly political mass strike in Chinese history. Meanwhile, anxious to do their bit for the national cause, Chinese students studying at universities across America besieged Congress and found an unusually receptive audience amongst Republicans who were only too happy to accuse Wilson of going soft on 'Japanese imperialism'.

On 10 June Prime Minister Qian Nengxun's cabinet collapsed, and a day later President Xu Shichang tendered his resignation.[35] A first round of detainees were released, but the nationalist protests continued unabated. On 24 June the Chinese government resorted to the humiliating expedient of announcing that its 'strategy' consisted of allowing the delegation in Paris to make up their own minds. Meanwhile, the most senior member of the delegation had retired to a suburban French sanatorium, leaving the rest of the team besieged in their hotel rooms on the Boulevard Raspail by a picket of enraged students. Independently, on 27 and 28 June first the Beijing government and then the Paris delegation decided that China could not sign the treaty.

III

The Japanese delegation signed the Versailles Treaty and Japan took its place as a member by right of the inner Council of the League of Nations. Its status as a major power was now undisputed. But the price that it had paid was steep. On the nationalist right the dual experience of the rejection of racial equality and the scorn heaped on Japan over its Shandong claim provoked a violent counter-reaction. In early 1919 General Ugaki Kazushige, a subordinate of Tanaka, commented: 'Britain and America seek, through the League of Nations, to tie down the military power of other nations whilst nibbling away at them through the use of their long suit, capitalism. There doesn't seem to be much difference between military conquest and capitalist nibbling.'[36] Japan must hone its sword to respond in its own way. In October 1921 three young Japanese military attachés met in Baden-Baden, Germany, to discuss the example provided by the European states for Japan. For these future leaders of right-wing Japanese militarism, Ludendorff's concept of a new era of Total War waged between huge global power blocs was one of the most inspiring concepts produced by World War I. For young Japanese military officers in Germany in the aftermath of the war, including Tojo Hideki, later the much-reviled leader of Japan in World War II, this was a future they envisioned for Japan in a struggle against the Western Powers.[37] They would fight at a vast material disadvantage, as Imperial Germany had done. They would compensate on the one hand by establishing an autarchic zone in China and on the other by rallying the army around an extreme samurai ethic, which depicted 'the way of the warrior (bushido) as the search for death'.[38] But this was not the mainstream response, even amongst nationalists who were hostile to the new Western order. Whatever one thought of the hypocrisy of the West, the force at its command demanded respect. Ugaki no less than Prime Minister Hara was convinced that 'for the forseeable future, the world will be an Anglo-American realm'.[39]

In China itself the rejection of the Versailles Treaty by Beijing was backed by a truly rare display of national unity. But it begged the question of how, beyond patriotic demonstrations, China was to secure a place for itself in the new international order. Fortunately for China, Beijing had declared war in 1917 not only on Germany but on the Habsburg Empire as well. Away from the high-stakes game being played at Versailles, in the arena of the smaller peace conferences in the Paris suburbs China could develop a more constructive diplomacy. Sticking to the position adopted since May, China insisted that the successor states to the Habsburg Empire forgo the privileges normally claimed by the Western Powers.[40] The fulfilment of Chinese wartime and post-war diplomacy came on 10 September 1919 when it signed the Treaty of Saint-Germain with Austria. This treaty, like the Treaty of Versailles, included the League of Nations Covenant in its preamble and gave China full rights of membership. At the first meeting of the League's General Assembly in December 1920, China, the most populous country on earth, was voted onto the Council by a huge majority.

A year earlier, in December 1919, China had successfully concluded its first international friendship treaty that explicitly provided for equality of status and ruled out extraterritoriality with the Bolivian Republic. By March 1920 China had established diplomatic contacts with the Weimar Republic. In June 1920 Beijing entered into a treaty with Persia on the Bolivian model. The following year, in May 1921, the negotiations with Berlin resulted in a trade treaty that provided for tariff autonomy for both sides. The freedom to set tariffs that was denied to China under the unequal treaties of the nineteenth century was denied to Germany under the Versailles Treaty. To student radicals like Mao Zedong the parallels between China's situation and that of the Weimar Republic were compelling.[41] Both were victims of Western imperialism. And Sun Yat-sen, the nationalist leader and long-time admirer both of Bismarck and Germany's organized capitalism, took this one step further. In 1923 he sought to lure the Weimar Republic into cooperation with Beijing by suggesting that 'to get rid of the yoke of Versailles there is no way better than the assistance of establishing a great, strong, modern army in China . . .'. China would be a 'sort of invisible force in the Far East' to be 'called to' Germany's aid.[42]

But it took considerable imagination to see in a Sino-German alliance a true means of escape for either country. What China needed was leverage in the Asian arena. In the chain of foreign oversight that the Western Powers were attempting to orchestrate around China, there was one missing link: Russia. With Russia excluded from the Versailles order and wracked by civil war, might Beijing use negotiations with Moscow to drive a wedge into the system of unequal treaties?

Already in July 1918, as the struggle over Brest-Litovsk was reaching its climax, Commissar Georgy Chicherin had announced that the Soviet regime renounced all claims to extraterritorial privilege in China. A year later the promise was repeated by Deputy People's Commissar Lev Karakhan. Invoking the language of the Petrograd peace formula of 1917, he promised that the Soviet regime renounced all 'annexations . . . any subjugation of other nations, and indemnities whatever'.[43] As the military fortunes of the Red regime recovered, the Kremlin was to think better of this offer. But for China it set a precedent. In the spring of 1920 a copy of Karakhan's original expansive statement was widely publicized in translation and caused a sensation. On 27 May 1920, in the so-called Yili Protocol signed between Chinese and Soviet negotiators in the Xianjiang region of the far west, the Soviets conceded to China the two demands that were refused by all the Western Powers: full freedom to set its own tariffs and Chinese jurisdiction over Russians in China. Soon afterwards Beijing unilaterally ended the Boxer indemnity payments to Russia. Next it withdrew recognition from the remnants of the Tsarist embassy in China and on 25 September 1920 Chinese troops took control of the Russian sector of the European concession in the Northern port city of Tianjin and hoisted the Chinese national flag.

At the same time, Beijing asserted control of its northeastern frontier by sending an armed detachment of police to remove the Russian officials from the courthouse in Harbin, from which they had administered justice over the entire area of operation of the Russian-owned Chinese Eastern Railway. The 1,400 miles of railway track that made up the final leg of the Trans-Siberian railway were the true strategic prize in North-East China. The takeover in Harbin was the prelude to a more aggressive assertion of Chinese control. In December, Beijing asserted its 'supreme control' over the railway and its management and excluded the Russian management from any 'political activity'.[44] It was a remarkable testament to the shift in the balance of power brought about by the Russian collapse that such demands could even have been contemplated, let alone conceded. Whether China would be able to make them permanent would depend both on the Western Powers, Japan and Russia.

18

The Fiasco of Wilsonianism

In presenting the text of the Versailles Treaty to the Senate on 10 July 1919, Woodrow Wilson chose words of extraordinary drama. 'The stage is set, the destiny disclosed. It has come about by no plan of our conceiving, but by the hand of God who led us into this way. We cannot turn back. We can only go forward, with lifted eyes and freshened spirit, to follow the vision. It was of this that we drew at our birth. America shall in truth show the way. The light streams upon the path ahead, and nowhere else.' 'Shall we or any other free people hesitate to accept this great duty?' 'Dare we reject it and break the heart of the world?'[1] The language was exalted but Wilson was not exaggerating. Both the victors and the vanquished looked to the United States as the pivot of the new order. As Wilson had prepared to leave Paris on 26 June, Lloyd George addressed to him a final despairing letter, imploring him to place the credit of the American government 'at the disposal of the nations for the regeneration of the world'.[2] But it was not only financial reconstruction that hinged on Washington. The Franco-German peace depended on the joint security guarantee of London and Washington. In Asia, Prime Minister Hara of Japan was hinging his foreign policy on Washington, whilst China looked to the League of Nations for redress. So too did the Germans, who had realized that though Wilson had disappointed them, only at the price of a signature could they call into existence the international structures through which the hated Versailles Treaty might be revised.

But by the time he arrived home in the US it was clear that Wilson would face a serious fight in Congress. The divided powers of the American constitution had preoccupied him since his earliest days as a political thinker. What had driven him into politics was a sense that the American nation state had reached a turning point that required creative presidential leadership. Since 1913 Wilson had used the presidency in new ways to drive congressional action and mobilize public opinion. He had established a new apparatus of national economic government, led first and foremost by the Federal Reserve. The war had led to state interference across American life. In 1919 what was put to the test was not only congressional ratification of the treaty but Wilson's entire political project. The paralysis produced by the stand-off between the White House and the Senate was compounded by a wide-ranging social and economic crisis, more severe than anything America had witnessed since the traumatic years of recession and populist mobilization in the 1890s. What was exposed at this moment of disaster was not only the central role of the United States in world politics, but also the frailty of the American state as the pivot of this new order. American history was no longer a domestic drama. The political and economic crises of post-war America had global ramifications.

I

Wilson's propagandists painted the 'Treaty Fight' as the second round in the great struggle between the President's idealism and the cynicism of 'old politics'.[3] The first round had been fought in Paris, the second would be contested at home. From the outset, Wilson was at a disadvantage. The concessions he had made to the demands of Japan and the Entente fatally undermined the legitimacy of the Versailles Treaty. Wilson's friends on the left deserted him in disillusionment. Even the progressives of the *New Republic* disowned the treaty. During September 1919, Henry Cabot Lodge, the Republican Senate leader, hounded Wilson through the Foreign Affairs Committee. To further his vendetta against the President, Lodge took evidence from every disaffected minority in America. He even took advantage of disillusioned Wilsonians such as the young William Bullitt, who aired in public the embarrassing divisions between Wilson and his Secretary of State, Robert Lansing.[4] It was a battle of attrition. Threatened by hypertension, the President put his life on the line. In an attempt to outflank the Senate and reestablish his personal bond with the American people, Wilson embarked on a gruelling nationwide speaking tour in defence of the treaty. In the intense heat of an Indian summer, the President's itinerary through the western states was cut short on 26 September by the first of a devastating series of strokes. As the treaty reached the crucial vote in the Senate in November, Wilson lay partially paralysed on his sickbed.

For critics of the President this narrative of heroic failure was itself symptomatic of Wilson's warped perception of reality. In the aftermath of the debacle, Lodge's star witness Bullitt sought solace on the analytic couch of Sigmund Freud. Together Bullitt and Freud co-authored a compelling psychobiography that analysed the failed President as a man trapped in an imaginary world of language woven by his domineering Presbyterian father.[5] To Republicans and Democrats interested in a compromise, the President was mulish. A majority in the Senate were ready to pass the treaty. But a two-thirds vote was needed. There was no doubt an irreconcilable, isolationist minority. But it was not these men who robbed Wilson of his peace. His truly dangerous opponents were the mainstream leadership of the Republicans, who could not reasonably be described as isolationist. They had favoured a far more aggressive stance in the war than Wilson. Even as he assaulted the Covenant in his rousing speech to the Senate on 12 August 1919, Lodge insisted in tones as strong as ever used by Wilson that the United States was 'the world's best hope'.[6] Like Teddy Roosevelt, he had at times been willing to consider a trilateral alliance with both Britain and France. In 1919 other prominent Republicans were still active supporters of the League of Nations. A two-thirds majority consisting of mainline internationalist Republicans such as Lodge and moderate Democrats would have been willing to pass the treaty with reservations, above all to Article X of the League Covenant that provided for collective assistance in case of aggression against members of the League. What they demanded was that Congress must have the final word in approving any collective enforcement action. Since the weakly worded Covenant could easily have been interpreted in this direction, it was Wilson himself who presented the ultimate obstacle to compromise. He insisted that the treaty must be accepted whole and complete, or not at all.

On 19 November at the first crucial Senate vote the Republicans defeated the treaty, whereupon on Wilson's instructions the Democratic minority blocked a motion to accept the treaty with reservations. For five further months the Senate agonized. But on 8 March 1920 Wilson reaffirmed his refusal to grant any concessions to the Republican majority, and on 19 March the Senate failed to find the requisite two-thirds majority for either the original or the amended treaty.

The failure to pass the treaty even in an amended version was undeniably in large part Wilson's doing. But it was far from obvious, even if the President had been willing to compromise, whether the reservations demanded by Lodge would have been acceptable to the Entente.[7] In this regard Article X was certainly not the main sticking point. The British had no more interest than Lodge in being dictated to by the League Council. More serious problems might well have arisen from Lodge's insistence that America could not be bound by any resolution in which the British Empire collectively had more than one vote. Lodge also wanted Japan's claim on Shandong overturned. The only way to have been sure of avoiding the impasse reached by the autumn of 1919 was for the Republicans to have been part of the negotiating team at Paris. Wilson was much criticized for personally leading the US delegation to Paris and for excluding any of the more difficult elements of the Republican Party from the talks. Again, personal vanity played its part. But the increasing savagery of the polemics in the elections of 1916 and 1918 made it hard to imagine a bipartisan delegation. In those elections foreign policy had been politicized as never before.

However, more was at stake in the Treaty Fight than party conflict. The differences between Wilson and the Republicans were not those between liberal internationalists and hidebound isolationists, but they were nevertheless real. Whereas Wilson saw the US overseeing a global order, the Republican vision of the peace was in key respects closer to that of the Europeans. To the vague commitments of the League Covenant, Lodge much preferred a continuation of America's wartime alliance with Britain and even with France. If America was to embark on radical new foreign commitments, it must be realistic about the constraints of its own polity. The wartime alliances had a compelling political rationale that had been hammered home to America's fickle, democratic electorate.[8] By contrast, the League of Nations was an ill-defined thing. Legally minded Republican internationalists such as Elihu Root took the wording of the Covenant more seriously than Wilson ever meant it.[9] They saw America as threatened by a series of legally binding obligations to an organization whose principles were unclear. The open-ended and general commitment entered into under Article X was not something that Congress should be asked to approve. The evidence suggests that Wilson in fact saw the League precisely as a way of disentangling America from the clutches of its Entente associates. As he insisted to the Senate leadership at a White House lunch in mid-August, all that Article X implied was a moral obligation.[10] If, however, the United States were to insist from the outset on bluntly asserting its sovereignty, it would lose the ability to lead the development of global opinion.[11]

As he recovered from his strokes and the shock of the Senate's first rejection of the treaty, Wilson in early 1920 gave every indication that he expected to resume that role of leadership. Between 7 and 30 October 1919 all the great powers recognized at Versailles – Italy, the British Empire, France and Japan – ratified the treaty with Germany. But this only began the long and complex process of enforcement. Furthermore, the question of the Adriatic still had to be settled, as did relations with the Ottoman Empire. Despite the fact that the Senate had not ratified the treaty with Germany and the United States had not been at war with the Ottoman Empire, Wilson claimed for himself once more the role of arbiter. Indeed, it seemed that as the confrontation with the Senate ground into its final round, it was all the more important for Wilson to act with assertive authority toward the outside world.

In February 1920 the President abruptly vetoed a compromise on the Fiume question brokered by Britain and France that he considered too favourable to Italy, threatening to withdraw altogether from engagement with Europe. Wilson then expressed his disagreement with the aggressive policy pursued by Britain in Turkey. But above all his pressure was directed against the French. On 9 March in an open letter to the Senate minority leader Gilbert M. Hitchcock, who was preparing for the final attempt to secure ratification, the President seemed to suggest that the contested Article X of the League Covenant was a guard as much against the resurgent militarism of France as it was against Germany. Though there were protests both from Paris and from the opposition in the Senate, Wilson did not shift from this position even when four days later there was a military coup – and not in France but in Germany. Despite the obvious menace of the Kapp putsch, Washington overrode the veto of Paris and approved the request by Berlin to move additional contingents of the Reichswehr and Freikorps into the Ruhr to put down the Red Army. When in April, France retaliated by occupying Frankfurt, Wilson's reaction was to withdraw from the

Senate the treaty guaranteeing France's security that some senators had wished to put in place of the failed peace treaty.[12]

For London and Paris the sudden re-emergence of this assertive Wilsonian diplomacy came as a considerable shock. We know with hindsight that Wilson's legacy was doomed. But as he himself appears to have seen it, the second rejection of the Versailles Treaty by the Senate in March 1920 and the clashes with France were merely part of an ongoing struggle in which as ever the domestic and international fronts were interconnected. The broken treaty gave him the possibility of leverage in Europe. A stand-off between the presidency and Congress was an in-built possibility of the American constitution.[13] At moments of crisis, Wilson believed, the role of the President was to act as the interpreter of the true will of the American people and to stake this personal vision against the partisanship of Congress. After the first clash with the Senate, Wilson seriously considered the unprecedented step of challenging the opposition group in the Senate to resign en masse, thus triggering a referendum by way of an election on the treaty issue. It was after that extraordinary idea was dropped that Wilson instead came to see the general election of 1920 as a 'great and solemn referendum' on America's future role in the world.[14] In the event he not only underestimated the uncertainty and insecurity he was injecting into the international arena. At home he overtaxed his personal charisma. He tragically overestimated his own physical strength. But, more fundamentally, in counting on the electorate to see him through, he failed to grasp the explosive social and economic legacy left by the war. By the autumn of 1919 it was not only Wilson's foreign policy but his vision of America's own future that was coming apart.

II

At the peak of his progressive enthusiasm in 1916, Wilson had promised to craft a new style of government that would be beyond politics as hitherto practised, that would be focused squarely on the everyday material concerns of people's lives.[15] The idea that a new focus on economic and social matters would lead to a depoliticization of public life was an improbable prospect at the best of times. In 1919 the after-effects of wartime mobilization combined with intense partisan rhetoric to turn wages, the control of industry and the condition of agriculture into objects of furious argument. On Wilson's return from Paris, in July 1919 only a few blocks away from the White House, entire African American neighbourhoods were aflame. Fifteen people were bludgeoned, shot and burned to death. In Chicago the death toll reached 38.[16] One thousand African American families were left homeless. In all, 25 American cities were convulsed in the summer of 1919 by the most widespread outburst of racial violence since the Civil War. The White gangs targeted symbols of wartime social change – African American servicemen and recent migrants to Northern cities.

Wilson was racially minded, but he profoundly disapproved of mob action and he understood how seriously it called into question America's claim to progressive leadership. A year earlier on 26 July 1918, after a threatening upsurge in lynching, he had issued a presidential appeal to state prosecutors denouncing mob rule as a 'blow at the heart of ordered law and humane justice'.[17] Writing as a historian, Wilson had justified the original Ku Klux Klan. But its formation was an act of self-defence in the aftermath of the Civil War, during what Wilson considered to have been a period of lawlessness, aided and abetted by the criminal folly of the radical Republicans in Congress.[18] In normal times, 'while the courts of justice are open and the governments of the States and the Nation are ready and able to do their duty', there was no excuse. 'Lawless passion' was precisely what America was fighting to defeat in Europe. 'Germany has outlawed herself among the nations because she has disregarded the sacred obligations of law and has made lynchers of her armies . . . How shall we commend democracy to the acceptance of other peoples,' Wilson went on, 'if we disgrace our own by proving that it is, after all, no protection to the weak?' Every lynching was a gift to German propaganda. 'They can at least say that such things cannot happen in Germany except in times of revolution, when law is swept away.'[19]

Faced with the nationwide race riots of 1919, the National Equal Rights League turned the point directly against Wilson. The black racial minority in the United States demanded the same protections that Wilson had 'forced Poland and Austria to undertake for their racial minorities'.[20] There was, of course, no possibility of any such thing. All Wilson was calling for was the proper enforcement of the law. The FBI for its part decided that its proper role, rather than prosecuting the racist ringleaders, was to track down Black radicals and their schemes of international subversion.[21] Racial fears mingled in the summer of 1919 with the all-pervasive Red Scare.

The Republican mid-term election campaign of 1918 had incited anti-Bolshevik agitation. The citywide general strike organized in Seattle in February 1919 was a nationwide sensation. The American authorities saw enemies everywhere. On 19 February a lone gunman wounded Georges Clemenceau in Paris, which provided the US Secret Service with the occasion for a dramatic domestic crackdown on International Workers of the World and suffragette militants.[22] On 2 June 1919 a bomb demolished the front porch of the house belonging to the Attorney General, A. Mitchell Palmer.[23] Simultaneously, bombs exploded in six other cities. Over the summer, hysteria spread nationwide. Appalling mob violence was directed at the activists of the IWW. On 30 July 1919 Palmer advised Wilson against releasing Eugene Debs, the venerable socialist and anti-war organizer, who in September 1918 had been sentenced to ten years on sedition charges. To release Debs, Palmer insisted, 'would be used by many opponents of the peace treaty as evidence of too great leniency toward law violators of the radical element . . .'. It might 'prejudice many people against the liberal labour provisions of the Treaty'.[24] Instead of clemency, Palmer spearheaded a campaign of investigations, arrests and deportations that culminated in the unprecedented round-up on 2 January 1920 of perhaps as many as three thousand suspected foreign-born radicals in 33 cities across America.[25]

It is conceivable, of course, that instead of this conservative turn the Wilson administration might have renewed its progressive purpose. Palmer himself was a veteran labour lawyer. An alliance with organized labour had been a key element in the 'New freedom' platform of 1912 and it was even more essential to Wilson's narrow election victory in 1916. Since 1917 the role played by the American Federation of Labour (AFL) under their union leader Samuel Gompers, as partners in the war effort, had seemed to promise a new position for organized labour both in relation to the state and to private business.[26] There were calls over the summer of 1919 for the Democrats to cement this relationship by passing a nationwide trade union recognition law. Talk of 'Industrial Democracy' and 'Reconstruction' were in the air. Nor was

Wilson opposed to using popular pressure to strengthen Federal control in key sectors. In July 1919 he confided to his brother-in-law Samuel E. Axson that 'it seems certain that some commodities will have to become the property of the state, the coal, the water powers and probably the railroads. Some people would call me a socialist for saying this', but this did not put Wilson off.[27] America's industrialists and their Republican friends, however, sensed weakness. Would the Democrats be willing to stand by organized labour, if employers raised the stakes and confronted the Federal government with the risk of serious civil strife?

The business counter-attack began with the end of the war. Already by December 1918, companies such as General Electric were rolling back the concessions granted in the previous 18 months. The apparatus of wartime industrial arbitration was stalled and then turned against the unions. The unions resisted, with a strike wave the likes of which had never been seen before in American history. In 1919 one out of every five industrial workers was involved in a stoppage. But they faced bad odds and nowhere more so than in the great bastion of anti-unionism – the steel industry. Ever since the epic Homestead strike of 1892, the industry had stood firm against recognizing trade unions as bargaining partners, and it upheld that position throughout the war. At the end of August 1919, despite appeals from President Wilson himself, 'Judge' Elbert Henry Gary of US Steel refused to agree to public arbitration. Desperate to avoid an open clash, the administration appealed to both sides. In the hope of calming nerves, Wilson promised an Industrial Conference to discuss 'fundamental means of bettering the whole relationship of capital and labor'.[28] But with the employers digging in, on 22 September a second great steel strike began. By the end of the week 365,000 workers were out. The employers responded with force. Industrial Pennsylvania was flooded with an army of 25,000 private security guards backing up the heavy-handed police. The US Steel town of Gary, Indiana, was placed under martial law.[29] Wilson's Industrial Conference met on 11 October amidst an intense campaign of intimidation. So lopsided was the climate of violence and denunciation that Gompers, the usually compliant boss of the AFL, stormed out.

On the same day, under pressure from the Secretary of Labor, mine workers and coal barons were brought together in Washington in the hope of forestalling a second major stoppage. But these talks too broke

down and the United Mine Workers (UMW) issued a strike call for
1 November. Wilson, who by this time had been confined to his sickbed
and was increasingly under the sway of Palmer, denounced the coal
strike as 'a grave moral and legal wrong', an attempted extortion ahead
of the freezing winter months.[30] Invoking wartime powers that were
supposed to have expired with the Armistice, Palmer barred the UMW
from involvement in the strike. This forced the AFL-CIO into an even
more confrontational position. Defying Palmer, it backed the
394,000 miners who had followed the strike call. But Palmer's legal
pressure was unrelenting and the American labour movement, like its
British counterpart, was unwilling to risk an all-out confrontation. On
11 November the UMW leadership was forced to concede that 'as
Americans ... we cannot fight our government'. After the Secretary of
Labour intervened to authorize a flat 14 per cent wage increase, the
miners returned to work.

They fared better than the steelworkers. After the loss of 20 lives and
over 112 million dollars in pay, the steel strike ended on 8 January
1920 with a complete victory for US Steel. It was a shock from which
the American labour movement was never to recover.[31] Talk of industrial democracy was abandoned in favour of the new managerial
discipline of 'industrial relations' and company unionism.[32] The coalition
between the Democratic Party and organized labour that had brought
Wilson victory in 1912 and 1916 was broken.

III

Attorney General Palmer ended 1919 with a New Year's Eve address in
which he promised an unrelenting struggle against the 'Red movement'
that was threatening the entire social order of America. It was not just
the barons of US Steel who were under threat. 'Twenty million people
in this country own Liberty bonds,' Palmer reminded his audience.[33]
'These the Reds propose to take away ... Eleven million people have
savings accounts in savings banks and 18.6 million people have deposits
in our national banks at which they aim.' This kind of exaggerated
demagoguery was soon to make Palmer a laughing stock. In 1920 the
Red Scare fizzled out as rapidly as the strike wave.

What did not dissipate so easily was the very real threat to the savings of millions of American families posed not by anarchists or foreign radicals but by the anonymous, all-pervasive force of inflation. By October 1919, even in America, the society best cushioned against the impact of the war, the cost of living index had risen by 83.1 per cent since 1913.[34] Up to the end of 1917, wages had lagged seriously behind. They caught up in 1918 under the pressure of the war effort.[35] But as inflation accelerated in 1919, real wages were once again eaten away. One could fight strikes with armies of private security thugs. Court injunctions would humble trade union leaders. One could offer concessions, even including an eight-hour day. Attorney General Palmer promised a crackdown on hoarders and speculators.[36] But none of this really addressed the grievances of tens of millions of people whose standard of living was threatened by the huge surge in prices. In May 1919, Massachusetts Democrats cabled Wilson in Paris reminding him that the 'citizens of the United States want you home to help reduce the high cost of living, which we consider far more important than the League of Nations'.[37] Their appeal was in vain. By the end of 1919 it took $2,000 a year to purchase a comfortable 'American' standard of living. At the time of the strike unskilled workers at US Steel struggled to make even the $1,575 that marked basic subsistence.[38] It was these facts, not Bolshevik subversion, that impelled the strike wave of 1919, in which a record 5 million American workers participated in 3,600 separate disputes.

The cause of this social and economic dislocation, in the United States as across the rest of the world, was not subversion or moral decrepitude, but the financial disequilibrium left by the war. The last Liberty Bond, the Victory Loan, was issued in the spring of 1919 in the hope of soaking up excess purchasing power and consolidating the government's finances. It brought in $4.5 billion. As during the war, however, these funds came in large part not out of savings but from bank credits, which only served to stoke inflationary pressure. In the course of 1919 the volume of notes in circulation surged by 20 per cent. Faced with such inflation, it was only to be expected that workers would organize to protect their standard of living.

The financial markets also were showing signs of unease. Throughout the autumn the Treasury struggled to refinance $3 billion in short-term certificates.[39] The markets were reluctant to commit to long-term loans, because they were expecting a fundamental change in monetary conditions – and they were expecting it soon. By the last weeks of 1919 it was not simply the President and Congress, or the Labour unions and the Attorney General, who were at loggerheads. Tension between the Treasury and the Federal Reserve Board had reached an extraordinary pitch. To attract long-term investors and to cool the markets the New York branch of the Federal Reserve was noisily demanding an increase in interest rates.[40] But throughout 1919 as inflation surged and gold drained out of the Fed's reserves, the Treasury resisted action. Its dilemma was that any large increase in interest rates would devalue the outstanding stock of Liberty Bonds, which carried an interest rate of only 4.25 per cent. To offer higher rates for new loans would drive down the resale value of Liberty Bonds, penalizing those who had committed their savings to the war effort. As Russell Leffingwell, the Assistant Secretary to the Treasury, made clear to the Fed Board on 4 September 1919, if the price of Liberty Bonds fell below 90 cents in the dollar, the administration could find itself facing unmanageable repercussions in Congress and a panic in the bond market. This was the hostage that had been given to fortune by the unprecedentedly wide dispersal of the bonds and the unsustainably low rate of interest at which they had been issued. Never before had the Federal government managed public debt on this scale. Before the war at most a few hundred thousand wealthy investors had held government bonds. Now the assets of millions of ordinary households were at stake. In the second half of 1919, despite its need for new money, the Treasury was forced to spend $900 million massaging the price of the Liberty Loans, by repurchasing outstanding bonds.[41]

From the vantage point of Europe, America might appear to be the only unencumbered centre of world finance. The dollar was the sole major international currency that could still boast a solid gold backing. But with inflation making it attractive to turn dollars into gold, by the end of 1919 the ratio of gold reserves to notes in circulation at the New York branch of the Federal Reserve had fallen to 40.2 per cent, within a whisker of the minimum required by law. Faced with an impending crisis, the governors of the New York Federal Reserve voted to suspend reserve requirements for a grace period of ten days. But the full Board of the Federal Reserve refused to permit this drastic step. Governor Strong, the dominant figure at the New York Fed, was outraged. It was the Treasury's refusal to allow a timely increase in interest rates that had put the New York banks in danger. He would 'loyally' carry out the instructions of the Treasury and Fed Board, 'but after this he would resign rather than continue such a policy'.[42]

On 26 November 1919 when the Fed Board met in Washington, Leffingwell replied with an extraordinary personal attack on Strong, accusing him of attempting 'to punish the Treasury of the United States for not submitting to dictation on the part of the Governor of the Federal Reserve Bank of New York'. Strong, Leffingwell alleged, was 'conspiring with the British to manipulate the trans-Atlantic gold flow to America's disadvantage'. Until 15 January 1920 the Treasury needed to borrow $500 million every fortnight. Until then there could be no thought of an increase in interest rates.[43] So uncertain was the Treasury of Strong's loyalty that they had Attorney General Palmer confirm that in the event of unauthorized, unilateral action by the New York bank, they had the power to relieve him of his position.

It did not come to that. In the long run the Treasury could not afford to continue subsidizing its existing creditors at the expense of new borrowing. On 2 January 1920 the Treasury offered the first batch of 12-month Treasury Certificates at the higher rate of 4.75 per cent. Three weeks later, Leffingwell completely reversed his previous position. The Treasury was now convinced that 'nothing but a drastic increase on commercial paper to 6% would curtail the situation'. America was 'dangerously near leaving the gold standard . . .'. Now it was the turn of the New York Fed to object. A sudden increase in interest rates of almost 50 per cent was 'unjust'. It would convey the impression either that 'the Federal Reserve board had lost its head or that conditions must be very critical'. It might incite a panic rather than calming the market. But Leffingwell was in a vindictive mood. 'If a panic in New York should break out, he would be glad of it.' With Treasury Secretary Carter Glass casting the decisive vote, rates were raised at a stroke to 6 per cent.[44] By June the New York discount rate hit 7 per cent. The Fed was barely seven years old. In the rest of the twentieth century it was never again to attempt a contraction of such severity (Fig. 2).

The deflationary impact was drastic. The abrupt tightening of credit tipped the American economy over a cliff. After continuing to accelerate to an annual inflation rate of 25 per cent in the first half of 1920, in the second half of the year the price level plunged by an annualized rate

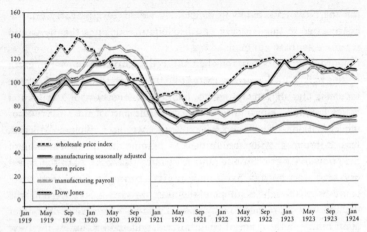

Figure 2. The Forgotten Recession: America's Post-War Shock, 1919–21

of 15 per cent. In the entire macroeconomic record of the US, this switchback is completely unique. In the Great Depression deflation was even sharper, but it did not follow a period of rapid inflation. In 1920 as prices fell, industrial output plummeted and unemployment shot up. By January 1921 the National Industrial Conference Board estimated that industrial unemployment topped 20 per cent.

But it was agriculture that suffered the worst. The terms of trade for American farmers collapsed and were not to recover for the rest of the twentieth century. In the 1890s the American political establishment had been profoundly shaken by a populist agrarian mobilization triggered by a similarly devastating deflation. William Jennings Bryan had seized control of the Democratic Party. If he had won the presidential election of 1896, he had pledged to take America off the gold standard. Wilson's institutional innovations of 1913 were supposed to have lain those demons to rest. The New Freedom with its combination of tariff reductions – benefiting export-oriented farmers and working-class consumers – and the new managerial competence of the Federal Reserve were supposed to have rebalanced American capitalism in a progressive direction. The switchback of 1919–20 revealed the fragility of those new institutions in the face of the enormous pressures created by the war. Not only was labour in revolt. As cotton prices collapsed, farmers resorted to 'night riding', threatening arson against ginneries and warehouses that paid inadequate prices. A new generation of populists organized in the cross-party 'Farm Bloc' tarred Wilson's Fed with responsibility for 'the crime of 1920'. One of the first actions of the incoming Republican Congress was a Joint Congressional commission of agricultural inquiry, to embarrass the outgoing Democrats.[45] Meanwhile, Wilson's former controller of currency, John Skelton Williams, fanned the storm of agrarian protest by alleging that the mishandling of the crisis and the collapse in farm prices were the work of a Wall Street cabal.[46]

Across the South and much of the West, the agrarian crisis fuelled the second coming of the Ku Klux Klan. Feeding off popular discontent across the American heartland and supercharged by a highly incentivized recruitment system, membership in the Klan surged from a few thousand in 1919 to as many as 4 million by 1924 – one in six, the Klan claimed, of the eligible white male population.[47] At their peak thousands of inductees were initiated en masse in torch-lit monster rallies. In northern Florida entire city neighbourhoods were cleared of their black inhabitants. In 1923 Texas, Alabama and Indiana all returned Klan candidates to the Senate. Southern Illinois was convulsed by white on white 'Klan wars'. Oregon's state politics were entirely under the spell of the local Grand Goblin. In Oklahoma the Klan's influence on the state legislature, court system and police force was such that the state governor was forced to resort to martial law.

In 1920 the dizzying succession of inflation and deflation set the scene for the electoral humiliation of the Democrats. Running for the Republicans, Warren Harding outscored his hapless Democratic opponent by 60 to 34 per cent. In the wake of that defeat the shrunken remnant of the Democratic Party became a vehicle for Klan influence across the country. At the 1924 election convention of the Democratic Party, the notorious 'Klanbake', the Klan caucus came close to derailing the party altogether, as they fought to prevent the nomination as a presidential candidate of the Catholic Al Smith, who stood on an anti-lynching platform. It took a record 103 ballots to defeat the Klan's preferred nominee, none other than William Gibbs McAdoo, Woodrow Wilson's son-in-law and wartime Treasury Secretary.[48]

IV

Wilson would linger on in Washington until his death in February 1924. But with his departure from the White House, so goes the familiar story, America's first wave of internationalism had broken. It was followed by an age of isolationism. But this terminology perpetuates contemporary polemics as historical misunderstanding. If, instead, we recognize Wilson for what he was – an exponent of turn-of-the-century high nationalism, bent on asserting America's exceptional claim to pre-eminence on a global scale – then what is more striking is the continuity between his administration and the Republicans who followed. Speaking in Boston in May 1920, just as the recession set in, Senator Warren G. Harding had coined the phrase that was to define not only his campaign but his presidency: 'America's present need is not heroics but healing; not nostrums but normalcy.' But he went on to add another telling line. What was called for was 'not submergence in internationality but sustainment of triumphant nationality'.[49] Triumphant nationalism is as apt a description of the policies of the Republican administrations in the 1920s as it was of Wilson's own administration. Triumphant national-ism was not inward-turning or isolationist. It was by definition addressed to an outside world, but it spoke in terms that were unilateral and exceptionalist.

In light of fierce contemporary struggles over the ethnic make-up of America, anxieties about foreign subversion and mounting unemploy-ment, it was no surprise that already in the autumn of 1920 Congress was actively discussing a 'genuine 100 percent American immigration law'.[50] Within weeks of his inauguration Harding approved a law that cut immigration from 805,228 in 1920 to 309,556 in 1921–2. Immigration from southern and eastern Europe and Asia was reduced to a trickle. In 1924 the cap was further lowered to 150,000 entrants per year. For centuries the New World had stood open to adventurous settlers. The damming up of transatlantic immigration marked the most decisive break between the liberal modernity of the nineteenth century and the increas-ing centrality of nation-state regulation in the twentieth century.

A less novel but nonetheless decisive reversal of liberalism occurred in trade policy. Whereas Wilson had sought to establish US leadership on the basis of a low-tariff policy, on 27 May 1921 Harding signed into effect an emergency law, followed within the year by the Fordney-McCumber tariff, which raised rates on average by 60 per cent.[51] In the name of non-discrimination the Federal government was authorized to use the threat of punitive tariffs to extract concessions from major trading partners.[52] Harding's successors would single out France for particular pressure. American protectionism was no novelty, of course. But the full implications of Fordney-McCumber become clear when we recall that France not only had a trade deficit with America, but that its government owed $3 billion to the US taxpayer.

How was America's assertive nationalism to be reconciled with its pivotal role in the international economy? If inter-Allied debts were to be serviced, if Germany was to pay even a modest amount of reparations, what the world needed was not protectionism but for the US to serve as an engine for global trade. If America wished to avoid this deepening entanglement, the obvious alternative, as Keynes had insisted, was for the net creditors, Britain and America, to forgive the debt, to deleverage. But that ran up against another radically novel feature of the situation. In 1912 the Federal government's debt stood at just over $1 billion. Seven years later, in 1919, the total debt burden of the Federal government had swollen to $30 billion. This was modest in relation to the size of the US economy. But of that sum, as much as one-third was actually foreign-owed war debt. Inter-governmental debt was not marginal to the US domestic discussion, it was a highly visible feature of the new world created by the war. In August 1919 Wilson's administration had unilaterally announced to the Entente a two-year moratorium on repayment. Lloyd George's government repeatedly appealed to Wilson to join Britain in a more expansive policy of debt write-down. But to no avail.

Meanwhile, over the winter of 1919–20 the fiasco of Wilsonian political economy was having an immediate impact on America's European debtors. The abrupt 50 per cent increase in the Federal Reserve's key interest rates delivered a deflationary shock to the entire world economy. After exporting $292 million of gold in 1919 and billions of dollars in credit, in 1920 new foreign credits dried up. Almost $800 million in gold surged back into the US. To compound this deflationary pressure, between 1918 and 1924 the United States ran a surplus of over $12.6 billion on trade account.[53] At a moment of intense political crisis, rather than serving as a dynamo of global trade, the Fed and the US Treasury were applying a massive, unilateral squeeze. Though Woodrow Wilson was passing from the scene a broken man, the fact of America's ascent remained an inescapable reality of the early twentieth century.

FOUR

The Search for a New Order

19

The Great Deflation

In the years that followed World War I the red hand of sedition was sighted from Boston to Berlin, from New Zealand to New York. It gripped even Latin America, which was otherwise largely immune to the intense violence of the early twentieth century. In Buenos Aires over New Year 1919, a bitter strike in a metalworking factory sparked the bloody confrontation of the Semana Tragica (7–15 January 1919), which claimed the lives of perhaps as many seven hundred people. Out of the anti-socialist and anti-Semitic agitation that followed there emerged the Liga Patriotica, which was to serve as the seedbed of the twentieth-century Argentinian right.[1] Throughout 1919 and 1920, paramilitaries associated with the Liga collaborated with the army and police in breaking strikes and intimidating trade union organizers, defending Argentina against the spectral threat of international revolution. Tens of thousands of leftist suspects were arrested. From the cosmopolitan Argentinian capital the politics of counter-revolution spread south to the very end of the inhabited world.

In the autumn of 1921 the notorious Tenth Cavalry regiment under the command of Lieutenant Colonel Hector Varela arrived in Patagonia to put down an insurgency amongst farm workers on the gigantic sheep haciendas of the desolate southern tip of the continent. In collaboration with local Welsh landlords and Leaguistas, the Tenth Cavalry in December 1921 murdered no fewer than 1,500 suspected labour activists. In the New Year Colonel Varela returned to Buenos Aires to be feted as a national saviour. Within a year he was gunned down by a German-born anarchist, Kurt Gustav Wilckens. Wilckens, who hailed from Schleswig, had come to Argentina by way of the coal mines of Silesia and Arizona, where he survived a brief but dangerous spell as an IWW organizer. Before Wilckens could receive his sentence, he himself was shot by Perez Milan, a Leaguist zealot, who had been smuggled into his jail by police sympathizers. The vendetta reached its conclusion only in 1925 when Perez Milan was gunned down by a Yugoslav-born fanatic who had been inspired by the Russian godfather of Argentinian anarchism, Germán Boris Wladimirovich.

It is an extraordinary tale. With variations it can be repeated across much of the world in the aftermath of World War I – a sense of a world coming apart, fantasies of conspiratorial communist influence, a pressing state of economic crisis, a wave of strikes and industrial conflict, fuelling drastic rhetorics of class conflict and violence on both sides. The nineteenth century had been haunted by revolution. Now was the moment, it seemed, that revolution had arrived. But outside Russia the far left was everywhere defeated.[2] Across the world, as in Argentina and the United States, the resources of the state and the property-owning classes were mobilized to defend established order aggressively. In Italy in 1922, in Bulgaria and Spain in 1923, a new type of authoritarian, paramilitary, anti-communist dictatorship was established. But in most places the violence ebbed away. The new authoritarianism, to which the left soon applied the generic label 'fascism', remained confined to the periphery. In most places, as in the United States, the Red Scare, anti-foreign witchhunts, and nightly gatherings under the sign of the burning cross, came in retrospect to seem like a carnivalesque distraction from the real business of restoring normalcy. That depended less on street-fighting and assassination than on addressing the deeper causes of both domestic and international disorder, above all the financial consequences of the war. As the United States demonstrated, this depended on breaking the inflationary wave. But the US role in this regard was not merely exemplary. It was the pivot of the world economy. The deflationary wave driven forward by America from the spring of 1920 was the true key to the 'world-wide Thermidor' of the 1920s, the main driver of the restoration of order, both domestically and internationally.[3] It is to this day probably the most underrated event in twentieth-century world history.

I

The inflation that followed the war in Germany is of course legendary. Poland and Austria were to suffer a similar fate. But until 1920 inflation was a generic experience of all the combatant and non-combatant states across the world. In Europe and Asia demand surged. Prices rose everywhere, with all but the United States having abandoned the gold standard. The relative value of currencies gives some measure of the dislocation. Relative to the dollar, by February 1920 sterling had fallen to as little as $3.40 to the pound, as compared to its pre-war parity of $4.92. The French franc collapsed from the supported rate of 5.45 francs to the dollar during the war to as little as 17.08 francs to the dollar at the end of April 1920.[4] The Italian lire plunged, driving up import prices and stoking inflation. In Asia, a huge surge in Chinese and Indian purchasing combined in 1919 to drive world silver prices to record levels. This resulted in a depreciation of the yen relative to its two major regional trading partners and a surge in Japanese exports.[5] These fluctuations were the expression of loose financial policy as governments continued to spend on post-war reconstruction, without taking the painful fiscal medicine.

This was perhaps most notable in Japan, which emerged as one of the real victors of the war, undamaged but with its status and economic capacity hugely increased. Prime Minister Hara's government was determined to capitalize on this boom. The era of so-called Taisho democracy was born on a wave of inflation and generous government spending. The budget projected a near doubling of government spending in the post-war years. The centrepiece of this splurge was an 800 million yen infrastructure programme for Japan's railways. Road building and school construction were other favourites of the conservative Seiyukai bloc. But the largest single increase was in military spending, propelled upward by the costs of the Siberian intervention and gigantic new naval plans.[6]

In France, at the other end of the spectrum from Japan in terms of war damage, inflation was also fuelled by reconstruction. The regular budget was balanced. But hanging over France was the huge deficit on the extraordinary expenditure account. Spending billions on the devastated areas helped to prevent a surge in unemployment as the army was demobilized. And in the first instance French bondholders showed themselves willing to subscribe truly remarkable amounts of money for the reconstruction.[7] The Bank of France was accommodating.[8] But how long could this be sustained?

As the inflationary boom gathered pace the anxiety caused by a surging cost of living was palpable. Rising prices threatened real wages and drove workers into the ranks of the trade unions. In 1919 and 1920 the French government was confronted with huge May Day strikes and threats of a general strike. In Italy the summer of 1919 ushered in a Biennio Rosso. On 30 August 1919 the Japanese Trade Union Congress was born under the sign of international progressivism. 'The world is changing and it is moving progressively forward, leaving only Japan behind,' the Japanese unionists declaimed.[9] Along with the eight-hour day, they demanded universal manhood suffrage, repeal of repressive police laws and democratization of education. Within a matter of months, the Hara government was deploying military police to deal with strikes in Tokyo and even at the Yawata works, the prestigious, state-owned birthplace of Japan's steel industry.[10] The sense of crisis was compounded in February 1920 by feverish parliamentary manoeuvring and popular mobilization in support of universal suffrage. No wonder that the conservative elder statesman Yamagata Aritomo opined: 'I am constantly and greatly apprehensive' of the 'confusion' and 'ferment' of 'chaos' that may result from the 'present difficulties in society caused by price rises'.[11]

In Britain too there was intense anxiety. Though Lloyd George's government enjoyed a huge majority in Parliament, this poorly reflected the actual balance of opinion in the country and was dangerously at odds with the extraordinary escalation of class conflict that threatened to destroy once and for all Britain's self-image as a peaceable kingdom. Following the alarming disorder in London and Glasgow over the winter of 1918–19, between 1919 and 1921 more days were lost in strikes in Britain than in revolutionary Germany or in Italy. This militancy in turn stoked a groundswell of bourgeois resentment toward the 'privileges' being conceded to the working class. As John Maynard Keynes advised the Treasury in February 1920, 'a continuance of inflationism and high prices will not only depress the exchanges but by their effect on prices will strike at the whole basis of contract, of security, and of the capitalist system generally'.[12] Meanwhile, Chancellor Austen Chamberlain

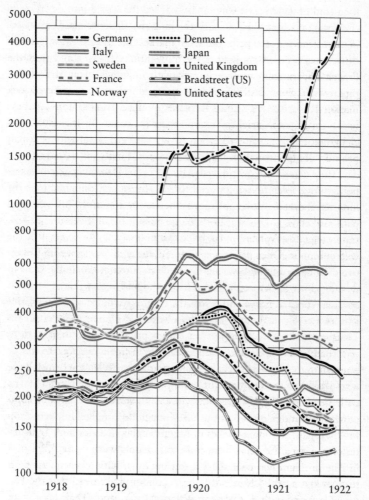

Figure 3. The Great Deflation (Logarithmic vertical scale; 1913 = 100)

fretted over the blackmail of the financial markets as week by week the Treasury struggled to refinance its floating debt.[13] The answer was clear. To restore order there must be a return to financial orthodoxy (Fig. 3).

Ahead of America, it was Japan that led the world into deflation in the spring of 1920. In February the long rise in silver prices reversed. Within a matter of months on Asian markets the price of gold in terms of silver doubled. By inverting the movement of 1919 this impelled a drastic appreciation of the yen relative to China's silver-backed currency. With export orders plunging, on 15 March 1920 the Tokyo stock market crashed.[14] Rice and silk prices plunged. Almost 170 Japanese banks faced panic-stricken runs on their accounts. By June 1920, the Tokyo stock exchange had fallen by 60 per cent against its post-war peak. By comparison with Japan, in the UK the deflationary adjustment was more clearly policy-induced. Already on 15 December 1919 Chamberlain had solemnly announced to the House of Commons that the long-term aim of British policy was the restoration of the pre-war gold parity of sterling. This was not the idle pursuit of prestige, or knee-jerk monetary conservatism, but a policy to uphold the good credit of the British Empire. Once parity was restored, the creditors to whom Britain owed billions of pounds would be repaid in currency worth the same in dollars as it was before the war. Those who had been willing to lend in sterling – both at home and across the empire – would suffer no greater loss as a result of the war than those who had chosen to invest in US Treasury bonds. The question was, what price would Britain have to pay, to uphold this claim to joint leadership in world finance? To enable a return to the pre-war exchange rate against the dollar, the British price level would have to be brought into line with that in the United States. In December 1919, UK prices stood at 240 relative to 1914, as compared to an index of 190 in the US. Though this implied a severe drop in UK prices, so long as prices in America remained elevated, Treasury officials judged the adjustment to be 'reasonably within reach'.[15]

The problem was that the US did not stay 'within reach'. As gold drained out of the US in early 1920, London had feared that the Fed might respond with an excessive deflationary squeeze. Their fears were more than realized. As American prices plummeted, the challenge of restoring sterling to its pre-war parity became ever more daunting. Britain not only had to close the gap between British and American wartime inflation. It now had to match the American deflation as well. In April

1920 the Bank of England followed the Federal Reserve in hiking interest rates and the budget brought in large tax increases on higher incomes and a spending cut of 30 per cent, leaving a 12 per cent surplus for debt repayment.[16] Prices plunged, interest rates increased, but nominal wages remained stubbornly high. Producers faced a ruinous surge in real costs, whilst debtors were plunged into negative equity. Bankruptcies followed en masse. By the autumn of 1920 the British economy was in free fall. Repeatedly, the Bank of England pleaded with the Federal Reserve to loosen its grip on the US economy. But the Fed refused. With specie surging back into America, instead of easing the pressure the Fed 'sterilized' the gold inflow, refusing to allow American credit to expand, resorting to accounting tricks to disguise the ample gold cover. Meanwhile, the situation in Britain reached such a pitch that the UK Treasury seriously considered the possibility of dumping its remaining gold reserve on New York, so as to shame the Fed into expanding the American money supply.[17]

The consequences of this deflation for the politics of post-war recovery in Britain were drastic. The ambitious plans for social expenditure, public housing and education reform promised in 1919 were consigned to the wastepaper basket. The disillusionment of the progressives with Lloyd George was complete. Between July 1920 and July 1921 unemployment amongst trade union members shot from 1 per cent to 23.1 per cent (Fig. 4). The balance of power in industrial relations had reversed. On 15 April 1921 Downing Street called out army and navy units to face down the last and most dramatic threat of a Triple Alliance strike.[18] Eleven battalions of infantry and three cavalry regiments, backed up by tanks, were readied for use in London.[19] But with the solidarity between the three most powerful unions disintegrating, the strike wave was broken. In 1922, with unemployment still close to 20 per cent, barely more than half a million workers were involved in industrial action, 80 per cent less than in 1919. There were those who wanted to press the deflationary 'counter-revolution' to its logical conclusion. Amongst Treasury officials there was talk of slashing pensions and cutting unemployment benefit to the 'barest minimum needed to prevent starvation'. But Chancellor Austen Chamberlain demurred. In the wake of the Great War the state could not deny its citizens a right to adequate support.[20] Given the levels of unemployment, the budgetary consequences of this new notion of entitlement were formidable. Whereas

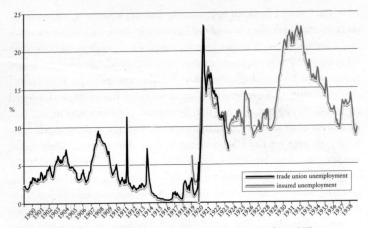

Figure 4. The 'Urshock' of the British Interwar: The First Spike in UK
Unemployment, 1920–21

before the war, total social services expenditure had never exceeded
4.7 per cent of GDP, the figure rose steadily throughout the 1920s to
almost double by 1930.

The United States, Britain and Japan were the worst affected by the
crisis, but deflation was a global phenomenon. Even in Germany, in the
wake of the Kapp putsch, in the summer of 1920 prices actually began
to fall, raising both hopes of a return to economic normality and fear of
a credit-crunch and British levels of unemployment. The question was
how far to push this reversal? Given the scale of their financial problems
and the pain of deflation, France, Italy and Japan opted for stabilization
rather than a punishing attempt to restore pre-war parities. In France
the Bloc national government acquired a black reputation on the left for
breaking two attempts in May 1919 and May 1920 to launch general
strikes. The French Chamber of Deputies of 1919, filled with grim-faced
veterans, superficially confirmed Wilsonian stereotypes. The American
ambassador, Hugh Campbell Wallace, reported to the State Department
that 'disappointment concerning America and the reported revival of
German militarism, which is laid at America's door, have produced a
distinct nationalist and militarist reaction'.[21] But Alexandre Millerand,
who took over as Prime Minister in a botched manoeuvre that was supposed to result in Clemenceau's elevation to the presidency but instead

resulted in his retirement, was no reactionary. He had served as the leader of the Socialist Party faction in parliament until 1899, when in the wake of the Dreyfus battle he took the decision to join the left-wing coalition cabinet that styled itself the Government of Republican Defence.[22] This willingness to engage in pragmatic reform earned him the hatred of the doctrinaires who had seized control of the French Socialist Party after 1904.

Taking office as Prime Minister in January 1920, Millerand conducted not a wholesale deflation but a limited monetary stabilization. Taxes were raised. Regular budgeted expenditure was contained, and Wilsonian accusations of French militarism to the contrary, this included military spending as well. Compared to the pre-war years, the manpower of the French Army was cut from 944,000 to 872,000 in 1920 and as little as 732,000 by 1922.[23] The Bank de France stopped the uncontrolled expansion of the money supply and inflation slowed to a halt. From a low of 17.08 to the dollar in April 1920, the franc recovered to 12.48 in December 1921.[24] But with reconstruction of the devastated regions the top propriety, Millerand never attempted a wholesale and sweeping roll-back of government spending. In Italy, where the labour unrest was amongst the most threatening in western Europe, Francesco Nitti's precipitate attempt to cut the bread subsidy cost him the premiership in June 1920.[25] It was not until 1921, with world commodity prices collapsing, that a new government headed by Giovanni Giolitti dared to eliminate the expensive subsidy.

In Japan, where the crisis had begun, there were conservatives who might have wished for a complete 'liquidation'. But the Bank of Japan judged it impossible to reverse the boom completely. An American or British-style deflation would have jeopardized much of the wartime industrial growth that had been fuelled by large-scale bank lending.[26] Instead, on 27 April 1920 a bank syndicate was formed to provide support to the stock market. In December 1920 an Imperial Silk Filiature company was established to buy up and freeze surplus silk stocks. In April 1921, to provide long-term stability for the rice-farming peasantry the Hara government put in place a comprehensive system of government purchasing and import regulation.

In the event, the refusal of these large economies to follow the UK and the US into wholesale deflation acted as a stabilizing force in the world economy.[27] One of the things that helped to make the worldwide crisis of 1920–21 less prolonged and severe than the 1929–33 recession was precisely that it was not uniform in its impact. But the fact that it was not experienced in the same way across the world economy was in itself significant. It made manifest the way in which the reconstruction of the world economy after World War I organized a new hierarchy. At the bottom were the basket cases en route to hyperinflation, the likes of Poland, Austria and Germany. They became wards of the 'money doctors' and international stabilization regimes, examples of a new form of diminished sovereignty.[28] At the top were the US and the UK, willing and able to carry through a headlong monetary contraction, reversing the monetary effects of the war. In the twilight between these extremes the majority of the world's states – France, Italy and Japan amongst them – were forced to settle for half-hearted stabilization. They avoided the worst of either hyperinflationary excess or bludgeoning deflation, but did so at the price of accepting a humbling second-tier position in the reconstituted economic order.

II

The net effect of the deflation that unfolded after 1920 was to tame the drama of post-war politics. Above all it broke the onrush of the labour movement. As unemployment surged and prices fell the momentum ebbed away from the trade unions. But its implications both domestic and international were more comprehensive than merely the crushing of the left. The deflation worked to contain the right as well. Whilst revolutionaries and paramilitaries traded blows on street corners, picket lines and in meeting halls, deflation acted as a force for strategic demobilization not only across the world but on both sides of the political divide. By the autumn of 1920, in the US Congress loud voices were calling for President Wilson's dramatic naval plans to be consigned to the dustbin of history along with the League of Nations. And given the pressures of deflation these calls were eagerly echoed in Britain as well as Japan.

Since the nineteenth century, Japanese advocates of imperial adventurism had always been able to count on popular patriotic enthusiasm. The huge surge in exports and foreign earnings during the war had added financial heft to the force of the Japanese military. By the end of 1919 the current account surplus accumulated since 1915 stood at 3 billion yen. Japan was now a net international creditor. And there were loud voices in Hara's Seiyukai government determined to continue this 'positive policy' into the post-war era. Japan must seize its chance to consolidate its escape from British tutelage and establish itself as the exclusive regional hegemon. But the conditions of 1914–18 were clearly exceptional. And the impact on Japan's domestic politics of the spectacular inflationary boom was deeply troubling. Amidst escalating food prices, the lack of enthusiasm for the army's intervention in Siberia was unmistakable. Reflecting on the anniversary of the rice riots in the autumn of 1919, the newspaper *Osaka Asahi Shimbun* editorialized: 'it is a fact that the attitude of the majority of our people is completely different from their attitude when they have met with so-called hardships in the past. Up to the present when the state had resorted to military force abroad ... the Japanese people have set aside their own needs and waxed wildly enthusiastic for the state ... now, however, while the authorities are clamouring about the great crisis overseas, the people are not asking "what will become of the country?"; they have risen to cry out "what will become of us?"' Despite the surge in national power, the majority of the people had 'fallen into circumstances too straitened to hope for honour or for glory'.[29]

With their policy of deflation Britain and America once more changed the rules of the game. In May 1921, Takahashi Korekijo, one of the Seiyukai's most aggressive advocates of growth, summarized the position in a top-secret memo. At Versailles, Japan had been recognized as a major power. But, so far, its claim to significance had rested on its military force. This was a fleeting advantage. The enduring foundation of power was economic. With their determination to restore the gold standard, America and Britain were reaffirming their leadership in the world economy. For Japan to adopt a deflationary policy would cut short the boom, but if wages and prices were not forced down, Japan's exporters would soon find themselves struggling to compete. As the balance of payments deteriorated, Japan would once more slide into dependence on foreign credits. The only way to make Japan a permanent member of the great-power club was to establish a platform for long-lasting economic prosperity on the basis of a truly harmonious relationship with China. But this required the definitive abandonment of militarist adventurism.[30] Whilst Takahashi and the

Seiyukai tolerated the army's interventionist ambition, amongst the opposition parties the anti-militarist consensus was overwhelming. In July 1921 the rump of pre-war liberalism, the Kokuminto Party, adopted the slogan that Japan should exchange militarism for industrialism.[31] In November of that year, on behalf of the liberal wing of the main opposition party, the Kenseikai, Ozaki Yukio launched an impassioned nationwide campaign against the ruinous costs of military spending. His pleas and those of tens of thousands of petitioners would be answered.[32] From a high of 65.4 per cent of government spending in 1922, defence expenditure was cut to less than 40 per cent between 1923 and 1927.[33]

In Britain too, as debt service and social spending rose, and as budgets plunged, it was military spending that was targeted.[34] The first round of budget cuts in April 1919 reduced UK spending on the army from £405 million to under £90 million. Imperial military expeditions and peace-keeping in Europe had to make do with £48 million.[35] Army manpower was slashed from 3.5 million to 800,000. By 1922 the army budget was down to £62 million. Sir Henry Wilson, the Chief of the Imperial General Staff, who had once deployed huge armies, found himself juggling battalions between Ireland, the Rhineland and Persia to meet one emergency after another.[36] Britain of course looked to its empire to make a contribution, but attempts to offload the cost of the imperial army on India met with fierce resistance.[37] In the Middle East, Britain's infamous policy of 'policing' insurgencies by means of aerial bombardment was adopted above all because it was cheap. The initial estimate for the military garrison of the Iraq Mandate had run to 30 battalions at a cost of £30 million. After the Cairo conference of March 1921, Winston Churchill decided he could manage with a budget of only £10 million so long as four infantry battalions based in Baghdad could be backed up by eight squadrons of bombers. The de Havilland DH9A bombers used in these operations could be had for as little as £3,000 apiece.[38]

These, however, were tactical adjustments. It was with regard to the navy that truly strategic decisions had to be taken. In the spring of 1919 as Britain and America clashed at Versailles, the Royal Navy had estimated its financial requirements for the coming year at £171 million. This was denied both on grounds of austerity and to avoid antagonizing the Americans. On 15 August the cabinet instructed the service departments to make their plans on the assumption that 'the British Empire would not be engaged in any great war during the next ten years'. For the navy this meant that spending was to be slashed to £60 million by 1920–21. The consequences were drastic. As the Admiralty pointed out: 'It must be clearly understood that Great Britain will no longer be supreme at sea . . . we shall be supreme in European waters, but as regards the seas as a whole the supremacy will be shared with the United States.'[39] Shared supremacy as the basis for a lasting global pacification had been the basic aspiration of the Lloyd George government since 1916. The Wilson administration had refused any such agreement, but given the financial legacy of the war, it was now being built into British strategy willy-nilly.[40]

III

The re-establishment of financial stability, symbolized by the restoration of the gold standard, was tied directly to policies of pacification, repressing expansionist energy on the right as well as the left. If the premise of conservative stability was accepted, it exerted discipline on every aspirant member, the United States and Britain no less than France or Japan. And in the crunching deflation of 1920–21 that pressure was certainly felt in America as well as Britain. But despite this basic symmetry, the position of the leading duo was nevertheless unique. They were setting themselves apart precisely by their willingness to make an investment in the creation of a new status quo. As the Versailles negotiations had made painfully evident, even amongst the victorious powers the starting conditions for the aspirant members of the new order were anything but equal.

France had suffered devastating war damage, leaving it dependent as never before. In 1920 the French Minister of Public Works estimated that thanks to the destruction of its northern mines France would have to import 50 million tons of coal, out of its annual requirement of 70 million. This was at a time when Britain had cut its supply to the world market from 80 million to only 33 million tons, of which France could count on at most 18 million, at escalating prices compounded by the depreciation of the franc.[41] French control of the Saar would provide it with 8 million tons annually. To make up the difference, Paris

demanded 27 million tons from the German mines in the Ruhr in reparations. But when German deliveries began in the spring of 1920, they
yielded less than half what was expected. Less tangible but no less pressing was the question of war debts. France's relations with Germany are
too often seen in simplistic terms as a struggle between two rival nationalisms on either side of the Rhine. In fact reparations politics were
determined by a complex web of influences that entangled Paris with
London and New York. The fact that this complex web remained largely
out of sight was itself an effect of Washington's power. Since the Paris
peace conference, Washington had used main force to keep the question
of linkage between reparations and war debts off the agenda. But from
the European point of view the question could not be dodged. Over the
summer of 1920 Paris had been seriously embarrassed by its inability to
repay minor credits owed to Spain and Argentina. Far more menacing
were the $250 million owed as its share of the first Entente loan con-
tracted through J. P. Morgan in 1915. To raise the necessary funds
France found itself borrowing on Wall Street at the humiliating rate of
8 per cent.[42] Whilst Washington stood back, for several weeks in early
1921 Paris teetered on the edge of default.

Since 1919 the policy preferred by the British government was for a
collective write-down of inter-Allied claims. But this had been vetoed by
the Wilson administration. In February 1920, despairing of any concessions from the US, the senior civil servants at the UK Treasury began to
think in radical terms. Britain should unilaterally implement its side of
the Keynes cancellation plan. Whilst honouring its debts to America,
London should renounce its claim on its former allies. Washington would
surely have no option but to match such a *beau geste*. The Foreign Office
applauded the suggestion, which would win goodwill for Britain 'for a
generation to come' and establish its 'incontestable moral leadership of
the world'. But the diplomats were too uncertain about the likely
response in Washington if London tried to 'shame the US into following
our example'.[43] The British certainly received no encouragement. The
Wilson administration did agree to extend the deferral of interest on
Britain's loans. But it made this conditional on a prior settlement of
reparations and a formal commitment to abstain from any future discrimination against America in the British Empire's trade policy.

Chancellor Austen Chamberlain reacted with indignation. The British Empire would accept no conditionality on its credit. Between the

governments of Britain and America, such terms should never have been put in writing. Britain must retain its absolute freedom of action. Sovereignty was paramount.[44] 'The American people are living in a different continent – I might say in a different world.' Chamberlain concluded: 'It is useless and worse than useless to criticize their insularity, blindness and selfishness, and it is not compatible with our dignity to appear as suitors pressing for a consideration which is not willingly given.'[45] Instead, by the end of the year a negotiating team was readied for bilateral debt talks in the American capital.

France did not have the financial cushion that allowed Britain to weigh up its options. The domestic costs of rebuilding northern France could, if necessary, be raised domestically through taxes, borrowing, or if this proved most expedient, by inflation, a tax on savers. The huge burden of France's foreign debt – $3 billion to America, $2 billion to Britain – had to be repaid in gold or dollars. Barring a miraculous surge in exports, which the US and the UK with their policies of aggressive deflation were doing nothing to promote, or a ruinous cut to essential imports, this foreign currency could only come from reparations. It was to consolidate France's claim to compensation that, following Millerand's accession to the presidency, Aristide Briand took the premiership in January 1921.[46] Like Millerand, Briand had started political life as a reform-orientated socialist and had since been ostracized by the left for his willingness to govern. By temperament an internationalist, as wartime premier he had been identified with the most aggressive French war aims. In 1921 he returned to power determined to impose the peace. This seemed all the more necessary since the Centre Party government that had taken office in Germany after the debacle of the Kapp putsch and the election of June 1920 seemed bent on provocation, encouraged it seemed by America's failure to back its former associates. When reparations talks opened in March 1921, Germany began with an absurdly low offer of 30 billion Goldmarks. From that point no compromise could be reached.

The Entente reacted with its last concerted display of power. On 13 March 1921 both British and French troops occupied bridgeheads in the industrial cities of Duisburg, Ruhort and Dusseldorf, and a customs boundary was erected separating the Rhineland from the rest of Germany. The French general staff had plans at the ready for an occupation of the entire Ruhr, but Briand wanted British backing before making any such move. Conscious of the risk they were running, the Germans responded by raising their offer to 50 billion Goldmarks, to which the British and French replied on 5 May with the London reparations ultimatum of 132 billion Goldmarks. Superficially enormous, the gap between the two offers was less than it at first appeared, since the Allied demand above 50 billion was to take the form of so-called Class C bonds. Barring a miraculous recovery in German exports, these would not be issued until 1957. On reasonable assumptions, the net present value of the settlement was 64 billion Goldmarks, or just over $15 billion.[47] At the same moment the Entente's collective indebtedness to the US stood at $10 billion. Unless America's claims were stretched out over a similarly long time period, this implied a painfully small margin to cover the up-front costs of reconstruction. For Germany the implications were undeniably dramatic. It would face enormous immediate payments and even if it managed to uphold the schedule for the next 35 years, its international credit would be questionable for generations to come. It had just one week to respond.

Since Wilson's ostentatious refusal to back French intervention in Frankfurt at the time of the Kapp putsch in March 1920 and the Senate's refusal to ratify the Versailles Treaty, Berlin's foreign policy had concentrated on luring America into returning to Europe to arbitrate a true 'peace of equals'. But faced with the crisis over reparations and the looming issue of Silesia, the boundaries of which were to be determined in 1921, the incoming Secretary of States Charles Evans Hughes had no desire to risk the role that Wilson had attempted to play. Two days before the ultimatum was to expire, on 10 May 1921 the German government collapsed.[48] As there had been in 1918 and 1919, there were now loud voices on the German right calling for a policy of confrontation. Their cynical calculation was that an Allied invasion of western Germany would trigger an upsurge of patriotic resistance and accomplish what the Kapp putsch had failed to do a year earlier. But in 1921, as it had done twice before, *raison d'état* prevailed. On 11 May, with 24 hours to go before the Allied deadline, a new coalition took office in Berlin. Again it was headed by a Centre Party politician, Joseph Wirth, the heir to Matthias Erzberger, as the leading voice of the popular wing of the party. His first order of business was to come to terms with the Entente. But this begged the question. Even if 'fulfilment' was politically desirable, could Germany pay? (Table 9).

Table 9. What Germany Paid, 1918–31 (billion 1913 marks)

	total peace treaty payments	national income	treaty burden (% national income)
1913		52	
1918	1.3	37	3.3
1919	1.1	32	3.1
1920	1.3	37	3.4
1921	3.4	40	8.2
1922	2.2	42	5.2
1923	0.9	36	2.4
1924	0.3	42	0.6
1925	1.1	48	2.2
1926	1.2	46	2.5
1927	1.6	54	2.8
1928	2.0	55	3.5
1929	2.3	56	4.0
1930	1.7	53	3.2
1931	1.0	47	2.1
1918–31 average	1.5	45	3.4
1924–31 average	1.4	50	2.8

NOTE (sources given in List of Figures):
Annual estimates are derived by reconciling Webb and Schuker and cross-checking against Bresciani-Turroni.

1918	Armistice deliveries from Schuker
1919	Residual of total 1918–24 costs from Schuker after subtraction of itemized payments for 1918 and 1920–24
1920–22	Quarterly treaty costs from Webb
1923	Ruhr occupation charges from Schuker
1924–31	Reparations item in the German balance of payments account (includes cash transfers, payments in kind and all other charges)
1929–30	Includes transfer of Young Plan loan

There was no straight line leading from reparations to the Ruhr crisis and hyperinflation of 1923. In the spring of 1920 following the defeat of the Kapp putsch, the Goldmark had strengthened against the dollar. Between March and July prices fell by 20 per cent and then stabilized. For a brief moment it seemed as though the Weimar Republic might be on the point of following the rest of the world in a deflationary financial consolidation. Given what was to come next, this cannot but appear attractive.[49] But with unemployment soaring in Britain, in the early 1920s an end to the post-war boom was regarded in Germany as a distinctly mixed blessing. There was great fear that Germany's precariously balanced political system would not withstand the kind of mass unemployment the British and American governments were inflicting on their populations. In any case, the reparations crisis of the spring of 1921 undid this temporary stabilization. After months of price stabilization, inflation resumed in June of that year and surged to double-digit figures in August. Nationalist economic opinion now insisted that excessive levels of reparations made any thought of stabilization absurd. France's real intention was to 'Ottomanize' Germany, to reduce it to the kind of international debt-slavery used to subordinate the bankrupt Chinese and Ottoman empires.

Nor can it be denied that successive demands on the reparations account were to play a major role in tumbling Germany into chaos. The frontloading of the reparations schedule in 1921 and 1922, reflecting the desperate French need for cash, put huge pressures on the Weimar Republic.[50] But to argue that there was nothing that Germany could do to improve a bad situation reflected not a realistic assessment but the unwillingness of nationalist opinion to come to terms with defeat.[51] Those who were most sincerely committed to the Republican project argued that Germany should put Britain and France in the wrong by pursuing responsible financial policies, thereby demonstrating the practical impossibility of fulfilment. As Allied experts, including Keynes, repeatedly pointed out, even if Germany could not restore pre-war conditions, then like Japan, France or Italy, it could certainly halt any further slide. Its price level would remain high, but at a suitably depreciated exchange rate it would be internationally competitive. This would provide a solid platform from which to renegotiate. If, on the other hand, Germany did not comply, what was there to hope for, but a descent into chaos, foreign occupation and civil war?

The problem was that even at a much lower exchange rate, the achievement of a durable stabilization required painful fiscal decisions. To find a democratic majority not only for stabilization but for reparations fulfilment was doubly difficult. There was in Germany, as in Britain, France and Japan, a powerful faction calling for stabilization on a pro-business platform. By rolling back the social gains of the revolution of 1918, reversing the eight-hour day, squeezing wages and lowering taxes, Germany would re-emerge as a global export champion. But this implied a political counter-revolution and despite the severe electoral setback of 1920, the Social Democratic Party was still the largest political party. As the general strike in response to the Kapp putsch had demonstrated, organized labour had a veto over the politics of the Republic. This blocked any decisive turn toward fiscal conservatism. But the Social Democrats also lacked the necessary majority for their own preferred option of steep progressive taxation and a wealth levy.

It was this political impasse that drove the slide into disaster. Inflation was the path of least resistance. The Wirth government clung to the rhetoric of reparations fulfilment. But it did so by printing cash and dumping it on the foreign exchanges. The result was a feverish domestic boom and a plunging exchange rate. By contrast with Britain and the US, up to the winter of 1922 unemployment in Weimar Germany was negligible. The bill was paid by the huge tax levied by inflation on Germany's savers. When that became unsustainable, the trigger was set for renewed confrontation.

IV

Reparations paid on such a transparently unsteady basis could not provide the financial security that France craved. Though the French share of the sum demanded under the London reparations ultimatum had a net present value of over $8 billion, the most that J. P. Morgan was able to raise on behalf of Paris in the spring of 1921 was $90 million at an embarrassing rate of 7.5 per cent.[52] As the third anniversary of the Armistice approached, France's situation was increasingly desperate. By the end of 1921 huge deferred interest payments would be due on its inter-Allied debts. Without some settlement of these sums enabling the restoration of French credit, there could be no talk of concessions on reparations, regardless of how desperate Germany's situation might become.

The mounting pressure in Europe was not lost on the incoming Harding administration. Charles Evans Hughes, the new Secretary of State, embodied a Republican version of the spirit of manifest destiny that had animated Wilson. He was, Teddy Roosevelt once quipped, 'the whiskered Wilson'.[53] Hughes believed, as Herbert Hoover, now serving as Commerce Secretary, had advised Wilson, that the best way to preserve American power was precisely to hold Europe at a distance. Since America did not want to take responsibility for actively policing the struggle in Europe, Washington should stand well back from the fray. Neutrality not only avoided the costs of entanglement. Upholding America's own claims was the best way of forcing the Europeans to a resolution. When the political passions of the old world had been humbled by financial pressure, markets would take over and private capital would lubricate a more lasting settlement.

This American strategy of distance was no doubt a reaction to the truly intractable situation in Europe. But it also responded to as impasse within the American state. The last 18 months of the Wilson presidency had demonstrated the bitter lesson of the limits to executive power. President Harding was widely seen as a creature of the Republican congressional majority. And though in the spring of 1921 his new administration showed a surprising degree of activism, it was not long before Congress delivered a shot across his bows.[54] In the autumn of that year, at the request of the President, Senator Boise Penrose introduced a bill into Congress that would have given the US Treasury authorization to conduct an activist foreign-debt policy – extending the payment period, authorizing debt swaps and part repayment in other obligations. Though the administration did not wish to offer the Europeans an immediate solution, it wanted to have the legal powers necessary to broker a deal should the opportunity arise. America's bankers, led by Benjamin Strong at the New York Fed, fully understood the need for an interlocking settlement. But in Congress the Farm Bloc saw things differently.[55] As Senator Ashhurst of Arizona put it, 'We saved Europe and our Christian civilization. But that does not imply now that the peril is past that we should feed the Europeans and allow them in their great cities to live in idleness and sometimes in luxury.'[56] A

Democratic opponent of war debt concessions was rather more specific, despite the bitter deflation pressing on the economy since the spring of 1920, 'we are taxing the American people as they have never been taxed before in the history of the republic ... If we collect but the interest upon these loans, we will of necessity reduce the taxation upon our own people by one-seventh.'[57]

On 24 October 1921 the Penrose Bill passed the House of Representatives, but only after having been turned on its head. Rather than authorizing the Treasury to broker strategic debt deals, it gave control over debt policy to a five-member Senate Commission and explicitly banned the use of any foreign bonds as means of repayment. In the aftermath, Governor Norman of the Bank of England complained resignedly to his friend Benjamin Strong at the New York Fed that Congress had created a 'ridiculous' roadblock. 'Having, let us suppose, steadied the exchanges by some reparations adjustment, we are immediately to see them unsteadied by inter-allied debt payments.'[58] But when word leaked to the press that the two central bankers were exchanging notes, it was enough to trigger a storm of indignation. Both the British and American governments were forced to issue denials that they harboured any plans for a transatlantic financial conference. The Senate rushed through a motion affirming that America would not cancel a cent of its claims on Europe.

20

Crisis of Empire

In Europe, Britain was the strongest power financially and the most stable politically. Further afield the war appeared to have ended as a triumph for the British Empire. Its rivals old and new were humbled, the Royal Navy ruled the waves, the armies of the empire were victorious in Europe and the Middle East (Table 10). But within a year of the Armistice the map of the British Empire came to resemble not so much a vista of power as a landscape of rebellion on which the sun never set.[1] The crisis of empire spanned the globe from the West Indies to Ireland, Egypt, Palestine, South Africa, India and Hong Kong.

The propaganda of the war with its appeal to the rights of small nations, self-determination and Wilson's 14 Points had created a common political language with which to make claims on London. Against this backdrop each protest vindicated others in their common appeal to the importance of this moment of history. At the same time the switchback of inflation and deflation swept through the colonial economy. As the cost of living surged, there was boiling labour unrest from Winnipeg to Bombay. In November 1919, facing a doubling of prices, stevedores in Trinidad demanded a 25 per cent wage increase and the eight-hour day.[2] In Sierra Leone in July 1919 the fivefold increase in the price of rice sparked unprecedented strikes.[3] In southern Rhodesia wartime inflation left the workforce barefoot and ragged, triggering strikes amongst railway workers, miners and public servants.[4]

But although inflation was destabilizing, when the deflation began in 1920 that too exacted a price. In West Africa the bursting of the post-war commodity bubble drove local businessmen into the ranks of the Pan African Congress.[5] As sterling rebounded from its lows against the dollar, gold prices plunged. The empire's main gold producers, the mines of

Table 10. Stretched Thin: Deployment of
British Imperial Forces, February 1920

	British	Indian Army
Germany	16,000	
Turkey	9,000	14,000
Egypt	6,000	20,000
Palestine	10,000	13,000
Mesopotamia	17,000	44,000

the South African Rand, faced a devastating blow to their corporate balance sheets. With wages being slashed and the white workforce diluted with black labour, on 10 March 1922 the white miners of the Rand rose in rebellion. To deal with the uprising, which at its peak involved tens of thousands of well-armed commandos, Prime Minister Smuts, the epitome of enlightened statesmanship, sent 20,000 troops, artillery, tanks and the airforce to bomb the strikers back to work.[6]

During the war, whilst Germany and Japan both struggled to formulate coherent strategic or political rationales for imperial expansion in Eurasia, it had seemed that Britain had successfully reinvented the formula of liberal empire. The British Empire, it seemed, would claim for itself a major place in the twentieth-century world as a self-sustaining and self-legitimating strategic unit. After 1919 that complacent scenario collapsed. London found itself struggling both to overcome resistance to its imperial rule and to mobilize the internal resources necessary to uphold its power. The international legitimacy and the strategic rationale of the empire were both in doubt as never before. The empire was to survive the crisis, but the challenge it had faced was like nothing it had ever experienced before. It brought Britain dangerously close to the edge of true political disaster.

I

Ireland offered a vision of imperial catastrophe in microcosm.[7] The results of the Khaki election in December 1918 confirmed the polarization brought about by Sinn Fein's suicidal Easter Uprising. The Unionists swept the board in Ulster. Sinn Fein dominated the entire rest of Ireland. London's moderate nationalist collaborators were driven out of politics. On 21 January 1919 nationalist MPs meeting in Dublin constituted the Dail Eirann, an Irish national parliament, and proclaimed a provisional government of the Irish Republic. Whilst a parallel state began to constitute itself across the South, the armed wing of republicanism, the Irish Republican Army (IRA), set itself the task of isolating and uprooting the infrastructure of British rule. By early 1920 Ireland was in the grip of an escalating guerrilla war, which over the next two years claimed the lives of 1,400 people in ambushes and reprisal shootings. In a country of only 3 million souls, casualties on such a scale were a terrible toll. (Magnified to the size of India it would have implied over 110,000 dead, in Egypt 14,000.) And it was as much the quality of the violence as the quantity that was shocking. From August 1920 the ordinary rule of civilian law was replaced by outright repression. Over 4,400 suspected IRA activists were detained without trial, again a vast number in relation to Ireland's population. Open sanction was given by the British cabinet to the assassination of IRA leaders and to reprisals including the burning of farms and other property. Martial law was declared across much of Ireland. But, given the lack of regular army and police units, London resorted to the deployment of brutish paramilitaries. By the summer of 1921 Field Marshal Henry Wilson, himself a co-conspirator in the Ulster mutiny plans of 1914, was calling for Ireland to be flooded with over 100,000 regular troops.[8]

In July 1921, Lloyd George used the threat of massive repression to force through a truce. But London was bluffing. A full-scale military occupation of Ireland would not only have placed an intolerable strain on Britain. It would have done incalculable political damage, both at home and abroad.[9] The fact that this escalation was avoided was due to concessions from moderates on all sides. The Tory Party in Britain made clear to the Ulster Unionists that they must finally concede Home Rule on the condition that the North remained a separate jurisdiction. The Irish nationalists swallowed a partition, a Council of Ireland in which Unionists had a voice, continued fealty to the British Empire, and British naval bases on Irish territory.

In December 1921 the Irish Free State was formally accorded Dominion status, 'in the community of nations known as the British Empire'.[10]

But this was not enough to bring peace. Sinn Fein's final burst of apocalyptic radicalism vented itself not on the British, but on their former comrades who had accepted the compromise. The resulting civil war within the Republic claimed more lives than the fight against the British. Taking the two wars together, the Irish death toll rose to levels comparable, in proportional terms, to that other great disaster of Britain's retreat from empire, India's partition in 1947. It was a humiliating ending to the effort to craft a liberal solution to the question of Irish self-determination that had preoccupied the British political class for fifty years. It stored up violence for the rest of the twentieth century. But Ireland never did become for Britain what Sinn Fein hoped it would, a true strategic liability. The nationalist strategy hinged on gaining recognition and support from Washington. But Wilson had refused to allow the Irish question to be raised at the Paris Peace Conference.[11] The subsequent civil war did much to discredit the extreme nationalists in the eyes of global opinion. London was able to contain the Irish question. The same could not be said for the self-inflicted wounds that resulted from the aggressive Middle Eastern policy of the Lloyd George coalition. Here Britain's ambitious pursuit of excessive imperial strategic goals provoked local resistance, outrage throughout the empire and a debacle of British policy in Europe.

II

From its opening in 1869 down to the Franco-British intervention of 1956, the Suez canal was to be a consistent focus of British strategic attention. But power could be exercised in different ways. It was the uneven momentum of the Great War that launched Britain on the most aggressive and disastrous phase of its career as a Middle Eastern power.[12] From the spring of 1918, faced with Germany's dramatic advance, Lloyd George's chief advisor Alfred Milner had advocated a retreat to the imperial periphery. If it was driven out of France, Britain would fight on from its offshore position, anchored in the North Sea, the Atlantic and through its bases dotted from end to end of the Mediterranean. By October 1918 British victory was complete on every front. In Palestine, in Syria, in Persia, even in the Caucasus, there seemed no limit to the expansion of British power. With the Bolsheviks hemmed in, London's main problem was its allies, France and the United States. At Versailles, France insisted on its claim to priority in Syria. Meanwhile, Lloyd George sought to lure America into accepting a mandate for an autonomous Armenian state. Washington dispatched investigative committees both to Palestine and Armenia to explore the possibility. Armenia became a personal hobby horse of Wilson. But the likely costs were obvious, the economic benefits minimal, and suspicion of British intrigue ran rife. Congress conclusively voted down the idea of an Armenian mandate along with the rest of the peace treaty in the spring of 1920.[13]

But not only did the British overestimate America's interest in the active sponsorship of self-determination. They seriously underestimated the force that this promise might acquire as a challenge to Britain's own power in the region, nowhere more so than in Egypt. In the 1880s Egypt had been at the centre of the new imperial competition in Africa. Britain had ousted both the Ottomans and the French from the country and secured dominance over the French-financed Suez canal. As war approached in 1914 there was talk of outright annexation. Instead, leaving open all possibilities, in December 1914 London declared a protectorate, whilst at the same time promising progress towards self-government.[14] This produced contradictory expectations. The French-orientated Egyptian elite took the liberal rhetoric of the Entente and the United States at face value, whereas Britain's most expansive imperialists expected the 'dissolution of the Ottoman Empire' to 'make Egypt the lodestar in any new Afro-Asian imperial constellation'.[15]

In 1918 the man who was rapidly emerging as the leader of the new nationalism, Sa'd pasha Zaghloul, a former Minister of Education and Minister of Justice, demanded representation at Versailles in the name of his patrician national delegation, or Wafd. The initial British response was one of contempt. When warned that they might soon be facing a conflagration, the British financial and judicial advisor, William Brunyate, responded that he 'would put out the fire by spitting on it'.[16] If Egyptian nationalism had remained confined to Zaghloul and his notable friends, that might have been enough. But over the winter of 1918–19 the cause gathered behind it a quite unprecedented popular coalition. By March 1919 the British faced a fully fledged, but largely non-violent, popular uprising in which politics and economics were mingled together.[17]

The dislocation of the Egyptian economy caused by its incorporation into the imperial war effort was one of the driving forces of this unrest.

Inflation was rampant. Prices had increased threefold and malnutrition was at alarming levels.[18] The cost of food hit the urban poor worst, but peasants too, who grew cotton for export, found themselves close to starvation. Yet as one Scandinavian diplomat commented, this was no mere food riot. It was the 'first time in modern Egyptian history that the whole of the native population has cooperated in a political movement'.[19] By March 1919, with Cairo in turmoil and Zaghloul in detention on Malta, the British were unable to find any significant Egyptian figure willing to serve as the head of a cooperative government. Martial law was declared whilst the hero of the victorious Palestine campaign, General Allenby, was hurriedly shipped in to serve as High Commissioner. But even the deployment of substantial British forces from their barracks in the Suez canal zone was not enough to restore order, as the government was paralysed by a nationwide civil service strike. In a symbolic display of national unity, Easter Sunday 1919 was celebrated jointly by Copts and Muslims.

Spitting was no longer enough to put out the fire. But London was determined to maintain its grip. At Versailles, Balfour and Lloyd George worked to extract recognition from France and the United States of their protectorate over Egypt.[20] Having secured its strategic grip, Zaghloul was released from his exile and in December 1919 a commission headed by Lord Milner arrived in Cairo to consider the 'form of constitution which, under the protectorate be best calculated to promote its peace and prosperity, the progressive development of self-governing institutions and the protection of foreign interests'.[21] Such patronizing language would have been provocative in 1914. Twelve months into a national rebellion it was entirely inadequate. Even Milner was forced to conclude that 'nationalism had established complete domination in Egypt over every social and articulate element. The country had become impossible to govern.'[22] By the summer of 1920 it was clear to those on the spot that Britain would have to negotiate over the continued presence of British military forces in an independent Egypt. As Milner reassured the British cabinet, though 'Egypt is truly the nodal point of our whole imperial system', it was not necessary for Britain to 'own it'. All that Britain needed was a 'firm foothold', which was provided by the recognition of Britain's right to station troops in the Suez canal zone whilst it consolidated its position on the upper reaches of the Nile in Sudan.[23] Indeed, Milner was willing to regard Egypt's independence as 'the most striking tribute to the efficacy of Great Britain's reforming work . . . The establishment of Egypt as an independent state in intimate alliance with Great Britain, so far from being a reversal of the policy with which we set out, would be the consummation of it . . . That we should attempt it at all, is evidence . . . of our good faith and of our confidence in the soundness of the work which we have been doing in Egypt . . .'[24] But Downing Street dragged its feet.

In February 1922 it took a threat of resignation by Allenby to force London to agree to acknowledge Egyptian independence and to end martial law. The problem was that, as in Ireland, Egyptian nationalism was already too strong to allow the British to feel comfortable with this compromise. In one election after another between 1923 and 1929 the Wafd won huge majorities for its moderate programme of national reform. Repeatedly, the British intervened to block its road to power, resulting in the suspension of Egypt's first liberal constitution and the installation in 1930 of a government sufficiently authoritarian to be able to square its limited vision of national independence with British interests. London extracted a heavy price for Cairo's limited sovereignty. The promise of democratic politics in Egypt was compromised at birth.

Britain's aggression toward Egyptian nationalism is even more puzzling given the lack of serious strategic threats in the region. Turkey and Germany were defeated. Russia was disarmed and America disinterested. Italy and France both looked to an Entente with Britain for their security and neither was in any position to mount a serious challenge to its pre-eminence. At times, indeed, it seemed as though the massive preponderance of Britain's forces was what carried it forward into further aggression. When T. E. Lawrence rode into Damascus alongside Amir Feisal and 1,500 horsemen in October 1918, it seemed that Britain was claiming patronage over territory that had already been allocated to the French in 1916. London insisted that it was simply making good on the promise to establish an independent Arab state. But it also burdened Feisal with responsibility for honouring the Balfour Declaration's promise of a Zionist homeland in Palestine, a project that by the autumn of 1919 was already arousing indignant Arab opposition.[25] Then, following the San Remo Conference in April 1920, as part of a new arrangement with France, the British abandoned their support for Feisal.[26]

Instead of Syria that was allocated to the French, Britain would base its position on Egypt and on a consolidated Iraqi state, a prospect which promptly aroused fierce tribal opposition in Mesopotamia. Heedless of this resistance, after the French had blasted out the Syrian nationalists with tanks and airpower, Feisal was switched from Damascus to Baghdad, whilst his brother was installed as king of Trans-Jordan.[27] The humiliation of the Arab political class reached its finale in March 1924 when the elected members of Iraq's constituent assembly were dragged into parliament by armed British guards to ratify the Anglo-Iraq Treaty that established Iraq's independence, but gave Britain control of its army and its finances.[28] A new order had been created in the Middle East, anchored on nominally independent Egypt and Iraq, but in fact based on a wilful disregard for political legitimacy, a lack that in turn rebounded on the moral foundation of the British Empire as a whole.[29]

London's aggression toward Turkey was even more naked and the consequences even more disastrous. By 1918 the dismantling of the Ottoman Empire had become official Entente policy. Turkey was to be left with Anatolia and eastern Thrace. By early May 1919 the Sultan was under Franco-British supervision in Istanbul. Some 40,000 British imperial troops were deployed along the railway lines of Anatolia. Greek troops established a brutal regime of occupation in Smyrna and Italian soldiers, in compensation for their disappointment in the Adriatic, were emplacing themselves on Aegean beachheads.[30] To the east autonomist movements were stirring amongst the Armenians and Kurds.[31] Insofar as Entente policy toward Turkey had had any political rationale, it consisted in the claim that through decrepitude and atrocity the Ottoman Empire had forfeited its right to historical existence.

However, what this ignored was the new force of Turkish nationalism. Though the killers of the Armenians in 1915 had discredited themselves, the March 1920 general elections for the Ottoman parliament returned a crushing majority for the nationalists. The British responded by occupying Istanbul, declaring martial law, and backing a Greek assault into the Anatolian interior. The nationalists withdrew to Ankara in the Anatolian highlands where a Grand National Assembly declared a national uprising. Heedless, the Western Powers pushed ahead. On 10 August 1920 the Sultan was forced to sign the humiliating provisions of the Treaty of Sèvres.[32] Lloyd George proclaimed that the Entente was 'releasing all non-Turkish populations from Turkish sway'. However, by putting his signature to the treaty, the Sultan also released the Turks from any loyalty to his dynasty. For the nationalist leader Ataturk it meant the 'passing of government . . . into the hands of the people'.

Over the summer of 1920 the Greek Army had made good headway in its invasion of Anatolia. But on 1 November in an unexpected turn of events the pro-monarchist Greek electorate repudiated the expansionist and liberal government of Eleftherios Venizelos. In bitter winter fighting the Greek advance was first halted and then driven back by the newly constituted army of Turkey's Grand National Assembly. In January 1921 the Assembly declared a new constitution and entered into a treaty with the Soviet Union. During the summer the Greek forces advanced once more. They drove to within 40 kilometres of Ankara, only for the Turkish national forces to rally around Ataturk, who inflicted a shattering defeat on the invaders in the three-week battle on the Sakarya river line.[33] As the Greeks began their long and bloody withdrawal to the coast in mid-September 1921, Lloyd George faced the shipwreck of his Middle Eastern policy. Britain's support for the Greeks had driven the Turks into an unlikely coalition with Russia. Meanwhile, the antagonism stirred up between Britain and France in the Middle East fractured the Entente and helped to unhinge Lloyd George's policy in Europe. Worst of all, Britain's aggression toward Turkey threatened to create an unmanageable situation in India.

III

The scale of the possible challenge to British rule in India had become clear in 1916 when Bal Gangadhar Tilak and Annie Besant launched their Home Rule agitation. In 1918 the promise of the Montagu Declaration and the containment of the threatening monetary crisis had served to hold unrest at bay. But, within the year, London quite suddenly found itself facing a mass movement on an imposing scale. In 1916 the crowds had numbered in the tens of thousands. By 1919 the anti-British movement ran into the millions. The new energy of the Indian National Congress and the Home Rule League no doubt owed much to the common denominator of economic distress. And it suited British administrators in the Raj only too well to blame the upsurge of rebellion in 1919 on economic factors. If it was hunger and frustration that were driving the Indians to revolt, then economic remedies would suffice. If a rising cost of living produced unrest, then deflation was the cure.[34]

Since before the war, Indian nationalists had been demanding the gold standard. In February 1920 London announced that they would have their wish. At the height of the post-war boom, the rupee was established on gold. Given the exaggerated rate chosen by the British, the result was not stability but a monetary squeeze, which by the summer of 1920 had drained India's currency reserves and triggered unrest amongst the business community. For the first time the Bombay bourgeoisie swung squarely behind the nationalist movement.[35] If the aim was to depoliticize economic issues, the strategy backfired. In any case, the tendency of the Raj administration to explain away unrest as economically motivated was itself part of their failure to come to terms with the true scale of the rebellion. Compounded of religious feeling and local resentments, melded with the radical energy of millions of dissatisfied students, workers and peasants, the uprising against the Raj was a whirlwind of heterogeneous elements. Economic grievances were one factor, but huge masses of the Indian population were now moved to political protest by outrage at the injustices of British rule.

In 1918, to persuade the conservative British provincial governors to accept the liberal provisions of the Montagu-Chelmsford reforms, a committee had been appointed under Sir Sidney Rowlatt to consider the need for wide-ranging post-war security measures. In January 1919, over the protests of Secretary of State Montagu, the government of India proposed to extend its emergency wartime powers indefinitely. India would, in effect, remain in a state of siege. The result was to trigger an unprecedented popular protest.[36] By early April, Bombay and Lahore were in uproar and Ahmedabad was under full martial law. On 10 April there began a wave of sweeping preventative arrests in Punjab. In Amritsar this sparked violent counter-demonstrations in which five Europeans were murdered and a female teacher was assaulted. With the White community in uproar, Brigadier Reginald Dyer was dispatched to Amritsar with 300 colonial troops. On 13 April, confronting a crowd of 20,000 who refused to disperse, he gave the order to fire and to continue firing. Ten minutes later 379 men, women and children lay dead. Hundreds more were wounded. Deaths in scuffles with British soldiers and imperial police were a regular occurrence throughout the post-war crisis of the empire. But the massacre at Amritsar set a new benchmark for violent repression, and Dyer clearly intended to drive the message home. Weeks of terror and humiliation followed.

In India, as in Ireland, it seemed that the point was rapidly approaching at which the tensions within imperial liberalism could no longer be sustained. Indian nationalists, including figures such as Gandhi who had sought an accommodation with the British, criticized the indiscipline of the protests that had given Dyer his excuse to act. But they could hardly be expected to sustain cooperation with a regime built on such naked and unapologetic force. For their part, Viceroy Chelmsford and the British cabinet could not distance themselves from their beleaguered and aggressive subordinates without a full inquiry. But their dismay was real. As Montagu commented to the Viceroy, 'our old friend, firm government, the idol of the club smoking room, has produced its invariable and inevitable harvest': violence, death and further radicalization.[37] Montagu was true to his personal convictions. In July 1920, presenting the results of the Amritsar inquiry to the House of Commons, he denounced the massacre as precisely the kind of shameful act of 'racial humiliation' that was calculated to bring the British Empire into ill repute. Dyer, he declared, had been proven guilty of 'terrorism' and 'prussianism'. To the embarrassment of the government whips, the reply from the Tory backbenches was an unseemly storm of racist bluster and anti-Semitic slur directed not at Dyer but at the Liberal Secretary of State.

If the outrage in the Hindu community was not enough, the British in early 1919 faced another threat. Safeguarding the Muslim minority population had long provided the British with a rationale for their presence in India. In 1916 this had been thrown into question by the Lucknow Agreement between the Indian National Congress and the Muslim League. By the spring of 1919, as the full severity of the peace terms with the Ottoman Empire became clear, Britain came instead to be seen, in Viceroy Chelmsford's own words, as the 'arch enemy of Islam'.[38] In the Khilafat movement, the formerly quiescent Muslim population rose in protest against the humiliating treatment being meted out to the Turkish Sultan, who as Caliph served as the anointed secular guardian of the Sunni faith. In February 1920 at the movement's conference in Bengal, long one of the hotbeds of anti-British protest, there was a majority not for reform of the Raj, but for a wholesale rebellion against British rule. Abdul Bari, one of the most radical pan-Islamist leaders, came close to calling for Jihad. Again and again Montagu and the British administration in India petitioned London to revise their policy toward the Turks, or at least to allow the government of India to take an independent stance, distancing the Raj from the attack on Turkey. But London refused. The result was to unite India against the British.

What gave Gandhi his pivotal role was precisely his unique ability to orchestrate this unprecedented coalition. In November 1919 he attended the all-India Khilafat conference in Delhi as the only representative of Hindu India. It was on that stage that he first advocated for India the strategy of non-cooperation he had first developed to protest anti-Asian racism in South Africa.[39] At the same time Gandhi's mass following transformed the staid assembly of the Indian National Congress. The Nagpur Congress of December 1920 was attended by a clamorous throng of 15,000 delegates. At Gandhi's insistence, Congress was reorganized so as to give recognition to the village as the 'basic institution' of Indian communal life. The effect was to empower the national leadership headed by Gandhi at the expense of the regional elites. Nor was gradual change any longer on the agenda. To the tumultuous applause of the assembly Gandhi promised self-rule, *Swaraj*, within the year. To achieve that goal Congress resolved to adopt not only constitutional methods, but any 'legitimate and peaceful means'.[40]

Whilst challenging British rule, Gandhi's insistence on non-violence played on the liberal aspirations still cherished by Secretary of State Montagu and the new Viceroy, Lord Reading. In December 1919 the Government of India Bill passed both houses of the British Parliament intact. With some reluctance Parliament approved the separate electorates agreed between Congress and the Muslim League.[41] Even after the Amritsar massacre the Congress meeting of December 1919 had still been willing to give grudging approval to Montagu's reforms. Gandhi himself had not yet rejected cooperation. It was the brutal terms of the Sèvres Treaty with Turkey, combined with the utterly inadequate official reaction to Dyer's massacre, that finally convinced Gandhi of London's lack of good faith. In August 1920 Congress declared its refusal to cooperate in the elections scheduled for November. The British had no option but to proceed anyway. They could not afford to disappoint those Indians who were still willing to cooperate with them. Amongst the Congress elite there was dismay at the emergence of Gandhi's new mass movement and over the winter of 1918–19 a faction of so-called 'moderates' had split away to form the National Liberal League. The constrained franchise under the Montagu-Chelmsford reforms suited them well.

By 1925, when the new constitution had begun to take on stable form, 8.258 million Indians were entitled to vote for Provincial Legislative councils. Some 1.125 million had a vote for the Indian Legislative Assembly, and an exclusive group of 32,126 dignitaries chose the members of the Council of State. Overall, less than 10 per cent of the adult male population were entitled to vote at any level.[42] Nevertheless, despite the boycott by Congress, the vast majority of the seats were contested by rival local factions, and the constituency of those mobilized was far wider than those enfranchised. In the first election in 1920, thanks to the Congress abstention, the Liberal League did well. The moderates who favoured compromise with the British had the dominant voice in the Assembly. The most surprising result was in Madras where the self-exclusion of the Hindu upper class allowed the non-Brahmin classes represented by the newly formed Justice Party to gain an unprecedented prominence, securing 63 of the 98 elected seats.

With local government in its entirety being transferred into Indian hands, Britain's imperial liberalism could finally claim to be delivering on its promises. Indian democracy had taken the first steps in its remarkable twentieth-century career. But the narrative of a 'British legacy of democracy' was losing its credibility almost before it began to be spun. The political event of 1920 was not India's first steps toward its own version of mass democracy, but the spectacular rise of anti-British non-cooperation. In India's first general election only 25 per cent of those entitled to vote at the provincial level did so, varying from 53 per cent of urban Hindus in Madras to less than 5 per cent amongst the highly politicized Muslim population of urban Bombay. As even British commentators were forced to admit, the result was to create quiescent councils that operated in 'an atmosphere of unreality.'[43]

The 'reality' of India's political situation in 1920 was defined by Gandhi's movement of popular resistance. For the British and Indian elite alike, it was a bewildering new world.[44] Gandhi's vision of Swaraj was in many ways deliberately utopian. It appealed to a future freed not only from the oppression of British rule, but from any modern state or economic order. It refused any vision of colonial development. It was at odds with the aspirations of the established nationalist elite and it was pilloried as absurdly anachronistic by India's emerging Communist movement. After 1945, despite his being acclaimed as spiritual leader of the Indian nation, Gandhi's communalist vision would be ruthlessly sidelined. Yet Gandhi's undeniable strength lay not only in his charisma, but also in his truly subtle understanding of political tactics. Day by day he gathered the forces of the uprising around himself, trying to gauge the possibility for increasing the pressure without provoking the British to the point where they had no option but to respond with lethal and massive force.[45] Non-cooperation was a deliberate effort to craft a revolution that avoided Lenin's headlong plunge toward a general conflagration or Sinn Fein's Irish version of the same. It was a strategy perfectly designed to probe the legitimacy of a liberal empire, to the tenets of which Gandhi himself had so recently subscribed.

Shocked by the horror of Amritsar and the calls for further blood that it provoked on both sides, Montagu and the Viceroy had sought to avoid any further escalation. But in London by the autumn of 1921 the cabinet was losing patience. As Lloyd George telegraphed to India, 'I am convinced that the time has passed for patience and toleration ... the majority of Indians are cooperating loyally in working the reforms, and it is essential that they should not be allowed to doubt which is the stronger, Gandhi or the British Raj ...'.[46] With the fate of both Ireland and Egypt in the balance, 'the British Empire' was 'passing through a very critical phase, and it will not survive unless it shows now in the most unmistakable fashion that it has the will and the power to ... deal conclusively with any who challenge its authority'. Lloyd George reminded Montagu and Reading that 'the views formed by the cabinet are based upon a very wide survey of our position throughout the world ...'. This was undoubtedly true. Imperial policy was world policy. But what the cabinet clearly lacked was any appreciation of the forces at work in India itself. Even amongst the India elite, the pressure for accelerated change was growing. Having lost the majority to Gandhi, the question was whether the British could sustain the cooperation even of the moderate minority. A failure to silence the radical nationalists would leave the moderates exposed. But a recurrence of Amritsar would create a situation as polarized as in Ireland.

When Congress declared a boycott of the state visit to India by Edward, Prince of Wales, over the winter of 1921–2, the moment for confrontation seemed to be fast approaching.[47] By January 1922, whilst massacres had been avoided, over 30,000 of Gandhi's non-cooperators had been arrested by the provincial authorities. Montagu's liberal policy of restraint and 'non-confrontation' was fraying. Desperate for a last-minute compromise in the third week of December 1921, Reading took up the idea of a constitutional Round Table. The risks were enormous. The Viceroy acted without approval either from London or the provincial governors and had every reason to expect howls of protest from both sides. The new electoral mechanism to which the Indian moderates had committed themselves was barely a year old. To be offering it up for revision so soon smacked of panic.

In the event, what rescued Reading over the New Year 1921–2 was an uncharacteristically rash move on Gandhi's part. Though there was substantial support for talks within the Congress leadership, Gandhi high-handedly turned down the offer of a Round Table.[48] This was Reading's salvation. Only days after he had issued his invitation, the entire idea was furiously condemned by Lloyd George and the provincial governors. If Gandhi had embraced the Viceroy's offer at precisely the moment when it was disowned by London, it would have created an unprecedented public divide between the governments of India and Britain. Instead, by January 1922 it was Gandhi who was left isolated. His rejection of talks confirmed an important element of the Indian political class in their suspicion that he was a dangerous populist radical. The tide was flowing back in favour of the British.

But to be talking in such terms was itself indicative of the extremity of the situation. By early 1922 it was evident to far-sighted imperial officials that for the foreseeable future Britain's grip on India would rest neither on grand political gestures, à la Montagu-Chelmsford, nor on the sort of show of force being demanded by London. What was needed was day-by-day improvisation. In mid-January 1922 the Home Department of the government of India delivered a remarkably subtle assessment. 'The struggle with Gandhi,' the officials commented, had 'always been a fight for position.' The policy of non-confrontation adopted by Reading and Montagu in the wake of Amritsar had risked handing the initiative to the nationalists, and in November and December 'the tactical advantage' had 'passed for a time to Gandhi'. But in early 1922 the officials sensed that 'moderate opinion' was 'showing distinct signs of veering round in favour of the government'. After

Gandhi's high-handed rejection of the Round Table, influential Indians would support his arrest, so long as the British chose the right moment. That moment would come when Gandhi openly declared his intention of overthrowing British rule. He had ended 1920 by promising *Swaraj* within a year. One year on, he had failed to deliver. '. . . (S)ooner or later', Britain's imperial tacticians noted, he would be 'forced into proclaiming mass civil disobedience . . . and then and then only, government will be in a position to enter on the final struggle with him . . . without the risk of alienating such support as we have in the country, and precipitating a crisis which would break the constitution'.[49]

In fact, the moment came very soon indeed. In February 1922, just as the truculence in London was reaching boiling point, Gandhi's grip failed him. After he had issued an open challenge to the government of India, thousands of young Indians began drilling in non-cooperation volunteer units. On 4 February, after police had violently dispersed a demonstration against the high cost of food at Chauri Chaura in Uttar Pradesh, the volunteers responded by burning down the police station, killing all 23 officers inside. London demanded Gandhi's immediate arrest. As Lloyd George blared: 'if there was an attempt to challenge our position in India, the whole strength of Britain would be put forward to maintain British ascendancy in India . . . with a strength and resolution that would amaze the world'. It was the same tactics of all or nothing that Lloyd George had used to intimidate the Irish. It was barefaced bluff, in India even more obviously than in Ireland.[50] There was certainly impatience on the part of the British public toward their 'ungrateful' Indian subjects. But there was no appetite whatsoever for an enormous campaign of repression. The India Office replied in more realistic terms. The government of India must make clear, Montagu insisted, not simply Britain's dominance but its commitment to India. It must be restated that it was a 'complete fallacy' for anyone to believe that Britain considered her 'mission in India as drawing to a close' or that London was 'preparing for a retreat'.

Gandhi himself was appalled by the violence at Chauri Chaura and on 12 February abruptly called off the civil disobedience campaign. As far as London was concerned he was now a wanted man, but even at this moment, at the urgent pleading of the Viceroy's moderate Indian collaborators, Reading held back. Gandhi must be arrested, but first the government of India should solidify its moral position by removing the basic grievance that had driven the Muslim population into Gandhi's arms. To restore its authority in India on liberal terms, the empire must reach a just peace with Turkey. Without gaining the backing of the full British cabinet, Montagu approved a statement to the press demanding for India a hearing on the question of Turkey. India's services in the Great War were undeniable. In Mesopotamia and Palestine, Indian Muslims had laid down their lives for the empire. On their behalf, the government of India insisted that there must be a withdrawal of all British and French forces from Constantinople, the traditional seat of the Khalif. The Sultan's 'suzerainty over the holy places' must be restored. The Greeks must withdraw altogether from Anatolia. And the final boundary line with Greece must preserve Ottoman Thrace for Turkey.[51]

Not surprisingly the Foreign Secretary, George Curzon, was outraged. That 'a subordinate branch of the British government 6000 miles away' should seek to dictate to London 'what line it thinks I ought to pursue' was 'quite intolerable'. If the government of India was 'entitled to express and publish its views about what we do in Smyrna or Thrace, why not equally in Egypt, the Sudan, Palestine, Arabia, the Malay peninsula or any other part of the Muslim world?' This question, which went to the heart of the problem of how to govern a global empire under democratic conditions, was never answered. Instead, on 9 March 1922 Montagu was forced to resign. The following day, without uproar, Gandhi was arrested. Within a week, the man with whom Montagu and Reading had hoped to negotiate a new foundation for a liberal empire was sentenced to six years in prison.

IV

The British Empire survived the crisis. In its wake, a conservative interpretation of imperial destiny was to hold sway for years to come. But it was a hollow victory. The conservatives had won. But they had not had to carry out the violent deeds of absolute domination that were discussed with such hard-boiled enthusiasm in saloon bars across the empire. In practice, it was the subtle tactical manoeuvring between the despised liberals in the colonial administration and the more sophisticated nationalists that saved Britain from having to repeat elsewhere on the vast stage of empire the grisly and discreditable escalation that in Ireland had threatened to open the door to disaster.[52] Liberalism saved the reactionaries from having to provide a full demonstration of how utterly untenable their position actually was. But in the process the liberal project itself suffered irreparable damage.

Up to the very end, Montagu insisted that his policy in India had been undone by the irrational aggression of the Turkophobes. Even in his last speech as Secretary of State for India to the House of Commons, he doggedly held fast to Lord Macaulay's famous justification of empire as a vehicle for progress. 'India should realize,' Montagu insisted, 'that, based on goodwill and partnership there are no rights that will be denied her by the British parliament . . . if India will believe in our good faith . . . if she will accept the offer that has been made to her by the British parliament, then she will find that the British Empire, for which so many Indians and Englishmen have so recently died, and which at this present moment is saving the world, will give her liberty not license, freedom but not anarchy, progress but not stampede, peace and the fulfillment of the best destinies that the future can offer.'[53] But Montagu ignored the contradictions repeatedly demonstrated by the liberal imperial model. Liberal visions were necessary to sustain empire in the sense that they offered fundamental justifications. But they were always likely to be reduced to painful hypocrisy by the real practices of imperial power and by the resistance of those subjected to empire.[54] In the 1850s the liberal vision of empire articulated in the 1830s had been swept away by the Indian mutiny. A full revolution of the cycle from liberalism to repression was avoided in India in 1917–22. But the oscillation between liberalism and reaction was now accelerating into a dizzying and unrelenting switchback that sapped the will of empire.[55]

Not, of course, that there was any realistic reassessment of the empire's predicament in the wake of the crisis of the early 1920s. Complacency came easily. The empire had weathered the storm. And this reinforced the sense in London that through 'timely redeployment' Britain's imperial operators would always be able to 'outflank', 'outmanoeuvre' and 'disarm' the forces of nationalist anti-imperialism. Crucially, the British expected the Hindu-Muslim pact of Lucknow to disintegrate, and as inter-communal violence resumed in the 1920s they were not disappointed. 'Deft political and constitutional footwork' and tactical finesse came to be seen as the defining characteristics of the masters of the empire.[56]

But what was the positive project of empire beyond the fact of having survived as the only truly global power? In the 1920s one answer was the promise of economic development to be realized within a global Commonwealth. But attractive though it may have been to conservatives and liberals alike, economic development required investments that London could ill afford.[57] In the 1920s loans continued to flow from the City of London to the world, but this increased Britain's dependence on funds from America. Furthermore, even if the resources could be found, would economic and social development and the creation of an educated indigenous middle class not simply accelerate the emergence of anti-imperial opposition? That was, after all, how liberals like Montagu interpreted the rise of nationalism in India. And as the fervent economic nationalism of the Indians revealed, the encouragement of national development and the wider vision of a global Commonwealth could easily come into conflict. Following in the footsteps of Canada, Australia and South Africa, one of the first demands of Congress had been for tariff protection against British imports. Political concessions to nationalism fragmented the economic coherence that was one of the empire's remaining justifications.

Even more explosive tensions were aroused by the question of immigration. Australia and Canada and the White settler minorities in Kenya and South Africa were happy to encourage White solidarity. But this meant excluding the 320 million people recorded as the total population of India from the right to migration or land purchase and perpetuating discrimination against the Indian diaspora throughout the empire, which numbered at least 2.5 million.[58] Gandhi had made his reputation fighting for Indian rights in South Africa before the war. In 1919 the demand for racial non-discrimination had been cut out of the League of Nations Covenant. But internally the British Empire could not escape the force of the point. As Lloyd George put it in July 1921 to the Imperial Conference: 'We are trying to build up a democratic empire on the basis of the consent of all the races that are inside it ... It really transfigures ... the human story. The British Empire will be a Mount of Transfiguration if it succeeds.'[59] The Commonwealth was to fall well short of such high aspirations, but it did vote over the furious protests of South Africa to affirm that there was an 'incongruity between the position of India as an equal member of the British Empire and the existence of disabilities upon British Indians' domiciled elsewhere in the empire.[60] In the event, in 1923 Kenya introduced new exclusions on Indian settlement, but in so doing, along with Australia, New Zealand, South Africa and Canada, and for that matter Britain itself, it put itself at odds with the very principle of equal treatment that was now acknowledged as a requirement of any consistent liberal vision of global empire.

If the tensions between autonomy and coherence, racial hierarchy and liberalism, were ever more apparent, the British Empire nevertheless enjoyed a collective sense of triumph after 1918. The solidarity of the war was not forgotten. In 1919, in the wake of Amritsar, an ill-timed jihad by the Afghans across the North-Western frontier helped the British to restore their standing as the defenders of India with Sikhs and Hindus in the Northern provinces. Faced with a more significant foreign threat, the Commonwealth would surely rally together again. But given the stark financial and strategic realities of the 1920s, even this begged the question. World War I had certainly demonstrated the empire's might. But it had also demonstrated that Britain's far-flung empire was vulnerable to regional challenges by well-organized nation states. If the question was not merely one of maintaining British rule against popular resistance from within, but of securing the empire's future as a global strategic unit, then even at the height of its power in November 1918 the idea of the empire standing alone was an illusion. In the absence of a truly powerful League of Nations, the empire's viability depended on coming to terms with the potential challengers of the future – Japan and Germany, the United States and a consolidated Soviet regime. But would a privileged relationship with one of these powers imply a dangerous antagonism toward the others, and were any of them in fact interested in an alliance with the British Empire?

21

A Conference in Washington

In the summer of 1921 the ceasefire in Ireland set the stage for a grand Imperial Conference.[1] The London Empire Conference, the first general imperial meeting for two years, was the matrix out of which the fully fledged idea of the British Empire as a Commonwealth emerged – enabling the newly formed Irish Free State to be squared with a continued claim to overarching imperial authority. But beyond the internal constitution of the empire, the overriding question of the moment was that of strategy. How was a Commonwealth stretched around the globe to protect itself? In 1918 the British Admiralty had proposed to answer this question by means of an imperial navy, jointly funded by contributions from each of the Dominions, with standard-ized training and a disciplinary code, participating on a footing of equality with the British Navy in an imperial naval staff.[2]

To sell the idea Admiral John Jellicoe was dispatched on an 18-month tour of the Dominions. For the Western Pacific he projected a fleet of eight battleships and eight battlecruisers, one of which would be con-tributed by New Zealand, four by Australia and the rest by Britain. It would be commanded from Singapore and fuelled by a network of oil dumps across the Indian Ocean and Western Pacific. If Jellicoe had had his way an integral part of the imperial fleet would have been a Royal Indian Navy, 'manned and maintained so far as is possible by the people of India'. Like the French idea of a League of Nations army, this vision of military internationalism was quickly shot down. The Dominions and the government of India were too jealous of their independence and too wary of the costs involved. But they did applaud in London in June 1921 when Arthur Balfour announced the construction of a massive base at Singapore, which, in case of emergency, would allow the British fleet to be deployed to the other side of the world.[3]

That redeployment, however, depended on the British Navy not being needed in home waters. With the German fleet at the bottom of Scapa Flow, if there was one thing on which the Dominions could agree, it was on the need to minimize any future commitments in Europe.[4] The French were regarded with suspicion, the 'restless natives' of eastern Europe with barely veiled contempt. 'Trouble on the continent' was precisely what the League of Nations was designed to deal with. It was left to Austen Chamberlain and Winston Churchill to remind Australia and Canada that the 'mother country' in fact had a vital interest in the security of its European neighbours. America's failure to ratify Versailles had left the security guarantee to France hanging in mid-air. From London's perspective, it was precisely the intractable conflicts in Europe that made it so crucial to find a strategic fix for the Pacific. Canada, not surprisingly, was a vigorous advocate of a special relationship with the United States. But could this be reconciled with the Anglo-Japanese alliance that since 1902 had served as the eastern buttress of the empire? And what could actually be expected from America? By 1921, Lloyd George was so frustrated with America's uncooperative stance in Europe that rather than dropping the Anglo-Japanese alliance he was tempted to reinforce it.

But quite how dangerous that might turn out to be was brought home in the spring of 1921 when Britain's ambassador in Washington, Auckland Geddes, had one of his first meetings with the incoming Secretary of States, Charles Evans Hughes. Hughes was a sophisticated progressive Republican. But he was also famous for his short temper. When Geddes stated London's reservations about dropping the Japanese alliance, Hughes lost his cool. 'You would not be here to speak for Britain!' Hughes ranted. 'You would not be speaking anywhere! England would not be able to speak at all. It is the Kaiser (all this in a grand crescendo moving to a shouted climax) – the Kaiser, who would be heard, if America seeking nothing for herself, but to save England, had not plunged into the war and (screamed) won it! And you speak of obligations to Japan.'[5] But if Britain dropped Japan, what assurances could America offer? Since 1919, Washington had resisted every effort to rope it into a bilateral partnership. The Imperial Conference concluded lamely that it would be ideal if London could somehow arrange to hustle both the United States and Japan into a tripartite alliance. But given the prevailing anti-Japanese sentiment in Washington, the chances of that were remote. Instead, in the summer of 1921 it seemed that it was London that would find itself being hustled.

On 8 July, to the dismay of Whitehall, Washington abruptly issued invitations not just to Britain but to the entire Entente to attend a conference to consider disarmament and the future of the Pacific.[6] The presumption of the Americans in inviting Britain on the same terms as Italy and France caused consternation in London.[7] Lloyd George and Churchill thought that Britain should refuse to attend. But given the empire's strategic dilemma, its profound interest in cooperation with Washington, the fact that Congress was about to debate the crucial question of inter-Allied debts, and that it was those same senators who were also demanding an end to the naval arms race, London really had no option.

I

The Assembly that met in Washington from 12 November 1921 to 6 February 1922 was in many ways a more dramatic expression of the new order than the Paris Peace Conference had been three years earlier. It was the first great-power conference ever to be held in the American capital. The stage for the opening session was the palatial headquarters of the Daughters of the American Revolution recently constructed just off the Mall. Business meetings were conducted in the neoclassical splendour of the Panamerican Union building. Assured of their domestic ascendancy, the Republicans outdid Wilson by making a show of bipartisanship. Given their experiences since 1919, the Europeans were wary. But unlike Wilson, the Republican administration chose to launch the conference amidst a refreshingly straightforward celebration of wartime solidarity. The first day of the conference was Remembrance Day, allowing the delegations to attend the inauguration of America's Monument to the Unknown Soldier, at which a nameless body dug from the battlefields of the Marne was solemnly reinterred in Arlington National Cemetery.

But above all, unlike Wilson who had made himself the aggressive spokesman of American naval power, the Harding administration had summoned the powers to Washington to discuss limitations on naval power. In the era before the bomber and the intercontinental ballistic missile, it was the battleship that was widely considered the great strategic weapon of modern war. With the German menace lifted from the Atlantic, naval disarmament would be coupled with an agreement on security in the Pacific, which in turn would be underpinned by an agreement between the United States, Britain and Japan to neutralize China, the decisive zone of pre-war imperialist competition. The political backing in the US for all three policies was solid. Wilson's compromise over Shandong was widely detested. Disarmament was popular. The savage deflationary crisis afflicting the US, Britain and Japan since the autumn of 1920 added further impetus. Through naval disarmament and a China settlement, the Washington Conference would reanimate the vision of the Open Door, creating an international space swept clean of militarism in which the free flow of American capital would unify and pacify.

Operating on familiar American territory, the Harding administration showed itself rather more adept than Wilson had been at controlling the conference table and bringing public opinion directly to bear. Compared to the solemnity of Versailles, the Washington Conference was a truly spectacular exercise in public diplomacy. After Harding had welcomed the delegations, Secretary of State Hughes rose to open the business. In the space of a few moments he outlined a plan that would banish oceanic naval warfare for a generation to come. He proposed immediately to end Wilson's battleship construction programme, to scrap hundreds of thousands of tons of capital ships, and to fix the ratio of the American, British and Japanese fleets at 5:5:3. Nor did he speak in generalities. To the amazement of the foreign delegations Hughes opened the conference by listing by name every ship in the three major navies that was suitable for scrapping, starting with America's own fleet. America would scrap 846,000 tons of naval shipping, leaving it with 501,000 tons. Britain would scrap 583,000 tons, leaving it with 604,000 tons of comparatively old ships. Japan would cut 449,000 tons, leaving it with 300,000 tons.[8]

Hughes achieved total surprise. The opening session, gushed one journalist, 'which was expected to consist only of formal addresses', was driven by a 'dynamic intensity such as had never been previously experienced at an international diplomatic gathering'. The contrast with Wilson's airy generalities was exhilarating.[9] 'The unprecedented clarity, definiteness and comprehensiveness of the concrete plan for naval disarmament . . . marked a new chapter in diplomatic history . . .'[10] As Hughes announced the immediate end to battleship construction, William Jennings Bryan, once Wilson's radical Secretary of State, could be seen leading the cheers from the press gallery. Ululating rebel yells were heard from the seats reserved for senators. The Europeans and Japanese were stunned. As Hughes read out his list, the naval experts on all sides could be seen giving involuntary nods of agreement. When Hughes finished, there were calls from the gallery for the leaders of France, Japan and Italy to give an immediate reply. It was more like a revolutionary convention than an international conference.

The force of the American opening was impressive, but the response was hardly less remarkable. On 15 November first the ageing and white-haired Lord Balfour and then the ramrod-straight Admiral Baron Kato Tomosaburō, Chief Plenipotentiary for Japan, gave their assent in principle to the terms that Hughes offered. The exact ratios of tonnage and ships and the question of Pacific fortifications were the subject of contentious discussion. But what was remarkable was the obvious willingness of two of the major contenders to settle one of the basic parameters of world power under American leadership. For Britain this meant abandoning the claim to absolute naval dominance that it had upheld for more than half a century. Scrambling to catch up with Hughes's PR stunt, on 18 November the British delegation announced that they had given instructions by telegraph to the shipyards on the Clyde to halt all work on four modern battleships of the Super-Hood class. That cancellation alone would save $160 million, enough to cover interest payments on Britain's war debts to America for a year.[11]

The reaction of the Japanese was even more surprising. In 1921, Western perceptions of Japan remained stubbornly simplistic. Earlier in the year John V. A. MacMurray, chief of the Far Eastern division of the State Department, had opined that the real power holders in Japan were an 'oligarchy of military clansmen' '. . . differing among themselves only in the degree to which their nationalistic aspirations are tempered by considerations of prudence in dealing with the rest of the world'.[12] A week before the Washington Conference opened, on 4 November 1921, Prime Minister Hara, himself a lifelong advocate of a cooperative relationship with the US, was stabbed to death. But it was an act of desperation, by an embittered loner. The conference itself provided further proof of the remarkable shift underway in Japanese politics. The advocates of pan-Asian aggression were in retreat. Hara was replaced as leader of the Seiyukai and as Prime Minister by Takahashi Korekiyo, who was even more firmly committed to cooperation with the West. Takahashi was a former governor of the Bank of Japan and former Finance Minister with close connections to banking circles both in London and on Wall Street. In the wake of the deflation of 1920–21 he was profoundly convinced that Japan must find a place for itself in a world order shaped by economic and financial power rather than military force. By the time of the conference, all the major parties of Taisho Japan favoured curbing military spending.[13] With naval expenditure accounting for almost a third of the budget it was a prime target.[14]

After much careful staff work the Japanese Navy, unlike the Japanese Army, had come to accept the principle of arms limitation, so long as it respected a minimum 70 per cent ratio between the Japanese and American fleets. In preliminary discussions over the summer of 1921 Admiral Katō Kanji, the chief technical advisor to the Japanese delegation, who was fluent in English and had extensive experience of inter-Allied cooperation during the war, expressed the view that a future great-power war was 'unthinkable' and that disarmament would be a great 'boon' given the stretched finances of both Japan and Britain. To the British attaché he rather unguardedly remarked that he hoped financial constraints would soon bring about the fall of the 'Military party' in Japan which continued to support the exorbitant demands of the army.[15] The problem at the Washington Conference was the gap between Hughes's scrapping list, which implied a 10:10:6 ratio, and the Japanese Navy's insistence on 70 per cent. Admiral Kanji put up stubborn resistance on this point, but he was overridden by the government in Tokyo that was willing to accept a ratio of 10:10:6, so long as it was offset by the addition of the cruiser *Mutsu*, a symbol of popular nationalism that had been paid for by popular subscription, and an American agreement not to establish menacing new naval bases in the Philippines or Guam. In light of Takahashi's strategic outlook, Japan had everything to gain from accepting a world order in which America and Britain acknowledged it as a third global power. This spared them the ruinous costs of an all-out military competition that Japan was, in any case, bound to lose.

Given this attitude in Tokyo, it seemed that Britain's strategic dilemma had been resolved. America's disarmament initiative opened the door to precisely the trilateral agreement that had seemed out of reach at the Imperial Conference only a few months earlier. The British Empire had escaped the choice between Japan and the United States, which in the summer of 1921 had appeared to hold the potential for disaster.[16] With Japan's position in the Pacific having been internationally acknowledged, the Anglo-Japanese Treaty could quietly be allowed to lapse. Instead, Britain and Japan collaborated in drafting an agreement providing for peaceful arbitration of all Pacific disputes.

Once more, however, this image of harmony was marred by the European question. The Pacific arbitration agreement was signed by a fourth power, France, which found itself in a far less satisfactory strategic position than the three main parties. From the French point of view it seemed, not without reason, that following the failure to create a stable North Atlantic system at Versailles, the British Empire was using the Washington Conference to escape its commitment to France in favour of sharing global hegemony with the United States. Wilson had withdrawn the security guarantee promised at Versailles. With the question of security on the Rhine and reparations unresolved, was France now to be expected to match the naval pact by accepting comprehensive restrictions on land armaments? The French were not assuaged by the American view that they should be satisfied with a third-tier navy, because that was all they would be able to afford for the foreseeable future.[17] It was Washington, after all, that was demanding a first claim against France's financial reserves.

Under intense pressure from patriotic opinion at home, Prime Minister Briand insisted that if France was to be barred from building the capital ships that befitted a great power, it could accept no limitations on cheap tactical substitutes, notably submarines.[18] This in turn provoked the British and Japanese into demanding exemptions for cruisers and destroyers. As Balfour frustratedly pointed out, the result was utterly counter-productive. Despite the demands of its empire, London was happy to acknowledge that it had a fundamental stake in French security. But as the Great War had demonstrated, Britain's capacity to support France depended above all on the Americans, whose patience with the old world was running out. For an American-hosted disarmament conference to have degenerated to the point at which the French and British were trading allegations about the uses of the French Navy in a cross-channel attack on Britain, was disastrous. After Versailles, it could not but seem that once again a visionary American initiative was being sabotaged by French resentment. What remained unspoken, of course, was the fact that Washington had ruled out any consideration of France's basic interests – either of an inter-Allied debt settlement, or of a European security guarantee.

However, despite the failure to deliver a truly comprehensive disarmament deal, there was no doubting the significance of the Washington Conference. America had resumed a role of leadership in global affairs. Japan's political class had responded constructively to the American line. Britain had accepted a profound realignment of its strategic position. Balfour described it as an event unparalleled in world history. This was no exaggeration. Never before had an empire of Britain's stature so explicitly and consciously conceded superiority in such a crucial dimension of global power. It deserves to stand as an early twentieth-century precursor to Mikhail Gorbachev's retreat from the escalation of the Cold War in the 1980s.

But was the Washington Conference also a disastrous miscalculation?[19] The Entente between Britain and the US was underpinned, despite many squabbles, by a shared interest in the status quo in the Atlantic. By contrast, the gamble taken in the Pacific was dramatic. The Four Power Agreement did not extend the intimacy of bilateral relations under the Anglo-Japanese Treaty. Large American investments flowed to Japan after 1921, but Washington and Wall Street never held the sway over Tokyo that London had enjoyed before 1914. Nor was the Pacific pact tied to the League of Nations. It hung in the air without any enforcement mechanism. Washington much reduced the striking power of the Japanese Navy. But following Hughes's cuts, neither the British nor the American navies would be in a position to operate in two oceans at once. The US Navy deployed three of its four task forces into the Pacific. The Royal Navy was more stretched. As a compromise, the most powerful squadron of battleships was stationed centrally in the Mediterranean.[20] In the case of a crisis it would race to the Western Pacific. But this would take two months and in the meantime it would leave Britain itself exposed. By deliberately unpicking the Anglo-Japanese alliance, did Washington set the stage for the disasters of the late 1930s, when the Western Powers failed to contain either

Mussolini's aggression in the Mediterranean or Japanese expansion in the Pacific?

It is an unfair question, but one that cannot reasonably be avoided. And it is a productive question because it points to the crucial significance of the 'sideshow' in Washington, the attempt alongside the global naval deal to arrive at a settlement for China. If pro-Western forces had the upper hand in Japan in 1921–2, this was in part the result of economic pressures and the changing of guard amongst the Japanese elite. But this strategic redirection was only conceivable against the backdrop of a relatively benign perception of Japan's security environment. The Soviet Union posed no immediate threat. Japan's intervention in Siberia was soon to come to an unheroic end. The decisive issue for Japan, therefore, was China. Whether or not the men of violence got the upper hand in Japan would depend crucially on whether it was possible to stabilize China-Japan relations.

II

After Versailles, the Washington Conference marked a further step in China's entrance into the global arena. If China was to be discussed, its representatives would be present and its voice would be heard. The conference offered a stage on which Wellington Koo and his colleagues enacted another act in the drama of patriotic self-assertion. The Chinese delegation seized the initiative on 16 November 1921 by laying out 10 proposals on questions of sovereignty and territorial settlement as the basis for any further discussion. Beijing now wanted a more far-reaching and substantive restoration of sovereignty. It wanted to revise the unequal treaties of the nineteenth century. In particular, it demanded the restoration of control over customs revenues and an end to the legal extraterritoriality of foreigners.[21] In one respect these demands were fully compatible with the American agenda. The Chinese were continuing their challenge to the spheres of interest model on which European and Japanese influence rested. With this, Washington concurred, and with the Americans appearing to set a clear course, the British hastily fell into line.

On 21 November the Washington Conference approved the so-called Root resolutions. These promised to 'respect the sovereignty, the independence and territorial and administrative integrity of China'. The Chinese delegation had wanted a specific commitment to the integrity of the Chinese Republic, but Japan thought it better not to prejudge the question of the Chinese constitution.[22] Nevertheless, this commitment went further than all previous guarantees in promising to uphold China's political as well as its territorial integrity. In what they regarded as a major concession, Britain persuaded Japan to evacuate all its troops from the hotly contested Shandong Peninsula. Japan promised China the right to buy out the German railway lease over a 15-year period. Here, too, Tokyo's retreat was in line with the strategic reorientation initiated by Hara and pushed forward by Takahashi.

A year earlier, in the summer of 1920, Tokyo had once again faced a crisis in its China policy. Its favoured warlord Duan Qirui had been ousted as Prime Minister for the second time by the Zhili faction led by Generals Wu Pei Fu and Cao Kun.[23] Amongst the Japanese army stationed in Manchuria, there were influential voices demanding that Japan's Manchurian client Chang Tso-lin should use this opportunity to extend his power in the north-east and even as far as Mongolia. But Chang's loyalty was suspect and Tokyo was still reeling from the huge upsurge in anti-Japanese feeling following the protests of 4 May 1919 over Shandong and Versailles. Following a conference on eastern strategy in May 1921, Tokyo resolved to reassert its defensive posture. Japan would hold fast to its special interest in the territories that lay to the north of the Great Wall and were thus outside China proper. But warlord Chang was to be discouraged from any aspirations to national leadership. Between Chang and the Zhili, Japan would attempt to preserve neutrality. A cooperative and mutually profitable economic relationship would be far more helpful in underwriting both China's and Japan's position in the new world order.[24] Japan's restless Manchurian army was put on the leash. At the Washington Conference, it was Kijuro Shidehara, the liberal-minded ambassador, who took charge of the Sino-Japanese negotiations and pushed them in a conciliatory direction, the line that he was to continue to personify for the next ten years.

The Chinese were not appeased by the Shandong settlement proposed at Washington.[25] Outside the conference there were angry demonstrations by Chinese Americans who sought to prevent their representatives from even continuing the talks. Since Versailles, however, the international mood had shifted. In Paris in 1919 China's position had attracted international sympathy. On that occasion it had been the Japanese who were in the dock. Since then, China's assertive nationalist diplomacy had unsettled the international community. The Western Powers were no friends of the Soviets, but China's efforts to exploit Russia's weakness in East Asia were viewed with unmitigated alarm. In October 1920, a year before the Washington Conference, Wellington Koo had reported from the US that the American media were treating China's abrogation of Russian rights as a 'preliminary step' toward the general abolition of all foreign privileges in China. According to opinion in the US, it was nothing less than a Bolshevik-instigated plot to 'attack the economic and political system of the capitalistic states'.[26] Wilson's last Secretary of State, Bainbridge Colby, opined ominously that 'by merely appearing to be subservient to the influence of the Russian communists, China would, it is to be feared, lose the friendly regard' of the international community and might well 'give an excuse for aggressions'. The need to safeguard strategic Russian assets such as the Chinese Eastern Railway was precisely the kind of excuse the Western Powers needed for intervention. On 11 October 1920 the diplomatic corps in China had addressed a note of collective protest to Beijing, insisting that the abrogation of Russia's rights should not be seen as setting any precedent. The Chinese reply was non-committal. The final treaty with the Russian government was pending. It would negotiate with the diplomatic corps over a modus vivendi, but would settle individual issues bilaterally.

When at Washington it was once again the Chinese who appeared to be obstructing a well-intentioned international settlement, there was less willingness than there had been in 1919 to overlook the disorder in Chinese domestic politics. In the first days of January 1921, as negotiations with the Japanese reached deadlock in Washington, the Beijing government installed by Chang Tso-lin was swept away by a tide of patriotic fervour orchestrated by the nationalists in the South and the Zhili.[27] At the end of April open warfare resumed between the major warlord blocs, which resulted after only a week of savage fighting in the decisive defeat of Chang and his retreat beyond the Great Wall to Manchuria. At the time of the Washington Conference, as one British diplomat pointed out scathingly, the Beijing government was in fact little more than a 'group of persons who call themselves a government but who have long ceased to function as such in the western sense of the term'.[28] Wellington Koo might put a brave face on things, but 'a delegation which represented Peking as a political unit would not and could not ... tell the truth about China'. Out of a 'mistaken sense of loyalty to Peking and an undue regard for "face"', China's diplomats were obscuring their country's 'real condition and needs'. What China needed was not patriotic grandstanding, by Western-educated mandarins, but an honest reckoning with its predicament and an earnest appeal for 'support and protection' to build a functioning state.[29] This was all very well, but what might such an internationally supported project of state-building in China entail? Washington's clear aim was to put an end to great-power competition in East Asia. But this did not imply the immediate recognition of China's equality.

As the conference in Washington dragged into its third month in January 1922, agreement was reached on the anodyne Nine Power Treaty that required all the major international powers to uphold the Open Door in China. This treaty mirrored the loan consortium that had finally been re-established with both Japan and America as members in May 1920.[30] Under the terms of the consortium, the United States, Britain, France and Japan agreed to abstain from rivalry in any financial ventures in China. In return, Beijing was expected to borrow only through the consortium. Thomas W. Lamont of J. P. Morgan referred to the partnership as a 'little League of Nations'.[31] In practice the main effect was to put an embargo on China loans, since cooperative deals were hugely complicated and no substantial political faction in China could be found willing to cooperate with the paternalist arrangements they required. In early 1922 US representative Jacob Gould Schurman spelled out to Beijing what Washington would expect in exchange for any substantial injection of funds. Control over the strategic Chinese Eastern Railway must be transferred to an international cartel. Schurman hinted darkly that 'he hoped that China would voluntarily request cooperation' since 'the powers would deplore using pressure against' it. To this the Foreign Ministry in Beijing simply refused to respond.[32] By 1922 no warlord, however unscrupulous, could comply with such radical foreign demands. It would have been political suicide.

Likewise, no progress was made over tariffs. China wanted control over its own tax revenues and the right to protect its own industries against foreign dumping. But the Washington Conference powers dragged their feet. With the end of the war, France, Italy, Belgium and Spain expected resumption of the payments on the Boxer indemnity. Given its own humiliating financial problems, France insisted on payment in pre-war gold currency, not depreciated modern francs. When Wellington Koo refused, Paris suspended ratification of the Washington Treaty. The state-building momentum that might have emerged from the conference was frittered away. Instead, the continuing disorder in the Chinese hinterland provided ample excuse to uphold the legal extra-territoriality claimed by foreigners. In May 1923, 19 foreign railway travellers were kidnapped in Lincheng.

As Secretary of State Hughes put it most pompously, these events had provided painful confirmation that the 'course of political development in China' had disappointed the expectations of 'those who had hoped that a fuller measure of opportunity for independent development would hasten ... the establishment of a governmental entity capable of fulfilling the international obligations correlative to the rights of sovereignty ...'.[33] Others jumped to rather more drastic conclusions. US representative Schurman suggested 'sweeping away ... the Chinese government' altogether and replacing it with 'an international agency'. When Washington refused to consider such a huge deployment of military force, Schurman retreated to arguing for international supervision of the Chinese railway system. The fact that radical 'students' and other 'champions of unabridged sovereignty of China will ... oppose it' would simply have to be ignored.[34]

The British representative at the Washington Conference, Victor Wellesley from the Foreign Office's Far Eastern Department, agreed that radical action was called for. 'Nothing can be more fatal than a display of weakness,' he opined. 'The prestige of the European races has been steadily declining in the Far East ever since the Russo-Japanese war and it has suffered a severe blow as the result of the Great War.' He too supported the idea of an international constabulary to take charge of the major traffic arteries across China. But as cooler heads in the Foreign Office immediately pointed out, in 1923 the idea of a collective expedition along the line of the Boxer intervention was out of the question. As one official in London commented in jaundiced tones, 'whereas in the days gone by we could make things uncomfortable for China or the Chinese, though we (still) could, they now know that we are not really prepared to do anything, and have called the bluff'.[35] He was surely right. The Washington Conference was both a dramatic demonstration of the global power hierarchy and a deliberate decision to deflate the currency of military power. The aim was to clear the way for economic forces to take the lead in reconstruction. But in the most troubled arenas of world power, in Asia and Europe, would that be enough?[36]

22

Reinventing Communism

America announced its entry into great-power politics at the highest level in 1905 when President Teddy Roosevelt arbitrated the Portsmouth Treaty that ended the Russo-Japanese War. When 16 years later his Republican successors welcomed the world to the Washington Conference, Japan was invited, as was China, but Russia was not. Though the Red Scare was over, there was no question of the Republicans being willing to host the Communists. But it was not just that they were excluded. In 1919 at Versailles the spectre of revolution had at least been seen as a menace. Two years later at Washington, the Soviets registered in the international balance only by way of the humiliating concessions that they were making to Beijing. The Soviet Union had survived. But its economy was in ruins and its attempts to spread the revolution had been contained, in large part through local counter-revolutionary action.[1]

This failure of the promise of revolution is an essential element in the story of post-war stabilization, and it is significant not only in a negative sense. Out of that failure the Communist movement developed a new long-range strategy of insurgency, not metropolitan but peripheral in its base, not based on the proletariat but appealing to the majority of the world's population, the peasantry. It was an ideological shift that marked a profound break with the nineteenth century, a wrenching reorientation within Marxist political thought at least as fundamental as anything that happened, for instance, to the tenets of bourgeois liberalism.[2] Whereas London and Washington were worrying about what self-determination might mean for the constitution of India or the Philippines, in Moscow the Comintern was recognizing the colonial and semi-colonial peasantry as one of the pre-eminent historical forces of the future.

I

In the aftermath of the war the international Communist movement had swung from anxiety to euphoria. The Third Communist International, the Comintern, which met for the first time during March 1919 in Moscow, was initially little more than a hastily improvised answer to the meeting of the Social Democratic International that had convened at Berne in February to celebrate Wilson and squabble over war guilt. At its inception the Comintern was not yet the disciplined, Moscow-centred organization that it was to become.[3] Along the lines of the pre-war Socialist International, it served as a multilateral meeting place for the Russian Communists and their comrades in the West. Its lingua franca was as much German as Russian. English and French were barely spoken. It reflected a vision of the global revolution as a gigantic all-encompassing blaze, not directed from Moscow but flaring up at many places at once, not defensive and contained but leaping aggressively from city to city. In 1919, true to Marxist orthodoxy, the centre of that firestorm was expected to be in the developed world. The strike waves in Britain and the United States were unprecedented. Even more promising was the situation in Germany, where the USPD had adopted the slogan 'All Power to the Soviets.' Most dramatic of all was the situation in Italy, where Socialist Party militants were spearheading a huge wave of strikes and peasant land occupations.[4] The central question was how these struggles were to be linked to the revolutionary centres in Russia.

The prospect of revolutionizing central Europe was what gave such significance to the uprising in the tiny, newly formed state of Hungary.[5] Hungary was in the unfortunate position of being both a new creation of the 1918 upheaval and, due to the privileged position it had enjoyed within the Habsburg Dual Monarchy, a defeated enemy of the Entente. It was thus perfectly placed for victimization. Its territory would ultimately be slashed by two-thirds. Not surprisingly, the first post-revolutionary government in Budapest, headed by President Mihaly Karolyi, was a keen exponent of Wilsonianism – of the 'peace without victory' variety. But the government was soon overwhelmed by punitive Allied demands and on 21 March 1919 Karolyi handed over power to a coalition nominally led by the Social Democrats but dominated by Hungary's tiny

Communist Party and its chief ideologue Bela Kun. Meanwhile the new Soviet government announced a dramatic programme of domestic reforms, but its main priority was to fight off the ambitions of Czechs and Romanians and to regain at least some of Hungary's pre-war territory. Coinciding as it did with the formation of a Soviet Republic in Munich on 6 April 1919 and the main crisis of the Versailles peace talks, the prospect of a revolutionary overthrow in central Europe created moments of panic in Paris and a thrill of excitement across the left wing of European socialism, above all in Italy.

A dramatic mobilization by the Hungarian Red Army raised its numbers to 200,000 men, including a brigade of international volunteers from Serbia, Austria and Russia, and on 20 July the revolutionary forces began an offensive due east into Romania across the Tisza River. Their hope was to connect with the Soviet forces that had taken Odessa and now dominated Ukraine. Aerial contact between Hungary and Soviet Russia had already been established in the spring. But unfortunately for the Hungarians at the crucial moment, the Red Army in the Ukraine suffered a setback against resurgent White forces. On 24 July, with the full weight of the Entente behind them, the Romanians counter-attacked. After hard fighting on 4 August the Romanian Army marched proudly down the grand boulevards of Budapest. Communism had been quashed.

There were those, Winston Churchill most prominent amongst them, who wanted to go further than this, to roll back the Bolshevik revolution itself. And by the spring of 1919, even though London and Paris had decided against full-scale intervention, the White forces of General Alexander Kolchak in Siberia and Anton Denikin in southern Russia had received enough materiel to pose a major threat to the survival of the Bolshevik regime. The White surge reached its high-water mark on 20 October 1919. With General Nikolai Yudenich's counter-revolutionary army advancing on the suburbs of Petrograd, Denikin driving towards Moscow from the south, and Kolchak on the march from Siberia, the possibility of simply putting an end to the Bolshevik regime looked more real than ever.[6] What saved Lenin and Trotsky was that they did not, in fact, face a united front. To have orchestrated a truly effective anti-Bolshevik campaign would have required not only substantial Western commitment, but, more importantly, a political resolution of the problem of self-determination, as well as a strategic decision on the future of Russia – the same problems that had reduced the strategists of Imperial Germany to embarrassing incoherence in the summer of 1918.

Over the summer of 1919 the Allies had extracted from Kolchak a commitment to hold elections for a new Constituent Assembly in Russia. But that was not enough for the Poles. Concerned about a resurgence of Russian nationalism, on 11 October Warsaw entered into furtive negotiations with the Soviets.[7] In exchange for Polish neutrality, the Bolsheviks ceded much of Belorussia and Lithuania. This arrangement allowed the Bolsheviks to redeploy over 40,000 troops against Yudenich, who was approaching Petrograd along the Baltic.[8] Combined with Trotsky's radical mobilization, which dragooned 2.3 million men into the Red Army, this was enough to tilt the balance. By mid-November the tide of the battle had turned. The Reds triumphed. Denikin and Kolchak were driven to flight. On 17 November 1919 Lloyd George announced to the House of Commons that London, after having spent almost half a billion dollars, was abandoning the attempt to break the Bolshevik regime by military force. The cost was too great and Britain really had no interest in restoring a legitimate and powerful Russian nation state. Echoing the German Foreign Secretary Richard von Kühlmann in the summer of 1918, Lloyd George reminded the House that a 'great, gigantic, colossal, growing Russia rolling onwards like a glacier towards Persia and the borders of Afghanistan and India' was the 'greatest menace the British Empire could be confronted with'. With the threat of revolution on the wane in western Europe, the better policy was to quarantine the Soviet regime behind a 'barbed wire fence'.[9]

Lloyd George's withdrawal had a devastating impact on the morale of the White forces, but it did not mean an end of the threats to the Soviet regime.[10] Over the winter of 1919–20 the Polish Ministry of War began preparing for the definitive settlement of the Russian question. The largest nationalist party in Poland, the National Democrats, were opposed to an offensive, preferring to defend a more compact, ethnically homogeneous territory. But Marshal Joseph Pilsudski, the dominant figure in the fragile Polish state, did not share their limited vision. Pilsudski dreamed of resurrecting the Polish-Lithuanian Commonwealth, which until the ravages of the Thirty Years War had blocked Muscovite expansion to the west. In alliance with an autonomous Ukraine, a new Polish super-state would anchor a cordon stretching from the Baltic to the Black Sea.[11] Pilsudski assumed this would appeal to London. But Lloyd George's government declined to give its backing to Polish aggression. The Poles had to make do with the anaemic support from the French and an alliance with the Ukrainian nationalists, who, following the German retreat from the Brest-Litovsk Treaty lines, had taken shelter in Galicia.[12] In exchange for the promise of eastern Galicia for Poland, Pilsudski threw Poland's weight behind Simon Petlura's bid to establish an independent Ukraine as a permanent part of the new order. It was a high-risk strategy, but Warsaw was convinced that the Red Army was preparing for a push west. Pilsudski would beat them to the punch.[13]

On 25 April 1920 the Polish-Ukrainian army attacked. On 7 May they took Kiev, enabling the surviving White Russian forces under General Pyotr Wrangel to stabilize a new base in the Crimea. Once more the Bolshevik regime seemed to confront an existential threat from the south. But the past three years had taken their toll on Ukraine. The arrival of Petlura and Pilsudski heralded the fifteenth change of regime in Kiev since January 1917. Hundreds of thousands of people had died at the hands of Germans, Austrians, White and Red Russian occupiers, amongst them 90,000 Jews who had been slaughtered in the worst series of pogroms since the Cossack uprising of the seventeenth century. The survivors were in no mood to raise a popular insurrection. In Russia, by contrast, the idea of Polish Lancers cantering through Kiev unleashed a storm of patriotic fury. With war hero Aleksei Brusilov in the lead, former Tsarist officers flooded into Trotsky's Red Army.[14]

The result was one of the climactic moments in modern European history. On 5 June 1920 the massed horde of General Semen Budennyi's Red Cavalry, 18,000-strong, smashed through the Polish lines, forcing a precipitate evacuation of Kiev. Only a month later, on 2 July, the brilliant Bolshevik commander and military theoretician Mikhail Tukhachevsky issued the order for the general advance. 'Over the corpse of White Poland lies the path to world conflagration ... On to Vilno, Minsk, Warsaw! Forward!' Egged on by their front commanders, Lenin and the Bolshevik leadership now believed that they 'stood at the turning point of the entire policy of the Soviet government'.[15] It was time to 'test with bayonets whether the socialist revolution of the proletariat had not ripened in Poland . . .'. The fact that the French were scrambling to prop up the Polish defences and that Britain was trying to mediate revealed that 'somewhere near Warsaw' lay 'the center of the whole contemporary

system of international imperialism ...'.[16] Through the conquest of
Poland they would 'shake' the entire structure to its foundations. The
Red Army would bring to life a 'completely new zone of proletarian
revolution against global imperialism'.

After Brest-Litovsk the Bolsheviks had moved their capital to the
relative safety of Moscow. Even in the summer of 1920 Lenin was
forced to travel incognito and at night, for fear of assassination. But, as
a show of defiance, the Second Congress of the Comintern held its opening session on 19 July 1920 in Petrograd before retreating to Moscow.
There, 217 delegates from 36 countries gathered under a large map of
Poland on which the latest advances of the Soviet armies were posted
hour by hour as news came in from the front.[17] In a mood approaching
'revolutionary delirium', Lenin cabled Stalin that 'the situation in the
Comintern was superb'. Together with Grigory Zinoviev and Nikolai
Bukharin he was looking forward to a revolutionary upsurge across
Italy, Hungary, Czechoslovakia and Romania.[18] Meanwhile German
comrades hoped that next year they would be able to host the Comintern in Berlin.[19]

II

It was against this backdrop of euphoric revolutionary expansion that
the Comintern underwent a first change. The unorganized, decentral-
ized revolutionary upsurge of 1919 had led to defeat in Hungary and
Germany. With the Red Army driving westwards, it was time for the
Russian revolution to assert command. Compared to the ineffectual
efforts of the western European socialists, Leninism had proven its
worth as a revolutionary doctrine. The Comintern would set new and
strict criteria for all its members. They must proclaim the dictatorship
of the proletariat as their immediate goal. There could be no compromise with democratic politics, now dubbed 'social-pacificism', or with
'bourgeois legality'. Whether in western Europe or America, Communists must recognize that they were 'entering the phase of civil war'.[20] As
a test of their revolutionary mettle they must commit to creating a 'parallel illegal organization' and prepare to mount a direct challenge to the
state by beginning mutinous subversion within the armed forces. If this
meant repression at the hands of the political police, so be it. The

Wilsonian nostrums so beloved of liberals and social democrats in 1918–19 were contemptuously swept aside. 'Without the revolutionary overthrow of capitalism no international court of arbitration, no agreement to limit armaments, no "democratic" reorganization of the League of Nations, will be able to prevent new imperialist wars.' In international affairs there was only one guiding principle: 'unconditional support to any Soviet republic in its struggle against counter-revolutionary forces'. Given that the moment of revolutionary truth was coming closer with every charge of the revolutionary Red cavalry, there was no time to lose. Within four months, all current members and aspirant members of the Communist International must decide: either for or against.[21]

Of the Comintern's 10 sessions at the 1920 Conference, eight were devoted to the difficult business of purifying the revolutionary forces of Europe. But befitting the radical mood, the second meeting of the Comintern also provided the forum for the first major debate of global strategy.[22] Given the frustration of revolutionary ambition in western Europe, the slogan of 'Asia first' found an articulate and eye-catching spokesman in the peripatetic Indian Marxist M. N. Roy. Roy had recently made his way to Russia by way of the United States and attended the Comintern conference as the representative of Mexico rather than India.[23] But it was to Asia, Roy argued, that the Comintern ought to direct its energies. It should work there to create its own base of revolutionary activism amongst the emerging working class in cities such as Bombay and the desperately poor stratum of peasants that constituted the huge mass of the Asian population. It was essential, Roy argued, for Communism to offer an alternative to the likes of Gandhi and the Indian National Congress, whom he regarded as bourgeois reactionaries. Despite its militant vigour, Roy's Third Worldism was too much for many of the older school. Giacinto Menotti Serrati, one of the most dogmatic Italian Marxists, answered with a classic assertion of Eurocentric orthodoxy. Revolution in Asia was impossible because there was no industrial working class. Asia must follow the European vanguard.

But Serrati was behind the times. Prominent Russians now felt that it was time to do more than merely recite the old religion of the *Communist Manifesto*, which, as Lenin pointed out, had been written 'under completely different circumstances'. Marxism was entering its fourth generation.[24] As the Bolsheviks had triumphantly demonstrated, twentieth-century revolutionaries needed to think for themselves, if necessary against Marx and Engels. Not that Lenin could entirely concur with Roy. 'Asia-first' was one-sided. The Comintern should not divert resources from Europe, the heartland of imperial power, at the very moment when the struggle appeared to be reaching its climax. But as Lenin had argued since 1916, the national liberation movements of the colonized world could make vigorous recruits to the revolutionary cause in the form of 'united anti-imperialist fronts'. Roy was unabashed as he pilloried any thought of alliances with 'bourgeois democracy'. So Lenin beat a tactical retreat that found the approval of the vast majority of the Comintern. United fronts would be adopted only in those cases where Communist parties could ally themselves with truly 'revolutionary' nationalist groupings. As the following years were to demonstrate, it was a distinction that was lethally difficult to draw in practice.

If the tactics of global revolution were contentious, on the main target the Comintern could easily agree. Great Britain had been the driving force behind anti-Bolshevik intervention since 1918. It was the dominant global empire. In 1920 it seemed that the 'Great Game' of imperial rivalry played out between Imperial Russia and Victorian Britain would give way to a new era of struggle in Central Asia. In April 1920 Commissar Stalin drove the Red Army into Azerbaijan. Based on Baku and its oil wells, the Communists launched a short-lived campaign to radicalize the Muslim population of Asia. In May, Soviet marines leapfrogged down the Caspian coastline and expelled the British from the Persian harbour town of Enzeli. Before they withdrew, the Soviet forces helped to found the Soviet Republic of Gilan in northern Persia as a challenge to the crumbling Teheran regime.[25] Composed of local warlords, Kurdish chieftains, anarchists and a smattering of radical intellectuals, the Gilan Republic's ideological inspiration came from Sultan Zade who outdid Roy in proclaiming a full-blown Asian revolution.

On 8 September 1920 at Baku, the Congress of Peoples of the East convened 1,900 delegates representing 29 nationalities and ethnic groups from across Persia, Armenia and Turkey.[26] At the opening ceremony they were treated to a protracted oration by Lenin's devoted follower and enthusiastic third-worldist, Zinoviev, who heralded an event 'previously unknown in the history of mankind' – the first gathering of representatives of hundreds of millions of oppressed peasants of the East, the men and women whom Zinoviev was delighted to hail as the 'mighty mass of our reserves', the 'foot soldiers' of the worldwide revolution.[27] To provide the necessary strategic base for their 'holy war ... against imperialist Britain', Moscow agreed a treaty of recognition with Afghanistan under which Kabul, in exchange for a substantial subsidy, promised not to enter into any agreement with Britain.[28] Meanwhile Comintern strategists imagined an anti-British combination consisting of Afghanistan, a pan-Turkic force led by Enver Pasha and a revolutionary 'Army of God', to be headed by Roy. Having redeployed to Tashkent, Roy set himself to raising a Muslim army that would add an extra dimension to the Khilafat movement challenging British rule in India.[29]

Despite the enthusiasm generated in 1920, the track record of the Comintern was not to be one of revolutionary success. For decades to come, recriminations over the Comintern's failure were to be the subject of bitter dispute between the different branches of the worldwide socialist movement. But such arguments beg the question. Certainly the period 1917–23 was one of convulsive disorder. But whether there was ever any realistic prospect of a general revolutionary overthrow is more than questionable. Accusations of failure deflect us from appreciating the more remarkable thing, which is the vision of global politics that the Comintern pursued. In terms of the sheer scale of its ambition it marked a high-water mark. For a generation before the war, the Socialist International had developed a regular pattern of joint meetings and collective decision-making by parties from across Europe and increasingly from around the world. Woodrow Wilson set the precedent for a politician seeking to appeal to a public on a global scale. Versailles and the League of Nations gathered the governments of the world. Britain was attempting to forge its empire into a world-spanning Commonwealth. At the Washington Conference a global structure of naval power had been settled by inter-governmental treaty.

But the Comintern attempted something far more radical. It tried to forge a worldwide political movement, with a common model of organization, a clear commitment to a list of doctrinal points, centrally controlled and directed toward a global action plan, which was itself based on a strategic, interconnected analysis of the class struggle at every major site on the globe. In secular politics no one had ever attempted anything like it before. Its only true precursor was the Catholic Church. It is hardly surprising that the concepts of the Comintern were crude and Eurocentric or that its tactical judgements went frequently and disastrously awry. The failures and frustrations of this project were over-determined. As it turned out, in 1920, it was not issues of conceptual subtlety or tactical finesse that were decisive, but a military misadventure.

As the Red Army advanced towards the West, Tukhachevsky threw an encircling right-hook along the Baltic coastline. By the second week of August his advanced guard was within 150 miles of Berlin.[30] With the Weimar Republic looking to resume diplomatic relations with the advancing Soviets, many East Prussian communities welcomed the Russian forces as a harbinger of the end of the hated Polish rule.[31] Cut off from resupply in the first weeks of August on the Vistula River line, Pilsudski made his stand. Exploiting the gaps that opened up between the northernmost pincer of the encirclement and the Soviet forces driving towards the outskirts of Warsaw, on 16 August 1920 he counter-attacked, driving north and then eastwards, deep into the rear of the Red Army. The result was a staggering reversal. By 21 August Tukhachevsky's entire front was disintegrating. To the south, after a futile siege of Lwow on 31 August, the Red Army units under the supervision of Political Commissar Stalin were defeated at Zamosc. In what was to be the last great cavalry battle of European history, General Budenny's 1st Red Cavalry Army was driven to flight by a brigade of Polish Uhlans, the descendants of the men who had ridden with Napoleon Bonaparte in 1812.

On 12 October 1920 Moscow agreed to an armistice and on 18 March 1921 it concluded the Treaty of Riga. The Baltic boundary with Russia drawn by the Germans in 1918 remained in place. The White Russian and Ukrainian states envisioned by Brest-Litovsk were partitioned between the Soviet regime and a hugely expanded Poland. It was, Lenin admitted, a crushing setback to the expansive hopes of the revolution. But it allowed the Soviet regime to consolidate its position and clarify its relations, notably with the British Empire. In March, London and Moscow concluded a trade treaty.[32] Meanwhile the last major White emplacement in the Crimea was driven to flight and the flames of anarchist rebellion in Ukraine were stamped out. The Soviet conquest of the Transcaucasus was completed by the end of February 1921 when the Georgian Republic was occupied by the Red Army.[33] On 28 December the Socialist Republics of Russia, Ukraine, Belorusse and Transcaucasus signed the treaty that created the Union of Soviet Socialist Republics. A continental revolutionary movement froze in the shape of a new kind of state.

As the Soviet regime consolidated its grip on most of the former territory of the Tsar, the Comintern's 21 Points were forced down the throat of the international socialist movement. In Germany this split the Independent Social Democratic Party, with the majority joining the ranks of the Communist Party, the rest returning to the ranks of the Social Democratic Party. In France likewise a Communist Party split away from the Socialist Party. The Italian Communist Party formed in January 1921. The newly hatched western European Communist movement committed itself to Lenin's uncompromising doctrine of class war precisely at the moment when in Europe the tradition of armed insurrection was definitely coming to an end. On 21 March 1921 Communists in the heavy industrial regions of central Germany launched a coup. Within days it ended in a humiliating fiasco. The same was to happen in 1923 in the abortive revolutionary mobilizations in Hamburg, Saxony and Thuringia. In Britain, France and Italy in 1920 and 1921 calls for general strikes all ended in disappointment. From November 1918 down to the present day, no frontal challenge to state power has ever succeeded in any Western state. In Central Asia too, the revolutionary elan of 1920 proved fleeting. The pan-Turkic hero Enver Pasha proved an unreliable ally. Rather than directing his energies toward an invasion of British India, he became the figurehead of a Central Asian rebellion against Soviet rule.[34] With Afghanistan likewise uncooperative, Roy's Islamic Army was disbanded.

The vision of revolution had gone through four phases since November 1918. As the war ended, Lenin had been on the defensive anxiously looking for ways to continue the balancing of Brest-Litovsk. In the spring of 1919 that had given way to the prospect of revolutions exploding like wildfires across Eurasia. When that was disappointed, the Comintern in 1920 took upon itself the task of orchestrating a global revolutionary campaign. Finally, after the renewed defeat of revolutionary hopes in Germany and Italy in 1921, Moscow came to see itself as pursuing a strategy of revolutionary defence. Rather than socialism being the animating force of a global uprising, or the strategic centre of a global campaign, it became the ideology of one state amongst others in a heterogeneous world system.[35]

For Communist activists across the world, the implications were drastic. In 1919 they had been agents of revolution in their own right. In 1920 they had submitted to the Comintern's discipline, but with the promise of imminent revolutionary success. Now they were required to subordinate themselves to the interests of the USSR in a brutal strategic clinch of indefinite duration. At the Third Meeting of the Comintern in June and July 1921, the subordination of all Communist parties to Soviet strategy was the sole substantive matter of discussion. With the major capitalist powers, notably Britain and its immediate neighbours, the Soviet state would seek coexistence. Outside Europe, the Communists would seek to collaborate with nationalist forces against imperialism. But as the bloody example of Turkey and Iran were soon to demonstrate, this involved huge risks for the Communist foot soldiers. Moscow insisted on maintaining good relations with Ataturk, regardless of the fact that he turned against the Turkish Communists as soon as he had disposed of the Greeks and the British.[36] Similarly the Iranian Communist Party was sacrificed to uphold relations with strongman General Reza Khan. The adventure of the revolutionary dialectic had entered its grimmest phase. Iron discipline and self-denial would establish themselves as the hallmarks of Communist revolutionary ethos.

III

It was this narrowing of revolutionary horizons that made China seem ever more crucial as an arena of revolutionary contest. At the Washington Conference, Chinese nationalists saw themselves as having been victimized not by one power singly but by a coalition of imperialists headed by the United States. The abstraction of imperialism 'in general' had taken on concrete form in the international banking consortium. The one state excluded from that oppressive combination was the Soviet Union. In 1919 and 1920 Chinese diplomacy had taken advantage of Russian weakness to roll back the privileges of the Tsarist regime. Now the tables were turned. With the Western Powers having affirmed their unwillingness to make substantial concessions, and with the Red Army re-establishing Moscow's grip over Siberia and Mongolia, the Soviets dispatched a delegation to Beijing for a new round of hard bargaining.

By 1924 this was to result in a substantial reassertion of Russian rights over the Manchurian railway system.[37] But the far bigger prize was the prospect of socialist revolution in China. Like the Japanese before them, Soviet policy toward China oscillated between two poles. They could limit themselves to establishing and defending a sphere of interest, potentially in alliance with other foreign powers. Or, more ambitiously, they could seek to hegemonize the entirety of China. The latter project required ideological justification. The best the Japanese had to offer was the weak and transparently self-serving brew of pan-Asianism. The Soviets were in a position to offer a rather more engaging set of formulae.

At the Congress of the Peoples of the East in Baku in September 1920, Zinoviev had been frustrated by the poor showing of the Chinese. In January 1922, in reaction to the Washington Conference, the Soviets called a new Congress of the Toilers of the Far East, attended by militants from Japan, India, Indonesia, Mongolia and Korea, as well as, for the first time, a large contingent of Communists from China.[38] There were disagreements over tactics, but concord at least on the need to distance the national revolution in China from any connection with the Western Powers. Nothing more was to be expected from the United States. The Chinese Communist Party in its first year was a tiny clique of intellectuals. But in the wake of high-profile strikes in Hong Kong and Canton, instructions were issued to begin engagement with workers' organizations.

In November 1922 at its Fourth Congress, the Communist International returned to the question of organizing the peasantry in 'oriental countries', formulating its 'general theses on the oriental question'. The central point of the new Comintern line was the need to draw the great mass of the rural population into national liberation struggles. The role of the Communist Party was to pressure the bourgeois-nationalist parties into adopting a revolutionary agrarian programme to appeal to the landless rural population.[39] Crucially, on 12 January 1923 the Comintern directed the Chinese Communist Party that 'The only serious national revolutionary group in China at present is the Kuomintang.'[40] With these words the Comintern for better or worse made the choice that none of the other foreign powers had been willing to make. It opted not just to acknowledge the significance of the Kuomintang, but to assist it in making a full-scale national revolution. This was affirmed by official Soviet diplomacy only a few weeks later when the Soviet ambassador to China, Adolphe Joffe, abandoned Beijing to meet with Sun Yat-sen in Shanghai, from where they issued a manifesto on future collaboration. In May this was followed by specific instructions designating the peasant problem as the central issue of the Chinese revolution. Along with their role in the cities, the Chinese comrades were enjoined to foment an agrarian revolt. This strategy was not to the taste of the founding members of the Chinese Communist Party, who were urban intellectuals fixated on the modern, industrial working class. But it brought to the fore a new cohort of organizers, including the young Mao Zedong, himself a son of the peasantry.

Nor was this new peasant-line confined to China. In October 1923 the Throne Room of the Kremlin played host to the First International Peasant Conference, attended by 158 delegates from 40 countries. Poland, Bulgaria and Hungary, as well as Mexico and the United States, were all represented. From Asia came Sen Katayama from Japan and Ho Chi Minh from Indochina. As Lenin hovered close to death over the winter of 1923–4, with Stalin lurking menacingly in the shadows, Trotsky, the hero of the Red Army, Zinoviev, the chief of the Comintern, and Bukharin, the theoretician and former Left Communist, vied for the limelight. Bukharin, who after Brest-Litovsk had counted on a peasant war to turn back the Germans, now reminded anyone who would listen that 'as long as the huge majority of the population of this world is peasants, the question of the struggle of the peasantry stands as one of the central questions of policy'.[41] Zinoviev for his part abandoned any talk of an exclusive proletarian dictatorship. He declared that the imperative to combine workers' revolution with peasant war was 'the most fundamental feature of Leninism', the 'most important discovery that Lenin made'. Zinoviev's latest revolutionary vision was to unhinge the European order by way of a Balkan uprising that would sweep westwards from Bulgaria and Yugoslavia.

But there was always another note that pervaded the talk of the peasantry and peasantism. Back in April 1923, at the 12th Congress of the Russian Communist Party, Zinoviev had defended the new line. In answer to those who accused him of deviating toward populism and agrarian interests, he responded. 'Yes we not only must deviate towards the peasantry, but we must bow and, if necessary, kneel before the economic needs of the peasants, who will follow us and give us complete victory.'[42] Along with Third Worldist revolutionary elan went a sense of realism, bordering on resignation, an acceptance that the 'true revolution', the proletarian revolution, as promised by the great prophets of the nineteenth century, was out of reach. Nor was this painful insight owed to the far-flung operations of the Comintern in China or in Poland. It was a bitter lesson taught by Russian reality.

IV

By early 1921, Trotsky and the Red Army had triumphed in the civil war. But victory had come at a heavy price. To avoid alienating the rural population, the Reds had abandoned any talk of collective farming, or the socialization of the land. The villagers were allowed to keep whatever land they had seized in 1917. This kept the peasants out of the clutches of counter-revolution. But it created a profound dilemma. Under the system of so-called 'war communism', the workers were paid almost entirely in ration entitlements. Already by 1918 the Russian currency had become virtually worthless. With the peasants in control of the land, as food supplies in the cities dwindled, the regime had no option but to resort to requisitioning, if necessary by force. The result was a terrifying downward spiral, in which peasant cultivation collapsed and the urban population, threatened with starvation, fled back to the countryside. The Soviet regime had won the civil war, but as a movement of proletarian revolution it had forfeited its *raison d'être*. Its international campaign of revolution had failed. And what was left of Russia was a far cry from what Marxism had promised. By the end of 1920 the population of Petrograd had plunged by 75 per cent and that of Moscow by almost half.

For Lenin himself there was one pre-eminent benchmark for the success of his regime: the Paris Commune of 1871, the originator of modern Communism. In early March 1921, as the Bolshevik regime prepared to celebrate the fiftieth anniversary of that revolutionary landmark at the 10th Party Congress, it was shaken by an event unprecedented in its own history. On 1 March the soldiers and sailors of the Kronstadt naval base outside Petrograd, one of the legendary sites of the 1917 revolution, rose up in rebellion against the Soviet regime. They issued a manifesto calling for free and fair elections to the Soviets, freedom of speech, the right of assembly for non-party members, the formation of free labour unions, the release of all socialist political prisoners and the independent investigation of the charges against all those incarcerated by the regime, the separation of party and state, the equalization of rations, and the granting of full freedom for production for small independent producers. Against this libertarian challenge the Bolsheviks responded as they had done consistently since November 1917, with massive force. With Tukhachevsky taking command, 50,000 Red Guards were hurled against Kronstadt. Perhaps as many as two thousand rebels were executed. Thousands more were jailed. By the time the 10th Party Congress had concluded, the tidy-up had begun.

On politics there could be no compromise. But on economic policy Lenin was willing to be flexible. The strategy of forced contributions had led to a disaster. Inflation was rampant. In the factories there was a veritable epidemic of absenteeism. On 21 March the sensation of the Communist Party conference was Lenin's proclamation of the so-called New Economic Policy. In towns and cities the strategy of total collectivization was reversed. Private property was permitted for businesses employing fewer than 20 workers. The coercive requisitioning of food was replaced by a regular tax that from 1924 was levied in cash. To restore confidence, a new gold-backed currency would be introduced.

By 1921, having abandoned its revolutionary invasion of Poland and its global campaign against the British Empire, and having retreated publicly, both at home and abroad, toward a compromise with capitalism, the Soviet regime appeared to the Western Powers less like a revolutionary threat than a failed state. As harvest season approached and a drought struck the weakened farmers of the Volga region, it became apparent that the New Economic Policy had come too late. The civil war had already cost well over a million dead. Now, in what had once been the bread basket of Europe, tens of millions were at risk of starvation. On 13 July, Lenin licensed the non-conformist writer Maxim Gorky to issue an international appeal for charity, not on behalf of worldwide revolution, but in the language of humanism, on behalf of 'the country of Tolstoy, Dostoyevsky, Mendeleyev ... Mussorgsky' and 'Glinka'. 'All honest people' across the world were to rally to his country's aid. This was no longer revolutionary internationalism. Without 'bread and medicine' Russia itself would die.[43]

23

Genoa: The Failure of British Hegemony

On 16 August 1921 Lloyd George addressed the House of Commons on the alarming news coming from Russia. The famine on the Volga was 'so appalling a disaster', Lloyd George declaimed, 'that it ought to sweep every prejudice out of one's mind and only appeal to one sentiment – pity and human sympathy'. The lives of 18 million people were immediately at risk. But to avoid politics in dealing with the Soviet regime was easier said than done. Combined with Lenin's announcement of the New Economic Policy in March 1921 and the retreat from a confrontational foreign policy, the famine was widely seen in the West as evidence that the Bolshevik regime might be nearing its end. Was it not significant that the appeal for assistance had been delivered by a committee of notable Russians, some of whom, like Maxim Gorky, were well-known critics of Lenin's regime? Might the Russian famine committee perhaps constitute the basis for a new provisional government?[1] In the autumn of 1921 the possibility seemed to come into view of a truly comprehensive European peace based on a taming of the Soviet regime and a reintegration of Russia. It was this vision that would tempt Lloyd George to undertake the boldest peace-making effort of the post-war period. It would prove a striking demonstration both of the self-confidence of British power and of its real limits.

I

Since the end of the Polish-Soviet War in the autumn of 1920, London had been seeking a modus vivendi that would restore trade with Russia and secure the borders of the British Empire. But this policy of détente had its limits. In return for aid and at least tacit recognition, the Soviet state must recognize its basic international obligations.[2] Above all it must come to terms over the billions of dollars owing to France and Britain on which it had defaulted at the time of Brest-Litovsk. A quarter of total French foreign investment was at stake. More than $4 billion was owed to upward of 1.6 million investors, many of them private stakeholders in Russian industry and railways. Britain's somewhat smaller share totalled $3.5 billion, which were overwhelmingly claims on the Russian government.[3] In October 1921 an international conference convened in Brussels to discuss a comprehensive Western response to the Soviet famine. With British leadership, the conference adopted a resolution under which aid to the Soviet Union was made conditional on acknowledgement of outstanding debts and the creation of 'conditions' within the Soviet territory that would allow trade to revive. International credit, the Brussels Conference insisted, 'must rest on confidence'.[4]

On 28 October the Soviet Commissar for Foreign Affairs, Georgy Chicherin, replied to the Brussels resolution that if the Western Powers were finally ready to include the Soviets as a legitimate member of a general peace settlement, the Soviet regime would be prepared to discuss honouring at least Russia's pre-war obligations. By that time, however, the Soviets had already found an alternative source of assistance. In Washington the news of the famine broke just as Secretary of State Charles Evans Hughes issued the invitations to the naval disarmament conference. This no doubt reinforced the State Department in its determination not to recognize the Soviet regime. But since the days of the Belgian relief operation, bringing succour to starving Europeans had become something of an American speciality. With world food markets in free fall, there were huge surpluses of grain to dispose of. Already in July 1921, Herbert Hoover, the master of emergencies, began to mobilize his well-proven Relief Administration. From Moscow's point of view, precisely because Washington was so squeamish about official contacts, American aid had definite attractions.[5] So long as Hoover was free to operate as he saw fit, there were minimal conditions attached. The scale of this American relief organization meant that Hoover could operate in Russia with no need for collaboration with the Soviet authorities.[6] On 18 August 1921, only two days after Lloyd George had issued his appeal for a common front, the Soviets accepted Hoover's offer of aid.[7] For the next 12 months, 10 million Russians were fed by America.

The Russian famine, however, was not the only crisis in the offing in the autumn of 1921. Two years after Versailles, the full bitterness of the peace was again souring Franco-German relations. In March 1921 the plebiscite in Silesia had delivered a predictably ambiguous result and triggered a Polish uprising. Combined with the continuing struggle over reparations, it made for an inflammable cocktail. Whilst the costs of reconstruction were ruining France's finances, the temporary monetary stabilization that had prevailed in Germany since 1920 was slipping dangerously.[8] Joseph Wirth's government professed itself ready to pay reparations, but to do so it was throwing printed money onto the exchanges. Though the Freikorps had been disbanded after their final fight with the Poles, the menace from the right continued. On 4 June 1921 whilst walking with one of his daughters, Philipp Scheidemann, the first Chancellor of the Weimar Republic, was attacked with cyanide gas. Scheidemann survived, but on 24 August the right-wing death squads struck again. This time they claimed the life of Matthias Erzberger. The nationalist right was settling a score that went back to the summer of 1917 when Erzberger and Scheidemann had led the Reichstag's first call for peace. The parties that backed the Republic understood the menace, but when the League in October 1921 awarded most of Upper Silesia and its heavy industry to Poland, they could not dissociate themselves from the patriotic groundswell. Chancellor Wirth's government, which in May 1921 had taken responsibility for fulfilling the London reparations ultimatum, resigned in protest. Wirth had no option but to form a new cabinet.

But the deadlock over reparations was now more severe than ever. German heavy industry exploited the indignation over Silesia to destroy an agreement brokered by Foreign Minister Walther Rathenau to pay France in kind with deliveries of coal. They also vetoed any increase in taxation on profits. Instead, the Reich was forced to enter into humiliating negotiations over the terms of a private international mortgage secured on the collective wealth of German business and large landowners. At a general meeting of German business leaders on 12 November 1921, led by Hugo Stinnes, the greatest baron of the Ruhr, the nationalist right wing demanded in return that the social promises of the revolutionary era, including the eight-hour day, should be repealed, and all the productive assets of the German state, including the Reichsbahn, the largest business organization in the world, should be privatized. No government could rule by democratic means on such a platform. But splintered as it was between the SPD, USPD and KPD, the left lacked the votes necessary to push through its own preferred solution, to pay for reparations by levying a steeply progressive tax on private wealth.

With the fiscal foundation of the German state in doubt, in the autumn of 1921 the markets signalled their mounting disbelief in the viability of fulfilment. From a previous low of 99.11 marks to the dollar, by the end of November the exchange rate had plunged to 262.96 marks. In Berlin the police had to be deployed to contain mobs of frantic shoppers desperate to stockpile imported food. As State Secretary Julius Hirsh of the Reich's Ministry for Economic Affairs put it: 'We do not stand before the question: an exchange rate with the dollar of 300 or 500? . . . we stand before the question of whether we can remain independent at all with our existing monetary conditions, whether we want to remain independent at all'.[9]

With the future of the Weimar Republic hanging in the balance, all sides in Germany looked for support abroad. Since America seemed determined not to intervene, by the end of 1921 it was Britain that came to be seen as Germany's saviour. In December both Walther Rathenau and Stinnes visited London to discuss options. Stinnes had extended his domestic vision of privatization to an extraordinary scheme under which an international syndicated loan would draw on Anglo-American capital to carry out a wholesale reorganization of the entire central European railway network.[10] In a system reminiscent of the foreign-operated railroads in China, Stinnes envisioned a privatized German Reichsbahn at the heart of an 'East European railroad community' incorporating Austrian, Polish and the Danubian main lines.[11] In discussions with Lloyd George, Stinnes and Rathenau widened their vision to take in Russia as well.[12] Since 1920, Soviet trade negotiators had been touting huge orders for railway equipment throughout Europe. Krupp had already secured a lucrative contract.[13] With Lenin having approved the allocation of 40 per cent of all Soviet gold reserves for the import of railway equipment, there was talk of the purchase of 5,000 new locomotives and 100,000 wagons. It was an import programme that dwarfed even the huge wartime contracts of the Tsarist era.[14] Beyond Hoover's food parcels, restoring the transport system was crucial to reintegrating Russia with the European economy. German industry could build the locomotives, but what it could not supply in 1921 was credit. For this they needed London.

The German appeal was well judged. By December 1921 the British cabinet had convinced itself that if reparations were allowed to tip Germany into crisis, the consequences for the whole of Europe 'would be disastrous beyond calculation'. With America on the sidelines, Britain would have to take the initiative.[15] The prospect of this British-German convergence was enough to trigger Paris into action. On 18 December 1921 Aristide Briand, the French Prime Minister, followed the Germans to Downing Street.[16]

Perhaps the impasse over reparations could be broken if Britain returned to the offer first made by Lloyd George in March 1919. Britain would revive the guarantee of French security that had lapsed when Congress failed to ratify the Versailles Treaty. France would make sufficient concessions to Germany to satisfy the Americans and the flow of credit would resume. A disaster would be avoided. The problem was to define the price that Britain would have to pay. What would be the scope of its security commitment to the French? London would not commit to coming to France's aid if it chose to intervene in a Polish-German war. Nor was there much enthusiasm in Britain for a bilateral military alliance with France. Briand had returned from the Washington Conference inspired by the idea of a regional pact for Europe akin to the four-power pact agreed with Japan regarding China's integrity, a solution he hoped would appeal to Washington.[17]

Lloyd George was moved to an even grander design. If the sticking point between Britain and France was the insecurity of France's allies in the East and the problem with Germany was reparations, Lloyd George proposed a scheme to stabilize and restore the economies of eastern Europe, including Russia. The insistent and claustrophobic French demand for a comprehensive bilateral security guarantee would be opened into a pacification of the entire continent.[18] In a single grand diplomatic bargain the Soviets would be persuaded to accept the conditions for economic assistance worked out at Brussels. On that basis, hundreds of millions of pounds would flood into the ruined Soviet Union, simultaneously bringing Russia back within the capitalist fold and funding a revival in German exports. Germany would earn the hard currency it needed to reliably service reparations, which in turn would restore France's credit in America. A regular payment by Germany to France of £50 million ($200–250 million) from the Russia trade should enable Paris to raise a loan of £700–800 million (c. $3.5 billion), which would go a long way toward resolving France's financial difficulties.[19] The unproductive struggle between Germany and France would be transformed into an expansive engine of continental economic growth. In a characteristic blend of opportunism and progressive ambition, Lloyd George also calculated that a diplomatic triumph would allow him to call a snap election, win a handsome victory for his wing of the Liberal Party, and escape the dependence on the Conservatives that had constrained him since the Khaki election. With Europe at peace, Lloyd George would outflank the rising Labour Party and re-establish himself as the master of the progressive centre ground.

With the British Empire holding the ring, the European economy would be restored, the spectre of Communism lifted, the conflict between Germany and France assuaged, and the political balance shifted back toward the centre-left. Lloyd George's breadth of strategic vision is all the more startling when we place it in its global context. His European initiative coincided over the winter of 1921–2 with the global naval agreement at the Washington Conference and the simultaneous resolution of multiple crises within the empire. As Lloyd George well understood, taming Gandhi, containing the Irish, and neutralizing Egyptian nationalism would remain tactical and short-lived successes if the wider strategic challenges of the Atlantic, Pacific and Eurasia were not addressed. What he was attempting was nothing less than a global fix for the post-war crisis of liberalism. One might, however, also turn this point on its head. The scope of Lloyd George's design indicates the dizzying scale that any truly comprehensive re-establishment of a liberal order would in practice have required. Nothing like this had ever been attempted. Given Britain's limited resources, the task was daunting.

II

On 4 January 1922 the Supreme Allied Council convened in Cannes and Lloyd George took the lead in asking for an economic and financial conference to be held within a matter of months to include both Germany and Russia. With regard to the Soviet Union, the Cannes

Conference passed a series of resolutions that amounted to the statement of a new vision of international order. States, the conference boldly declared, would not dictate to each other their internal systems of ownership, internal economy or government. But foreign investment depended on recognition of property rights, governments must acknowledge public debts, there had to be impartial legal systems and secure currency conditions, and there must be no subversive propaganda. On the basis of this manifesto for neutering any threat to the capitalist order, the Soviets would be readmitted to the international community.[20] On 8 January 1922 Moscow agreed to accept an invitation to a European conference. Side-stepping the failed Wilsonian construction of the League of Nations, of which neither Germany nor the Soviet Union was a member, the British and French invited the other interested powers to a summit meeting in the Italian city of Genoa.

Germany was delighted with the British approach. Chancellor Wirth exclaimed to the British ambassador Lord D'Abernon that 'Germany is England's advance post on the continent, or I shall say an advance post of Anglo-Saxon civilization. Like you, like America, we must have exports, only by trade can we live. That must be the policy of all three countries.'[21] But the German idea of a benign Anglo-American financial hegemony over Europe was a fantasy. Washington had no intention of providing any encouragement for Lloyd George's vision. Food aid was one thing, but Washington regarded the idea of direct talks with the Soviets as anathema and refused the invitation to Genoa. In France as well the manner in which British power was being exercised was hugely sensitive. To the critics of Prime Minister Briand, the British idea of a general European security pact seemed less suited to protecting France than to offering Germany immunity against any vigorous enforcement of the Versailles Treaty. The invitation to the Soviets remained controversial so long as France's loans remained unpaid.[22] To invite both of the pariah states to the same conference on friendly terms seemed nothing short of suicidal.

On 12 January 1922 the restless centre-right majority in the French Chamber of Deputies ousted Briand in favour of Raymond Poincaré. The new French Prime Minister is often caricatured as a narrow-minded chauvinist. He soon became the object of a concerted propaganda campaign sponsored by Germany and the French Communist Party to paint him as a warmonger, whose secret diplomacy with Imperial Russia had been the true cause of war in August 1914.[23] This historical interpretation found eager adherents amongst latter-day Wilsonians in the anglophone world.[24] For Poincaré, however, no less than for Clemenceau, Millerand and Briand, the pursuit of an Entente with Britain was the priority. His vision of European security, however, was different from the Washington Conference model.

On 23 January 1922 Poincaré presented London with the proposal for a 30-year military convention offering mutual guarantees against Germany. From Lloyd George's point of view this was a disaster. As he reminded Poincaré, he had always been committed to the alliance between France and Britain. Even at the height of imperialist tension at the time of the Fashoda crisis in 1898, Lloyd George had denounced the folly of conflict between the 'two democracies'. Now Lloyd George warned Poincaré of the hostility of the opposition Liberals and Labour in Britain, who were set firm against any continental entanglement.[25] If the British and French democracies were to turn against each other, it would set the stage for the 'greatest disaster in the history of Europe'.[26] Lloyd George's pleas, however, were in vain. Poincaré knew that the British Prime Minister had staked his reputation on the conference that was now scheduled for Genoa in April. This gave him leverage.

As the clock ticked toward the Genoa Conference, with France desperately fending off claims from its foreign creditors and Germany on the brink of bankruptcy, Europe's financial impasse was reaching a new crisis point. As Poincaré came into office, the Reparations Commission granted Germany a provisional postponement of payments, but only on the condition that Berlin submit a comprehensive programme of fiscal consolidation for approval by the Commission.[27] Overriding the violent opposition of German business, the Wirth government complied with the Allied demand. It agreed to raise taxes, levy compulsory internal loans, collect customs duties in gold, raise the domestic price of coal and hike rail rates, grant autonomy to the Reichsbank and impose currency controls to prevent capital flight.[28] A major element of the fiscal consolidation was the long-promised cut to food subsidies, which would save billions of marks but would require a crunching 75 per cent increase in bread prices. The political costs were obvious.

In early February 1922 Chancellor Wirth faced the only major strike by public-sector workers in German history. Initially, he wanted to take a tough line by deploying the emergency powers provided by the Weimar constitution. But even Carl Severing, who had mastered the Communist uprising in the Ruhr in 1920 and was now serving as Prussia's tough Interior Minister, shrank at the prospect of nationwide confrontation. 'The consequence will be food shortages and plundering. The Reichswehr will then have to be employed as a last resort, and then civil war will be at hand.'[29] Though this was avoided, the reparations instalment due on 18 March 1922 drained the foreign-exchange reserves of the Reichsbank to the barest minimum. On 21 March 1922 the Reparations Commission announced that Germany could suspend all payments until 15 April, but in return it must now agree to fiscal consolidation within a matter of weeks. An additional 60 billion marks in taxes were to be voted through the Reichstag by the end of May. Germany's public finances were, in effect, placed under international supervision. From Paris, the German reparations negotiators warned Berlin that it should not overreact. The threats issued on 21 March were in fact a watered-down version of even more far-reaching demands made by the French. In Paris there was once again talk of 'ottomanizing' Germany.[30] But that was exactly what the German government took the new demands to be – a fundamental assault on German sovereignty, a renewed threat to relegate Germany to the second or third rank, in what had once been politely dubbed the family of nations. If it was, in fact, Poincaré and not Lloyd George who was setting the terms, the entire rationale that had led Rathenau and Stinnes to London in December 1921 was in question.[31]

With increasing desperation Stresemann and Rathenau looked across the Atlantic to the United States. As Rathenau put it in the Reichstag, 'never before has a nation held the fate of a continent so inescapably in its hand as does America at this moment'.[32] But Rathenau's appeal elicited no reaction from Washington. The Harding administration refused to budge from the position that Hoover had first outlined for the Wilson administration in May 1919. The best way to force the Europeans to come to a satisfactory resolution was American non-intervention. Europe's reparations crisis, like the deflationary economic crisis of 1920, would have to run its course before the logic of business-led reconstruction could take hold.[33]

III

By contrast with the sensational opening to the Washington Conference, Lloyd George's conference in Genoa began anti-climactically. The complex bargain to be brokered did not lend itself to the kind of startling offer with which Secretary of State Hughes had surprised the world. America's absence and Poincaré's decision to stay away gave leadership to Britain, but it also endangered the negotiations from the start. Lloyd George was reduced to opening proceedings on 14 April 1922 with the rather lame quip that since it was a Genoese citizen, Christopher Columbus, who had once discovered America for Europe, 'he hoped that this city might now rediscover Europe for the Americans'.[34] Relations between France and Britain were strained, with Poincaré insisting that there could be no discussion of reparations. Italy was no substitute for France as a partner in power. With Fascist squads running rampant across the countryside, a dangerous power vacuum had opened in Rome, which within the year would open the door to Benito Mussolini's ascent to power. Meanwhile Japan was invited to Genoa as a matter of course, but unlike at Washington no vital Japanese interests were engaged. The Germans were resentful and tactless. The Soviet delegation was the real sensation of the conference.

There was much talk at Genoa that the international gathering marked a new era in European politics, the first genuine, all-inclusive peace conference since the end of the war. But if this was the case, it was profoundly disillusioning. There was no hiding the distaste that many in London felt for the compromises they were themselves proposing.[35] In private letters and diary entries, the British delegation vented their alienation in visceral terms. Rathenau, the head of the German delegation and one of the leading lights of the Weimar Republic, was dismissed as a 'bald-headed Jewish degenerate'. The Bolsheviks appeared to the British as though 'they had stepped out of a Drury Lane pantomime ... Chicherine looks the degenerate he is, and of course except for himself and Krassin ... they are all Jews'. 'It is very unpleasant,' another remarked, 'to reflect that the main interest here is centered on the future relations between them and ourselves.'[36]

In the opening exchanges of the conference Chicherin set out to embarrass his hosts by claiming for the Soviet Union the mantle of an advocate of peace and disarmament.[37] It was a softer line of internation-alism than that pushed by the Comintern when it had demanded that its European affiliates prepare for civil war.[38] But when it came to the negotiations over the terms of Soviet readmission to the international community, the bargaining was hard. The Western Powers insisted on the rights of their creditors. The Soviets countered by delivering a repara-tions bill for 50 billion gold roubles ($3.6 billion) to cover the damage done by Allied intervention in the civil war. The Cannes agenda, with its contradictory promise of non-interference combined with the demand for the protection of property rights, was enough by itself to have derailed the Genoa Conference. But the question of how fresh capitalist invest-ment could be reconciled with socialism was never seriously broached. The discussions never got past the problem of outstanding international debts. Would Russia pay? Some compromise seemed possible on the basis of trading forgiveness of inter-Allied war debts in exchange for the acknowledgement of pre-war Tsarist liabilities. But the Soviets were, in any case, not committed to reaching a deal. The radicals in the delegation headed by Adolphe Joffe were more than happy to fall back on the Len-inist formula of 'divide and conquer'.

Moscow's fundamental objective was to forestall Lloyd George's fan-tasy of a British-French-German consortium to hegemonize Russia. They found a partner in the Germans, whose confidence in Lloyd George's grand bargain had been profoundly shaken by the reparations crisis of March and who were themselves haunted by the fear that the real purpose of the conference was not to broker a general peace, but to rebuild the encircling anti-German alliance. This idea had been nourished by conservative elements in the German Foreign Office who favoured a Russo-German agreement.[39] At Genoa these fears were heightened by alarming reports that France and Britain might help Russia to repay the Tsarist debts by backing Moscow's reparations claims against Ger-many. When news reached Rathenau of exclusive conversations between the Russians and the Western Powers, this was enough to panic the Ger-man delegation. At all costs they must forestall a new anti-German coalition.

Early on the morning of Easter Sunday, 16 April, Rathenau aban-doned his previous advocacy of an agreement with the West and accepted an invitation to join the Soviet delegation for separate talks at their villa on the outskirts of Genoa.[40] By 6.30 that evening, having signed the so-called Rapallo Treaty, the German and Soviet delegations had derailed the entire conference. Lloyd George's bold initiative, rather than producing a Europe-wide security order, had opened the door to a treaty of mutual recognition and cooperation between the two pariahs, Germany and the Soviet Union. As Lloyd George himself acknowledged, 'With an aggregate population of over two hundred millions the combination of Germany's technical skill with Russia's resources in raw materials and man-power' posed a 'terrible danger to [the] peace of Europe'.[41] For France it was a truly terrifying prospect. It is indicative of the mistrust suffusing Genoa that Paris immediately jumped to the conclusion that London had plotted this Russo-German alignment from the start.[42] In fact, it was a catastrophe for Lloyd George. The grand design of reconciling Germany and France by way of Russia had exploded.

Though the Washington Conference was regarded as a qualified success and Genoa was viewed as an unmitigated disaster, what both grand designs had in common was their tendency to underestimate the forces committed to disrupting the post-war status quo. London, Paris and Washington imagined that the nationalist urge could be tamed by financial hegemony. Consortia were constructed to oversee and supervise the finances and transport infrastructure of China and Russia.[43] Great business opportunities no doubt beckoned. But without state guarantees of the old kind, secured by spheres of interest and promises of extra-territoriality, it turned out that private bankers were reluctant to extend substantial loans. For all the politicking around the China consortium, no money flowed. Without the participation of the United States, the idea of subjecting the Soviet Union to a capitalist consortium was stillborn. The Western Powers underestimated the force of nationalism in China. At Genoa, ironically, the Western delegations were concerned that if they pressed too hard they might precipitate the replacement of the Soviet Communist regime by an aggressively nationalist one.[44] Though the situation of the Soviet regime was no doubt serious, this was nonetheless a misjudgement. Lenin's New Economic Policy was a tactical adjustment rather than a strategic retreat. Moscow's cynical exploitation of Herbert Hoover's aid was not a sign of surrender, but a demonstration of its will to survive at whatever cost. It certainly had no intention of allowing London to orchestrate a unified capitalist consortium aimed at Russia's subordination.[45]

Though nominally professing its commitment to fulfilment, the German government was sorely tempted to throw itself in with the club of insurgents. The Rapallo Treaty with the Soviets was of a piece with Germany's diplomatic ties to Republican China. It was loudly applauded by Ataturk in Turkey.[46] Of course, Germany's financial situation was grave, but to associate itself with the Soviet Union, Republican China or the insurgent Turks in the league of pariahs, was a self-indulgent nationalist fantasy. Versailles was built on the assumption of German sovereignty. In August 1921 Washington had formally ended the state of war by concluding a separate and extremely favourable peace with the Weimar Republic. Britain clearly wished for the reintegration of Germany into both the international economic and political system. France's anxiety could easily have been exploited to Germany's advantage. All Lloyd George needed was Germany's continued commitment to the Versailles process. The side deal at Rapallo delivered the opposite. If it harkened back to the Realpolitik of the Bismarck era, this was Realpolitik without the substance. If Rapallo was something else, not a carefully calculated power play, but a rallying cry, a gesture of national resistance, it begged the question. How far were the Germans willing to go?[47]

What it might mean was spelled out in blood on 20 June 1922 when a right-wing hit squad gunned down the industrialist Walther Rathenau outside his Grunewald villa. With pro-Republican demonstrators in the streets, the markets gave their verdict. In the week following Rathenau's killing, the mark plunged from 345 against the dollar to 540.[48] Would the German right wing risk civil war and economic chaos in a showdown with the Western Powers? This question had hung in the air since the Armistice. In the wake of Genoa it was precisely such an act of resistance that was to cost Lloyd George the premiership and demonstrate the vanity of any British-led attempt to restore order in Europe.

IV

In the weeks ahead of the Genoa Conference, Lloyd George had had to ride out the clash between his Secretary of State for India, Edwin Montagu, and his Foreign Secretary George Curzon over the arrest of Gandhi and the terms that London would propose to Turkey for a peace in the eastern Mediterranean. Weakened by the disaster at Genoa, London now faced a comprehensive crisis of its policy not only in Europe but also in the Near East. Already by the end of 1921 it was clear that the Greeks had no chance of defeating Ataturk's nationalist forces. Seeking an escape from the Entente's botched policy toward the Ottoman Empire, France had sought an accommodation with Ankara already in March 1921. London attempted to work out its own face-saving withdrawal. But with the French on the sidelines, the Soviets bolstered by their new alliance with Germany and the reconquest of Anatolia in his sights, Ataturk refused any compromise.[49] In the late summer of 1922 the Greeks made an ill-judged attempt to restore their position by occupying Constantinople and holding the Ottoman capital to ransom. But Ataturk was not intimidated, the Ottomans had forfeited any claim to Turkish loyalty. On 26 August 1922 Ataturk began an advance towards the Aegean coastline that culminated on 9 September in the sack of Smyrna and the terror-stricken evacuation of the Greek population. The Turkish forces then wheeled north and drove to within a few miles of the Entente zone of occupation on the Turkish side of the straits. In mid-September 1922, with their Greek allies put to flight, 5,000 Entente troops stationed at Chanak on the western end of the straits found themselves facing the rampant Turkish Army.

For London withdrawal was not an option. In the wake of the climb-down in Ireland, the uprising in India, challenges to its authority across the Middle East, and the fiasco at Genoa, London could ill afford any further loss of face. The British forces dug in and Curzon desperately appealed to France and to the empire. But when Curzon met Poincaré in Paris the two fell to trading accusations of betrayal.[50] The reply from the Dominions was, if anything, even more crushing. South Africa failed to respond to London. As far as Canada was concerned, the Washington Conference had taken care of the fundamental strategic concerns of the empire. Australia was furious that London called on it for help only in the midst of a crisis and expressed no enthusiasm for a re-enactment of Gallipoli.[51] The distintegration of Lloyd George's grand strategy left Britain isolated not just in Europe but within its own empire.

When, on 23 September 1922, a battalion-strength detachment of Turkish troops entered the neutralized buffer zone within full view of the British forces, London ordered an ultimatum to be delivered demanding their immediate withdrawal. Britain and nationalist Turkey were on the point of full-scale war.[52] The prospect was daunting, not only because the Turks outgunned the British on the spot, but because behind Ataturk, as behind Germany at Rapallo, stood the Soviet Union. The Soviets were believed to have offered submarines with which to break the Royal Navy's stranglehold of the eastern Mediterranean. On 18 September British naval forces were ordered to sink any Soviet vessels that approached them. To make matters worse, a week earlier the Greek Army rebelled against the 'pro-German' king they blamed for the disaster in Anatolia. This was no fascist takeover *avant la lettre*. The aim of the coup was to restore Lloyd George's great ally, the pro-Western Prime Minister Eleftherios Venizelos. But this meant riding roughshod over the will of the Greek electorate.

At no point, until the confrontation with Hitler over the Sudetenland, was Britain closer to entering a major war. And Lloyd George's position was based on bluff. If fighting had broken out, the British would almost certainly have been overwhelmed.[53] Perhaps not surprisingly the British commander on the spot chose not to deliver the aggressive ultimatum. On 11 October 1922 an armistice was negotiated. War was averted. But the government could no longer be saved. Just over a week later, on 19 October, restless Tory backbenchers toppled the Prime Minister, ending Lloyd George's astonishing 16 years in cabinet. He was to be the last Liberal Prime Minister of modern Britain. The chief priority of the new Tory government was to disengage as far as possible from foreign entanglements. After six months of tortuous negotiations, the Eastern Question was finally put to rest with the Treaty of Lausanne in July 1923.[54] The plans for the division of Anatolia originating in the London Treaty of 1915 and the Sykes-Picot agreement of 1916 were definitively abandoned. France and Britain settled their differences. The Turkish nation state was established as the only truly robust pillar of the disastrous post-war settlement in the eastern Mediterranean. Since 1919 the Greco-Turkish conflict had claimed 50,000 military fatalities and left tens of thousands more wounded. The civilian casualties of ethnic cleansing on both sides ran into the hundreds of thousands. The peace set an ominous new precedent in requiring the 'exchange' of 1.5 million ethnic Greeks for half a million Turks.

Even before the Chanak crisis, London's European diplomacy had reached breaking point. With Germany on the brink of default and France under massive pressure from the United States, London made one last effort to maintain the initiative. In an uncharacteristically rash move the Foreign Secretary, Arthur Balfour, put his name to a unilateral, but conditional, offer to forgive all financial claims against former allies, except for the amount demanded by the United States from Britain.[55] The unilateral British cancellation, which had been repeatedly suggested in 1920 and 1921, might well have sent a powerful signal. But the Balfour note of 1922 managed to look manipulative rather than generous. It made demands on France whilst putting America in the dock. It was rejected by both.[56] In January 1923 the new Tory government abandoned the search for a comprehensive financial settlement. Leaving reparations to the French, London negotiated a bilateral settlement of its war debts with Washington. Britain would repay $4.6 billion to the US over a 62-year period at an average yearly interest of 3.3 per cent.[57] The annual payment of over $160 million was more than it had cost to service the entire British national debt before the war. It was equivalent to the national education budget, or two-thirds of the cost of the navy, enough over 62 years to rehouse the entire city slum population of the UK.[58] Prime Minister Andrew Bonar Law, who had lost two sons in the war, was so incensed at these terms that he withdrew from the cabinet discussion and threatened to resign.

Though bitterly resented in London, this was considerably more generous than the tough guidelines laid down by the congressional committee in early 1922.[59] It took very strong appeals from the Harding administration to persuade the Senate to agree even to this deal. As far as American policy was concerned, it confirmed the new order emerging in the wake of the Anglo-American naval agreement at Washington. As Hoover put it, the debt settlement with London allowed American policy to separate Britain, 'a state of great paying power and pacific intentions', from the policy to be pursued towards states of continental Europe, including France, 'of low paying power, and still steeped in the methods of war'.[60]

24

Europe on the Brink

Less than a week after the shocking news of the Soviet-German deal at Rapallo, the newly formed Congressional World War Debt Funding Commission presented Paris with an official request to submit plans for repayment of the $3.5 billion owed by France to America.[1] Three days later, on 24 April 1922, Prime Minister Poincaré addressed a rally in his home town of Bar Le Duc.[2] Whatever its desire for an Entente with Britain and America, he declared, France reserved the right to act against Germany and to do so if necessary with force. Over the summer the State Department dispatched Jack Morgan to Europe in the hope that a private loan might ease the reparations imbroglio.[3] But Poincaré swept the bankers aside.[4] If there was no movement on inter-Allied debts, there could be no concessions on reparations. Morgan did not judge. France might be right to prefer military action to a financial stabilization of Germany, but in that case there could be no question of further loans. American investors could not be expected to 'buy into a quarrel'.[5]

Whereas Lloyd George over the winter of 1921–2 had hoped to use economics to bridge the violent antagonisms that divided Europe, France was now bracing itself to use force to adjust the terms of the financial settlement. An act of state violence was cashed out in remarkably stark terms. Paris calculated that the cost of sending the French Army into the Ruhr, the heartland of West German industry, would be as little as 125 million francs. The return from the exploitation of the Ruhr's coal mines could be as much as 850 million gold francs per annum. As it turned out, the military occupation of western Germany did offer France a substantial return.[6] But it also provoked a crisis that pushed the German nation state to the brink of collapse and forced Britain and the United States to re-engage with European politics. There were risks to France as well. A confrontation with Germany would antagonize its allies and provoke speculative attacks against the French currency. But the status quo offered France no safety.

I

The French did not want to act alone. The Entente remained at least notionally the anchor of French policy. On Armistice Day 1922 Georges Clemenceau came out of retirement to embark on a last transatlantic voyage in the hope of gaining public support for an American intervention on France's behalf. On 21 November, speaking to a New York audience, he asked 'Why did you go to war? Was it to help others preserve democracy? What have you gained? You accuse France now of militarism, but you did not do so when French soldiers saved the world. There can be no doubt that Germany is preparing a new war. Nothing can stop that except a close entente among America, Great Britain and France.'[7] Whilst Clemenceau struck a chord with the crowds of New York, behind the scenes American diplomats were seeking to pull France back to the negotiating table. But with Congress stubborn on the war-debt issue, the Harding administration was boxed in. On 29 December, following what he would later claim was 'the voice of God', Secretary of State Hughes addressed the meeting of the American Historical Association at New Haven, Connecticut.[8] He offered the most that Washington dared. There would be no renewed political or financial engagement by America with its wartime associates. But America would send commissioners to attend a European meeting of financial experts to determine Germany's capacity to pay.[9] This was no longer enough for the French. By the end of November, Poincaré's cabinet had resolved that on the occasion of the next German default the French Army would enforce the Treaty of Versailles.

How would the other members of the Entente respond? Given Germany's spoliation, the Belgians could be counted upon to support reparations enforcement. The British were standing back. As of October 1922 Italy had a new Prime Minister in the form of Benito Mussolini. Il Duce was a mercurial character, a former socialist and paramilitary gang leader. The activity of his *squadistri* since 1919 could not but be distasteful to anyone committed to the rule of law. But by 1922 Mussolini was distancing himself from the more disreputable elements of his own movement and he clearly enjoyed the backing of some of the most influential groups in Italian society. Whatever else one might say about them, the Fascists were solidly anti-Communist. Above all, from the French point of view, Mussolini's entire career was built on his war record. No one had been more vocal in his railings against 'peace without victory'. Worries about the aggressive impulses of Fascism would come later. In 1923 Mussolini was not about to stand in the way of French enforcement action against Germany.[10] That was all that Paris needed to know.

On 11 January 1923 crowds of resentful German civilians watched in ominous silence as the French Army of the Rhine, accompanied by a battalion of Belgian infantry and a token team of Italian engineers, marched into the Ruhr. The invasion was a dramatic statement of France's military preponderance in Europe. The French advance guard included a substantial mobile contingent with tanks and truck-born infantry. The French general staff wanted the option of making a deep thrust across the north German plain. But instead of any such free-wheeling military operation, upward of 60,000 French soldiers pitted themselves against the civilian population of the Ruhr in a brutal and unequal struggle. By March the Ruhr and Rhineland were isolated administratively from the rest of Germany. In the French parliament, André Maginot, himself a crippled war veteran, called for the Ruhr to be razed to the ground, to inflict on Germany what Germany had done to northern France.[11] However, Poincaré was determined not to ruin the Ruhr, but to extract coal from it.

The Germans responded with passive resistance. Miners refused to dig and the railways would not run. Of 170,000 Reichsbahn staff in the Ruhr, only 357 agreed to work for France. In retaliation, railway workers and public employees along with their families were summarily expelled from the zone of occupation, often with no more than a few hours' notice – altogether 147,000 men, women and children.[12] Four hundred railwaymen were sentenced to lengthy prison sentences for acts of sabotage. Eight died in scuffles with the occupying forces. To deter attacks, handpicked German hostages were assigned to every train carrying coal to France.[13] In total, at least 120 Germans lost their lives.[14] This was a small fraction of the thousands of civilians executed by the

Kaiser's armies in Belgium and northern France during the war. But the violence of the occupation justified German observers in their contention that the new order was one in which the line between war and peace had become hopelessly blurred. What did it mean to be at peace, if an essential part of the German nation state could be occupied by military force and its population subjected to brutal reprisals? If this was peace, what was war?

On 16 January 1923 the Berlin government declared official support for the Ruhr resistance. The consequences for the Reich's finances and for the German economy were ruinous. The exchange rate plunged from 7,260 marks to the dollar to a low of 49,000. The price of imported essentials such as food and raw materials surged. To halt the slide, the Reich threw its last remaining foreign exchange onto the currency markets, buying up marks to sustain their value artificially. The major industrial groupings and trade unions were persuaded at least temporarily to suspend disbelief and to freeze their wages and prices.[15] But Germany's situation was evidently untenable. With the Ruhr out of action Germany needed foreign exchange even to import coal. On 18 April the dykes broke. The mark plunged, reaching 150,000 to the dollar by June. With bundles of currency being disbursed in the Ruhr, by 1 August the mark had reached 1 million to the dollar. Whereas double-digit inflation since 1921 had helped to keep Germany out of the global recession, the hyperinflation of 1923 caused paralysis (Table 11). Amidst the great steelworks and mineshafts of the Ruhr, the population starved as peasants refused to sell their crops for worthless money. Three hundred thousand famished children had to be evacuated to Germany from the Ruhr, where panic-stricken food riots left dozens dead and hundreds injured.[16] But Germany itself offered no more than relative safety. As the mark plunged to 6 million to the dollar at the end of August, perhaps as many as 5 million workers, a quarter of the workforce, were either laid off or on short-time.

First in March, and then more seriously in June, the Germans appealed for British and American mediation. But both countries were loath to act. For Secretary of State Hughes, 'America was the only point of stability in the world and . . . for this reason, we absolutely could not make any move unless it would surely be successful'. After Wilson's fiasco, the Harding administration would not risk finding itself caught between the Europeans and Congress.[17] Hughes had no desire to tangle

Table 11. Germany's Slide into Hyperinflation, 1919–23

	job-seekers per 100 openings (quarterly average)	month-to-month wholesale price inflation (quarterly average)	monthly steel production, 000 tons (quarterly average)	nominal domestic debt (billion 1913 marks)	real value of domestic debt (billion 1913 marks)	quarterly Versailles Treaty costs (million 1913 marks)	budget balance excluding Versailles (million 1913 marks)	budget balance (million 1913 marks)
I 1919	187	4	518	151	54	0	0	0
II 1919	159	4	501	162	50	0	−3393	−3393
III 1919	149	17	704	169	32	0	−1998	−1998
IV 1919	171	18	654	174	17	0	−780	−780
I 1920	173	31	608	178	11	0	−348	−348
II 1920	182	−7	694	195	14	−393	−795	−1188
III 1920	218	3	753	220	15	−441	−1206	−1647
IV 1920	214	−1	790	230	16	−402	−339	−741
I 1921	245	−2	813	233	18	−543	348	−195
II 1921	209	1	758	257	18	−849	−966	−1815
III 1921	158	16	839	280	12	−960	−270	−1230
IV 1921	149	20	922	310	9	−1017	102	−915

I 1922	159	16	961	330	6	-843	345	-498
II 1922	115	9	972	349	4	-696	399	-297
III 1922	118	61	974	484	1	-354	-231	-585
IV 1922	179	76	999	1403	1	-333	-492	-825
I 1923	309	62	889	1986	0	-393	-663	-1056
II 1923	297	67	631	8048	1	-252	-837	-1089
III 1923	369	1293	312	54130	0	-156	-5490	-5646
IV 1923	1070	13267	270	5119160061	0	na	na	na

with a Senate in which the internationalists were now split between Anglophiles and Francophiles, and strong-arm nationalists of the Teddy Roosevelt variety, who sympathized with Poincaré, clashed with a growing pro-German faction.[18] As Hughes remarked to the British ambassador Lord D'Abernon, in tones reminiscent of 'peace without victory', France and Germany would each have to 'enjoy its own bit of chaos' until they would be willing to reach a 'fair settlement'.[19] Indeed, so reminiscent were Hughes's views of those that the British representatives had encountered from the American delegation in Paris in 1919 that senior members of the British government fell unconsciously into the habit of referring to the Secretary of State as 'Wilson'.[20]

Meanwhile, Britain had withdrawn from a position at the very centre of European affairs to a position of deliberate abstention. To the new, all-Tory government it seemed that the greater the distance they kept from their turbulent neighbours on the continent the better. In June 1923 Parliament was persuaded to vote additional funds to more than double the establishment of the newly formed Royal Air Force, the principal mission of which was to deter a French attack on Britain.[21] But though they did not want to back Poincaré, neither Washington nor London leapt to Germany's assistance. On 20 July, in response to the latest German call for help, London suggested a joint approach to the reparations question. But when Poincaré insisted that Germany must first call off passive resistance and Berlin refused, London and Washington withdrew to the sidelines.[22]

How long could they stay there? If the situation on the Rhine was not bad enough, over the summer of 1923 the world was treated to its first display of Fascist aggression. On 27 August an international commission attempting to demarcate the boundaries of Greece and Albania was ambushed by Greek bandits. An Italian general and his staff were murdered. When the Greeks refused to pay Mussolini's exorbitant compensation demand, or to allow Italians to take charge of the murder investigation, Italy's new Prime Minister sent his fleet to bombard and then to occupy the Ionian island of Corfu, killing 15 civilians. The Greeks appealed to the League of Nations. Finally, London was shocked out of its detached complacency. Foreign Secretary George Curzon, fresh from having finalized the Lausanne peace settlement with Ataturk and determined to prevent another flare-up in the Mediterranean, denounced Italy's 'conduct' as 'violent and inexcusable'.[23] The British

Embassy in Rome wired to London in panic-stricken tones that Mussolini was a 'mad dog, who may do infinite harm before he is dispatched'. The Italian dictator was 'capable of any ill-considered and reckless action which might even plunge Europe into war'.

Unlike the Ruhr crisis, which was a matter pertaining directly to the Versailles Treaty, the violence in the Ionian Islands was precisely the kind of incident that the League of Nations was designed to de-escalate. Corfu was viewed as a test by all sides. Mussolini did not hide his scorn for a 'League which placed Haiti and Ireland on equality with great powers, which showed impotence in questions of Greco-Turkish conflict, Ruhr or Saar, and reserved its activities for encouraging socialist attacks on Fascisti Italy'.[24] In reply, the British Foreign Office seriously weighed the possibility of imposing full-scale sanctions on Italy. However, a full naval blockade proved too cumbersome. It would have required not only a mobilization of the entire British fleet but the collaboration of all of Italy's neighbours. Nor could it be effective without America. Furthermore, given the unresolved situation in the Ruhr, France had no interest in antagonizing Mussolini. Paris vetoed any attempt to take the issue to the League and insisted that the question be resolved instead through the Conference of Ambassadors in Paris. Their verdict, swiftly delivered on 8 September, was widely considered a travesty of justice for the tough terms it imposed on Greece. But at least Mussolini's attempt to annex Corfu had been foiled. Furthermore, the kack-handed negotiations of the ambassadors strengthened the critics of old-school diplomacy, who insisted that the League must play a greater role in the future. Despite his open contempt for the League, Mussolini was too sensitive a politician not to realize the seriousness of the international indignation he had provoked. Until the more general collapse of the international order in the early 1930s, Corfu marked the limit of his aggression.

Whilst the Corfu crisis was contained, in Germany the crisis escalated sharply. On 13 August 1923, with the population of the Ruhr on the point of starvation, the centre-right government of Chancellor Wilhelm Cuno resigned. Gustav Stresemann took office as Chancellor of a cross-party coalition of national solidarity. Stresemann's accession to power in 1923 was the defining moment in his remarkable trajectory from wartime imperialist ideologue to the architect of a new German foreign policy. The key to Stresemann's understanding of the world was his belief in the central role of American economic power.[25] During the war this had led him to demand that Germany must create for itself an American-sized greater economic sphere in central Europe. In defeat, like his Japanese counterparts, Stresemann came around to the view that America's rise to power was initiating an entirely new era in which Germany's only realistic policy was to accommodate itself to American hegemony and to seek a place for itself as a valued market and invest-ment vehicle for American capital. In August 1923 Stresemann at first hoped that by drawing the Americans and British back into European politics he might be able to avoid capitulating to the French. But Poin-caré had made his conditions clear and neither Washington nor London hurried to Germany's aid.

Berlin was faced with an appalling dilemma. Should the Republic preserve its national honour by continuing to support resistance in the Ruhr even if this came at the price of risking total national disintegra-tion? Or should it seek to come to terms with France? After five weeks of agonizing discussion, on 26 September the Berlin government gave in. The cabinet decided that it would end official support for the Ruhr and seek to meet French demands as best it could. Following the Armis-tice of November 1918 and acceptance of the Versailles terms in June 1919, the autumn of 1923 witnessed Germany's third capitulation and it unleashed a period of truly existential crisis. In 1918 and 1919 Erzberger and the Social Democrats had at least been able to present acceptance of the peace as part of the process of overcoming the Wilhelmine past. They had been united by bonds of wartime patriotism. When a French army marched into the Ruhr, the population had rallied around the Republic as they had around the Wilhelmine Empire in August 1914, only for their hopes to be dashed once more. Across the steel cities of the Ruhr in the autumn of 1923 German police as well as French tanks were required to restrain the outraged population.[26]

The French had won. As Poincaré had promised, the Ruhr occupa-tion had paid dividends. The costs of the operation up to the end of September had come to 700 million francs, against revenues from the Ruhr of 1 billion francs.[27] But France had done far more than vindicate its military power and gain economic advantage. The entire structure of the post-war order was in play. On the French side the possibilities that had been shut down by Clemenceau at Versailles were reopened. Per-haps, after all, France did not have to accept the sovereignty of an integral

German nation.[28] Having shrunk from the task in 1919, in early October 1923 France was presented with a second chance to construct a radically new map of Europe, a second Westphalian peace, which would return to 1648 in founding European security on the disintegration of Germany.

Jacques Bainville, the most penetrating conservative critic of the 1919 peace, was known to exercise considerable influence over Poincaré. On 21 October separatist putsches with more or less overt French sponsorship were launched all along the western rim of Germany, in Aachen, Trier, Koblenz, Bonn and the Palatinate.[29] In practice none of these uprisings had any popular following. When not chaperoned by French troops, German separatists were liable to be lynched. But by the autumn of 1923 the most dangerous threat to the Reich's integrity came not from French intrigue but from within. Germany's long-simmering civil war was coming back to the boil.[30] Since 1920, when the Comintern had demanded that all its members should prepare for civil war, the German Communist Party had been drilling a paramilitary organization. In October 1923 when the leader of the party, Heinrich Brandler, was summoned to Moscow for instructions, he claimed to have at his disposal a force of over 113,000 men.[31]

To coincide with the anniversary not of the German revolution of 1918 but the Bolshevik seizure of power in 1917, the date for the Communist uprising in Germany was set at 9 November 1923.[32] Following a miscommunication with revolutionary headquarters, the local party in the port city of Hamburg launched an ill-prepared uprising on 23 October, which was quickly put down. But Moscow was undaunted. Mobile units of the Red Army were moved to the Polish border along with every available German-speaking officer. In Germany the main body of Communist militancy was massing in the industrial regions in the centre of the country.[33] Worryingly for Berlin, in early October the state government of Saxony was taken over by a United Front coalition headed by left-wing Socialists but including Communist Party ministers who were taking instructions directly from Moscow.[34] On 17 October, under the emergency laws in force since the surrender of 26 September, 60,000 Reichswehr troops were moved into the region. The Reich suspended the authority of the Socialist government and the much-touted Communist militia were rapidly overwhelmed.

Following only weeks after the surrender to France, the result of the Saxon intervention was to throw German politics once more into crisis.

Having been abandoned by the right wing in September, Stresemann's coalition was now deserted by the Socialist Party, which departed in protest against the Reich's lopsided action against the left. The centre-right now had to govern alone, but as far as Stresemann was concerned there was no choice. He had to act against the left in Saxony so as to preserve his grip on the situation in Bavaria, where an even more menacing threat had arisen on the far right. Following the end of the fighting against the Poles in Silesia in 1921, Bavaria had become the rallying place for German admirers of Mussolini.[35] Since the spring of 1923 the youthful rabble-rouser Adolf Hitler had risen to prominence as one of the loudest advocates of a bloody struggle with the French. Invoking the Russian decision to torch their own capital in the face of Napoleonic occupation in 1812, Hitler demanded that the Ruhr must become Poincaré's Moscow on the Rhine.[36] With the brown-shirted stormtroops of the National Socialist German Workers' Party (NSDAP) at his back, Hitler was clearly waiting for his chance to mount a coup, and it was far from obvious how Bavaria's highly conservative state government would react. There was talk of a Bavarian anti-communist crusade against Saxony. In desperation, Chancellor Stresemann appealed to the Reichswehr, only for its commander, General Hans von Seeckt, to reply that whereas he was happy to intervene against the Red Guards in Saxony, he could not order his troops to fire on their Bavarian comrades. There were well-founded rumours in Berlin that Seeckt himself was weighing up the Bonapartist option of putting paid to the Weimar Republic with a 'whiff of grapeshot'.

Despite his personal sympathy for the agenda of the nationalist right, Stresemann was convinced that no authoritarian government could possibly broker the international settlement on which Germany's future depended. By fomenting internal disorder, the conspirators placed in jeopardy the value he held most deeply, the integrity of the Reich itself. Challenging the right wing of his own party, the German People's Party (DVP), to give him their wholehearted backing, Stresemann announced on 5 November 1923 'this week will decide whether the Vaterlaendische Verbaende (nationalist paramilitary associations) will risk a battle'. Were they to challenge the authority of the Reich, the result would be 'civil war' and the 'loss of the Rhine and Ruhr' to the French-backed separatists. To preserve the Reich there must be order at home. He was 'sick and tired' of irresponsible intrigue and the blackmail of the business and agrarian interests who had brought on the hyperinflationary disaster. If the nationalist stormtroops marched on Berlin, Stresemann would stand his ground. They would have to 'shoot' him down in the Reich's Chancellery, where as the head of government he had a 'right to be'.[37]

Berlin was saved from this scenario, by Hitler's impatience and the internecine rivalries of the Bavarian right. On 9 November 1923 it was not the Communists but Hitler and his SA-men with General Erich Ludendorff in their midst who marched through the streets of Munich, to be met with the 'whiff of grapeshot' delivered by the Bavarian police. Hitler fled ignominiously from the scene. The challenge to the Weimar Republic from the right as well as the left had been defeated. Over the next 15 months of incarceration Hitler was to arrive at the conclusion that was also dawning on the Comintern in Moscow: a violent seizure of power was out of the question in modern Germany. If he was to destroy 'the system', Hitler would have to do so from within.

But it was not only the extremists who learned from this crisis. At the very heart of events in 1923 was Konrad Adenauer, the Centre Party Mayor of Cologne, the capital of the Rhineland. After 1949, as the first Chancellor of the Federal Republic, Adenauer would do more than any other individual to shape the West German success story. But already, thirty years earlier, with the British Army occupying his city, Adenauer had made himself into the spokesman for a daring vision of West European pacification. Rather than separating the Rhineland from the Reich, as was advocated by the traitorous collaborators of the French, Adenauer proposed splitting his westward-facing region from the authoritarian grip of Prussia. Prussia's presence in the west of Germany was an unfortunate legacy of the Congress of Vienna, which had sought to erect a buffer against France. The result had been to unbalance the constitution of Germany, out of whose population of 65 million, 42 million were subjects of Prussia. Under Adenauer's federalist vision, an autonomous Rhineland state with 15 million industrious, cosmopolitan inhabitants would give the Reich the balance it needed to steer toward an accommodation with its western neighbour. By breaking the grip of Prussia, an intact German nation state could be reconciled with a peaceful European order.[38]

In 1919 Adenauer had hoped that such a vision would appeal to Britain, which could surely have no interest in the Rhineland becoming a 'French colony'.[39] By 1923, despairing of the British, Adenauer hoped that his plan would appeal to France. Rather than subsidizing a general strike, the German government would pay the coal mines of the Ruhr to make reparations deliveries to France.[40] By the end of 1923 the leading coal and steel baron of the Ruhr, Hugo Stinnes, was lobbying Berlin to approve a megamerger of all the major steel interests in the Ruhr as the economic basis for a 'new state structure' that would have a 'mediating role between France and Germany'.[41] Unlike Gustav Stresemann, who continued to look to Washington and Wall Street, Adenauer and Stinnes had arrived at the conclusion that no 'significant help' was to be 'expected either from America or England'. To the German ambassador in Washington, Stinnes sketched the vision of a 'continental block' based on the Ruhr and the Rhineland that would resist 'Anglo-Saxon' hegemony.[42] Stinnes was now convinced that the entire post-war order was the result of an Anglo-American diktat and threatened that when 'international capitalism attempted to suck Germany out ... the youth of Germany would take up arms'.[43] Emotionally satisfying though such talk might be, it was profoundly out of season. At this moment, the culminating point of the post-war crisis, everything had once more come to pivot on the United States.

II

In the autumn of 1923, with Mussolini on the loose in the Mediterranean, talk of a division of Germany, a new Westphalian peace and Franco-German rapprochement on the Rhine, with Nazis and Communists contending for power, and Stresemann, Ludendorff, Hitler and Adenauer all on the scene simultaneously, it was as though the entire drama of western European history for the next two generations was to be compressed into a matter of months. All the options, from Communist and Fascist coups to the total dismemberment of Germany, were on the table. Would the door swing open already in 1923 to the comprehensive disaster of 1945? If the French and Belgians were enacting revenge for the brutal German occupation of 1914, Hitler's fantasies of a Moscow on the Rhine prefigured the fiery hell that was to consume the Ruhr between 1943 and 1945. Given this remarkable flash of premonition, the outcome of the crisis of 1923 is all the more significant. The order created in 1919 proved more resilient than anyone expected.

In the spring of 1923 the Europeans were certainly enjoying the 'bit of chaos' prescribed by Secretary of State Hughes. But whereas he seemed to expect this to result in a stalemate that would set the stage for America to arbitrate a reasonable solution, in fact the Ruhr crisis had ended in a French victory. Germany was prostrate as never before. It was the prospect of what France might do with its victory that forced the United States and Britain to re-enter the European game. America could not stand by as France divided up Germany or collaborated with the likes of Stinnes in creating a powerful industrial complex that might one day overshadow even America's economic might.[44] On 11 October Hughes reaffirmed the terms of his New Haven speech of the previous December. The United States would extend its backing to an expert inquiry. This was eagerly taken up by London.[45] The question was how the French would respond.

Their reaction was telling. Although he certainly relished France's second victory over Germany, Poincaré, like Clemenceau before him, was above all concerned to found French security on an Anglo-American alliance. Despite the fact that Germany was prostrate at France's feet and a strategy of disintegration was being weighed in Paris, Poincaré never delivered the *coup de grâce*. It was obvious that separatism had little or no support in Germany. Poincaré was wary of the self-interested business schemes of Stinnes and his French counterparts in heavy industry. He did not want to see the French Republic reduced to the plaything of the interest groups that the Weimar Republic had become. After Hitler's coup attempt it was clear that France risked finding itself face to face with an enraged nationalist dictatorship.[46] But finally and most importantly, it was clear that any open attack on German sovereignty would end France's hope of building a new alliance with Britain and the United States.

Rejecting both the ultra-aggressive advocates of Rhineland separation and the Adenauer-Stinnes proposal for a bilateral Franco-German deal, Poincaré agreed to allow committees of experts including prominent Americans to reconsider Germany's reparations payment schedule. The pill was sweetened by misleading hints from London that Washington might be on the point of permitting war debts to be discussed.[47] In fact, no such deal was ever on offer. The French for their part, despite threats from the US, vetoed any discussion of the reparations total. The questions put to the expert committees were indirect: How could reparations be made compatible with stabilizing the German budget and the

German currency? Unlike in 1919, the American government would not be officially present in Paris, but the State Department chose the two US delegates who would chair the main expert committees. Charles Dawes, the leader of the delegation, was a Republican banker from Chicago who on the basis of his war record was considered to be friendly to the French. He was seconded by Owen D. Young, a Wilsonian internationalist, who as chairman of General Electric had close links to Germany through its sister corporation, AEG. As Hughes advised the US Embassy in Paris, the choice of Dawes and Young was in part decided by the fact that despite their interest in Europe, neither of them had ever advocated cancellation of inter-Allied war debts.[48]

The plan that came to bear Dawes's name was worked out in the early months of 1924. It was based on the idea that since Germany had evaporated away its internal debt, if it imposed taxes equal to those of its neighbours then it should be able to generate a cash surplus with which to finance its reparations obligations.[49] The fact that for every debtor relieved by the German inflation there was also an offsetting financial loss was not part of the calculation. Nor did the obvious damage that German productive capacity had suffered during the Ruhr occupation and the hyperinflation enter into the narrowly financial discussions. The Dawes Plan did, however, recognize what was a key problem, the destabilizing effect on the currency markets of exchanging huge quantities of Reichsmarks for dollars. In future, a resident reparations agent would see to it that Berlin's transfers did not unduly destabilize the markets. Funds that could not be safely exchanged would be held on account in Germany, in the name of the creditors. The Dawes committees were not authorized to modify the final reparations total set by the London ultimatum in May 1921. But they did specify a new payments schedule, which by stretching the payments until the 1980s considerably lightened the burden on Germany. After weeks of haggling, Young managed to persuade the French to accept an annuity rising to 2.5 billion Reichsmarks after a grace period of five years.[50]

Given the fact that Germany was on the point of total collapse, this benign outcome is most surprising. France's willingness to accept the Dawes Plan is even more so. But once Anglo-American experts took charge of the discussion, the result was to a degree predictable. It was all the more so given the dramatic shift in the complexion of British politics. Ahead of the Genoa Conference in 1922, Lloyd George had warned

Poincaré of the mounting anti-European mood amongst the opposition Liberals and Labour Party in Britain. In 1923 the combination of the Ruhr crisis and the Corfu incident confirmed his worst fears. Across the entire spectrum of British party politics, a latter-day Wilsonian conception of the Anglo-American role in international affairs came to the fore. In retrospect, to many on the liberal left Britain's entanglement in European affairs through the Entente with Russia and France came to seem a disastrous mistake. The July crisis of 1914, Versailles, and now the Ruhr crisis were the predictable consequences. To bring stability, Britain and the Commonwealth should stand offshore, shoulder to shoulder with the United States, helping through the good offices of the League of Nations and the sound counsel of experts to calm the violence of the continent.

This was natural terrain for both the Liberals and the Labour Party. It was also a conception strongly favoured by the Dominions and thus agreeable to many in the Tory Party. As they had made clear during the Chanak crisis, the empire had no taste for intervention.[51] The outcome of the snap general election held on 6 December 1923 confirmed this new British mood. The Tory Party suffered a disastrous defeat. The big winners were the Asquithian Liberals, the men of Keynes's disposition who since 1916 had favoured a compromise peace, precisely because they, like Wilson, wanted to avoid any unnecessary entanglement between Britain and either Europe or America.

But the party that actually took office in December 1923 was the Labour Party, a composite of middle-class socialists, radical liberals and a phalanx of organized labour, headed by Ramsay MacDonald, who as an out-and-out Wilsonian had during the war suffered insults and political ostracism for his support of a 'peace without victory'.[52] Including the Prime Minister, the first Labour cabinet included 15 ministers who were members of the Union of Democratic Control (UDC), the British pressure group that had corresponded on intimate terms with Wilson as he devised his first peace programme over the winter of 1916–17. Then it had seemed as though it would take the overturning of the existing political order in Europe to achieve their goal. For Downing Street to be occupied by the Labour Party was not a revolution. But it was certainly a political upheaval of dramatic proportions.

As Lloyd George had warned, the new mood in London had serious implications for France. Throughout 1923 Ramsay MacDonald had denounced France's pursuit of reparations as a will-o'-the-wisp. Germany's surrender in the Ruhr was for him the strangulation of a 'broken and disarmed' country by a 'well-armed and powerful country', not a 'success', but a triumph for 'evil'.[53] The only route to peace, he confided to his diary, was to ensure that France was 'reasonable' and ceased 'her policy of selfish vanity'.[54] Philip Snowden, Labour's first Chancellor of the Exchequer, spoke of the Ruhr occupation as the attempted 'enslavement' by France 'of sixty or seventy million of the best educated and most industrious and most scientific people'. E. D. Morel, the UDC activist who had turned his muck-raking instincts against the 'Black Horror on the Rhine' allegedly perpetrated by Senegalese troops, now inveighed against France's effort 'to tear the lungs and heart out of the living body of Germany'.[55]

In France, Poincaré over the winter of 1923–4 was still riding a wave of patriotic enthusiasm, but the currency markets were not confident that France could continue the occupation of the Ruhr in the face of British and American opposition.[56] By December 1923 the pre-war exchange rate of 5.18 francs to the dollar was no more than a fond memory.[57] During the Ruhr occupation the franc had depreciated more than 30 per cent, reaching 20 to the dollar. In early January 1924 Poincaré won a huge vote of confidence in the French Chamber of Deputies. But the parliamentarians were more hesitant when it came to fiscal consolidation. There was no majority for austerity.

Finally on 14 January, just as the delegations were assembling in Paris to begin the Dawes Plan negotiations, the French stock exchange was gripped by a 'grande peur'.[58] Fearing a collapse of the Bourse, Poincaré demanded decree powers to push through the necessary budget cuts and tax increases. The parliamentary majority that had sustained the Ruhr intervention ruptured. The left denounced Poincaré's call for decree powers as an attack on the Republican constitution and demanded a heavy levy on capital, not on wages.[59] Unconvinced by this display, the markets let the franc slide from 90 against the pound early in the year to as little as 123 francs to the pound. To the American ambassador Myron Herrick, Poincaré admitted that he feared the franc might follow the mark 'into oblivion'.[60] But Washington was not sympathetic. As one State Department official noted, 'the franc has fallen very opportunely and the result has been a great increase of reasonableness in this country'.[61]

On 29 February Poincaré agreed to end the Ruhr occupation in

17. 'Red Scare' cartoon by William Allen Rogers showing the expiring Russian bear on a stretcher being carried by allegorical figures of Czechoslovakia, Britain, Japan and America, while the lizard-like Lenin and Trotsky look on, 1918

18. Japanese Red Cross nurses returning from the Siberian intervention, 1919

19. Risking Peace: Matthias Erzberger (*sitting left*) and advisors discussing the future of Danzig, March 1919

20. Patriotic, anti-Japanese protestors in Shanghai, spring 1919

21. Unemployment rally, London, January 1921

22. An old woman being escorted to vote in the Upper Silesia plebiscite, March 1921

23. Normalcy: Warren Harding and Calvin Coolidge

24. The Washington Naval Conference, November 1921

25. Gandhi Day, Delhi, July 1922

26. French troops guarding the entrance hall to the Coal Syndicate, the Ruhr, January 1923

27. Lenin's funeral, Moscow, January 1924

28. Ku Klux Klan
parade, Washington
DC, 1926

29. Architect of peace in East Asia: Japan's Foreign Minister Kijuro Shidehara

30. General Chiang Kai Shek being greeted by crowds in Hankow, 1927

31. Architects of peace in Europe: Aristide Briand and Gustav Stresemann, September 1926

32. Crowds gathering outside the London Stock Exchange after the Gold Standard had been suspended, 21 September 1931

exchange for guarantees of German good behaviour. As a quid pro quo he wanted American support, and he got it. J. P. Morgan was given State Department approval for a $100 million credit. Pressured by the American move, the Bank of England chipped in a short-term loan. This double commitment allowed the Bank of France to pull off a remarkable recovery. Buoyed by the sudden influx of dollars and sterling the franc surged, inflicting substantial losses on bearish speculators. For the Poincaré government this was a triumphant defensive stand, a *Verdun financier*. But Morgan's loan was for no more than six months. Its renewal on a long-term basis was conditional on an effort by the French Chamber of Deputies to stabilize the country's finances fully. Six weeks later, on 11 May, the French electorate recovered its balance. Recoiling from the nationalist emotion of November 1919, it restored the left-republican majority that had been the norm before the war. The *Cartel de Gauche* (Cartel of the Left) government claimed victory. Poincaré, now excoriated as the architect of futile brutality in the Ruhr, resigned.

The new government, headed by Edouard Herriot of the left Radicals, the grouping that Clemenceau had once called home, came into office with a programme of progressive social reforms, including an extension of the eight-hour day, public sector unionization and income tax increases.[62] The Socialists gave their backing in the Chamber of Deputies, though they refused the responsibility of government. In foreign policy, Herriot reaffirmed the principles of internationalism upon which the likes of Léon Bourgeois had long insisted as essential to French republicanism. Paris hoped this would please London and Washington. There would be no more of Poincaré's aggression. But with Poincaré also went the calm in the financial markets. Within days of the left taking office, the franc resumed its alarming slide. The evidence suggests that this was a 'natural' adjustment to the overvaluation achieved by Poincaré. But to the French left it could not but seem that Herriot was being crushed against a *mur d'argent* (wall of money).

To make matters worse, over the summer of 1924 the full consequences of the design of the Dawes Plan dawned on the Herriot government. Under the terms of the plan, the process of reparations settlement was to be lubricated by a large international loan headed by Wall Street. However, the loan was not to go to London or to Paris, but to the government of Germany. Both British and American banks had demonstrated their willingness to lend to France, even under distressed circumstances. Lending to Germany was a novel proposition and for Jack Morgan certainly a distasteful one.[63] But the State Department was insistent. The result was to split the coalition between the Entente and Wall Street established in 1915. To establish Germany as a viable borrower required Morgan's to insist on priority for its bondholders over the claims of the French government. Investors needed to be assured that in case of reparations default, France would not send its troops back into the Ruhr. Not only was French fiscal policy subject to the scrutiny of financial markets, its foreign policy would be as well.

Of course, taming French foreign policy was the aim of the State Department. But the structure of the Dawes Plan allowed the American government to vanish into the background. As Secretary of State Hughes put it to the German ambassador Otto Wiedfeldt on 2 July 1924, Washington would neither guarantee the Dawes Plan nor could it assume responsibility for any loan to Germany. Any such commitment 'would arouse partisan controversy in the United States and engender a destructive legislative-executive struggle over the control of foreign policy. The US government . . . could play a much more constructive role by rendering disinterested advice, helping to reconcile European positions, and encouraging the mobilization of private capital . . .'[64] Hughes was actually in Europe in the summer of 1924 but not in his capacity as Secretary of State. He travelled as a member of a delegation of the American Bar Association. His advice to the American ambassador to Britain, Frank B. Kellogg, was nevertheless unambiguous: If the French government were to demand the right to impose military sanctions on Germany, 'you might then say that while you could not speak for the Government of the United States . . . on the basis of your knowledge of views of American investment public, that under those conditions the loan could not be floated in the United States'.[65]

The Herriot government thought it had reason to expect solidarity from its comrades in the British Labour Party. But given the Wilsonian orientation of MacDonald, the effect was rather the reverse. There were expressions of barely contained excitement in Downing Street as the 'French militarists' were humbled by the plunging franc.[66] On 23 July 1924 Prime Minister Herriot and his Minister of Finance, Étienne Clémentel, the one-time advocate of inter-Allied economic integration, were reduced to pleading with J. P. Morgan to accept the retention of at least basic elements of the Versailles Treaty. The Reparations Commission must retain the right to declare default. To ensure German compliance French troops must stay in the Ruhr for at least two further years.

Over the weeks that followed, Herriot was forced to concede both points. At Young's suggestion, the commission remained nominally sovereign in deciding German default. But when considering any such case the Americans would have the right to send a delegate to join the commission. Any decision to declare a default would have to be unanimous and would be referred to an arbitral commission, chaired by an American. In the unlikely case that sanctions were agreed on, the financial claims of Dawes creditors would have absolute priority. Behind the scenes more direct forms of pressure were applied. In August 1924 with anxiety again mounting about the franc, Paris appealed to J. P. Morgan to renew the $100 million loan granted in March. Morgan's made clear that it was willing to do so, but only if France pursued a determined fiscal consolidation combined with a 'peaceful foreign policy'. Again the bankers got their way. Under an American-brokered compromise, France agreed to withdraw from the Ruhr within a year.

Of course, the rescue of German democracy from the crisis of 1923 was a very real achievement of transatlantic diplomacy and it demanded sacrifices from all sides. Gustav Stresemann is often described as a *Vernunftrepublikaner* and it is probably true that he remained a monarchist at heart. But if *Vernunft* is taken to imply merely cynical calculation, this does not do him justice. The *Vernunft* that came to the fore in the battle to stabilize the Weimar Republic was 'reason of state' in a fuller sense. On 29 March 1924, when he addressed the national conference of the German National People's Party (DNVP) in Hanover, Stresemann pointed out that it would be the easiest thing to become the most popular man in the country by joining Hitler in demanding that Germany should march with the Kaiser's 'black white red banner across the Rhine'. But such populism would be profoundly irresponsible.[67] The 'cry for a dictator' was the worst 'political dilettantism'.[68] The right wing of his party, the heirs to the National Liberals of Bismarck's day, might be attracted by the idea of marginalizing the SPD and making common cause with the radical nationalists of the DNVP, all the more so when the latter ran the Social Democrats close in the May 1924 general election, emerging as the second party in the Reichstag. But in the midst of the delicate Dawes Plan negotiations, Stresemann rejected any such move. The pan-German rhetoric of the DNVP, laced with liberal doses of anti-Semitism, was not suitable 'for export'.[69] Only a responsible Republican politics could preserve a minimum of order at home and working relations with Britain and the United States.

But German stabilization was not built on Stresemann's skilful politics alone. It required painful spending cuts and tax increases. This was where the question of dictatorship became truly pressing. To break out of the deadlock of the interest groups that had impelled the inflation, the government, with SPD support, had invoked the presidential powers of Friedrich Ebert.[70] The deflation they imposed after November 1923 was savage and brought huge cuts both in public sector staffing and real wages. But it was not one-sided. In real terms the Reich's tax take quintupled between December 1923 and the New Year. The German business community never reconciled itself to the Republic's high level of social spending. But this balancing was deliberate. Like Stresemann and the austere Finance Minister Hans Luther, Hjalmar Schacht, the dynamic banker brought in to head the Reichsbank after the debacle of hyperinflation, was committed above all to restoring the authority of the German state, both within and without. For Schacht the Reichsbank was the 'one economic power position from which the state is in a position to successfully fight the assault of the special interests'.[71] After years of corporate excess and disastrous inflation, 'the German business community' would have to learn, he insisted, 'to obey, not to command'.[72]

But however determined this programme of domestic consolidation, following the Reichstag election results of May 1924, not even the votes of the SPD were sufficient to carry the constitutional amendments necessary to ratify the Dawes Plan, which included an international mortgage on the Reichsbahn. Over a quarter of the German electorate had voted for the far right – 19 per cent for the DNVP, almost 7 per cent for Hitler's NSDAP. Almost 13 per cent had opted for the Communists. The two-thirds majority would have to include at least some deputies from the DNVP, intransigent foes of the Versailles Treaty and the progenitors of the 'stab in the back' legend. So concerned were the foreign powers that the American ambassador Alanson Houghton intervened directly in German party politics, summoning leading figures in the DNVP to explain bluntly that if they rejected the Dawes Plan, it would be one hundred years before America ever assisted Germany again. Under huge pressure from their business backers, on 29 August

1924 enough DNVP members defected to the government side to ratify the plan. In exchange, the Reich government offered a sop to the nationalist community by formally renouncing its acceptance of the war-guilt clause of the Versailles Treaty.

Nevertheless, on 10 October 1924 Jack Morgan bit his tongue and signed the loan agreement that committed his bank along with major financial interests in London, Paris and even Brussels to the 800-million Goldmarks loan.[73] The loan was to apply the salve of business common sense to the wounds left by the war. And it was certainly an attractive proposition. The issuers of the Dawes Loan paid only 87 cents on the dollar for their bonds. They were to be redeemed with a 5 per cent premium. For the 800 million Reichsmarks it received, Germany would service bonds with a face value of 1.027 billion.[74]

But if Morgan's were bewildered by the role they had been forced to play, this speaks to the eerie quality of the reconfiguration of international politics in 1924. The Labour government that hosted the final negotiations in London was the first socialist government elected to preside over the most important capitalist centre of the old world, supposedly committed by its party manifesto of 1919 to a radical platform of nationalization and social transformation. And yet in the name of 'peace' and 'prosperity' it was working hand in glove with an avowedly conservative administration in Washington and the Bank of England to satisfy the demands of American investors, in the process imposing a damaging financial settlement on a radical reforming government in France, to the benefit of a German Republic, which was at the time ruled by a coalition dominated by the once notorious annexationist, but now reformed Gustav Stresemann.

'Depoliticization' is a euphemistic way of describing this tableau of mutual evisceration.[75] Certainly, it had been no plan of Wilson's New Freedom to raise Morgan's to such heights. In fact, even Morgan's did not want to own the terms of the Dawes settlement. Whereas Wilson had invoked public opinion as the final authority, this was now represented by the 'investing' public, for whom the bankers, as financial advisors, were merely the spokesmen. But if a collective humbling of the European political class had been what lay behind Wilson's call for a 'peace without victory' eight years earlier, one can't help thinking that the Dawes Plan and the London Conference of 1924 must have had him chuckling in his freshly dug grave. It was a peace. There were certainly no European victors.

25

The New Politics of War and Peace

In June 1927 Gustav Stresemann, then the German Foreign Minister, rose before the packed Aula of Oslo University to deliver his Nobel Peace Prize acceptance speech.[1] His words were broadcast to audiences across Norway, Sweden and Denmark. Stresemann was honoured along with Aristide Briand and Austen Chamberlain for their collective efforts in steering their countries toward what was widely hailed as the first true peace of the post-war era – the Locarno Security Pact which had been negotiated within a year of the Dawes Plan and ratified at Geneva on 14 September 1926. Locarno was a status quo pact, solemnly guaranteeing the borders of western Europe. Stresemann made no secret of the fact that it was harder for the vanquished to accept than for the victors. It was precisely his track record as a standard-bearer of German imperialism and cheerleader for unrestricted U-boat warfare that made the occasion so significant. But his rhetoric was sincere. Locarno meant, he declaimed, the realization of a common European dream, the Carolingian vision that '*Treuga Dei*, the peace of God' might prevail on the Rhine, 'where for centuries bloody wars have raged . . .'. And he assured his audience: 'The youth of Germany can be won over to the same cause. Youth sees its ideal of individual physical and spiritual achievement in the peaceful competition of the Olympic Games and, I hope, in technical and intellectual development as well . . . Germany faces this future with a stable nation . . . based upon hard work . . . and upon a vital spirit which strives for peace in accordance with the philosophies of Kant and Fichte.'

In the second half of the 1920s such post-political visions were not the stuff of ridicule. They counted as Realpolitik.[2] What other lesson was one to draw from the decade-long crisis between 1914 and 1924?

The era in which great-power war could be reckoned a reasonable tool of policy, other than in self-defence, was surely over. What did anyone have to show for the lives lost and the billions spent since 1914? Britain had won a great victory but then frittered away its credit in a disastrous series of post-war affairs at Amritsar, in Ireland, in the Middle East. The Italians had raged against their mutilated victory. Mussolini had attacked Corfu but could not hold it. The Japanese had been presented with a heaven-sent opportunity to fulfil their imperialist dreams in Russia and China, but had been unable to capitalize on them. The Germans had won a great victory in the East, but had been unable to consolidate a legitimate peace. In the West they had been forced to accept defeat not once but three times. And what did the French, who had defeated them most recently in 1923, have to show for their victory?

There was not one single reason for this frustration of power. But there were certain patterns. Whether on the battlefield or on the home front, whether on the docks of Shanghai, the fields of Ukraine or the steel mills of the Ruhr, war was no longer contained. The costs, even of victory, were exorbitant. Self-determination might be hard to define and harder to realize, but pretensions to imperial overlordship were quickly resented and loudly denounced. At home, resources for imperial adventures had always been scarce. The war had made them scarcer and democracy had imposed real constraints, both in terms of the priorities of government expenditure and the legitimation of rule. Finally, the competition between the powers in military, economic and political terms acted as a fundamental countervailing force. The fetters that shackled the international 'chain gang' together were real.[3] As Britain found to its detriment in the Middle East, seemingly low-cost acquisitions in one arena could come at a very high price in another strategic venue, whether that be on the Rhine or in Bengal.

But if there was one common denominator in all these frustrations it was the overshadowing of the European power states – a model originating in seventeenth-century Europe and imported to Asia by Japan – by the challenges of a new era and the rise in the form of the United States of a different focus of economic, political and military authority. As a memo compiled by the British Foreign Office put it in November 1928: 'Great Britain is faced in the United States of America with a phenomenon for which there is no parallel in our modern history – a state twenty-five times as large, five times as wealthy, three times as populous, twice as ambitious, almost invulnerable, and at least our equal in prosperity, vital energy, technical equipment, and industrial science. This state has risen to its present state of development at a time when Great Britain is still staggering from the effects of the superhuman effort made during the war, is loaded with a great burden of debt, and is crippled by the evil of unemployment.' However frustrating it might be to search for cooperation with the United States, the conclusion could not be avoided: 'in almost every field, the advantages to be derived from mutual co-operation are greater for us than for them'.[4] If this was true for Britain and its empire, it was all the more so for all the other, once great powers. The question it posed for all of them was the same. If confrontation was not an option, what would be the terms of 'mutual cooperation' under this new dispensation?

I

One of the decisions of the ill-starred Genoa Conference that was overshadowed by the eclat of the Rapallo Treaty in April 1922 was a resolution to return to a common gold-exchange standard. Washington's engagement with the Dawes Plan and the establishment of the new Reichsmark on gold in 1924 demonstrated that this was now a common transatlantic priority. Gold was the anchor of normalcy restored, a guarantee of the financial order. But as experience since 1920 had shown, the consequences were bound to be painful.[5] Any settlement of the monetary order was tied to an agreement on both domestic and international debts. Germany's situation, in this respect, was peculiar in that its domestic debt burden had been evaporated by hyperinflation. Though it was burdened with reparations, the country's international balance sheet was otherwise a clean slate. It was not, like Britain, France or Italy, saddled with heavy inter-Allied debts. Meanwhile, Germany's once prosperous businesses and its well-run cities offered plenty of first-class collateral.

The result was that the stabilization of the Weimar Republic was underpinned after 1924 by a dramatic influx of American credit, offered to private business and all levels of government other than the bankrupt Reich.[6] The fact that this influx of capital implied a deficit on the trade account, upward pressure on prices and wages, and an uncompetitive exchange rate was of little concern, so long as the money flowed. The fact that there might in due course be a reckoning was not even unwelcome from Stresemann's point of view. In the event of a crisis Berlin hoped to be able to play its new American creditors against the reparations claims of Britain and France. Debts owed to America would become a lever of revision.[7] As Stresemann remarked in an unbuttoned moment in 1925: 'One must simply have enough debts; one must have so many debts that, if the debtor collapses, the creditor sees his own existence jeopardized.'[8]

In the wake of the fiasco of Lloyd George's European policy in 1922, Britain had washed its hands of the European debt and reparations imbroglio. The war debt settlement with the United States in January 1923 was painful, but it restored Britain's credit. Since 1920, the Treasury and Bank of England had been applying sustained deflationary pressure. From the point of view of the US, after Germany was secured under the Dawes Plan, pushing Britain back to the gold standard was the next priority. If Britain rejoined, the empire and much of the rest of the European and Latin American economy would follow. Ramsay MacDonald's Labour government hesitated, hearing evidence from critics such as the former Chancellor Reginald McKenna and his chief advisor John Maynard Keynes. Unless there was a pick-up in inflation in the United States, the final convergence to parity between the British and American price levels would be agonizing. Though the UK had recovered from the depths of the 1920–21 recession, and the trade unions were quiescent by October 1924, Britain was in the grips of a full-blown Red Scare. The left wing of the Labour Party called for the nationalization of the Bank of England and the right-wing *Daily Mail* circulated rumours of Soviet subversion.

On 29 October 1924, Britain's first Labour government was ousted by a Conservative landslide led by Stanley Baldwin. With the City of London looking for a system that was permanently 'knave proof' and the United States threatening to lever away Canada and South Africa, on 28 April 1925 Winston Churchill, as Chancellor of the Exchequer, made the announcement that Britain would resume gold-convertibility.[9] By the end of the year 35 currencies worldwide were either officially convertible into gold or had been stabilized for at least a year. As one of its contemporary critics observed, it was the 'most comprehensive' effort at concerted international economy policy 'the world had ever seen'. Fragile peripheral economies such as Austria, Hungary, Bulgaria, Finland, Romania and Greece 'literally starved themselves to reach the golden shores'.[10]

In Britain, the effect was not quite so severe, but the return to gold at the pre-war rate further reduced the competitiveness of the export-oriented staple industries, notably coal mining. Over the winter of 1925–6 a rancorous dispute between mine owners and workers sparked British industrial militancy back into life. On 4 May 1926 the TUC dared to do what it had shrunk from doing in the aftermath of the war. It declared a general strike. On the first day 1.75 million workers stayed away from work. It was a huge stoppage by any standard and it sent ripples of excitement through the international socialist movement. Back in 1920 it might have been enough to force the government's hand. But the Tories in 1926 had a solid parliamentary majority. Britain was no longer the supplier of last resort to all of Europe. Coal was now coming plentifully out of German and Polish mines. The Conservatives had had many months to prepare for the confrontation with the miners. The trade unions were weakened by six years of mass unemployment. Their solidarity was fragile. With workers drifting back to work en masse, already by 11 May the TUC was suing for peace. It was to be the final spasm of the great wave of labour unrest that had begun in the years before World War I. In Moscow the defeat was seen as a clear sign of the passing of the post-war phase of revolutionary activism.[11]

With Britain leading the deflationary drive, the question was posed to its former partners in the Entente. In 1920 Italy, Japan and France had chosen not to follow Britain and the US in their deflationary push. Would they conform to the restored gold standard? Italy's war debt burden relative to its income was the heaviest of all the Entente powers. Prime Minister Francesco Nitti and the other struggling liberal governments of the post-war period had pleaded for concessions from Washington, but in vain. By contrast, Mussolini's regime could count on considerable sympathy in the State Department and on Wall Street.[12] In November 1925 Italy's well-connected Finance Minister, the industrialist Guiseppe Volpi, concluded an extremely favourable war debt deal, opening the door to a flow of new credit from Wall Street (Table 12).[13] This allowed Italy to ride out the turbulence in foreign exchange markets in 1926 and to peg the lira to the pound at 90 in August 1926, the prevailing rate at the moment when Mussolini had taken power four

Table 12. Coming to Terms with Washington: War Debt Agreements, 1923–30

debtor	date of agreement	date from which debt was funded	total annuities payable ($ million)	% of total debt owed	effective rate of interest on debt
Finland	1 May 1923	14 Dec 1922	22	82	3.31
Great Britain	18 Jun 1923	15 Dec 1925	11,106	82	3.31
Hungary	25 Apr 1924	15 Dec 1933	5	82	3.31
Lithuania	22 Sep 1924	15 Jun 1924	15	82	3.31
Poland	14 Nov 1924	15 Dec 1922	482	32	3.31
Belgium	18 Aug 1925	15 Jun 1925	728	54	1.79
Latvia	24 Sep 1925	15 Dec 1922	16	32	3.31
Czechoslovakia	13 Oct 1925	15 Jun 1925	313	80	3.33
Estonia	28 Oct 1925	14 Dec 1922	38	82	3.31
Italy	14 Nov 1925	15 Jun 1925	2,408	32	0.41
Romania	4 Dec 1925	15 Jun 1925	123	89	3.32
France	29 Apr 1926	15 Jun 1925	6,848	50	1.64
Yugoslavia	3 May 1926	15 Jun 1925	95	79	1.03
Greece	10 May 1929	1 Jan 1928	38	34	0.25
Austria	8 May 1930	1 Jan 1928	25	40	
total			22,262		2.135

years earlier. Fascism had stopped the slide. And unlike in Britain, in Fascist Italy there was no general strike to fear. Mussolini's *squadristi* had done their work in the street battles of 1920–22. In 1927 the full force of the dictatorship was used to impose a 20 per cent wage cut.

Japan's return to the gold standard was ill-starred.[14] In 1923, after three years of deflation, the yen had come within striking distance of its pre-war exchange rate against the dollar, only for Japan to be hit on 1 September by one of the most devastating earthquakes in modern history. With 140,000 dead, half a million homeless, and a large part of urban Japan in ruins, the Bank of Japan was forced to respond with emergency credit measures. Foreign currency drained out of the country and after ten years of accumulating foreign assets, Japan was forced in January 1924 to resort to a loan brokered by J. P. Morgan at the punitive rate of 6.5 per cent. Reminiscent of pre-war terms, it was dubbed the 'national humiliation loan'.[15] No less clearly, the loan marked the definitive shift in Japan's source of finance from London to New York.[16] Three years later the general move toward gold-standard restoration took Japan once more back to the pre-war rate only for disaster to strike again, this time in the form of a major banking crisis that forced the closure of three dozen banks. In 1927, with the currency trading at a comfortable discount to its pre-war parity, the new expansively minded Seiyukai government decided to suspend any further attempt toward a gold-standard return so that it might concentrate on the growing Nationalist challenge in China. Japanese national development, if necessary with state involvement, was the priority. As in Mussolini's Italy, Wall Street interests led by J. P. Morgan fell into line with remarkable complacency (Table 13).

France's experience was rather more painful. In November 1924, as the Dawes loan for Germany was pushed through, J. P. Morgan asked the State Department for permission to consolidate Prime Minister Poincaré's short-term loan of $100 million. But Washington had other priorities. There would be no more credit for France until it had put its domestic finances in order and settled the repayment of the $3.5 billion owing in inter-Allied debts. As of April 1925 the Coolidge administration imposed a complete loan embargo, starting with the cancellation of a large loan to the city of Paris. That same month Édouard Herriot's ill-fated *Cartel de Gauche* government was defeated in the French Senate, ushering in a period of political and financial instability that ended only at the end of November 1925 when Aristide Briand returned as Prime Minister. He promptly sought a debt agreement with Washington. The resulting Mellon-Berenger accord provided for complete repayment over 60 years at a concessionary rate of 1.6 per cent. The initial annual payment would be $30 million.

Anxious to secure the deal, Andrew Mellon had the proposal approved by the US House of Representatives, but when the plan was put before the French public in the early summer of 1926 the patriotic backlash was dramatic. The Mellon-Berenger accord was denounced as 'servitude with hard labour and for life'. Briand was accused of having 'put a noose around the throat of France'. In July, 25,000 French veterans marched in silent protest against the 'vultures of international finance'.[17] The US ambassador Myron T. Herrick reported that American bankers were evacuating their families from Paris for fear of a hot summer of anti-Americanism. On 21 July, as nationalist protest surged across Paris, with thousands modelling themselves on Mussolini's blackshirts, the franc, which in 1914 had stood proudly at 25.22 to the pound, plunged to 238.50. In annualized terms, in July 1926 French inflation hit 350 per cent.[18] With rumours circulating of a right-wing coup possibly to be led by Marshal Pétain, the Republican political class rallied. Poincaré took office once more at the head of a cross-party coalition including his predecessor Herriot and four other former prime ministers.[19] Briand returned as Foreign Secretary. A constitutionally autonomous public debt agency was established to guarantee repayment to France's domestic creditors.[20] Confidence rebounded and on 17 August the franc hit 179 to the pound and continued to rise.

In December 1926 the franc was stabilized at the aggressively priced exchange rate of 124 to the pound, or roughly 25 to the dollar.[21] This inflicted a heavy loss on France's domestic creditors. It increased the cost of imported goods into the country, but it also helped to bolster exports and made it extremely attractive to purchase French assets, bringing an unprecedented flow of gold to Paris. The stabilization not only asserted the durability of the French Republic. Poincaré was drawing conclusions from the humiliating settlement imposed on France after its victory in the Ruhr. Back in 1924 France's financial weakness had laid it at the mercy of Britain and America. In the autumn of 1926, however, the gold flowing into the Bank of France helped, as its governor put it, to 'reinforce in international relations the prestige and

Table 13 Doux Commerce: US Private Long-Term Foreign Investment, December 1930 (million $)

	direct investment	portfolio total	portfolio government guaranteed	portfolio private	total	% of world total
Austria	17	98	93	5	115	0.7
Belgium	65	189	189	0	254	1.6
France	162	310	300	10	472	3.1
Germany	244	1177	801	376	1421	9.1
Hungary	10	109	49	60	119	0.7
Italy	121	280	171	109	401	2.6
Poland	53	124	124	0	177	1.1
UK	497	144	144	0	641	3.9
total Europe	1468	3461	2567	894	4929	31.4
Africa	115	3	3	0	118	0.7
China	130	0	0	0	130	0.8
Dutch E Indies	66	135	135	0	201	1.3
Japan	62	383	241	142	445	2.8
Philippines	82	85	71	14	167	1.1
total Asia	420	603	447	156	1023	6.5

Australia and NZ	155	264	262	2	419	2.7
Canada	2049	1893	1270	623	3942	25.2
Mexico	694	0	0	0	694	4.4
Cuba	936	131	127	4	1067	6.8.
Argentina	359	449	449	0	808	5.2
Brazil	210	347	344	3	557	3.5
Chile	441	260	260	0	701	4.5
Colombia	130	172	144	28	302	1.9
Peru	125	75	75	20	300	1.3
Venezuela	247	0	0	0	247	1.6
total Latin America	3634	1610	1575	35	5244	33.5
adjusted total					15170	

independence of the country'.[22] Poincaré chose rather more dramatic language. Through their 'internal effort' his French countrymen would free themselves from the 'yoke of Anglo-Saxon finance'.[23] By the summer of 1927 Paris had accumulated gold and foreign exchange reserves totalling $540 million. It did not match the $6 billion France owed Britain and the United States in war debts, but it was a useful *masse de manoeuvre* with which to counterbalance any financial pressure, particularly from the Bank of England.[24]

II

The Washington treaties in 1921 had halted the arms race in capital ships. In 1924 the Dawes Plan, whilst setting the stage for the economic restoration of the post-war system, defanged the Versailles Treaty. In effect, it precluded any further use of the French Army to ensure compliance. But this begged the question. Who or what would provide for the security of Europe? In the autumn of 1924, to compensate the French for the humiliation dealt to them over the Dawes Plan, Prime Minister Ramsay MacDonald joined Édouard Herriot at the League of Nations to launch a plan to beef up the League Covenant with a compulsory arbitration procedure, backed by an automatic sanctions regime and a major new disarmament initiative. But the momentum behind the so-called Geneva Protocols dissipated when Britain's first Labour government was toppled in October 1924. Though the incoming Conservative Foreign Secretary, Austen Chamberlain, was a true Francophile, the rest of the Tory cabinet did not want to shackle Britain to a system of compulsory League arbitration.

Furthermore, the Geneva Protocols had produced a startlingly hostile reaction from Washington. Rather than welcoming the European initiative, Secretary of State Charles Evans Hughes responded that given the stiffness of the proposed sanctions mechanism, the United States would have to regard the League as potentially hostile.[25] The US would not tolerate a maritime blockade unilaterally imposed by the British and French navies, even if this had the backing of the League of Nations. For the British the jeopardy in which they had found themselves during 1916, facing a potentially hostile United States in a transatlantic stand-off, had come to seem a nightmare that they must avoid at all costs.[26] The only solution agreeable to Hughes was for Washington to be given a veto over the implementation of any League sanctions. But as Chamberlain pointed out, that would be to place Washington on a par with the collective authority of the League and would thus confer on the United States the status of a 'super-State ... a court of appeal from all proceedings of the League'. When Britain's ambassador in America, Sir Esme Howard, replied that 'we all have to face facts sometime', Chamberlain shot back that 'there is a difference between recognition of a fact and public proclamation of its consequences'.[27]

Chamberlain himself would have preferred to renew the offer of a bilateral British security guarantee for France. This was strongly supported by the British chiefs of staff. In a fiercely worded memorandum in February 1925, Britain's senior soldiers insisted that it was misleading to regard such a promise as a concession to France. It was a matter of essential British self-interest and 'only incidentally a question of French security . . .'. The war had revealed that 'The true strategic frontier of Great Britain is the Rhine; her security depends entirely upon the present frontiers of France, Belgium and Holland being maintained and remaining in friendly hands.'[28] The problem was that the French would not be satisfied with a Rhine guarantee. They wanted comprehensive military backing for the frontiers of eastern Europe. This was too much for London to contemplate. The return to the gold standard required maximum economy, not even greater commitments.[29] Instead, on 20 March 1925, London announced that it was taking up a proposal made by Germany for a Rhineland security pact. This would guarantee the western borders of Europe and normalize relations with Germany by bringing it into the League. It would also have the effect of ensuring that Germany remained firmly bound to the 'system of the West'.[30] The terrifying Rapallo scenario of a Russo-German alliance would be banished.

The results of this process of compromise were the Locarno Treaties, ratified in September 1926. Notoriously, though they secured Europe's western boundaries, they left the question of the eastern frontiers open. Germany and Poland remained unreconciled. The road to German expansion in the East was not barred shut. But as a great-power security system this was not the chief deficiency of the treaties. The real problem was not in the East, but in the West. The basic question was the attitude of America. Without backing from America, could Britain and France really contain German aggression whether directed eastwards or westwards? In 1927 it was Paris that took the initiative to try to re-engage the United States with Europe. On 7 April, the tenth anniversary of America's entry into the war, Aristide Briand proposed to Washington a bilateral security treaty between France and the US.[31] The State Department was loath to enter into any such special relationship. But given the prevailing public sentiment, the Coolidge administration could hardly deny the attractiveness of a non-aggression pact. As a substitute, in December 1927 Secretary of State Frank Kellogg proposed a multilateral pact to renounce war.[32]

On the afternoon of 27 August 1928, with Kellogg himself in attendance, 15 powers gathered in Paris to endorse a treaty that required its signatories to 'condemn recourse to war for the solution of international controversies, and renounce it as an instrument of national policy in their relations with one another'. It was the first time since 1870 that a German Foreign Minister had been officially received at the Quai d'Orsay.[33] The Germans had hoped to include the Soviets in the signing ceremony, but that was too much for Washington. Nevertheless the Soviet Union became the first to ratify what became known as the Kellogg-Briand Pact.[34] In the course of 1928, no fewer than 33 powers signed on. By 1939, its signatories had reached 60 in number. It was the crowning glory of the new ideology of peace that dominated the late 1920s, a vision of the 'world existing in peace' as 'normal and normative', a world in which war was redefined as nothing less than a criminal 'aberration'.[35] Easily ridiculed, overwhelmed during the following generation by terrifying violence, the Kellogg-Briand Pact was not without historical vindication. In 1945, when the Allies were formulating the indictment of the Nazi leadership before the International Military Tribunal at Nuremberg, the main charge against the defendants was neither the familiar canon of war crimes codified in the nineteenth century, nor the relatively novel concept of crimes against humanity, let alone genocide, which as yet barely featured in the minds of international lawyers. The central point of the indictment drawn up by the American prosecutors was Nazi Germany's violation of Kellogg-Briand, its crimes against peace.

The difference was that in 1945 the United States appeared as the conquering champion of a new era of internationalism. In 1928 both the French and the British had reason to read the Kellogg-Briand peace pact as an American evasion. How was it to be enforced? Washington had given no approval for British naval action. It had insisted that the pact be kept at a distance from the League. This did nothing to calm French anxiety. In 1923 Poincaré had responded to the Anglo-American refusal to take seriously France's security needs by occupying the Ruhr. Now France opted to work around the American roadblock through European cooperation. In September 1926, after welcoming Germany as a full member of the League of Nations, Foreign Minister Briand held secret talks with Gustav Stresemann.[36] Since Germany could access American capital markets and France could not, it was proposed that the Reich should launch a large loan on Wall Street, allowing it to make a large down payment to France. In exchange, France would return the Saar coal mines and accelerate the withdrawal of its troops from the Rhineland.

If the aim of American policy was to drive France and Germany toward a rational solution to their differences, one might have expected Washington to welcome the so-called 'Thoiry initiative'. But instead it chose to interpret the Franco-German proposal as an aggressive move to form a debtors' cartel. The State Department vetoed the plan. Germany could borrow on its own behalf. But if it was to borrow for France, Poincaré must first persuade the French parliament to swallow a distasteful war debt deal. Indeed, to raise the pressure further, Washington gave notice that unless the Mellon-Berenger debt deal was finally ratified, it would present France in 1929 with a demand in cash for $400 million. True to his policy of reasserting France's credibility, Poincaré did not blink. A titanic two-week struggle in the Chamber of Deputies in July 1929 over the American war debts was the last act of his political career. It broke his health and forced him into retirement at the age of 69, but ratification of Mellon-Berenger put the seal on the restoration of French credit-worthiness.[37]

Britain too was torn between conflicting impulses. There was intense frustration in Baldwin's Conservative government over continuing American challenges to the legality of naval blockade. The UK Treasury fumed over every instalment of the war debts. By 1928 there were the rumblings of a strategic realignment. Perhaps London's gamble on a strategic relationship with America had been a mistake. Perhaps Britain would do better to rally the empire as a counterweight to the United States. Or perhaps Britain ought to join France in pushing for a consolidated European bloc, including Germany and the Benelux countries. But London hesitated. Any move away from Washington was fraught with risks. If Britain were to pit the empire against the United States, the likely result would be the defection of Canada, which as part of the new and fuller conception of Dominion status had been granted permission to open its own embassy in Washington. If, on the other hand, Britain chose to pursue the European option, this would give enormous leverage to Germany. As the Foreign Office recognized, the United States was 'a phenomenon for which there is no parallel' in Britain's 'modern history'. The advantages to Britain of cooperating with the US were vast, whereas confrontation was unthinkable.[38] Like the French, the British government resolved not to back away, but instead to attempt to consolidate the transatlantic relationship.[39]

This resolve was only reinforced when Labour under Ramsay MacDonald took office for a second time after the general election of 30 May 1929. As a convinced Atlanticist and Francophobe, MacDonald's overriding priority was to patch up relations with the United States. He was all the more enthusiastic to be dealing with the quintessential exponent of interwar progressivism, the freshly elected Herbert Hoover. As Trotsky mockingly remarked, it was no longer Anglo-French talks that mattered: 'If you want to discuss *seriously* then take the trouble to cross the Atlantic.'[40] MacDonald became the first of a long line of European statesmen eager to inaugurate his term in office with a trip to America. In October 1929 at the President's rustic retreat at Rapidan Camp in Virginia, sitting on opposite ends of a tree trunk, out of earshot of the panic on Wall Street, Hoover and MacDonald settled the agenda for what the newspapers promised would be a new, comprehensive naval disarmament conference to be hosted in London early in 1930.[41]

III

Robust as these structures appeared to be and resilient in the face of disappointment, if the Locarno Treaty was one anchor of the post-war order and the Pacific treaties signed at Washington were the other, then a striking feature of this new geopolitics was that it was incomplete. 'In between' Locarno and Washington loomed the Eurasian land mass dominated by the Soviet Union. Conversely, as seen from the point of view of Moscow, the marches of the new world order – Poland and China – appeared in the mid-1920s as twin arenas in the ongoing struggle between revolution and counter-revolution. In this struggle Moscow was on the defensive. The fact that Poland's borders with Germany were ostentatiously excluded from the Locarno Treaty was no doubt cause for anxiety in Warsaw. But when Marshal Pilsudski staged a *coup d'état* in May 1926, it was in Moscow that the alarm bells rang.[42] The Soviets only too well remembered his aggression six years earlier.

Pilsudksi, however, was now in defensive mode. His aim was to maintain the balance within the multi-ethnic Polish state, to uphold the status quo between Poland and the Soviet Union and Germany, and to do everything possible to modernize the Polish economy and the military. It was indicative of the balance of forces in the mid-1920s that Pilsudski estimated, quite correctly as it turned out, that neither Russia nor Germany would have the strength to mount an attack on Poland in the next ten years. It was no doubt alarming that Germany and the Soviet Union had followed up on Rapallo in April 1926 by concluding a neutrality and non-aggression pact. But unlike the non-aggression pact between those two countries in 1939, this one was truly defensive. Berlin's main aim was to signal that it would play no part in a Polish attack on Russia instigated by France and Britain. Stresemann showed no inclination to resume the dangerous balancing game of Rapallo. When Soviet invective against Poland escalated to an alarming extent in the summer of 1927, Germany acted as a go-between, assuring the Soviets that Britain and France had no aggressive intentions and warning Moscow against any precipitate action of its own.[43]

With the West apparently stabilized, the question looming over the Comintern was whether in Asia too it faced a roadblock. Britain had restored its grip on India. Relations between the Western Powers and Japan were from the Soviet point of view alarmingly amicable. But China remained unsettled. At Versailles and Washington, Japan and the Western Powers had demonstrated their refusal to take Chinese nationalism seriously. The question was who would take advantage of this situation. In September 1924 factional fighting once more erupted along the eastern seaboard of China. But this was no ordinary warlord skirmish.[44] For the first time Chinese generals deployed modern, World War I weaponry on a large scale. The Zhili faction and the 'Jade General' Wu

Peifu, who took the Yangtzi valley in October 1924, seemed poised to assert their control across China. Given the bellicosity of Wu Peifu this was alarming both to the Western Powers and Japan. Japan's Western-oriented Foreign Minister Kijuro Shidehara, a protégé of Marquis Saionji, wanted to avoid an open breach with the Washington principles, but the Zhili faction had to be stopped. Instead of unleashing the Japanese Army, Tokyo poured weapons into the armouries of Zhang Zoulin, the Manchurian warlord, and used huge bribes to break up the Zhili faction.[45] By 1925 Wu Peifu's coalition was disintegrating and as the momentum of unification reversed, Chinese politics degenerated once more into discreditable and murderous incoherence.

Washington heartily disliked Wu Peifu's nationalism. Meanwhile for France and Britain the chaos in China was not the worst of all worlds.[46] They could live with disorder so long as they could guard their spheres of interest and no Nationalist challenger emerged. But Wu Peifu's incursions into the south had put their interests in play as well. On 30 May 1925 British police in the Shanghai concession opened fire on patriotic Chinese demonstrators, killing a dozen and wounding scores more. This gratuitous display of violence sparked an upsurge in patriotic sentiment not seen since 4 May 1919. Within weeks more than 150,000 workers in Shanghai had joined a protest strike. The result was to throw open the door to a force more menacing even than Wu Peifu – the Guomindang and the Comintern.

In the north of China the warlords drew their advisors and increasingly sophisticated armouries from the vast surplus stocks of the Entente. By contrast from early 1923 onward, following the Sun-Joffe Declaration, the Nationalists looked to Moscow. On 6 October the revolutionary activist Mikhail Borodin arrived in Canton to provide on-the-spot guidance in the reconstruction of the Nationalist movement as a mass party.[47] At the first modern National Congress of the Guomindang Party in January 1924, 10 per cent of the delegates and 25 per cent of the central executive committee members were Communist. Sun Yat-sen opened the conference with a proclamation of anti-imperialism. As a sign of respect the Congress adjourned for three days to mourn Lenin's death that month. The Soviets reciprocated amply. To make good on Lenin's vision of a United Front, they dispatched over 1,000 advisors and $40 million in funds to back their new allies, a far larger commitment of revolutionary resources than Moscow had ever attempted in Europe. On the Soviet model, the Guomindang set about constructing a politicized military. The Soviet civil-war hero Vasily Blyukher acted as chief military advisor. Sun Yat-sen dispatched his up-and-coming new military leader Chiang Kai-shek for training to Moscow. To indoctrinate the rank and file, party cells were organized within each military unit. A newly founded military academy on Whampoa Island was to shape a young generation of Nationalist military leaders. The school's political commissar was Zhou Enlai, who had joined the Communist Party and become a loyal agent of the Comintern whilst on a work-study scholarship to Paris and Berlin in 1919.

Modernizing militarism had been the stock in trade of Chinese warlord politics since the era of Yuan Shi-kai, the first President of the Republic of China. The truly distinctive contribution of the Communists was to widen the social imagination of Chinese nationalism. When over the winter of 1923–4 the Guomindang base in Canton was threatened by the forces of a regional warlord, Borodin urged a radical programme of mass mobilization. He recommended a decree expropriating the landed gentry and distributing land to peasants, as well as an eight-hour day for industrial labour and a minimum wage. Out of concern for his middle-class support, Sun Yat-sen refused to concede Borodin's more inflammatory demands. But for the first time social demands had been coupled to the Guomindang's Nationalist agenda. In June 1925 Nationalist activists in Canton helped to sustain a massive strike by a quarter of a million workers in Hong Kong, as well as a protracted and highly effective boycott of trade with the British concession.[48] In the 500-mile corridor that stretched north from Canton to Wuhan and beyond, a peasant rebellion was brewing.[49] Under the influence of Communist organizer Peng Pai, the Guomindang's farmers' bureau began developing a programme for the mass base of the party.[50] The Guomindang established an agrarian leadership school, which from May 1926 was directed by the young Hunanese revolutionary Mao Zedong.[51] By the end of the first year of its efforts, Mao could claim 1.2 million peasants in the ranks of the new organization.[52]

With the northern warlords having eviscerated each other, over the summer of 1925 Blyukher and his Chinese collaborators worked out what the Russian dubbed the 'The Great Guomindang Military Plan' – a coordinated military campaign to extend the influence of the Guomindang from its southern base in Guangdong province, north into the Yangtze river valley. From there they might strike towards Beijing.[53] This was a campaign of unprecedented scale, involving the unification of two-thirds of China, a territory inhabited by as many as 200 million people and ruled by five major warlord groupings, who could, as they had shown in 1924, mobilize formidable armies amounting to 1.2 million soldiers, whereas the Nationalists mustered only 150,000.[54] Even with the Zhili in disarray, this was not a venture to be undertaken lightly. At first the Nationalists hoped that a conference of warlords might bring unification without armed struggle. That prospect evaporated with Sun Yat-sen's untimely death in March 1925, which both robbed the unification conference of its obvious figurehead and unsettled Moscow's influence within the Guomindang.

Though Sun committed his party in his testament to continuing the alliance with the Soviets, it was now split between a left wing, closer to the Chinese Communist Party, and a military wing headed by Chiang Kai-shek. In March 1926 Chiang showed his hand by launching a political coup within the Nationalist leadership in Canton, rolling back the influence of the Communists and having himself appointed head of the National Revolutionary Army. Believing that there was no time to lose, the Comintern decided to go over to the offensive. Leon Trotsky, who was urging that the Chinese Communists should exit the Guomindang and establish their own military base amongst the peasantry and workers of Guangdong, was overridden. With Stalin and Bukharin to the fore, the Comintern threw itself wholeheartedly into preparations for the decisive Northern Expedition.[55]

In the short term the result was a triumph. Whilst the prospects of revolution may have been fading in Europe with the British general strike, between June and December 1926 the Chinese National Republican Army (NRA) waged an unprecedentedly well-organized and successful campaign that brought most of central and southern China under Nationalist control. Blyukher and his staff coordinated operational planning. Soviet pilots provided air cover. Leading Chinese Communists gave political direction to the more left-leaning divisions of the NRA. In many provinces the campaign against the warlords was carried forward on a tide of peasant rebellion.[56] The young Mao invoked the image of a 'fierce wind, or tempest, a force so swift and violent that no power, however great, will be able to hold it back'.[57]

After a 38-day siege, on 10 October 1926, the fifteenth anniversary of the 1911 revolution, the National Revolutionary Army took the city of Hankou-Wuchang, where the revolution had begun. The Western Powers were unsettled as never before. Already in April 1926, London had withdrawn recognition from what remained of the Chinese government in Beijing.[58] Now on 18 December, in an effort to respond to the Nationalist surge, the British Embassy issued a public memorandum acknowledging that the 'situation which exists in China today is ... entirely different from that which faced the powers at the time they framed the Washington treaties'.[59] The great powers must 'abandon the idea that the economic and political development of China can only be secured under foreign tutelage'. They must come to terms with the demands of the Chinese Nationalists for treaty revision.[60]

But how far would the British go toward accommodating Nationalist demands? Almost immediately the limits of flexibility were put to the test. On 4 January 1927 after weeks of unrest, a Chinese crowd backed up by Republican troops faced down a detachment of British marines and occupied the British concession in Hankou-Wuchang. Dexterous manoeuvring on the spot avoided bloodshed, but the shock to the British was dramatic. There were those in London, Churchill among them, who called for immediate retaliation. But Foreign Secretary Austen Chamberlain was well aware how 'deeply pacific' was the attitude of the British public and how badly any aggressive action would be received in Washington: 'only by ... patience, only by making clear to everyone how earnestly' Britain was 'seeking a peaceful solution', and 'how liberal' its 'policy was', would it be possible to mobilize the necessary force, if British strategic interests were truly threatened.[61]

The strategic asset over which Britain would stand its ground was Shanghai. The city was the hub of British commerce in East Asia. Hundreds of millions of pounds were at stake. On 17 January 1927 the British cabinet decided to deploy 20,000 troops to China, backed up by a formidable display of naval power, including three cruisers, gunboats and a flotilla of destroyers. Altogether by February, 35 warships from 7 nations were assembled in Shanghai. Along the coastline of China the

Royal Navy had a fleet of 2 light aircraft carriers, 12 cruisers, 20 destroyers, 12 submarines and 15 river gunboats.[62]

The stage seemed set for confrontation. Inside the Guomindang the Communists were again tightening their grip. The Chinese Communist Party (CCP) had grown from a tiny handful of intellectuals to a party of 60,000 activists concentrated in the big cities of central and southern China. Defying the West's show of force, the Nationalist armies were marching relentlessly towards the coast. On 21 March NRA forces entered Shanghai. This triggered a Communist-led uprising in an attempt to turn the imminent victory of nationalism against Chiang Kai-shek in a revolutionary direction.[63] Though clashes with the Western Powers were avoided in Shanghai, three days later on 24 March the NRA occupied Nanjing, triggering a wave of rioting.[64] American and British warships at anchor on the Yangtze responded by shelling the city, inflicting a heavy loss of life. But with several Westerners having been killed, the British Consulate damaged and the consul-general wounded, was this enough? Britain had the military potential in Shanghai to respond with real force.

On 11 April a threatening message was sent both to General Chiang and the Nationalist authorities in Wuhan. When the left Guomindang government in Wuhan gave an uncompromising response, the battelines seemed drawn.[65] However, at that moment the power struggle between Communist, left- and right-wing factions within the Guomindang came to a head. From Moscow, the Comintern was calling for their comrades to oust General Chiang. But he had no intention of being outflanked. In March 1927 Chiang had ordered the disarmament of the Communist militia in the army divisions under his command. On the day after the protest by the Western Powers about the 'outrages' in Nanjing, before the powerful Shanghai trade union movement could organize resistance, Chiang delivered his decisive blow.[66]

On 12 April, declaring that the Chinese revolution must liberate itself from Russian tutelage, he launched a bloody anti-Communist purge in Shanghai. With the Japanese keen to support Chiang's anti-Communist drive and the Americans refusing to condone the use of force, London backed down. The Chinese Communist Party, having integrated its organization into that of the Guomindang, was defenceless. When the left wing of the Guomindang in Wuhan turned against them as well, their position was hopeless. Of the 60,000 Chinese Communists in the spring of 1926, by the end of 1927 no more than 10,000 were still alive. In the countryside the White Terror claimed the lives of hundreds of thousands of insurgent peasants.[67] What was left of the rural organization was destroyed in Mao's ill-fated 'autumn harvest' uprising in Hunan in September 1927.[68] A year later in July 1928, after Beijing had fallen to the regular forces of the NRA, the United States recognized Chiang's government with its capital in Nanjing, granting it full rights to set its own tariff duties, one of the long-standing demands of Chinese nationalism.[69]

For Moscow the events in China were shattering. Twice in the space of seven years – first in Poland in August 1920 and then in China in the spring of 1927 – the Soviet regime had seemed poised to achieve a stunning revolutionary breakthrough, only to suffer crushing defeat. And to Moscow's fevered geopolitical imagination it was obvious that events in Poland and China were interconnected. The common denominator was British imperialist intrigue. Within weeks of the disaster in Shanghai, on 12 May 1927 Scotland Yard raided the offices of the Soviet trade delegation in London. Claiming to have found incriminating evidence, the Tory government severed diplomatic relations with the Soviet Union. Rumours of war took on an added urgency when on 7 June the Soviet envoy in Warsaw was assassinated by a White Russian terrorist. Was this another Sarajevo?[70] With a war scare sweeping Moscow and the Communist Party torn by bitter in-fighting between Stalinist and Trotskyite factions, the sense of crisis reached a new height in October when it became clear that harvest procurement was failing. As in the civil war, the peasants were on strike. In 1920–21 Lenin had faced a similar constellation. Huge ambition for revolutionary expansion and socialist construction had crashed into a wall of violent Western opposition and the threat of famine. With NEP and peaceful coexistence, Lenin had taken one step back.

To do so again in 1927 would be a betrayal of what had been achieved since that strategic retreat. For Stalin it would be a dangerous concession to his opponents, who were now looking for a showdown. He would not retreat. Trotsky and Zinoviev were exiled. But what did going forward mean? In 1925 it had been Trotsky and the left opposition who had urged more rapid industrialization. Now, in response to the war scare of the summer of 1927, the Politburo appropriated their agenda. By the end of the year a gigantic programme of industrialization was recast as the Five Year Plan and underpinned with a coercive programme of rural collectivization. Stalin was embarking on an utterly unprecedented programme of economic and social transformation that would in a matter of years give the Soviet state full and direct control over the mass of the peasantry.[71] It was, as Trotsky put it, a 'hazardous bureaucratic super-industrialization' hedged with economic and political risks.[72] By the early 1930s this voluntarist bid for growth at any price would unleash a hellish famine and a violent war against the peasantry, whilst putting the Soviet Union's foreign policy on the defensive. It was no coincidence that Stalin eagerly embraced the Kellogg-Briand Pact. For the foreseeable future the construction of 'socialism in one country' required peace.

IV

If there was any power other than the Soviet Union more exposed to the strategic uncertainty in East Asia in the late 1920s, it was Japan. And there were plenty of voices in Japanese politics and the military who demanded an assertive response. Since the early 1920s the relative moderation of Japanese policy had been underpinned by a belittling depreciation of the potential of Chinese nationalism. In light of the forces mobilized by Wu Peifu in 1924 and the even greater momentum of the Northern Expedition, this came to seem dangerously complacent. Nevertheless, in the face of right-wing outrage Foreign Minister Shidehara stuck to the policy of non-aggression that had been pursued since 1921. In the spring of 1927, when both Britain and the United States confronted the Chinese Nationalists with armed force, Japan stayed its hand.[73] In the Japanese Navy the sense of humiliation was so intense that one of the lieutenants involved in the evacuation of Japanese citizens from Nanjing committed hara-kiri in protest.[74] Why was Japan not defending its interests? Meanwhile, whilst China was recovering its strength, Japan's crucial foothold in Manchuria, was suffering from neglect.[75] In the late 1920s the Japanese settler population of Manchuria numbered only 200,000, increasing by no more than 7,000 every year. By comparison, annual in-migration of land-hungry Chinese to Manchuria peaked in 1927 at 780,000. Barring truly decisive political action, Japanese overlordship had no future even in its designated sphere of interest.

In April 1927, with Japan's economy in crisis and China on the march, the liberal government that had stuck so doggedly to a policy of conciliation was brought down.[76] The conservative Seiyukai Party took office headed by former chief of staff and China-hand General Tanaka, who announced his determination to take a firmer stance. By reinforcing Japan's military position in Shandong and Manchuria, whilst courting Chiang Kai-shek, Tanaka hoped that the Chinese might eventually be persuaded to accept a de facto separation of the territory north of the Great Wall. What Tanaka did not dare to do was break with the Western Powers even when the NRA began a major offensive to the north in April 1928. Despite repeated clashes between the NRA and Japanese troops, in which thousands of Chinese were killed, Tanaka bit his tongue and officially acknowledged to Washington China's sovereignty over Manchuria.

For Japanese nationalist extremists this was too much.[77] On 4 June 1928 radical officers within Japan's Manchurian army assassinated the warlord Chang Tso-lin as he was fleeing Beijing ahead of the arrival of the NRA. The assassins hoped thereby to provoke a clash with the warlord's army, thus paving the way for full Japanese annexation of Manchuria. But they were to be disappointed. Whilst the NRA occupied Beijing and completed the Nationalist unification of China, in Manchuria Chang Tso-lin was succeeded by his son Chang Hsueh-liang. The 'Young Marshal' avoided open confrontation with the Japanese Army but soon revealed himself to be a Chinese patriot in the new mould. In December, ignoring the Japanese, he placed the three Manchurian provinces under the sovereignty of the Nationalist government in Nanjing, which was now officially recognized by both the United States and Great Britain.

Prime Minister Tanaka's policy was in tatters. Unable either to confront or to accommodate the Chinese, he came to seem like a 'Don Quixote of the East', an old-school samurai out of time.[78] When his cabinet finally collapsed in July 1929, it was replaced not by a government of Nationalist radicals, but by their chief opponents, the Constitutional People's Government Party, or Minseito. Their agenda was reformist not confrontational. Japan must ratify Kellogg-Briand, take up the Anglo-American invitation to naval disarmament talks in London, complete the liberalization of its domestic politics, and resume the push toward the gold standard. In February 1930 these Asian counterparts to Gustav Stresemann received a resounding majority from Japan's democratized electorate.[79] Even with Stalin and Chiang Kai-shek on the march, the advocates of aggression in Asia had not yet made their case.

26

The Great Depression

The Great Depression was the event that would shatter this surprisingly resilient system of international order. But this disintegrative effect was not immediately obvious. The initial impact of the downturn, like that of the recession of 1920–21, was not to blow the world apart but to tighten the constraints of the existing order. Indeed, it was a sign of how far the new norms had become entrenched that in 1929, unlike in 1920, deflation was pursued in every major country of the world. It was not just Britain and the United States that chose deflation but France, Italy and Germany. In a remarkable expression of their conformity to international expectations, Japan's newly installed liberal government took their country onto the gold standard in January 1930, backed by a large loan brokered by J. P. Morgan. The question that critics have asked ever since is why the world was so eager to commit to this collective austerity. If Keynesians and monetarist economists can agree on one thing, it is the disastrous consequences of this deflationary consensus. Were ignorant central bankers to blame, or an atavistic attachment to the memory of the gilded age?[1] Or did the experience of inflation in the wake of World War I create an anti-inflationary bias even among the better-placed countries, the United States and France, which ought to have acted as counterweights to the downward pressure on Britain, Germany and Japan?[2] More political interpretations suggest that deflation provided fiscal hawks with a welcome opportunity to roll back the concessions made to labour in the tumultuous aftermath of the war.[3]

What all these explanations underestimate is the wider political investment in the restored international order of the 1920s. This went beyond fear of inflation, or a conservative desire to cut welfare. The gold standard was tied to visions of international cooperation that went beyond technical discussions amongst central bankers. At the real pressure points in the international system the gold standard was 'knave proof' not just with regard to big-spending, inflation-minded socialists. The 'golden fetters' also constrained the militarists. Indeed, given Washington's veto over any tougher collective security system, an embedded market-based liberalism was the only significant guard against the resurgence of imperialism. A cyclical recession, even one that brought mass unemployment and bankruptcy, was a small price to pay to uphold an international order that was the best hope of peace as well as economic progress. It was one of the tragic ironies of the Great Depression that constructive policies of international cooperation became so tightly entangled with economic policies of austerity. The perverse consequence was that advocates of 'positive' economic policy found themselves gravitating toward the insurgent nationalist camp.

I

The stage was set by the Young Plan. With the shadows of a recession already in the offing, on 11 February 1929 a new round of reparations negotiations opened in Paris. They were presided over by Owen D. Young, Charles Dawes's deputy in 1924. It was a triumph of Stresemannian diplomacy that the call for the talks had come not from the Germans but from the Americans. They had reason to fear that once Berlin's reparations liability increased under the payments schedule of the Dawes Plan, this would crowd out Germany's private debts to Wall Street. The negotiations that were concluded a year later in the Second Hague Conference of January 1930 were a mixed success.[4] In form at least, the Young Plan promised to defuse the reparations issue by depoliticizing the payments system. But substantively, thanks to the refusal of Washington to allow any joint discussion of war debts and reparations, the outcome was a disappointment.

Given Washington's intransigence, which became ever more marked as the Hoover administration came into office in March 1929, France and Britain could concede a reduction of Germany's reparations payments of no more than 20 per cent.[5] Their room for manoeuvre was small. As reparations were reduced, the claims on them by the United States loomed ever larger. In 1919 the ratio of reparations claims to war debts owed to the US had stood at a comfortable 3:1. The effect of America's dogged debt diplomacy and Germany's revisionism regarding the Versailles Treaty was to reduce that cushion. Britain and France increasingly functioned as conduits for a cycle of payments that ran from the United States to Germany and back again. After the Young Plan, France retained only 40 per cent of its reparations payments, Britain barely 22 per cent. The rest was passed on to the United States for war debts. As Trotsky put it in typically drastic terms: 'From the financial shackles on Germany's feet, there extend solid chains which encumber the hands of France, the feet of Italy and the neck of Britain. MacDonald, who nowadays fulfills the duties of keeper to the British lion, points with pride to this dog collar, calling it the best instrument of peace.'[6] It was more than mere coincidence that the sum of $2 billion paid to the United States in war debts by 1931 was almost exactly the total of credits advanced to Germany from the US by the early 1920s.[7] Funds were being recycled. But it was precisely that cycle that was put under immense strain by the Young Plan. The result of the Plan was to normalize Germany's debts, but by the same taken to make the burden more transparent and to pin responsibility more directly on Berlin.[8]

The nationalist reaction was to rally around a protest referendum. This offered Adolf Hitler a chance to re-energize his movement, which after its disastrous setback in the Reichstag elections of 1928 seemed to be slipping back into obscurity.[9] But once more the insurgents were defeated. The no vote gained only 14 per cent. Once more the nationalist Reichstag deputies voted shamefacedly to give the Young Plan the super-majority it needed for ratification. As Allied troops withdrew from the Rhineland five years ahead of time, it was another victory for practical diplomacy.

It was congruent with this image of a returning normality that in restoring German sovereignty the Young Plan tightened the regime of financial orthodoxy. The transfer protection system, which had been overseen in Berlin since 1924 by an American reparations agent, was wound up. Henceforth Germany was responsible for managing its own balance of payments. It would make its payments not to the Reparations Commission but to a new international clearing house, the Bank of International Settlements. That would require a fresh fiscal discipline, but for German conservatives this was far from unwelcome. In March 1930, having shed the Social Democrats from the broad-based coalition that had taken office in 1928, the Centre Party government of Heinrich Brüning embarked on the long haul of restructuring the Weimar state.[10] The ultimate goal was to overturn the Versailles Treaty, but the means of achieving that revisionist objective were conformist. Germany would escape the coils of political debt by restoring its competitiveness. From the purge of deflation it would re-emerge as it had been before 1914, a champion exporter in a world economy finally freed from the financial legacies of the war.

While Germany was preoccupied with reparations over the winter of 1929–30, Britain and America were preparing for the renewal of global disarmament. On 21 January 1930 amid the splendour of the House of Lords, the major powers convened for the Second London Naval Conference. The opening ceremony was broadcast live by radio all over the world, causing a sensation in Japan 5,000 miles away. For the first time a truly global public participated simultaneously in a single media event.[11] The timing was dictated by the expiration of the 10-year system agreed in Washington. In 1931, barring a new agreement, Britain, the US and Japan were poised to build a total of 39 battleships at an estimated price tag of $2 billion. The limitations of battleships agreed in Washington had not stopped the construction since 1922 of almost a million tons of cruisers, destroyers and submarines. A huge naval appropriation bill was before Congress. All this was flagrantly at odds with the deflationary demands of the moment. Instead, the Big Three agreed in London to go beyond battleships to adopt truly comprehensive naval arms limitations.

The agreement by the Hamaguchi government on 2 April 1930, namely to accept a compromise ratio just short of 10:10:7 for cruisers and other auxiliary vessels, was the breakthrough of the conference. Even more than at Washington in 1921, this was a triumph for Japan's civilian politicians and diplomats over the military, who by this point were preoccupied with China and had lost any confidence in America's good faith. But whatever one's strategic assessment, about the common deflationary imperative there was no doubt. Hoover's administration estimated that the US had saved $500 million.[12] Given the cruiser construction it had undertaken since 1921, for Japan the conference was tantamount to a complete naval holiday. In total over the next six years the Japanese Navy would add only 50,000 tons of new ships. The navy lobby was incensed. With the big-spending Seiyukai opposition in support, they turned the London Naval Conference into the 'most significant constitutional battle' since the beginning of the Taisho era in 1913.[13] But despite the resignation of Admiral Katō Kanji, the Naval Chief of Staff, and at least one ritual suicide amongst the junior officers, Prime Minister Osachi Hamaguchi stood his ground.[14] The pressure for budget cuts was unrelenting. He had a large parliamentary majority at his back and could count on the support of the veteran, pro-Western liberal Prince Saionji as president of the emperor's Privy Council.[15] In the face of challenges from all sides, Hamaguchi's government continued to align itself with London and Washington on security policy as well as the gold standard. To celebrate the ratification of the London naval treaty, on 28 October 1930 in a synchronized worldwide radio event broadcast to audiences in all three countries, Hamaguchi of Japan, Prime Minister Ramsay MacDonald and President Herbert Hoover took turns to praise this milestone in international peace.

As had been the case nine years earlier, it was the French who were made to seem the uncooperative party at the London talks.[16] But they had reason to fear that their security interests were being ignored. With a navy barely one-third the size of that of Britain or America, the French would be forced to choose between defending their Atlantic coastline and guarding the Mediterranean against Mussolini, who was openly scornful of the entire disarmament process. Not that France was asking to compete with Britain or the United States. On the contrary, its priority was to link disarmament to more specific security commitments than those offered by either the League of Nations or the Kellogg-Briand Pact. If London and Washington desired naval disarmament, France wanted what remained of the Royal Navy to be firmly committed to its defence.

To the latter-day Wilsonians in MacDonald's second Labour government, this was as distasteful as ever. As far as MacDonald was concerned, the Great War had been as much the result of Franco-Russian intrigue as of German aggression.[17] It was imperative that Britain never again be placed in the position in which it had found itself during 1916, when entanglements in Europe caused the country to risk everything in a fruitless clash with a progressive American President. Though the conference in 1930 was being hosted in London, it was the American delegation that decided its outcome. If the key to European security was the willingness of the British to back the force of the French Army with a smothering naval blockade, then America's approval was indispensable. Britain would make no promises to France that would risk antagonizing America.

On 24 March 1930, desperate to pull the conference back from the 'brink of a precipice', the American Secretary of State, Henry Stimson, offered that if France would consent to disarmament, the United States would consider a consultative pact, under which it would commit itself to making clear its position in advance of any Franco-British blockade.[18] This went far further than Secretary of State Hughes had been willing to go in 1924, and Stimson acted without backing from the State Department or President Hoover. His proposal was never put before the Senate. But this minimal concession, which suggested at least the possibility of American approval for British action on France's behalf, was enough to enable the French to agree not to derail the conference. The unfortunate effect of this struggle, however, was to paint France in dark colours precisely at the moment when it desperately needed British cooperation.

In the wake of the frustrating Young Plan negotiations, the movement for European integration that had experienced a first flush of enthusiasm after the Ruhr crisis moved back to the forefront of discussion.[19] In light of America's uncompromising stance over war debts, in June 1929 at a meeting in Madrid, Briand and Stresemann had discussed a vision of a European bloc large enough to withstand American economic competition and capable of releasing itself from dependence on Wall Street.[20] In a speech on 5 September 1929, using the League of Nations as his stage, Briand seized the initiative: The European members of the League must move toward a closer union. The toothless peace pact that bore his name was not enough. Given the obvious downward trend in the world economy and the looming prospect of further American protectionism, Briand's first approach was to propose a system of preferential tariff reductions. But this economic approach met with such hostility that over the winter he moved to a different tack.

In early May 1930, within weeks of the conclusion of the ticklish London Naval Conference, the French government circulated a formal proposal to all 26 of the other European member states of the League of Nations. Paris called upon its fellow Europeans to realize the implications of their 'geographical unity' to form a conscious 'bond of solidarity'.[21] Specifically, Briand proposed a regular European conference with a rotating presidency and a standing political committee. The ultimate aim would be a 'federation built upon the idea of union and not of unity'. 'Times have never been more propitious nor more pressing,' Briand concluded, 'for the starting of constructive work of this kind ... It is a decisive hour when a watchful Europe may ordain in freedom her own fate. Unite to live and prosper!'

II

When news reached Briand on 3 October 1929, barely a month after his European speech, of Gustav Stresemann's death, it is said that the French Premier exclaimed that they should order a second coffin for him. There was no doubt that Stresemann's departure from the scene followed by Heinrich Brüning's rise to the Chancellorship in Berlin at the head of a right-wing minority cabinet signalled an alarming development in German politics. Brüning was no Erzberger. The echoes of the days of the Reichstag majority were now very faint. The disappointment of the outcome of the Young Plan pushed more confrontational attitudes to the fore in Germany. But this might not have mattered if Britain had decided to throw its weight behind Briand's proposal. At the London Naval Conference the cooperation of Britain and America had been enough to hold France and Japan in line. A Franco-British combination might have set the terms in Europe. Not only was Britain a naval superpower but unlike France it was a champion importer. Faced with America's recalcitrant protectionism, access to the markets of Britain and its empire was a truly powerful bargaining chip.[22]

But the face of the Labour government was set squarely against any cooperation with France, and it was this that let Germany off the hook. Despite the enthusiastic approval given to Briand's proposal by 20 of its 26 recipients, including all the smaller countries of Europe except for Hungary and Ireland, both London and Berlin let the proposal drop. On 8 July 1930 Brüning's cabinet concluded smugly that the most appropriate response to the historic French initiative should be to offer it a 'first-class funeral'.[23]

What London did not appreciate was that by stymying France it was opening the door to disaster. Again and again since 1918 the German political class had rallied itself to find a majority for painful but necessary acts of compliance. Rapallo and the Ruhr had demonstrated the disastrous consequences of confrontation. But in 1930 the willingness to conform began to fray once more. Stresemann's successor as Foreign Minister, the Bismarckian nationalist Julius Curtius, had already declared that he intended to 'rebalance' Germany's foreign policy toward the East. In 1931 a large export credit guaranteed by the Reich quadrupled German exports to the Soviet Union, making Germany into by far the largest trading partner of Stalin's regime.[24] In the summer of 1930 Berlin had strengthened its links to Fascist Italy, France's main rival in the Mediterranean. In early July as the last French troops withdrew from the Rhineland, Curtius embarked on his masterstroke. He initiated top-secret negotiations with Vienna over a possible Austro-German *Zollverein* (customs union). Kept secret until the spring of 1931, it was to be this German initiative that unleashed the first true landslide of the Great Depression.

That a government headed by Brüning should have initiated this disastrous train of events was tragic but predictable. Brüning was a nationalist but not unusual in this respect.[25] He was certainly no fascist sympathizer. His aspirations for the Reich were conservative. His economics were liberal. His goal was to restore something like the Wilhelmine golden age. On the part of a rich and powerful nation this combination might have been innocuous. But given Germany's vulnerable position, a vigorous national liberalism was a dangerous cocktail. The economic adjustment that the Weimar Republic had to undertake was severe. Between 1929 and 1931 Germany veered from a looming trade deficit to a substantial trade surplus largely by slashing domestic demand for imports. In the summer of 1930 the presidential decree powers of Field Marshall Hindenburg were invoked not to impose dictatorship, but to enforce deflationary compliance with the rules of the international game. The rise of unemployment to 4 million over the winter of 1930–31 was the predictable consequence. To offset the collapse in domestic demand Germany needed exports. It was not illogical to seek closer economic relations with Austria. But Briand's European plan offered a far larger market. And to cushion the agony of the deflation, Germany needed all the help from the international community that it could get.

Under such circumstances, for Brüning to have engaged in clandestine talks with Vienna, which violated if not the letter then the spirit of as many as three post-war peace treaties, was a high-risk strategy to say the least. To have done so as a sop to the nationalist far right, which after the Reichstag election of September 1930 was coming under the sway of Hitlerism, was deeply irresponsible. The essence of Stresemann's strategy had been the subtle calculation that the best way to widen Germany's room for manoeuvre was precisely to avoid open confrontation. Brüning's more aggressive approach had the reverse effect. By dangling nationalist fantasies, rather than widening his room for manoeuvre he narrowed it, piling up on both domestic and international pressure.

On 20 March 1931 the announcement of the Austro-German customs-union plan exploded onto the pages of the international press.[26] Earlier in the year, to reward Germany's conformity to the gold standard, France had been preparing to open the Paris money markets to German borrowing.[27] Now Berlin seemed bent on confrontation. To make matters worse, neither the British nor American governments showed any sign of wanting to rein Brüning in. So long as its Most Favoured Nation status was preserved, the United States had no objection to the consolidation of the fragile states of central Europe.[28] This was alarming for Paris. But thanks to Poincaré's policy of stabilization, it was now in a far stronger position. By 1931 France's undervalued currency and strong balance of payments had enabled it to accumulate 25 per cent of the world's gold reserves, second only to the United States, vastly more than Britain had ever held even in its pomp as the maestro of the gold standard orchestra. As financial speculation hit Austria in May and then spread to Germany, there were rumours that Paris was deliberately encouraging the sell-off. But there was no need for that. The deflation was taking its toll. The bankruptcy of the Viennese Kreditanstalt and the trouble that hit the Danat bank in Germany were dangerous but predictable side effects of a severe deflationary adjustment. Germany's balance of payments was highly unstable. And Brüning himself seemed quite determined to spook the markets. On 6 June, having been invited to visit MacDonald at Chequers, the German Chancellor used the occasion to denounce the next instalment due under the Young Plan as a 'tribute payment'.

Under these circumstances it was not surprising that gold and foreign currency began to drain out of the German financial system. Since 1924 German policy had been waiting for this moment. Would the country be able to use its debtor relationship with America to unhinge its reparations obligations? There was no doubt that Wall Street was seriously exposed. All told, American investors had $2 billion tied up in

Germany. Since January 1931 Stimson had been warning of the serious risk to America if there was a German collapse.[29] But to imagine that the President was at the behest of the bankers was to repeat the mistake made by Berlin in their fateful U-boat decision of January 1917. Hoover was no friend of the Wall Street barons, and the voters of the Midwest were even less so. It was not until 19 June, with desperate telegrams arriving from London, that Hoover finally agreed to act. The next day he announced a plan to freeze all political debts, both reparations and inter-Allied war debts. Announced on a Saturday, on the following Monday 22 June the Berlin stock market was in a frenzy of bullish trading, only for the bubble to be abruptly pricked when France refused to fall into line.

This French veto caused outrage in London and Washington, and the sounds of protest have echoed down to the present through historical writing. According to the most influential interpreter of the Great Depression, France's unwillingness to cooperate with Hoover's rescue effort in June 1931 revealed the true weakness of the interwar system. What was at fault 'was not lack of US leadership. It was the failure of cooperation, specifically French unwillingness to go along.'[30] At the time, the language was less restrained. In London, gallophobic conspiracy theories were rife. Prime Minister MacDonald raged that 'France has been playing its usual small-minded and selfish game over the Hoover proposals. Its methods are those of the worst Jews ... Germany cracks while France bargains.' In Washington, Under-Secretary of State William Castle concluded 'that the French are the most hopeless people in the world'.[31] Hoover hinted darkly that for the future he could see only the possibility of an Anglo-German alignment, possibly including the United States, against France.[32]

The expostulation was all the greater for the fact that the net cost to America of Hoover's moratorium was larger than it was for either Britain or France. Since those countries made up through the cancellation of war debts much of what they lost through the cancellation of reparations, their net contribution amounted to no more than one-third of the total. According to one set of contemporary calculations, Germany was relieved of £77 million per annum in reparations payments, whilst the United States forfeited £53.6 million in war-debt payments. But to the French this political arithmetic was lopsided. If America was footing most of the bill, this reflected the fact that France had made round after round of concessions on reparations not reciprocated by Washington.

Nor were reparations merely a matter of money. If that was what they had become, this was thanks to the Dawes Plan and the Young Plan, each of which had been a French retreat. Again and again France had called for the creation of an international security system to replace the provisions agreed at Versailles. But this had been vetoed by Washington. Instead, Britain and America had collaborated to found a new order on nothing but disarmament and the rules of the international financial markets. As France had experienced during its time of crisis between 1924 and 1926, the force of those constraints was real, certainly as far as any cooperative player of the system was concerned. Whether Germany was a cooperative player remained an open question. France for its part had fallen into line. With the stabilization of the franc in 1926, the agreement to the Young Plan and the Mellon-Berenger war-debt deal in 1929, it had paid the price. Now, as the result of a crisis that the Germans had brought upon themselves, America was unilaterally asserting its right to declare an emergency and overturn the rules of its own game. In Paris the reaction was one of disbelief and shock. Hoover had acted without prior consultation. He was, one newspaper screamed, treating France like Nicaragua.[33] This time, however, unlike in 1923–4, it was France that could afford to bargain, transferring the risk to Germany and its creditors. It was not until 6 July that France agreed to allow the Reich to take shelter under Hoover's moratorium (Table 14).

In the meantime Germany's financial system had collapsed. Its banks were closed. A moratorium was imposed on its short-term trade debt to Britain, Holland and Switzerland. The Reichsbank continued to uphold the parity of its currency in terms of gold, but to all intents and purposes Germany had been driven off the gold standard. The Reich had nationalized all private holdings of gold and foreign currency and imposed exchange controls. Brüning could credit himself with having forced the suspension of reparations, but in every other respect this first effort to assert national interest and to escape the constraints of the international order had ended in catastrophe. To obtain Hoover's financial protection Brüning even had to publicly announce Germany's abstention from any new military spending for the duration of the moratorium.[34] What Brüning had demonstrated was that for a country as vulnerable as Germany an assertive nationalist posture was incompatible with membership in the international economy. One could draw two conclusions. Conservatives shrank back to conformity. In December

Table 14. The Effects of the Hoover Moratorium on
'Political Debts', June 1931 (000 £)

	suspended receipts	suspended payments	net loss/gain
United States	53,600	–	(53,600)
Great Britain	42,500	32,800	(9,700)
France	39,700	23,600	(16,100)
Italy	9,200	7,400	(1,800)
Belgium	5,100	2,700	(2,400)
Romania	700	750	50
Yugoslavia	3,900	600	(3,300)
Portugal	600	350	(250)
Japan	600	–	(600)
Greece	1,000	650	(350)
Canada	900	–	(900)
Australia	800	3,900	3,100
New Zealand	330	1,750	1,420
South Africa	110	–	(110)
Egypt	90	–	(90)
Germany	–	77,000	77,000
Hungary	–	350	350
Czechoslovakia	10	1,190	1,180
Bulgaria	150	400	250
Austria	–	300	300

1931 Brüning used decree powers to force through another round of compulsory wage and price cuts. But this strategy was not only agonizing. It begged the question of how much longer there would be an international economic or political order to which to conform. More radical nationalists drew the conclusion that if nationalism and economic liberalism could not be combined, then the reassertion of national interest would have to be truly comprehensive – economic, as well as strategic and political.[35]

III

In Japan too the struggle over the strategy of conformity was heating up. Prime Minister Hamaguchi's commitment to the disarmament talks at the London Naval Conference had outraged the navy lobby. Now, in Geneva, the League of Nations was preparing a second round that might curb the army too. Was the deflation of 1930, like the Anglo-American retrenchment of 1920–21, to usher in another lost decade for imperialist ambition? Since the politicians seemed so terrifyingly blind to the peril in which Japan found itself, for the nationalist radicals the moment for action had come. In October 1930 Hamaguchi was mortally wounded by an assassin. Over the following months other prominent representatives of establishment internationalism were killed, including the liberal Finance Minister, Inoue Junnosuke, and the head of the Mitsui business conglomerate, Dan Takuma.

But assassination was not enough. The key was China. In 1928 the radicals had assassinated northern warlord Chang Tso-lin without triggering the sought-for crisis. In 1931 they would go one better. They would stage a Chinese attack on Japan. On 18 September a bomb, planted by Japan's own renegade soldiers, exploded under a Japanese railway line immediately adjacent to one of the military bases commanded by the 'Young Marshal'. Within 24 hours the Japanese Army had launched its response. Some 500 radical nationalist troops seized the regional capital of Mukden in Manchuria. Having brought the rest of the Kwantung army behind them, within weeks three entire Chinese provinces were under Japanese control. The right wing had broken into the open. If they had their way, Japan's strategic dilemma would be resolved by force, severing the territory north of the Great Wall from China proper. Furthermore, if Japan's mainstream political parties would not cooperate and if the newly democratized electorate would not fall into line, then there would have to be a comprehensive 'reconstruction' at home as well.

But despite the upheaval in Manchuria, the desired escalation once more failed to materialize.[36] The Chinese Nationalists withdrew from the challenge and Japan's diplomats swarmed out to limit the damage. Japan's government enjoyed considerable goodwill. Unlike Brüning's

Austrian customs-union proposal, the Mukden provocation was clearly the work of rogue soldiers. In any case, there was merit from the point of view of the Western Powers in Japan consolidating its grip on Manchuria – rather than Stalin. Moscow for its part showed every sign of wanting to avoid a clash. Even as the economic crisis escalated in 1931, a handful of right-wing extremists were not yet capable of shaking loose the international system. Germany could be quarantined. It would take a further shock to the heart of the global financial system to open the door to disaster. As deflation ate its way across the world, precisely such a crisis was brewing.

Over the weekend of the Mukden incident on 19–20 September 1931 the eyes of the world were focused less on North-East Asia than on London. Following the disaster in Germany, pressure had begun to build on the Bank of England.[37] Since 1929, despite a new wave of misery across much of industrial Britain, Ramsay MacDonald's Labour government had conformed without question to the imperatives of the gold standard. With sterling under pressure the demands of the Bank of England and the City of London were remorseless. In August, out of a budget of £885 million they recommended cuts of £97 million, of which £81 million were to come from unemployment and social services. The dole, on which millions of unemployed and their families subsisted, was to be cut by 30 per cent. New York and Paris rallied round, but the Bank of England wanted a showdown with the Labour cabinet and secretly encouraged potential American and French lenders to stiffen their conditions. Though there was unanimity on the principle of upholding the gold standard, MacDonald acknowledged to his colleagues that what they were being asked for was the 'negation of everything that the Labour Party stood for'.

When the cabinet failed to achieve complete unanimity, MacDonald resigned and formed a cross-party National Government, which, shorn of the dangerous socialists, announced large tax increases and spending cuts. It was not enough. On Friday 18 September, despite assistance both from the New York Federal Reserve and the Banque de France, London gave up the fight. The Bank of England was far from being in the position that had confronted Berlin over the summer. But it had no desire to end up there either. Even with the help of an emergency loan from New York and Paris, by midday on Monday 21 September the Bank of England would have been forced to contemplate truly drastic action. Instead, MacDonald agreed to make the humiliating admission that sterling was departing the gold standard.

Unlike the Mukden incident, this was a truly global event, causing banks to fail in America and panic in Berlin. For a day, it displaced the Manchurian scandal from the headlines even in Tokyo. The gold standard was the frame of discipline and coordination that Washington and London had made into the anchor of post-war stabilization. As sterling plunged, Britain was followed by the empire and all of its smaller trading partners. The initial reaction to the suspension of the gold standard was one of shock. But, within a year as the pound stabilized at a new and far more competitive level, Britain's National Government, still headed by MacDonald, would discover that for a country with some degree of international credibility, a free-floating exchange rate offered not disaster but the possibility of a creative reinvention of economic liberalism.[38] With its banking system intact, low interest rates delivered an effective stimulus to the British recovery. When compared to either the US or continental Europe, the British experience of the 1930s was far from dismal.

But Britain's discovery of what Keynes was to dub 'real liberalism' had wider consequences. Sterling's plunge put huge pressure on Britain's trading partners. And the pressure was only further increased when the empire adopted protectionism in February 1932. This was not the first protectionist move. Nor was it the worst. The justly infamous Smoot Hawley tariff had been log-rolled through Congress in June 1930. But from the Americans protectionism was to be expected. Britain's devaluation and tariff signalled a regime break. Since the repeal of the Corn Laws in the 1840s, Britain had been the pillar of free trade. Now it was responsible for initiating the death spiral of protectionism and beggar-thy-neighbour currency wars that would tear the global economy apart. As a senior British official admitted, 'no country ever administered a more severe shock to international trade' than Britain did with its combination of devaluation and the turn to protectionism.[39]

On top of the wave of assassinations and the desperate aggression of the Kwantung army, it was this spectacular and sudden collapse of the framework of the international economy that undid the efforts by Japanese liberals to hold the line. As 1931 came to a close, in the Diet the Foreign Office official, Manchuria-hand and fascist sympathizer Matsuoka Yosuke demanded to know: 'It is a good thing to talk about economic foreign policy but we must have more than a slogan. Where are the fruits? We must be shown the benefits of this approach.'[40] If even the British Empire was turning inwards, Japan must take urgent steps to create its own trade bloc. If in Ramsay MacDonald's Britain the end of the gold standard had brought low-interest mortgages for suburban home-building, in Japan the stakes were higher. The decision to return to gold in 1930 was directly associated with disarmament. As soon as Japan abandoned the gold standard in December 1931, Finance Minister Korekijo Takahashi came under huge pressure from the military. Facing a resurgent China and the menace of Soviet industrialization, with the Japanese public stirred by the Mukden incident into a patriotic fervour not seen since 1905, the military were determined to break the constraints of the 1920s. Between 1930 and 1934 the defence budget doubled. In 1935, when Takahashi refused a further increase, he was hacked to death by right-wing zealots. By 1937, having ruptured the naval limits agreed in London, Japan's military spending had risen to five times its level in 1930.[41]

In the super-heated strategic environment of East Asia, the link between the financial crisis of 1931 and the military escalation that was to follow was remarkably direct. In Europe and across the Atlantic the breakdown was more incremental. After 1931, France and Italy remained on the gold standard. The result was not to 'activate' policy, as in Japan, but to confine France and Italy within an ever-tightening deflationary straitjacket. The fact that this was combined in Mussolini's case with expansive foreign-policy ambitions was one of the truly disabling irrationalities of his regime. Largely as a result, the Italian armed services never came close to getting what they needed to fulfil the Duce's dreams of conquest. Given its enormous gold holdings, France for its part had little reason to leave the gold standard, despite the deflationary pressure. The deflation did not begin to take a really severe toll until 1932.

It was in Germany that the situation now became truly unbearable. It could not devalue because it was pinned down by its huge burden of foreign debt denominated in dollars, the weight of which would increase if the value of the Reichsmark fell. Unlike the Bank of England, the Reichsbank had no reserves with which to ward off the speculative attacks that were bound to follow a departure from gold. Furthermore, Washington made clear that it preferred to see Germany hunker down behind the exchange controls and debt moratoria put in place over the summer. That way it could at least continue to service its debts to Wall Street. Meanwhile, the consequences for German trade of upholding its gold parity whilst Britain devalued were nothing short of catastrophic. Up to September 1931 Brüning's cabinet could at least claim that its harsh deflationary policy had produced a gain in export competitiveness. Now, clinging to the wreckage of a disintegrating gold standard, Germany's exports suffered one blow after another. By the end of 1931, as unemployment surged from 4 to 6 million and a wave of bankruptcies shook German industry, the deflation consensus splintered. If there was no international system left to which to conform, what was the rationale for another wave of government-decreed wage and price cuts? Across Germany, cliques of experts, business interests and politicians began to rally around the call for a concerted policy of national economic salvation.

One wing of this debate congregated around the trade union movement, but another wing entertained increasingly prominent guests from the anti-Young Plan campaign and from Hitler's National Socialist Party. In the summer of 1932 with a work-creation programme emblazoned on its banners, the Nazis swept to a dramatic election victory. Hitler's party scored 37 per cent of the national vote, just short of the Socialist Party's triumph in the National Assembly election of January 1919. The right wing was well short of a majority. The DNVP for its part was ailing. And in the second general election, in November 1932, the Nazi vote began to ebb. But it was this breakthrough over the desperate winter of 1931–2 that made Hitler into a candidate for the Chancellorship. When the effort to consolidate a conservative regime under Franz von Papen or a military directorate under General von Schleicher failed, in January 1933 it was Hitler who was next in line to head a nationalist coalition.[42]

But though the military class and economic groups such as agrarians might have little to lose in abandoning internationalism, other influential groups, notably big business, were slower to relinquish the promises of the 1920s. For countries such as Japan and Germany multilateral trade, underwritten by Britain, had been the bedrock of their economic development. Could one really contemplate a departure from such a foundational element of world order? The Mukden incident in East Asia was clearly dangerous. But none of the parties had chosen to turn it into a *casus belli*. A new round of disarmament talks had begun at Geneva in February 1932.[43] In Europe in June of that year the reparations issue had finally been resolved at the Lausanne Conference. France was upholding the monetary orthodoxy. Britain and Japan's departure from the gold standard was serious, but perhaps not irrevocable. As of the summer of 1932 there were some signs of an economic rebound. A major conference was scheduled to meet in the summer of 1933 in London. On its agenda was the reconstruction of the world economy, and in addressing that issue one question was decisive: where stood the United States?

IV

In 1928 Herbert Hoover's landslide election victory had seemed to put the final stamp of authority on the restored post-war order. Hoover was the great engineer of progressivism and his response to the initial shocks of 1929 was in character.[44] In October he partnered with MacDonald in the cause of disarmament. At home he urged his contacts in America's business circles and trade associations to respond to the crisis by bringing forward private investment. But such measures were unavailing in the face of a huge collapse in confidence and domestic spending. Hoover, the master of foreign disasters, the harbinger of American affluence, the emblem of progressive efficiency and self-satisfaction, found himself humiliated by a home-grown catastrophe, a devastating return of the instability that had plagued the US economy in the late nineteenth century.[45] It was not that the President did not understand the basic rationale for countercyclical government spending. The problem was that the Federal government budget at 3 per cent of GDP was too small to exercise any stabilizing effect. Nor could Hoover prevent Congress passing the outrageous Smoot-Hawley tariff. Meanwhile, despite the urging of the White House, the Fed sacrificed the stability of the banking system to its pursuit of radical deflation. Following Britain's departure from gold in September 1931, 522 American banks with deposits to the tune of $705 million failed. And even worse was to follow.

In early February 1933 as America awaited a new President, a menacing bank run started in Louisiana. By 3 March it had reached the heart of the world financial order in New York. In desperation, New York State appealed to Washington for federal action. But Hoover's presidential powers expired that day and Franklin Roosevelt, his successor, refused to cooperate. Before daybreak on 4 March 1933, with no guidance from the national government, the Governor of New York took the decision to shut the centre of the global financial system. In the face of the worst global economic crisis in modern history the American state had absented itself.

The first priority of FDR's new administration was to remedy that impression. Democracy must be seen to govern.[46] The New Deal introduced a radically new conception of the role of the Federal government. After the revolution, and the Civil War of the 1860s, the United States was about to undergo its third moment of founding.[47] Hoover himself had already taken dramatic steps to increase the scope of Federal government support for the economy with the creation of the Reconstruction Finance Corporation, which by the summer of 1932 had been authorized to borrow up to $3 billion. Further dramatic steps were to follow. But this turn to 'constructive' policy in the United States was, as elsewhere, associated with a throwing off of international obligations. It was not in the aftermath of World War I but in reaction to the disillusionment of the 1920s and the Great Depression that full-throated isolationism came truly to the fore in American politics.[48] The nationalist turn of American policy in the first phase of FDR's administration completed the process of disintegration set in motion by the shock delivered by Britain in 1931.

Since the 1870s the gold standard had been the flagship of respectable politics in America. The struggle over gold had defined the new breed of progressives in the 1890s, whose legacy both Wilson and Hoover had inherited. But by the spring of 1933 America's gold reserves were so severely depleted and its banking system was so badly shaken that on 19 April Roosevelt announced America's departure from the gold standard. The decision created a platform of financial stability for the recovery in the United States.[49] But on top of exorbitant tariffs the sudden depreciation of the dollar made it extraordinarily difficult to export to the US.[50] In addition, after investor confidence recovered, funds surged back into New York, draining liquidity from the rest of the world.

As the summer approached, America's inward turn put in jeopardy the World Economic Conference that Britain and France were arranging in London, and it did so precisely at the moment when the situation in Germany was revealing its dangers. Publicly, Hitler's coalition was espousing a message of peace and national reconstruction. It did not dare to make an immediate, barefaced break with the international order. But it was a badly kept secret that rearmament was as essential to Hitler's government as roadworks. Meanwhile, Hjalmar Schacht, who had lent his expertise and authority to the anti-Young Plan campaign, returned as Hitler's President of the Reichsbank. He immediately departed for Washington, where he hoped to arrange a suspension of Germany's debt service. When he was rebuffed, on 9 June 1933, three days before the delegates of 66 nations were to assemble in London, Schacht declared a unilateral moratorium. As the conference convened, the head of the German delegation, Alfred Hugenberg, further embarrassed himself by making drastic demands for the return of colonial assets and openly touting the idea of an anti-Communist pact against Stalin. But in the summer of 1933 Germany's atrocious new government was a sideshow. The business of the World Economic Conference was dominated by the question of whether America, France and Britain could come to an agreement on how to manage the violent fluctuations of the dollar and sterling against the franc, now the lead currency on gold. Throughout June the negotiators moved close to a stabilization agreement. But on 3 July Roosevelt issued his 'bombshell telegram', denouncing any effort to stabilize the American currency as irrelevant to the business of achieving recovery. The dollar would float to whatever level suited the US economy, regardless of its impact on the rest of the world. Berlin took the hint. In October, Hitler withdrew the German delegation from the League of Nations disarmament talks and announced a near total default on all its outstanding international obligations.

As Germany and Japan simultaneously embarked on a comprehensive break with the post-war order – in strategy, politics and economics – who would oppose them? The formidable world-dominating coalition of 1919, which still seemed able to hold the ring as recently as 1930, had collapsed. In 1931 France and Britain had reluctantly accepted Hoover's moratorium. In the summer of 1932 at the Lausanne Conference they had granted Germany a permanent end to reparations. They had done so on the understanding that there would be no further demands for inter-Allied debt repayment. But Congress had never approved Hoover's moratorium. When he showed signs of wanting to make it permanent, Hoover was immediately reprimanded. In December 1931 American lawmakers decided to remind the world that it was 'against the policy of Congress that any of the indebtedness of foreign countries to the United States should in any manner be cancelled or reduced'. Given that Hoover's moratorium had been transparently motivated by the desire not to shield London and Paris, but to save Wall Street's investment in Germany, and that his intervention discriminated one-sidedly against the reparations creditors, British diplomats were dumbfounded. In the words of the British ambassador to Washington, Sir Ronald Lindsay, the incident had been an 'exhibition of irresponsibility, buffoonery, and ineptitude that could hardly be paralleled by the Haitian legislature'.[51]

A generation earlier it had been the irresponsibility of parliaments like the one in Haiti that had warranted interventions by US marines throughout the Caribbean. Now finding themselves at the mercy of what appeared to be an irresponsible legislature in Washington, it was London and Paris that did the unthinkable. By the end of 1933 the governments of both Britain and France, once pillars of the global financial system and eager members of a democratic alliance with the United States, had suspended payment on billions of dollars of debt they owed to the people of the US. Only tiny Finland continued to honour its debts to America in full. As Ramsay MacDonald, the most pro-American of British prime ministers, put it in his diary on 30 May 1934: 'Payments that would upset [the] financial order (such as it is) would be treason to the whole world. We have to take upon ourselves the thankless task of putting an end to the folly of continuing to pay.'[52]

Conclusion

Raising the Stakes

World War I had seen the first effort to construct a coalition of liberal powers to manage the vast unwieldy dynamic of the modern world. It was a coalition based on military power, political commitment and money. Layer by layer, piece by piece, issue by issue, that coalition had disintegrated. The price that the collapse of this great democratic alliance would exact defies estimation. The failure of the democratic powers opened a strategic window of opportunity in the early 1930s. We know what nightmarish forces would tear through that window. In Berlin the Jewish pogroms began in the spring of 1933. Party government in Japan ended in the spring of 1932 after an all-out paramilitary-style assault on the headquarters of the Conservative Party, the Seiyukai. After years of posturing Mussolini finally slaked his thirst for blood in 1935 when he launched his assault on Abyssinia. But amongst the aggressive and insurgent members of the 'chain gang',[1] Germany, Japan and Italy were second or third movers.

The first movers, as they had been since 1917, were the heirs of Lenin. Stabilization in Europe and Asia in the early 1920s had been built on the ground of their failure. In 1926–7, through their sponsorship the Great Northern Expedition, the Soviets delivered the first truly telling blow to the post-war order, making painfully obvious the failure of Japan and the Western Powers to come to terms with Chinese nationalism. When the Chinese Communists themselves were massacred by Chiang Kai-shek, a second process of transformation was initiated within the Soviet Union. Having crushed Trotsky and the domestic opposition, Stalin launched a programme of internal reconstruction without precedent. This process of collectivization and industrialization that uprooted tens of millions of people in a gigantic burst of development reveals something fundamental about the international order which had emerged in the 10 years since World War I. To those who sought to challenge that order, it seemed truly formidable.

Too often and too easily we write 'interwar history' as though there was a seamless continuity between the phase on which we have concentrated here, 1916–1931, and what came after in the 1930s. There were continuities of course. But the most important is that of a dialectical reaction and supersession. Not only Stalin, but the Japanese, German and Italian insurgents of the 1930s were impelled in their radical energy by a sense that at their first attempt they had failed. The Western Powers might squabble and prevaricate. Knowing the costs of full-scale war, both political and economic, they shrank from it. But they did not shrink from fear of failure. In a direct confrontation Britain, France and the United States were to be feared. In 1930 at the London Naval Conference, as they traded battleships, cruisers, destroyers and submarines, neither the Russians nor the Germans had a navy to barter with. The positions of Japan and Italy were second and third tier. As Stalin reiterated to factory managers in February 1931, at the height of the first, agonizing Five Year Plan: 'To slacken the pace would mean to lag behind, and those who lag behind are beaten. We do not want to be beaten ... We have lagged behind the advanced countries by fifty to a hundred years. We must cover that distance in ten years. Either we'll do it or we will go under.'[2]

What Stalin articulated was not merely the common sense of an age of global competition. After World War I his was the characteristic perspective of those who had been made to feel what backwardness meant in the global power game, who had lived through the disappointment of the revolutionary elan, and witnessed the overwhelming force of Western capitalism mobilized against Imperial Germany, the main challenger of the nineteenth century. The men whom Lenin had hailed as the champions of organized modernity, Rathenau, Ludendorff and company, had put up a brave fight, but they had gone down to defeat. What was needed was something even more radical. Over the next generation Stalin's refrain was to be reiterated by planners and politicians in Japan, Italy and Germany and – as decolonization began – in India, China, and dozens of other post-colonial states.

Once again we are, in some ways, too familiar with the story of the 1930s to appreciate the drama of what was occurring. We speak of an armaments race, as though what Japan, Germany and the Soviet Union were engaged in was akin to the dreadnought naval arms race of an earlier era. In fact, the rearmament drives of 1930s Japan and Nazi Germany were, like the efforts of Stalin's Soviet Union, comparable to nothing ever seen in the three-hundred-year history of modern militarism. As a share of national income, by 1938 Nazi Germany was spending five times what Imperial Germany had spent during its arms race with Edwardian Britain, and the GDP at Hitler's command by 1939 was almost 60 per cent greater than that available to the Kaiser. In constant prices the resources lavished on the Wehrmacht in the late 1930s were at least seven times greater than those received by Germany's military in 1913. This was the compliment collectively paid by all of the insurgents of the 1930s to the force of the status quo. They knew the power arrayed against them. They knew that during the era of World War I the more conventionally minded efforts of Japan and Germany to escape the limits of their national power had run aground (Table 15). It would take something unprecedented.

There were those of course who hoped that new technologies, notably the aircraft, might provide an avenue of escape from the inexorable logic of materiel. But as Japan, Germany and Italy were all to find to their cost, air war was pre-eminently a field of attritional combat dominated by economics and technology. Up to 1945 there were two global naval powers – Britain and the United States. With his famous announcement in May 1940 of a US airforce of 60,000 planes, Roosevelt made clear that in the age of airpower the United States would claim sole pre-eminence. The cities of Germany and Japan would feel its terrible force, followed by those of Korea, Vietnam, Cambodia and many more.

But the would-be insurgents had not only economics and military power with which to contend. The challenge was political as well. The lesson of the first decades of the twentieth century was not simply, as is so often asserted, that democracies were weak. Though they no doubt had their weaknesses, they were vastly more resilient than the monarchies or aristocratic regimes that they replaced. The more strategic point was that the advent of mass democracy appeared to make certain kinds of power politics increasingly problematic. The comfortable half-way and quarter-way houses of the late nineteenth century, the Bismarckian constitutions, the limited franchises of Britain, Italy and Japan, had all collapsed in on themselves in the course of World War I. Before they did

Table 15. The Rising Cost of Confrontation: Military Spending before World War I Compared to the 1930s

military spending as share of GDP		before World War I		before World War II					
		1870–1913 average	1913	1928	1930	1932	1934	1936	1938
status quo, liberal powers	USA	0.7	0.9	0.7	0.9	1.4	1.1	1.4	1.4
	France	3.0	4.2	2.8	4.6	4.9	4.8	5.9	6.8
	UK	2.6	3.0	2.4	2.3	2.4	2.5	3.5	6.5
	weighted average	1.7	2.0	1.6	1.8	3.1	3.5	4.4	9.4
1930s challengers	Japan	5.0	5.0	3.1	3.0	5.2	5.6	5.6	23.0
	Russia	3.9	4.2	6.2	2.3	8.2	5.4	7.8	10.7
	Germany	2.6	3.3	0.9	0.9	1.1	4.7	10.5	14.6
	weighted average	3.5	3.9	3.0	4.1	8.3	10.8	14.6	19.6
absolute level of military expenditure relative to 1913 level		1870–1913 average	1913	1928	1930	1932	1934	1936	1938
status quo, liberal powers	USA	50	100	127	117	240	197	240	259
	France	58	100	90	35	144	149	182	225
	UK	72	100	90	84	101	109	155	290
	weighted average	61	100	99	110	153	146	187	259
1930s challengers	Japan	72	100	111	119	229	258	275	1308
	Russia	61	100	151	62	304	220	324	472
	Germany	53	100	30	27	42	191	459	698
	weighted average	60	100	100	59	194	216	366	697

so, the Reichstag and the Japanese Diet had acted as real checks on the ambitions of German and Japanese imperialists. The default that emerged everywhere as the norm, from Japan to the United States, was a comprehensive or near-comprehensive manhood suffrage and, in the case of new states, national republicanism. These constitutions were often still thin and weakly established. But the popular demands that they reflected were real and made it hard to sustain truly large-scale imperial expansion under anything approximating to liberal conditions.

The choice as it increasingly appeared to nationalist insurgents was between supine, democratic conformism and national self-assertion driven by a new form of domestic authoritarianism. There could be, it seemed, no compromise. This was in no way a traditional formula. Insofar as the insurgents themselves had a historical model, it was Bonaparte and he was hardly a traditionalist. The authoritarian movements of the interwar period and the regimes they spawned were a novel answer produced in response to the dramatic changes in international and domestic politics. But this challenge developed gradually. Throughout the 1920s dictatorships like that of Mussolini were still very much the exception and confined to the periphery. Neither the Polish nor the Spanish dictatorship of the 1920s was conceived of as permanent. It was only in the 1930s, in their all-out drives to challenge the status quo, that Stalinism, Nazism and Japanese imperialism would shed any inhibition. The new imperialism was unprecedented and uninhibited in its aggression both toward the domestic population and that of other countries. Hypocrisy was one crime that Nazism would not be accused of.

But what gave the insurgents their chance to undertake their doomed effort at revolt? As we saw in the first part of this book, World War I was won by a coalition that appeared to demonstrate a new level of international cooperation. The United States and the Entente acted together militarily. They combined their economic resources and sought to articulate certain common values. In the aftermath, France, Britain, Japan, and for a time Italy as well, looked to consolidate those relationships. The United States was the crucial factor in all those calculations. The League of Nations that emerged from the Versailles negotiations did serve down to the 1930s as a new forum for international politics. It was no coincidence that every major European initiative of the 1920s revolved around Geneva. But the League without its great political inspiration, the American President, became symbolic of the truly defining feature of the new era – the absent presence of US power. America was, as one British internationalist put it, the 'ghost at all our feasts'.[3]

Woodrow Wilson had, of course, intended for America to exert its influence from within the League of Nations. But as he had made clear with his 'peace without victory' speech in January 1917, he had no desire to place the United States at the head of anything like an international coalition. Already at Versailles he was pulling away from his wartime associates. The actual structure that emerged by the early 1920s was an ironic fulfilment of Wilson's ambition. As Austen Chamberlain pointed out in 1924, America's absence from the League, combined with Britain and France's dependence on it, had the effect of making America into a de facto 'super-State', exercising a veto over the combined decisions of the rest of the world.[4] Nothing less was the ambition both of Wilson and his Republican successors.

The entire story told in this book – from 'peace without victory' down to the Hoover moratorium of 1931 – is inflected by this basic impulse on behalf of successive United States administrations: to use America's position of privileged detachment, and the dependence on it of the other major world powers, to frame a transformation in world affairs. The 'revolution' in Europe and Asia that was as yet far from complete must be allowed to run its full course. This was in many respects a liberal and progressive project according to the terms defined by the US. Peace between the great powers, disarmament, commerce, progress, technology, communication were its watchwords. But fundamentally, in its view of America itself, in its conception of what might be asked of America, the project was profoundly conservative.

Wilson and Hoover had wished a revolutionary transformation upon the rest of the world, the better to uphold their ideal of America's destiny. However, theirs was a conservatism that did not look forward to MacCarthyism and the Cold War but instead backwards to the nineteenth century. In the half-century before 1914, no country had experienced the conflicts produced by 'uneven and combined development' more violently than America. After the traumatic blood-letting of the Civil War, the gilded age had promised a new unity and stability. The central purpose of two generations of American progressives was to hold at bay the disruptive ideologies and social forces of the twentieth century, so as not to disturb this new American equilibrium. The fragility of that vision was exposed by Wilson's humiliation in Congress, by the panic of the Red Scare and the sudden deflationary recession of 1920–21. With the return of 'normalcy' conservative order appeared to have been restored, only to be struck in 1929 by the most devastating economic crisis of all time. By 1933 the idea that America could be exempted from the maelstrom of twentieth-century history had collapsed from within. Billions of dollars were lost in Europe. In Asia, America's efforts to stabilize the world at arm's length were reduced to tatters. The Kellog-Briand style of internationalism without sanctions threatened to discredit the very idea of 'new diplomacy'.

One reaction was a true isolationism. The New Deal in its early phase was hostage to this impulse. It manifested, as one historian has put it, 'the great isolationist aberration'.[5] Domestic change was bought at the price of international withdrawal. But as the international challenges of the 1930s intensified, Roosevelt's administration did not stand aside. Out of the New Deal would emerge an American power state capable of exerting influence on a global stage in a far more positive, interventionist sense than anything seen in the aftermath of the First World War. But that militarized great power status was precisely the destiny from which progressives of Wilson's and Hoover's stripe had hoped to escape. For all America's new power, the disconcerting conclusion could not be escaped. The US was as much moved by the jarring, unpredictable momentum of the 'chain gang' as it was a mover.

In 1929, when introducing his proposal for European integration, Aristide Briand acknowledged the radicalism of what the new world demanded. 'In all the wisest and most important acts of man there was always an element of madness or recklessness,' he insisted.[6] This typically elegant and dialectical phrase provides a striking framework for the recurring debates about the history we have traversed here. With hindsight it is, of course, easy for self-stylized realists to criticize progressive visions of interwar order as symptomatic of the delusions of liberal idealism and as doleful overtures to appeasement. But hindsight deceives as well as it clarifies. As has been presented here, the restless search for a new way of securing order and peace was the expression not of deluded idealism, but of a higher form of realism. The search for international coalition and cooperation was the only appropriate response to the experience of uneven and combined development, to life in the international 'chain gang'. These were the calculations of a new type of liberalism, a Realpolitik of progress. It is a drama all the more moving for the fact that it remains an open, unfinished history, no less a challenge for us today.

Notes

EPIGRAPHS

1. W. Wilson, 'The Reconstruction of the Southern States', *Atlantic Monthly*, January 1901, vol. lxxxvii, 1–15.
2. J. M. Keynes, 'Mr Churchill on the Peace', *New Republic*, 27 March 1929.

THE DELUGE: THE REMAKING OF WORLD ORDER

1. *The Times*, 27 December 1915, issue 41047, 3.
2. Reichstag, *Stenographischer Bericht*, vol. 307, 850 ff, 5 April 1916, 852.
3. W. S. Churchill, *The Gathering Storm* (Boston, MA, 1948), vii.
4. W. S. Churchill, *The Aftermath* (London, 1929), 459.
5. G. L. Weinberg (ed.), *Hitler's Second Book* (New York, 2006).
6. See the works collected at http://www.marxists.org/archive/trotsky/works/.
7. The central preoccupation of C. Schmitt, *Positionen und Begriffe im Kampf mit Weimar-Genf-Versailles 1923–1939* (Berlin, 1940).
8. The phrase was popularized by D. Chakrabarty, *Provincializing Europe* (Princeton, NJ, 2000), who borrowed it from H.-G. Gadamer, most likely from 'Karl-Jaspers-Preis Laudatio für Jeanne Hersch', *Heidelberger Jahrbücher* 37 (1993), 151–8. Gadamer himself located this impression in the early years of his childhood in the aftermath of World War I.
9. Two highly sophisticated responses are M. Hardt and A. Negri, *Empire* (Cambridge, MA, 2001), and C. S. Maier, *Among Empires: American Ascendancy and Its Predecessors* (Cambridge, MA, 2006).
10. L. Trotsky, 'Is the Slogan "The United States of Europe" a Timely One?' http://www.marxists.org/archive/trotsky/1924/ffyci-2/25b.htm.
11. A. Hitler, 'Zweites Buch' (unpublished), 127–8.
12. There is a kindred relation here to 'power transition' and 'bargaining' theories of war developed by political scientists, such as A. F. K. Organski and J. Kugler, *The War Ledger* (Chicago, IL, 1980).
13. Amongst 'power transition' theories of war, the factor of risk-acceptance is

stressed by W. Kim and J. D. Morrow, 'When Do Power Shifts Lead to War?', *American Journal of Political Science* 36, no. 4 (November 1992), 896–922.

14. On the political stakes engaged even at the beginning of the war see H. Strachan, *The First World War* (London, 2003).

15. F. R. Dickinson, *World War I and the Triumph of a New Japan, 1919–1930* (Cambridge, 2013), 87.

16. L. Trotsky, 'Perspectives of World Development', http://www.marxists.org/archive/trotsky/1924/07/world.htm.

17. L. Trotsky, 'Disarmament and the United States of Europe', 4 October 1929, http://www.marxists.org/archive/trotsky/1929/10/disarm.htm.

18. F. Meinecke, *Machiavellism: The Doctrine of Raison d'État and its Place in Modern History*, trans. Douglas Scott (New Haven, CT, 1957), 432.

19. C. Schmitt, *The Nomos of the Earth in the International Law of the Jus Publicum Europaeum* (New York, 2006).

20. For a comprehensive historical corrective see P. W. Schroeder, *The Transformation of European Politics, 1763–1848* (Oxford, 1994).

21. S. Falasca-Zamponi, *Fascist Spectacle: The Aesthetics of Power in Mussolini's Italy* (Berkeley, CA, 1997), 163.

22. A. J. Mayer, *Wilson vs Lenin: Political Origins of the New Diplomacy, 1917–1918* (New York, 1964); N. Gordon Levin, *Woodrow Wilson and World Politics* (Oxford, 1968).

23. L. Trotsky, 'Perspectives on World Development', http://www.marxists.org/archive/trotsky/1924/07/world.htm.

24. L. Trotsky, 'Europe and America', February 1924, http://www.marxists.org/archive/trotsky/1926/02/europe.htm.

25. Ibid.

26. See, for instance, the data compiled for the OECD by Angus Maddison, http://www.theworldeconomy.org/.

27. The modern classic being P. Kennedy, *The Rise and Fall of the Great Powers* (London, 1987).

28. J. Darwin, *Empire Project: The Rise and Fall of the British World-System, 1830–1970* (Cambridge, 2009).

29. D. Bell, *The Idea of Greater Britain* (Princeton, NJ, 2009).

30. E. J. Eisenach, *The Lost Promise of Progressivism* (Lawrence, KS, 1994), 48–52.

31. A distinction deliberately blurred by the capacious notion of 'informal empire' introduced by John Gallagher and Ronald Robinson, 'The Imperialism of Free Trade', *The Economic History Review*, second series, VI, no. 1 (1953), 1–15.

32. W. A. Williams, *The Tragedy of American Diplomacy* (New York, 1959).

33. A self-consciousness beautifully captured by V. de Grazia, *Irresistible Empire: America's Advance Through Twentieth-Century Europe* (Cambridge, MA, 2005).

34. To give just one highly influential example, E. Hobsbawm, *Age of Extremes* (London, 1994).

35. Of which by far the most influential was R. S. Baker, *Woodrow Wilson and the World Settlement* (New York, 1922).

36. See its use even in accounts critical of Wilson, for example T. A. Bailey, *Woodrow Wilson and the Lost Peace* (New York, 1944), 154–5.

37. American radical critics of Wilson concluded that there had been no 'failure' at Versailles, but that upholding the vested interests of the established order was always the true purpose of the peace; see T. Veblen, Editorial from 'The Dial', 15 November 1919, in Veblen, *Essays in Our Changing Order* (New York, 1934), 459–61.

38. This is the basic storyline of A. Mayer's oeuvre, threading through *The Persistence of the Old Regime: Europe to the Great War* (New York, 1981), *Wilson versus Lenin: Political Origins of the New Diplomacy, 1917–1918* (New York, 2nd ed., 1964), *Politics and Diplomacy of Peacemaking* (New York, 1967), and *Why Did the Heavens Not Darken? The 'Final Solution' in History* (New York, 1988).

39. M. Mazower, *Dark Continent: Europe's Twentieth Century* (London, 1998), has been hugely influential.

40. J. L. Harper, *American Visions of Europe* (Cambridge, 1994).

41. D. E. Ellwood, *The Shock of America* (Oxford, 2012).

42. For different flavours of this kind of theorizing see P. Kindleberger, *The World in Depression: 1929–1939* (Berkeley, CA, 1973), R. Gilpin, 'The Theory of Hegemonic War', *The Journal of Interdisciplinary History* 18, no. 4 (Spring 1988), 591–613, and G. Arrighi, *The Long Twentieth Century: Money, Power, and the Origins of Our Times* (London, 1994).

43. J. Ikenberry, *After Victory: Institutions, Strategic Restraint, and the Rebuilding of Order after Major Wars* (Princeton, NJ, 2001).

44. C. A. Kupchan, *No One's World: The West, the Rising Rest, and the Coming Global Turn* (Oxford, 2012).

45. C. Bright and M. Geyer, 'For a Unified History of the World in the Twentieth Century', *Radical History Review* 39 (September 1987), 69–91, M. Geyer and C. Bright, 'World History in a Global Age', in *American Historical Review* 100 (October 1995), 1034–60, and M. Geyer and C. Bright, 'Global Violence and Nationalizing Wars in Eurasia and America: The Geopolitics of War in the Mid-Nineteenth Century', *Comparative Studies in Society and History* 38, no. 4 (October 1996), 619–57.

46. J. Hobson, *Imperialism: A Study* (London, 1902).

47. For an excellent recent survey see A. D'Agostino, *The Rise of Global Powers: International Politics in the Era of the World Wars* (Cambridge, 2012).

48. N. Smith, *American Empire: Roosevelt's Geographer and the Prelude to Globalization* (Berkeley, CA, 2003).

49. M. Nebelin, *Ludendorff* (Munich, 2010).

50. D. Fromkin, *The Peace to End all Peace* (New York, 1989).

51. For this argument the book owes much to A. Iriye, *After Imperialism: The Search for a New Order in the Far East, 1921–1931* (Cambridge, MA, 1965).

52. D. Gorman, *The Emergence of International Society in the 1920s* (Cambridge, 2012).

53. As in earlier work I remain deeply indebted to M. Berg, *Gustav Stresemann. Eine politische Karriere zwischen Reich und Republik* (Göttingen, 1992).

54. N. Bamba, *Japanese Diplomacy in a Dilemma* (Vancouver, 1972), 360–66.

55. L. Trotsky, *Perspectives of World Development* (1924), http://www.marxists.org/archive/trotsky/1924/07/world.htm.

56. A. Hitler, *Mein Kampf* (London, 1939), vol. 2, chapter 13.

57. In deep agreement with R. Boyce, *The Great Interwar Crisis and the Collapse of Globalization* (London, 2009).

58. For a short introduction see A. Stephanson, *Manifest Destiny: American Expansionism and the Empire of Right* (New York, 1995).

59. Eisenach, *Lost Promise*, 225.

60. A theme most recently developed by D. E. Ellwood, *The Shock of America* (Oxford, 2012). For an insightful critique, see T. Welskopp and A. Lessoff (eds), *Fractured Modernity: America Confronts Modern Times, 1890s to 1940s* (Oldenbourg, 2012).

61. A conclusion reached from a very different direction by G. Kolko, *The Triumph of Conservatism: A Reinterpretation of American History, 1900–1916* (New York, 1963).

62. J. T. Sparrow, *Warfare State: World War II Americans and the Age of Big Government* (New York, 2011).

63. Douglas Steeples and David O. Whitten, *Democracy in Desperation: The Depression of 1893* (Westport, CT, 1998).

64. The best short introduction remains A. S. Link, *Woodrow Wilson and the Progressive Era 1910–1917* (New York, 1954).

65. W. C. Widenor, *Henry Cabot Lodge and the Search for an American Foreign Policy* (Berkeley, CA, 1983).

66. B. Knei-Paz, *The Social and Political Thought of Leon Trotsky* (Oxford, 1978).

67. V. I. Lenin, 'The Chain Is No Stronger Than Its Weakest Link', *Pravda* 67, 9 June (27 May) 1917; *Lenin: Collected Works* (Moscow, 1964), vol. 24, 519–20.

68. S. Hoffmann, *Gulliver's Troubles, or the Setting of American Foreign Policy* (New York, 1968), 52. For other political science elaborations of 'uneven and combined development' see R. Gilpin, *War and Change in World Politics* (Cambridge, 1981).

I WAR IN THE BALANCE

1. Amongst recent histories see H. Strachan, *The First World War* (London, 2003), and D. Stevenson, *1914–1918: The History of the First World War* (London, 2004).

2. N. A. Lambert, *Planning Armageddon: British Economic Warfare and the First World War* (Cambridge, MA, 2012).

3. S. Roskill, *Naval Policy Between the Wars* (New York, 1968 and 1976), vol. 1, 80–81.

4. H. Nouailhat, *France et Etats-Unis: Aout 1914–Avril 1917* (Paris, 1979), 349–55.

5. C. Seymour (ed.), *The Intimate Papers of Colonel House* (London, 1926), vol. 1, 312–13.

6. A. S. Link (ed.) et al., *The Papers of Woodrow Wilson* [hereafter *PWW*], 69 vols (Princeton, NJ, 1966–94), vol. 36, 120.

7. J. J. Safford, *Wilsonian Maritime Diplomacy 1913–1921* (New Brunswick, NJ, 1978), 67–115.

8. P. O. O'Brian, *British and American Naval Power: Politics and Policy, 1900–1936* (Westport, CT, 1998), 117.

9. R. Skidelsky, *John Maynard Keynes: A Biography*, 3 vols (New York, 1983–2000), vol. 1, 305–15.

10. K. Burk, *Britain, America and the Sinews of War, 1914–1918* (London, 1985), and H. Strachan, *Financing the First World War* (Oxford, 2004).

11. K. Neilson, *Strategy and Supply: The Anglo-Russian Alliance 1914–1917* (London, 1984), 106–12.

12. M. Horn, *Britain, France, and the Financing of the First World War* (Montreal, 2002).

13. Nouailhat, *France*, 368.

14. S. Broadberry and M. Harrison (eds), *The Economics of World War I* (Cambridge, 2005).

15. A classic account is H. Feis, *Europe: The World's Banker 1870–1914* (New York, 1965).

16. R. Chernow, *The House of Morgan: An American Banking Dynasty and the Rise of Modern Finance* (New York, 2001).

17. J. M. Keynes, *The Collected Writings of John Maynard Keynes*, vol. 16 (London, 1971–89), 197.

18. P. Roberts, '"Quis Custodiet Ipsos Custodes?" The Federal Reserve System's Founding Fathers and Allied Finances in the First World War', *The Business History Review* 72 (1998), 585–620.

19. E. Sanders, *Roots of Reform* (Chicago, IL, 1999) and A. H. Meltzer, *A History of the Federal Reserve* (Chicago, IL, 2002–3).

20. W. L. Silber, *When Washington Shut Down Wall Street: The Great Financial Crisis of 1914 and the Origins of America's Monetary Supremacy* (Princeton, NJ, 2007).

21. N. Ferguson, *The Pity of War: Explaining World War I* (London, 1998).

22. A. Offer, *The First World War: An Agrarian Interpretation* (Oxford, 1991).

23. For a survey see D. E. Ellwood, *The Shock of America* (Oxford, 2012).

24. J. Banno, *Democracy in Prewar Japan: Concepts of Government 1871–1937* (London, 2001), 47.

25. W. Wilson, *Congressional Government: A Study in American Government* (PhD thesis, Johns Hopkins University, 1885).

26. D. T. Rodgers, *Atlantic Crossings: Social Politics in a Progressive Age* (Cambridge, MA, 1998).

27. W. Wilson, 'Democracy and Efficiency', *Atlantic Monthly* (March 1901), 289.

28. T. Raithel, *Das Wunder der inneren Einheit* (Bonn, 1996).

29. T. Roosevelt, *America and the World War* (New York, 1915).

30. J. M. Cooper, *The Warrior and the Priest: Theodore Roosevelt and Woodrow Wilson* (Cambridge, MA, 1983), 284–5.

31. W. Wilson, *A History of the American People* (New York, 1902), and J. M. Cooper, *Woodrow Wilson: A Biography* (New York, 2009).

32. *PWW*, vol. 57, 246.

33. W. Wilson, 'The Reconstruction of the Southern States', *Atlantic Monthly*, January 1901, 1–15.

34. R. E. Hannigan, *The New World Power: American Foreign Policy, 1898–1917* (Philadelphia, PA, 2002), 45–8.

35. R. S. Baker and W. E. Dodd (eds), *The Public Papers of Woodrow Wilson* (New York, 1925–7), vol. 1, 224–5.

36. T. J. Knock, *To End All Wars: Woodrow Wilson and the Quest for a New Order* (Princeton, NJ, 1992), 77.

37. *PWW*, vol. 37, 116.

38. *PWW*, vol. 40, 84–5.

39. *PWW*, vol. 41, 183–4, and repeated in February 1917, see ibid., 316–17.

40. B. M. Manly, 'Have Profits Kept Pace with the Cost of Living?', *Annals of the American Academy of Political and Social Science* 89 (1920), 157–62.

41. M. J. Pusey, *Charles Evans Hughes* (New York, 1951), vol. 1, 335–66.

42. *The Memoirs of Marshal Joffre*, trans. T. B. Mott (London, 1932), vol. 2, 461.

43. P. v. Hindenburg, *Aus Meinem Leben* (Leipzig, 1920), 180–81.

44. G. Ritter, *Staatskunst und Kriegshandwerk* (Munich, 1954–68), vol. 3, 246.

45. G. E. Torrey, *Romania and World War I* (Lasi, 1998), 174.

46. S. Miller, *Burgfrieden und Klassenkampf: Die deutsche Sozialdemokratie in Ersten Weltkrieg* (Düsseldorf, 1974), 263–4.

47. D. French, *The Strategy of the Lloyd George Coalition, 1916–19* (Oxford, 1995), and M. G. Fry, *Lloyd George and Foreign Policy* (Montreal, 1977).

48. Keynes, *The Collected Writings* (18 October 1916), vol. 16, 201.

49. Brilliantly set out in G.-H. Soutou, *L'Or et le Sang: Les Buts de guerre économique de la Première Guerre Mondiale* (Paris, 1989), 365–72, 398–9.

50. *Papers Relating to the Foreign Relations of the United States: Lansing Papers* (Washington, DC, 1940), vol. 1, 306–7.

51. Seymour (ed.), *Intimate Papers*, vol. 2, 129.

52. Fry, *Lloyd George*, 219.

53. Neilson, *Strategy and Supply*, 191; A. Suttie, *Rewriting the First World War: Lloyd George, Politics and Strategy 1914–1918* (London, 2005), 85.

2 PEACE WITHOUT VICTORY

1. V. I. Lenin, 'Imperialism, the Highest Stage of Capitalism', in V. I. Lenin, *Selected Works* (Moscow, 1963), vol. 1, 667–766.

2. On the left Lenin was arguing against theories of so-called ultra-imperialism, see K. Kautsky, 'Der Imperialismus', *Die Neue Zeit* 32, no. 2 (1914), 908–22. For a recent revival of this theory see A. Negri and M. Hardt, *Empire* (Cambridge, MA, 2001).

3. A. S. Link (ed.) et al., *The Papers of Woodrow Wilson* [hereafter *PWW*], 69 vols (Princeton, NJ, 1966–94), vol. 40, 19–20. For an illuminating revisionist narrative of America's entry into the war, see J. D. Doenecke, *Nothing Less Than War: A New History of America's Entry into World War I* (Lexington, KY, 2010).

4. *PWW*, vol. 40, 77.

5. P. Roberts, '"Quis Custodiet Ipsos Custodes?" The Federal Reserve System's Founding Fathers and Allied Finances in the First World War', *Business History Review* 72 (1998), 585–620.

6. H. Nouailhat, *France et Etats-Unis: Aout 1914–Avril 1917* (Paris, 1979), 382.

7. J. Siegel, *For Peace and Money* (Oxford, 2014, forthcoming), chapter 4.

8. G.-H. Soutou, *L'Or et le Sang: Les Buts de guerre économique de la Première Guerre Mondiale* (Paris, 1989), 373–8; J. Wormell, *The Management of the Public Debt of the United Kingdom* (London, 2000), 222–41.

9. J. H. von Bernstorff, *My Three Years in America* (New York, 1920), 317.

10. T. J. Knock, *To End All Wars: Woodrow Wilson and the Quest for a New Order* (Princeton, NJ, 1992), 110. On reactions in Russia see *Papers Relating to the Foreign Relations of the United States: Lansing Papers* [hereafter *FRUS: Lansing Papers*] (Washington, DC, 1940), vol. 2, 320–21.

11. 'President Wilson and Peace', *The Times* (London), Friday 22 December 1916, 9; 'French Public Opinion', *The Times* (London), 23 December 1916, 7.

12. Nouailhat, *France*, 393.

13. D. French, *The Strategy of the Lloyd George Coalition, 1916–1918* (Oxford, 1995), 34.

14. Ibid., 38.

15. J. M. Keynes, *Collected Writings of John Maynard Keynes*, vol. 16 (London, 1971).

16. *The New York Times*, 23 January 1917; *PWW*, vol. 40, 533–9.

17. Knock, *To End All Wars*, comes closest to grasping this, but treats the speech uncritically as a manifesto of progressivism. In the critical vein of the New Left is N. Levin, *Woodrow Wilson and World Politics* (New York, 1968), 260.

18. J. Cooper, *The Warrior and the Priest: Woodrow Wilson and Theodore Roosevelt* (Cambridge, MA, 1983).

19. C. Seymour (ed.), *The Intimate Papers of Colonel House* (London, 1926), vol. 2, 412.

20. *PWW*, vol. 40, 533–9.

21. Bernstorff, *My Three Years*, 390–91.

22. *The New York Times*, 23 January 1917.

23. *PWW*, vol. 41, 11–12.

24. *The New York Times*, 23 January 1917.

25. 'Labour in Session', *The Times* (London), 23 January 1917, 5.

26. 'War Aims of Labour', *The Times* (London), 24 January 1917, 7.

27. *The New York Times*, 24 January 1917.

28. Nouailhat, *France*, 398.

29. Bernstorff, *My Three Years*, 286.

30. Ibid., 371.

31. 'Aufzeichnung über Besprechung 9.1.1917', in H. Michaelis and E. Schraepler (eds), *Ursachen und Folgen. Vom deutschen Zusammenbruch 1918 und 1945* (Berlin, 1958), vol. 1, 146–7.

32. K. Erdmann (ed.), *Kurt Riezler. Tagebücher, Aufsaetze, Dokumente* (Göttingen, 1972), 403–4.

33. M. Weber, *Gesammelte politische Schriften* (Tübingen, 1988).

34. As Lansing put it to Wilson on 2 February 1917, *FRUS: Lansing Papers*, vol. 1, 591–2.

35. K. Burk, 'The Diplomacy of Finance: British Financial Missions to the United States 1914–1918', *The Historical Journal* 22, no. 2 (1979), 359.

36. On the history of Atlanticism see M. Mariano, *Defining the Atlantic Community* (New York, 2010).

37. M. G. Fry, *Lloyd George and Foreign Policy*, vol. 1, *The Education of a Statesman: 1890–1916* (Montreal, 1977), 34.

38. See D. Lloyd George, *The Great Crusade: Extracts from Speeches Delivered during the War* (London, 1918).

39. R. Hanks, 'Georges Clemenceau and the English', *The Historical Journal* 45, no. 1 (2002), 53–77.

40. *PWW*, vol. 42, 375–6. For Tardieu's own understanding of the challenges facing this relationship see A. Tardieu, *France and America: Some Experiences in Cooperation* (Boston, MA, 1927).

41. *PWW*, vol. 41, 136, 256 and 336–7.

42. Ibid., 89, 94, 101, and *PWW*, vol. 42, 255.

43. *PWW*, vol. 41, 120.

44. M. Hunt, *Ideology and US Foreign Policy* (New Haven, CT, 1987), 129–30. Seeking to link Wilson to the Cold War, Hunt overemphasizes the importance of the Commune as opposed to the great revolution of 1789.

45. See *Burke's Speech on Conciliation with the Colonies*, in Robert Andersen (ed.) with an introduction by Woodrow Wilson (Boston, MA, 1896), xviii.

46. W. Wilson, 'The Character of Democracy in the United States', in idem, *An Old Master and Other Political Essays* (New York, 1893), 114–15.

47. Wilson, 'Democracy and Efficiency', *Atlantic Monthly* LXXXVII (1901), 289.

48. Wilson, *The Character of Democracy*, 115.

49. Ibid., 114.

50. *PWW*, vol. 40, 133.

51. E. Mantoux, *The Carthaginian Peace* (New York, 1952), 50.

52. The best biographies remain D. Watson, *Georges Clemenceau: A Political Biography* (London, 1976), and G. Dallas, *At the Heart of a Tiger: Georges Clemenceau and His World 1841–1929* (London, 1993).

53. G. Clemenceau, *American Reconstruction, 1865–1870* (New York, 1969), 226.

54. W. Wilson, *A History of the American People* (New York, 1901), vol. 5, 49–53.

55. Clemenceau, *American Reconstruction*, 84.

56. The similarity between Clemenceau's and Roosevelt's positions on peace and justice was remarked upon by Clemenceau already in 1910 in lectures collected in G. Clemenceau, *Sur La Democratie* (Paris 1930), 124–5.

57. E. Benton, *The Movement for Peace Without Victory during the Civil War* (Columbus, OH, 1918), and J. McPherson, *This Mighty Scourge* (Oxford, 2007), 167–86.

58. Roosevelt waited until Wilson refused to act on Germany's aggression before unleashing this tirade. 'PEACE WITHOUT VICTORY MEANS PEACE WITHOUT HONOR', in *Poverty Bay Herald* XLIV, 20 March 1917, 8. See E. Morrison (ed.), *The Letters of Theodore Roosevelt* (Cambridge, MA, 1954), 1162–3.

59. *PWW*, vol. 41, 87.

60. *FRUS: Lansing Papers*, vol. 2, 118–20.

61. *PWW*, vol. 41, 201 and 283.

62. Ibid., 123 and 183–4.

63. Zimmermann to Bernstorff on 19 January 1917, in Michaelis and Schraepler, *Ursachen und Folgen*, vol. 1, 151–2.

64. Quoted in F. Katz, *The Secret War in Mexico: Europe, the United States and the Mexican Revolution* (Chicago, IL, 1981), 359–60.

65. W. Rathenau, *Politische Briefe* (Dresden, 1929), 108.

66. A. S. Link, *Woodrow Wilson and the Progressive Era 1910–1917* (New York, 1954), 275.

67. *PWW*, vol. 42, 140–48.

3 THE WAR GRAVE OF RUSSIAN DEMOCRACY

1. N. Saul, *War and Revolution: The United States and Russia, 1914–1921* (Lawrence, KS, 2001), 97–98.

2. The best recent narrative is O. Figes, *A People's Tragedy: The Russian Revolution 1891–1924* (London, 1996).

3. Snapshots of the popular mood in M. Steinberg, *Voices of Revolution, 1917* (New Haven, CT, 2001).

4. A. S. Link (ed.) et al., *The Papers of Woodrow Wilson* [hereafter *PWW*], 69 vols (Princeton, NJ, 1966–94), vol. 41, 425–7.

5. *PWW*, vol. 41, 440, and *Papers Relating to the Foreign Relations of the United States: Lansing Papers* [hereafter *FRUS: Lansing Papers*] (Washington, DC, 1940), vol. 1, 626–8, 636.

6. Wilson's declaration of war, 2 April 1917.

7. Quoted in M. Winock, *Clemenceau* (Paris, 2007), 418–19.

8. For a vivid account see N. Sukhanov, *The Russian Revolution, 1917: A Personal Record* (London, 1955), 202–3.

9. Sukhanov, *Russian Revolution*, 240–41.

10. W. Roobol, *Tsereteli – A Democrat in the Russian Revolution: A Political Biography* (The Hague, 1976); M. Khoundadze, *La révolution de février 1917: La social-démocratie contre le bolchevisme, Tsertelli face à Lenine* (Paris, 1988); R. Abraham, *Alexander Kerensky: The First Love of the Revolution* (London, 1987).

11. V. I. Lenin, 'Letter to *Pravda* on 7 April 1917', in V. I. Lenin, *Collected Works* (Moscow, 1964), vol. 24, 19–26.

12. J. H. von Bernstorff, *My Three Years in America* (London, 1920), 383.

13. D. Stevenson, 'The Failure of Peace by Negotiation in 1917', *The Historical Journal* 34, no. 1 (1991), 65–86.

14. S. Miller, *Burgfrieden und Klassenkampf: Die deutsche Sozialdemokratie im Ersten Weltkrieg* (Düsseldorf, 1974), 283–98.

15. *PWW*, vol. 42, MacDonald to Wilson, 29 May 1917, 420–22.

16. J. Turner, *British Politics and the Great War: Coalition and Conflict 1915–1918* (New Haven, CT, 1992).

17. L. Gardner, *Safe for Democracy: The Anglo-American Response to Revolution, 1913–1923* (Oxford, 1987), 138; A. Suttie, *Rewriting the First World War: Lloyd George, Politics, and Strategy, 1914–1918* (Houndmills, 2005), 191–4.

18. S. Carls, *Louis Loucheur and the Shaping of Modern France 1916–1931* (Baton Rouge, FL, 1993), 43–4, 50–51.

19. C. Seton-Watson, *Italy from Liberalism to Fascism 1870–1925* (London, 1979), 468–71.
20. *Der Interfraktioneller Ausschuss, 1917/18* [hereafter IFA], eds E. Matthias and R. Morsey (Düsseldorf, 1959), vol. 1, 3–13.
21. M. Epstein, *Matthias Erzberger and the Dilemma of German Democracy* (Princeton, NJ, 1959).
22. *IFA*, vol. 1, 15.
23. I. Sinanoglou, 'Journal de Russie d'Albert Thomas: 22 avril–19 juin 1917', *Cahiers du Monde Russe et Soviétique* 14, no. 1/2 (1973), 86–204, and J. Winter, *Socialism and the Challenge of War* (London, 1974), 243–59.
24. Wade, *Russian Search for Peace*, 79–80.
25. *FRUS: Lansing Papers*, vol. 2, 332 and 338.
26. *PWW*, vol. 43, 465–70 and 487–9; see also *PWW*, vol. 42, 140–41.
27. *PWW*, vol. 42, 365–7.
28. Ibid., 385.
29. J. J. Wormell, *Management of the National Debt in the United Kingdom, 1900–1932* (London, 2000), 249–59.
30. J. Terraine, *White Heat: The New Warfare 1914–18* (London, 1982), 218.
31. D. French, *The Strategy of the Lloyd George Coalition, 1914–1918* (Oxford, 1995), 101–23.
32. B. Millman, *Managing Domestic Dissent in First World War Britain* (London, 2000).
33. V. I. Lenin, 'Peace Without Annexations and the Independence of Poland as Slogans of the Day in Russia', http://www.marxists.org/archive/lenin/works/1916/feb/29.htm.
34. V. I. Lenin, 'The Discussion on Self-Determination Summed Up, July 1916', in V. I. Lenin, *Collected Works*, (Moscow, 1963), vol. 22, 320–60.
35. V. I. Lenin, 'The Petrograd City Conference of the R.S.D.L.P. 14–22 April 1917', in ibid., *Collected Works* (Moscow, 1964), vol. 24, 139–66.
36. *FRUS: Lansing Papers*, vol. 2, 340–41; L. Bacino, *Reconstructing Russia: U.S. Policy in Revolutionary Russia, 1917–1922* (Kent, OH, 1999).
37. L. Heenan, *Russian Democracy's Fatal Blunder: The Summer Offensive of 1917* (New York, 1987).
38. A. Kerensky, *The Kerensky Memoirs* (London, 1965), 285.
39. H. Herwig, *The First World War: Germany and Austria-Hungary 1914–1918* (London, 1997), 338.
40. M. Thompson, *The White War: Life and Death on the Italian Front 1915–1919* (New York, 2008), 294–327.
41. H. Hagenlücke, *Deutsche Vaterlandspartei* (Düsseldorf, 1997).
42. Abraham, *Kerensky*, 257.
43. Ibid., 305.
44. R. Service, *Lenin: A Biography* (London, 2000), 304.

45. O. Radkey, *Russia Goes to the Polls: The Election to the All-Russian Constituent Assembly, 1917* (Ithaca, NY, 1989), 63.

46. *PWW*, vol. 43, 471–2.

47. Ibid., 523.

48. Ibid., 509.

49. Ibid., 523–5.

50. O. Radkey, *The Agrarian Foes of Bolshevism: Promise and Default of the Russian Socialist Revolutionaries, February to October 1917* (New York, 1958), 85.

51. Ibid., 88.

4 CHINA JOINS A WORLD AT WAR

1. W. Wheeler, *China and the World War* (New York, 1919), 100.

2. A. S. Link (ed.) et al., *The Papers of Woodrow Wilson* [hereafter *PWW*], 69 vols (Princeton, NJ, 1966–94), vol. 41, 108–12.

3. G. Xu, *China and the Great War* (Cambridge, 2005), 162–3.

4. For a savage critique of the memorandum by Frank Goodnow of Columbia, see B. Putnam Weale, *The Fight for the Republic in China* (New York, 1917), 142–90; J. Kroncke, 'An Early Tragedy of Comparative Constitutionalism: Frank Goodnow and the Chinese Republic', *Pacific Rim Law and Policy Journal* 21, no. 3 (2012), 533–90.

5. W. Kirby, 'The Internationalization of China: Foreign Relations at Home and Abroad in the Republican Era', *The China Quarterly* 150, 'Special Issue: Reappraising Republican China' (1997), 433–58.

6. D. Kuhn, *Die Republik China von 1912 bis 1937* (Heidelberg, 2004), 89.

7. T.S. Chien, *The Government and Politics of China* (Cambridge, MA, 1950), 75–6.

8. S. Craft, *V. K. Wellington Koo and the Emergence of Modern China* (Lexington, KY, 2004), 40–41.

9. J. Sheridan, *China in Disintegration: The Republican Era in Chinese History, 1912–1949* (New York, 1977), 69.

10. N. Bose, *American Attitudes and Policy to the Nationalist Movement in China (1911–1921)* (Bombay, 1970), 105.

11. Xu, *China and the Great War*, 213.

12. S. Schram (ed.), *Mao's Road to Power: Revolutionary Writings 1912–1949: The Pre-Marxist Period*, vol. 1, *1912–1920* (New York, 1992), 104.

13. N. Pugach, *Paul S. Reinsch: Open Door Diplomat in Action* (Millwood, NY, 1979), 226.

14. *PWW*, vol. 41, 177.

15. Ibid., 175.

16. Ibid., 185.

17. N. Kawamura, *Turbulence in the Pacific: Japanese–US Relations During World War I* (Westport, CT, 2000), 66.

18. C. Tsuzuki, *The Pursuit of Power in Modern Japan 1825–1995* (Oxford, 2000).

19. F. Dickinson, *War and National Reinvention: Japan in the Great War 1914–1919* (Cambridge, MA, 1999).

20. L. Gardner, *Safe for Democracy: The Anglo-American Response to Revolution, 1913–1923* (Oxford, 1987), 83; Xu, *China and the Great War*, 94–7.

21. K. Kawabe, *The Press and Politics in Japan* (Chicago, IL, 1921); F. R. Dickinson, *World War I and the Triumph of a New Japan, 1919–1930* (Cambridge, 2013), 52.

22. Dickinson, *War and National Reinvention*, 150–65.

23. M. Schiltz, *The Money Doctors from Japan: Finance, Imperialism, and the Building of the Yen Bloc, 1895–1937* (Cambridge, MA, 2012), 135–54.

24. P. Duus, *Party Rivalry and Political Change in Taisho Japan* (Cambridge, 1968), 97–9.

25. P. Duus (ed.), *The Cambridge History of Japan*, vol. 6, *The Twentieth Century* (Cambridge, 1988), 280.

26. Weale, *Fight*, 206.

27. Quoted in Pugach, *Reinsch*, 226.

28. Wheeler, *China and the World War*, 71.

29. *PWW*, vol. 41, 186.

30. *PWW*, vol. 42, 53–4.

31. *Papers Relating to the Foreign Relations of the United States: Lansing Papers* [hereafter *FRUS: Lansing Papers*] (Washington, DC, 1940), vol. 2, 19–32, and Y. Zhang, *China in the International System, 1918–1920* (Basingstoke, 1991), 203.

32. M. Bergere, *Sun Yat-Sen* (Stanford, CA, 1998), 271.

33. Wheeler, *China and the World War*, 51.

34. 'American Press Tributes to Dr Wu Ting-Fang', *China Review* 3 (1922), 69–72.

35. Xu, *China and the Great War*, 241.

36. *PWW*, vol. 42, 466.

37. Wheeler, *China and the World War*, 94.

38. *The New York Times Current History*, vol. 13, *The European War* (New York, 1917), 353.

39. Wheeler, *China and the World War*, 173–4.

40. *FRUS: Lansing Papers*, vol. 2, 432–3.

41. Kawamura, *Turbulence in the Pacific*, 91–2.

42. Xu, *China and the Great War*, 226–7.

43. G. McCormack, *Chang Tso-Lin in Northeast China, 1911–1928: China, Japan and the Manchurian Idea* (Stanford, CA, 1977).

44. Dickinson, *War and National Reinvention*, 223.

45. *PWW*, vol. 42, 60–64.

46. Pugach, *Reinsch*, 236.

47. M. Metzler, *Lever of Empire: The International Gold Standard and the Crisis of Liberalism in Prewar Japan* (Berkeley, CA, 2005), 108–9.

5 BREST-LITOVSK

1. F. Fischer, *Griff nach der Weltmacht: Die Kriegszielpolitik des Kaiserlichen Deutschland, 1914–18* (Düsseldorf, 1961).

2. J. Wheeler-Bennett, *Brest-Litovsk: The Forgotten Peace, March 1918* (London, 1938).

3. For a history of Ober Ost written entirely in the shadow of the Third Reich see V. Liulevicius, *War Land on the Eastern Front: Culture, National Identity, and German Occupation in World War I* (Cambridge, 2000).

4. V. I. Lenin, 'The Debate on Self-Determination Summed Up', in V. I. Lenin, *Collected Works* (Moscow, 1964), vol. 22, 320–60.

5. V. I. Lenin, 'Statistics and Sociology', in V. I. Lenin, *Collected Works* (Moscow, 1964), vol. 23, 271–7.

6. T. Snyder, *The Reconstruction of Nations: Poland, Ukraine, Lithuania, Belarus, 1569–1999* (New Haven, CT, 2003).

7. 'Hitch in Negotiations: German Delegates Point to Peoples Who Desire . . .', *The New York Times*, 31 December 1917.

8. *Der Interfraktioneller Ausschuss, 1917/18* [hereafter *IFA*], eds E. Matthias and R. Morsey (Düsseldorf, 1959), vol. 1, 213–402.

9. Heinz Hagenlücke, *Deutsche Vaterlandspartei* (Düsseldorf, 1996).

10. *IFA*, vol. 1, 635.

11. W. Ribhegge, *Frieden für Europa: Die Politik der deutschen Reichstagsmehrheit, 1917–18* (Essen, 1988), 228–9.

12. M. Llanque, *Demokratisches Denken im Krieg: Die deutsche Debatte im Ersten Weltkrieg* (Berlin, 2000), 207.

13. A. Vogt, *Oberst Max Bauer, Generalstabsoffizier im Zwielicht, 1869–1929* (Osnabrück, 1974), 108.

14. K. Erdmann (ed.), *Kurt Riezler: Tagebücher, Aufsaetze, Dokumente* (Göttingen, 1972).

15. W. Ribhegge, *Frieden für Europa. Die Politik der deutschen Reichstagsmehrheit 1917/18* (Berlin, 1988), 228–9.

16. P. Gatrell, *A Whole Empire Walking: Refugees in Russia during World War I* (Indiana, IN, 2005).

17. Hagenlücke, *Vaterlandspartei*, 204.

18. I. Geiss, *Der polnische Grenzstreifen 1914–1918: Ein Beitrag zur deutschen Kriegszielpolitik im Ersten Weltkrieg* (Lübeck, 1960), 129.

19. For the Erzberger jibe see Ribhegge, *Frieden*, 173–5. For the SPD response, ibid., 228–9.

20. P. Theiner, *Sozialer Liberalismus und deutsche Weltpolitik. Friedrich Naumann im Wilhelminischen Deutschland (1860–1919)* (Baden-Baden, 1983), 242–58.

21. M. Berg, *Gustav Stresemann und die Vereinigten Staaten von Amerika: weltwirtschaftliche Verflechtung und Revisionspolitik, 1907–1929* (Baden-Baden, 1990), 43.

22. *IFA*, vol. 1, 11.

23. R. Service, *Lenin: A Biography* (Düsseldorf, 2000), 321–5.

24. Fischer, *Griff*, 299–300.

25. Fischer, *Griff*, 299–300.

26. J. Snell, 'The Russian Revolution and the German Social Democratic Party in 1917', *Slavic Review* 15, no. 3 (1956), 339–50; see also *IFA*, vol. 1, 631–2.

27. S. Miller, *Burgfrieden und Klassenkampf: Die deutsche Sozialdemokratie im Ersten Weltkrieg* (Düsseldorf, 1974), 228–9.

28. K. Epstein, *Matthias Erzberger and the Dilemma of German Democracy* (Princeton, NJ, 1959), 219–20, 237.

29. On the renegotiation of sovereignty more generally see M. Koskenniemi, *The Gentle Civilizer of Nations: The Rise and Fall of International Law 1870–1960* (Cambridge, 2002), 172.

30. S. D. Krasner, *Sovereignty: Organized Hypocrisy* (Princeton, NJ, 1999).

31. Miller, *Burgfrieden*, 351.

32. Wheeler-Bennett, *Brest*, 117–20.

33. G. Kennan, *Russia Leaves the War: Soviet-American Relations, 1917–1920* (Princeton, NJ), vol. 1, 136.

34. C. Seymour (ed.), *The Intimate Papers of Colonel House* (Boston, MA, 1926–8), vol. 3, 264–85.

35. W. Hahlweg (ed.), *Der Friede von Brest-Litowsk. Ein unveröffentlichter Band aus dem Werk des Untersuchungsauschusses der deutschen verfassungsgebenden Nationalversammung und des deutschen Reichstages* (Düsseldorf, 1971), 150–53.

36. A. May, *The Passing of the Habsburg Monarchy, 1914–1918* (Philadelphia, PA, 1966), vol. 1, 458.

37. *IFA*, vol. 2, 86.

38. Full text in Hahlweg, *Der Friede*, 176.

39. Summarized in V. I. Lenin, 'Theses on the Question of the Immediate Conclusion of a Separate and Annexationist Peace, 7 January 1918', in V. I. Lenin, *Collected Works* (Moscow, 1972), vol. 26, 442–50.

40. Wheeler-Bennett, *Brest*, 145.

41. L. Gardner, *Safe for Democracy: The Anglo-American Response to Revolution, 1913–1923* (Oxford, 1987), 160.

42. E. Manela, *The Wilsonian Moment: Self-Determination and the International Origins of Anticolonial Nationalism* (Oxford, 2007), 19–53.

43. B. Unterberger, *The United States, Revolutionary Russia, and the Rise of Czechoslovakia* (Chapel Hill, NC, 1989), 94-5.

44. For this and what follows, see A. S. Link (ed.) et al., *The Papers of Woodrow Wilson* [hereafter *PWW*], 69 vols (Princeton, NJ, 1966-94), vol. 45, 534-9.

45. *Papers Relating to the Foreign Relations of the United States: Lansing Papers* (Washington, DC, 1940), vol. 2, 348.

46. See the devastating critique in Kennan, *Russia Leaves the War*, 255-72.

47. C. Warvariv, 'America and the Ukrainian National Cause, 1917-1920', in T. Hunczak (ed.), *The Ukraine 1917-1921: A Study in Revolution* (Cambridge, MA, 1977), 366-72.

48. *PWW*, vol. 45, 534-9.

49. D. Woodward, *Trial by Friendship: Anglo-American Relations, 1917-1918* (Lexington, KY, 1993), 153-4.

50. B. Unterberger, 'Woodrow Wilson and the Russian Revolution', in A. Link (ed.), *Woodrow Wilson and a Revolutionary World* (Chapel Hill, NC, 1982), 54.

6 MAKING A BRUTAL PEACE

1. J. Reshetar, *The Ukrainian Revolution, 1917-1920: A Study in Nationalism* (Princeton, NJ, 1952), 53-4.

2. W. Stojko, 'Ukrainian National Aspirations and the Russian Provisional Government', in T. Hunczak (ed.), *The Ukraine 1917-1921: A Study in Revolution* (Cambridge, MA, 1977).

3. P. Borowsky, *Deutsche Ukrainepolitik 1918 unter besonderer Berücksichtigung der Wirtschaftsfragen* (Lübeck, 1970), 21-5.

4. E. Carr, *The Bolshevik Revolution, 1917-1923* (London, 1966), vol. 1, 301.

5. W. Hahlweg (ed.), *Der Friede von Brest-Litowsk: Ein unveröffentlichter Band aus dem Werk des Untersuchungsausschusses der deutschen verfassunggebenden Nationalversammlung und des deutschen Reichstages* (Düsseldorf, 1971), 299.

6. Hahlweg, *Friede*, 332, an English rendition in J. Wheeler-Bennett, *Brest-Litovsk: The Forgotten Peace, March 1918* (London, 1938), 161-3.

7. The most famous tragic interpretation is that offered by the German sociologist Max Weber in a speech delivered in early 1919, 'Politics as a Vocation'. Significantly, to arrive at his tragic conclusions Weber distorts Trotsky's meaning by quoting only a fragment of his first sentence; see Peter Lassman and Ronald Speirs (eds), *Weber: Political Writings* (Cambridge, 1994), 310.

8. M. D. Steinberg, *Voices of Revolution, 1917* (New Haven, CT, 2001), 262-73.

9. W. H. Roobol, *Tsereteli – A Democrat in the Russian Revolution: A Political Biography* (The Hague, 1977), 181-2.

10. J. Bunyan and H. Fisher (eds), *The Bolshevik Revolution 1917–1918: Documents and Materials* (Stanford, CA, 1934), 369–80.

11. M. Gorky, *Untimely Thoughts* (New Haven, CT, 1995), 124–5.

12. R. Pipes, *The Russian Revolution* (New York, 1990), 554.

13. V. I. Lenin, 'People from Another World', in V. I. Lenin, *Collected Works* (Moscow, 1972), vol. 26, 431–3.

14. J. Siegel, *For Peace and Money* (Oxford, 2014, forthcoming), chapter 5.

15. C. Bell and B. Elleman, *Naval Mutinies of the Twentieth Century: An International Perspective* (London, 2003), 45–65.

16. P. Scheidemann, *Der Zusammenbruch* (Berlin, 1921), 70–71.

17. *Der Interfraktioneller Ausschuss, 1917/18* [hereafter *IFA*], eds E. Matthias and R. Morsey (Düsseldorf, 1959), vol. 2, 188–93.

18. Wheeler-Bennett, *Brest-Litovsk*, 209–11.

19. K. Liebknecht, *Politische Aufzeichnungen aus seinem Nachlass* (Berlin, 1921), 51, cited in L. Trotsky, *My Life* (New York, 1960), 378.

20. G.-H. Soutou, *L'Or et le Sang: Les Buts de guerre économique de la Première Guerre Mondiale* (Paris, 1989), 661–3.

21. Wheeler-Bennett, *Brest-Litovsk*, 171.

22. Pipes, *Russian Revolution*, 591.

23. Quoted retrospectively in V. I. Lenin, 'Peace or War, 23 February 1918', in V. I. Lenin, *Collected Works* (Moscow, 1972), vol. 27, 36–9.

24. R. Debo, *Revolution and Survival: The Foreign Policy of Soviet Russia 1917–1918* (Toronto, 1979), 120–21.

25. Wheeler-Bennett, *Brest-Litovsk*, 226–9.

26. *IFA*, vol. 2, 250.

27. Ibid., 163.

28. For this and the following, W. Baumgart and K. Repgen, *Brest-Litovsk* (Göttingen, 1969), 58–66.

29. The Kaiser's words were: 'bolshewiki tiger, kesseltreiben abschiessen'.

30. Baumgart and Repgen, *Brest-Litovsk*, 61.

31. Ibid., 62.

32. Ibid., 66.

33. R. von Kühlmann, *Erinnerungen* (Heidelberg, 1948), 548.

34. I. Geiss, *Der polnische Grenzstreifen, 1914–1918. Ein Beitrag zur deutschen Kriegszielpolitik im Ersten Weltkrieg* (Lübeck, 1960), 132–4.

35. M. Hoffmann, *War Diaries and Other Papers* (London, 1929), vol. 1, 205.

36. R. Pipes, *Russia under the Bolshevik Regime* (New York, 1994), 27–8, 52.

37. Pipes, *Russian Revolution*, 588.

38. Debo, *Revolution*, 124–46.

39. Wheeler-Bennett, *Brest-Litovsk*, 245.

40. Pipes, *Russian Revolution*, 594.

41. V. I. Lenin, 'Political Report of the Bolshevik Central Committee, 7 March 1918. Seventh Congress of the Russian Communist Party: Verbatim Report

6–8 March 1918', in V. I. Lenin, *Collected Works* (Moscow, 1972), vol. 27, 85–158.

42. R. Service, *Lenin: A Political Life* (Bloomington, IN, 1985), 327–30.

43. V. I. Lenin, 'Extraordinary Fourth All-Russia Congress of Soviets, 14–16 March 1918', in V. I. Lenin, *Collected Works* (Moscow, 1972), vol. 27, 169–201.

44. W. Ribhegge, *Frieden für Europa: Die Politik der deutschen Reichstagsmehrheit, 1917–18* (Essen, 1988), 264–5.

45. *Der Interfraktioneller Ausschuss, 1917/18*, eds E. Matthias and R. Morsey (Düsseldorf, 1959), vol. 2, 285–91; S. Miller, *Burgfrieden und Klassenkampf: Die deutsche Sozialdemokratie im Ersten Weltkrieg* (Düsseldorf, 1974), 368.

46. Wheeler-Bennett, *Brest-Litovsk*, 304–7.

47. Ribhegge, *Frieden*, 268.

48. *IFA*, vol. 2, 303.

49. Stevenson, *With Our Backs to the Wall* (London, 2011), 42, 53–4.

50. W. Churchill, *The World Crisis, 1916–1918* (New York, 1927), vol. 2, 132.

51. W. Goerlitz (ed.), *Regierte Der Kaiser? Kriegstagebücher, Aufzeichnungen und Briefe des Chefs des Marinekabinetts Admiral George Alexander von Mueller, 1914–1918* (Göttingen, 1959), 366.

52. Erich Ludendorff, *My War Memories* (London, 1919), vol. 2, 602.

53. Max von Baden, *Erinnerungen und Dokumente* (Stuttgart, 1968), 242–3.

7 THE WORLD COME APART

1. W. Baumgart, *Deutsche Ostpolitik 1918. Von Brest-Litowsk bis zum Ende des Ersten Weltkrieges* (Vienna and Munich, 1966), 40.

2. S. F. Cohen, *Bukharin and the Bolshevik Revolution: A Political Biography 1888–1938* (London, 1974).

3. 'The Chief Task of Our Day', *Izvestia VTsIK*, no. 46, 12 March 1918, in V. I. Lenin, *Collected Works* (Moscow, 1972), vol. 27, 159–63.

4. For this and following, *Seventh Congress of the Russian Communist Party: Verbatim Report*, 6–8 March 1918, in ibid., 85–158.

5. Baumgart, *Deutsche Ostpolitk*, 36. This telltale admission was later removed from the official Moscow edition of Lenin's collected works.

6. R. Pipes, *The Russian Revolution* (New York, 1990), 603–5.

7. P. E. Dunscomb, *Japan's Siberian Intervention, 1918–1922* (Plymouth, 2011), 40.

8. F. R. Dickinson, *War and National Reinvention: Japan in the Great War, 1914–1919* (Cambridge, MA, 1999), 57 and 197.

9. J. Morley, *The Japanese Thrust into Siberia, 1918* (New York, 1957), 53.

10. Dickinson, *War*, 183–4.

11. Dunscomb, *Siberian Intervention*, 42–3.

12. Dickinson, *War*, 196.

13. S. Naoko, *Japan, Race and Equality: The Racial Equality Proposal of 1919* (London, 2003), 109.

14. C. Tsuzuki, *The Pursuit of Power in Modern Japan, 1825–1995* (Oxford, 2000), 206.

15. G. Kennan, *Russia Leaves the War: Soviet-American Relations, 1917–1920* (Princeton, NJ), vol. 1, 272–3.

16. B. M. Unterberger, 'Woodrow Wilson and the Russian Revolution', in *Woodrow Wilson and a Revolutionary World*, ed. Arthur S. Link (Chapel Hill, NC, 1982), 61.

17. Kennan, *Soviet-American*, 480.

18. C. Seymour (ed.), *The Intimate Papers of Colonel House* (Boston, MA, 1926–8), vol. 3, 399.

19. Pipes, *Russian Revolution*, 598–9.

20. Morley, *The Japanese Thrust*, 140–41.

21. N. Kawamura, *Turbulence in the Pacific: Japanese-US Relations during World War I* (Westport, CT, 2000), 116; A. S. Link (ed.) et al., *The Papers of Woodrow Wilson*, 69 vols (Princeton, NJ, 1966–94).

22. House at least did, recognizing the existence of 'two parties in Japan', see Seymour (ed.), *Intimate Papers*, vol. 3, 415.

23. U. Trumpener, *Germany and the Ottoman Empire 1914–1918* (Princeton, NJ, 1968), 249.

24. See the exchange between Erzberger, Kühlmann and Hertling in June 1918, in *Der Interfraktioneller Ausschuss, 1917/18* [hereafter *IFA*], eds E. Matthias and R. Morsey (Düsseldorf, 1959), vol. 2, 410.

25. R. G. Hovanissian, *Armenia on the Road to Independence, 1918* (Berkeley, CA, 1967), 175.

26. Baumgart, *Ostpolitik*, 181.

27. Ibid., 193–4.

28. Hovannisian, *Armenia on the Road to Independence*, 184.

29. A policy acknowledged in Reichstag committee, *IFA*, vol. 2, 519.

30. Trumpener, *Germany*, 256–7.

31. R. G. Suny, *The Making of the Georgian Nation* (Bloomington, IN, 1994), 192.

32. Baumgart, *Ostpolitik*, 269.

33. P. Borowsky, *Deutsche Ukrainepolitik, 1918* (Lübeck 1970).

34. As Erzberger insisted in discussion with German authorities in Ukraine, *IFA*, vol. 2, 407.

35. See the explanation given to the Reichstag majority in *IFA*, vol. 2, 404.

36. Max Hoffmann, *War Diaries and Other Papers* (London, 1929), vol. 1, 209.

37. T. Hunczak, 'The Ukraine under Hetman Pavlo Skoropadskyi', in idem., *The Ukraine: A Study in Revolution, 1917–1921* (Cambridge, MA, 1977), 61–81.

38. A. F. Upton, *The Finnish Revolution 1917–1918* (Minneapolis, MN, 1980).

39. C. J. Smith, *Finland and the Russian Revolution 1917–1922* (Athens, GA, 1958), 78.

40. Stanley G. Payne, *Civil War in Europe 1905–1940* (Cambridge, 2011), 30.

41. Pipes, *Russian Revolution*, 612–15.

42. Baumgart, *Ostpolitik*, 37.

43. R. H. Ullman, *Anglo-Soviet Relations 1917–1921*, vol. 1, *Intervention and the War* (Princeton, NJ, 1961), 177.

44. Baumgart, *Ostpolitik*, 267–8.

45. '"Left-Wing" Childishness', written April 1918, first published 9, 10, 11 May 1918 in *Pravda*, nos 88, 89, 90; Lenin, *Collected Works* (Moscow, 1972), vol. 27, 323–34.

46. Baumgart, *Ostpolitik*, 264.

47. *Russian American Relations March 1917–March 1920* (New York, 1920), Doc. 73, 152–3.

48. Ibid., Doc. 91, 209.

49. D. W. McFadden, *Alternative Paths: Soviets and Americans 1917–1920* (Oxford, 1993), 122.

50. Baumgart, *Ostpolitik*, 70.

51. Ibid., 129.

52. Ibid., 183.

53. K. Epstein, *Matthias Erzberger and the Dilemma of German Democracy* (Princeton, NJ, 1959), 239–40.

54. Borowsky, *Deutsche Ukrainepolitik*, 190–92.

55. See Gothein, *IFA*, vol. 2, 289.

56. See his protests against interference in Lithuanian education, *IFA*, vol. 2, 388.

57. Epstein, *Erzberger*, 242.

58. W. Baumgart and K. Repgen (eds), *Brest-Litovsk* (Göttingen, 1969), 100. The Reichstag majority had resisted the German intervention from the outset, see *IFA*, vol. 2, 316–17.

8 INTERVENTION

1. R. H. Ullman, *Anglo-Soviet Relations, 1917–1921* (Princeton, NJ, 1962), vol. 1, 169.

2. C. Seymour (ed.), *The Intimate Papers of Colonel House* (Boston, MA, 1926–8), vol. 3, 410.

3. R. Pipes, *The Russian Revolution* (New York, 1990), 558–65.

4. B. M. Unterberger, *The United States, Revolutionary Russia and the Rise of Czechoslovakia* (Chapel Hill, NC, 1989), 124–7.

5. *Papers Relating to the Foreign Relations of the United States: Lansing Papers* (Washington, DC, 1940), vol. 2, 126–8, 139–41 and 364.

6. L. Gardner, *Safe for Democracy: The Anglo-American Response to Revolution, 1913–1923* (Oxford, 1987), 186.

7. Quoted in Unterberger, *United States*, 235.

8. Quoted in T. J. Knock, *To End All Wars: Woodrow Wilson and the Quest for a New Order* (Princeton, NJ, 1992), 161.

9. I. Somin, *Stillborn Crusade: The Tragic Failure of Western Intervention in the Russian Civil War 1918–1920* (New Brunswick, NJ, 1996), 40.

10. Ullman, *Anglo-Soviet*, 222.

11. Ibid., 305.

12. Ibid., 221–2.

13. Pipes, *Russian Revolution*, 633–5.

14. W. Baumgart, *Deutsche Ostpolitik 1918. Von Brest-Litowsk bis zum Ende des Ersten Weltkrieges* (Vienna and Munich, 1966), 85.

15. Ibid., 85–6.

16. F. Fischer, *Griff nach der Weltmacht: Die Kriegszielpolitik des Kaiserlichen Deutschland, 1914–18*, (Düsseldorf, 1961), 836–40.

17. *Der Interfraktioneller Ausschuss, 1917/18* [hereafter *IFA*], eds E. Matthias and R. Morsey (Düsseldorf, 1959), vol. 2, 400–01.

18. Baumgart, *Ostpolitik*, 139.

19. M. Kitchen, *The Silent Dictatorship: The Politics of the German High Command under Hindenburg and Ludendorff, 1916–1918* (London, 1976), 204.

20. *IFA*, vol. 2, 413–18.

21. Quoted in W. Ribhegge, *Frieden für Europa: Die Politik der deutschen Reichstagsmehrheit, 1917–18* (Essen, 1988), 299.

22. *IFA*, vol. 2, 447–65.

23. Ibid., 426–8.

24. Ibid., 517.

25. Ibid., 474.

26. Pipes, *Russian Revolution*, 638–9.

27. Pipes, *Russian Revolution*, 653–6; Baumgart, *Ostpolitik*, 232.

28. A. J. Mayer, *Furies: Violence and Terror in the French and Russian Revolutions* (Princeton, NJ, 2000), 273–4.

29. Ibid., 277.

30. Lenin speech to All-Russia Central Executive Committee, Fifth Convocation, 29 July 1918, in V. I. Lenin, *Collected Works* (Moscow, 1965), vol. 28, 17–33.

31. K. Helfferich, *Der Weltkrieg* (Berlin, 1919), vol. 3, 466.

32. Rosa Luxemburg, 'The Russian Tragedy', *Spartacus*, no. 11, 1918.

33. *IFA*, vol. 2, 505–6.

34. Baumgart, *Ostpolitik*, 109.

35. Pipes, *Russian Revolution*, 664–6; Baumgart, *Ostpolitik*, 111–13.

36. The effort by G.-H. Soutou, *L'Or et le Sang. Les Buts de guerre économique de la Première Guerre Mondiale* (Paris, 1989), 706–8, to read the supplementary Brest Treaty as a preliminary to Rapallo is far too generous to Lenin. However, he is right that the economic terms were hardly punitive.

37. M. Kitchen, *The Silent Dictatorship: The Politics of the German High Command under Hindenburg and Ludendorff, 1916–1918* (New York, 1976), 242; Baumgart, *Ostpolitik*, 201.

38. Pipes, *Russian Revolution*, 666.

39. R. Pipes, *Russia under the Bolshevik Regime* (New York, 1994), 53–5.

40. *IFA*, vol. 2, 476–9.

41. Baumgart, *Ostpolitik*, 313–15.

42. *IFA*, vol. 2, 474–9, 500–01.

43. Helfferich, *Weltkrieg III*, 490–92.

44. *IFA*, vol. 2, 517.

45. Baumgart, *Ostpolitik*, 318–19.

46. C. Tsuzuki, *The Pursuit of Power in Modern Japan, 1825–1995* (Oxford, 2000), 206.

47. In whole-hearted agreement with Pipes, *Russian Revolution*, 668–70, who however oversimplifies the German position.

9 ENERGIZING THE ENTENTE

1. D. Stevenson, *With Our Backs to the Wall: Victory and Defeat in 1918* (London, 2011).

2. See for a typical assessment the comments by an anguished conservative under-secretary at the time of Germany's parliamentarization in September 1918, *Der Interfraktioneller Ausschuss, 1917/18*, eds E. Matthias and R. Morsey (Düsseldorf, 1959), vol. 2, 773–8.

3. M. Knox, *To the Threshold of Power, 1922/33*, vol. 1, *Origins and Dynamics of the Fascist and National Socialist Dictatorships* (Cambridge, 2007), 143–231.

4. L. V. Smith, S. Audoin-Rouzeau and A. Becker, *France and the Great War* (Cambridge, 2003).

5. P. O'Brien, *Mussolini in the First World War: The Journalist, The Soldier, The Fascist* (Oxford, 2005).

6. G. Clemenceau, 'Discours de Guerre', Chambre des Députés, Assemblée Nationale, Paris (8 March 1918).

7. D. Watson, *Georges Clemenceau: A Political Biography* (London, 1976), 275–92.

8. G. Clemenceau, *Demosthenes* (New York, 1926).

9. W. A. McDougall, *France's Rhineland Diplomacy 1914–1924* (Princeton, NJ, 1978), 17–25.

10. H. J. Burgwyn, *The Legend of the Mutilated Victory: Italy, the Great War, and the Paris Peace Conference, 1915–1919* (Westport, CT, 1993).

11. C. Seton-Watson, *Italy from Liberation to Fascism, 1870–1925* (London, 1967), 485.

12. D. Rossini, *Woodrow Wilson and the American Myth in Italy* (Cambridge, MA, 2008), 125–31.

13. For a brilliant near-contemporary account see L. Hautecoeur, *L'Italie sous le Ministère Orlando 1917–1919* (Paris, 1919), 83–110.

14. C. Killinger, *Gaetano Salvemini: A Biography* (Westport, CT, 2002).

15. K. J. Calder, *Britain and New Europe 1914–1918* (Cambridge, 1976), 180–82.

16. G. A. Heywood, *Failure of a Dream: Sidney Sonnino and the Rise and Fall of Liberal Italy 1847–1922* (Florence, 1999).

17. H. Nicolson, *Peacemaking, 1919* (London, 1933), 167.

18. S. Di Scala, *Vittorio Orlando* (London, 2010), 119; Rossini, *Woodrow Wilson*, 142–6.

19. For all of what follows the indispensable reference is J. Darwin, *The Empire Project: The Rise and Fall of the British World System, 1830–1970* (Cambridge, 2009).

20. J. Grigg, *Lloyd George: War Leader, 1916–1918* (London, 2002), 61.

21. For a brilliant overview see R. Fanning, *Fatal Path: British Government and Irish Revolution, 1910–1922* (London, 2013).

22. J. P. Finnan, *John Redmond and Irish Unity, 1912–1918* (Syracuse, NY, 2004).

23. C. Duff, *Six Days to Shake an Empire* (London, 1966).

24. J. S. Mortimer, 'Annie Besant and India 1913–1917', *Journal of Contemporary History* 18, no. 1 (January 1983), 61–78.

25. H. F. Owen, 'Negotiating the Lucknow Pact', *The Journal of Asian Studies* 31, no. 3 (May 1972), 561–87.

26. A. Rumbold, *Watershed in India, 1914–1922* (London, 1979), 64.

27. Ibid., 73.

28. B. R. Tomlinson, *The Political Economy of the Raj, 1914–1947: The Economics of Decolonization in India* (London, 1979).

29. Rumbold, *Watershed*, 71–2.

30. P. Robb, 'The Government of India and Annie Besant', *Modern Asian Studies* 10, no. 1 (1976), 107–30.

31. H. Owens, *The Indian Nationalist Movement, c. 1912–1922: Leadership, Organisation and Philosophy* (New Delhi, 1990), 85.

32. R. Kumar, *Annie Besant's Rise to Power in Indian Politics, 1914–1917* (New Delhi, 1981), 115.

33. B. Millman, *Managing Domestic Dissent in First World War Britain* (London, 2000), 170.

34. H. C. G. Matthew, R. I. McKibbin and J. A. Kay, 'The Franchise Factor in the Rise of the Labour Party', *The English Historical Review* 91, no. 361 (October 1976), 723–52.

35. The indispensable reference remains M. Pugh, *Electoral Reform in War and Peace, 1906–1918* (London, 1978).

36. Ibid., 103.

37. J. Lawrence, 'Forging a Peaceable Kingdom: War, Violence, and Fear of Brutalization in Post-First World War Britain', *Journal of Modern History* 75, no. 3 (2003), 557–89.

38. D. H. Close, 'The Collapse of Resistance to Democracy: Conservatives, Adult Suffrage, and Second Chamber Reform, 1911–1928', *The Historical Journal* 20, no. 4 (December 1977), 893–918.

39. Pugh, *Electoral Reform*, 136.

40. S. S. Holton, *Feminism and Democracy: Women's Suffrage and Reform Politics in Britain, 1900–1918* (Cambridge, 1986), 149.

41. Pugh, *Electoral Reform*, 75.

42. Darwin, *Empire Project*, 353.

43. Ibid., 348.

44. Rumbold, *Watershed*, 88.

45. S. D. Waley, *Edwin Montagu: A Memoir and an Account of his Visits to India* (London, 1964), 130–34.

46. R. Danzig, 'The Announcement of August 20th, 1917', *The Journal of Asian Studies* 28, no. 1 (November 1968), 19–37; R. J. Moore, 'Curzon and Indian Reform', *Modern Asian Studies* 27, no. 4 (October 1993), 719–40.

47. Waley, *Montagu*, 135.

48. Ibid., 137–8.

49. H. Tinker, *The Foundations of Local Self-Government in India, Pakistan and Burma* (London, 1954), 112–61.

50. All of the following are from E. Montagu and F. Chelmsford, *The Constitution of India Under British Rule: The Montagu-Chelmsford Report* (New Delhi, 1992).

51. D. A. Low, *Lion Rampant: Essays in the Study of British Imperialism* (London, 1973).

52. T. R. Metcalf, *Ideologies of the Raj* (Cambridge, 1997), 225–6.

53. M. Gandhi, *Collected Works* (New Delhi, 1999), vol. 17, 'Appeal for Enlistment 22 June 1918'.

54. S. Sarkar, *Modern India, 1885–1947* (Madras, 1983), 150.

55. Kumar, *Annie Besant*, 112–13.

56. Manela's imaginative construction of an Indian Wilsonian moment relies heavily on the lone figure of Lala Lajpat Rai; see E. Manela, *The Wilsonian Moment: Self-Determination and the International Origins of Anticolonial Nationalism* (Oxford, 2007), 84–97.

57. S. Hartley, *The Irish Question as a Problem in British Foreign Policy, 1914–1918* (Basingstoke, 1987), 107.

58. Finnan, *Redmond*, 190.

59. A. S. Link (ed.) et al., *The Papers of Woodrow Wilson* [hereafter *PWW*], 69 vols (Princeton, NJ, 1966–94), vol. 42, 24–5 and 41–2.

60. M. Beloff, *Imperial Sunset: Britain's Liberal Empire, 1897–1921* (London, 1969), vol. 1, 316.

61. Hartley, *The Irish Question*, 147–8.

62. Ibid., 153.

63. *PWW*, vol. 42, 542. Wilson himself had requested these reports, see *PWW*, vol. 43, 360–61.

64. Hartley, *Irish Question*, 134.

65. Ibid., 175.

66. Ibid., 178.

67. House of Lords parliamentary debates, May 1917, 170.

68. Hartley, *Irish Question*, 172 and 191.

69. J. Gallagher, 'Nationalisms and the Crisis of Empire, 1919–1922', *Modern Asian Studies* 15, no. 3 (1981), 355–8.

70. E. Monroe, *Britain's Moment in the Middle East, 1914–1971* (Baltimore, MD, 1981), 26–35.

71. B. C. Bush, *Britain, India, and the Arabs, 1914–1921* (Berkeley, CA, 1971).

72. H. Luthy, 'India and East Africa: Imperial Partnership at the End of the First World War', *Journal of Contemporary History* 6, no. 2 (1971), 55–85.

73. A reversal brought into brilliant focus by Darwin, *Empire Project*, 311–17.

74. D. R. Woodward, *Trial by Friendship: Anglo-American Relations, 1917–1918* (Lexington, KY, 1993), 174.

75. J. Kimche, *The Unromantics: The Great Powers and the Balfour Declaration* (London, 1968), 66.

76. J. Renton, *The Zionist Masquerade: The Birth of the Anglo-Zionist Alliance, 1914–1918* (Houndsmill, 2007); L. Stein, *The Balfour Declaration* (London, 1961).

77. M. Levene, 'The Balfour Declaration: A Case of Mistaken Identity', *The English Historical Review* 107, no. 422 (January 1992), 54–77.

78. J. Reinharz, 'The Balfour Declaration and Its Maker: A Reassessment', *The Journal of Modern History* 64, no. 3 (September 1992), 455–99; R. N. Lebow, 'Woodrow Wilson and the Balfour Declaration', *The Journal of Modern History* 40, no. 4 (December 1968), 501–23.

79. Grigg, *Lloyd George*, 308–9.

80. Ibid., 336–7.

81. D. Lloyd George, *The Great Crusade: Extracts from Speeches Delivered During the War* (New York, 1918), 176–86 (5 January 1918).

82. C. Seymour (ed.), *The Intimate Papers of Colonel House* (Boston, MA, 1926–8), vol. 3, 341.

10 THE ARSENALS OF DEMOCRACY

1. W. L. Silber, *When Washington Shut down Wall Street: The Great Financial Crisis of 1914 and the Origins of America's Monetary Supremacy* (Princeton, NJ, 2007).

2. H. Strachan, *The First World War*, vol. 1, *To Arms* (Oxford, 2001).

3. V. Lenin, '"Left-Wing" Childishness', April 1918, in V. I. Lenin, *Collected Works*, vol. 27 (Moscow, 1972), 323–34.

4. For an example of Rathenau's influence see A. Dauphin-Meunier, 'Henri de Man et Walther Rathenau', *Revue Européenne des Sciences Sociales* 12, no. 31 (1974), 103–20.

5. G. Feldman, *Army, Industry and Labour in Germany, 1914–1918* (Oxford, 1992).

6. T. S. Broadberry and M. Harrison (eds), *The Economics of World War I* (Cambridge, 2005); K. D. Stubbs, *Race to the Front: The Material Foundations of Coalition Strategy in the Great War, 1914–1918* (Westport, CT, 2002).

7. J. Terraine, *White Heat: The New Warfare 1914–1918* (London, 1982).

8. D. L. Lewis, *The Public Image of Henry Ford* (Detroit, MI, 1976), 70–77, 93–5.

9. R. Alvarado and S. Alvarado, *Drawing Conclusions on Henry Ford* (Detroit, MI, 2001), 82.

10. C. S. Maier, *In Search of Stability: Explorations in Historical Political Eonomy* (Cambridge, 1987), 19–69, and J. Herf, *Reactionary Modernism: Technology, Culture and Politics in Weimar and the Third Reich* (Cambridge, 1984).

11. D. R. Woodward, *Trial by Friendship: Anglo-American Relations, 1917–1918* (Lexington, KY, 1993), 130–49.

12. Y.-H. Nouailhat, *France et Etats-Unis: août 1914–avril 1917* (Paris, 1979), 250–62.

13. This is the repeated refrain of the official report, B. Crowell, *America's Munitions 1917–1918* (Washington, DC, 1919).

14. J. H. Morrow, *The Great War in the Air: Military Aviation from 1909 to 1921* (Washington, DC, 1993), 338.

15. Woodward, *Trial by Friendship*, 118–19.

16. R. Sicotte, 'Economic Crisis and Political Response: The Political Economy of the Shipping Act of 1916', *The Journal of Economic History* 59, no. 4 (December 1999), 861–84.

17. E. E. Day, 'The American Merchant Fleet: A War Achievement, a Peace Problem', *The Quarterly Journal of Economics* 34, no. 4 (August 1920), 567–606.

18. Woodward, *Trial by Friendship*, 136.

19. Ibid., 155, 159.
20. *Papers Relating to the Foreign Relations of the United States: Lansing Papers* (Washington, DC, 1940), vol. 2, 205.
21. D. Rossini, *Woodrow Wilson and the American Myth in Italy* (Cambridge, MA, 2008), 100–03.
22. A. Salter, *Allied Shipping Control* (Oxford, 1921).
23. F. Duchêne, *Jean Monnet: The First Statesman of Interdependence* (New York, 1994).
24. A. Kaspi, *Le Temps des Américains. Le concours américain à la France en 1917–1918* (Paris, 1976), 253–65, speaks of a 'victoire ignorée'.
25. G. D. Feldman, 'Die Demobilmachung und die Sozialordnung der Zwischenkriegszeit in Europa', *Geschichte und Gesellschaft*, 9. Jahrg., vol. 2 (1983), 156–77.
26. E. Roussel, *Jean Monnet 1888–1979* (Paris, 1996), 67.
27. C. P. Parrini, *Heir to Empire: United States Economic Diplomacy, 1916–1923* (Pittsburgh, PA, 1969), 31–2.
28. J. J. Safford, *Wilsonian Maritime Diplomacy* (New Brunswick, NJ, 1978), 149.
29. Salter, *Allied Shipping*, 165–74.
30. W. Churchill, *The World Crisis, 1916–1918* (London, 1927), vol. 2, 195.
31. R. Skidelsky, *John Maynard Keynes: Hopes Betrayed, 1883–1920* (London, 1983), vol. 1, 342; K. Burk, *Britain, America and the Sinews of War* (Boston, MA, 1985).
32. A. S. Link (ed.) et al., *The Papers of Woodrow Wilson* [hereafter *P W W*], 69 vols (Princeton, NJ, 1966–94), vol. 43, 136.
33. Skidelsky, *John Maynard Keynes*, vol. 1, 345.
34. R. Ally, *Gold and Empire: The Bank of England and South Africa's Gold Producers, 1886–1926* (Johannesburg, 1994), 31.
35. *P W W*, vol. 43, 390–91, 424–5.
36. Ibid., 34, 44, and 223–30, 326–33.
37. Ally, *Gold and Empire*, 34–41.
38. D. Kumar (ed.), *The Cambridge Economic History of India* (Cambridge, 1983), and M. Goswami, *Producing India* (Chicago, IL, 2004), 209–41.
39. H. S. Jevons, *The Future of Exchange and the Indian Currency* (London, 1922), 190–200.
40. H. Tinker, *The Foundations of Local Self-Government in India, Pakistan and Burma* (London, 1954), 96.
41. G. Balachandran, *John Bullion's Empire: Britain's Gold Problem and India Between the Wars* (London, 1996), 54–9.
42. Jevons, *The Future*, 206; F. L. Israel, 'The Fulfillment of Bryan's Dream: Key Pittman and Silver Politics, 1918–1933', *Pacific Historical Review* 30, no. 4 (November 1961), 359–80.
43. Balachandran, *John Bullion's Empire*, 58.

44. I. Abdullah, 'Rethinking the Freetown Crowd: The Moral Economy of the 1919 Strikes and Riot in Sierra Leone', *Canadian Journal of African Studies* 28, no. 2 (1994), 197–218.

45. T. Yoshikuni, 'Strike Action and Self-Help Associations: Zimbabwean Worker Protest and Culture after World War I', *Journal of Southern African Studies* 15, no. 3 (1989), 440–68.

46. M. A. Rifaat, *The Monetary System of Egypt: An Inquiry into its History and Present Working* (London, 1935).

47. A. E. Crouchley, *The Economic Development of Modern Egypt* (London, 1938).

48. P. H. Kratoska, 'The British Empire and the Southeast Asian Rice Crisis of 1919–1921', *Modern Asian Studies* 24, no. 1 (February 1990), 115–46.

49. M. Lewis, *Rioters and Citizens: Mass Protest in Imperial Japan* (Berkeley, CA, 1990).

50. J. C. Ott, *When Wall Street Met Main Street: The Quest for an Investors' Democracy* (Cambridge, MA, 2011), 64–135.

51. J. C. Hollander, 'Certificates of Indebtedness in Our War Financing', *The Journal of Political Economy* 26, no. 9 (November 1918), 901–08; C. Snyder, 'War Loans, Inflation and the High Cost of Living', *Annals of the American Academy of Political and Social Science* 75 (January 1918), 140–46; A. Barton Hepburn, J. H. Hollander and B. M. Anderson, Jr, 'Discussion of Government's Financial Policies in Relation to Inflation', *Proceedings of the Academy of Political Science in the City of New York* 9, no. 1 (June 1920), 55–66.

52. A. H. Hansen, 'The Sequence in War Prosperity and Inflation', *Annals of the American Academy of Political and Social Science* 89 (May 1920), 234–46.

53. C. Gilbert, *American Financing of World War I* (Westport, CT, 1970), 200–19.

54. E. B. Woods, 'Have Wages Kept Pace with the Cost of Living?', *Annals of the American Academy of Political and Social Science* 89 (May 1920), 135–47.

55. B. D. Mudgett, 'The Course of Profits during the War', and B. M. Manly, 'Have Profits Kept Pace with the Cost of Living?', *Annals of the American Academy of Political and Social Science* 89 (May 1920), 148–62.

11 ARMISTICE: SETTING THE WILSONIAN SCRIPT

1. J. D. Morrow, *The Great War: An Imperial History* (London, 2005), 246–7.

2. D. Stevenson, *With Our Backs to the Wall: Victory and Defeat in 1918* (London, 2011).

3. W. Ribhegge, *Frieden für Europa: Die Politik der deutschen Reichstagsmehrheit, 1917–18* (Essen, 1988), 312.

4. See the crucial meetings of September 1918 documented in *Der Interfrak-*

tioneller Ausschuss, 1917/18 [hereafter *IFA*], eds E. Matthias and R. Morsey (Düsseldorf, 1959), vol. 2, 494–788.

5. *IFA*, vol. 2, 541.

6. Michael Geyer, 'Insurrectionary Warfare: The German Debate about a *Levée en Masse* in October 1918', *The Journal of Modern History* 73, no. 3 (September 2001), 459–527.

7. K. Helfferich, *Der Weltkrieg* (Berlin, 1919), vol. 3, 536–7.

8. *IFA*, vol. 2, 485.

9. M. Erzberger, *Der Völkerbund. Der Weg zum Weltfrieden* (Berlin, 1918).

10. *IFA*, vol. 2, 615–16.

11. Ibid., 626–7.

12. F. K. Scheer, *Die Deutsche Friedensgesellschaft (1892–1933): Organisation, Ideologie und Politische Ziele. Ein Beitrag zur Geschichte des Pazifismus in Deutschland* (Frankfurt, 1981), 331–2.

13. *IFA*, vol. 2, 530.

14. Ibid., 779–82.

15. A. S. Link (ed.) et al., *The Papers of Woodrow Wilson* [hereafter *PWW*], 69 vols (Princeton, NJ, 1966–94), vol. 42, 433. Reinforced by House, see C. Seymour (ed.), *The Intimate Papers of Colonel House* (Boston, MA, 1928), vol. 3, 130–38.

16. *PWW*, vol. 58, 172.

17. D. R. Woodward, *Trial by Friendship: Anglo-American Relations, 1917–1918* (Lexington, KY, 1993), 210.

18. Ibid., 218–19.

19. *PWW*, vol. 53, 338.

20. *PWW*, vol. 51, 415.

21. C. M. Andrew and A. S. Kanya, 'France, Africa, and the First World War', *The Journal of African History* 19, no. 1 (1978), 11–23.

22. See the sympathetic evaluation of their options by Tasker Bliss, the American representative on the Supreme War Council, in *Papers Relating to the Foreign Relations of the United States: Lansing Papers* (Washington, DC, 1940), vol. 2, 288.

23. *PWW*, vol. 43, 172–4.

24. Most influentially J. M. Keynes, *The Economic Consequences of the Peace* (London, 1919), 60.

25. Nicolson notes the basic duality of intention that underpinned and undermined the peace, but fails to consider the circumstances of the Armistice that created it, see H. Nicolson, *Peacemaking, 1919* (New York, 1965), 82–90.

26. P. Krüger, 'Die Reparationen und das Scheitern einer deutschen Verständigungspolitik auf der Pariser Friedenskonferenz im Jahre 1919', *Historische Zeitschrift* 221, no. 2 (October 1975), 326–72.

27. T. J. Knock, *To End All Wars: Woodrow Wilson and the Quest for a New Order* (Princeton, NJ, 1992), 170–72.

28. Ibid., 176.

29. See E. Morison (ed.), *The Letters of Theodore Roosevelt* (Cambridge, MA, 1951), vol. 1, 378–81. On Roosevelt's concern that Lloyd George not break with Wilson, see ibid., vol. 1, 289.

30. Knock, *To End All Wars*, 176. See the Cabot Lodge and Roosevelt correspondence in C. Redmond (ed.), *Selections from the Correspondence of Theodore Roosevelt and Henry Cabot Lodge 1884–1918* (New York, 1925), vol. 2, 542–3.

31. Knock, *To End All Wars*, 180.

32. Ibid., 178.

33. J. M. Cooper, *Breaking the Heart of the World: Woodrow Wilson and the Fight for the League of Nations* (Cambridge, 2001), 39.

34. Redmond, *The Letters of Theodore Roosevelt*, vol. 1, 394–5.

12 DEMOCRACY UNDER PRESSURE

1. A. S. Link (ed.) et al., *The Papers of Woodrow Wilson* [hereafter *PWW*], 69 vols (Princeton, NJ, 1966–94), vol. 53, 366.

2. R. Olson, *The Emergence of Kurdish Nationalism and the Sheikh Said Rebellion, 1880–1925* (Austin, TX, 1989), 28–9.

3. R. M. Coury, *The Making of an Egyptian Arab Nationalist: The Early Years of Azzam Pasha, 1893–1936* (Reading, 1998), 159.

4. E. Manela, *The Wilsonian Moment: Self-Determination and the International Origins of Anticolonial Nationalism* (Oxford, 2007).

5. M. Geyer, 'Zwischen Krieg und Nachkrieg', in A. Gallus (ed.), *Die vergessene Revolution* (Göttingen, 2010), 187–222.

6. A. Mayer, *Politics and Diplomacy of Peacemaking: Containment and Counterrevolution at Versailles, 1918–1919* (London, 1968).

7. V. I. Lenin, 'Report at a Joint Session of the All-Russia Central Executive Committee: The Moscow Soviet, Factory Committees and Trade Unions, October 22 1918', in V. I. Lenin, *Collected Works* (Moscow, 1974), vol. 28, 113–26.

8. E. Mawdsley, *The Russian Civil War* (London, 2007).

9. M. Gilbert, *Winston S. Churchill*, vol. 4, *The Stricken World, 1917–1922* (London, 1975), 234.

10. J. M. Thompson, *Russia, Bolshevism, and the Versailles Peace* (Princeton, NJ, 1966).

11. The following quotes are from Document 129 in C. K. Cumming and W. W. Pettit (eds), *Russian-American Relations, March 1917–March 1920* (New York, 1920), 284–9.

12. Gilbert, *Churchill*, vol. 4, 230.

13. M. J. Carley, 'Episodes from the Early Cold War: Franco-Soviet Relations, 1917–1927', *Europe-Asia Studies* 52, no. 7 (November 2000), 1,276.

14. Document 127, 'Russian-American Relations', 281.

15. As brilliantly observed by Soutou, the Western reorientation of the leading circles in Germany began not in 1923 but already in the autumn of 1918, in G.-H. Soutou, *L'Or et le Sang: Les Buts de guerre économique de la Première Guerre Mondiale* (Paris, 1989), 745.

16. R. Luxemburg, 'What Does the Spartacus League Want?', *Die Rote Fahne*, 14 December 1918, and *The Russian Revolution* (written 1918, published Berlin, 1922).

17. K. Kautsky, *Terrorismus und Kommunismus* (Berlin, 1919).

18. H. A. Winkler, *Arbeiter und Arbeiterbewegung in der Weimarer Republik* (Berlin, 1984), vol. 1.

19. R. Luxemburg, 'The National Assembly', *Die Rote Fahne*, 20 November 1918.

20. G. D. Feldman, *The Great Disorder: Politics, Economics, and Society in the German Inflation, 1914–1924* (Oxford, 1997).

21. C. Mathews, 'The Economic Origins of the Noskepolitik', *Central European History* 27, no. 1 (1994), 65–86.

22. G. Noske, *Von Kiel bis Kapp. Zur Geschichte der deutschen Revolution* (Berlin, 1920), 68.

23. W. Wette, *Gustav Noske* (Düsseldorf, 1987), 289–321.

24. Mayer, *Politics and Diplomacy*, 373–409; A. S. Lindemann, *The 'Red Years': European Socialism Versus Bolshevism, 1919–1921* (Berkeley, CA, 1974); G. A. Ritter (ed.), *Die II Internationale 1918/1919. Protokolle, Memoranden, Berichte und Korrespondenzen* (Berlin, 1980), vols 1 and 2.

25. *PWW*, vol. 53, 574.

26. D. Marquand, *Ramsay MacDonald* (London, 1997), 248–9; C. F. Brand, 'The Attitude of British Labor Toward President Wilson during the Peace Conference', *The American Historical Review* 42, no. 2 (January 1937), 244–255.

27. Ritter, *Die II Internationale*, vol. 1, 208–85.

28. Ibid., vol. 1, 230–43.

29. See Hoover's incongruous enthusiasm for the USPD in *Two Peacemakers in Paris: The Hoover-Wilson Post-Armistice Letters, 1918–1920* (College Station, TX, 1978), 128–9 and 135–41.

30. Ritter, *Die II Internationale*, 288–377.

31. The opposite position of the necessity of SPD-USPD unity is crisply articulated by S. Miller, *Burgfrieden und Klassenkampf: Die deutsche Sozialdemokratie im Ersten Weltkrieg* (Düsseldorf, 1974), 320.

32. D. Tanner, *Political Change and the Labour Party, 1900–1918* (Cambridge, 1990), 393–7; R. McKibbin, *Parties and People, England 1914–1951* (Oxford, 2010), 30.

33. J. Turner, *British Politics and the Great War: Coalition and Conflict, 1915–1918* (New Haven, CT, 1992), 319.

34. Marquand, *MacDonald*, 236.

35. M. Pugh, *Electoral Reform in War and Peace, 1906–1918* (London, 1978), 176–7.

36. M. Cowling, *The Impact of Labour, 1920–24* (Cambridge, 1971).

37. Tanner, *Political Change*, 403–4.

38. L. Haimson and G. Sapelli, *Strikes, Social Conflict, and the First World War* (Milan, 1992); C. Wrigley, *Challenges of Labour: Central and Western Europe 1917–1920* (London, 1993); B. J. Silver, *Forces of Labor: Workers' Movements and Globalization since 1870* (Cambridge, 2003).

39. C. Wrigley, *Lloyd George and the Challenge of Labour: The Post-War Coalition, 1918–22* (Hemel Hempstead, 1990).

40. B. Millman, *Managing Domestic Dissent in First World War Britain* (London, 2000), 263.

41. Wrigley, *Lloyd George and the Challenge of Labour*, 223.

42. Turner, *British Politics*, 314.

43. Wrigley, *Lloyd George and the Challenge of Labour*, 82.

44. Ibid., 204.

45. E. Morgan, *Studies in British Financial Policy, 1914–1925* (London, 1952).

46. L. Ross, 'Debts, Revenues and Expenditures and Note Circulation of the Principal Belligerents', *The Quarterly Journal of Economics* 34, no. 1 (November 1919), 168.

47. R. E. Bunselmeyer, *The Cost of the War, 1914–1919: British Economic War Aims and the Origins of Reparations* (Hamden, CT, 1975), 106–48.

48. E. Johnson and D. Moggridge (eds), *The Collected Writings of John Maynard Keynes* (Cambridge, 2012), vol. 16, 418–19.

49. B. Kent, *The Spoils of War* (Oxford, 1991), and D. Newton, *British Policy and the Weimar Republic 1918–1919* (Oxford, 1997).

50. M. Daunton, *Just Taxes: The Politics of Taxation in Britain, 1914–1979* (Cambridge, 2002), 69–72.

51. D. P. Silverman, *Reconstructing Europe after the Great War* (Cambridge, MA, 1982), 71.

52. Soutou, *L'Or et Le Sang*, 806–28.

53. L. Blum, *L'Oeuvre de Léon Blum*, 3 vols (Paris, 1972), vol. 1, 278.

54. E. Clémentel, *La France et la politique économique interalliée* (Paris, 1931), 343.

13 A PATCHWORK WORLD ORDER

1. A. S. Link (ed.) et al., *The Papers of Woodrow Wilson* [hereafter *PWW*], 69 vols (Princeton, NJ, 1966–94), vol. 53, 550.

2. T. J. Knock, *To End All Wars: Woodrow Wilson and the Quest for a New Order* (Princeton, NJ, 1992), 224.

3. The most influential being R. S. Baker, *Woodrow Wilson and the World*

Settlement (New York, 1922), which shaped A. Mayer, *Wilson vs. Lenin: Political Origins of the New Diplomacy, 1917–1918* (New York, 1964).

4. C. Schmitt, *Positionen und Begriffe im Kampf mit Weimar-Genf-Versailles, 1923–1939* (Hamburg, 1940); T. Veblen, 'Peace', in *Essays in Our Changing Order* (New York, 1934), 415–22, criticized the Covenant as a defunct expression of Woodrow Wilson's mid-Victorian liberalism.

5. *PWW*, vol. 55, 175–77.

6. *PWW*, vol. 53, 336–7.

7. *Journal officiel de la République française* (Paris, 1918), 29 December 1918, vol. 50, 3,732ff.

8. *PWW*, vol. 53, 571.

9. Amongst the few to recognize this, W. R. Keylor, 'France's Futile Quest for American Military Protection, 1919–22', in M. Petricioli and M. Guderzo (eds), *Une Occasion manquée? 1922: La reconstruction de L'Europe* (Frankfurt, 1995), 62.

10. G. Clemenceau, *Grandeur and Misery of Victory* (New York, 1930), 202. A reference to Blaise Pascal picked up in G. Dallas, *At the Heart of a Tiger: Clemenceau and His World 1841–1929* (London, 1993), 481. See also his 1910 speech on democracy and war in G. Clemenceau, *Sur la Démocratie: neuf conférences* (Paris, 1930), 117–34.

11. D. Demko, *Léon Bourgeois: Philosophe de la solidarité* (Paris, 2001); C. Bouchard, *Le Citoyen et l'ordre mondial 1914–1919* (Paris, 2008); S. Audier, *Léon Bourgeois: Fonder la solidarité* (Paris, 2007).

12. P. J. Yearwood, *Guarantee of Peace: The League of Nations in British Policy* (Oxford, 2009), 139.

13. F. Meinecke, *Machiavellism: The Doctrine of Raison d'Etat and its Place in Modern History* (New Haven, CT, 1962), 423–4, and Schmitt, *Positionen*.

14. F. R. Dickinson, *War and National Reinvention: Japan in the Great War 1914–1919* (Cambridge MA, 1999), 212–18.

15. L. Connors, *The Emperor's Adviser: Saionji Kinmochi and Pre-War Japanese Politics* (Oxford, 1987), 60–66.

16. S. Naoko, *Japan, Race and Equality: The Racial Equality Proposal of 1919* (London, 2003), 61.

17. *PWW*, vol. 53, 622; M. Macmillan, *Peacemakers: The Paris Conference of 1919 and its Attempt to End War* (London, 2001), 154–5.

18. D. H. Miller, *The Drafting of the Covenant* [hereafter *DC*] (New York, 1928), vol. 2, 64–105.

19. *DC*, vol. 1, 138.

20. Ibid., 146–7. The phrase is Eyre Crowe's; see H. Nicolson, *Peacemaking, 1919* (London, 1933), 226.

21. *DC*, vol. 1, 162.

22. Ibid., 152.

23. Ibid., 160.

24. Ibid., 160–62.

25. Knock, *To End All Wars*, 218.

26. *DC*, vol. 1, 160.

27. Ibid., 166.

28. Ibid., 165.

29. Ibid., 165.

30. Ibid., 167.

31. *DC*, vol. 2, 303.

32. *DC*, vol. 1, 216–17.

33. *DC*, vol. 2, 294.

34. Ibid., 293.

35. Ibid., 264.

36. Ibid., 297.

37. *DC*, vol. 1, 262.

38. *PWW*, vol. 57, 126–7.

39. S. Bonsal, *Unfinished Business* (New York, 1944), 202–17.

40. A. Anghie, *Imperialism, Sovereignty and the Making of International Law* (Cambridge, 2004); M. Mazower, *No Enchanted Palace: The End of Empire and the Ideological Origins of the United Nations* (Princeton, NJ, 2009).

41. Yearwood, *Guarantee*, and G. W. Egerton, *Great Britain and the Creation of the League of Nations* (Chapel Hill, NC, 1978).

42. *PWW*, vol. 53, 427.

43. Ibid., 320–21.

44. J. W. Jones, 'The Naval Battle of Paris', *Naval War College Review* 62 (2009), 77–89.

45. The confusion of America's position was admitted by the administration's own advisory staff; *PWW*, vol. 57, 180.

46. Ibid., 91–2.

47. Egerton, *Great Britain and the League*, 158.

48. R. Dingman, *Power in the Pacific: The Origins of Naval Arms Limitation, 1914–22* (Chicago, IL, 1976), 86–7; *PWW*, vol. 57, 142–4, 216–17.

14 'THE TRUTH ABOUT THE TREATY'

1. J. Bainville, *Les Conséquences politiques de la paix* (Paris, 1920), 25.

2. The narrative that has extended down to M. Macmillan, *Peacemakers: The Paris Conference of 1919 and its Attempt to End War* (London, 2001).

3. M. Trachtenberg, *Reparation in World Politics: France and European Economic Diplomacy, 1916–1923* (New York, 1980), 48–52.

4. Perhaps the most vivid and self-conscious record of this cycle is H. Nicolson, *Peacemaking, 1919* (London, 1933); A. Lentin, *Lloyd George, Woodrow Wilson and the Guilt of Germany* (Leicester, 1984), and A. Lentin, *Lloyd*

George and the Lost Peace: From Versailles to Hitler, 1919–1940 (Basingstoke, 2001).

5. Bainville, *Conséquences*, 25–9.

6. G. Clemenceau, *Grandeur and Misery of Victory* (New York, 1930), 144–207.

7. A. Thiers, *Discours parlementaire: 3eme partie 1865–1866* (Paris, 1881), 645–6.

8. Clemenceau, *Grandeur*, 185.

9. C. Clark, *Iron Kingdom: The Rise and Downfall of Prussia, 1600–1947* (London, 2006); P. Schroeder, *The Transformation of European Politics, 1763–1848* (Oxford, 1994), and P. Schroeder, *Austria, Great Britain, and the Crimean War: The Destruction of the European Concert* (Ithaca, NY, 1972).

10. A. S. Link (ed.) et al., *The Papers of Woodrow Wilson* [hereafter *PWW*], 69 vols (Princeton, NJ, 1966–94), vol. 54, 466.

11. M. Beloff, *Imperial Sunset*, vol. 1, *Britain's Liberal Empire, 1897–1921* (London, 1969, and Basingstoke, 1989), 289–90.

12. W. McDougall, *France's Rhineland Diplomacy, 1914–1924: The Last Bid for a Balance of Power in Europe* (Princeton, NJ, 1978).

13. For a German view see B. Wendt, 'Lloyd George's Fontainebleau Memorandum', in U. Lehmkuhl, C. Wurm and H. Zimmermann (eds), *Deutschland, Grossbritannien, Amerika* (Wiesbaden, 2003), 27–45. For the anti-French atmosphere, see J. Cairns, 'A Nation of Shopkeepers in Search of a Suitable France: 1919–40', *The American Historical Review* 79 (June 1974), 714.

14. *PWW*, vol. 57, 50–61.

15. A. Tardieu, *The Truth About the Treaty* (London, 1921).

16. N. Angell, *The Great Illusion* (New York, 1910).

17. J. Horne and A. Kramer, 'German "Atrocities" and Franco-German Opinion, 1914: The Evidence of German Soldiers' Diaries', *The Journal of Modern History* 66 (1994), 1–33; I. Hull, *Absolute Destruction: Military Culture and the Practices of War in Imperial Germany* (Ithaca, NY, 2005).

18. I. Renz, G. Krumeich and G. Hirschfeld, *Scorched Earth: The Germans on the Somme 1914–18* (Barnsley, 2009).

19. J. M. Keynes, *The Economic Consequences of the Peace* (London, 1919), 126–8.

20. F. W. O'Brien, *Two Peacemakers in Paris: The Hoover-Wilson Post-Armistice Letters, 1918–1920* (College Station, TX, 1978), 65.

21. *PWW*, vol. 57, 120–30, 316.

22. D. Stevenson, 'France at the Paris Peace Conference', in R. Boyce (ed.), *French Foreign and Defence Policy, 1918–1940* (London, 1998), 10–29.

23. G. Dallas, *At the Heart of a Tiger: Clemenceau and His World, 1841–1929* (London, 1993), 566.

24. See for instance the critique of these compromises by Poincaré, *PWW*, vol. 58, 211–14.

25. *PWW*, vol. 57, 279.

26. W. Wilson, *The Public Papers of Woodrow Wilson* (New York, 1927), 523.

27. Nicolson, *Peacemaking*, 32.

28. P. Mantoux, *The Deliberations of the Council of Four*, trans. and ed. A. S. Link (Princeton, NJ, 1992), vol. 1, 144–5.

29. S. Wambaugh, *Plebiscites Since the World War* (Washington, DC, 1933), vol. 1, 33–62, 206–70.

30. P. Wandycz, *France and her Eastern Allies, 1919–1925* (Minneapolis, MN, 1962).

31. Mantoux, *Deliberations*, vol. 2, 452–5.

32. E. Mantoux, *The Carthaginian Peace – Or the Economic Consequences of Mr. Keynes* (London, 1946).

33. J. Hagen, 'Mapping the Polish Corridor: Ethnicity, Economics and Geopolitics', *Imago Mundi: The International Journal for the History of Cartography* 62 (2009), 63–82.

34. R. Blanke, *Orphans of Versailles: The Germans in Western Poland, 1918–1939* (Lexington, KY, 1993).

35. A. Demshuk, *The Lost German East: Forced Migration and the Politics of Memory, 1945–1970* (Cambridge, 2012).

36. *Papers Relating to the Foreign Relations of the United States: Lansing Papers* [hereafter *FRUS: Lansing Papers*] (Washington, DC, 1940), vol. 2, 26.

37. Clemenceau, *Grandeur*, 162–3.

38. *FRUS: Lansing Papers*, vol. 2, 27.

39. *PWW*, vol. 57, 151.

40. R. Boyce, *The Great Interwar Crisis and the Collapse of Globalization* (Basingstoke, 2009), 52–5.

41. A. Orzoff, *Battle for the Castle: The Myth of Czechoslovakia in Europe, 1914–1948* (Oxford, 2009).

42. D. Miller, *Forging Political Compromise: Antonin Svehla and the Czechoslovak Republican Party, 1918–1933* (Pittsburgh, NJ, 1999); W. Blackwood, 'Socialism, Czechoslovakism, and the Munich Complex, 1918–1948', *The International History Review* 21 (1999), 875–99.

43. A. Polonsky, *Politics in Independent Poland, 1921–1939: The Crisis of Constitutional Government* (Oxford, 1972).

44. T. Snyder, *The Reconstruction of Nations: Poland, Ukraine, Lithuania, Belarus, 1569–1999* (New Haven, CT, 2003).

45. D. Durand, 'Currency Inflation in Eastern Europe with Special Reference to Poland', *The American Economic Review* 13 (1923), 593–608.

46. N. Davies, 'Lloyd George and Poland, 1919–20', *Journal of Contemporary History* 6 (1971), 132–54.

47. D. L. George, *Memoir of the Peace Conference* (New Haven, CT, 1939), vol. 1, 266–73.

48. Boyce, *Great Interwar Crisis*, 51.

49. M. Mazower, 'Minorities and the League of Nations in Interwar Europe', *Daedalus* 126 (1997), 47–63.

50. Wambaugh, *Plebiscites*, vol. 1, 249.

51. G. Manceron (ed.), *1885: Le tournant colonial de la République: Jules Ferry contre Georges Clemenceau, et autres affrontements parlementaires sur la conquête coloniale* (Paris, 2006).

52. As supposed for instance by F. Meinecke, *Machiavellism: The Doctrine of Raison d'Etat and its Place in Modern History* (New Haven, CT, 1962), 432.

53. C. Schmitt, *Positionen und Begriffe im Kampf mit Weimar-Genf-Versailles, 1923–1939* (Hamburg, 1940).

15 REPARATIONS

1. H. Winkler, *Arbeiter und Arbeiterbewegung in der Weimarer Republik, 1918–1924* (Berlin, 1987), 185.

2. C. Schmitt, *Positionen und Begriffe im Kampf mit Weimar-Genf-Versailles, 1923–1939* (Hamburg, 1940).

3. G. D. Feldman, *The Great Disorder: Politics, Economics, and Society in the German Inflation, 1914–1924* (Oxford, 1993), 434.

4. M. Horn, *Britain, France, and the Financing of the First World War* (Montreal, 2002).

5. D. Artaud, *La Question des dettes interalliées et la reconstruction de l'Europe, 1917–1929* (Lille, 1978).

6. G.-H. Soutou, *L'Or et le Sang: Les Buts de guerre économique de la Première Guerre Mondiale* (Paris, 1989), 777–805.

7. G. Rousseau, *Étienne Clémentel* (Clermont-Ferrand, 1998), 18; P. Rabinow, *French Modern: Norms and Forms of the Social Environment* (Chicago, IL, 1995), 325, suggests the apt designation as 'middling modernism'.

8. E. Clémentel, *La France et la politique économique interalliée* (Paris, 1931).

9. M. Trachtenberg, *Reparation in World Politics: France and European Economic Diplomacy, 1916–1923* (New York, 1980), 5.

10. W. McDougall, 'Political Economy versus National Sovereignty: French Structures for German Economic Integration after Versailles', *The Journal of Modern History* 51 (1979), 4–23.

11. E. Roussel, *Jean Monnet* (Paris, 1996), 33–44.

12. F. Duchène, *Jean Monnet* (New York, 1994), 40; J. Monnet, *Memoirs* (London, 1978), 75.

13. R. S. Baker, *Woodrow Wilson and the World Settlement* (New York, 1922), vol. 3, 322.

14. W. R. Keylor, 'Versailles and International Diplomacy', in M. Boemeke, R. Chickering and E. Glaser (eds), *The Treaty of Versailles: A Reassessment After 75 Years* (Washington, DC, 1998), 498.

15. F. W. O'Brien, *Two Peacemakers in Paris: The Hoover-Wilson Post-Armistice Letters, 1918–1920* (College Station, TX, 1978), 4.

16. Ibid., 156–61.

17. Trachtenberg, *Reparations*, 34.

18. S. Lauzanne, 'Can France Carry Her Fiscal Burden?', *The North American Review* 214 (1921), 603–9.

19. A. Lentin, *The Last Political Law Lord: Lord Sumner* (Cambridge, 2008), 81–104; R. E. Bunselmeyer, *The Cost of the War, 1914–1919: British Economic War Aims and the Origins of Reparation* (Hamden, CT, 1975).

20. P. M. Burnett, *Reparation at the Paris Peace Conference* (New York, 1940), vol. 1, Document 211, 777.

21. Ibid., Document 210, 776.

22. Ibid., Document 246, 857–8.

23. Ibid., Document 234, 824, and Document 262, 898–903.

24. *Two Peacemakers*, 118–19.

25. J. M. Keynes, *Revision of the Treaty* (London, 1922), 3–4.

26. Summarized brilliantly in E. Mantoux, *The Carthaginian Peace; or, The Economic Consequences of Mr. Keynes* (New York, 1952).

27. V. Serge, *Memoirs of a Revolutionary* (Oxford, 1963), 102, and L. Trotsky, *The First Five Years of the Communist International* (Moscow, 1924), vol. 1, 351.

28. N. Ferguson, *Paper & Iron: Hamburg Business and German Politics in the Era of Inflation, 1897–1927* (Cambridge, 1995).

29. E. Johnson and D. Moggridge (eds), *The Collected Writings of John Maynard Keynes* (Cambridge, 2012), vol. 16, 156–84.

30. R. Skidelsky, *John Maynard Keynes: Hopes Betrayed, 1883–1920* (London, 1983), vol. 1, 317.

31. J. M. Keynes, *The Economic Consequences of the Peace* (London, 1919), 5, reiterated 253.

32. Ibid., 146–50.

33. Ibid., 269.

34. Artaud, *La Question des dettes interalliées*, vol. 1, 116.

35. D. P. Silverman, *Reconstructing Europe after the Great War* (Cambridge, MA, 1982), 32.

36. A. Tardieu, *The Truth About the Treaty* (Indianapolis, IN, 1921), 344.

37. Silverman, *Reconstructing Europe*, 39.

38. Keynes, *Collected Writings*, vol. 16, 422.

39. Ibid., 426–7.

40. Keynes, *Economic Consequences*, 283–8.

41. Keynes, *Collected Writings*, vol. 16, 428–36.

42. Ibid., 434.

43. Silverman, *Reconstructing Europe*, 36.

44. A. Orde, *British Policy and European Reconstruction after the First World War* (Cambridge, 1990), 57.

45. Hoover to Wilson, 11 April 1919, *Two Peacemakers*, 112–15.

46. Baker, *Woodrow Wilson*, vol. 3, 344–6.

47. Ibid., 373–5.

48. L. Gardner, *Safe for Democracy: The Anglo-American Response to Revolution, 1913–1923* (Oxford, 1987), 247; F. Costigliola, *Awkward Dominion: American Political, Economic, and Cultural Relations with Europe, 1919–1933* (Ithaca, NY, 1987), 35.

49. *Two Peacemakers*, 196–203.

50. B. D. Rhodes, 'Reassessing "Uncle Shylock": The United States and the French War Debt, 1917–1929', *The Journal of American History* 55 (March 1969), 791.

51. Silverman, *Reconstructing Europe*, 171, 205–11.

16 COMPLIANCE IN EUROPE

1. A. Hitler, *Mein Kampf* (Munich, 1925–7).

2. H. J. Burgwyn, *The Legend of the Mutilated Victory: Italy, the Great War, and the Paris Peace Conference, 1915–1919* (Westport, CT, 1993), 300.

3. S. Falasca-Zamponi, *Fascist Spectacle* (Berkeley, CA, 1997), 32, 163–4.

4. For Mussolini see A. Mayer, *Politics and Diplomacy: Containment and Counter-Revolution at Versailles, 1918–1919* (New York, 1967), 206–7, and P. O'Brien, *Mussolini in the First World War: The Journalist, the Soldier, the Fascist* (Oxford, 2005), 151. For Hitler, *Mein Kampf*, 712–13.

5. Mayer, *Politics and Diplomacy*, 219–20.

6. *Papers Relating to the Foreign Relations of the United States: Lansing Papers* (Washington, DC, 1940), vol. 2, 89–90.

7. H. Nicolson, *Peacemaking, 1919* (London, 1933), 161.

8. A. S. Link (ed.) et al., *The Papers of Woodrow Wilson* [hereafter *PWW*], 69 vols (Princeton, NJ, 1966–94), vol. 57, 614.

9. Burgwyn, *The Legend*, 256–8.

10. *PWW*, vol. 57, 432–3.

11. *PWW*, vol. 58, 19.

12. *PWW*, vol. 57, 527.

13. *PWW*, vol. 58, 7.

14. D. Rossini, *Woodrow Wilson and the American Myth in Italy* (Cambridge, MA, 2008), 117–23.

15. Ibid., 131.

16. *PWW*, vol. 58, 142.

17. Ibid., 47.

18. *PWW*, vol. 57, 70.

19. *PWW*, vol. 58, 4.

20. Ibid., 59.

21. Ibid., 91–3.

22. Burgwyn, *Legend*, 281.

23. Nicolson, *Peacemaking*, 319.

24. *PWW*, vol. 58, 143.

25. D. J. Forsyth, *The Crisis of Liberal Italy* (Cambridge, 1993), 205.

26. L. Hautecoeur, *L'Italie sous le Ministère Orlando, 1917–1919* (Paris, 1919), 209–10.

27. M. Knox, *To the Threshold of Power, 1922/33: Origins and Dynamics of the Fascist and National Socialist Dictatorships* (Cambridge, 2007), vol. 1, 307–10.

28. G. Salvemini, *The Origins of Fascism in Italy* (New York, 1973), 230.

29. Akten der Reichskanzlei Das Kabinett Scheidemann (AdR DKS), Nr 66, 303.

30. Ibid., 303–06.

31. Ibid., 8 May 1919, 306, and AdR DKS Nr 70, 12 May 1919, 314–16.

32. P. Scheidemann, *The Making of a New Germany* (New York, 1928), 24–5.

33. AdR DKS Nr 15, 63, and Nr 20, 85–91. See also K. Kautsky, *Wie der Weltkrieg Entstand* (Berlin, 1919).

34. AdR DKS Nr 79, 19 May 1919, 350–51.

35. AdR DKS Nr 67, 9 May 1919, 308.

36. AdR DKS Nr 80, 20 May 1919, 354.

37. Ibid., 20 May 1919, 358–9, Nr 86, 26 May 1919, 375, Nr 87, 26 May 1919, 379–80.

38. AdR DKS Nr 84, 23 May 1919, 368–9.

39. P. Krüger, 'Die Reparationen und das Scheitern einer deutschen Verständigungspolitik auf der Pariser Friedenskonferenz im Jahre 1919', *Historische Zeitschrift* 221 (1975), 336–8.

40. L. Haupts, *Deutsche Friedenspolitik, 1918–19: eine Alternative zur Machtpolitik des Ersten Weltkrieges* (Düsseldorf, 1976), 329–72.

41. Compare Keynes's estimate of the real value of the German counter-offer with his own proposed reparations figure, which adopted the same figure of $7.5 billion but provided for no interest. J. M. Keynes, *The Economic Consequences of the Peace* (London, 1919), 223, 262.

42. In *The Deliberations of the Council of Four (March 24–June 28, 1919): Notes of the Official Interpreter, Paul Mantoux*, trans. and ed. by Arthur S. Link and Manfred F. Boemeke (Princeton, NJ, 1991), vol. 2, 462–6, Foch gave a figure of 39, which were the equivalent of 44 regular divisions, allowing for the double-strength of the US divisions.

43. H. Mühleisen, 'Annehmen oder Ablehnen? Das Kabinett Scheidemann, die Oberste Heeresleitung und der Vertrag von Versailles im Juni 1919. Fünf Dokumente aus dem Nachlaß des Hauptmanns Günther von Posek', *Vierteljahrshefte für Zeitgeschichte* 35 (1987), 419–81.

44. AdR DKS Nr 107, 11 June 1919, 445.

45. AdR DKS Nr 114, 20 June 1919.

46. AdR DKS Nr 111, 14 June 1919.

47. AdR DKS Nr 113, 469–75.

48. AdR DKS Nr 99, 3 June 1919.

49. AdR DKS Nr 113, 17 June 1919, 475.

50. AdR DKS Nr 105, 10 June 1919, 105.

51. AdR DKS Nr 114, 20 June 1919, 485–6.

52. AdR DKS Nr 118, 18 June 1919, 506.

53. AdR DKS Nr 100, 4 June 1919, 419–20.

54. For the following narrative see A. Luckau, 'Unconditional Acceptance of the Treaty of Versailles by the German Government, June 22–28, 1919', *The Journal of Modern History* 17 (1945), 215–20.

55. G. Noske, *Von Kiel bis Kapp: zur Geschichte der deutschen Revolution* (Berlin, 1920), 147–56, and W. Wette, *Gustav Noske: eine politische Biographie* (Düsseldorf, 1987), 461–93.

56. AdR DKS Nr 118, 501–02.

57. AdR DKS Nr 114, 20 June 1919, 491.

58. AdR DKS Nr 3, 23 June 1919, 10.

59. *Two Peacemakers in Paris: The Hoover-Wilson Post-Armistice Letters, 1918–1920*, ed. with commentaries by Francis William O'Brien (College Station, TX, 1978), 168–73; Nicolson, *Peacemaking*, 362–4.

60. Wette, *Noske*, 506–17.

61. See the narrative of the coup in AdR KBauer Nr. 183, 653–6, Nr 186–92, 667–83, Nr 218, 771–91.

62. AdR KBauer Nr 204, 710–25.

63. AdR KBauer, Nr 215, 760–62. See the highly critical account in G. Eliasberg, *Der Ruhrkrieg von 1920* (Bonn, 1974).

64. H. A. Turner, *Stresemann and the Politics of the Weimar Republic* (Princeton, NJ, 1963), 43–91.

65. M. Berg, *Gustav Stresemann und die Vereinigten Staaten von Amerika: Weltwirtschaftliche Verflechtung und Revisionspolitik, 1907–1929* (Baden-Baden, 1990), 102.

17 COMPLIANCE IN ASIA

1. The story is told from the American and Chinese point of view in E. Manela, *The Wilsonian Moment: Self-Determination and the International Origins of Anticolonial Nationalism* (Oxford, 2007), 99–117, 177–96.

2. L. Connors, *The Emperor's Adviser: Saionji Kinmochi and Pre-War Japanese Politics* (Oxford, 1987), 60–71.

3. Y. S. Sun, *The International Development of China* (New York, 1922).

4. Y. Zhang, *China in the International System, 1918–1920* (Basingstoke, 1991), 105.

5. N. S. Bose, *American Attitudes and Policy to the Nationalist Movement in China, 1911–1921* (Bombay, 1970), 157–9.

6. L. Gardner, *Safe for Democracy: The Anglo-American Response to Revolution, 1913–1923* (Oxford, 1987), 230.

7. Zhang, *China*, 55.

8. S. G. Craft, *V. K.: Wellington Koo and the Emergence of Modern China* (Lexington, KY, 2004), 49–50.

9. S. Naoko, *Japan, Race and Equality: The Racial Equality Proposal of 1919* (London, 2003), 49–50.

10. N. Kawamura, *Turbulence in the Pacific: Japanese-U.S. Relations during World War I* (Westport, CT, 2000), 140.

11. Y. Ozaki, *The Autobiography of Ozaki Yukio* (Princeton, NJ, 2001), 330–36.

12. On the ambiguities of mass politics in the period see A. Gordon, *Labor and Imperial Democracy in Prewar Japan* (Berkeley, CA, 1991).

13. Naoko, *Japan*, 19.

14. M. Lake and H. Reynolds, *Drawing the Global Color Line: White Men's Countries and the International Challenge of Racial Equality* (Cambridge, 2008).

15. A. S. Link (ed.) et al., *The Papers of Woodrow Wilson* [hereafter *PWW*], 69 vols (Princeton, NJ, 1966–94), vol. 57, 239–40.

16. Ibid., 247, 264.

17. Naoko, *Japan*, 29–31.

18. *PWW*, vol. 57, 285.

19. As was made clear to Balfour by Makino, see *PWW*, vol. 58, 179.

20. Kawamura, *Turbulence*, 147.

21. *PWW*, vol. 57, 554.

22. D. H. Miller, *The Drafting of the Covenant* (New York, 1928), vol. 1, 103.

23. *PWW*, vol. 57, 584 and 618.

24. *PWW*, vol. 58, 165.

25. Connors, *Emperor's Adviser*, 74.

26. *PWW*, vol. 58, 112–13.

27. Craft, *Wellington Koo*, 56; *PWW*, vol. 57, 615–26.

28. *PWW*, vol. 58, 130, 183–4.

29. Zhang, *China*, 88–9.

30. R. Mitter, *A Bitter Revolution: China's Struggle with the Modern World* (Oxford, 2004).

31. J. Chesneaux, F. Le Barbier and M.-C. Bergère, *China from the 1911 Revolution to Liberation*, trans. P. Auster and L. Davis (New York, 1977), 65–9.

32. D. Kuhn, *Die Republik China von 1912 bis 1937: Entwurf für eine politische Ereignisgeschichte* (Heidelberg, 2004), 142.

33. Zhang, *China*, 79.

34. Chesneaux et al., *China*, 67–8.

35. Zhang, *China*, 75–99.

36. Y. T. Matsusaka, *The Making of Japanese Manchuria, 1904–1932* (Cambridge, MA, 2001), 241.

37. L. A. Humphreys, *The Way of the Heavenly Sword: The Japanese Army in the 1920s* (Stanford, CA, 1995), 175.

38. Ibid., 41.

39. Matsusaka, *The Making*, 241.

40. Zhang, *China*, 139–41.

41. S. R. Schram and N. J. Hodes (eds), *Mao's Road to Power: Revolutionary Writings 1912–1949* (New York, 1992), vol. 1, 321–2, 337, 357–67, 390, and vol. 2, 159–60, 186–8.

42. W. C. Kirby, *Germany and Republican China* (Stanford, CA, 1984), 35.

43. B. A. Ellman, *Diplomacy and Deception: The Secret History of Sino-Soviet Diplomatic Relations, 1917–1927* (London, 1997), 25.

44. Zhang, *China*, 157.

18 THE FIASCO OF WILSONIANISM

1. A. S. Link (ed.) et al., *The Papers of Woodrow Wilson* [hereafter *PWW*], 69 vols (Princeton, NJ, 1966–94), vol. 61, 426–36.

2. Ibid., 225.

3. Compare R. S. Baker, *Woodrow Wilson and the World Settlement* (New York, 1922), and L. E. Ambrosius, *Woodrow Wilson and the American Diplomatic Tradition: The Treaty Fight in Perspective* (Cambridge, 1987).

4. *The New York Times*, 'Bullitt Asserts Lansing Expected the Treaty to Fail', 13 September 1919.

5. W. C. Bullitt and S. Freud, *Thomas Woodrow Wilson: A Psychological Study* (Boston, MA, 1967).

6. *The New York Times*, 'Lodge Attacks Covenant and Outlines 5 Reservations; Assailed by Williams', 13 August 1919.

7. Ambrosius, *Woodrow Wilson*, xxx.

8. W. C. Widenor, *Henry Cabot Lodge and the Search for an American Foreign Policy* (Berkeley, CA, 1980).

9. *The New York Times*, 'Qualify Treaty on Ratification, Says Elihu Root', 22 June 1919.

10. *PWW*, vol. 42, 340–44.

11. T. J. Knock, *To End All Wars: Woodrow Wilson and the Quest for a New Order* (Princeton, NJ, 1992), 267.

12. M. Leffler, *The Elusive Quest: America's Pursuit of European Stability and French Security, 1919–1933* (Chapel Hill, NC, 1979), 15.

13. W. Lippmann, 'Woodrow Wilson's Approach to Politics', *New Republic*, 5 December 1955; T. Bimes and S. Skowronek, 'Woodrow Wilson's Critique of Popular Leadership: Reassessing the Modern-Traditional Divide in Presidential History', *Polity* 29 (1996), 27–63.

14. K. Wimer, 'Woodrow Wilson's Plan for a Vote of Confidence', *Pennsylvania History* 28 (1961), 2–16, and R. L. Merritt, 'Woodrow Wilson and the "Great and Solemn Referendum", 1920', *The Review of Politics* 27 (1965), 78–104.

15. See the series of speeches given between August and December 1916 in *PWW*, vol. 40.

16. A. Hagedorn, *Savage Peace: Hope and Fear in America, 1919* (New York, 2007), 297–322.

17. A. Hart (ed.), *Selected Addresses and Public Papers of Woodrow Wilson* (New York, 1918), 270.

18. W. Wilson, *A History of the American People* (New York, 1902), vol. 5, 59–64.

19. Hart (ed.), *Selected Addresses*, 271.

20. *The New York Times*, 26 November 1919.

21. T. Kornweibel, *'Seeing Red': Federal Campaigns against Black Militancy, 1919–1925* (Bloomington, IN, 1998).

22. *The New York Times*, 'President Cheered from Pier to Hotel', 25 February 1919.

23. Hagedorn, *Savage Peace*, 218–25.

24. *PWW*, vol. 62, 58.

25. *The New York Times*, 'Raid from Coast to Coast', 3 January 1920; R. K. Murray, *Red Scare: A Study in National Hysteria, 1919–1920* (Minneapolis, MN, 1955).

26. J. A. McCartin, *Labor's Great War: The Struggle for Industrial Democracy and the Origins of Modern American Labor Relations* (Chapel Hill, NC, 1997).

27. J. Cooper, *The Warrior and the Priest: Woodrow Wilson and Theodore Roosevelt* (Cambridge, MA, 1983), 264.

28. *PWW*, vol. 64, 84.

29. Commission of Enquiry, the Interchurch World Movement, 'Report on the Steel Strike of 1919' (New York, 1920); D. Brody, *Labor in Crisis: The Steel Strike of 1919* (New York, 1965).

30. *PWW*, vol. 63, 600.

31. D. Montgomery, *The Fall of the House of Labor: Workplace, the State, and American Labor Activism, 1865–1925* (New Haven, CT, 1988).

32. McCartin, *Labor's Great War*, 199–220.

33. *The New York Times*, 'Palmer Pledges War on Radicals', 1 January 1920.

34. R. K. Murray, *The Politics of Normalcy: Governmental Theory and Practice in the Harding-Coolidge Era* (New York, 1973), 3, and idem., *The Harding*

Era: Warren G. Harding and His Administration (Minneapolis, MN, 1969), 82.

35. B. M. Manly, 'Have Profits Kept Pace with the Cost of Living?', *Annals of the American Academy of Political and Social Science* 89 (1920), 157–62, and E. B. Woods, 'Have Wages Kept Pace with the Cost of Living?', *Annals of the American Academy of Political and Social Science* 89 (1920), 135–47.

36. *The New York Times*, 'Palmer Has Plan to Cut Living Cost', 17 December 1919, 19.

37. *The New York Times*, 'Urge President to Return', 24 May 1919, 4.

38. Interchurch World Movement, 'Report', 94–106.

39. H. L. Lutz, 'The Administration of the Federal Interest-Bearing Debt Since the Armistice', *The Journal of Political Economy* 34 (1926), 413–57.

40. M. Friedman and A. J. Schwartz, *A Monetary History of the United States, 1867–1960* (Princeton, NJ, 1963), 222–6.

41. A. Meltzer, *A History of the Federal Reserve* (Chicago, IL, 2003), vol. 1, 94–5.

42. Friedman and Schwartz, *Monetary History*, 227.

43. Meltzer, *History*, 101–2.

44. Friedman and Schwartz, *Monetary History*, 230.

45. Meltzer, *History*, 127.

46. *The New York Times*, 'Williams Strikes at High Interest', 11 August 1920, 24, and 'Bank Convention Condemns Williams', 23 October 1920, 20.

47. J. Higham, *Strangers in the Land: Patterns of American Nativism, 1860–1925* (New Brunswick, NJ, 1988); N. K. MacLean, *Behind the Mask of Chivalry: The Making of the Second Ku Klux Klan* (Oxford, 1995).

48. J. C. Prude, 'William Gibbs McAdoo and the Democratic National Convention of 1924', *The Journal of Southern History* 38 (1972), 621–8.

49. F. E. Schortemeier, *Rededicating America: Life and Recent Speeches of Warren G. Harding* (Indianapolis, IN, 1920), 223.

50. Higham, *Strangers*, 309.

51. R. Boyce, *The Great Interwar Crisis and the Collapse of Globalization* (Basingstoke, 2003), 88.

52. Leffler, *Elusive Quest*, 44.

53. Boyce, *Great Interwar Crisis*, 178.

19 THE GREAT DEFLATION

1. S. M. Deutsch, *Counter-Revolution in Argentina, 1900–1932: The Argentine Patriotic League* (Lincoln, NB, 1986).

2. R. Gerwarth and J. Horne (eds), *War in Peace: Paramilitary Violence in Europe after the Great War* (Oxford, 2012).

3. C. S. Maier, *Recasting Bourgeois Europe: Stabilization in France, Germany, and Italy in the Decade after World War I* (Princeton, NJ, 1975), 136.

4. E. L. Dulles, *The French Franc, 1914–1928: The Facts and their Interpretations* (New York, 1929), 120–21.

5. M. Metzler, *Lever of Empire: The International Gold Standard and the Crisis of Liberalism in Prewar Japan* (Berkeley, CA, 2005), 118–33.

6. L. Humphreys, *The Way of the Heavenly Sword: The Japanese Army in the 1920s* (Stanford, CA, 1995), 44; P. Duus (ed.), *The Cambridge History of Japan*, vol. 6, *The Twentieth Century* (Cambridge, 1988), 277.

7. R. Haig, *The Public Finances of Post-War France* (New York, 1929), 70–88.

8. B. Martin, *France and the Après Guerre, 1918–1924: Illusions and Disillusionment* (Baton Rouge, FL, 1999), 35–6.

9. F. R. Dickinson, *War and National Reinvention: Japan in the Great War, 1914–1919* (Cambridge, MA, 1999), 230.

10. P. Duus, *Party Rivalry and Political Change in Taisho Japan* (Cambridge, MA, 1968), 141.

11. M. Lewis, *Rioters and Citizens: Mass Protest in Imperial Japan* (Berkeley, CA, 1990), 82.

12. C. Wrigley, *Lloyd George and the Challenge of Labour: The Post-War Coalition, 1918–22* (Hemel Hempstead, 1990), 81.

13. M. Daunton, *Just Taxes: The Politics of Taxation in Britain, 1914–1979* (Cambridge, 2002), 76–7.

14. Metzler, *Lever of Empire*, 133.

15. G. Balachandran, *John Bullion's Empire: Britain's Gold Problem and India Between the Wars* (London, 1996), 96.

16. A. C. Pigou, *Aspects of British Economic History, 1918–1925* (London, 1945), 149.

17. Balachandran, *John Bullion's Empire*, 93, 109–12.

18. K. Jeffery (ed.), *The Military Correspondence of Field Marshal Sir Henry Wilson, 1918–1922* (London, 1985), 253.

19. A. Clayton, *The British Empire as a Superpower, 1919–39* (Basingstoke, 1986), 103.

20. R. Middleton, *Government versus the Market: The Growth of the Public Sector, Economic Management, and British Economic Performance, 1890–1979* (Cheltenham, 1996), 199, 311–35.

21. M. Leffler, *The Elusive Quest: America's Pursuit of European Stability and French Security, 1919–1933* (Chapel Hill, NC, 1979), 14.

22. M. Milbank Farrar, *Principled Pragmatist: The Political Career of Alexandre Millerand* (New York, 1991).

23. D. Artaud, 'La question des dettes interalliées', in M. Petricioli and M. Guderzo (eds), *Une occasion manquée? 1922: La reconstruction de l'Europe* (New York, 1995), 89.

24. Dulles, *French Franc*, 130.

25. F. H. Adler, *Italian Industrialists from Liberalism to Fascism* (Cambridge, 1995), 165.

26. Metzler, *Lever of Empire*, 134; Duus, *Cambridge History*, 461; Lewis, *Rioters*, 246.

27. C.-L. Holtfrerich, *The German Inflation, 1914–1923* (Berlin, 1986).

28. M. Flandreau (ed.), *Money Doctors: The Experience of International Financial Advising, 1850–2000* (London, 2003).

29. Duus, *Party Rivalry*, 111.

30. Metzler, *Lever of Empire*, 129, 160.

31. Humphreys, *Heavenly Sword*, 61.

32. I. Gow, *Military Intervention in Prewar Japanese Politics: Admiral Katō Kanji and the 'Washington System'* (London, 2004), 85.

33. F. R. Dickinson, *World War I and the Triumph of a New Japan, 1919–1930* (Cambridge, 2013), 115–16.

34. M. Beloff, *Imperial Sunset*, vol. 2, *Dream of Commonwealth, 1921–42* (Basingstoke, 1989), 27.

35. K. Jeffery, *The British Army and the Crisis of Empire* (Manchester, 1984), 13–23.

36. K. Jeffery, *The Military Correspondence of Field Marshal Sir Henry Wilson, 1918–1922* (London, 1985), 197–201.

37. K. Jeffery, '"An English Barrack in the Oriental Seas"? India in the Aftermath of the First World War', *Modern Asian Studies* 15 (1981), 369–86.

38. Clayton, *The British Empire as a Superpower, 1919–1939*, 20.

39. S. Roskill, *Naval Policy Between the Wars* (New York, 1968), vol. 1, 215–16.

40. J. Ferris, *The Evolution of British Strategic Policy, 1919–26* (Basingstoke, 1989), 54–63.

41. Maier, *Recasting*, 195.

42. D. P. Silverman, *Reconstructing Europe after the Great War* (Cambridge, MA, 1982), 215–20.

43. Ibid., 149.

44. R. Self, *Britain, America and the War Debt Controversy: The Economic Diplomacy of an Unspecial Relationship, 1917–1941* (London, 2006), 29.

45. National archive, CAB 24/116 CP 2214.

46. G. Unger, *Aristide Briand: Le ferme conciliateur* (Paris, 2005).

47. Maier, *Recasting*, 241–9.

48. G. D. Feldman, *The Great Disorder: Politics, Economics, and Society in the German Inflation, 1914–1924* (Oxford, 1993), 338–41.

49. It is the counterfactual explored in N. Ferguson, *Paper and Iron: Hamburg Business and German Politics in the Era of Inflation, 1897–1927* (Cambridge, 1995).

50. S. B. Webb, *Hyperinflation and Stabilization in Weimar Germany* (Oxford, 1988).

51. N. Ferguson, 'Constraints and Room for Manoeuvre in the German Inflation

of the Early 1920s', *The Economic History Review* New Series 49 (1996), 635–66.

52. Silverman, *Reconstructing Europe*, 224–5.

53. M. J. Pusey, *Charles Evans Hughes* (New York, 1951), vol. 1, 350.

54. N. A. Palmer, 'The Veterans' Bonus and the Evolving Presidency of Warren G. Harding', *Presidential Studies Quarterly* 38 (2008), 39–60.

55. Artaud, 'La question', in Petricioli and Guderzo (eds), *Occasion manquée*, 87.

56. S. A. Schuker, 'American Policy Towards Debts and Reconstruction', in C. Fink (ed.), *Genoa, Rapallo and European Reconstruction in 1922* (Cambridge, 1991), 98.

57. M. Leffler, 'The Origins of Republican War Debt Policy, 1921–1923: A Case Study in the Applicability of the Open Door Interpretation', *The Journal of American History* 59 (1972), 593.

58. A. Orde, *British Policy and European Reconstruction after the First World War* (Cambridge, 1990), 173–4.

20 CRISIS OF EMPIRE

1. J. Gallagher, 'Nationalisms and the Crisis of Empire, 1919–1922', *Modern Asian Studies* 15 (1981), 355–68.

2. W. F. Elkins, 'Black Power in the British West Indies: The Trinidad Longshoremen's Strike of 1919', *Science and Society* 33 (1969), 71–5.

3. I. Abdullah, 'Rethinking the Freetown Crowd: The Moral Economy of the 1919 Strikes and Riot in Sierra Leone', *Canadian Journal of African Studies/ Revue Canadienne des Études Africaines* 28, no. 2 (1994), 197–218.

4. T. Yoshikuni, 'Strike Action and Self-Help Associations: Zimbabwean Worker Protest and Culture after World War I', *Journal of Southern African Studies* 15, no. 3 (April 1989), 440–68.

5. D. Killingray, 'Repercussions of World War I in the Gold Coast', *The Journal of African History* 19 (1978), 39–59; A. Olukoju, 'Maritime Trade in Lagos in the Aftermath of the First World War', *African Economic History* 20 (1992), 119–35; A. Olukoju, 'Anatomy of Business-Government Relations: Fiscal Policy and Mercantile Pressure Group Activity in Nigeria, 1916–1933', *African Studies Review* 38 (1995), 23–50.

6. R. Ally, *Gold and Empire: The Bank of England and South Africa's Gold Producers, 1886–1926* (Johannesburg, 1994); J. Krikler, 'The Commandos: The Army of White Labour in South Africa', *Past and Present* 163 (1999), 202–44; A. Clayton, *The British Empire as a Superpower, 1919–39* (Basingstoke, 1986), 241–4; J. Krikler, *White Rising: The 1922 Insurrection and Racial Killing in South Africa* (Manchester, 2005).

7. C. Townsend, *The British Campaign in Ireland, 1919–1921* (Oxford, 1975).

8. W. Wilson, *Letters*, 250, 266–72.

9. J. Lawrence, 'Forging a Peaceable Kingdom: War, Violence, and Fear of Brutalization in Post-First World War Britain', *The Journal of Modern History* 75, no. 3 (September 2003), 557–89.

10. M. Beloff, *Imperial Sunset: Britain's Liberal Empire, 1897–1921* (London, 1969), vol. 1, 314.

11. M. Hopkinson, 'President Woodrow Wilson and the Irish Question', *Studia Hibernica* 27 (1993), 89–111.

12. An essential guide is J. Darwin, *Britain, Egypt and the Middle East: Imperial Policy in the Aftermath of War, 1918–1922* (London, 1981).

13. W. Stivers, *Supremacy and Oil: Iraq, Turkey, and the Anglo-American World Order, 1918–1930* (Ithaca, NY, 1982), 45–50.

14. M. W. Daly (ed.), *The Cambridge History of Egypt* (New York, 1998), vol. 2, 246–7.

15. Ibid., 247–8. On the lack of British cultural influence see Beloff, *Imperial Sunset*, vol. 2, 44.

16. J. Berque, *Egypt: Imperialism and Revolution* (New York, 1972), 305.

17. M. Badrawi, *Ismail Sidqi, 1875–1950* (Richmond, VA, 1996), 14.

18. M. A. Rifaat, *The Monetary System of Egypt* (London, 1935), 63–4; A. E. Crouchley, *The Economic Development of Modern Egypt* (London, 1938), 197.

19. Berque, *Egypt*, 316.

20. Ibid., 318.

21. J. L. Thompson, *A Wider Patriotism: Alfred Milner and the British Empire* (London, 2007), 184–95.

22. Berque, *Egypt*, 315–16.

23. Gallagher, 'Nationalisms', 361.

24. Cited in E. Kedourie, *The Chatham House Version and Other Middle-Eastern Studies* (London, 1970), 121.

25. L. Stein, *The Balfour Declaration* (New York, 1961), 640–45.

26. E. Monroe, *Britain's Moment in the Middle East, 1914–1956* (Baltimore, MD, 1963), 65–6.

27. Q. Wright, 'The Bombardment of Damascus', *The American Journal of International Law* 20 (1926), 263–80; D. Eldar, 'France in Syria: The Abolition of the Sharifian Government, April–July 1920', *Middle Eastern Studies* 29 (1993), 487–504.

28. Stivers, *Supremacy and Oil*, 84, and E. Kedourie, 'The Kingdom of Iraq: A Retrospect', in Kedourie, *Chatham House Version*, 236–85.

29. Beloff, *Imperial Sunset*, vol. 1, 347.

30. I. Friedman, *British Miscalculations: The Rise of Muslim Nationalism, 1918–1925* (New Brunswick, NJ, 2012), 252.

31. B. Gökay, *A Clash of Empires: Turkey between Russian Bolshevism and British Imperialism, 1918–1923* (London, 1997).

32. B. Lewis, *The Emergence of Modern Turkey* (Oxford, 1961), 247–51.

33. Gökay, *Clash of Empires*, 131.

34. G. Balachandran, *John Bullion's Empire: Britain's Gold Problem and India Between the Wars* (London, 1996).

35. B. R. Tomlinson, *The Political Economy of the Raj, 1914–1947: The Economics of Decolonization in India* (London, 1979).

36. J. Brown, *Gandhi's Rise to Power: Indian Politics, 1915–1922* (Cambridge, 1972), 161.

37. Ibid., 231.

38. Friedman, *British Miscalculations*, 229.

39. Brown, *Gandhi*, 202.

40. P. Woods, *Roots of Parliamentary Democracy in India: Montagu-Chelmsford Reforms, 1917–1923* (Delhi, 1996), 139–40.

41. A. Rumbold, *Watershed in India, 1914–1922* (London, 1979), 160–93.

42. W. R. Smith, *Nationalism and Reform in India* (New Haven, CT, 1938), 108–9.

43. Ibid., 118–19.

44. Brilliantly elucidated in G. Pandey, 'Peasant Revolt and Indian Nationalism: The Peasant Movement in Awadh, 1919–1922', in R. Guha (ed.), *Subaltern Studies* (Delhi, 1982–9), vol. 1, 143–91.

45. D. A. Low, 'The Government of India and the First Non-Cooperation Movement 1920–22', *The Journal of Asian Studies* 25 (1966), 247–8.

46. Rumbold, *Watershed*, 266–7.

47. See the report by General Rawlinson to Wilson in Wilson, *Letters*, 306–7.

48. Woods, *Roots*, 157–69.

49. Low, 'Government of India', 252.

50. Rumbold, *Watershed*, 294.

51. Ibid., 301–3.

52. Monroe, *Britain's Moment*, 69–70.

53. D. Waley, *Edwin Montagu* (New Delhi, 1964), 270.

54. K. Mantena, *Alibis of Empire: Henry Maine and the Ends of Liberal Imperialism* (Princeton, NJ, 2010).

55. D. A. Low, *Lion Rampant: Essays in the Study of British Imperialism* (London, 1973), 157.

56. These are characterizations offered by J. Darwin, 'Imperialism in Decline?', *Historical Journal* 23 (1980), 657–79.

57. Cooper's analysis of the French dilemma is highly pertinent, see F. Cooper, *Colonialism in Question: Theory, Knowledge, History* (Berkeley, CA, 2005). See also Low, *Lion Rampant*, 70–72.

58. H. Tinker, *Separate and Unequal: India and the Indians in the British Commonwealth, 1920–1950* (Vancouver, 1976), 43–77.

59. Woods, *Roots*, 232.

60. Beloff, *Imperial Sunset*, vol. 1, 312–13; Waley, *Montagu*, 258; Beloff, *Imperial Sunset*, vol. 2, 30.

21 A CONFERENCE IN WASHINGTON

1. W. R. Louis, *British Strategy in the Far East, 1919–1939* (Oxford, 1971), 50–78; M. Beloff, *Imperial Sunset: Britain's Liberal Empire, 1897–1921* (London, 1969), vol. 1, 318–24.

2. N. Tracy, *The Collective Naval Defence of the Empire, 1900–1940* (London, 1997).

3. S. Roskill, *Naval Policy Between the Wars* (New York, 1968), vol. 1, 271–90.

4. Beloff, *Imperial Sunset*, vol. 1, 332–43.

5. L. Gardner, *Safe for Democracy: The Anglo-American Response to Revolution, 1913–1923* (Oxford, 1987), 307–9.

6. T. H. Buckley, *The United States and the Washington Conference, 1921–1922* (Knoxville, TN, 1970), 30–37.

7. M. G. Fry, *Illusions of Security: North Atlantic Diplomacy, 1918–1922* (Toronto, 1972), 144–51.

8. Roskill, *Naval Policy*, vol. 1, 311.

9. As noted by Lansing, who attended; see Buckley, *The United States*, 74.

10. 'The Arms Conference in Action', *Current History* 15, 3 December 1921, i.

11. Ibid., xxxii.

12. A. Iriye, *After Imperialism: The Search for a New Order in the Far East, 1921–1931* (Cambridge, MA, 1965), 14.

13. L. Humphreys, *The Way of the Heavenly Sword: The Japanese Army in the 1920s* (Stanford, CA, 1995), 46.

14. Buckley, *United States*, 59.

15. I. Gow, *Military Intervention in Prewar Japanese Politics: Admiral Katō Kanji and the 'Washington System'* (London, 2004), 82–101.

16. Fry, *Illusions of Security*, 154–86.

17. *Papers Relating to the Foreign Relations of the United States: Lansing Papers* (Washington, DC, 1922), vol. 1, 130–33.

18. B. Martin, *France and the Après Guerre, 1918–1924: Illusions and Disillusionment* (Baton Rouge, FL, 1999), 87–9.

19. E. Goldstein and J. Maurer (eds), *The Washington Conference, 1921–22: Naval Rivalry, East Asian Stability and the Road to Pearl Harbour* (London, 1994).

20. Roskill, *Naval Policy*, vol. 1, 354.

21. D. Wang, *China's Unequal Treaties: Narrating National History* (Oxford, 2005).

22. 'Arms Conference', *Current History* 15, 383–4.

23. G. McCormack, *Chang Tso-lin in Northeast China, 1911–1928: China, Japan, and the Manchurian Idea* (Stanford, CA, 1977), 52–66.

24. M. Metzler, *Lever of Empire: The International Gold Standard and the Crisis of Liberalism in Prewar Japan* (Berkeley, CA, 2005), 129.

25. E. S. K. Fung, *The Diplomacy of Imperial Retreat: Britain's South China Policy, 1924–1932* (Hong Kong, 1991), 18–25.

26. Y. Zhang, *China in the International System, 1918–1920* (Basingstoke, 1991), 184–5.

27. W. King, *China at the Washington Conference, 1921–1922* (New York, 1963), 18–19.

28. Goldstein and Maurer, *Washington Conference*, 263.

29. See the opinions discussed in King, *China*, 38–9.

30. Metzler, *Lever of Empire*, 127.

31. Gardner, *Safe for Democracy*, 313.

32. Ibid., 313.

33. Iriye, *After Imperialism*, 29.

34. Gardner, *Safe for Democracy*, 318–19.

35. Ibid., 320.

36. R. A. Dayer, *Bankers and Diplomats in China, 1917–1925* (London, 1981), 155–61.

22 REINVENTING COMMUNISM

1. M. Lewin, *Lenin's Last Struggle* (New York, 1968).

2. As R. Hofheinz, *The Broken Wave: The Chinese Communist Peasant Movement, 1922–1928* (Cambridge, MA, 1977), 3, acutely remarked: 'Not many realize today that the consciously articulated idea of peasant revolution is only a few decades old.'

3. A. S. Lindemann, *The Red Years: European Socialism versus Bolshevism, 1919–1921* (Berkeley, CA, 1974), 48–68.

4. C. S. Maier, *Recasting Bourgeois Europe: Stabilization in France, Germany, and Italy in the Decade after World War I* (Princeton, NJ, 1975), 113–74; F. H. Adler, *Italian Industrialists from Liberalism to Fascism* (New York, 1995), 165–8; G. Salvemini, *The Origins of Fascism in Italy* (New York, 1973), 206–8.

5. P. Pastor (ed.), *Revolutions and Interventions in Hungary and its Neighbor States, 1918–1919* (Boulder, CO, 1988).

6. C. Kinvig, *Churchill's Crusade: The British Invasion of Russia, 1918–1920* (London, 2006), 283–5.

7. N. Davies, *White Eagle, Red Star: The Polish-Soviet War, 1919–1920* (London, 1972), 71–6.

8. R. Pipes, *Russia under the Bolshevik Regime* (New York, 1994), 91–2.

9. Davies, *White Eagle, Red Star*, 90–91.

10. C. E. Bechhofer, *In Denikin's Russia and the Caucasus, 1918–1920* (London, 1921), 120–22.

11. T. Snyder, *The Reconstruction of Nations: Poland, Ukraine, Lithuania, Belarus, 1569–1999* (New Haven, CT, 2003), 63–139.

12. G. A. Brinkley, 'Allied Policy and French Intervention in the Ukraine, 1917–1920', in T. Hunczak (ed.), *The Ukraine, 1917–1921: A Study in Revolution* (Cambridge, MA, 1977), 345–51.

13. N. Davies, 'The Missing Revolutionary War', *Soviet Studies* 27 (1975), 178–95.

14. Pipes, *Russia under the Bolshevik Regime*, 179–83.

15. T. Fiddick, 'The "Miracle of the Vistula": Soviet Policy versus Red Army Strategy', *The Journal of Modern History* 45 (1973), 626–43.

16. For the British response see M. Beloff, *Imperial Sunset: Britain's Liberal Empire, 1897–1921* (London, 1969), vol. 1, 328–9.

17. J. Degras (ed.), *The Communist International: Documents, 1919–1943* (London, 1956–65), vol. 1, 111–13.

18. Pipes, *Russia under the Bolshevik Regime*, 177.

19. O. Ruehle, 'Report from Moscow', http://www.marxists.org/archive/ruhle/1920/ruhle01.htm.

20. Lindemann, *Red Years*, 102–219.

21. Degras, *The Communist International, 1919–1943*, 166–72.

22. J. Jacobson, *When the Soviet Union Entered World Politics* (Berkeley, CA, 1994), 51–8.

23. J. P. Haithcox, *Communism and Nationalism in India: M. N. Roy and Comintern Policy, 1920–1939* (Princeton, NJ, 1971).

24. S. White, *Britain and the Bolshevik Revolution: A Study in the Politics of Diplomacy, 1920–1924* (London, 1979), 120.

25. S. Blank, 'Soviet Politics and the Iranian Revolution of 1919–1921', *Cahiers du Monde russe et soviétique* 21 (1980), 173–94.

26. S. White, 'Communism and the East: The Baku Congress, 1920', *Slavic Review* 33 (1974), 492–514.

27. J. Riddell (ed.), *To See the Dawn: Baku, 1920 – First Congress of the Peoples of the East* (New York, 1993), 47–52.

28. Ibid., 232.

29. Jacobson, *When the Soviet Union*, 77.

30. N. Davies, 'The Soviet Command and the Battle of Warsaw', *Soviet Studies* 23 (1972), 573–85.

31. H. G. Linke, 'Der Weg nach Rapallo: Strategie und Taktik der deutschen und sowjetischen Außenpolitik', *Historische Zeitschrift* 264 (1997), 63.

32. Beloff, *Imperial Sunset*, vol. 1, 328–9.

33. Pipes, *Russia under the Bolshevik Regime*, 134, 164.

34. S. R. Sonyel, 'Enver Pasha and the Basmaji Movement in Central Asia', *Middle Eastern Studies* 26 (1990), 52–64.

35. Beautifully outlined in Jacobson, *When the Soviet Union*.

36. B. Gökay, *A Clash of Empires: Turkey between Russian Bolshevism and British Imperialism, 1918–1923* (London, 1997), 148–9.

37. B. A. Elleman, *Diplomacy and Deception: The Secret History of Sino-Soviet Diplomatic Relations, 1917–1927* (Armonk, NY, 1997).

38. P. Dukes, *The USA in the Making of the USSR: The Washington Conference, 1921–1922, and 'Uninvited Russia'* (New York and London, 2004), 57–61.

39. J. K. Fairbank and D. Twitchett (eds), *The Cambridge History of China*, vol. 12, *Republican China, 1912–1949, Part 1* (Cambridge, 1983), 541.

40. A. J. Saich, *The Origins of the First United Front in China: The Role of Sneevliet (Alias Maring)* (Leiden, 1991).

41. G. D. Jackson, *Comintern and Peasant in Eastern Europe, 1919–1930* (New York, 1966), 93.

42. Ibid., 60.

43. *Papers Relating to the Foreign Relations of the United States: Lansing Papers* (Washington, DC, 1921), vol. 2, 805.

23 GENOA: THE FAILURE OF BRITISH HEGEMONY

1. B. M. Weissman, *Herbert Hoover and Famine Relief to Soviet Russia, 1921–1923* (Stanford, CA, 1974), 15–16.

2. A. Orde, *British Policy and European Reconstruction after the First World War* (Cambridge, 1990), 162.

3. S. White, *The Origins of Détente: The Genoa Conference and Soviet-Western Relations, 1921–1922* (Cambridge, 1985), 26–7.

4. Orde, *British Policy*, 163; C. Fink, *The Genoa Conference: European Diplomacy, 1921–1922* (Chapel Hill, NC, 1984), 6.

5. P. Dukes, *The USA in the Making of the USSR: The Washington Conference, 1921–1922, and 'Uninvited Russia'* (New york and London, 2004), 71.

6. B. Patenaude, *The Big Show in Bololand: The American Relief Expedition to Soviet Russia in the Famine of 1921* (Stanford, CA, 2002).

7. C. M. Edmondson, 'The Politics of Hunger: The Soviet Response to Famine, 1921', *Soviet Studies* 29 (1977), 506–18.

8. G. D. Feldman, *The Great Disorder: Politics, Economics, and Society in the German Inflation, 1914–1924* (Oxford, 1993), 346–412.

9. Ibid., 388.

10. G. D. Feldman, *Hugo Stinnes: Biographie eines Industriellen 1870–1924* (Munich, 1998), 720–38.

11. Orde, *British Policy*, 177.

12. R. Himmer, 'Rathenau, Russia, and Rapallo', *Central European History* 9 (1976), 146–83.

13. H. G. Linke, 'Der Weg nach Rapallo: Strategie und Taktik der deutschen und sowjetischen Außenpolitik', *Historische Zeitschrift* 264 (1997), 82.

14. A. Heywood, *Modernising Lenin's Russia: Economic Reconstruction, Foreign Trade and the Railways* (Cambridge, 1999), 6.

15. Orde, *British Policy*, 170–78.
16. B. Martin, *France and the Après Guerre, 1918–1924: Illusions and Disillusionment* (Baton Rouge, LA, 1999), 96.
17. *Documents on British Foreign Policy, 1919–1939*, 1st ser. [hereafter *DBFP*] (London, 1974), vol. 13–14, 57–8. A shift recently emphasized by P. Jackson, 'French Security and a British "Continental Commitment" after the First World War: A Reassessment', *English Historical Review* CCXVI (2011) 519, 345–85. For the wider background to this shift see A.-M. Lauter, *Sicherheit und Reparationen. Die französische Öffentlichkeit, der Rhein und die Ruhr (1919–1923)* (Essen, 2006), 232–42, 286–90.
18. The development of this design is charted in December 1921 and January 1922 in *DBFP*, vol. 9.
19. White, *The Origins*, 45.
20. Orde, *British Policy*, 180–82.
21. Feldman, *Great Disorder*, 382.
22. Martin, *France*, 97–126.
23. J. Keiger, *Raymond Poincaré* (Cambridge, 1997), 279–83.
24. *The New Republic*, 8 March 1922, 30–33.
25. *DBFP*, vol. 19, 171–2.
26. *Ibid.*, 300.
27. Martin, *France*, 128; Feldman, *Great Disorder*, 383.
28. Feldman, *Great Disorder*, 410–31.
29. Ibid., 421.
30. Ibid., 431–4.
31. C. S. Maier, *Recasting Bourgeois Europe: Stabilization in France, Germany, and Italy in the Decade after World War I* (Princeton, NJ, 1975), 282–3; M. Berg, *Gustav Stresemann und die Vereinigten Staaten von Amerika: Weltwirtschaftliche Verflechtung und Revisionspolitik, 1907–1929* (Baden-Baden, 1990), 108–9.
32. Fink, *Genoa*, 83–6.
33. W. Link, *Die Amerikanische Stabilisierungspolitik in Deutschland, 1921–1932* (Dusseldorf, 1970), 174.
34. *DBFP*, vol. 19, 342.
35. White, *The Origins*, 82–94.
36. *DBFP*, vol. 19, 393.
37. Ibid., 348–51.
38. White, *The Origins*, 107–9.
39. Fink, *Genoa*, 60.
40. R. Himmer, 'Rathenau, Russia and Rapallo', *Central European History* 9 (1976), 146–83.
41. J. Siegel, *For Peace and Money* (Oxford, 2014, forthcoming), chapter 5.
42. Fink, *Genoa*, 174–5.
43. A parallel not lost on the Soviets, see White, *The Origins*, 110.

44. For Lloyd George's warnings about Ottomanizing the Soviet Union see *DBFP*, vol. 19, 377–8.

45. Linke, 'Der Weg', 77.

46. B. Gökay, *A Clash of Empires: Turkey between Russian Bolshevism and British Imperialism, 1918–1923* (London, 1997), 119.

47. Berg, *Stresemann*, 109; Maier, *Recasting*, 284.

48. Feldman, *Great Disorder*, 450.

49. Gökay, *Clash of Empires*, 119.

50. J. C. Cairns, 'A Nation of Shopkeepers in Search of a Suitable France: 1919–40', *The American Historical Review* 79, no. 3 (June 1974), 720.

51. M. Beloff, *Imperial Sunset: Britain's Liberal Empire, 1897–1921* (London, 1969), vol. 2, 79–80.

52. Z. Steiner, *The Lights that Failed: European International History, 1919–1933* (Oxford, 2005), 113–20.

53. J. R. Ferris, *The Evolution of British Strategic Policy, 1919–26* (Basingstoke, 1989), 120.

54. Gökay, *Clash of Empires*, 164.

55. D. P. Silverman, *Reconstructing Europe after the Great War* (Cambridge, MA, 1982), 179–80.

56. R. Self, *Britain, America and the War Debt Controversy: The Economic Diplomacy of an Unspecial Relationship, 1917–41* (London, 2006), 36–54.

57. B. D. Rhodes, 'Reassessing "Uncle Shylock": The United States and the French War Debt, 1917–1929', *The Journal of American History* 55, no. 4 (March 1969), 793.

58. A. Turner, 'Keynes, the Treasury and French War Debts in the 1920s', *European History Quarterly* 27 (1997), 505.

59. M. P. Leffler, *The Elusive Quest: America's Pursuit of European Stability and French Security, 1919–1933* (Chapel Hill, NC, 1979), 69.

60. Link, *Stabilisierungspolitik*, 175.

24 EUROPE ON THE BRINK

1. B. Martin, *France and the Après Guerre, 1918–1924: Illusions and Disillusionment* (Baton Rouge, LA, 1999), 132–50.

2. A.-M. Lauter, *Sicherheit und Reparationen: die französische Öffentlichkeit, der Rhein und die Ruhr (1919–1923)* (Essen, 2006), 292–301.

3. *Papers Relating to the Foreign Relations of the United States: Lansing Papers* [hereafter *FRUS: Lansing Papers*] (Washington, DC, 1922), vol. 1, 557–8.

4. W. Link, *Die amerikanische Stabilisierungspolitik in Deutschland 1921–32* (Düsseldorf, 1970), 122–47.

5. S. A. Schuker, 'Europe's Banker: The American Banking Community and European Reconstruction, 1918–1922', in M. Petricioli and M.Guderzo (eds),

Une Occasion manquée 1922: la reconstruction de l'Europe (Frankfurt, 1995), 56.

6. P. Liberman, *Does Conquest Pay? The Exploitation of Occupied Industrial Societies* (Princeton, NJ, 1996), 87–98.

7. Martin, *France*, 156; *The New York Times*, 'Clemenceau Feels So Sure of Success He's a "Boy" Again', 23 November 1922, 1–3.

8. M. J. Pusey, *Charles Evans Hughes* (New York, 1951), vol. 2, 581–2.

9. C. E. Hughes, *The Pathway of Peace: Representative Addresses Delivered during his Term as Secretary of State (1921–1925)* (New York, 1925), 57; Link, *Stabilisierungspolitik*, 168–74.

10. W. I. Shorrock, 'France and the Rise of Fascism in Italy, 1919–23', *Journal of Contemporary History* 10 (1975), 591–610.

11. Martin, *France*, 165.

12. C. Fischer, *The Ruhr Crisis, 1923–1924* (Oxford, 2003), 86–107.

13. Ibid., 176.

14. G. Krumeich and J. Schröder (eds), *Der Schatten des Weltkrieges: Die Ruhrbesetzung, 1923* (Essen, 2004), 207–24.

15. G. D. Feldman, *The Great Disorder: Politics, Economics, and Society in the German Inflation, 1914–1924* (Oxford, 1993), 637–69; C. S. Maier, *Recasting Bourgeois Europe: Stabilization in France, Germany, and Italy in the Decade after World War I* (Princeton, NJ, 1975), 367–76.

16. Feldman, *Great Disorder*, 705–66.

17. P. Cohrs, *The Unfinished Peace after World War I* (Cambridge, 2006), 88; M. Leffler, *The Elusive Quest: America's Pursuit of European Stability and French Security, 1919–1933* (Chapel Hill, NC, 1979), 86; B. Glad, *Charles Evans Hughes and the Illusions of Innocence: A Study of American Diplomacy* (Urbana, IL, 1966), 219–23.

18. S. Adler, *The Uncertain Giant, 1921–1941: American Foreign Policy Between the Wars* (New York, 1965), 75.

19. *FRUS: Lansing Papers*, 1923, vol. 2, 56.

20. W. Louis, *British Strategy in the Far East, 1919–1939* (Oxford, 1971), 104.

21. M. Howard, *The Continental Commitment: The Dilemma of British Defence Policy in the Era of the Two World Wars* (London, 1972), 81–4.

22. Link, *Stabilisierungspolitik*, 179–87.

23. P. Yearwood, *Guarantee of Peace: The League of Nations in British Policy, 1914–1925* (Oxford, 2009), 253.

24. Ibid., 264–5.

25. M. Berg, *Gustav Stresemann und die Vereinigten Staaten von Amerika: weltwirtschaftliche Verflechtung und Revisionspolitik, 1907–1929* (Baden-Baden, 1990).

26. Fischer, *The Ruhr Crisis*, 230.

27. Martin, *France*, 188.

28. H.-P. Schwarz, *Konrad Adenauer: A German Politician and Statesman in a Period of War, Revolution, and Reconstruction* (Oxford, 1995), vol. 1, 171–94.

29. Feldman, *Great Disorder*, 768.

30. R. Scheck, 'Politics of Illusion: Tirpitz and Right-Wing Putschism, 1922–1924', *German Studies Review* 18 (1995), 29–49.

31. A. Wirsching, *Vom Weltkrieg zum Buergerkrieg? Politischer Extremismus in Deutschland und Frankreich, 1918–1933/39. Berlin und Paris im Vergleich* (Munich, 1999), 238.

32. D. R. Stone, 'The Prospect of War? Lev Trotskii, the Soviet Army, and the German Revolution in 1923', *The International History Review* 25, no. 4 (December 2003), 799–817.

33. G. Feldman, 'Bayern und Sachsen in der Hyperinflation 1922', *Historische Zeitschrift* 238 (1984), 569–609.

34. D. Pryce, 'The Reich Government versus Saxony, 1923: The Decision to Intervene', *Central European History* 10 (1977), 112–47.

35. Feldman, *Great Disorder*, 774.

36. K. Schwabe (ed.), *Die Ruhrkrise 1923: Wendepunkt der internationalen Beziehungen nach dem Ersten Weltkrieg* (Paderborn, 1985), 29–38.

37. Feldman, *Great Disorder*, 776–7.

38. G. Schulz (ed.), *Konrad Adenauer 1917–1933* (Cologne, 2003), 203–32, and K. D. Erdmann, *Adenauer in der Rheinlandpolitik nach dem Ersten Weltkrieg* (Stuttgart, 1966).

39. Schulz, *Konrad Adenauer 1917–1933*, 346.

40. Maier, *Great Disorder*, 393.

41. Feldman, *Great Disorder*, 825.

42. Ibid., 661.

43. Berg, *Stresemann*, 160, 168–9, 171.

44. Link, *Stabilisierungspolitik*, 206–7.

45. A. Orde, *British Policy and European Reconstruction after the First World War* (Cambridge, 1990), 244.

46. Krumeich and Schroeder (eds), *Der Schatten*, 80.

47. J. Bariéty, *Les Relations Franco-Allemands aprés la Première Guerre Mondiale* (Paris, 1977), 263–5.

48. Berg, *Stresemann*, 159.

49. Leffler, *Elusive Quest*, 94–5.

50. Ibid., 99.

51. Yearwood, *Guarantee of Peace*, 273–89.

52. D. Marquand, *Ramsay MacDonald* (London, 1997), 297–305.

53. *The Times*, 'MacDonald on Ruhr', 12 February 1923, 12, and 'Mr. MacDonald On Ruhr "Success"', 26 September 1923.

54. Marquand, *MacDonald*, 333; *The Times*, 'Labour and Allied Debts', 13 December 1923.

55. J. C. Cairns, 'A Nation of Shopkeepers in Search of a Suitable France: 1919–40', *The American Historical Review* 79, no. 3 (June 1974), 721.

56. Martin, *France*, 189–92.

57. S. A. Schuker, *The End of French Predominance in Europe: The Financial Crisis of 1924 and the Adoption of the Dawes Plan* (Chapel Hill, NC, 1976), 28, 53–7.

58. E. L. Dulles, *The French Franc, 1914–1928: The Facts and their Interpretation* (New York, 1929), 170–74.

59. Martin, *France*, 232–3; Maier, *Recasting*, 460–71.

60. Leffler, *Elusive Quest*, 97.

61. Feldman, *Great Disorder*, 829.

62. D. Neri-Ultsch, *Sozialisten und Radicaux – eine schwierige Allianz* (Munich, 2005).

63. Leffler, *Elusive Quest*, 100–04.

64. Ibid., 105.

65. *FRUS: Lansing Papers*, 1924, vol. 2, 28–30; B. Glad, *Charles Evans Hughes and the Illusions of Innocence: A Study in American Diplomacy* (Urbana, IL, 1966), 227.

66. Schuker, *End of French Predominance*, 103.

67. J. Wright, *Gustav Stresemann: Weimar's Greatest Statesman* (Oxford, 2002), 275.

68. Scheck, 'Politics of Illusion'.

69. Feldman, *Great Disorder*, 801.

70. T. Raithel, *Das Schwierige Spiel des Parlamentarismus: Deutscher Reichstag und französische Chambre des Députés in den Inflationskrisen der 1920er Jahre* (Munich, 2005), 196–341.

71. Feldman, *Great Disorder*, 822–3.

72. Ibid., 815, 802.

73. Leffler, *Elusive Quest*, 111.

74. W. McNeil, *American Money and the Weimar Republic: Economics and Politics on the Eve of the Great Depression* (New York, 1986), 33.

75. Cohrs, *Unfinished Peace*.

25 THE NEW POLITICS OF WAR AND PEACE

1. See The Nobel Peace Prize speech at www.nobelprize.org/nobel_prizes/peace/laureates/1926/stresemann-lecture.html.

2. On the development of 'pacificism as Realpolitik' in Germany see L. Haupts, *Deutsche Friedenspolitik, 1918–1919* (Dusseldorf, 1976).

3. S. Hoffmann, *Gulliver's Troubles, or the Setting of American Foreign Policy* (New York, 1968), 53.

4. *Documents on British Foreign Policy, 1919–1939* [hereafter *DBFP*], series 1a, vol. 5, ed. E. L. Woodward and Rohan Butler (London, 1973), 857–75; B. McKercher, *The Second Baldwin Government and the United States, 1924–1929: Attitudes and Diplomacy* (Cambridge, 1984), 174.

5. W. Link, *Die amerikanische Stabilisierungspolitik in Deutschland 1921–32* (Düsseldorf, 1970), 223–41.

6. W. McNeil, *American Money and the Weimar Republic: Economics and Politics on the Eve of the Great Depression* (New York, 1986).

7. A. Ritschl, *Deutschlands Krise und Konjunktur, 1924–1934: Binnenkonjunktur, Auslandsverschuldung und Reparationsproblem zwischen Dawes-Plan und Transfersperre* (Berlin, 2002).

8. A. Thimme, 'Gustav Stresemann: Legende und Wirklichkeit', *Historische Zeitschrift* 181 (1956), 314.

9. R. Boyce, *British Capitalism at the Crossroads, 1919–1932* (New York, 1987), 66–78.

10. K. Polanyi, *The Great Transformation: The Political and Economic Origins of Our Times* (Boston, MA, 1944), 27.

11. G. Gorodetsky, 'The Soviet Union and Britain's General Strike of May 1926', *Cahiers du monde russe et soviétique* 17, no. 2/3 (1976), 287–310; J. Jacobson, *When the Soviet Union Entered World Politics* (Berkeley, CA, 1994), 169–72.

12. J. Diggins, 'Flirtation with Fascism: American Pragmatic Liberals and Mussolini's Italy', *The American Historical Review* 71, no. 2 (1966), 487–506.

13. S. Romano, *Guiseppe Volpi et l'italie moderne: Finance, industrie et état de l'ère giolittienne à la deuxième guerre mondiale* (Rome, 1982).

14. G. Allen, 'The Recent Currency and Exchange Policy of Japan', *The Economic Journal* 35, no. 137 (1925), 66–83.

15. M. Metzler, *Lever of Empire: The International Gold Standard and the Crisis of Liberalism in Prewar Japan* (Berkeley, CA, 2005), 149.

16. R. A. Dayer, *Bankers and Diplomats in China, 1917–1925: The Anglo-American Relationship* (London, 1981), 178.

17. B. D. Rhodes, 'Reassessing "Uncle Shylock": The United States and the French War Debt, 1917–1929', *The Journal of American History* 55, no. 4 (March 1969), 787–803.

18. On the fascist movement in France in the 1920s see K.-J. Müller, '"Faschismus" in Frankreichs Dritter Republik?', in H. Möller and M. Kittel (eds), *Demokratie in Deutschland und Frankreich, 1918–1933/40* (Munich, 2002), 91–130.

19. T. Raithel, *Das schwierige Spiel des Parlamentarismus: Deutscher Reichstag und französische Chambre des Députés in den Inflationskrisen der 1920er Jahre* (Munich, 2005), 480–519.

20. D. Amson, *Poincaré: L'acharné de la politique* (Paris, 1997), 352–3.

21. R. M. Haig, *The Public Finances of Post-War France* (New York, 1929), 173.

22. R. Boyce, *The Great Interwar Crisis and the Collapse of Globalization* (Basingstoke, 2009), 165.

23. M. P. Leffler, *The Elusive Quest: America's Pursuit of European Stability and French Security, 1919-1933* (Chapel Hill, NC, 1979), 153.

24. R. Boyce, *British Capitalism at the Crossroads, 1919-1932* (New York, 1987), 144-6.

25. P. Yearwood, *Guarantee of Peace: The League of Nations in British Policy, 1914-1925* (Oxford, 2009), 342.

26. M. Beloff, *Imperial Sunset: Britain's Liberal Empire 1897-1921* (London, 1969), vol. 2, 140, citing *DBFP*, series 1a, III, 734.

27. Yearwood, *Guarantee*, 342.

28. Boyce, *Great Interwar Crisis*, 133.

29. J. R. Ferris, *The Evolution of British Strategic Policy, 1919-26* (Basingstoke, 1989), 158-78.

30. Yearwood, *Guarantee*, 355.

31. G. Unger, *Aristide Briand: Le ferme conciliateur* (Paris, 2005), 532-7.

32. P. O. Cohrs, *The Unfinished Peace after World War I: America, Britain and the Stabilisation of Europe, 1919-1932* (Cambridge, 2006), 448-76.

33. J. Wheeler-Bennett, *Information on the Renunciation of War, 1927-1928* (London, 1928), 56.

34. Jacobson, *When the Soviet Union*, 247.

35. A. Iriye, *The Cambridge History of American Foreign Relations*, vol. 3, *The Globalizing of America, 1913-1945* (Cambridge, 1993), 103-06.

36. Cohrs, *Unfinished Peace*, 378-409.

37. J. Keiger, *Raymond Poincaré* (Cambridge, 1997), 337-40.

38. McKercher, *The Second Baldwin Government and the United States, 1924-1929*, 174.

39. Beloff, *Imperial Sunset*, vol. 2, 142-3.

40. L. Trotsky, 'Disarmament and the United States of Europe' (October 1929) http://www.marxists.org/archive/trotsky/1929/10/disarm.htm

41. D. Marquand, *Ramsay MacDonald* (London, 1997), 507.

42. Z. Steiner, *The Lights that Failed: European International History, 1919-1933* (Oxford, 2005), 510-18.

43. Jacobson, *When the Soviet Union*, 183-8, 224-9.

44. A. Waldron, *From War to Nationalism: China's Turning Point, 1924-1925* (Cambridge, 1995).

45. J. Fairbank (ed.), *The Cambridge History of China*, vol. 12, *Republican China, 1912-1949. Part 1* (Cambridge, 2008), 314-15; L. Humphreys, *The Way of the Heavenly Sword: The Japanese Army in the 1920s* (Stanford, CA, 1995), 130.

46. Dayer, *Bankers*, 186-7.

47. C. Martin Wilbur and J. Lien-Ying, *Missionaries of Revolution: Soviet Advisers and Nationalist China, 1920-1927* (Cambridge, MA, 1989), 90-100.

48. E. Fung, *The Diplomacy of Imperial Retreat: Britain's South China Policy, 1924–1931* (Hong Kong, 1991), 42–54.

49. R. Hofheinz, *The Broken Wave: The Chinese Communist Peasant Movement, 1922–1928* (Cambridge, MA, 1977).

50. Wilbur and Lien-Ying, *Missionaries of Revolution*, 108–12; P. Zarrow, *China in War and Revolution, 1895–1949* (London, 2005), 216–21.

51. R. Karl, *Mao Zedong and China in the Twentieth-Century World: A Concise History* (Durham, NC, 2010), 29.

52. S. Schram (ed.), *Mao's Road to Power: Revolutionary Writings, 1912–1949* (New York, 1994), vol. 2, 421.

53. J. Solecki and C. Martin Wilbur, 'Blücher's "Grand Plan" of 1926', *The China Quarterly* 35 (1968), 18–39.

54. H. Kuo, *Die Komintern und die Chinesische Revolution* (Paderborn, 1979), 148.

55. B. Elleman, *Moscow and the Emergence of Communist Power in China, 1925–1930* (London, 2009), 23–36.

56. Karl, *Mao Zedong*, 30.

57. Schram (ed.), *Mao's Road to Power*, vol. 2, 430.

58. S. Craft, *V. K. Wellington Koo and the Emergence of Modern China* (Lexington, KY, 2004), 86.

59. *Papers Relating to the Foreign Relations of the United States: Lansing Papers* (Washington, DC, 1926), vol. 1, 924; A. Iriye, *China and Japan in the Global Setting* (Cambridge, MA, 1992), 99–101.

60. Fung, *Diplomacy*, 100–11.

61. Ibid., 131–2.

62. A. Clayton, *The British Empire as a Superpower, 1919–39* (Basingstoke, 1986), 207–8.

63. Zarrow, *China*, 236–7.

64. M. Murdock, 'Exploiting Anti-Imperialism: Popular Forces and Nation-State-Building during China's Northern Expedition, 1926–1927', *Modern China* 35, no. 1 (2009), 65–95.

65. Fung, *The Diplomacy of Imperial Retreat*, 137–44.

66. Kuo, *Komintern*, 202–17.

67. Karl, *Mao Zedong*, 33.

68. Hofheinz, *The Broken Wave*, 53–63.

69. Craft, *Wellington Koo*, 92.

70. M. Jabara Carley, 'Episodes from the Early Cold War: Franco-Soviet Relations, 1917–1927', *Europe-Asia Studies* 52, no. 7 (2000), 1,297.

71. L. Viola, *The War Against the Peasantry, 1927–1930: The Tragedy of the Soviet Countryside* (New Haven, CT, 2005), 9–56.

72. L. D. Trotsky, 'The New Course in the Economy of the Soviet Union'(March 1930), http://www.marxists.org/archive/trotsky/1930/03/newcourse.htm

73. P. Duus (ed.), *The Cambridge History of Japan*, vol. 6: *The Twentieth Century* (Cambridge, 1988), 286–2.

74. Humphreys, *Heavenly Sword*, 136–42.

75. W. F. Morton, *Tanaka Giichi and Japan's China Policy* (New York, 1980), 71.

76. K. Colegrove, 'Parliamentary Government in Japan', *The American Political Science Review* 21, no. 4 (1927), 835–52.

77. Humphreys, *Heavenly Sword*, 122–57.

78. N. Bamba, *Japanese Diplomacy in a Dilemma* (Vancouver, 1972), 134.

79. T. Sekiguchi, 'Political Conditions in Japan: After the Application of Manhood Suffrage', *Pacific Affairs* 3, no. 10 (1930), 907–22.

26 THE GREAT DEPRESSION

1. M. Friedman and A. Schwartz, *A Monetary History of the United States, 1867–1960* (Princeton, NJ, 1963), and K. Polanyi, *The Great Transformation: The Political and Economic Origins of our Times* (Boston, MA, 1944), 21–44.

2. B. Eichengreen, *Golden Fetters: The Gold Standard and the Great Depression, 1919–1939* (Oxford, 1992), and A. Meltzer, *A History of the Federal Reserve* (Chicago, IL, 2003), vol. 1.

3. H. James, *The German Slump: Politics and Economics, 1924–1936* (Oxford, 1986).

4. Z. Steiner, *The Lights that Failed: European International History, 1919–1933* (Oxford, 2005), 470–91; P. Heyde, *Das Ende der Reparationen* (Paderborn, 1998), 35–77; P. Cohrs, *The Unfinished Peace after World War I: America, Britain and the Stabilisation of Europe, 1919–1932* (Cambridge, 2006), 477–571.

5. S. Schuker, 'Les États-Unis, la France et l'Europe, 1929–1932', in J. Bariéty (ed.), *Aristide Briand, la Société des Nations et l'Europe, 1919–1932* (Strasbourg, 2007), 385.

6. L. Trotsky, 'Disarmament and the United States of Europe' (October 1929) http://www.marxists.org/archive/trotsky/1929/10/disarm.htm

7. S. Adler, *The Uncertain Giant, 1921–1941: American Foreign Policy Between the Wars* (New York, 1965), 79.

8. A. Ritschl, *Deutschlands Krise und Konjunktur 1924–1934: Binnenkonjunktur, Auslandsverschuldung und Reparationsproblem zwischen Dawes-Plan und Transfersperre* (Berlin, 2002).

9. B. Fulda, *Press and Politics in the Weimar Republic* (Oxford, 2009), 144–6.

10. H. Mommsen, *The Rise and Fall of Weimar Democracy* (Chapel Hill, NC, 1996).

11. F. R. Dickinson, *World War I and the Triumph of a New Japan, 1919–1930* (Cambridge, 2013), 185–6.

12. Adler, *Uncertain Giant*, 130.

13. R. Sims, *Japanese Political History Since the Meiji Renovation: 1868–2000* (London, 2001), 150.

14. I. Gow, *Military Intervention in Prewar Japanese Politics: Admiral Katō Kanji and the 'Washington System'* (London, 2004), 249–66, and J. W. Morley (ed.), *Japan Erupts: The London Naval Conference and the Manchurian Incident, 1928–1932* (New York, 1984).

15. L. Connors, *The Emperor's Adviser: Saionji Kinmochi and Pre-War Japanese Politics* (Oxford, 1987), 117–26; T. Mayer-Oakes (ed.), *Fragile Victory: Saionji-Harada Memoirs* (Detroit, IL, 1968).

16. R. Boyce, *The Great Interwar Crisis and the Collapse of Globalization* (Basingstoke, 2009).

17. Schuker, 'États-Unis', 393.

18. W. Lippman, 'An American View', *Foreign Affairs* 8, no. 4 (1930), 499–518; R. Fanning, *Peace and Disarmament: Naval Rivalry and Arms Control, 1922–1933* (Lexington, KY, 1995), 125.

19. W. Lipgens, 'Europäische Einigungsidee 1923–1930 und Briands Europaplan im Urteil der deutschen Akten (Part 2)', *Historische Zeitschrift* 203, no. 1 (1966), 46–89. For a prominent example of this enthusiasm see former Prime Minister E. Herriot's *Europe* (Paris, 1930).

20. Boyce, *Great Interwar Crisis*.

21. Société des Nations, *Documents relatifs à l'organisation d'un régime d'Union Fédérale Européenne*, Séries de publ. questions politique, VI (Geneva 1930), 1–16.

22. Boyce, *Great Interwar Crisis*, 258–72.

23. W. Lipgens, 'Europäische Einigungsidee 1923–1930 und Briands Europaplan im Urteil der deutschen Akten (Part 2)', *Historische Zeitschrift* 203, no. 2 (1966), 341.

24. H. Pogge Von Strandmann, 'Großindustrie und Rapallopolitik. Deutsch-Sowjetische Handelsbeziehungen in der Weimarer Republik', *Historische Zeitschrift* 222, no. 2 (1976), 265–341; R. Spaulding, *Osthandel and Ostpolitik: German Foreign Trade Policies in Eastern Europe from Bismarck to Adenauer* (Oxford, 1997), 267–9.

25. W. Patch, *Heinrich Brüning and the Dissolution of the Weimar Republic* (New York, 1998).

26. T. Ferguson and P. Temin, 'Made in Germany: The German Currency Crisis of 1931', *Research in Economic History* 21 (2003), 1–53.

27. Heyde, *Das Ende*, 130–44.

28. Schuker, 'États-Unis', 394.

29. Boyce, *Great Interwar Crisis*, 305.

30. Eichengreen, *Golden Fetters*, 278.

31. Boyce, *Great Interwar Crisis*, 307–08.

32. Schuker, 'États-Unis', 395.

33. Heyde, *Das Ende*, 208–16.

34. *The New York Times*, 'Germany Pledges a Holiday on Arms', 6 July 1931.

35. A. Tooze, *Wages of Destruction: The Making and Breaking of the Nazi Economy* (London, 2006).

36. C. Thorne, *The Limits of Foreign Policy: The West, the League and the Far Eastern Crisis of 1931–1933* (London, 1972).

37. Boyce, *Great Interwar Crisis*, 314–22.

38. Eichengreen, *Golden Fetters*, 279–316.

39. N. Forbes, *Doing Business with the Nazis* (London, 2000), 99.

40. K. Pyle, *The Making of Modern Japan* (Lexington, MA, 1978), 139.

41. J. Maiolo, *Cry Havoc: How the Arms Race Drove the World to War, 1931–1941* (London, 2010), 31.

42. Tooze, *Wages of Destruction*, 1–33; R. Evans, *The Coming of the Third Reich* (London, 2003).

43. Steiner, *The Lights*, 755–99.

44. D. Kennedy, *Freedom from Fear* (Oxford, 1999), 70–103.

45. Cohrs, *Unfinished Peace*, 581–7.

46. I. Katznelson, *Fear Itself: The New Deal and the Origins of Our Time* (New York, 2013).

47. B. Ackerman, *We the People*, vol. 2, *Transformations* (Cambridge, MA, 1998).

48. R. Dallek, *Franklin Roosevelt and American Foreign Policy, 1932–1945* (Oxford, 1979), 23–100.

49. C. Romer, 'What Ended the Great Depression?', *The Journal of Economic History* 52, no. 4 (1992), 757–84.

50. S. Schuker, *American 'Reparations' to Germany, 1919–1933* (Princeton, NJ, 1988), 101–5.

51. R. Self, *Britain, America and the War Debt Controversy: The Economic Diplomacy of an Unspecial Relationship, 1917–1941* (London, 2006), 74.

52. R. Self, 'Perception and Posture in Anglo-American Relations: The War Debt Controversy in the "Official Mind", 1919–1940', *The International History Review* 29, no. 2 (2007), 286.

CONCLUSION: RAISING THE STAKES

1. S. Hoffmann, *Gulliver's Troubles, or the Setting of American Foreign Policy* (New York, 1968), 53.

2. J. Stalin, *Collected Works* (Moscow, 1954), vol. 13, 41–2.

3. H. Nicolson, *Peacemaking, 1919* (London, 1933), 108.

4. P. Yearwood, *Guarantee of Peace: The League of Nations in British Policy, 1914–1925* (Oxford, 2009), 342.

5. S. Adler, *The Uncertain Giant, 1921–1941: American Foreign Policy Between the Wars* (New York, 1965), 150.

6. R. Boyce, *The Great Interwar Crisis and the Collapse of Globalization* (Basingstoke, 2009), 251.

Index

Page references in *italic* indicate figures and tables. These are also listed in full after the Contents.

585

United States of America – *cont.*

debts 298, 299, 302, 304, 349,
366, 367, 440, 467–70, 468,
473, 496–7, 498, 506–7; and
the Washington Conference
400–401; and the Washington
Naval Conference 11; Wilson
and the Socialists 240; Wilson
on French freedom 276–7

German-Americans 43

and Germany: and American
business interest 320; anti-
American Mexican alliance
proposal 65–6; and the
armistice 220–31; breaking of
diplomatic relations (February
1917) 89; Dawes Plan 453–61,
464, 497; derailment of
Wilson's 'peace without victory'
52, 56–8; and the French
invasion of the Ruhr 443–6,
448, 459; German embassy in
Washington 56; Germany's
Atlanticist internationalism
221–2; and the Great
Depression 495–6; Hitler's
concerns over the US 6, 7;
Hoover moratorium 498,
502–3, 507; and reparations
293–5, 297–304, 441, 453–61,
495–6, 498, 506; severing of
diplomatic relations 59;
stabilization of Weimar
Republic after 1924 by US
credit 461, 464–5; Stresemann's
policy of accommodation 448;
Thoiry initiative 473; U-boat
campaign 24, 45, 48, 57–8, 64,
66; US debts 498, 502–3,
506–7; US private long-term
investment (December 1930)
476, 495–6; and Wilson's 14
Points manifesto 122–3, 134,

143, 144, 145, 198, 224, 226,
227, 228, 230, 233, 327;
Wilson's demand for Kaiser's
abdication 224, 225; Wilson's
unilateral negotiations with
Berlin 222–5, 229, 231

gold 344, 345, 349, 359, 505;
standard 38, 345, 346, 355,
363, 505

growth in power through the war
6–7, 11

and the Hague Convention 267

Harding administration 348–9,
372, 432, 439, 441, 443; and
the Washington Conference
396–7, 401

hegemonic crisis model 18–20, 26

Hoover administration 488

image 41

immigration law 348

and India 210

industry 41; industrial action
(1919) 247, 341–2, 343, 409;
Industrial Conference 341

interest rates 344–5, 349

invisible influence on post-war
international order 3–4,
515–16

isolationism 348, 505, 517

and Italy *see* Italy: and the US

and Japan *see* Japan: and the US

Jewish-Americans 43

and the Ku Klux Klan 339, 347

labour movement 43, 340–42

and the League of Nations 267,
336–7; and the absent presence
of US power 515–16; and
Article X of Covenant 335,
336–7; and Britain 258,
259–61, 266, 268–70, 271, 455;
and Geneva Protocols 470–71;
and the need for the US to
dissociate from former allies

ALLEN LANE
an imprint of
PENGUIN BOOKS

Recently Published

John Gray, *The Soul of the Marionette: A Short Enquiry into Human Freedom*

Emily Wilson, *Seneca: A Life*

Michael Barber, *How to Run a Government: So That Citizens Benefit and Taxpayers Don't Go Crazy*

Dana Thomas, *Gods and Kings: The Rise and Fall of Alexander McQueen and John Galliano*

Steven Weinberg, *To Explain the World: The Discovery of Modern Science*

Jennifer Jacquet, *Is Shame Necessary?: New Uses for an Old Tool*

Eugene Rogan, *The Fall of the Ottomans: The Great War in the Middle East, 1914-1920*

Norman Doidge, *The Brain's Way of Healing: Stories of Remarkable Recoveries and Discoveries*

John Hooper, *The Italians*

Sven Beckert, *Empire of Cotton: A New History of Global Capitalism*

Mark Kishlansky, *Charles I: An Abbreviated Life*

Philip Ziegler, *George VI: The Dutiful King*

David Cannadine, *George V: The Unexpected King*

Stephen Alford, *Edward VI: The Last Boy King*

John Guy, *Henry VIII: The Quest for Fame*

Robert Tombs, *The English and their History: The First Thirteen Centuries*

Neil MacGregor, *Germany: The Memories of a Nation*

Uwe Tellkamp, *The Tower: A Novel*

Roberto Calasso, *Ardor*

Slavoj Žižek, *Trouble in Paradise: Communism After the End of History*

Francis Pryor, *Home: A Time Traveller's Tales from Britain's Prehistory*

R. F. Foster, *Vivid Faces: The Revolutionary Generation in Ireland, 1890-1923*

Andrew Roberts, *Napoleon the Great*

Shami Chakrabarti, *On Liberty*

Bessel van der Kolk, *The Body Keeps the Score: Mind, Brain and Body in the Transformation of Trauma*

Brendan Simms, *The Longest Afternoon: The 400 Men Who Decided the Battle of Waterloo*

Naomi Klein, *This Changes Everything: Capitalism vs the Climate*

Owen Jones, *The Establishment: And How They Get Away with It*

Caleb Scharf, *The Copernicus Complex: Our Cosmic Significance in a Universe of Planets and Probabilities*

Martin Wolf, *The Shifts and the Shocks: What We've Learned - and Have Still to Learn - from the Financial Crisis*

Steven Pinker, *The Sense of Style: The Thinking Person's Guide to Writing in the 21st Century*